The Reception of Paul and Early Christian Initiation

This book breaks new ground in New Testament reception history by bringing together early Pauline interpretation and the study of early Christian institutions. Benjamin A. Edsall traces the close association between Paul and the catechumenate through important texts and readers from the late second century to the fourth century to show how the early Church arrived at a widespread image of Paul as the apostle of Christian initiation. While exploring what this image of Paul means for understanding early Christian interpretation, Edsall also examines the significance of this aspect of Pauline reception in relation to interpretive possibilities of Paul's letters. Building on the analysis of early interpretations and rhetorical images of the Apostle, Edsall brings these together with contemporary scholarly discourse. The juxtaposition highlights longstanding continuity and conflict in exegetical discussions and dominant Pauline images. Edsall concludes with broader hermeneutical reflections on the value of historical reception for New Testament Studies.

Benjamin A. Edsall is Research Fellow at the Australian Catholic University. He is the author of *Paul's Witness to Formative Early Christian Instruction* (2014) and of numerous articles in journals such as *New Testament Studies*, *Vigiliae Christianae*, and the *Journal of Theological Studies*.

The Reception of Paul and Early Christian Initiation

History and Hermeneutics

BENJAMIN A. EDSALL

Australian Catholic University, Melbourne

CAMBRIDGE
UNIVERSITY PRESS

University Printing House, Cambridge CB2 8BS, United Kingdom

One Liberty Plaza, 20th Floor, New York, NY 10006, USA

477 Williamstown Road, Port Melbourne, VIC 3207, Australia

314–321, 3rd Floor, Plot 3, Splendor Forum, Jasola District Centre,
New Delhi – 110025, India

79 Anson Road, #06-04/06, Singapore 079906

Cambridge University Press is part of the University of Cambridge.

It furthers the University's mission by disseminating knowledge in the pursuit of
education, learning, and research at the highest international levels of excellence.

www.cambridge.org
Information on this title: www.cambridge.org/9781108471312
DOI: 10.1017/9781108558525

First published 2019

Printed and bound in Great Britain by Clays Ltd, Elcograf S.p.A.

A catalog record for this publication is available from the British Library.

Library of Congress Cataloging-in-Publication Data
Names: Edsall, Benjamin A., 1982– author.
Title: The reception of Paul and early Christian initiation : history and
hermeneutics / Benjamin Edsall, Australian Catholic University, Melbourne.
Description: New York: Cambridge University Press, 2019. |
Includes bibliographical references.
Identifiers: LCCN 2018048291 | ISBN 9781108471312 (hardback) |
ISBN 9781108457620 (pbk.)
Subjects: LCSH: Paul, the Apostle, Saint – Influence. | Catechumens – History –
Early church, ca. 30–600. | Catechetics – History – Early church, ca. 30–600. |
Initiation rites – Religious aspects – Christianity – History. | Church history –
Primitive and early church, ca. 30–600 – Sources. | Christianity – Origin.
Classification: LCC BR195.C38E37 2019 | DDC 227/.0609015–dc23
LC record available at https://lccn.loc.gov/2018048291

ISBN 978-1-108-47131-2 Hardback

For my parents,
who taught me to read

Contents

Preface

I believe that Fredrick Buechner was on to something when he wrote, "at its heart, most theology...is essentially autobiography."[1] Though this book is not a work of theology, strictly speaking, its shape and argument certainly reflect developments in my own thinking about theology, philosophy, and history that have taken place slowly over the last decade or so. (I also think that Beuchner's view describes the works of the interpreters examined here, though a defense of that will have to wait until later.) Those who know me will have little difficulty, I think, in spotting this. What started as the pursuit of a simple historical account of a particular aspect of Pauline reception has slowly become something more ambitious: an attempt to situate these early readers within contemporary scholarly discussions in order to reframe the relationship between New Testament Studies (as it is often practiced) and "reception history." We shall see if I was successful.

All projects of this size require the support of institutions and colleagues to come to completion, and that is no less the case here. Many have offered valuable feedback at various times, though only a few can be mentioned here. My colleagues in the Institute for Religion and Critical Inquiry (IRCI) at Australian Catholic University (ACU) have been exceptionally generous with their time and helpful in their feedback. Matthew Crawford and Michael Champion never failed to provide guidance in the world of late antique Christianity and ancient philosophy. Matt was also my go-to resource for all questions pertaining to Syriac or Armenian. Edward Jeremiah endured the task of proofreading all my Greek and

---

[1] Frederick Buechner, *The Alphabet of Grace* (New York: Harper One, 2007), 3.

Latin translations and, in addition to saving me from awkward phrasing (some of which no doubt I neglected to change sufficiently) and typos, he offered incisive and substantive suggestions on how to clarify and improve difficult passages. Chris Jacobs-Vandegeer and Alda Balthrop-Lewis graciously read and commented on the final chapter. The award for scholar most put-upon by this project, however, goes to Stephen Carlson, who was there at its start and consistently provided incisive criticisms on every chapter. Many thanks are also due to Frank Moloney for welcoming me to ACU and providing support and guidance up to and well beyond his retirement. The research leadership at the IRCI – Wayne McKenna (DVCR), James McLaren, and David Runia – have supported this project from the start, by enabling me to attend conferences to road-test the material and by allowing me to spend seven months in Berlin to finish the initial draft of the manuscript.

My time in Germany was generously funded by the Alexander von Humboldt-Stiftung, which enabled not only me but my whole family to flourish while we were there. Jens Schröter, at Humboldt Universität zu Berlin, was a gracious host and provided very helpful feedback on my work, especially Chapters 7–8. I am grateful for his hospitality, support, feedback, and enthusiasm for this project, as well as for the welcome from other colleagues there, in particular Konrad Schwarz and Christine Jacobi.

As one trained in New Testament Studies, it is hard to avoid the feeling that I am trespassing on others' domains while covering such a wide range of interpreters and issues. For that reason I am indebted to experts in these areas who have taken the time to read and comment on drafts of my chapters: Michael Champion (again) on Clement; Peter Martens on Origen; Wendy Mayer on John Chrysostom; and A. K. M. Adam on hermeneutics. David Lincicum offered helpful comments on my discussion of F. C. Baur (along with broader comments on the manuscript), as did Simeon Zahl on my discussion of Luther and Erasmus. Matyáš Havrda read an earlier related version of the material about Clement and offered extremely useful feedback; Judith Kovacs kindly corresponded with me about her work on Pauline reception; and Christoph Markschies supplied some helpful bibliographical suggestions in relation to Origen. Early on in the project, a valuable conversation with Markus Bockmuehl pushed me to begin thinking harder about the hermeneutical significance of reception.

The initial research for this project, focusing in particular on the *Acts of Paul*, was presented at SBL in Atlanta (2015, chaired by Christopher

M. Hays). The material on Clement was first road-tested at the Rome Seminar hosted by ACU and convened by Lewis Ayres (2016), and a summary of the whole project was presented in Berlin in October 2017, convened by Jens Schröter together with Tobias Nicklas and Joseph Verheyden. I am thankful to the organizers and conveners of these seminars for the opportunity to try out a few of the arguments present in this volume.

Finally, I owe a huge debt of thanks to my family. They have traveled around the world with me over the last four years, from Oxford to Melbourne to Berlin and back to Melbourne again, and they have done so with incredible spirits. I simply could not have done this without their support. The book is dedicated to my parents, who did not put in much work on the project, but did put in the much harder work of raising me.

I

Introduction

And I Paul, the least of the apostles, give you bishops and presbyters these commands concerning the canons. Those who are first approaching the mystery of piety, let them be led by the deacons to the bishop or the presbyters.[1]

This is a book about the reception of the Apostle Paul – doubly so, in fact. On the one hand, it primarily explores an important but unappreciated aspect of the early reception of Paul that shaped his developing profile in the early Church from the late second century through the fourth century: namely, the close link forged between the Apostle and the catechumenate. On the other hand, it is about the reception of Paul in the sense that it provides the occasion to offer some broader reflections on the meaning and contemporary value of reception-historical approaches to Paul. The question, then, is not only "what happened when the early Christians read about Paul?" but also "what, if anything, do these early readings mean for interpreters of Paul today?" The epigraph above is the starting point for this double investigation, which is perhaps best introduced simply by jumping in, beginning at the end of the development to be traced in subsequent chapters.

---

[1] CA 8.32 (ed. Marcel Metzger, *Les constitutions apostoliques*, 3 vols., SC 320, 329, 336 (Paris: Cerf, 1985–1987)) – Κἀγὼ Παῦλος ὁ τῶν ἀποστόλων ἐλάχιστος, τάδε διατάσσομαι ὑμῖν τοῖς ἐπισκόποις καὶ πρεσβυτέροις περὶ κανόνων. Οἱ πρώτως προσιόντες τῷ μυστηρίῳ τῆς εὐσεβείας διὰ τῶν διακόνων προσαγέσθωσαν τῷ ἐπισκόπῳ ἢ τοῖς πρεσβυτέροις. Note that all translations of primary and secondary literature are my own unless otherwise noted. For the most part, I will only list the edition for the first citation.

1.1 PAUL AT THE END OF THE FOURTH CENTURY

Sometime toward the end of the fourth century, an anonymous ecclesial leader, perhaps in Syria, compiled a work we know as the *Constitutiones apostolorum*. To produce this new church order document, the writer incorporated revised versions of at least three previous prominent church order documents that were already circulating in Syria: the *Didache*, the *Didascalia apostolorum*, and the *Traditio apostolica*. Although the compiler evidently had Arian theological tendencies, the treatises he appropriated were not themselves Arian, a fact that led him to recast and update his sources to fit with his theology and ecclesial praxis.[2]

In book 8 of this rather sprawling work, each of the apostles is brought forward – in roughly Matthean order (Matt. 10:2–4) – to declare their own canons for the Church. Paul, who is inserted after Matthias, begins his declamation with the epigraph that opens this chapter (*CA* 8.32):

And I Paul, the least of the apostles, command you, bishops and presbyters, these things concerning the canons. Those who are first approaching the mystery of piety, let them be led by the deacons to the bishop or the presbyters.

What follows is a discussion of the catechetical process, providing particular guidance on which vocations are suitable for baptism (with the repeated phrase "let one cease or let one be cast away") and how best to assess the character of one requesting baptism.[3]

As we shall see in the next chapter, this concern for moral preparation is part and parcel of the catechumenate throughout its development into the fourth century. In fact, the material for this section of the *Constitutiones apostolorum* is drawn from the *Traditio apostolica*, which contains an important witness to the development of the catechumenate in the third century. The discussion of catechesis and baptism there supplies many details about Christian initiation lacking from other church order documents appropriated by the editor of the *Constitutiones*

---

[2] See the discussion of sources in Metzger, *Constitutions*, vol. I, pp. 14–18 (who also notes the use of the *Canones apostolorum* in *CA* 8.47; see also F. X. Funk, *Didascalia et constitutiones apostolorum* (Paderborn: Ferdinand Schönigh, 1905–1906), vol. I, pp. xviii–xix; Edward J. Yarnold, "Baptismal catechesis," in Cheslyn Jones, Geoffrey Wainwright, and Edward Yarnold (eds.), *The Study of Liturgy* (London: SPCK, 1978), pp. 59–60; Paul F. Bradshaw, *The Search for the Origins of Christian Worship: Sources and Methods for the Study of Early Liturgy*, 2nd edn (New York: Oxford University Press, 2002), pp. 84–86) and the theology of the text in Metzger, *Constitutions*, vol. II, pp. 10–39.

[3] *CA* 8.32 *passim* – παυσάσθω ἢ ἀποβαλλέσθω.

apostolorum, including the concern for the vocation of initiates. Paul's presence, however, is particularly notable in *CA* 8.32 because it has been *added* to the underlying source material by the late fourth-century editor.[4]

In the majority of church rules, the voices of the apostles are combined near the beginning for the weight of their unified authority. For example, in the proem of the third-century *Didascalia*, the author writes with the collective authority of "the twelve apostles...with Paul the apostle to the Gentiles and James the bishop" of Jerusalem.[5] The *Traditio apostolica* appears to have had a similar literary artifice at the beginning, though the fragmentary state of the manuscript tradition at that point makes certain determinations of how the apostles were referred to and which of them were included difficult.[6] What is much less common, however, is the presence of individual apostolic voices. But for the compiler of the *Constitutiones apostolorum*, just as Peter, the chief apostle, has become responsible for the canons regarding the appointment of bishops (*CA* 8.4), Paul has become the apostle of initiation, directing the late fourth-century readers in the principal moral tasks of the catechumenate.

---

[4] It is also worth noting that, while Paul's name does appear at the beginning of the *Didascalia apostolorum*, he is not a regular fixture in Church order documents. He (and his influence) is famously absent in the *Didache*. The Sahidic witness to the *Traditio apostolica* (*TA*), included in the *Apostolic Church Order*, omits Paul, as do the *Canones apostolorum*, transmitted in the same manuscript; Paul de LaGarde, *Aegyptica* (Gottingen: Arnold Hoyer, 1883), 209–238. It simply mentions "the apostles," who transmit the canons to the church via "Clement." Moreover, the *Canons of Hippolytus* address the catechumenate, but are not associated with Paul (Paul F. Bradshaw (ed.), *The Canons of Hippolytus*, trans. Carol Bebawi, Grove Liturgical Study 50 (Bramcote, Notts.: Grove Books, 1987)).

[5] *Didasc. apost.* Proem, in Arthur Vööbus (ed.), *The Didascalia Apostolorum in Syriac*, 4 vols., CSCO 401, 402, 407, 408 (Louvain: Secrétariat du Corpus SCO, 1979), pp. 9–10; see also the second title to the *Didache* – Διδαχὴ κυρίου διὰ τῶν δώδεκα ἀποστόλων τοῖς ἔθνεσιν.

[6] Further discussion of these textual issues are in Chapter 2.3.5 below. See also the comments on the introduction in Paul F. Bradshaw *et al.*, *The Apostolic Tradition: A Commentary*, Hermeneia (Minneapolis: Fortress, 2002), pp. 20–23. Moreover, the Sahidic witness to the *TA* is part of an ostensibly continuous text with the preceding *Apostolic Church Order*, which begins: "These are the canons of our fathers, the holy apostles of our Lord Jesus Christ (ⲛⲁⲓ ⲛⲉ ⲛⲕⲁⲛⲱⲛ ⲛ̄ⲛⲉⲛⲉⲓⲟⲧⲉ ⲉⲧ ⲟⲩⲁⲁⲃ ⲛⲁⲡⲟⲥⲧⲟⲗⲟⲥ ⲙ̄ⲡⲉⲛϫⲟⲉⲓⲥ ⲓⲏⲥⲟⲩⲥ ⲡⲉⲭⲣⲓⲥⲧⲟⲥ), which were appointed for the church. 'Rejoice, oh our sons and daughters, in the name of our Lord Jesus Christ!' said John with Matthew, Peter, Andrew, Philip, Simon, James, Nathaniel, Thomas, Cephas, Bartholomew, and Judas the brother of James" (de LaGarde, *Aegyptica*, p. 239). The full manuscript is presented by de LaGarde, while the newer corrected edition and translation of Walter Till and Johannes Leipoldt, *Der koptische Text der Kirchenordnung Hippolyts*, TU 58 (Berlin: Akademie, 1954), reproduces only the text of the *TA*.

On its own, this text would merely be an interesting piece of trivia: which apostle gets which church canon? It is *not* on its own, however. Around the same time that the *Constitutiones apostolorum* was being compiled, a certain Euthalius appears to have been shaping his own edition of Paul's letters, which included a number of paratextual features: chapter titles (κεφάλαια-τίτλοι), book summaries (ὑποθέσεις), and prologues (πρόλογοι) for each block of texts – Paul's letters, Acts, and the Catholic Epistles.[7] According to Eric Scherbenske, both the manuscript edition and the paratextual features were designed with "catechetical and paraenetic" goals in view.[8] The author makes this clear at the end of the Prologue to Paul's letters. "Thus the book as a whole includes every aspect of proper way of life arranged according to progress."[9]

This purpose, however, is not only that of Euthalius but is also presented as the purpose of the Pauline epistles themselves. As he says earlier in the Epitome to Paul's letters, "the letter to the Romans contains a catechism of Christ, in particular through an argument based on natural reasoning. This is why it is placed first, as a letter written to people whose devotion was new."[10] In fact, he claims that the first five letters

---

[7] Unfortunately, almost nothing about either the author (Euthalius or Evagrius?), the date (somewhere between the fourth and sixth centuries?), or the scope (only Paul's letters or already including Acts and the Catholic Epistles?) of the original work is agreed on among scholars. The recent discussion of these matters in Vemund Blomkvist, *Euthalian Traditions: Text, Translation and Commentary*, TU 170 (Berlin: De Gruyter, 2012), pp. 1–8, is judicious. He concludes later that "At the present stage of research only conjectures [*viz.* on these introductory matters] can be made" (p. 242). Even so, a plausible case has recently been made for placing the origin of the Euthalian Apparatus in the last decades of the fourth century; see Eric W. Scherbenske, *Canonizing Paul: Ancient Editorial Practice and the Corpus Paulinum* (New York: Oxford University Press, 2013), pp. 118–122, who follows the analysis of Louis Charles Willard, *A Critical Study of the Euthalian Apparatus*, ANT 41 (Berlin: De Gruyter, 2009), pp. 111–127. Furthermore, Blomkvist has suggested that the final form of the Apparatus need not be the work of a single author, proposing that perhaps the first volume with the Pauline apparatus served as the original work, later expanded by another writer to include Acts and the Catholic Epistles (Blomkvist, *Euthalian Traditions*, pp. 4, 242–243).

[8] Scherbenske, *Canonizing Paul*, p. 135; see also pp. 142, 158–159, *et passim*.

[9] *Prologus* 708A, edited in Blomkvist, *Euthalian Traditions* (trans. modified from Blomkvist) – οὕτως ἡ πᾶσα βίβλος περιέχει παντοῖον εἶδος πολιτειῶν κατὰ προσαύξησιν. This passage is noted in Scherbenske, *Canonizing Paul*, p. 142.

[10] *Prologus* 701A (trans. Blomkvist): περιέχει οὖν ἡ πρὸς Ῥωμαίους ἐπιστολὴ κατήχησιν εἰς Χριστόν, καὶ μάλιστα διὰ τῆς ἐκ φυσικῶν λογισμῶν ἀποδείξεως, διὸ πρώτη τέτακται, οἷα δὴ πρὸς ἀρχὴν ἔχοντας εἰς θεοσέβειαν γραφεῖσα.

of the Pauline corpus – from Romans to Ephesians – are dedicated to "first principles for catechumens" and "introductions for believers."[11] Moreover, one might argue that even Paul's biography itself, presented in the *Prologus* (696A–701A), is based on an ideal model of repentance, conversion, and salvation.[12] Of course, as is the case for the authors discussed later, catechesis is not the only thing that Euthalius' Paul is interested in. Nevertheless, it is an important aspect of his work and the ongoing function of his letters.

At first glance, the representation of Paul in the *Consitutiones apostolorum* and the Euthalian Apparatus may appear to contemporary scholars as simple anachronisms, unsupported by the textual resources of Paul's letters. For instance, while "Paul" speaks about the function of the "bishop" (ἐπίσκοπος) in *CA* 8.32, scholars today normally differentiate between Paul's varied and limited use of terms such as ἐπίσκοπος to denote community leaders and later developments of fixed church offices.[13] Any portrayal of Paul that implicates him in such a strict ecclesial hierarchy is bound to strike many modern readers as strange, to say nothing of the fact that such an image of Paul and the other apostles is far more harmonious than many scholars today would accept.[14] Second, it may appear out of place for Paul to offer apostolic canons on the

---

[11] Ibid.: καὶ εἰσὶν αὗται...ἀρχαὶ κατηχουμένων, πιστῶν εἰσαγωγαί. Similar comments on the catechetical quality of Ephesians (though with a different evaluation of Colossians) can be found in Euthalius *Hypoth.* 761C; cf. 765C on Colossians.

[12] This is the argument of Scherbenske, *Canonizing Paul*, p. 124. See also his comments on p. 173: "Euthalius predicated his edition of the *Corpus Paulinum* on education, both preliminary and advanced. This pedagogical goal was articulated in and developed by means of the paratextual components of his edition. Foremost among the instructional aspects of these paratexts was Euthalius's emphasis on exemplarity and mimesis, prominently displayed in the prologue's epitomes of Paul's letters and his *bios*."

[13] E.g., David G. Horrell, *An Introduction to the Study of Paul*, 2nd edn (London and New York: T. & T. Clark, 2006), pp. 134–135. See also the discussion in Benjamin L. White, "The traditional and ecclesiastical Paul of 1 Corinthians," *Catholic Biblical Quarterly*, 79, no. 4 (2017), 651–669; and John S. Kloppenborg, "Pneumatic democracy and the conflict in *1 Clement*," in Mark Grundeken and Joseph Verheyden (eds.), *Early Christian Communities Between Ideal and Reality*, WUNT I/342 (Tübingen: Mohr Siebeck, 2015), pp. 61–81. The distinction between the Spirit-led communities and organized offices is normally more nuanced in current discussion than in the epochal debate between Sohm and Harnack; see the discussion in Jörg Frey, "Ämter," in Friedrich Wilhelm Horn (ed.), *Paulus Handbuch* (Tübingen: Mohr Siebeck, 2013), pp. 408–412, and Udo Schnelle, *Paulus. Leben und Denken*, 2nd edn, De Gruyter Studium (Berlin: De Gruyter, 2014), pp. 621–623.

[14] This theme is picked up again in more detail below in Chapter 7.

preparation of candidates for baptism when he appears to claim in 1 Corinthians 1:17 that he was not sent to baptize at all: his task was proclamation. In fact, this tension – between Paul's apparent disavowal of baptism and the clear importance of baptism and baptismal preparation in the (early) Church – generates an interpretive problem, even anxiety in some cases, for early and contemporary readers that is addressed in various ways. Furthermore, the catechetical and pedagogical structuring of Paul's letters presented by Euthalius runs counter to the prevailing view among Pauline scholars that each letter ought to be treated primarily as an *ad hoc* act of communication, deeply marked by its historical exigency and only later compiled into a collection.[15] Indeed, from this perspective it is hard to avoid the impression that, were he able to read it, the Apostle Paul would be rather surprised to find himself portrayed as he is in these works.

And yet, the presentation of Paul in these late fourth-century works is not mere anachronism. It is the culmination of a process of Pauline interpretation that begins near the end of the second century and is not without its undergirding textual resources within Paul's letters. The themes of moral preparation for and progress within the Christian life, mimetic and paradigmatic appeals to Paul's biography, and a link between Paul and the other apostles will appear repeatedly in the chapters that follow. The association between Paul and early Christian initiation, casting his ministry and letters as paradigmatic for catechetical praxis, is bound up with broader ecclesiological and pedagogical goals for writers from the second century to the fourth. Attempting to understand their goals and methods will take us a long way toward appreciating this association. For now, though, we must let the contrast stand between this late fourth-century Paul and the Apostle familiar to us from historical scholarship, as we move on to other introductory matters.

---

[15] The debate over the reason for Romans is emblematic of this general shift, on which see esp. the essays in Karl Paul Donfried (ed.), *The Romans Debate* (Edinburgh: T. & T. Clark, 1991). This point stands even for those like Trobisch who argue that Paul's own copies of his letters formed the basis for the later *Corpus Paulinum*; see David Trobisch, *Die Entstehung der Paulusbriefsammlung. Studien zu den Anfängen christlicher Publizistik* (Göttingen: Vandenhoeck & Ruprecht, 1989). A notable exception to this trend is Brevard S. Childs, *The Church's Guide for Reading Paul: The Canonical Shaping of the Pauline Corpus* (Grand Rapids: Eerdmans, 2008), whose arguments have not gained wide traction within the field.

1.2 ABOUT PAULINE RECEPTION

Although the first work devoted specifically to the reception and influence of Paul in the Church appeared in the 1880s, Otto Pfleiderer's *Lectures on the Influence of the Apostle Paul on the Development of Christianity*, it was not until the landmark works by Andreas Lindemann and Ernst Dassmann in 1979 that interest in Pauline reception truly began to gain momentum.[16] Lindemann's and Dassmann's works represent a shift in the field, principally in their attempt to overturn the long dominant narrative stemming from F. C. Baur that the early Church had to rescue Paul from the Gnostics in their Catholicizing project – what Ben White refers to as the "Pauline captivity" narrative.[17] Given that detailed accounts of scholarship on Pauline reception are available elsewhere, I will not reproduce one here.[18] Rather, I want simply to highlight a few important considerations arising from work on (Pauline) reception which help to situate the present study and contributed to its shape.

1.2.1 Reception and (Mis)Interpretation

Perhaps the most decisive shift in studies of Pauline reception during the twentieth century has been away from the question of whether or

---

[16] Otto Pfleiderer, *Lectures on the Influence of the Apostle Paul on the Development of Christianity, Delivered in London and Oxford in April and May, 1885*, 3rd edn, trans. J. Frederick Smith (London: Williams and Norgate, 1897); Andreas Lindemann, *Paulus im ältesten Christentum. Das Bild des Apostels und die Rezeption der paulinischen Theologie in der frühchristlichen Literatur bis Marcion*, BHT 58 (Tübingen: Mohr Siebeck, 1979); Ernst Dassmann, *Der Stachel im Fleisch. Paulus in der frühchristlichen Literatur bis Irenäus* (Münster: Aschendorff, 1979). Other important works from before 1979 are Eva Aleith, *Paulusverständnis in der alten Kirche*, BZNW 18 (Berlin: De Gruyter, 1937); Karl Hermann Schelkle, *Paulus, Lehrer der Väter. Die altkirchliche Auslegung von Römer 1–11*, 2nd edn (Düsseldorf: Patmos, 1956); Maurice F. Wiles, *The Divine Apostle: The Interpretation of St. Paul's Epistles in the Early Church* (Cambridge: Cambridge University Press, 1967); and Elaine H. Pagels, *The Gnostic Paul: Gnostic Exegesis of the Pauline Letters* (Philadelphia: Fortress Press, 1975).

[17] Benjamin L. White, *Remembering Paul: Ancient and Modern Contests over the Image of the Apostle* (New York: Oxford University Press, 2014), p. 20 and *passim*. Lindemann's work was particularly influential, and was supported largely independently by David K. Rensberger, "As the apostle teaches: the development of the use of Paul's letters in second century Christianity," unpublished Ph.D. thesis, Yale University (1981). Work on specific early Christian writers also developed the Lindemann/Dassmann line of argumentation: e.g., Rolf Noormann, *Irenäus als Paulusinterpret. Zur Rezeption und Wirkung der paulinischen und deuteropaulinischen Briefe im Werk des Irenäus von Lyon*, WUNT II/66 (Tübingen: Mohr Siebeck, 1994).

[18] Useful accounts can be found in Lindemann, *Paulus im ältesten Christentum*, pp. 6–10 (for a discussion of earlier scholarship, though he omits Wiles); Rensberger, "Apostle," pp. 3–53; and particularly White, *Remembering Paul*, pp. 20–69.

not early readers got Paul "right" toward an effort to understand *why* they interpreted Paul in the way they did. In 1936, Heinrich Seesemann summed up the then dominant view of early Christian Pauline interpretation: "everyone knows that Paul was misunderstood very soon in the early Church."[19] At the end of the 1960s, Ernst Käsemann still considered it uncontroversial to claim that Paul's "characteristic theology" had little success in the early Church, though sentiments were already shifting away from such evaluations.[20] Seesemann himself had noted that the more productive question was "how" the early Church had "misunderstood" Paul. Maurice Wiles was one of the first to highlight clearly the methodological problem inherent in passing judgment on early Pauline interpretations. He wrote:

the question that immediately arises in our minds is the question "How far then did the early commentators give a true interpretation of Paul's meaning?" Yet the very form in which the question arises is not without danger. It implies the assumption that we have a true interpretation of Paul's meaning – or at least a truer one than that of those whom we have studied – in the light of which theirs may be tested and judged. It may be so; but we as much as they are children of our own times and there may well be aspects of Pauline thought to which we are blinded by the particular presuppositions and patterns of theological thinking in our own day. If therefore we seek to pass judgement on other interpreters it can only be in the recognition that we also stand in need of judgement, even and perhaps especially when we are least conscious of that need.[21]

---

[19] H. Seesemann, "Das Paulusverständnis des Clemens Alexandrinus," *Theologische Studien und Kritiken* 107 (1936), 312: "Daß Paulus in der Alten Kirche sehr bald mißverstanden wurde, ist allbekannt." I will return to this again in Chapter 7 below. Similar judgments can be found in Walther Völker, "Paulus bei Origenes," *Theologische Studien und Kritiken* 102 (1930), 258–279; and Aleith, *Paulusverständnis* (summarizing her conclusion on pp. 119–122). Pfleiderer stated that "It was Luther in whom the spirit of Paulinism first re-appeared in all its power, successfully bursting the fetters of Catholicism"; Pfleiderer, *Influence*, p. 273.

[20] Ernst Käsemann, "The theological problem presented by the motif of the body of Christ," in *Perspectives on Paul*, trans. Margaret Kohl (London: SCM, 1971), p. 115. Though Käsemann elsewhere explicitly indicates his debt to F. C. Baur, his comments here are reminiscent of Adolf von Harnack's judgment that Paul's letters were not the *basis* for early theological development (except for Marcion) but simply a "ferment" which generated a series of reactions; see Adolf Harnack, *History of Dogma*, vol. 1, trans. Neil Buchanan (Boston: Roberts Brothers, 1895), p. 136 (see also pp. 89–90), and see the discussion of Harnack's view in Rensberger, "Apostle," pp. 22–24. This interpretation of Paul is well detailed in White, *Remembering Paul*, pp. 20–41.

[21] Wiles, *The Divine Apostle*, p. 132.

Though he does not cite Wiles, Andreas Lindemann made similar observations about the dangers of treating contemporary Pauline understanding as the measuring rod for early readers.[22]

Scholars have by and large taken this point to heart, exploring the ways in which early readers engaged in creative uses of Pauline materials within their own historical contexts and in the light of their own interpretive needs.[23] This has led to an emphasis among some scholars on the constructive element of Pauline interpretation, reflected clearly in the title of Richard Pervo's work, *The Making of Paul*.[24] Others, while acknowledging this aspect of Pauline reception, also emphasize the roles of memory and tradition in shaping early Pauline presentations.[25] In a programmatic article, Daniel Marguerat argued that there are "three poles" of early Pauline reception – documentary, biographical, and doctoral – among which early representations and appropriations of Paul can be construed.[26] This "should permit the modulation of the relationship with

---

[22] Lindemann, *Paulus im ältesten Christentum*, pp. 3, 72.

[23] See the comments in Rensberger, "Apostle," p. 57; Margaret M. Mitchell, *The Heavenly Trumpet: John Chrysostom and the Art of Pauline Interpretation* (Louisville: Westminster John Knox Press, 2002), pp. 18–22; Margaret M. Mitchell, *Paul, the Corinthians, and the Birth of Christian Hermeneutics* (Cambridge: Cambridge University Press, 2010), p. 12; White, *Remembering Paul*, pp. 68–69; Jennifer R. Strawbridge, *The Pauline Effect: The Use of the Pauline Epistles by Early Christian Writers*, SBR 5 (Berlin: De Gruyter, 2015), pp. 55–56. With respect to the Hebrew Bible, see the comments in Brennan W. Breed, "What can a text do? Reception history as an ethology of the biblical text," in Emma England and William John Lyons (eds.), *Reception History and Biblical Studies: Theory and Practice*, Library of Hebrew Bible 615/Scriptural Traces 6 (London: Bloomsbury, 2015), pp. 100–101. Nevertheless, some scholars repeat the trope of a misunderstood Paul, even if in a softened form. Peter Kohlgraf, *Die Ekklesiologie des Epheserbriefes in der Auslegung durch Johannes Chrysostomus. Eine Untersuchung zur Wirkungsgeschichte paulinischer Theologie*, Hereditas 19 (Bonn: Borengässer, 2001), pp. 355–366, and Matthias Westerhoff, *Das Paulusverständnis im Liber Graduum*, PTS 64 (Berlin: De Gruyter, 2008), pp. 212–213, presume a traditional, justification-centric Paul against which they measure later interpretations; while James D. G. Dunn, *Neither Jew nor Greek: A Contested Identity*, Christianity in the Making 3 (Grand Rapids: Eerdmans, 2015), measures early Pauline reception against his own construal of Pauline theology (see my review in *Australian Biblical Review* 64 (2016)).

[24] Richard I. Pervo, *The Making of Paul: Constructions of the Apostle in Early Christianity* (Minneapolis: Fortress Press, 2010).

[25] So White, *Remembering Paul*, and, more optimistically with reference to the "historical" Paul, Alexander N. Kirk, *The Departure of an Apostle: Paul's Death Anticipated and Remembered*, WUNT II/406 (Tübingen: Mohr Siebeck, 2015).

[26] Daniel Marguerat, "Paul after Paul: a (hi)story of reception," in *Paul in Acts and Paul in His Letters*, WUNT 310 (Tübingen: Mohr Siebeck, 2013), p. 6, originally published as Daniel Marguerat, "Paul après Paul: une histoire de réception," *New Testament Studies* 54, no. 3 (2008), 317–337.

the writings of Paul, depending on whether one is situated in the realm of intertextuality ('doctoral' pole) or of the construction of a biographical memory."[27] In other words, particularly for the first and early second centuries, Marguerat shows that the Pauline letters constituted only one stream of Pauline tradition and so they cannot be taken as determinative for "Paulinism" as a whole.[28] Paul's self-presentation in his letters and, according to his own testimony (e.g., 1 Cor. 9:19–22), in person was itself multifaceted, and it appears that "the different roles accorded to the apostle correspond" to his manifold "self-comprehension."[29] These observations indicate how deep is the difficulty of comparing the "historical" Paul with early Christian images of Paul. If, in Margaret Mitchell's excellent phrase, "the marvelous malleability" of Paul extends back through his reception into his own works, deciding which Paul to use as the benchmark for the "real" Paul becomes very difficult.[30] Rather than providing grounds simply to abandon historical-critical readings of Pauline texts, however, this fact points toward the value of a hermeneutically nuanced approach, one in which the reception, interpretation, and appropriation of Paul's persona and letters also feature as meaningful contributions to understanding the Apostle and his writings, rather than as an optional add-on for those with extra time on their hands.

These points will receive further reflection and expansion in Chapters 7 and 8. At present it is enough simply to note that this shift in studies of Pauline reception has in fact taken place and shapes the present study in a particular way. If the dominant recent trend has been to focus on the plurality and constructive quality of Pauline reception, there have also been some who have reacted by emphasizing the tight continuity between the historical figure of Paul and his early reception.[31] The present study, though, adopts a middle path: acknowledging the developments and shifts in the reception of Paul, and noting the constructive elements in early interpretation, while attending to the way in which this reception

---

[27] Marguerat, "Paul after Paul," p. 21.

[28] Ibid., p. 6.

[29] Ibid., p. 14. See the similar comments about the plurality of *Paulusbilder* in Samuel Vollenweider, "Paulus zwischen Exegese und Wirkungsgeschichte," in Moisés Mayordomo-Marín (ed.), *Die prägende Kraft der Texte. Hermeneutik und Wirkungsgeschichte des Neuen Testaments*, Stuttgarter Bibelstudien 199 (Stuttgart: Verlag Katholisches Bibelwerk, 2005), pp. 153–154.

[30] Mitchell, *Heavenly Trumpet*, p. 20.

[31] So esp. Kirk, *Departure*, who uses the language of "family resemblance" to link various portrayals of Paul's death in the late first and second centuries; see also Brian J. Arnold, *Justification in The Second Century*, SBR 9 (Berlin: De Gruyter, 2017).

reflects back upon contours and potentialities of the canonical profile of Paul and, therefore, informs our contemporary interpretive discourse.[32]

There is a further point to be made about early interpreters, however, that will need to be borne in mind throughout the book. As has long been recognized, if not always appreciated in practice, early Christian readers of Paul were not reading *only* Paul.[33] As Eva Aleith noted in 1937, the early Church "did not want to be Petrine or Pauline but rather apostolic."[34] That is to say, while contemporary scholarship including the present study focuses on early interpretations of Paul, these early readers were not strictly Pauline interpreters; they were not concerned with understanding his letters or theology (to say nothing of a more limited set of "authentic" letters), except insofar as they functioned within a broader set of authoritative texts and traditions with which they were presumed to fit.[35] Therefore, any attempt to trace, for instance, Origen's treatment of Paul is necessarily to focus on only part of the story; his image of Paul is bound up with his reading of a range of other scriptural texts as well as his institutional, intellectual, and historical contexts. To forget this fact is to risk holding early Pauline interpreters to contemporary historiographical or exegetical standards foreign to their own interpretive contexts.

1.2.2 Pauline Images and the Catechumenate

A second important element of Pauline reception, which has come to the fore since Lindemann's work and is related to the shift noted above,

[32] My approach here is similar in certain respects to the recent work of Stephen Chester, which was unfortunately published well after the majority of the present study was completed. He argues that reading Paul with the Reformers is not simply a matter of ignoring their constructive interpretation in favor of repetition but of critical engagement with their readings in relation with contemporary analysis of Paul's letters; Stephen J. Chester, *Reading Paul with the Reformers: Reconciling Old and New Perspectives* (Grand Rapids: Eerdmans, 2017).

[33] Marcion, of course, is the partial exception that proves the rule.

[34] Aleith, *Paulusverständnis*, p. 119: "Die Institution der alten Kirche will nicht petrinisch oder paulinisch sein, sondern apostolisch"; see also Völker, "Paulus," p. 258: "Der Paulinismus bildet hier nur einen Einschlag, nur einen Faktor neben ganz anderen Faktoren, und der nicht immer ganz leichte Gedankengang des Apostels wird die Zurückhaltung weiter Kreise nur gesteigert haben."

[35] Marcion may again be the exception that proves the rule here. Others among the so-called "gnostic" groups also highly valued other apostolic figures and related texts such as John (e.g., Heracleon's commentary on John; the *Apocryphon* of John). It has been argued that the fourth-century Priscillian *Canones* represents the earliest attempt to outline a specifically Pauline theology; see T. J. Lang and Matthew R. Crawford, "The origins of Pauline theology: paratexts and Priscillian of Avila's *Canons on the Letters of the Apostle Paul*," *New Testament Studies* 63, no. 1 (2017), 125–145.

is the significance of early Christian images of Paul (their *Paulusbilder*) for the interpretation of his letters and the presentation or appropriation of the Apostle.[36] By "images of Paul" I refer not to actual visual material culture – though that certainly has a place, particularly in late antiquity, from which we have many more examples of early Christian art – but rather to *verbal images* of the Apostle.[37] Recent work, particularly by Margaret Mitchell and Andreas Heiser, has demonstrated the variety of ways in which rhetorical depictions of Paul serve to bolster exegetical arguments, lend weight to homiletic and paraenetic appeals, and supply precedent for early Christian practices.[38] Such images of Paul are constructed in a variety of ways, through description of his physical attributes or activities, through speech in character, through contextualizing his writings or activities in contemporary terms, and through the network of relations with other Christian teachers or communities within which he is situated. These *Paulusbilder* most often have roots in Paul's letters, whatever else they draw on in addition, though they need not always cite or allude to the letters even while playing an important part in the rhetorical power of Pauline interpretations throughout the early Church.[39]

One image of Paul that was widespread in antiquity, and is widely acknowledged among scholars, is that of Paul the teacher. This role is usually connected with his activities as preacher of the gospel, though occasionally distinguished, with Paul being regularly identified as a (if

---

[36] See Lindemann, *Paulus im ältesten Christentum*, pp. 36–113, *pace* Rensberger, "Apostle," pp. 56–57.

[37] The depictions of Paul in the central mosaics of the Neonian and Arian baptistries in Ravenna (fifth–seventh centuries), for instance, are intriguing examples of Pauline reception connected with baptism and with the other apostles; see the discussion in Robin M. Jensen, *Living Water: Images, Symbols and Settings of Early Christian Baptism*, VC Sup 105 (Leiden: Brill, 2011), pp. 108–112 and *passim*, with possible catechetical resonances noted on p. 264.

[38] Mitchell, *Heavenly Trumpet*, who focuses on John Chrysostom's depictions of Paul; and Andreas Heiser, *Paulusinzenierung des Johannes Chrysostomus. Epitheta und ihre Vorgeschichte*, STAC 70 (Tübingen: Mohr Siebeck, 2012), whose work on Pauline epithets covers the whole period of Pauline reception prior to Chrysostom as well as the fourth-century bishop himself. These works are engaged with in more detail in subsequent chapters, particularly Chapter 6.

[39] See the comments in Vollenweider, "Paulus," pp. 153–154. Others who emphasize the importance of Pauline images include David L. Eastman, *Paul the Martyr: The Cult of the Apostle in the Latin West* (Atlanta: SBL, 2011) (whose work does include material culture); Ben C. Blackwell, "Paul and Irenaeus," in Michael F. Bird and Joseph R. Dodson (eds.), *Paul and the Second Century*, LNTS 412 (London: T. & T. Clark, 2011), pp. 190–206; Marguerat, "Paul after Paul," pp. 1–21; and White, *Remembering Paul*.

not the) paradigmatic teacher among the apostles.[40] This arises explicitly within the Pauline corpus itself: in 2 Timothy 1:11 Paul is described as "preacher, apostle *and teacher*."[41] As is well known, this image is put to various uses within the early Church, whether establishing precedent for one's own teaching practice or combatting opposing views by pitching Paul as the defender of the Church against heresy.[42] Notably, Jennifer Strawbridge has pointed out that 1 Corinthians 2:6–16, which is tightly connected with Paul's image as teacher, is the most cited Pauline pericope in the pre-Constantinian Church.[43]

Despite the wide recognition of this dominant Pauline image, discussions of it rarely note the frequent links with the catechumenate or other early Christian institutional pedagogical or homiletical contexts.[44] In his 2007 work, *Kaiserzeitliche christliche Theologie und ihre Institutionen*,

---

[40] Relevant ancient material is covered in Chapters 3–7 below. Emphasis on Paul's role as teacher in the early Church can be found in Schelkle, *Paulus*; Lindemann, *Paulus im ältesten Christentum*; Alberto Viciano, "Das Bild des Apostels Paulus im Kommentar zu den paulinischen Briefen des Theodoret von Kyros," *Studia Patristica* 25 (1993), 176–188; Mitchell, *Heavenly Trumpet*; James W. Aageson, *Paul, the Pastoral Epistles, and the Early Church* (Peabody, MA: Hendrickson, 2008); Pervo, *Making of Paul*; Andrew M. Bain, "Tertullian: Paul as teacher of the Gentile churches," in Bird and Dodson, *Paul and the Second Century*, pp. 207–225; Heiser, *Paulusinszenierung*; Judith L. Kovacs, "Reading the 'divinely inspired' Paul: Clement of Alexandria in conversation with 'heterodox' Christians, simple believers, and Greek philosophers," in Veronika Cernuskova, Judith L. Kovacs, and Jana Plátová (eds.), *Clement's Biblical Exegesis: Proceedings of the Second Colloquium on Clement Of Alexandria (Olomouc, May 29–31, 2014)*, VC Sup 139 (Leiden: Brill, 2017), pp. 325–343; and John David Penniman, *Raised on Christian Milk: Food and the Formation of the Soul in Early Christianity*, Synkrisis (New Haven: Yale University Press, 2017).

[41] Ulrich Luz, *Theologische Hermeneutik des Neuen Testaments* (Neukirchen-Vluyn: Neukirchener, 2014), p. 437, makes this observation in the context of describing the hermeneutical "impulse" that arises from the Pauline corpus, in which tensions between "inclusive" and "exclusive" impulses provide the ground for hermeneutical reflection and give rise to a multiplicity of Pauline interpretations.

[42] See also the summary comments in Lindemann, *Paulus im ältesten Christentum*, pp. 112–113. For establishing precedent for early Christian ministries, see the discussions of Clement, Origen, and John Chrysostom in Chapters 4–6 below.

[43] Strawbridge, *Pauline Effect*, 24.

[44] Synchronic studies of specific interpreters tend to fare better on this count. For instance, Mitchell, *Heavenly Trumpet*, repeatedly returns to the homiletic context of Chrysostom's interpretations and mentions catechetical aims in passing (one might also mention here David Rylaarsdam, *John Chrysostom on Divine Pedagogy: The Coherence of His Theology and Preaching*, Oxford Early Christian Studies (Oxford: Oxford University Press, 2014)). Francesca Cocchini, *Il Paolo di Origene. Contributo alla storia della recezione delle Epistole paoline nel III secolo*, Verba Seniorum 11 (Rome: Edizioni Studium, 1992), similarly highlights links between Origen's involvement in homiletic or academic contexts and his Pauline interpretation.

however, Christoph Markschies compellingly demonstrates the subtle but important ways in which different ecclesial and pedagogical institutions within early Christianity shaped theological development.[45] His study, which does not itself discuss the impact of institutions on scriptural interpretation, nevertheless serves as a call for further work on the theological impact of early Christian institutions. These institutional contexts shaped the lived experience of those who inhabited them, and their influence can be seen in a variety of subtle ways.[46] As will become clear in the course of this study, the impact of the catechumenate on the interpretation of Paul is one particularly clear example of this.

In the late second century a range of pre-baptismal practices began to coalesce into a more formalized catechumenate, acquiring a set of increasingly (though never entirely) standardized practices and recognized roles and responsibilities for those involved.[47] The catechumenate represented a formalized liminality for those entering the Christian community, within which their access to certain resources and rites was regulated and their moral progress evaluated. In this process, those in the vague penumbra of the interested-but-not-committed that surrounded early Christian communities were brought into a formal and increasingly articulated relationship with the community of the baptized, participating in an institution which gave shape to the space between conversion and baptism.

Two of these terms, in particular, require a brief working definition. "Conversion" in antiquity, as today, is an immensely contested concept.[48]

---

[45] Christoph Markschies, *Kaiserzeitliche christliche Theologie und ihre Institutionen. Prolegomena zu einer Geschichte der antiken christlichen Theologie* (Tübingen: Mohr Siebeck, 2007), now translated as Christoph Markschies, *Christian Theology and Its Institutions in the Early Roman Empire: Prolegomena to a History of Early Christian Theology*, trans. Wayne Coppins, BMSEC (Waco, TX: Baylor, 2015). Citations in what follows are from the English translation unless otherwise noted.

[46] For a working definition of "institution," see below, pp. 15–16.

[47] The evidence for this is presented in some detail in Chapter 2 below.

[48] Since the epochal work of Arthur Darby Nock, *Conversion: The Old and the New in Religion from Alexander the Great to Augustine of Hippo* (Oxford: Oxford University Press, 1933), debates continue about the dynamics of conversion in relation to intellect, praxis, and social standing. See the recent discussion in Veronika Niederhofer, *Konversion in den Paulus- und Theklaakten. Eine narrative Form der Paulusrezeption*, WUNT II/459 (Tübingen: Mohr Siebeck, 2017), pp. 7–11, whose whole volume demonstrates that conversion in the second century was a multistage process (p. 245). The conversion to a "way of life" associated with philosophical conversions was famously articulated in Pierre Hadot, *Philosophy as a Way of Life: Spiritual Exercises from Socrates to Foucault*, ed. Arnold I. Davidson (Malden, MA: Blackwell, 1995), and is seen now Ilinca Tanaseanu-Döbler, *Konversion zur Philosophie in der Spätantike. Kaiser Julian und Synesios von Kyrene* (Stuttgart: Franz Steiner, 2008), who focuses in particular on Neoplatonism in the late fourth and early fifth centuries. More generally, see Lewis R. Rambo, *Understanding*

The purpose here is not to break new ground on that debate but simply to clarify the terminology with which I frame the catechumenate and Christian initiation in what follows. The term "conversion," as used here, signifies simply a person's initial decision in favor of Christian faith and praxis, which is accompanied by their articulation of intent to join the community. In a full sense, conversion in early Christianity involved a change in one's social group and a shift in religious praxis (e.g., avoiding public sacrifices), in addition to the intellectual assent which accompanied these changes. One's "conversion" to Christianity was not complete in a limited sense until one had been baptized and therefore fully initiated into the community, while in another sense this completed initiation signifies only the first step in a life of spiritual progress.[49] The catechumenate, moreover, problematizes any easy binary of "in" or "out" of the Christian community because catechumens were simultaneously in and out, members of a Christian community while not fully initiated or integrated into their religious or liturgical practices. Some intellectual, practical, and social change had already taken place in order for a person to become a catechumen – a conversion – though these changes were not yet complete. Occasionally I refer to this as "initial conversion" to keep a more robust notion of conversion from fading entirely from view.

It is important to note here that the language of "institution" is used broadly to denote "any collectively accepted system of rules (procedures, practices) that enable us to create institutional facts…The creation of an institutional fact is, thus, the collective assignment of a status function."[50] That is to say, in the terms used above, the catechumenate as an "institutional fact" entails the collective acceptance of its practices as well as the recognition of its function within the community. The roles, status, and responsibilities of those involved are also fundamental parts of this social arrangement.[51] In the case of the catechumenate, the terminology

---

Religious Conversion (New Haven: Yale University Press, 1993) who emphasizes the malleable quality of "religious conversion" across times and religious groups.

[49] See also the brief discussion of various related conversion terminologies in Niederhofer, *Konversion*, pp. 8–12. The notion of an ongoing need for spiritual progress is explored in more detail in relation to Clement, Origen, and John Chrysostom, in their respective chapters below.

[50] John R. Searle, "What is an institution?," *Journal of Institutional Economics* 1, no. 1 (2005), 21–22.

[51] The language of "social arrangement" echoes the account of "institutions" provided by Gert Melville and Shmuel Eisenstadt (see the discussion in Markschies, *Christian Theology*, pp. 20–29, esp. pp. 23–24). The language of "social arrangement" is at least partially formulated to avoid the implication that institutions must be formally or legally ratified in order to count as such.

by which it is discussed develops over time and varies between writers. As early as Clement of Alexandria, discussions of the catechumenate orbit closely around the Greek κατηχέω and cognates, though catechesis is not uniquely nor exclusively connected with such terminology. Identifying references to the catechumenate therefore requires further considerations of the ritual, liturgical, and exegetical contexts of such terminology. To that end, each writer's vocabulary is investigated within its specific historical and institutional contexts.[52]

1.3 ABOUT THE PRESENT STUDY

These shifts – away from passing judgment on early readers and toward a recognition of the hermeneutical significance of Pauline reception and Pauline images – have proven important for the present study. The image of Paul as a catechist, which links him with early Christian institutions and practices surrounding initiation, supplies the unifying thread linking writings from the *Acts of Paul* to the Euthalian Apparatus. Further, these texts are not examined for their fidelity to some reconstructed Pauline figure, but rather for the way in which they draw on Pauline resources in their presentation of the Apostle and in response to their own historical needs. Put in concrete terms, it is not a question of whether the *Consitutiones apostolorum* got Paul "right" when the compiler depicted him presenting the canons on the catechumenate. Rather, it is a question of understanding *why* Paul is depicted in that way, including the textual and institutional resources that undergird that image.

The first task is to trace the development of the catechumenate, which is the purpose of Chapter 2. The debates surrounding the origin of the catechumenate require that I provide the framework of its historical development before attempting to situate the reception of Paul within it. As noted, it is at the end of the second century and beginning of the third that the various practices and concerns associated with Christian initiation coalesce into to a recognizable institutional shape. Consequently it is there that we find the first evidence for the connection between Paul

---

[52] Notably, by the time one reaches Tertullian at the turn of the third century, the Greek terminology was already being taken into Latin and, shortly thereafter, into Coptic, as technical language referring to catechetical instruction and practices; further discussion of specific works is in Chapter 2 below.

and the catechumenate and so it provides the starting point for the investigation of Pauline interpretation that follows.

Chapters 3–6 trace the link between Paul and the catechumenate from the late second century through the end of the fourth century. Beginning with the *Acts of Paul*, I argue that already in that narrative format Paul's image is being shaped in light of the emerging catechetical practices. This comes out particularly clearly in Paul's interactions with Thecla, though it is also present in a variety of other subtle ways throughout the narrative. Chapter 4 turns to Clement of Alexandria to highlight the ways in which his image of Paul is cast in light of his larger pedagogical and catechetical goals. Paul's letters, furthermore, provide a crucial resource for the formulation of Clement's larger framework for the Christian life of spiritual growth. In the course of this discussion, Clement's treatment of Paul is situated in relation to his Valentinian and proto-orthodox interlocutors and their reading of the Pauline resources most important to the Alexandrian teacher. Following Clement, the study turns to Origen's catechetical presentation of Paul in Chapter 5. In addition to Origen's treatment of the catechumenate, we must come to terms with his homiletic and academic institutional contexts. Origen sees in Paul's ministry and letters a paradigm for his own work, establishing the place and function of catechetical instruction and its relation to further spiritual maturity and knowledge. Chapter 6 focuses on John Chrysostom, whose images of Paul serve a wide range of ends in his homiletical work. The focus of this investigation, however, is of course to illuminate the way in which Paul is cast as the paradigmatic arch-catechist, associated with even the most recent developments in the catechumenate of the late fourth century. Although Chrysostom provides the fullest example of Paul's image as catechist, there are other fourth-century writers who associate Paul and his letters with the catechumenate who are briefly discussed at the end of that chapter. This discussion, then, ends where the present chapter started, with a catechetical Paul who can plausibly be portrayed as delivering apostolic canons on initiation in the *Constitutiones apostolorum* and whose very textual corpus can be identified as fundamentally catechetical in the Euthalian Apparatus.

Focusing on the interpretive movements and concerns among these texts and authors gives the present argument a distinctive shape. The majority of work on Pauline reception since 1979 has concerned itself with the earliest stages of Pauline reception, from the so-called Deutero-Pauline letters and Acts up to Irenaeus and perhaps the *Acts of Paul*. It is within the context of these first two centuries that arguments for the impact of (social) memory on Pauline images, including Ben White's discussion of tradition, tend to function.[53] Daniel Marguerat's account of Pauline reception and his appeal to the ongoing significance of orally circulating memories or traditions is also described within that period, terminating with the *Acts of Paul*.[54] If we consider Marguerat's "poles" in relation to the texts covered here and in Chapters 3–6, however, it quickly becomes apparent that the modulation between them is less a matter of clarifying different streams of Pauline tradition than it is about understanding that different aspects of the Pauline profile are being woven together. In the majority of works to be examined, the biographical and doctoral poles are combined and reworked. In fact, even the documentary pole, which Marguerat reserves for the collection, copying, and reconfiguring of Paul's letters, is notably present in the composition of 3 Corinthians (later included in the *Acts of Paul*) or the reproduction of Paul's texts in homilies and commentaries, which bring in biographical and doctoral materials as well. The Euthalian Apparatus may well be the clearest combination of all three of Marguerat's poles, since it reproduces the Pauline text, configures it for catechetical and pedagogical purposes, and includes prefaces, *kephalaia*, and summaries, which draw on Paul's biography and doctrine, alongside the text.

When one moves beyond the reach of Marguerat's analysis of these "poles," however, the hermeneutical weight of Pauline images shifts somewhat. In an important sense, the author of the *Acts of Paul*, Clement, Origen, and John Chrysostom are in the same boat as modern interpreters: namely, forced to rely on the resources within Paul's textual corpus, including a broader emerging canonical profile, and their contemporary interpretive traditions to construct their images of Paul. As we shall see, they are particularly attentive to the contours and resources of Paul's letters and it is this fact that leads to the discussion in the final two chapters, where the bulk of the hermeneutical discussion is located.

In Chapter 7, I situate the early catechetical readings of Paul within the exegetical debates of contemporary scholarship. The chapter begins with

---

[53] Of course, unlike memory, White's discussion of tradition has the potential to reach well beyond the scope of genuine (or plausible) appeals to memory, as in the influential work of H.-G. Gadamer, to which I will return in Chapter 8; see White, *Remembering Paul*, pp. 70–79 and *passim*.

[54] Marguerat, "Paul after Paul," pp. 1–21. Although he does not engage with him, Marguerat's historical framing is reminiscent of Bockmuehl's account of "living memory," extending to Irenaeus; see Markus N. A. Bockmuehl, *Seeing the Word: Refocusing New Testament Study* (Grand Rapids: Baker Academic, 2006), pp. 161–188. Notably, Kirk, *Departure*, has argued that the *Acts of Paul* demonstrate a striking lack of genuine Pauline memory in relation to the narrative of Paul's death.

a summary of the previous material designed to draw the various threads together and illuminate not only the image of Paul the catechist, but also the Pauline texts that repeatedly supply the foundation for that image and further aspects of his profile that it entails.[55] I then turn to these Pauline passages and situate the early readings within contemporary exegetical discourse. This highlights the ongoing value of engaging with ancient interpreters. The relation of the broader catechetical image of Paul is then brought into juxtaposition with contemporary images of Paul, particularly represented by the image of a confrontational and independent Paul prevalent today. This image, I argue, can be traced with particular clarity back to F. C. Baur, and then to the debate between Luther and Erasmus. It is there that we see the now familiar confrontational Paul deliberately contrasted with the ecclesiological and pedagogical image of Paul that is so closely associated with early catechetical presentations of the Apostle.

The final chapter closes the study with more general hermeneutical reflections arising from the historical work in Chapters 3–6 and the juxtaposition of old and new in Chapter 7. Rather than offering a fully articulated hermeneutical account of interpretation, the goal of the chapter is to expand the above comments into a proposed framework within which historical and contemporary readings can be mutually informative, even when separated on historical, traditional, or philosophical terms. Readings emerge as iterations of Pauline interpretation, actualizations of textual potentialities. Any particular reading, then, embodies possible, but not necessary, configurations of Pauline resources, illuminating the contours of the texts in question. Such a perspective helps to frame our understanding of contemporary Pauline studies as one further aspect of Pauline reception, as we try to catch sight of the scholarly field in its historical contingency. This (admittedly) highly compressed formulation will be expanded in the Conclusion.

In terms of the questions that began this chapter, the bulk of the present argument is devoted to ascertaining "what happened" when early readers of Paul interpreted his letters in the context of early Christian initiation. It is to this task that I turn now, beginning with the difficult question of the origin and development of the catechumenate.

---

[55] The repetition here is also for those readers who are most interested in the hermeneutical argument of the present volume in Chapters 1, 7–8 and who are therefore inclined to skip or only skim the detailed arguments in Chapters 3–6.

2

Catechesis and the Catechumenate:
A Historical Sketch

> The history of patristic catechesis remains to be written. This is a simple outline. Its goal is to introduce readers to a field of exceptional richness and demonstrate its interest.[1]

This chapter aims to provide a rough account of the development of the catechumenate – in the above words of Cardinal Daniélou, a "simple outline." Although some of this material will be revisited and expanded in subsequent chapters, the present sketch provides a broad framework within which the authors discussed later can be situated. Gathering this material in a single narrative of development, moreover, helps to illuminate certain trends, convergences of practices or concerns, that arise through time and between locales. The argument as a whole, then, is strengthened by the cumulative weight of the various authors who bear witness to the development of the catechumenate. Even with evidence of some broad similarities, though, each writer examined in Chapters 3–6 frames the catechumenate in terms of their own particular concerns and theological or ecclesiological views – from concerns about moral fortitude and endurance to broader pedagogical visions of spiritual growth or attaining divine virtues.

If the present sketch is "simple" in one sense, the complexity of the sources and historical ambiguities is much less so. It is not possible, as some used to think, to argue for a common catechetical form reaching

---

[1] Jean Daniélou and Régine du Charlat, *La catéchèse aux premiers siècles*, École de la foi (Paris: Fayard-Mame, 1968), p. 11: "L'histoire de la catéchèse patristique reste à écrire. Il s'agit ici d'une simple ébauche. Elle a pour but d'introduire à un domaine d'une exceptionnelle richesse et d'en montrer l'intérêt."

back to the New Testament and extending in more or less unbroken form into the fourth century.[2] More recent critical assessments have tended to push texts that bear witness to a formal catechumenate later, as in the case of the *Traditio apostolica*, which has been severed from its Hippolytan connection, thereby removing a crucial support for much earlier work.[3] What follows will, I hope, supply a critically plausible account of the catechumenate that is able to engage the various scholarly debates, without requiring their resolution in every instance.

As noted in Chapter 1, when I speak of the development of the "catechumenate," I mean the process whereby a vague liminal penumbra around the early Christian communities became an institutional fact, with recognized rules, roles, and expectations.[4] The term "catechesis" (and cognates) began to refer to the instruction of those inhabiting this liminal space in the late second century but it was not clearly and widely used as a technical term until the fourth century, and even then some flexibility and variety remained.[5] The practices that would come to define the catechumenate – enrollment, moral examination, instruction, fasting, etc. – were variously practiced in relation to Christian initiation throughout the second century. In due course, I will describe this in terms of "emerging" catechetical practices which begin to converge

---

[2] Such is the impression supplied by standard surveys of the material in Daniélou and du Charlat, *La catéchèse*; Michel Dujarier, *A History of the Catechumenate: The First Six Centuries*, trans. Edward J. Haasl (New York: Sadlier, 1979); and still, in a subtle way, even in Paul L. Gavrilyuk, *Histoire du catéchuménat dans l'Église ancienne*, trans. Françoise Lhoest, Nina Mojaïsky, and Anne-Marie Gueit, Initiations aux pères de l'église (Paris: Cerf, 2007). See further below, pp. 22–25 on the New Testament material.

[3] Christoph Markschies, "Wer schrieb die sogenannte *Traditio apostolica*? Neue Beobachtungen und Hypothesen zu einer kaum lösbaren Frage aus der altkirchlichen Literaturgeschichte," in Wolfram Kinzig, Christoph Markschies, and Markus Vinzent (eds.), *Tauffragen und Bekenntnis. Studien zur sogenannten "Traditio apostolica," zu den "Interrogationes de fide" und zum "Römischen Glaubensbekenntnis"*, AKG 74 (Berlin and New York: De Gruyter, 1998), pp. 1–74; Maxwell E. Johnson, *The Rites of Christian Initiation: Their Evolution and Interpretation*, rev. and expanded edn (Collegeville, MN: Liturgical Press, 2007). See also the further discussion below, pp. 44–48.

[4] The language of "institutional fact" is drawn from Searle, "Institution," pp. 1–22. See further in Chapter 1.2.2 above. Questions about the early shape of this "liminal penumbra," its relation to the debated category of "God fearers," etc. cannot be broached here. For an exploration of some proposed analogues to the catechumenate in Greek, Roman, and Jewish sources, see Benjamin A. Edsall, "Clement and the catechumenate in the late second century," in Lewis O. Ayres and Clifton Ward (eds.), *Rise of the Christian Intellectual*, AZK (Berlin: De Gruyter, forthcoming).

[5] Note the flexibility of this terminology in, e.g., John Chrysostom's exegesis of 1 Cor. 1:17 (*Hom. in 1 Cor.* 3.3). See further in Chapter 6.1.2 below and see also Lampe *s.v.* κατηχέω.

into a widely recognizable form toward the end of the second century, flourishing in both East and West in the fourth and fifth centuries.

For the present survey, with the language of "catechesis" and associated catechetical practices I refer to instruction specifically associated with the preparation for baptism and the Christian life. According to this view, the majority of catechesis occurs between conversion and baptism, though some basic instruction often continued briefly for the recently baptized neophytes.[6] In this way catechesis is, properly speaking, *peri*-baptismal, rather than (restrictively) *pre*-baptismal, even if the latter does often capture its main feature. On the other hand, for the writers surveyed in this study, baptism marked the end of one's liminal status as a catechumen in a decisive way.[7] As for the content of catechesis, as far as we are able to discern, it overlaps substantially with evangelistic proclamation and homiletic exhortation, though directed toward different ends. A defining feature is that it commences *after* one has already expressed belief or interest in joining a Christian community and is oriented toward baptism.

The sketch here will begin with the New Testament materials which, despite the absence of any clear catechetical pattern, nevertheless provide important vocabulary and imagery for later discussions of catechesis. I then turn to the emerging and converging catechetical practices of the second century up to Irenaeus ("A Quiet Beginning") before turning to the appearance of the catechumenate in fuller form in the late second century ("A Burst of Activity"). The discussion closes with an overview of the catechetical institutions in the fourth century, when preachers like John Chrysostom faced a new phenomenon: a church full of catechumens.

2.1 (NO) CATECHESIS IN THE NEW TESTAMENT

Despite the erudite efforts of scholarship in the early twentieth century, particularly in the works of Alfred Seeberg, Philip Carrington, and Edward Selwyn, attempts to discover a catechetical framework underlying the

---

[6] See also the comments on "conversion" on pp. 14–15 above.

[7] This view continued into the seventh century, as evidenced by Isidore of Seville, noted in Gavrilyuk, *Histoire*, p. 22. Isidore writes, "'Catechumen' is applied to the one who as yet listens to the doctrine of faith and has not yet received baptism." ('Catechumenus' dictus pro eo, quod adhuc doctrinam fidei audit, necdum tamen baptismum recepit; *Etym.* 7.14.7–8, in Wallace Martin Lindsay (ed.), *Isidori Hispalensis episcopi Etymologiarum sive Originvm libri XX*, vol. 1 (Oxford: Clarendon, 1911).) He also goes on to distinguish between a catechumen as *auditor* and as *conpetens*, a distinction that came into practice in the third and fourth centuries (see below, pp. 61–62).

New Testament texts have largely failed to convince.[8] While it is certainly true that instruction of various sorts was important for the establishment and spread of the early Church, there is no clear evidence for a liminal phase of community membership between conversion and baptism.[9] What evidence there is points in a different direction.

According to the book of Acts, baptism normally followed immediately upon conversion. In Acts 2, Peter's harangue of the gathered Pentecost crowd results in the apparently immediate baptism of several thousand people (Acts 2:41). There is no space for liminal membership, instruction or moral examination; devotion to the apostles' teaching occurs here *after* baptism (v. 42).[10] Similarly, after a brief conversation with an Ethiopian eunuch, Philip grants his request for baptism (8:26–39).[11] Perhaps even more telling is the baptism of Simon Magus. He is impressed by Philip's preaching and general presence, believes, and is baptized in evidently short order (8:9–13). When Peter and John travel north to mediate the Holy Spirit to the new converts in Antioch, Simon falls afoul of the apostles and evidently is excluded from the community owing to his being "bitter bile" and "enchained to injustice" (εἰς γὰρ χολὴν πικρίας καὶ σύνδεσμον ἀδικίας ὁρῶ σε ὄντα; 8:23). There was evidently no space for a vetting of Simon's "intention" (ἐπίνοια, v. 22) prior to baptism. Other parts of the narrative confirm this general pattern.

---

[8] Alfred Seeberg, *Der Katechismus der Urchristenheit* (Leipzig: Deichert, 1903); Alfred Seeberg, *Die Didache des Judentums und der Urchristenheit* (Leipzig: Deichert, 1908); Philip Carrington, *The Primitive Christian Catechism: A Study in the Epistles* (Cambridge: Cambridge University Press, 1940); Edward Gordon Selwyn, *The First Epistle of St. Peter: The Greek Text with Introduction, Notes and Essays* (London: Macmillan and Co., 1958). On these and other attempts, see Benjamin A. Edsall, "*Kerygma*, catechesis and other things we used to find: twentieth-century research on early Christian teaching since Alfred Seeberg (1903)," *Currents in Biblical Research* 10, no. 3 (2012), 410–441.

[9] For a recent account of early Christian teaching, see Benjamin A. Edsall, *Paul's Witness to Formative Early Christian Instruction*, WUNT II/365 (Tübingen: Mohr Siebeck, 2014). Ulrich Neymeyr, *Die christlichen Lehrer im zweiten Jahrhundert. Ihre Lehrtätigkeit, ihr Selbstverständnis und ihre Geschichte*, VC Sup 4 (Leiden: Brill, 1989), p. 1, states the obvious well: "Da Jesus Christus das Christentum als Lehrer vermittelt hatte, machten es sich die frühen Christen zur Aufgabe, das Christentum ebenfalls zu lehren, sie wurden selbst zu Lehrern des Christentums." See also Gavrilyuk, *Histoire*, pp. 21–22.

[10] The use of this and other Acts material as precedent for later Valentinian catechetical practice by Bas van Os, "Baptism in the bridal chamber: the Gospel of Philip as a Valentinian baptismal instruction," unpublished Ph.D. thesis, Groningen (2007), 24–25 is therefore problematic. Gavrilyuk, *Histoire*, pp. 32–33, is similarly problematic, though he notes on p. 31 the looseness of his language here.

[11] The apparent irregularity of this baptismal practice in view of later expectations is picked up as early as Irenaeus *Haer.* 4.23.2; see the *Excursus* in Chapter 4 below.

Notably, there is no material elsewhere in other New Testament texts to challenge the portrayal in Acts. Pauline passages such as 1 Corinthians 3:1–2 and Romans 6:17, though, do suggest a progression in teaching despite a lack of other indications of institutionalized liminality or specific peri-baptismal roles and responsibilities.[12] Indeed, as Paul notes in 1 Corinthians 3, the Corinthians are *still* not ready for solid food despite their baptism sometime before and their demonstration of spiritual gifts. Nevertheless, the images of foundational teaching and a progressive maturation become important for later catechetical discussions, particularly for Clement and Origen. Hebrews 6:1–2 perhaps suggests the closest analogue for later developing catechetical practice. It speaks of a "beginning discourse about Christ" (ὁ τῆς ἀρχῆς τοῦ Χριστοῦ λόγος) that includes repentance, faith, baptism, and laying-on of hands along with eschatological resurrection and judgment.[13] And yet, although these elements reappear later in specifically catechetical contexts,[14] such a brief summary hardly presents a clear picture of the process of initiation. There is no indication of a period of instruction or moral evaluation (formalized or otherwise) which takes place after "faith in God" and in preparation for "baptisms."[15] As Paul Gavrilyuk notes in relation to the New Testament evidence as a whole, "If we were to define the catechumenate for this chapter only as instruction prior to baptism, we would find that in the

---

[12] These passages were favorites in earlier form-critical approaches to this issue: see Seeberg, *Der Katechismus*, pp. 1–5; Seeberg, *Didache*, p. 5.

[13] Heb. 6:1–2: "Therefore, leaving the introductory discourse about Christ, let us press on to the most perfect, not laying the foundation again: repentance from dead works, faith upon God, teaching of baptism, laying-on of hands, resurrection of the dead and eternal judgment."

[14] It is interesting to note, however, that a late date for Hebrews could well put it near some other evidence to be considered below. On the vexing issues of the date and provenance of Hebrews, see Dunn, *Neither Jew nor Greek*, pp. 91–96 (with earlier bibliography there), who dates it to around 86 CE. The various historical contexts for Hebrews – Jewish, Roman, and Christian (in addition to spatial contexts) – are explored in Gabriella Gelardini and Harold W. Attridge (eds.), *Hebrews in Contexts*, AJEC 91 (Leiden: Brill, 2016); the contributions on the Roman imperial context by Rüpke and Maier agree on a Flavian connection, c. 69–96 CE.

[15] The plural βαπτισμῶν in v. 2 is difficult. In Hebrews, the singular βαπτισμός never occurs, though the plural is used again in Heb. 9:10 in reference to the symbolic value of ritual washings in the Law (cf. Mark 7.4). Elsewhere in the New Testament and Apostolic Fathers, the term is only ever used in the singular. Although it might seem reasonable for "teaching of baptisms" to precede baptism itself, this was demonstrably not the case for some even in the fourth century (as in Cyril of Jerusalem's *Mystagogical Catechesis* – see further below, pp. 63–64); in the absence of any further specification as to the contents of this teaching, it is difficult to be sure when it might have occurred.

New Testament canon one rarely speaks of it."[16] In fact, if one takes note of the institutional element implicit in the concept of the "catechumenate," one in which initial liminal community status has become formalized and recognized as an institutional fact, one cannot properly speak of the catechumenate at all.[17] It is not until the second century that we gain sight of the practices that would become the catechumenate.

2.2 A QUIET BEGINNING: THE SECOND CENTURY

2.2.1 *Didache* (Syria)

Probably somewhere in the Roman east, perhaps in Syria, an unknown author compiled a document shortly after the turn of the second century that probably constitutes the oldest of the "church orders" – the *Didache*.[18] This manual begins with ethical instruction covering the "two

---

[16] Gavrilyuk, *Histoire*, p. 31: "Si pour définir le catéchuménat nous avions pris dans ce chapitre le seul enseignement précédant le baptême, nous aurions alors découvert que, dans le canon néotestamentaire, on en parle rarement." In including the New Testament as a witness to the catechumenate, Gavrilyuk follows a practice that reaches back at least to Heinrich Julius Holtzmann, "Die Katechese der alten Kirche," in *Theologische Abhandlungen. Carl von Weizsäcker zu seinem siebzigsten Geburtstag gewidmet* (Freiburg: Mohr, 1892), pp. 62–66, and includes Seeberg, *Der Katechismus*; Daniélou and du Charlat, *La catéchèse*; and Dujarier, *Catechumenate*. Victor Saxer, *Les rites de l'initiation chrétienne du IIe au VIe siècle. Esquisse historique et signification d'après leurs principaux témoins*, Centro italiano di studi sull'alto Medioevo 7 (Spoleto: Centro italiano di studi sull'alto Medioevo, 1988), is a notable exception to this trend, and note the criticism of this in A. Turck, "Aux origines du catéchuménat," *Revue des sciences philosophiques et théologiques* 48 (1964), 21–22.

[17] See Turck, "Aux origines," p. 27: "Quand on parle de catéchuménat, il faut entendre une institution bien précise: institution d'Église, qui vise à préparer au baptême en commun ceux que, justement, l'on appelle catéchumènes, tout d'abord par un enseignement structuré appelé catéchèse, mais aussi par tout un ensemble de disciplines et de rites."

[18] The date and provenance of the *Didache* are normally reconstructed on the basis of its relationship with other early Jewish and Christian paraenesis (e.g., the "two ways" material in 1QS 4, Matthew, *Ep. Barnabas*; see John S. Kloppenborg, "*Didache* 1.1–6.1, James, Matthew, and the Torah," in Andrew F. Gregory and Christopher M. Tuckett (eds.), *Trajectories through the New Testament and the Apostolic Fathers* (Oxford: Oxford University Press, 2007), pp. 193–221) and later "church orders" such as the *Didascalia apostolorum* and the *Constitutiones apostolorum* (see Bradshaw, *Search*, pp. 73–97). These issues cannot be sorted out here. Suffice it to say that I find Tuckett's arguments for dependence on Matthew persuasive (Christopher M. Tuckett, "The *Didache* and the Synoptics once more: a response to Aaron Milavec," *Journal of Early Christian Studies* 13, no. 4 (2005), 509–518), effectively putting it around the turn of the second century. The notable alternative to this is treating the *Didache* as independent but contemporary with the production of Matthew; see Clayton N. Jefford, "Social locators as a bridge between the *Didache* and Matthew," in Gregory and Tuckett (eds.), *Trajectories*,

ways" (*Did.* 1–6), followed by a discussion of baptism (7), fasts and prayer (8), the eucharist (9–10, 14), teachers, prophets, and travelers (11–13), bishops and deacons (15), and an eschatological coda (16). What is important here is *Didache 7*.

> Now concerning baptism, baptize in this way: after declaring all these things, baptize in the name of the Father and the Son and the Holy Spirit in living water... Before baptism, let the baptizer and the baptizand fast along with any others who are able. But command the baptizand to fast for one or two days.[19]

While many scholars see clear catechetical teaching in the *Didache*, especially in the "two ways" material of *Didache* 1–6,[20] the text as a whole is much more complex. In the first place, as Jonathan Draper notes, "catechesis would have been delivered orally by a teacher," such that the material in *Didache* 1–6 is more easily described in terms of an *aide-mémoire* for the leader.[21] Furthermore, this leader is specifically addressed by the imperatives in 7:1–4: "baptize," "let the baptizer fast," and "command."

---

pp. 245–264. Keeping it relatively early is the discussion of wandering prophets in *Did.* 11–13, but note that Neymeyr, *Die christlichen Lehrer*, pp. 141–149, shows the practice of wandering teachers to continue into the middle of the third century. On its paraenetic similarities with *Barnabas* and Jewish paraenesis like that in 1QS 4, see Jean-Paul Audet, "Literary and Doctrinal Relationships of the 'Manual of Discipline'," in *The Didache in Modern Research*, trans. Jonathan A. Draper, AGJU 37 (Leiden: Brill, 1996), pp. 129–147; and Huub van de Sandt, "Baptism and holiness: two requirements authorizing participation in the *Didache's* eucharist," in Jonathan A. Draper and Clayton N. Jefford (eds.), *The Didache: A Missing Piece of the Puzzle in Early Christianity* (Atlanta: SBL, 2015), pp. 151–153.

[19] *Did.* 7:1, 4 (in Bart D. Ehrman (ed.), *The Apostolic Fathers*, LCL 24–25 (Cambridge, MA: Harvard University Press, 2003)): Περὶ δὲ τοῦ βαπτίσματος, οὕτω βαπτίσατε· ταῦτα πάντα προειπόντες, βαπτίσατε εἰς τὸ ὄνομα τοῦ πατρὸς καὶ τοῦ υἱοῦ καὶ τοῦ ἁγίου πνεύματος ἐν ὕδατι ζῶντι...πρὸ δὲ τοῦ βαπτίσματος προνηστευσάτω ὁ βαπτίζων καὶ ὁ βαπτιζόμενος καὶ εἴ τινες ἄλλοι δύνανται· κελεύεις δὲ νηστεῦσαι τὸν βαπτιζόμενον πρὸ μιᾶς ἢ δύο. Note that CA 7.22 lacks the phrase ταῦτα πάντα προειπόντες, which Audet takes to mean that it was not originally part of the *Didache*: Jean-Paul Audet, *La Didachè: Instructions des Apôtres*, Études Bibliques (Paris: Gabalda, 1958), *ad loc.*). See further below, p. 27.

[20] E.g., Dietmar Wyrwa, "Religiöses Lernen im zweiten Jahrhundert und die Anfänge der alexandrinischen Katechetenschule," in Beate Ego and Helmut Merkel (eds.), *Religiöses Lernen in der biblischen, frühjüdischen und frühchristlichen Überlieferung*, WUNT 1/180 (Tübingen: Mohr Siebeck, 2005), p. 273. The bibliography on the "two ways" material is enormous; see Huub van de Sandt and David Flusser, *The Didache: Its Jewish Sources and Its Place in Early Judaism and Christianity*, CRINT 3:5 (Assen: Royal Van Gorcum; Minneapolis: Fortress Press, 2002), for a starting point.

[21] See Jonathan A. Draper, "Vice catalogues as oral-mnemonic cues: a comparative study of the two ways tradition in the *Didache* and parallels from the perspective of oral tradition," in Tom Thatcher (ed.), *Jesus, the Voice, and the Text: Beyond The Oral and the Written Gospel* (Waco, TX: Baylor University Press, 2008), p. 112. If Draper is correct about this, then it has potentially wide-ranging significance for determining the date and

But does *Didache* 7 signify that the preceding chapters constitute catechesis? On the one hand, a pre-baptismal emphasis on ethical teaching is certainly in keeping with other developments discussed below.[22] On the other hand, if Draper is right that the *Didache* serves primarily as a reminder for an already knowledgeable reader, then "these things" need not be restricted to literary reference points and may refer rather to pre-baptismal declarations by the priest and believer (note the plural προειπόντες) rather than to *Didache* 1–6. Later appropriations of the *Didache* in "church order" documents like the *Constitutiones apostolorum* (7.22) do not preserve this link between baptism and the "two ways" material. In the context of the single *Didache* manuscript (Codex Hierosolymitanus), the phrase "after declaring all these things" is the only textual element that would identify such teaching as specifically associated with baptism.[23] We should be cautious, therefore, in associating the *Didache* and the catechumenate. Undoubtedly, it is *de facto* associated with emerging catechetical practices, at least insofar as it is concerned with pre-baptismal preparation by fasting, another often-recurring feature. But, aside from the two days of fasting, there is no indication of a formal liminal space between conversion and baptism or how long such a period of baptismal preparation might be. For our purposes, then, *Didache* 7 is at best *suggestive* of an early development related to liminal community membership in which one is instructed (in ethical matters?) prior to being baptized.

2.2.2 *Shepherd of Hermas* (Rome)

In Rome in the middle of the second century, perhaps at around the same time that the *Didache* was being compiled, another hint of developing

---

provenance of the text, which he does not himself draw out. Can one expect an *aide-mémoire* to contain theological or ritual developments when the "performance" of it will be carried out by a knowledgeable teacher? Criteria for measuring "primitivity" would need to be drastically reevaluated and the geographical and temporal range would need to be expanded. See also Bradshaw's comments that church order documents are best conceived as "living documents": Bradshaw, *Search*, pp. 91–92; and see p. 45 below.

[22] So Eugene Paul, *Geschichte der christlichen Erziehung*, vol. 1: *Antike und Mittelalter* (Freiburg: Herder, 1993), p. 43; see also Van de Sandt, "Baptism and holiness," pp. 151–156, who emphasizes the evident ethical importance of moral purity as a baptismal prerequisite in the *Didache*.

[23] See the comments in Christopher M. Tuckett, "The *Didache* and the writings that later formed the New Testament," in Andrew F. Gregory and Christopher M. Tuckett (eds.), *The Reception of the New Testament in the Apostolic Fathers* (Oxford: Oxford University Press, 2005), pp. 83–86, regarding matters of word-order preservation and the implications of treating the *Didache* as a composite document.

catechetical practices emerges in the *Shepherd of Hermas*.[24] Hermas'
third vision is a famously elaborate metaphor in which he sees a building
being constructed on water from various types of stone (*Vis.* 3.2).[25]
The building is, of course, the Church and the stones are explained as
corresponding to different groups of people (3.3–7). The stones used
are brought up from the water to be fitted in the tower. One group,
described at the very end of the vision, are those "falling near the water
and not able to roll into the water, although wanting to roll and enter the
water."[26] These stones are later identified as "those who hear the word
and desire to be baptized in the name of the Lord. Then, when the true
purity is mentioned to them, they change their mind and go back after
their wicked desires."[27] These stones, then, represent people who have
made a decision in favor of Christianity, who have already converted in
the sense described earlier, before being fully instructed or baptized.[28]
During this initial period between conversion and baptism, those desiring
to be baptized are made aware of the requirements of "true purity," a
phrase likely including sexual purity though not exhausted by it.[29] This

---

[24] The date of the *Shepherd of Hermas* is difficult to establish and is related to one's evaluation of the Muratorian fragment, which extends beyond the scope of the present inquiry.
Several scholars place it around the middle of the second century, with varying ranges
on either side (e.g. Saxer, *Les rites*, p. 49; Neymeyr, *Die christlichen Lehrer*, p. 9), though
Carolyn Osiek, *Shepherd of Hermas: A Commentary*, Hermeneia (Minneapolis: Fortress
Press, 1999), p. 20, concludes her discussion by arguing for "an expanded duration of
time beginning perhaps from the very last years of the first century through most of the
first half of the second century." See also the comments in Norbert Brox, *Der Hirt des
Hermas. Übersetzt und erklärt*, KAV 17 (Göttingen: Vandenhoeck & Ruprecht, 1991),
pp. 22–25.

[25] This is perhaps related to the building imagery in 1 Cor. 3:9–15, which is picked up
enthusiastically by Origen in his homilies on Joshua. The text and numbering used here
is according to Ehrman, *The Apostolic Fathers*.

[26] *Vis.* 3.2: ἑτέρους δὲ πίπτοντας ἐγγὺς ὑδάτων καὶ μὴ δυναμένους κυλισθῆναι εἰς τὸ ὕδωρ,
καίπερ θελόντων κυλισθῆναι καὶ ἐλθεῖν εἰς τὸ ὕδωρ.

[27] *Vis.* 3.7: οὗτοί εἰσιν οἱ τὸν λόγον ἀκούσαντες καὶ θέλοντες βαπτισθῆναι εἰς τὸ ὄνομα τοῦ
κυρίου· εἶτα ὅταν αὐτοῖς ἔλθῃ εἰς μνείαν ἡ ἁγνότης τῆς ἀληθείας, μετανοοῦσιν καὶ πορεύονται
πάλιν ὀπίσω τῶν ἐπιθυμιῶν αὐτῶν τῶν πονηρῶν. See also the discussion in Osiek, *Shepherd*,
p. 74; Saxer, *Les rites*, pp. 51–52. Brox, *Der Hirt*, p. 137, refers to this group specifically
as "Katechumenen."

[28] See the discussion of conversion terminology, pp. 14–15 and n. 48.

[29] Note that in *Sim.* 9, where this vision is recast, it is explicitly *virgins* who are in charge
of building the tower, and rejected stones are those "seduced by women" (ἀνεπείσθησαν
ὑπὸ τῶν γυναικῶν; *Sim.* 9.13). Elsewhere in Hermas, similar terminology refers to purity
from unspecified sins (ἁγνεία, *Mand.* 4.3; *Sim.* 5.6 also with ἁγνῶς) and purity in carrying
out ministries (ἁγνῶς, *Vis.* 3.5; *Sim.* 9.25–27). In *Sim.* 9.16, the issue of ἁγνεία comes up
again, but in connection with those who died in "purity" before the coming of Jesus.
This terminology should be taken also in the context of concern for sexual sin in *Vis.*
1.1, in addition to the concern in early Christianity more widely. LSJ *s.v.* ἁγνεία, ἁγνός,

requirement is too much for the candidates and they do not carry through their initial intention.[30] It would seem that this group of people was large enough to warrant mention in the vision, but their formal relationship to the church is not clarified.[31] Victor Saxer is correct, then, to say that the *Shepherd of Hermas* is "silent regarding the catechumenate" insofar as the term designates a formalized institutional fact.[32] What does come briefly into view, however, is a hint of pre-baptismal moral instruction that takes place between "hearing the word" and baptism. So the outlines of liminal community membership become visible in Syria and Rome.

2.2.3 Justin Martyr (Rome)

In the middle of the second century, the philosopher Justin was teaching and writing in Rome.[33] Emerging catechetical concerns and practices noted in the *Didache* and Hermas are also present in Justin's writings, though a clear view of a formalized catechumenate does not yet emerge from his work.

In the first place, we are told in the *Acta Iustini* that Justin taught above the baths of Myrtius during his time in Rome and that he taught the "true message" to anyone who was interested.[34] This was evidently a sort of

and ἀγνότης notes the often sexual undertone of the terms. Osiek, *Shepherd*, p. 74, notes that "'The purity of truth'…is obscure; it probably means the call to keep chastity (not celibacy) or at least moral integrity." This concern for pre-baptismal purity is related to the problem of post-baptismal repentance in Hermas, on which see recently Mark Grundeken, "Baptism and Μετάνοια in the *Shepherd of Hermas*," in Mark Grundeken and Joseph Verheyden (eds.), *Early Christian Communities between Ideal and Reality*, WUNT I/342 (Tübingen: Mohr Siebeck, 2015), pp. 127–142, and see further below, pp. 88–89, in relation to the *Acts of Paul*.

[30] Brox, *Der Hirt*, p. 547, among others, notes the emphasis on moral aspects of baptismal preparation in Hermas.

[31] Brox, *Der Hirt*, pp. 137–138, argues that this group was a reality for the author, whose presentation is rooted in the actual ritual practices surrounding baptism. See also Wyrwa, "Religiöses Lernen," p. 274, who notes the role of teachers in baptismal preparation, but does not discuss the passage in question here.

[32] Saxer, *Les rites*, p. 55: "Pour conclure, on retiendra que le *Pasteur* d'Hermas est muet sur le catéchuménat.…"

[33] While Justin's *Dialogue* is associated with Ephesus by Eusebius (*Hist. ecct.* 4.18.6), Neymeyr rightly notes that "die Lehrtätigkeit Justins in Rom am besten bezeugt ist"; Neymeyr, *Die christlichen Lehrer*, p. 16.

[34] *Acta Iust.* 3.3: Ἰουστῖνος εἶπεν· Ἐγὼ ἐπάνω μένω τοῦ Μυρτίνου βαλανείου παρὰ πάντα τὸν χρόνον ὃν ἐπεδήμησα τὸ δεύτερον τῇ Ῥωμαίων πόλει· οὐ γινώσκω δὲ ἄλλην τινὰ συνέλευσιν εἰ μὴ τὴν ἐκεῖ. καὶ εἴ τις ἐβούλετο ἀφικνεῖσθαι παρ' ἐμοί, ἐκοινώνουν αὐτῷ τῶν τῆς ἀληθείας λόγων; text in Herbert Musurillo, *The Acts of the Christian Martyrs: Introduction, Texts and Translations*, OECT (Oxford: Clarendon, 1972), pp. 42–60. On the location of

independent philosophical school after the manner of other self-appointed free teachers.[35] If the report in the *Acta* is accurate, of the six students questioned by Rusticus alongside Justin, three were already Christians before coming to listen to Justin's teaching.[36] Ulrich Neymeyr takes the silence of the others to indicate that Justin had converted them,[37] but, whether or not this is the case, Justin's school itself was evidently not focused on Christian initiation. All of those questioned with Justin were Christians who continued to come and hear his lectures. Irenaeus tells us that Tatian was a "hearer" (ἀκροατής) of Justin (*Haer.* 1.28.1), though it is not clear whether he means that Justin converted Tatian, using "hearer" in its later technical sense, or whether he was using the term in the generic sense to denote a regular philosophical audience member.[38] Justin's own teaching activities, then, do not appear particularly concerned with Christian initiation, despite their explicitly Christian motivation and content.[39]

Justin's school, note the detailed argument in Harlow Gregory Snyder, "'Above the Bath of Myrtinus': Justin Martyr's 'school' in the city of Rome," *Harvard Theological Review* 100, no. 3 (2007), 335–362, and the continued skepticism of such specificity in Tobias Georges, "Justin's school in Rome: reflections on early Christian 'schools'," *Zeitschrift für Antikes Christentum* 16, no. 1 (2012), 79.

[35] For arguments that Justin's school was analogous to other philosophical schools, see the recent discussions in Jörg Ulrich, "What do we know about Justin's 'school' in Rome?," *Zeitschrift für Antikes Christentum* 16, no. 1 (2012), 62–74; Georges, "Justin's School," pp. 75–87; and Peter Gemeinhardt, "In search of Christian Paideia: education and conversion in early Christian biography," *Zeitschrift für Antikes Christentum* 16, no. 1 (2012), 88–98. See also Wyrwa, "Religiöses Lernen," p. 276; Markschies, *Christian Theology*, pp. 72–74; and Peter Lampe, *Christians at Rome in the First Two Centuries: From Paul to Valentinus*, ed. Marshall D. Johnson, trans. Michael Steinhauser (London: Continuum, 2003), pp. 276–279.

[36] *Acta Iust.* 4.5–8, in recensions A and B. Note, however, the hesitation about the usefulness of the *Acta Iustini* in Ulrich, "Justin's 'school'," p. 64.

[37] Neymeyr, *Die christlichen Lehrer*, p. 27. In contrast, Gemeinhardt, "In Search," pp. 88–98, claims that Justin's "pupils bluntly denied that Justin himself was responsible for their becoming Christians," which we have noted only applies strictly to three students.

[38] See Justin *Dial.* 2.4 (a "hearer" of a Pythagorean teacher; in Philippe Bobichon (ed.), *Justin Martyr, Dialogue avec Tryphon. Édition critique, traduction, commentaire*, 2 vols., Paradosis 47/1–2 (Fribourg: Éditions universitaires de Fribourg, 2003)); Diog. Laert. *Vitae* 8.46 (regarding Pythagorean pupils; in H. S. Long (ed.), *Diogenis Laertii vitae philosophorum*, 2 vols. (Oxford: Clarendon Press, 1964)); and Pseudo-Plutarch *Vitae* 840B (Aeschines as "hearer" of Isocrates and Plato; in J. Mau (ed.), *Plutarchi moralia*, vol. 5.2.1 (Leipzig: Teubner, 1971)) and 841B (Lycurgus as "hearer of Plato the philosopher"). See also the comments on Porphyry in Aaron P. Johnson, *Eusebius*, Understanding Classics (London: I. B. Taurus, 2014), p. 53. Tatian's references to Justin in his *Oratio* do not connect him with Tatian's conversion. Ulrich, "Justin's 'school'," p. 64, notes that such "terminology is anything but specific."

[39] Neymeyr, *Die christlichen Lehrer*, p. 29 (followed by Paul, *Geschichte*, p. 45), argues that Justin's school was private insofar as he "unterrichtete aus eigener Initiative" but

Nevertheless, in his famous discussion of early Christian conversion, Justin does reveal emerging catechetical practices. In *Apologia* 1.61.1–2, he states "as many as are persuaded and believe that what we teach and say is true, and promise to be able to live accordingly, are taught to pray and ask God while fasting for the forgiveness of previously committed sins, while we pray and fast with them."[40] After this prayer and fasting, the candidates are baptized (τὸ ἐν τῷ ὕδατι τότε λουτρὸν ποιοῦνται; 1.61.3), and considered to be "illuminated" when they have repented from their sins and have had the name of God pronounced over them (1.61.10–12). This rather compressed account provides a view of Christian initiation strikingly similar to that provide by Hermas. In the first place, there is a conversion that is followed by an intention to be baptized, which is to say, there is something more than intellectual assent. This persuasion also produces in the newly converted person the motivation to live in accordance with the new-found truth and so occasions further teaching, here concerning fasting, prayer, and repentance.[41] At this point, similarities with *Didache* 7 arise, insofar as fasting features as a baptismal prerequisite.

Even so, as noted earlier, while this passage bears witness to a variety of emerging catechetical practices, it still falls somewhat short of revealing an institutional catechumenate. Justin is describing conversion in general terms and does not himself clearly denote the liminal phase of the transition as a distinctive "step" formally recognized in the community. If his comments are suggestive, they are also too brief to say more

that he "stand dabei in lebendigem Kontakt zur Gemeinde der Christen in Rom"; see also the conclusion of Georges, "Justin's School," p. 80. This Roman Christian community extended beyond the practice of Justin in his philosophical school. I find this to be a more satisfactory depiction than that of Lampe, *Christians at Rome*, p. 376, who argues that Justin ran a philosophical school with a strong religious component but was not at all connected with other early Christian communities in Rome, because he does not even know about them. This leads Lampe to argue that Justin's "school" itself engaged in all the activities of evangelization, instruction, communal worship, eucharist, etc. without recourse to any larger community. To my mind this presses the notice in *Acta Iust.* 3.3 too far. There is room for some middle ground between Lampe's arguments and those for an early Roman monarchial episcopate; note the final "open questions" regarding the relationship of Justin's school with the larger ecclesial structures in Ulrich, "Justin's 'school'," pp. 72–73.

[40] *Apologia* 61.2: ὅσοι ἂν πεισθῶσι καὶ πιστεύωσιν ἀληθῆ ταῦτα τὰ ὑφ' ἡμῶν διδασκόμενα καὶ λεγόμενα εἶναι, καὶ βιοῦν οὕτως δύνασθαι ὑπισχνῶνται, εὔχεσθαί τε καὶ αἰτεῖν νηστεύοντες παρὰ τοῦ θεοῦ τῶν προημαρτημένων ἄφεσιν διδάσκονται, ἡμῶν συνευχομένων καὶ συννηστευόντων αὐτοῖς; text in Charles Munier (ed. and trans.), *Justin. Apologie pour les chrétiens. Introduction, texte critique, traduction et notes*, SC 507 (Paris: Cerf, 2006).

[41] See also Saxer, *Les rites*, pp. 57–58.

than that this stage is a passing moment in Justin's picture of the singular movement of initiation marked by the ritual of fasting.[42]

2.2.4 Irenaeus (Gaul)

Moving further west, Irenaeus of Lyon offers a glimpse of the subtle convergence of emerging catechetical practices, though the catechumenate does not quite appear clearly in his writings. Although some want to press his *Demonstratio* (c. 190 CE) into service as containing Irenaeus' catechetical material,[43] that work does not indicate that such was its purpose.[44] Unfortunately for contemporary scholars, Irenaeus' discussion of Christian initiation is much more laconic than that. Despite his emphasis on the "rule of truth," he himself gives only the barest outline of the sort of foundational doctrine he has in mind. The institutional context for such instruction, moreover, is not illuminated, though a few items can be extrapolated.[45]

[42] See the comments in Gavrilyuk, *Histoire*, p. 82: "Le laconisme de Justin et le silence des autres auteurs ne nous permettent pas d'en déduire que la catéchèse au milieu du IIe siècle était fait d'étapes très différenciées. Justin ne dit rien directement ni de la séquence ni du contenu de la catéchèse." See also Wyrwa, "Religiöses Lernen," pp. 277–278.

[43] As in Daniélou and du Charlat, *La catéchèse*, pp. 89–102, and Gavrilyuk, *Histoire*, pp. 82–89. See also Adelin Rousseau, *Irénée de Lyon. Démonstration de la prédication apostolique*, SC 406 (Paris: Cerf, 1995), p. 50, though the term "catechetique" does not feature heavily in the analysis of the text and he identifies only *Dem.* 3b–7 with the "rule of faith" and so with pre-baptismal instruction.

[44] Daniélou's appeal to the opening lines – "We send you as it were a manual of essentials [Daniélou: mémoire sur les points capitaux], that by little you may attain to much, learning in short space all the members of the body of the truth, and receiving in brief the demonstration of the things of God. So shall it be fruitful to your own salvation, and you shall put to shame all who inculcate falsehood, and bring with all confidence our sound and pure teaching to everyone who desires to understand it" (*Dem.* 1; trans. J. A. Robinson) – is not sufficient to demonstrate that the material in the *Demonstratio* was intended for pre-baptismal instruction, though undoubtedly some of it has made its way into such instruction at various times in history. In the absence of such a general purpose statement, material in the *Demonstratio* must be taken on a case by case basis. Indeed, J. A. Robinson early on stated that "It is in no sense a manual for catechumens: it is a handbook of Christian Evidence, though its form is not controversial"; J. Armitage Robinson, *St. Irenaeus: The Demonstration of Apostolic Preaching*, Translations of Christian Literature IV: Oriental Texts (London: SPCK, 1920), p. 2. His view has been firmly vindicated and surpassed by Susan L. Graham, "Structure and purpose of Irenaeus' *Epideixis*," *Studia Patristica* 36 (2001), 210–221, who argues that the proper framework for the text is ancient εἰσαγωγή and a concern for "continuing education" (pp. 219–220 and n. 42). Note that later for Origen, however, such "introductory" concerns are closely related to the catechumenate.

[45] Notably, Irenaeus' general silence on initiatory teaching and practices is reflected in Victor Saxer's omission of him from his otherwise comprehensive survey.

In the first place, the "rule of truth" is, according to Irenaeus, "received through baptism" (διὰ τοῦ βαπτίσματος; *Haer.* 1.1.9).[46] The "rule" itself appears to contain a number of foundational doctrinal commitments – that there is one creator God, that one son of God came in flesh, the Holy Spirit's activity in inspiring the prophets, and a coming resurrection and judgment (*Haer.* 1.1.10) – which fortifies the church against "knowledge, falsely so-called."[47] The meaning of Irenaeus' prepositional phrase is difficult, however, since one does not normally associate the baptismal act itself with passing on doctrinal instruction. On the face of it, Irenaeus associates foundational teaching with initiation in a way that suggests catechetical practice: those who have already decided to join the community are instructed in the basics.[48] Elsewhere, he may indicate that both doctrinal and moral instruction are prerequisites for baptism. In discussing Philip's baptism of the Ethiopian eunuch (4.23.2), Irenaeus supports his immediate baptism, noting that "he had been previously instructed (*praecatechizatus*) by the prophets" such that "he was not ignorant of God the Father nor of the ordering of one's way of life (*conversationis dispositionem*)."[49] Shortly after this, Irenaeus explains Paul's claim to have worked harder than everyone else by noting the relative ease by which Jews could be instructed (*catechizatio*) from scripture, while the Apostle was forced to begin his instruction (*primo catechizabat*) by combatting idolatry, passing on basic monotheistic and christological doctrines, and prohibiting numerous vices (*Haer.* 4.24.1).[50] I should

---

[46] Text in Adelin Rousseau and Louis Doutreleau, *Irénée de Lyon. Contre les hérésies I*, 2 vols., SC 263–264 (Paris: Cerf, 1979).

[47] *Dem.* 6 contains a similar summary of essential doctrine, where the "rule of faith" (հաւատոյ կանոն/πίστεως κανών) mentioned in *Dem.* 3 is presented in its proper "order" (կարգի/τάξις; see also Rousseau, *Démonstration*, pp. 35, 90). "And this is the order of our faith [կարգի հաւատոյ մերոյ]..." (text in Karapet Ter Mekerttchian and S. G. Wilson, "S. Irenaeus, Εἰς ἐπίδειξιν τοῦ ἀποστολικοῦ κηρύγματος, The proof of the apostolic preaching with seven fragments, Armenian version," *Patrologia Orientalis* 12 (1919), 655–746).

[48] In Alistair Stewart's recent treatment of Irenaeus' use of the "rule of truth" in baptismal confessions, he takes it "as axiomatic that the rule of faith was the basis for catechetical direction," though he does not argue for anything beyond a general "catechetical process" nor does he note the moral aspect present in Irenaeus' account as well; see Alistair Stewart, "'The rule of truth...which he received through baptism' (*Haer.* I.9.4): Catechesis, Ritual, and Exegesis in Irenaeus's Gaul," in Sara Parvis and Paul Foster (eds.), *Irenaeus: Life, Scripture, Legacy* (Minneapolis: Fortress Press, 2012), pp. 151–158.

[49] Text in Adelin Rousseau, B. Hemmerdinger, and Louis Doutreleau, *Irénée de Lyon. Contre les hérésies IV*, SC 100 (Paris: Cerf, 1965).

[50] The presence of catechesis terminology in the Greek fragments of *Against Heresies* (3.12.7; Frag. 13) suggests that the Latin translator need not be doubted here. On the significance of Irenaeus' reading of Paul, see Chapter 4 below.

emphasize here that it is the relation between *catechizo* terminology, foundational doctrinal instruction, and baptism in these passages which points toward catechetical practices, rather than simply the occurrence of the term itself.

Irenaeus, then, demonstrates a remarkable convergence of emerging catechetical practices which operate at the level of assumptions for him. Once one decides to join the Christian community, the path to baptism includes moral and doctrinal instruction, as it appears to do for Hermas and Justin. Further, Irenaeus is the first to bring catechesis language into connection with the initial phase of Christian teaching. His use is by no means fixed or unambiguous.[51] But his use is still suggestive of catechetical developments that are taking place below the surface. These practices emerge from writers across the Roman Mediterranean, from Syria to Gaul. There are few indications by this point that these convergences have risen to the status of an institution, entailing a recognized status with acknowledged rules of conduct and practices. Irenaeus does not mention the practice of pre-baptismal fasting, nor are other ritual elements associated with catechesis in view during this period. For that scholars must wait until the work of Irenaeus' younger contemporary, Clement of Alexandria.

2.3 A BURST OF ACTIVITY: THE EARLY THIRD CENTURY

In the last decade of the second century and the first decades of the third century, the catechumenate as an institution becomes visible in Alexandria, Carthage, Syria, and Rome. This explosion of evidence in different locations is made more remarkable by the absence of any explanation of the *fact* of catechesis: it is everywhere assumed as a regular feature of community life which needs only proper definition and structure, not introduction. This point suggests that these writers saw a strong continuity between an earlier, less formalized period of liminal membership and their increasingly regulated catechumenate. That is, at the very least, they would likely have viewed any difference as one of degree rather than kind.[52]

---

[51] See his use in 3.12.7, which appears to refer simply to hearing a report (this time through scripture); the Latin translator read κατηχεῖτο as *audierat*. The use of the term in 3.12.15, on the other hand, may suggest a specific connection between catechesis language and initial instruction.

[52] One might also argue that in the light of this explosion of evidence, Irenaeus' and Justin's earlier accounts should be treated as allusive references to an already institutional

2.3.1 Clement of Alexandria

Discussing the place of the catechumenate in the work of Clement Alexandrinus may at first appear as a controversial move against the common view that Clement was never involved with an Alexandrian catechetical school. Nevertheless, as argued in some detail later, Clement cared a great deal for the catechumenate and its place in his pedagogical vision of the Christian life. In the present chapter, however, all I hope to establish is that Clement knew of a catechumenate and spoke of it in ways consonant with widespread (e.g., previous and contemporary) practice. Before turning to the evidence from Clement's own writing, it will be helpful to address Eusebius' view that Clement inherited leadership of a "school" for catechesis from his teacher Pantaenus.[53]

Since the work of Gustave Bardy in 1937, the presence of a catechetical school in Alexandria under the leadership of Pantaenus and (then) Clement has been vigorously debated.[54] Bardy's principle argument was that Pantaenus and Clement directed philosophical schools rather than catechetical schools and that the ambiguities in Eusebius' account of their lives indicates that the historian extrapolated a succession narrative from partial information.[55] Bardy claimed that, although catechesis likely was happening in Alexandria at the time, Pantaenus and Clement were not engaged in it.[56]

catechumenate and that it was only their apologetic aims and mode of writing that kept them from expanding on the catechumenate more fully.

[53] *Hist. eccl.* 5.10.4: "Now indeed, after many successes, Pantaenus led the school in Alexandria until he died, interpreting by the living voice and in writing the treasures of the divine decrees" (ὃ γε μὴν Πάνταινος ἐπὶ πολλοῖς κατορθώμασι τοῦ κατ' Ἀλεξάνδρειαν τελευτῶν ἡγεῖται διδασκαλείου, ζώσῃ φωνῇ καὶ διὰ συγγραμμάτων τοὺς τῶν θείων δογμάτων θησαυροὺς ὑπομνηματιζόμενος); 6.6.1: "When Clement succeeded Pantaenus, he led the catechesis in Alexandria at that time, so that Origen was also one of his students" (Πάνταινον δὲ Κλήμης διαδεξάμενος, τῆς κατ' Ἀλεξάνδρειαν κατηχήσεως εἰς ἐκεῖνο τοῦ καιροῦ καθηγεῖτο, ὡς καὶ τὸν Ὠριγένην τῶν φοιτητῶν γενέσθαι αὐτοῦ); text in Gustave Bardy, *Eusèbe de Césarée. Histoire ecclésiastique*, 3 vols., SC 31, 41, 55 (Paris: Cerf, 1952–1958).

[54] Gustave Bardy, "Aux origines de l'école d'Alexandrie," *Recherches de science religieuse* 27 (1937), 65–90; see also the concise account of the debate in Wyrwa, "Religiöses Lernen," pp. 280–282.

[55] Evidence marshaled for his view includes: Clement is the only known student of Pantaenus and he was already a Christian before they met; Eusebius is inconsistent about whether Clement succeeded Pantaenus or worked at the same time as him; Clement's teaching is too advanced for catechumens; Origen could not have been a catechumen in the school since he was given his basic instruction by his father and would have been baptized before attending Clement's lectures. See Bardy, "Aux origines," pp. 78–84.

[56] Bardy, "Aux origines," p. 82; see also the comments on p. 88: "A qui succède-t-il [*viz.* Origen, in his role as a catechist]? Nous n'en savons rien. Il est vraisemblable qu'il a eu des

While Bardy's general position has been widely accepted, his arguments have also faced some criticism.[57] For instance, his strict opposition between "independent" teaching and official teaching sanctioned by a bishop[58] has rightly been critiqued for its lack of nuance.[59] In the late second and early third centuries, when the monarchial episcopal structure had not yet achieved complete hegemony,[60] the distinction is not easy to clarify. It is plausible that one could not be subordinated to the authority of a bishop while also not being independent of the "nascent ecclesiastical institution."[61] The strong rejoinders from Annewies van den Hoek and Alain Le Boulluec, among others, arguing that Clement was in fact engaged in catechesis, draw heavily from Clement's own writings to demonstrate his knowledge of the catechumenate and offer new light on Eusebius' account.[62] Even so, it is not clear that Clement's engagement in catechesis justifies Eusebius' account of a catechetical school, as such.[63]

prédécesseurs; mais ceux-ci ont été des catéchistes obscurs et sans renom, humblement attachés à leur besogne élémentaire."

[57] Bardy's view has been followed and augmented by, e.g., Roelof van den Broek, "The Christian 'school' of Alexandria in the second and third centuries," in Jan Willem Drijvers and Alasdair A. MacDonald (eds.), *Centers of Learning: Learning and Location in Pre-Modern Europe and the Near East* (Leiden: Brill, 1995), pp. 39–47, and Clemens Scholten, "Die alexandrinische Katechetenschule," *Jahrbuch für Antike und Christentum* 38 (1995), 16–37, who is more optimistic about the credibility of Eusebius but ultimately excludes the school under Origen from being a catechetical school. He concludes, "Die Bezeichnung 'Katechetenschule' sollte man, weil mißverständlich, aufgeben. Die alexandrinische Einrichtung ist keine Anstalt zur Vorbereitung der Taufbewerber, sondern die theologische Hochschule der dortigen Kirche"; Scholten, "Katechetenschule," p. 37.

[58] Bardy, "Aux origines," p. 82.

[59] See Neymeyr, *Die christlichen Lehrer*, p. 86–87, followed by Paul, *Geschichte*, pp. 52–53; and see Alain Le Boulluec, "Aux origines, encore, de l'"école' d'Alexandrie," in *Alexandrie antique et chrétienne. Clément et Origène* (Paris: Institut d'Études Augustiniennes, 2012), p. 38.

[60] On Rome, see esp. the arguments of Lampe, *Christians at Rome*, though he perhaps reifies community divisions too firmly. On Alexandria, see Neymeyr, *Die christlichen Lehrer*, pp. 87–89. Bardy himself argues that Demetrius used Origen to aid in consolidating the authority of the bishop (Bardy, "Aux origines," p. 87).

[61] See Alain Le Boulluec, "Clément d'Alexandrie," in Bernard Poudern (ed.), *Histoire de la littérature grecque chrétienne des origines à 451*, vol. 3: *De Clément d'Alexandrie à Eusèbe de Césarée* (Paris: Les Belles Lettres, 2017), p. 66, for the quote and the sentiment.

[62] Annewies van den Hoek, "The 'catechetical' school of early Christian Alexandria and its Philonic heritage," *Harvard Theological Review* 90, no. 1 (1997), 59–87, and Le Boulluec, "Clément," pp. 65–72; see also Wyrwa, "Religiöses Lernen," pp. 297–298.

[63] Note the reluctant affirmation of this point in Eric F. Osborn, *Clement of Alexandria* (Cambridge: Cambridge University Press, 2005), pp. 19–24, who generally follows Van den Hoek, "'Catechetical' school," pp. 59–87. Le Boulluec, "Clément," pp. 70–71, argues that keeping Eusebius' "school" terminology is fine so long as we do not think of it in terms of a rule of succession or as being controlled by the authority of the bishop.

At a minimum, Clement is plausibly seen as a Christian philosophical teacher for whom the catechumenate was one concern within a larger pedagogical vision.[64] As Victor Saxer put it, the catechumenate "shows through his work in filigree."[65] In the rest of this section I want only to identify the presence of a few lines of filigree that can be expanded in subsequent discussion.

In his *Paedagogus*, Clement writes a handbook for Christian instruction, aimed primarily at other teachers who could find in it a resource for their own work.[66] Speaking about this work after the fact he states,

> The *Paedagogus*, which we divided into three books, already presented the guidance and nourishment from childhood, that is the way of life that grows out of catechesis with faith and, for those enrolled to be men, prepares the soul imbued with virtue for the reception of gnostic understanding.[67]

---

[64] See the treatment of Clement and Origen as "free teachers" by Christoph Markschies, focused on the appropriation of Greco-Roman educational structure and pedagogy by early Christians; Markschies, *Christian Theology*, pp. 188–189 and *passim*, building on the arguments in Scholten, "Katechetenschule," pp. 16–37. The "freedom" of Clement (and Origen's) teaching from ecclesial structures is disputed, however; see above and see further Le Boulluec, "Aux origines," p. 38; Wyrwa, "Religiöses Lernen," p. 298; and Jutta Tloka, *Griechische Christen – Christliche Griechen. Plausibilisierungsstrategien des antiken Christentums bei Origenes und Johannes Chrysostomos*, STAC 30 (Tübingen: Mohr Siebeck, 2005), p. 96.

[65] Saxer, *Les rites*, p. 101: "Clément, non plus, ne parle pas d'institution, mais celle-ci, en filigrane, transparaît à travers son oeuvre."

[66] This view, cogently presented by Neymeyr, *Die christlichen Lehrer*, p. 55 (building on the arguments of Knauber), effectively accounts for the pedagogical features of the text while also allowing one to take seriously the consistent use of the first person plural (e.g., *Paed.* 1.2.6.5; 1.5.12.1) that places Clement in the same category as his intended readers (*pace* Adolf Knauber, "Ein frühchristliches Handbuch katechumenaler Glaubensinitiation: der Paidagogos des Clemens von Alexandrien," *Münchener Theologische Zeitschrift* 23, no. 4 (1972), 318–320, who argues that this should be read as a rhetorical commonplace); see also the similar comments in Le Boulluec, "Aux origines," p. 34. This view also allows helpful insights from other pro-catechetical readings of the *Paedagogus*, such as those of Saxer, *Les rites*; Van den Hoek, "'Catechetical' school," pp. 59–87; and Wyrwa, "Religiöses Lernen," pp. 271–306. The challenge to this view in Marco Rizzi, "The literary problem in Clement of Alexandria: a reconsideration," *Adamantius* 17 (2011), 154–163, based on observations that the *Paedagogus* was written with a wider audience in mind, is intriguing but need not point beyond a sort of handbook of basic Christian instruction, which focuses on healing the soul and needs to be widely accessible.

[67] *Strom.* 6.1.1.3 – φθάσας δὲ ὁ Παιδαγωγὸς ἡμῖν ἐν τρισὶ διαιρούμενος βίβλοις τὴν ἐκ παίδων ἀγωγήν τε καὶ τροφὴν παρέστησεν, τουτέστιν ἐκ κατηχήσεως συναύξουσαν τῇ πίστει πολιτείαν καὶ προπαρασκευάζου-σαν τοῖς εἰς ἄνδρας ἐγγραφομένοις ἐνάρετον τὴν ψυχὴν εἰς ἐπιστήμης γνωστικῆς παραδοχήν; text in Annewies van den Hoek and Claude Mondésert, *Clément d'Alexandrie: Les Stromates, Stromate IV*, SC 463 (Paris: Cerf, 2001). Knauber, "Ein frühchristliches Handbuch," p. 313 argued that the implications of this passage had not been sufficiently appreciated by previous scholarship.

A similar division of teaching appears in the *Paedagogus* itself. "For catechesis leads to faith and faith is taught at baptism by the Holy Spirit."[68] This catechesis clearly precedes baptism and is inextricably linked with it;[69] the instruction follows a previous stage of teaching identified elsewhere by Clement as *pro-catechesis* or "first instruction."[70] His concern for catechetical instruction is primarily aimed at moral formation. As Clement puts it, the *telos* of this kind of pedagogy is the improvement of the soul, while the teacher is only later concerned with reasoned discourse.[71] The content of the *Paedagogus* bears this out: after the more theological introduction and foundation in book 1, books 2 and 3 cover all manner of practical issues from eating and drinking, to the use of ointments, to sex, to personal adornment, etc.[72] These instructions are studded with biblical references bolstering Clement's instructions designed as the preparatory formation for baptism and the subsequent Christian life.

[68] *Paed.* 1.6.30: Ἡ μὲν γὰρ κατήχησις εἰς πίστιν περιάγει, πίστις δὲ ἅμα βαπτίσματι ἁγίῳ παιδεύεται πνεύματι; text in Henri-Irénée Marrou, Marguerite Harl, Claude Mondésert, and Chantal Matray (eds.), *Clément d'Alexandrie. Le pédagogue*, 3 vols., SC 70, 108, 158 (Paris: Cerf, 1960–1970).

[69] See the discussion in Neymeyr, *Die christlichen Lehrer*, pp. 51–52; see also A. Turck, "Catéchein et catéchésis chez les premiers pères," *Revue des sciences philosophiques et théologiques* 47, no. 3 (1963), 367–369, and pace André Méhat, *Étude sur les "Stromates" de Clément d'Alexandrie*, Patristica Sorbonensia 7 (Paris: Éditions du Seuil, 1966), p. 302 ("Rien dans Clément ne permet de l'entendre en ce sens" (*viz.* "la catéchèse…représente l'enseignement du minimum nécessaire pour donner un contenu à la foi du candidat")). See further in Chapter 4.1 below.

[70] *Prot.* 10.96.2 (προκατηχέω; text in Claude Mondésert, *Clément d'Alexandrie. Le protreptique*, 2nd edn, SC 2 (Paris: Cerf, 1949)) and see also *Strom.* 5.8.48.9 (ὁ ἐκ κατηχήσεως τῆς πρώτης εἰς αὔξησιν ἀνδρός; text in Alain Le Boulluec and Pierre Voulet (eds.), *Clément d'Alexandrie. Les Stromates. Stromate V*, 2 vols., SC 278–279 (Paris: Cerf, 1981)); Van den Hoek, "'Catechetical' school," pp. 68–69; Neymeyr, *Die christlichen Lehrer*, pp. 52–53. Rizzi, "Literary problem," pp. 157–158, notes that in the prologue to the *Paedagogus*, Clement treats the prior προτρεπτικός as "a sort of preliminary step, a call by the Logos to convert and to leave ancient customs (ἤθη) in order to attain the new ethical habits of the Christians, which are shown specifically by Clement's *Paedagogus.*"

[71] Improvement of the soul, *Paed.* 1.1.1.4: "The goal of him [*viz.* the Pedogogue] is to improve the soul, not to teach"(…ᾗ καὶ τὸ τέλος αὐτοῦ βελτιῶσαι τὴν ψυχήν ἐστιν, οὐ διδάξαι). The role of the teacher, *Paed.* 1.1.2.1: "And indeed this same Logos is able to teach, but does not do so now" (καίτοι καὶ διδασκαλικὸς ὁ αὐτός ἐστι λόγος, ἀλλ' οὐ νῦν). See the similar characterization in Knauber, "Ein frühchristliches Handbuch," p. 317; Saxer, *Les rites*, pp. 73–74; Neymeyr, *Die christlichen Lehrer*, p. 52; Paul, *Geschichte*, pp. 52–53; Gavrilyuk, *Histoire*, p. 128; and, without explicit reference to catechesis, Rizzi, "Literary problem," p. 158.

[72] See the discussion of the outline and thematic unity of the *Paedagogus* in Le Boulluec, "Clément," pp. 96–101.

From these brief passages, then, some important information can be deduced. Clement presumes the existence of catechesis as a specific step in the Christian life which finds its place in each of his (extant) major works. It was concerned primarily with moral formation, as is familiar at this point in the investigation, and Clement devoted a three-volume work to providing teaching relevant to catechesis. Nevertheless, as his comments in *Strom.* 6.1.1.3 indicate, the content of this moral and practical instruction would also be relevant for those newly baptized or other immature Christians, a point that will recur later in the full discussion of Clement.[73]

2.3.2 *Passio Perpetuae et Felicitatis* (Carthage)

In Carthage just after the turn of the third century (203 CE), the martyrdom of a group of Christians brought the catechumenate into striking view. In the opening editorial comments of the *Passio Perpetuae et Felicitatis*, the reader is told that those apprehended by the local authorities were "young catechumens" (*adolescentes catechumeni*), among whom was a certain Vibia Perpetua, a highborn woman, whose brother was also a catechumen.[74] Perpetua's own account begins at her initial trial as a catechumen, during which she declares "I cannot say I am anything other than what I am: a Christian."[75] Whatever else is at stake in this declaration, it signifies her membership in the Christian community, a membership for which she and the others are willing to die, before being finally baptized. This is an indication that a conversion has already taken place and that Perpetua and the others are inhabiting a liminal space within the Christian community at the time of their arrest. Some days after this trial and before the final arrest, Perpetua and the others are baptized, completing the process of initiation.[76]

---

[73] Gavrilyuk, *Histoire*, pp. 127–128, notes this in passing. Le Boulluec, "Clément," pp. 101–103, suggests that, while the *Paedagogus* may have originated in the instruction of baptismal candidates, it also appears to exceed this limited task and envision a wider (wealthy and educated) Christian readership.

[74] *Pass. Perp.* 2.1; Latin and Greek text in Thomas J. Heffernan, *The Passion of Perpetua and Felicity* (New York: Oxford University Press, 2012). On the background of Perpetua, see e.g., Petr Kitzler, "*Passio Perpetuae* and *Acta Perpetuae*: between tradition and innovation," *Listy filologické* 130, no. 1–2 (2007), 7 and n. 18; Heffernan, *Passion*, p. 21.

[75] *Pass. Perp.* 3.2: "ego aliud me dicere non possum nisi quod sum, Christiana." For present purposes, the differences between the Greek and Latin manuscript tradition are not significant.

[76] *Pass. Perp.* 3.5; on the timing of these proceedings and possible legal framework for the sentence, see Saxer, *Les rites*, pp. 132–133. Heffernan, *Passion*, p. 177, argues that in the subsequent vision Perpetua had not yet been fully initiated into "the sacramental Mysteries of the church," though it is unclear what he means by this. It is true that no

Perhaps even more striking in relation to the present question, though, are the actions of Saturus. During Perpetua's first vision, concerning the ladder and the serpent, she is preceded by Saturus, who is introduced into the narrative for the first time at that point. We are told, perhaps by way of editorial insertion, that, although Saturus was absent when the catechumens were arrested, he voluntarily handed himself over "for us, because he had taught us."[77] This explanation, "because he had taught us," is taken by several scholars to indicate that Saturus was in charge of instructing this group of catechumens.[78] This explanation would make sense of his voluntary incarceration as well as elucidating why Saturus plays such a leading role both in the first vision of the martyrdom and in the martyrdom itself. If this reading is correct, it signifies that by 203 CE in Carthage, catechumens were a recognizable group of Christians, between conversion and baptism, and that they had a specific teacher who was deeply concerned for their continued endurance under duress. It is notable that Saturus is not identified with a particular office, which may indicate that he did not hold one, but nevertheless engaged in the instruction of catechumens.

2.3.3 Tertullian (Carthage)

In the same context, Tertullian bears further witness to the catechumenate in Carthage at the turn of the third century, providing several additional details on timing and attendant practices.[79]

Eucharist celebration was narrated at the baptism account, but the notice is very brief and it is not clear either that one could separate one from the other in this period nor that if one had been baptized but had not celebrated the Eucharist one would be considered to be somehow *less* initiated than others.

[77] *Pass. Perp.* 4.5: "ascendit autem Saturus prior, qui postea se propter nos ultro tradiderat (quia ipse nos aedificauerat [αὐτοῦ γὰρ καὶ οἰκιδομὴ ἦμεν]), et tunc cum adducti sumus, praesens non fuerat"; see Heffernan, *Passion*, p. 177, for a defense of the editorial insertion view.

[78] Geoffrey D. Dunn, *Tertullian*, The Early Church Fathers (London and New York: Routledge, 2004), p. 16, and Kitzler, "*Passio*," p. 6, call him a "catechist," while Heffernan, *Passion*, p. 177, calls him "their teacher and spiritual guide." Somewhat strangely, Saxer, *Les rites*, makes no mention of Saturus' role as a teacher. This notice is downplayed by Carolyn Osiek, "Perpetua's husband," *Journal of Early Christian Studies* 10, no. 2 (2002), 287–290, who argues that Saturus was actually Perpetua's husband.

[79] Cf. the comments on Tertullian in Daniélou and du Charlat, *La catéchèse*, pp. 44–45; E. Dekkers, *Tertullianus en de geschiedenis der liturgie*, Catholica VI-2 (Brussels: Kinkhoren; Desclée de Brouwer, 1947), pp. 164–173; and Saxer, *Les rites*, pp. 122–125. Gavrilyuk, *Histoire*, intersperses his comments on Tertullian in his discussion of the *Traditio apostolica*. Wyrwa, "Religiöses Lernen," p. 278, notes that "im letzten Drittel des 2. Jahrhunderts setzt die volle Institutionalisierung des Katechumenates ein, die in Karthago durch Tertullian…bezeugt wird."

Tertullian refers to *catechumeni* as one of the groups in the church in his discussion of military honors (*Cor.* 2.1)[80] and he addressed his tractate *De baptismo* at least partially to those who were about to be baptized.[81] This group is also referred to as "hearers" (*audientes*), as they may have been as early as Hermas.[82] In *De baptismo* Tertullian gives an extended theological and scriptural defense of baptism while also supplying details concerning the mechanics and order of baptism (*Bapt.* 6–8), views on the delay of baptism (18), and the relation between preaching and baptism (14).[83]

For present purposes, the order of baptismal rituals is not of primary importance.[84] What are more instructive are the views on the catechumenate that indicate its structure, timing, and status within the community. In the first place, as with the witness of the *Passio Perpetuae*, Tertullian makes it clear that baptism follows on from prior teaching. As he states: "For preaching comes first, baptizing later, assuming that preaching has preceded."[85] He does not illuminate what kind of teaching ought to precede baptism, but it almost certainly included the expected baptismal confessions.[86] Although he does not clearly distinguish

[80] Text in E. Kroymann, "De Corona," in E. Dekkers (ed.), *Corpus Christianorum*, Series Latina 1 (Turnhout: Brepols, 1954), pp. 1037–1065.

[81] *Bapt.* 20.1, 5 (text in Ernest Evans (ed.), *Tertullian's Homily on Baptism* (London: SPCK, 1964)). Adhémar D'Alès, *La théologie de Tertullien*, Bibiotheque de théologie historique (Paris: Beauchesne, 1905), p. 324: "Les rites de l'initiation chrétienne sont décrits dans le traité du baptême, dédié aux catéchumènes et aussi aux fidèles insuffisamment instruits." Neymeyr, *Die christlichen Lehrer*, pp. 126–127, notes that this fact does not clearly demonstrate that Tertullian ever served as an instructor for catechumens.

[82] E.g., *Paen.* 6.20: "Thus hearers ought to *desire* baptism, not *expect* it" (Itaque audientes optare intinctionem, non praesumere oportet; text in Charles Munier (ed.), *Tertullien. La pénitence*, SC 316 (Paris: Cerf, 1984)); see §2.2.2 above for a discussion of Hermas' reference to "hearers of the word." This changes by the late fourth century; see Metzger, *Constitutions*, vol. II, p. 91.

[83] The general structure of the baptismal rite evident in *De baptismo* is confirmed in his *Cor.* 3.2–4.

[84] *Bapt.* 4, 6–7, 20 indicate that baptism was preceded by fasting, praying (20), and blessing the water (4), followed by the chrism and the laying-on of hands (6–7).

[85] *Bapt.* 14.2: "Nam et prius est praedicare, posterius tinguere si prius praedicatum"; see also *Paen.* 6.1, in which he refers to the novices who have begun to wet their ears with divine addresses: "sed praecipue novitiolis istis inminet, qui cum maxime incipiunt divinis sermonibus aures rigare."

[86] He refers to a pre-baptismal renunciation of the devil in *Spec.* 4.1 (see Marie Turcan (ed.), *Tertullian. Les spectacles (De spectaculis)*, SC 332 (Paris: Cerf, 1986)) and *Cor.* 3.2; see also the discussion in Saxer, *Les rites*, pp. 127–132. Holtzmann, "Die Katechese," p. 66, argues that Tertullian's allusions suggest that "der Bekenntnissact bei der Taufe" took the form of a *responsio*.

between different stages of the catechumenate or indicate its length,[87] Tertullian does argue for the value of delaying baptism "according to the person's character, attitude or even age."[88] As he argues earlier, a person who sins after baptism is "appointed for the fire."[89] It appears, then, that Tertullian's major concern for catechumens is moral preparedness, a time for baptizands to demonstrate their intention and ability to leave aside sin and live up to the community's standards.[90]

Further, the danger of inappropriate baptism is not only directed toward the baptismal candidates, but also toward their sponsors (*sponsores*). Tertullian here provides the first mention we have of the practice of sponsorship that becomes ubiquitous in the church orders and in the practice of the fourth century, though he does not elaborate on the process.[91] He notes that the delay of baptism is designed not only to prove the baptizands, but also to spare the sponsors, who would be imperiled by the later lapsing of the newly baptized member.[92]

Finally, Tertullian notes that baptism, the culmination of the catechumenate, was associated particularly with certain days. He notes,

The Passover is the most sacred day for baptism...Besides that, Pentecost is the most favorable period for arranging the washings...On the other hand, every day belongs to the Lord: every hour, every time is suitable for baptism. If there is a difference in solemnity, there is no difference with respect to grace.[93]

Tertullian provides analogical justifications from the life of Jesus and the story of the earliest church which may indicate that his affiliation of

---

[87] See Saxer, *Les rites*, pp. 124–125, and already Dekkers, *Tertullianus*, p. 165, and Holtzmann, "Die Katechese," p. 86, who also notes that Cyprian reflects a similarly undifferentiated catechumenate.

[88] *Bapt.* 18.4: "itaque pro cuiusque personae condicione ac dispositione, etiam aetate, cunctatio baptismi utilior est, praecipue tamen circa parvulos." See the further discussion of this in relation to the *Acts of Paul* in Chapter 3 below and note Tertullian's rejection of delayed baptism if it is used as an excuse for sin; *Paen.* 6.2–4; see also comments in Dekkers, *Tertullianus*, pp. 164–165.

[89] *Bapt.* 8.5: "itaque igni destinatur, sicut et homo cum post baptismum delicta restaurat."

[90] See also Cyprian *Test.* 3.98 (in R. Weber (ed.), "Ad Quirinum; Ad Fortunatum," in *Sancti Cypriani Episcopi Opera*, CCSL III.1 (Turnhout: Brepols, 1972), pp. li–216), entitled "Catecuminum peccare iam non debere," which cites Paul's comments in Rom. 3:8.

[91] See the discussion in Dekkers, *Tertullianus*, pp. 212–213.

[92] *Bapt.* 18.4: "quid enim necesse, si non tam necesse est, sponsores etiam periculo ingeri, qui et ipsi per mortalitatem destituere promissiones suas possunt et proventu malae indolis falli?"

[93] *Bapt.* 19.1–3: "Diem baptismo sollemniorem pascha praestat...exinde pentecoste ordinandis lavacris laetissimum spatium est...ceterum omnis dies domini est: omnis hora, omne tempus habile baptismo. si de sollemnitate interest, de gratia nihil refert."

baptism with these days was not yet common practice.[94] On the other hand, his softening of these same links by undermining any intrinsic connection between solemnity and grace may indicate that the connection between Pascha and baptism (and Pentecost by association) was already in place and that Tertullian wanted to reemphasize the importance of the event apart from calendrical considerations. In either case, the catechumenate – with its beginning processes of sponsorship and its final rituals of prayer, fasting, and ultimately baptism – was evidently becoming oriented around a developing Christian calendar, providing the liminal community members not only a status and practices but a place within the community's liturgical calendar.[95]

2.3.4 *Epistula Clementis* (Syria)

At some point in the late second or third century, a pseudepigraphal letter ostensibly from Clement of Rome to James the brother of Jesus (*Ep. Clem.* 1.1) was composed, probably in Syria, which stands generally in the tradition of church orders.[96] The text says little about the existence or practice of the catechumenate, claiming that it would be too much to explore the details (*Ep. Clem.* 13.3). It does, however, indicate clearly that there is a catechumenate in which there was a recognized role for "catechists" (οἱ κατηχοῦντες) who were to meet certain standards of

---

[94] On the origins of Christian Pentecost celebration, see esp. Gerard Rouwhorst, "The origins and evolution of early Christian Pentecost," *Studia Patristica* 35 (2001), 309–322, and Roger T. Beckwith, *Calendar and Chronology, Jewish and Christian: Biblical, Intertestamental and Patristic Studies*, AGAJU 33 (Leiden: Brill, 1996), pp. 51–70, in addition to the older work of Robert Cabié, *La Pentecôte. L'évolution de la Cinquantaine pascale au cours des cinq premiers siècles*, Bibliothèque de liturgie (Tournai: Desclée, 1965). It would seem likely, following Rouwhorst, that Pentecost was a relatively recent addition to the Western liturgical calendar, but note the mention of Pentecost in the *Acts of Paul*, below (pp. 86–87).

[95] See Wyrwa, "Religiöses Lernen," p. 278, whose argument for novelty and reliance on the *Traditio apostolica* is nevertheless somewhat undercut by the present argument.

[96] The date of this text is notoriously difficult, though a *terminus ante quem* is provided by Rufinus, who notes in the preface of his translation of the *Recognitions*, "Indeed, there is a letter in which the same Clement, writing to James the brother of the Lord, relates the death of Peter, and that he left him as successor of his chair and teaching (*cathedrae et doctrinae suae*), and in which was enclosed even the whole ecclesiastical order." (*Rec.* preface, lines 48–49). See the discussion on the tradition of the Clementine writings in Graham Stanton, "Jewish Christian elements in the pseudo-Clementine writings," in Oskar Skarsaune and Reidar Hvalvik (eds.), *Jewish Believers in Jesus* (Peabody, MA: Hendrikson, 2007), pp. 309–313. Neymeyr, *Die christlichen Lehrer*, p. 155, treats the *Epistula Clementis* as part of second-century Syrian Christianity.

learning and character. In the first place, in 14.2, the author lists ecclesial officers in descending hierarchical order, including "catechists" after deacons.[97]

Let the catechists instruct, having first been instructed, because the work concerns human souls. For it is necessary that the teacher of the lessons adapt to the many views of the students. Therefore, it is necessary that the catechist be learned and blameless and mature and fearless, just as you yourselves will know Clement, who is going to provide instruction after me.[98]

The practice of teachers adapting to their students was commonly advocated in antiquity and the concern with ψυχή ἀνθρώπων further links this with ancient concerns with psychagogy.[99] Notably, this same connection is taken up in other discussions of the catechumenate, particularly in the work of Clement, Origen, and John Chrysostom. The further requirements for catechists build on this tradition and would be further elucidated in later instructions. Even with such a brief passage, and despite the baffling differentiation between the authorial voice and Clement, the ostensible author, the *Epistula Clementis* bears witness to a catechumenate which evidently entails the formal recognition of catechetical teachers within the community. This takes place (probably) in Syria around the same time that the catechumenate becomes visible in Alexandria, Carthage, and, perhaps, Rome, to where we now turn.

2.3.5 *Traditio apostolica* (Rome?)

In turning to the *Traditio apostolica*, we encounter the first full discussion of the catechumenate as such. Unfortunately, it is a text and discussion fraught with difficulty. To begin, the *Traditio apostolica* is only available in early translations which disagree about the order of initiation,

---

[97] See the discussion in Neymeyr, *Die christlichen Lehrer*, pp. 155–156.

[98] *Ep. Clem.* 13.1–3: Οἱ κατηχοῦντες πρῶτον κατηχηθέντες κατηχείτωσαν· ὅτι περὶ ψυχῆς ἀνθρώπων τὸ ἔργον· πρὸς γὰρ τὰς πολλὰς τῶν μανθανόντων γνώμας συναρμόζεσθαι δεῖ τὸν τῶν λόγων ὑφηγητήν. πολυμαθῆ οὖν καὶ ἀνεπίληπτον πέπειρόν τε καὶ ἄδειλον τὸν κατηχοῦντα εἶναι δεῖ, ὡς αὐτοὶ εἴσεσθε Κλήμεντα μετ' ἐμὲ κατηχεῖν μέλλοντα; text in J. Irmscher, F. Paschke, and B. Rehm (eds.), *Die Pseudoklementinen I. Homilien*, 2nd edn, GCS (Berlin: Akademie, 1969).

[99] E.g., Pseudo-Plutarch *Lib. ed.* 9B–C; Quintillian *Inst. or.* 1.1. On the philosophical side of things, with reference to Paul, see further Clarence E. Glad, *Paul and Philodemus: Adaptability in Epicurean and Early Christian Psychagogy*, NovT Sup 81 (Leiden: Brill, 1995). The issue of adaptability to one's audience is a common theme in rhetorical discussions from Plato and Aristotle, through Cicero and Quintillian, as well as appearing in a variety of other contexts; see Edsall, *Paul's Witness*, pp. 20–29.

among other things. Moreover, while the above heading lists Rome as its provenance, the link is increasingly difficult to maintain.[100] I have done so here largely because a small majority of scholars still favor a tenuous connection, where the matter is decided at all.[101] There is a third problem posed by the *Traditio apostolica*: "church order" documents that are expected to be functionally normative are particularly susceptible to being updated. As is often noted, these texts are "living literature" in the sense that each new production, a new copy or a new translation, is likely to update the liturgical or ritual processes for the time of the scribe.[102] This means that, although it would seem that the Sahidic and related witnesses maintain earlier readings in the section relevant for this discussion, there is reason to think that each text we have differs from the lost Greek work.[103] The position adopted here is that the text now known as the *Traditio apostolica* is representative of widespread catechetical practices in the early third century which were deeply influential on subsequent practice across the Mediterranean, but that certain elements

[100] For criticisms, see Bradshaw, *Search*, pp. 80–83, and wider discussion throughout Bradshaw *et al.*, *The Apostolic Tradition* (e.g., pp. 64–66). Bradshaw has recently restated his criticisms of scholarship on the *TA* in Paul F. Bradshaw, "Conclusions shaping evidence: an examination of the scholarship surrounding the supposed *Apostolic Tradition* of Hippolytus," in Paul van Geest, Marcel Poorthuis and Els Rose (eds.), *Sanctifying Texts, Transforming Rituals: Encounters in Liturgical Studies* (Leiden: Brill, 2017), pp. 13–30.

[101] See, in order of decreasing confidence, Saxer, *Les rites*, p. 109; Wyrwa, "Religiöses Lernen," p. 278; Alistair Stewart-Sykes, "*Traditio apostolica*: The Liturgy of Third-Century Rome and the Hippolytean School or Quomodo historia liturgica conscribenda sit," *St Vladimir's Theological Quarterly* 48, no. 2 (2004), 233–248; Allen Brent, *Hippolytus and the Roman Church in the Third Century: Communities in Tension Before the Emergence of a Monarch-Bishop*, VC Sup 31 (Leiden: Brill, 1995), pp. 459–465; Johnson, *Rites*, pp. 96–97, 102–105. Markschies, "Wer schrieb," p. 73, notes that an anonymous *Grundschrift* that has been later reworked does not allow for certain decisions on these issues; see also Bradshaw, "Conclusions," pp. 20–22. A survey of those who favored Hippolytan authorship, which is associated with a Roman provenance, can be found in J. A. Cerrato, "The association of the name Hippolytus with a church order now known as the *Apostolic Tradition*," *St Vladimir's Theological Quarterly* 48, no. 2 (2004), 181–183.

[102] So Anders Ekenberg, "Initiation in the *Apostolic Tradition*," in David Hellholm, Tor Vegge, Øyvind Norderval, and Christer Hellholm (eds.), *Ablution, Initiation, and Baptism: Late Antiquity, Early Judaism, and Early Christianity*, vol. 2, BZNW 176 (Berlin: De Gruyter, 2011), pp. 1011–1012; Johnson, *Rites*, p. 102; Stewart-Sykes, "Traditio apostolica," p. 241 n. 21; Bradshaw, *Search*, pp. 91–92.

[103] See esp. the lucid textual discussion in Ekenberg, "Initiation," pp. 1012–1018, see also Markschies, "Wer schrieb," pp. 3–13, and the earlier work in Bernard Botte (ed.), *Hippolytus. La tradition apostolique, d'après les anciennes versions*, 2nd edn, SC 11 bis. (Paris: Cerf, 1984).

of this "living" document may have been updated in the course of transmission. The material concerning the catechumenate is present in similar form across the various witnesses (excepting the Latin, which is only a partially preserved palimpsest), which suggests that it was also present in the (early) third-century archetype, even if the order of the discussion and certain details remain uncertain.

Even so, as noted, the *Traditio apostolica* is the first extant work to provide a detailed outline of the catechetical process, from entry rituals to final baptismal culmination.[104] The relevant section begins with the heading "Concerning those new people who will give their assent to the faith."[105] These are first admitted as "hearers of the word" (ⲉⲥⲱⲧⲙ̄ ⲉⲡϣⲁϫⲉ) after being publicly questioned by the teachers in the community concerning their status and profession (15–16). Those who bring the candidates for questioning are themselves questioned concerning the postulants' ability to "hear the word."[106] After determining that none of the prohibited professions are practiced by the postulant, they are officially admitted to the catechumenate, which lasts for three years, though "the time shall not be judged but rather it is the conduct that will be judged."[107]

Once admitted, the catechumens are to participate in the regular teaching of the community, though they nevertheless inhabit a marginal space. When the teaching is finished they must separate from the believers to pray, and women are principally to be separated from the men during this prayer time. Further, the ritual kiss of peace is not to be shared by catechumens, "for their kiss is not yet pure."[108] Only the faithful (ⲙ̄ⲡⲓⲥⲧⲟⲥ) are to greet one another, evidently in some official fashion, and after the time of prayer the teacher is to lay hands on the catechumens and pray before dismissing them (*TA* 19.1).

When the three-year period is complete the catechumens enter the final preparation for baptism after a second interview with the candidate

---

[104] See the discussions in Gavrilyuk, *Histoire*, pp. 95–120; Saxer, *Les rites*, pp. 109–119; and the brief treatment in Wilhelm Geerlings, "Traditio apostolica = Apostolische Überlieferung," in *Zwölf-Apostel-Lehre; Apostolische Überlieferung*, Fontes Christiani 1 (Freiburg: Herder, 1991), pp. 180–191.

[105] *TA* 15: ⲉⲧⲃⲉ ⲛⲣⲱⲙⲉ ⲛ̄ⲃ̄ⲣ̄ⲣⲉ ⲛⲁⲓ ⲉⲧⲛⲁϯ ⲙ̄ⲡⲉⲩⲟⲩⲟⲓ ⲉϩⲟⲩⲛ ⲉⲧⲡⲓⲥⲧⲓⲥ. The numbering follows that of Bradshaw *et al.*, *The Apostolic Tradition*, though the paragraphs in the Coptic manuscript begin at §40; the Coptic edition used is Till and Leipoldt, *Kirchenordnung*.

[106] *TA* 15.3: ⲁⲩⲱ ⲙⲁⲣⲟⲩⲉⲣ ⲙⲛ̄ ϩⲁⲣⲟⲟⲩ ⲛ̄ϭⲓ ⲛⲉⲛⲧⲁⲩⲉⲛⲧⲟⲩ ⲉϩⲟⲩⲛ ϫⲉ ⲉⲛⲉ ⲟⲩⲉⲛ ϭⲟⲙ ⲙ̄ⲙⲟⲟⲩ ⲉⲥⲱⲧⲙ̄ ⲉⲡϣⲁϫⲉ.

[107] *TA* 17.2: ⲙⲉⲩⲕⲣⲓⲛⲉ ⲙⲡⲉⲭⲣⲱⲛⲟⲥ ⲁⲗⲗⲁ ⲡⲉⲧⲣⲟⲡⲟⲥ ⲙ̄ⲙⲁⲧⲉ ⲡⲉⲧⲟⲩⲛⲁⲕⲣⲓⲛⲉ ⲙ̄ⲙⲟϥ ⲙ̄ⲙⲁⲧⲉ.

[108] *TA* 18.3: "When they cease praying, they shall not give the peace for their kiss is not yet pure" (ⲉⲩϣⲁⲛⲟⲩⲟⲱ ⲇⲉ ⲉⲩϣⲗⲏⲗ ⲙ̄ⲡⲉⲧⲣⲉⲩϯ ⲉⲓⲣⲏⲛⲏ ⲙ̄ⲡⲁⲧⲉⲧⲉⲩⲡⲉⲓ ⲅⲁⲣ ϣⲱⲡⲉ ⲉⲥⲟⲩⲁⲁⲃ).

and their sponsors.[109] This interview is concerned primarily with the catechumen's conduct:

> their lives will be investigated about whether they lived honorably while catechumens – whether they honored widows, whether they visited the sick, whether they completed any good deed – and when those who brought them bear witness about them,[110] that they lived in this manner, let them hear the gospel.[111]

It is not clear how long this final period lasts, though it must have been at least a week to allow for daily exorcisms, washing on the fifth day, and a fasting vigil on Friday or Saturday before baptism on Sunday.[112]

This full discussion of the catechumenate contains elements seen elsewhere, such as the pre-baptismal fasting noted by the *Didache*, Justin Martyr, and Tertullian, and the importance of sponsors noted by Tertullian. Teachers play an important role here, though no actual teaching is identified beyond implicit moral teaching against which the catechumens are finally measured.[113] As Maxwell Johnson notes, "Formation…had more to do with an apprenticeship in learning to *live* as Christians rather than in doctrinal instruction."[114] Similar importance is given to teachers by Clement of Alexandria, Tertullian, the *Epistula Clementis*, and, in a more emotionally evocative key, the *Passio Perpetuae*. Moreover, the importance of teaching is signaled by calling catechumens "hearers of the

---

[109] Johnson's claim – that the three-year notice here and "perhaps" a forty-day Egyptian practice (which he argues is preserved in *Can. Hippol.* 12) are the only clear indications for the extent of pre-baptismal preparation before 325 (Johnson, *Rites*, p. 201) – is not accurate. Some have attempted to relate comments by Clement of Alexandria to this same three-year catechumenate (*Strom.* 2.18.96.1–2; see Dujarier, *Catechumenate*, p. 43), though this is disputed. Johnson, *Rites*, pp. 64–66, argues that the absence of the three-year period from the *Canones Hippolyti* 12, the earliest development of the *Traditio apostolica*, makes its attestation in the latter suspect. On the other hand, the absence of other, even later, attestations of a three-year catechumenate are notable and bring their own difficulties of interpretation. See below on the witness of the Synod of Elvira (c. 306–314 CE).

[110] I follow Till and Leipoldt's correction here to read the masculine singular ϩⲁⲣⲟⲟϥ ϫⲉ ⲁϥⲉⲓⲣⲉ as ϩⲁⲣⲟⲟⲩ ϫⲉ ⲁⲩⲉⲓⲣⲉ, following the Boharic witness and in line with the surrounding syntax; Till and Leipoldt, *Kirchenordnung*, p. 14.

[111] *TA* 20.1–2: …ⲉⲁⲩϩⲉⲧϩⲉⲧ ⲡⲉⲩⲃⲓⲟⲥ ϫⲉ ⲉⲛⲉ ⲁⲩⲱⲛϩ ϩⲛ̄ ⲟⲩⲙⲛ̄ⲧⲥⲉⲙⲛⲟⲥ ⲉⲩⲟ ⲛ̄ⲕⲁⲧⲏⲭⲟⲩⲙⲉⲛⲟⲥ ϫⲉ ⲉⲛⲉ ⲁⲩⲧⲁⲉⲓⲉ ⲛⲉⲭⲏⲣⲁ ϫⲉ ⲉⲛⲉ ⲁⲩϭⲉⲙ ⲡϣⲓⲛⲉ ⲛ̄ⲛⲉⲧϣⲱⲛⲉ ϫⲉ ⲉⲛⲉ ⲁⲩϫⲉⲕ ϩⲱⲃ ⲛⲓⲙ ⲉⲃⲟⲗ ⲉⲛⲁⲛⲟⲩϥ ⲁⲩⲱ ⲉⲣϣⲁⲛⲛⲉⲛⲧⲁⲩⲉⲛⲧⲟⲩ ⲉϩⲟⲩⲛ ⲉⲣ ⲙⲛ̄ⲧⲣⲉ ϩⲁⲣⲟⲟⲩ ϫⲉ ⲁⲩⲉⲓⲣⲉ ⲛ̄ⲧⲉⲓϩⲉ ⲉⲓⲉ ⲙⲁⲣⲟⲩⲥⲱⲧⲙ̄ ⲉⲡⲉⲩⲁⲅⲅⲉⲗⲓⲟⲛ.

[112] *TA* 20.3–10. See also the discussion of this final timeline in Saxer, *Les rites*, p. 114; Bradshaw *et al.*, *The Apostolic Tradition*, pp. 110–111; and Gavrilyuk, *Histoire*, pp. 108–112.

[113] See Saxer, *Les rites*, p. 111.

[114] Johnson, *Rites*, p. 98, emphasis original.

word," which notably correlates with other Roman descriptions perhaps as early as Hermas and also with Tertullian's account.[115] The *Traditio apostolica*, then, contains practices otherwise seen individually in places ranging from Carthage to Syria within a full ritual framework for initiation. Thus, from the early third century, the catechumenate had evidently attained the level of an institutional fact in communities across key centers of the Mediterranean.

2.3.6 Valentinian Initiation (Rome etc.)

There is growing agreement in recent scholarship on "gnostic" groups[116] that Valentinian, Marcionite, and perhaps even Sethian initiation practice did not differ markedly from that of proto-orthodox groups.[117] The initiatory practices about which we have the most information are those of the Valentinians, whose movement began in Rome in the middle of the second century with Valentinus and continued to grow and spread through much of the third century.[118]

In general outline, Valentinian initiation proceeded from catechesis and preparatory discipline to anointing, baptismal confessions, and the immersion itself, which was possibly followed by further anointing or laying-on of hands and a celebration of the eucharist.[119] Clement of Alexandria preserves an earlier Valentinian account of baptism in his *Excerpta ex Theodoto*. In *Exc.* 78.2, Clement's source states,

---

[115] See further the discussion of "hearers" in Origen's works below, p. 57.

[116] See the discussion of the term "gnostic" below, p. 93 n. 2.

[117] See respectively Einar Thomassen, *The Spiritual Seed: The Church of the "Valentinians"*, NHMS 60 (Leiden: Brill, 2006), pp. 398–405 and *passim*; Eve-Marie Becker, "Taufe bei Marcion: eine Spurensuche," in David Hellholm, Tor Vegge, Øyvind Norderval, and Christer Hellholm (eds.), *Ablution, Initiation, and Baptism: Late Antiquity, Early Judaism, and Early Christianity*, vol. 2, BZNW 176 (Berlin: De Gruyter, 2011), pp. 871–894; and John D. Turner, "From baptismal vision to mystical union with the One: the case of the Sethian Gnostics," in April D. De Conick, Gregory Shaw and John Douglas Turner (eds.), *Practicing Gnosis: Ritual, Magic, Theurgy, and Liturgy in Nag Hammadi, Manichaean and Other Ancient Literature: Essays in Honor of Birger A. Pearson*, NHMS 85 (Leiden: Brill, 2013), pp. 411–431. For what follows, I am particularly indebted to the analyses of Thomassen.

[118] Valentinianism was popular in both the eastern and the western Roman empire, reaching into Latin-, Greek-, Coptic-, and Syriac-speaking populations. See Thomassen, *Spiritual Seed*, pp. 491–508, for a survey of Valentinian witnesses in the west and east. Note also the popularity of Valentinianism among Syriac-speaking Christians, traced in Arthur Vööbus, *History of Asceticism in the Syrian Orient: A Contribution to the History of Culture in the Near East* (Louvain: Secrétariat du Corpus SCO, 1958), pp. 54–61.

[119] See the synoptic account in Thomassen, *Spiritual Seed*, pp. 386–394.

It is not the bath alone that frees, but also knowledge: Who were we? What have we become? Where were we? Where have we been thrown in? Where do we hasten? From what are we rescued? What is birth? What is rebirth?[120]

Thomassen argues that "[w]hat we have here...are the headings of a Valentinian baptismal catechism."[121] Whether or not such a strong statement can be sustained – and directly corroborating evidence is unfortunately lacking – it nevertheless remains the case that a baptizand would require prior instruction to know the answer to these questions. Clement further preserves what appears to be a reference to baptismal renunciation of evil spirits[122] and a trinitarian baptismal formula based on Matthew 28:19 that was viewed as a "seal."[123] The renunciation is related to further preparatory practices including fasting, supplications, prayers, laying-on of hands, and genuflections.[124] These practices are designed to purify one's soul from the unclean spirits that could otherwise undergo baptism *with* the candidate and thereby be incurable (83). The sources in the *Excerpta* also note the practice of anointing (82.1–2), though it is not specified whether it is a pre- or post-baptismal unction.

A similar structure of initiation is present in the (possibly) third-century *Tripartite Tractate* (NHC I,5),[125] in which a believer must first be

---

[120] Ἔστιν δὲ οὐ τὸ λουτρὸν μόνον τὸ ἐλευθεροῦν, ἀλλὰ καὶ ἡ γνῶσις, τίνες ἦμεν, τί γεγόναμεν· ποῦ ἦμεν, [ἢ] ποῦ ἐνεβλήθημεν· ποῦ σπεύδομεν, πόθεν λυτρούμεθα· τί γέννησις, τί ἀναγέννησις. Text in François Sagnard (ed.), *Clément d'Alexandrie. Extraits de Théodote*, SC 23 (Paris: Cerf, 1970).

[121] Thomassen, *Spiritual Seed*, p. 338. See also Sagnard, *Extraits*, p. 202; Saxer, *Les rites*, pp. 67–68.

[122] *Exc.* 77.1: "we renounce the wicked Rulers, since life [is] according to Christ, which he alone rules" (ἀποτασσομένων ἡμῶν ταῖς πονηραῖς Ἀρχαῖς, ζωὴ δὲ κατὰ Χριστόν, ἧς μόνος αὐτὸς κυριεύει). See also Thomassen, *Spiritual Seed*, p. 337.

[123] *Exc.* 76.3–4 (baptizing in the name of the Father, Son, and Spirit for rebirth); 80.3 (being sealed through the three names, Father, Son and Spirit); Thomassen, *Spiritual Seed*, pp. 333–334, 337. See also Sagnard, *Extraits*, p. 204; Saxer, *Les rites*, pp. 69–70. Both Sagnard and Thomassen note the connection between these two passages.

[124] *Exc.* 84.1: "Therefore [there are] fasts, supplications, prayers, the laying-on of hands, genuflections, since the soul is rescued 'from the world' 'from the mouth of lions'" (Διὰ τοῦτο νηστεῖαι, δεήσεις, εὐχαί, <θέσεις> χειρῶν, γονυκλισίαι, ὅτι ψυχὴ 'ἐκ κόσμου' καὶ 'ἐκ στόματος λεόντων' ἀνασῴζεται). Saxer, *Les rites*, p. 68, notes these in contrast with Clement's lack of such detail concerning his own baptismal practices (p. 74).

[125] See the discussion in Harold W. Attridge and Elaine H. Pagels, "The Tripartite Tractate: 1,5:51.1–138.27," in Harold W. Attridge (ed.), *Nag Hammadi Codex I (The Jung Codex): Introductions, Texts, Translations, Indices*, Nag Hammadi Studies 22, 23 (Leiden: Brill, 1985), vol. 1, p. 178, who place it among the "western" Valentinian tradition and note a particular connection with Heracleon. Thomassen, *Spiritual Seed*, pp. 46–58, on the other hand, argues on the basis of its soteriology that the *Tripartite Tractate* is an example of "eastern" Valentinian thought, on par with that in *Excerpta ex Theodoto*.

instructed and make a confession of faith before being baptized into the
Father, Son, and Holy Spirit.[126] Like the source for Clement's *Excerpta*
(and, as we shall see later, for Clement himself), for the author of the
Tractate knowledge is fundamental to salvation and is linked directly
with the things maintained in faith.[127] Baptism is supplied with numerous
other names which elucidate its significance in different ways and, in
light of criticisms from Irenaeus (*Haer.* 1.21.3) and others, perhaps the
most notable is "the bridal chamber" (ⲙⲁ ⲛϣⲉⲗⲉⲉⲧ).[128] The author of the
Tractate, then, envisions a single baptism for those who hear and believe
the truth about God, confess it, and are then baptized. The anthropological division of humanity into three groups – the spiritual, the physical, and the material (ϯⲡⲛⲉⲩⲙⲁⲧⲓⲕⲏ ⲙⲛ ϯⲯⲩⲕⲓⲕⲏ ⲙⲛ ϯⲥⲩⲗⲓⲕⲏ) – is not in
view in his discussion of baptism because only the first group can receive
salvation, while those in the second group act as "servants or helpers of
the church."[129]

In addition to possible Valentinian liturgical fragments (NHC XI,2A–
E) and two notable inscriptions,[130] the *Gospel of Philip* (NHC II,3) is
often viewed as a valuable source for Valentinian initiation in the late

---

[126] *Trip. tract.* 127.25–128.5: "Concerning the baptism which is supreme (ⲡⲓⲃⲁⲡⲧⲓⲥⲙⲁ
ⲉⲧϣⲟⲟⲡ ϩⲛ̄ⲛ ⲟⲩⲙⲛ̄ⲧϫⲁⲉⲓⲥ), into which the whole ones will descend and in which they
abide: there is no other baptism except this one alone (ⲙⲛ ϭⲉⲃⲁⲡⲧⲓⲥⲙⲁ ⲥⲁ ⲡⲉⲧⲙ̄ⲙⲉⲩ
ⲟⲩⲁⲉⲉⲧϥ̄), which is redemption (ⲡⲥⲱⲧⲉ), into God, the Father, the Son and the Holy
Spirit, when the confession comes about through faith (ϯϩⲟⲙⲟⲗⲟⲅⲓⲁ ⲁⲃⲁⲗ ϩⲓⲧⲛ̄ⲛ ⲟⲩⲛⲁϩⲧⲉ)
in these names, which are the one name of the gospel, and when they believe the things
which they were told, that they are [true]. And from this, those who believe that they
are [true] will receive their salvation." The translation here reflects the analysis of
Thomassen, *Spiritual Seed*, pp. 353–354, which differs slightly from that of Attridge
and Pagels, "Tripartite Tractate," vol. I, p. 323, and vol. II, pp. 475–476.

[127] *Trip. tract.* 128.15–20: "the father, God, whom they confess in faith and who provided
their union with him in knowledge" (ⲡⲓⲱⲧ ⲡⲛⲟⲩⲧⲉ ⲡⲉⲉⲓ ⲛ̄ⲧⲁⲩⲣ̄ ϩⲟⲙⲟⲗⲟⲅⲓ ⲙ̄ⲙⲁϥ ϩⲛ̄ⲛ
ⲟⲩⲛⲁϩⲧⲉ ⲁⲩⲱ ⲡⲉⲉⲓ ⲉⲛ̄ⲧⲁϩϯ ⲛ̄ⲛⲟⲩⲙⲟⲩⲝϭ ⲛⲙ̄ⲙⲉϥ ϩⲛ̄ⲛ ⲟⲩⲥⲁⲩⲛⲉ).

[128] *Trip. tract.* 128.34–35: "It [*viz.* baptism] is also called 'bridal chamber' " (ⲥⲉ ⲙⲟⲩⲧⲉ ⲁⲣⲁϥ
ⲁⲛ ϫⲉ ⲙⲁ ⲛϣⲉⲗⲉⲉⲧ).

[129] Thomassen, *Spiritual Seed*, p. 57.

[130] See ibid., pp. 350–353, 355–360. On the "bridal chamber inscription" (NCE 156), see
now H. Gregory Snyder, "A second-century Christian inscription from the Via Latina,"
Journal of Early Christian Studies 19, no. 2 (2011), 157–195; and on the liturgical
fragments and their "Valentinian" character, see the varying views in Hugo Lundhaug,
"Evidence of 'Valentinian' ritual practice? The *Liturgical Fragments* of Nag Hammadi
Codex XI (NHC XI,2a–e)," in Kevin Corrigan and Tuomas Rasimus (eds.), *Gnosticism,
Platonism and the Late Ancient World*, NHMS 82 (Leiden: Brill, 2013), pp. 225–243,
and Antti Marjanen, "A salvific act of transformation or a symbol of defilement?
Baptism in the *Valentinian Liturgical Readings* (NHC XI,2) and in the *Testimony of
Truth* (NHC IX,3)," in ibid., pp. 245–259.

second century.[131] Key ideas such as the "bridal chamber" (ογΝγΜφωΝ) and reference to anointing and baptism can be read to fit with the presentations of Valentinian initiation seen in the *Excerpta ex Theodoto* and the *Tripartite Tractate*,[132] though it is not clear that one should harmonize these accounts since each has its own emphases. For example, while the *Tripartite Tractate* explicitly equates baptism with the "bridal chamber," the witness of the *Gospel of Philip* is not so clear and any ritual equation appears to be with the chrism over baptism.[133] Although there is no explicit mention of pre-baptismal instruction in the *Gospel of Philip*, the importance of knowledge and the concern for suitable instruction throughout appear to presuppose catechesis of some sort.[134]

[131] In different ways: e.g., Thomassen, *Spiritual Seed*, pp. 341–349; Van Os, "Baptism in the bridal chamber"; Minna Heimola, *Christian Identity in the Gospel of Philip*, Publications of the Finnish Exegetical Society 102 (Helsinki: The Finnish Exegetical Society, 2011); and Hans-Martin Schenke, "Das Evangelium nach Phillipus (NHC II,3)," in Hans-Martin Schenke, Ursula Ulrike Kaiser, Hans-Gebhard Bethge, Katharina Stifel, and Catherine Gärtner (eds.), *NHC I–XIII, Codex Berolinensis 1 und 4, Codex Tchacos 3 und 4*, Nag Hammadi Deutsch: Studienausgabe (Berlin: Akademie Verlag, 2013), pp. 140–163.

[132] See esp. *GPhil.* 60, 67.28–31: "The Lord did everything in a mystery, one baptism and one chrism and one eucharist and one redemption and one bridal chamber" (ⲁⲡϫⲟⲉⲓⲥ ⲣ̄ϩⲱⲃ ⲛⲓⲙ ϩⲛ̄ⲟⲩⲙⲩⲥⲧⲏⲣⲓⲟⲛ ⲟⲩⲃⲁⲡⲧⲓⲥⲙⲁ ⲙⲛ̄ⲟⲩⲭⲣⲓⲥⲙⲁ ⲙⲛ̄ⲟⲩⲉⲩⲭⲁⲣⲓⲥⲧⲓⲁ ⲙⲛ̄ⲟⲩⲥⲱⲧⲉ ⲙⲛ̄ⲟⲩⲛⲩⲙⲫⲱⲛ). There is also mention of descending and ascending in the water (51, 64.22–23) and perhaps an allusion to baptismal disrobing (86, 75.23–26); see also the comments in Heimola, *Christian Identity*, pp. 22–31, and Thomassen, *Spiritual Seed*, pp. 346–348. The earlier analysis of Eric Segelberg, "The Coptic-Gnostic Gospel according to Philip and its sacramental system," *Numen* 7 (1960), 191–194, 197–198 remains illuminating, despite his problematic argument for five distinct Valentinian sacraments. His is the observation that the indefinite articles should in this case be taken to indicate singular instances.

[133] See the subtle discussion of the various uses of "bridal chamber" imagery in Heimola, *Christian Identity*, pp. 149–165, who surveys the identification of the bridal chamber with initiation as a whole (so Thomassen, *Spiritual Seed*, pp. 341–342, who also includes the eucharist as part of the initiation process, though it is not so associated in the *Gospel of Philip*), with the holy kiss (so Segelberg, "Coptic-Gnostic Gospel," pp. 197–198), with spiritual and actual marriage (see Jacques-É. Ménard, "L'évangile selon Philippe' et l'"exégèse de l'âme'," in Jacques-É. Ménard (ed.), *Les Textes de Nag Hammadi. Colloque du Centre d'Histoire des Religions (Strasbourg, 23–25 octobre 1974)*, NHS 7 (Leiden: Brill, 1975), pp. 60–64, who argues that marriage is "sacramental" for the *Gospel of Philip* and is the referent of the language of "children of the bridal chamber"), and with the eucharist (so Elaine H. Pagels, "Ritual in the Gospel of Philip," in John D. Turner and Anne McGuire (eds.), *The Nag Hammadi Library After Fifty Years: Proceedings of the 1995 Society of Biblical Literature Commemoration*, NHMS 44 (Leiden: Brill, 1997), p. 286).

[134] Instruction targeted to learners' status is found in *GPhil.* 100 (81.8–15); see Heimola, *Christian Identity*, pp. 33, 123, and Thomassen, *Spiritual Seed*, p. 349. The witness of the *GPhilip* is further complicated by the fact that it may well have been treated as "living

The material from Theodotus, the *Tripartite Tractate*, and the *Gospel of Philip* attend to the various rites and the theology of baptism while any discussion of catechesis remains largely implicit. Nevertheless, these texts are suggestive of a catechumenate among Valentinian groups at the end of the second or early third century, that is, around the same time similar developments took place elsewhere in the Church. Tertullian mentions the presence of "catechumens" among the Valentinians (and others), though his comments are difficult to correlate exactly with information available from other sources. In his tractate against the "heretics," Tertullian is concerned with a lack of ecclesial order: the "heretics" mix catechumens with the baptized such that "the catechumens are perfected before they are taught," perhaps a reference to pre-baptismal eucharist.[135] Unfortunately, Tertullian is not clear about which heretics he has in mind here, and his previous lumping together of Marcion, Valentinus, and Apelles makes it difficult to interpret.[136] Elsewhere he is concerned not with a lack of ecclesial order but with excessive secrecy on the part of the Valentinians. They "teach by persuading" rather than plainly making their doctrines known.[137] He claims that they operate on the pattern of the Eleusinian mystery cult, keeping their teaching secret from those who want to join and maintaining a five-year vetting period.[138]

literature" and updated such that the initiatory practices in the Nag Hammadi text reflect a fourth-century rather than a late second-century context: see Hugo Lundhaug, *Images of Rebirth: Cognitive Poetics and Transformational Soteriology in the Gospel of Philip and the Exegesis on the Soul*, NHMS 73 (Leiden: Brill, 2010), pp. 10–15, 162, and Hugo Lundhaug, "Begotten, not made, to arise in this flesh: the post-Nicene soteriology of the *Gospel of Philip*," in Eduard Iricinschi, Lance Jenott, Nicola Denzey Lewis, and Philippa Townsend (eds.), *Beyond the Gnostic Gospels: Studies Building on the Work of Elaine Pagels*, STAC 82 (Tübingen: Mohr Siebeck, 2013), pp. 235–271. Bas van Os has argued that GPhilip is a Valentinian catechetical handbook and, although his arguments are not without problems (see comments in Heimola, *Christian Identity*, pp. 30–31 and the entirely contrary account in Martha Lee Turner, *The Gospel According to Philip: The Sources and Coherence of an Early Christian Collection* (Leiden and New York: Brill, 1996)), the comparanda cited by Van Os could also suggest a text updated with baptismal practices represented in the fourth-century works of Cyril of Jerusalem, Gregory of Nyssa, and Ambrose of Milan.

[135] *Prae. haer.* 41.4: "Ante sunt perfecti catechumeni quam edocti"; text from François Refoule (ed.), *Tertullien. Traité de la prescription contre les hérétiques*, SC 46 (Paris: Cerf, 1957).

[136] *Prae. haer.* 10.7–8.

[137] He claims the opposite for "truth": "veritas autem docendo persuadet non suadendo docet" (*Val.* 1.4; text from Jean-Claude Fredouille (ed.), *Tertullien. Contre les valentiniens*, 2 vols, SC 280–281 (Paris: Cerf, 1981)).

[138] *Val.* 1.1–2: "nam et illa Eleusinia, haeresis et ipsa Atticae superstitionis, quod tacent, pudor est. idcirco et aditum prius cruciant diutius initiant quam consignant, cum epoptas ante quinquennium instituunt..." but see the comments in Thomassen, *Spiritual*

It would appear that the Valentinian catechumenate as an institution, if it is discernible at all, arises at the same time as does the catechumenate visible in Clement's and Tertullian's writings. From the evidence available, catechetical and baptismal practice among the Valentinians did not diverge significantly from that of proto-orthodox churches, except perhaps in one respect. The discussions surveyed here, though concerned with moral issues elsewhere, do not mention moral instruction or vetting as part of the preparation for baptism.

2.3.7 Origen from Alexandria to Caesarea

The final piece of evidence for the catechumenate in the third century CE to be discussed here comes from and concerns Origen. A more detailed treatment of Origen's institutional contexts in Caesarea, where he produced the majority of his writings, will be provided in Chapter 5. In the present section, however, two points need to be made: first that there remains reason to think that Origen was involved in catechetical instruction in Alexandria – despite certain well-known difficulties in Eusebius' account – and second that his own writings witness to the existence of the catechumenate in Caesarea. What Origen's witness adds to this survey, then, is a further geographic point of reference. His move from Alexandria to Caesarea was attended by no evident adjustment of his views on the practice of Christian initiation, and the ease of his movement attests to the significant degree of liturgical and practical continuity between churches in Alexandria and Caesarea. In other words, Origen's witness to the catechumenate, building on that of Clement and others, suggests something of the spread of a common institutional framework familiar across the Roman Mediterranean by the middle of the third century, also attested in the witnesses to the *Traditio apostolica*.

According to Eusebius, Origen was appointed to leadership of the Alexandrian "catechetical school" in 203–204 CE by bishop Demitrius.[139]

Seed, pp. 387–388, who notes that the five-year period might only refer to Tertullian's characterization of the Eleusinian mysteries.

[139] According to Eusebius' chronology (*Hist. eccl.* 6.3.3, 8) it happened when he was eighteen, in 203–204 CE. Pierre Nautin has argued that this is better dated to 211 CE or shortly after, making Origen roughly twenty-six years old: see Pierre Nautin, *Origène. Sa vie et son œuvre*, Christianisme antique 1 (Paris: Beauchesne, 1977), p. 417 and *passim*. Nautin's chronology is generally followed by Van den Broek, "Christian 'school'," p. 44, though others such as Henri Crouzel, *Origen*, trans. A. S. Worrall (Edinburgh: T. & T. Clark, 1989), pp. 10–14, and Scholten, "Katechetenschule," p. 19, find it too ingenious.

As noted, however, Eusebius' account contains some difficulties. Although he refers to the institution as τὸ τῆς κατηχήσεως διδασκαλεῖον (*Hist. eccl.* 6.3.3) and informs us that Origen alone was entrusted with ἡ τοῦ κατηχεῖν διατριβή (6.3.8) after having himself sat at the feet of Clement for ἡ κατ᾽ Ἀλεξάνδρειαν κατήχησις (6.6.1), he elsewhere indicates that the subjects covered by Origen were more in line with standard Greco-Roman higher education.[140] Within Eusebius' chronology this account follows on from Origen's division of the catechetical school, reserving the more advanced students for himself while leaving the basic instruction in the charge of his former pupil Heraclas.[141] Even the language used here, however, may be read within the framework of Greco-Roman education: "introduction" (εἰσαγωγή) was a standard aspect of ancient pedagogy throughout the Mediterranean.[142] Furthermore, Eusebius himself preserves a letter by Origen to Alexander of Jerusalem, evidently written from Alexandria, in which Origen discusses his own activities and those of Heraclas without any indication that catechesis featured among their teaching duties.[143] Other evidence could be added.[144] Clemens Scholten concludes his influential study by stating that "one should give up the designation 'catechetical school' because it is misleading. The Alexandrian establishment is

---

[140] See *Hist. eccl.* 6.18.2–4; see further Chapter 5.2.1 below and see also Nautin, *Origène*, pp. 49–53, who argues that Eusebius constructed this passage using Origen's letter to Gregory as a source. If this is correct, it has implications for our understanding of Origen's teaching activity more broadly, since Eusebius would be using a letter normally associated with Origen's Caesarean period to describe his teaching in Alexandria. Note also Marco Rizzi, "La scuola di Origene tra le scuole di Caesarea e del mondo tardoantico," in Osvalda Andrei (ed.), *Caesarea Maritima e la scuola origeniana. Multiculturalità, forme di competizione culturale e identità christiana* (Brescia: Morcelliana, 2013), pp. 105–119, who situates Origen's work within the framework of epideictic – i.e., public – philosophy in the second and third centuries.

[141] *Hist. eccl.* 6.15.1: ...τῷ [*viz.* Heraclas] μὲν τὴν πρώτην τῶν ἄρτι στοιχειουμένων εἰσαγωγὴν ἐπιτρέψας, αὐτῷ [*viz.* Origen] δὲ τὴν τῶν ἐν ἕξει φυλάξας ἀκρόασιν.

[142] See Scholten, "Katechetenschule," p. 22. Note that a similar pedagogical framework has been proposed both for Irenaeus' *Demonstratio* and for Eusebius' *Eclogae propheticae*, on either side of Origen chronologically; see respectively Graham, "Structure," pp. 210–221, and Johnson, *Eusebius*, pp. 54–73.

[143] Origen *apud* Eusebius *Hist. eccl.* 6.19.12–14; see Pierre Nautin, *Lettres et écrivains chrétiens des IIe et IIIe siècles*, Patristica 2 (Paris: Cerf, 1961), pp. 126–129, and the critical assessments in Scholten, "Katechetenschule," pp. 21–22, and Van den Broek, "Christian 'school'," p. 46.

[144] Eusebius claims that Origen introduced uneducated students to philosophical schools of thought (*Hist. eccl.* 6.18.4), and Origen's *Epistula ad Gregorium* 4 extols the value of Greek and Roman learning. See also Gregory Thaumaturgus *Pan.* 8 and Scholten, "Katechetenschule," p. 25.

no institution for the preparation of baptismal candidates, but rather a theological *Hochschule* for the church there."[145]

Nevertheless, there remain reasons not to dismiss a catechetical reading of Eusebius' account out of hand. Indeed, it can absorb the above criticisms to a certain extent insofar as one is able to trust his notice that Origen had split the school according to the level of the students (*Hist. eccl.* 6.15.1), reserving the more advanced students for himself.[146] In splitting the school in this way, Origen would have extended its pedagogical scope to reach beyond basic catechesis or even more general introductory exhortation regarding the Christian way of life. Further, this point accounts for the fact that some of Origen's students were evidently already believers, as attested by his letter to Alexander.[147] That Origen was recruited by Demetrius and that his subsequent work was related to the ecclesial community in Alexandria need not stand in tension with the philosophical content of his advanced teaching.[148] His connection with the church is borne out not only by the clear concerns of his own writings, but by his conflict with Demetrius and the fallout which forced

---

[145] Scholten, "Katechetenschule," p. 37: "Die Bezeichnung 'Katechetenschule' sollte man, weil mißverständlich, aufgeben. Die alexandrinische Einrichtung ist keine Anstalt zur Vorbereitung der Taufbewerber, sondern die theologische Hochschule der dortigen Kirche." He is followed particularly by Markschies, *Christian Theology*, p. 81. Note the criticisms of Scholten's thesis in Peter Gemeinhardt, "Glaube, Bildung, Theologie: ein Spannungsfeld im frühchristlichen Alexandria," in Tobias Georges, Felix Albrecht, and Reinhard Feldmeier (eds.), *Alexandria*, COMES 1 (Tübingen: Mohr Siebeck, 2013), pp. 450–451, among others.

[146] This notice is taken seriously by Manlio Simonetti, "Origene Catecheta," *Salesianum* 41 (1979), p. 299; Attila Jakab, "Alexandrie et sa communauté chrétienne à l'époque d'Origène," in Lorenzo Perrone (ed.), *Origeniana Octava*, BETL 164 (Leuven: Peeters, 2003), p. 99; Wyrwa, "Religiöses Lernen," p. 287; Tloka, *Griechische Christen*, pp. 118–119; Anders-Christian Jacobsen, "Conversion to Christian philosophy: the case of Origen's school in Caesarea," *Zeitschrift für Antikes Christentum* 16, no. 1 (2012), 146. See also Gemeinhardt, "Glaube, Bildung, Theologie," pp. 453–454, and Alfons Fürst, *Origenes. Grieche und Christ in römischer Zeit* (Stuttgart: Anton Hiersemann, 2017), pp. 5–6, who nevertheless do not connect Heraklas' work explicitly with catechesis.

[147] See the comments in Gavrilyuk, *Histoire*, p. 141: "Origène ne refusait jamais d'admettre dan son école celui qui voulait recevoir une instruction uniquement philosophique, espérant que par la même occasion, l'homme se convertirait au christianisme." He goes on to state "Soulignons que l'enseignement à l'école ne cessait pas avec le baptême mais qu'il passait alors à un stade supérieur" (p. 155).

[148] The intervention of Demetrius in Origen's Alexandrian work is accepted by the majority of scholars, even among those who reject the presence of catechesis within Origen's work. See Tloka, *Griechische Christen*, pp. 122–124; Rizzi, "La scuola di Origene," pp. 112–113; Gemeinhardt, "Glaube, Bildung, Theologie," p. 151.

him to move to Caesarea.[149] It is also important that Eusebius' account of Origen's engagement in catechetical instruction in Alexandria works cumulatively with the witness of Clement discussed earlier. Insofar as Clement's writings contain evidence of the catechumenate in Alexandria, they provide further reason to see Origen's familiarity and engagement with catechesis as plausible.

A middle position between accepting or rejecting Eusebius' account is possible, then, in which the Alexandrian διδασκαλεῖον under Origen's leadership fulfilled several functions, from basic to in-depth theological instruction, in which catechumens would be able to learn foundational doctrines to the extent of their intellectual competence and moral preparation.[150] Eusebius' emphasis on the catechetical element of the instruction would therefore be restrictive but not simply wrong; there is no reason to assume that he is attempting a total description of the school's scope. For present purposes, any remaining ambiguity on this matter is not an insuperable difficulty. It is perhaps best mitigated by the way in which Origen's own writings display both a recognition of and an engagement with the catechumenate that, as we shall see in due course, shapes his reading of the Apostle Paul.

Although there is no clear indication of duration or specifically catechetical sessions devoted purely to pre-baptismal instruction,[151] nevertheless Origen clearly indicates that catechumens constituted a distinct group who were undergoing fundamental moral formation and instruction as a preparation for the Christian life. Writing from Caesarea, Origen responds to Celsus' criticism that Christians only teach their ideas among the uneducated, immature, and stupid, arguing that in fact the opposite is the case. Rather than Christians sharing their teachings

---

[149] See the comments in Tloka, *Griechische Christen*, p. 96. Note also that the entire thrust of Ronald E. Heine, *Origen: Scholarship in the Service of the Church*, Christian Theology in Context (New York: Oxford University Press, 2010), emphasizes Origen's connection with and concern for the church.

[150] This *via media* has been represented recently in Heine, *Origen*, pp. 60–64; see also Pier Angelo Gramaglia, "Battesimo," in Adele Monaci Castagno (ed.), *Origene dizionario. La cultura, il pensiero, le opere* (Rome: Città Nuova, 2000), pp. 45–46, and Wyrwa, "Religiöses Lernen," pp. 286–291. Jutta Tloka concludes her discussion on a similarly affirmative note regarding Origen's engagement in catechesis in Alexandria: "Aus dem dargestellten Befund ergibt sich, daß Origenes' Anfänge als christlicher Lehrer mit größter Wahrscheinlichkeit in der Katechese zu suchen sind"; Tloka, *Griechische Christen*, p. 121. The importance of Origen's efforts at philosophical education for his Pauline interpretation will be explored in Chapter 5 below.

[151] See Gavrilyuk, *Histoire*, p. 155, and note that catechetical instruction appears to have largely taken place in homiletical contexts; see further in Chapter 5.2.2, below.

with just anyone, it is the philosophers, and especially the Cynics, who teach indiscriminately to the crowd.[152] Christians, on the other hand, first carefully examine the souls of those who want to "hear" and warn each person individually. Then,

When the hearers, before entering into fellowship, appear to have advanced with respect to their desire to live honorably, at that time they introduce them. They form a *particular class of those now beginning and being introduced* who have not yet received the symbol of their purification. But there is another class of those who, to the best of their ability, have made good their decision to desire nothing except what is approved by Christians.[153]

These two groups of Christians ought to be read not as two stages of the catechumenate, as Origen makes clear subsequently, but rather as a way to describe the difference between catechumens and full members of the community: the former are still receiving introductory teaching (εἰσαγωγή) and have thus far only expressed a desire to live a pure life but that remains a work in progress, not yet actualized fully in baptism as a "symbol of purification."[154] Some from the latter group, who are already baptized, are responsible for vetting the "lives and conduct" of those who want to join the church, "improving them daily."[155] Origen's description

---

[152] *Cels.* 3.50.16–19: Καὶ οἱ φιλόσοφοί γ᾽ ἂν εὔξαιντο ἀγείρειν τοσούτους ἀκροατὰς λόγων ἐπὶ τὸ καλὸν παρακαλούντων· ὅπερ πεποιήκασι μάλιστα τῶν Κυνικῶν τινες, δημοσίᾳ πρὸς τοὺς παρατυγχάνοντας διαλεγόμενοι; text from Marcel Borret (ed.), *Origène. Contre Celse,* 5 vols., SC 132, 136, 147, 150 (Paris: Cerf, 1967–1976).

[153] *Cels.* 3.51.7–14 (emphasis added): ἐπὰν δοκῶσιν αὐτάρκως οἱ ἀκροαταὶ πρὶν εἰς τὸ κοινὸν εἰσελθεῖν ἐπιδεδωκέναι πρὸς τὸ θέλειν καλῶς βιοῦν, τὸ τηνικάδε αὐτοὺς εἰσάγουσιν, ἰδίᾳ μὲν ποιήσαντες τάγμα τῶν ἄρτι ἀρχομένων καὶ εἰσαγομένων καὶ οὐδέπω τὸ σύμβολον τοῦ ἀποκεκαθάρθαι ἀνειληφότων, ἕτερον δὲ τὸ τῶν κατὰ τὸ δυνατὸν παραστησάντων ἑαυτῶν τὴν προαίρεσιν οὐκ ἄλλο τι βούλεσθαι ἢ τὰ Χριστιανοῖς δοκοῦντα.

[154] Saxer, *Les rites,* pp. 153, 187, notes the link between "purification" and baptism in Origen. A similar account of restricted access to the "mysteries" based on moral progress is given slightly later in *Cels.* 3.59.25–29; see also 3.56.19–27. Gavrilyuk, *Histoire,* p. 154, rightly notes that Origen does not maintain a strict division between two classes of catechumens, while Saxer, *Les rites,* pp. 152–153, argues that Origen does bear witness to a two-step catechetical process (pre-catechumenate and catechumenate) which is differentiated by moral progress. While Origen clearly does envision a differentiated Christian community related to spiritual and moral advancement (see Chapter 5.3.2 below), he does not clearly correlate it with stages of the catechumenate.

[155] *Cels.* 3.51.15–19: "Among them [*viz.* the class of believers] are some appointed to inquire into the lives and conduct of those who come forward, so that they might hinder those who engage in infamous activities from coming to the common assembly and, receiving those who do not do such things with their whole soul, they might improve them daily" (παρ᾽ οἷς εἰσι τινὲς τεταγμένοι πρὸς τὸ φιλοπευστεῖν τοὺς βίους καὶ τὰς ἀγωγὰς τῶν προσιόντων, ἵνα τοὺς μὲν τὰ ἐπίρρητα πράττοντας ἀποκωλύσωσιν ἥκειν ἐπὶ τὸν κοινὸν αὐτῶν σύλλογον τοὺς δὲ μὴ τοιούτους ὅλῃ ψυχῇ ἀποδεχόμενοι βελτίους ὁσημέραι κατασκευάζωσιν).

appears to have some similarities with the practice of sponsorship as mentioned by Tertullian and described in the *Traditio apostolica* – with members of the Christian community who are responsible for an initial assessment and who evidently bring those whom they can vouch for to join the catechumenate – though he does not elaborate on it. Further, the concern for a proper *modus vivendi* continues the catechetical concern from the early second century.[156]

One place where the catechumenate comes to the fore in Origen's work is in his homilies. Many times he addresses catechumens directly.[157] For example, when Origen comes to the story of Jesus' baptism during his homilies on Luke, a discussion of catechesis and initiation makes an appearance. Origen notes that baptism is "for the remission of sins" and then addresses the catechumens directly.

Come, catechumens! Do penance, so that you might obtain baptism "for the remission of sins." "For the remission of sins": he accepts baptism who has ceased to sin. For if someone comes to the washing while sinning, there is no remission of sins for him…Spend some time in good company. Keep yourself clean from all dirt and vices and then there will be remission of sins for you when you begin to condemn your own sins.[158]

It is clear from these passages, then, that Origen has in view a formalized catechumenate. It has a recognized place in the community, with official teachers involved in catechesis. There are hints of formal entry praxis, such as the use of sponsors, sustained penitence, moral formation, and teaching,[159] which culminate in baptism and full membership

---

[156] Heine, *Origen*, p. 50, notes that Gregory Thaumaturgus also emphasized Origen's primary concern to "form character." On Gregory's *Oration* to Origen, see Chapter 5.2.1.

[157] E.g., *Hom. in Jesu* 4.1, 26.2; *Hom. in Num.* 26.4.1; *Hom. in Ezek.* 6.5 (editions supplied in Chapter 5). On the composition of Origen's audience, see esp. Adele Monaci Castagno, *Origene predicatore e il suo pubblico* (Milan: Franco Angeli, 1987), who notes Origen's attention to catechumens on pp. 68, 83, and *passim*. Origen finds the crossing of the Red Sea particularly useful for a typology of Christian initiation: see the comments in Saxer, *Les rites*, pp. 158–159; Dujarier, *Catéchumenate*, pp. 33–34; and Wyrwa, "Religiöses Lernen," pp. 288–289; see further in Chapter 5 below.

[158] *Hom. in Luc.* 21.4: "Venite catechumeni, agite paenitentiam, ut *in remissionem peccatorum* baptisma consequamini. *In remissionem peccatorum* ille accipit baptisma, qui peccare desistit. Si quis enim peccans ad lavacrum venit, ei non fit remissio peccatorum.…Facite aliquid temporis in conversatione bona, mundos vos a cunctis sordibus vitiisque servate, et tunc vobis remissio peccatorum fiet, quando coeperitis et ipsi propria pecata contemnere" (text from Henri Crouzel, François Fournier, and Pierre Périchon (ed.), *Origène. Homélies sur S. Luc*, SC 87 (Paris: Cerf, 1962)). See also the discussion in Saxer, *Les rites*, p. 161, and Gavrilyuk, *Histoire*, p. 154.

[159] See *Hom. in Iud.* 5.6, where this elementary teaching is included alongside moral formation for catechumens.

in the church community. In short, the catechumenate is an institutional fact, and this appears to be so in both Alexandria and Caesarea, with no evidence that Origen adapted his understanding of the institution from one place to the next. The convergence of catechetical praxis traced here, at least in general terms, is also testified to by Origen's teaching activity, which spanned multiple locations in the first half of the third century.

Following Origen, there is a gap in our evidence for the catechumenate until the fourth century.[160] Persecution and the increased urgency of certain christological debates appear to have pushed extended discussions of initiation out of the extant texts, though certainly not out of practice in the various churches. When we catch sight of the catechumenate again in the fourth century, we see it in its golden period.

2.4 THE FLOWERING OF CATECHESIS IN THE FOURTH CENTURY

In the first decades of the fourth century, a synod met in Elvira (present-day Granada in Spain) and addressed several issues of church order after a period of persecution.[161] A number of different problems are addressed in the resulting canons – from abuses among church leaders (§§19–20), to women, marriage, and sex (§§8–10, 12–17), to church attendance (§21) – but particularly notable is the way in which the catechumenate features as a presumed part of church life.[162] At stake is not the existence or nature of the catechumenate in general, but rather how to deal with special cases that impinge on the catechumenate. For example, how ought the churches deal with those who are appointed as *flamines*? "Likewise, if *flamines* are catechumens and they abstain from offering

---

[160] In fact, for a view of the catechumenate in any real detail we must wait until Cyril of Jerusalem's *Catecheses ad illuminandos*, delivered in 350/351 CE. Note that this gap is evident also in the material covered in Saxer, *Les rites*, and see the chronological chart of relevant sources in Daniélou and du Charlat, *La catéchèse*, pp. 263–265.

[161] Eckhard Reichert, *Die Canones der Synode von Elvira. Einleitung und Kommentar* (Hamburg: Hamburg University, 1990), pp. 22–23, dates the Synod between the end of the Diocletian persecution (306 CE) and the beginning of the Synod of Arles (314 CE). He argues that it is impossible to determine who called for the synod and why, based on the sparse information available (pp. 35–40). See also the earlier (and more optimistic) discussion in Alfred W. W. Dale, *The Synod of Elvira and Christian Life in the Fourth Century: A Historical Essay* (London: Macmillan, 1882), p. 57.

[162] Whether or not §§22–81 are original or added later is not relevant to my argument since the catechumenate features in §§1–21. See the discussion in Reichert, *Synode*, p. 49, and Hamilton Hess, *The Early Development of Canon Law and the Council of Serdica*, OECS (Oxford: Oxford University Press, 2002), pp. 41–42.

sacrifices, after a period of three years it is determined that they should be admitted to baptism."[163] Other special issues pertaining to catechumens included the issue of separation from spouses (§10) and what to do if a female catechumen were to contract a serious illness (*graviter fuerit infirmata*) during her five-year catechumenate (§11).[164] Similar "special case" treatment of the catechumenate is given in 325 CE in the Nicene canons as well.[165]

Given the explosion of relevant surviving material from the fourth century, the purpose of this final section is not to trace the fourth-century catechumenate in all its nuance and variation. There were, of course, local variations and shifts in each local practice throughout the century. Nevertheless, the fact of the catechumenate did not change and there are large-scale similarities that pertain across the Mediterranean, facts which permit a general outline of the structure and qualities of the catechumenate in this period. Therefore, rather than treating each author individually as I have done above, I will indulge in a more synthetic account here.

The fourth century brought numerous changes to the lot of the Church in the Roman world. It is difficult, for instance, to overestimate the significance of Constantine's conversion and appropriation of Christianity as the state *religio* for the shape of Christianity. With the persecution – which held an important place in the early Christian imagination – officially over, there was now a large influx of new converts. It is likely that, at least in some places, the number of catechumens outnumbered the baptized members, partially because of a shift in common practice in which Christian families would enroll their children as catechumens who would then not be baptized until much later.[166]

---

[163] §4: "Item flamines si fuerint catechumeni et se a sacrificiis abstinuerint, post triennii tempora placuit ad baptismum admitti debere"; text in Reichert, *Synode*.

[164] There is no further comment on the extended period of the catechumenate for women (*Intra quinquennii autem tempora*) in relation to the three-year period noted for *flamines* (*post triennii tempora*), which appears to be limiting that period to the normal male catechumenate time-span, since it appears unlikely that pagan priests would be given a shorter catechumenate than others. This formalized discrepancy is not evident elsewhere. See also the mentions of catechumens in §§38, 45, 67–68, 73. Reichert, *Synode*, p. 103, interprets this five-year period as a result of some (otherwise unspecified) failure. He notes "Ein Zussammenhang mit den Verfehlungen aus Canon 10 ist möglich, aber nicht zwingend." This does not easily account for the fact that §11 is limited to women, nor that its specific content relates not to failure but to sickness.

[165] See Nicene canons §§2, 11–12, 14, text in William Bright (ed.), *The Canons of the First Four General Councils of Nicaea, Constantinople, Ephesus and Chalcedon: With Notes*, 2nd edn (Oxford: Clarendon, 1892).

[166] Augustine is a famous example of this: see *Conf.* 1.11.17; 2.3.6 (speaking of his father as a catechumen; text in L. Verheijen (ed.), *Augustinus: Confessionum libri XIII*, CCSL

These new catechumens were received within the two-level structure of the catechumenate already identified in the *Traditio apostolica*. After joining the catechumenate for an indeterminate period of time, the final stage of baptismal preparation – accompanied by specific catechetical lectures and attendant rituals such as exorcisms – was only entered by enrolling one's name, usually before the major feast days.[167] In particular, as already noted by Tertullian, baptism was associated with Easter and so the final catechetical stage became closely associated with Lent, which had recently been widely adopted.[168] This enrollment was often accompanied by an interview between the bishop, the candidate, and their sponsors.[169]

27 (Turnhout: Brepols, 1981)). See also the various discussions in Louis-Lucien Rochat, *Le catéchuménat au IVme siècle d'après les catéchèses de St. Cyrille de Jérusalem* (Geneva: Taponnier & Studer, 1875), pp. 50–53; Thomas M. Finn, *The Liturgy of Baptism in the Baptismal Instructions of St. John Chrysostom*, The Catholic University of America Studies in Christian Antiquity 15 (Washington, D.C.: Catholic University of America Press, 1967), pp. 33–34; Reiner Kaczynski (ed.), *Johannes Chrysostomus. Catecheses Baptismales = Taufkatechesen*, Fontes Christiani 6 (Freiburg: Herder, 1992), pp. 73–74; William Harmless, *Augustine and the Catechumenate* (Collegeville, MN: Liturgical Press, 1995), pp. 51–56; Philippe de Roten, *Baptême et mystagogie. Enquête sur l'initiation chrétienne selon s. Jean Chrysostome*, Liturgiewissenschaftliche Quellen und Forschungen 91 (Münster: Aschendorff, 2005), pp. 11–27; Jaclyn LaRae Maxwell, *Christianization and Communication in Late Antiquity: John Chrysostom and His Congregation in Antioch* (Cambridge and New York: Cambridge University Press, 2006), pp. 121–124; and Gavrilyuk, *Histoire*, pp. 187–198, 223–225.

[167] Cyril of Jerusalem uses the term ὀνοματογραφία (*Procat.* 1; see also ὄνομά σου ἐνεγράφη, 4) and refers to his listeners as οἱ ἀπογραφέντες (5); John Chrysostom similarly addresses his listeners as οἱ εἰς τὸ ἴδιον τοῦ Χριστοῦ ἀπογραψάμενοι (*Cat.* 7.1); Augustine speaks of it as "giving his name" ("Inde ubi tempus advenit, quo me nomen dare oportet," *Conf.* 9.6.14) which also corresponds with Egeria's account in *Itin.* 45.1. See also the discussion in Edward J. Yarnold, "The fourth and fifth centuries," in Cheslyn Jones, Geoffrey Wainwright, and Edward Yarnold (eds.), *The Study of Liturgy* (London: SPCK, 1978), p. 97, and Roten, *Baptême et mystagogie*, pp. 188–190.

[168] On the development of Lent, see Jan Willem Drijvers, *Cyril of Jerusalem: Bishop and City*, VC Sup 72 (Leiden; Boston: Brill, 2004), p. 54. This is true from Jerusalem to Antioch to Rome: see Harmless, *Augustine*, pp. 61–69, 94–98; Josef Knupp, *Das Mystagogieverständnis des Johannes Chrysostomus*, ed. Anton Bodem and Alois M. Kothgasser, Benediktbeurer Studien 4 (Munich: Don Bosco, 1995), pp. 43–49; Gavrilyuk, *Histoire*, pp. 190–191. Cyril of Jerusalem mentions a forty-day period for instruction in *Procat.* 4; see Saxer, *Les rites*, pp. 196–201.

[169] See the helpful discussion in Drijvers, *Cyril of Jerusalem*, p. 87, who notes the relevance of Egeria *It.* 45.2–46.5; see also John Chrysostom's address to sponsors (οἱ ἀναδεχόμενοι) in *Cat.* 1.15. It is not clear that an interview with sponsors was in place in every location. There is no discussion of *sponsores* in Ambrose or Augustine related to baptismal instruction.

Once admitted into the final stage of instruction, being now φωτιζόμενοι or *competentes*, candidates were provided with frequent catechetical instruction. It appears that the catechetical emphasis on a (multi-year) moral vetting period evident throughout the third century shifted onto the Lenten period as one of repentance and moral formation.[170] For instance, Cyril of Jerusalem considers it possible that some are approaching baptism simply for social advantage.

It is possible that you come with a different motivation. For it is possible that a man desires to earnestly pursue a woman and comes for that reason. The same point applies also to women. And a slave often wants to please his master, a friend his friend. I avail myself of that bait and accept you, coming with a wicked motivation but about to be saved by a good hope. Perhaps you did not know where you have come nor what kind of net has taken hold of you. You have become entangled within ecclesiastical nets. Be caught! Do not flee![171]

Just prior to this startling statement, Cyril describes his listeners as those whose souls are muddied with sins and this appears not merely as a theological judgment on the pre-baptized soul.[172] In light of the above citation this seems to be a comment on the moral state of those who have already passed the first phase of the catechumenate. Ambrose of Milan devoted his Lenten instructions to daily moral teaching and John Chrysostom devoted roughly half of his catechetical lectures one year to issues of behavior including female clothing, attendance at pagan festivals, and taking oaths.[173] These approaches are all the more notable

---

[170] The evidence from Syrian Christianity at this time is less clear on the formal structure of the catechumenate. Nevertheless, Aphrahat emphasizes the link between baptism and moral preparation (*Dem.* 7.18–23; see D. Ioannes Parisot (ed.), *Aphraatis Sapientis Persae Demonstrationes I–XXII*, Patrologia Syriaca 1.1 (Paris: Firmin-Didot, 1894)) and references to catechumens may be found in Ephrem's commentary on Paul's letters; see further in Chapter 6 below.

[171] Cyril of Jerusalem *Procat.* 5 (text from W. C. Reischl and J. Rupp (eds.), *Cyrilli Hierosolymorum archiepiscopi opera quae supersunt omnia* (Hildesheim: Olms, 1967)): Ἐγχωρεῖ σε καὶ προφάσει ἄλλῃ ἐλθεῖν· ἐγχωρεῖ γὰρ καὶ ἄνδρα βούλεσθαι γυναικὶ καθικετεῦσαι, καὶ διὰ τοῦτο προσελθεῖν· ἀντιστρέφει καὶ ἐπὶ γυναικῶν τὸ ὅμοιον ὁ λόγος· καὶ δοῦλος πολλάκις δεσπότῃ, καὶ φίλος φίλῳ ἀρέσαι ἠθέλησε. Δέχομαι τὸ δέλεαρ τοῦ ἀγκίστρου, καὶ καταδέχομαί σε, κακῇ προαιρέσει μὲν ἐλθόντα, ἐλπίδι δὲ ἀγαθῇ σωθησόμενον. Ἴσως οὐκ ᾔδεις ποῦ ἔρχῃ, οὐδὲ ποία σε σαγήνη λαμβάνει· γέγονας εἴσω δικτύων ἐκκλησιαστικῶν· ζωγρήθητι· μὴ φύγῃς·

[172] *Procat.* 4: Ἐγχωρεῖ δέ σε βεβορβορωμένην ἔχοντα τὴν ψυχὴν ἁμαρτίαις.

[173] Ambrose *Myst.* 1 (O. Faller (ed.), *Ambrosius. Explanatio symboli, De sacramentis, De mysteriis, De paenitentia, De excessu fratris, De obitu Valentiniani, De obitu Theodosii*, vol. IV, CSEL 73 (Salzburg: Österreichischen Akademie der Wissenschaften, 1955)); John Chrysostom *Cat.* 6.25–47. See also Harmless, *Augustine*, p. 94, on Ambrose; Saxer, *Les rites*, pp. 245–250, and Gavrilyuk, *Histoire*, pp. 228–230, on Chrysostom.

when compared with the views of previous writers such as Tertullian or Origen, for whom the approach to baptism was predicated on already rejecting sinful practices.

Beyond moral instruction, however, the catechetical lectures also focused on theological instruction, particularly with the practical goal of teaching the catechumens the "symbol" of faith.[174] This instruction was considered to be too advanced for outsiders, including catechumens still in the first stage, and was therefore restricted to the *competentes*.[175] A notable example of this doctrinal emphasis is in Gregory of Nyssa's *Oratio catechetica*. A guide for catechists, it devotes only the final small section to moral issues, while the enormous bulk of it is devoted to theological issues. Topics in these Lenten catechetical lectures included God, the incarnation, the Holy Spirit, eschatology, or even baptism, though this was typically reserved for a new stage of catechesis developed in the fourth century: mystagogy.[176]

While the language of "mystery" had a long tradition in early Christianity,[177] mystagogy developed particularly in the fourth century alongside the increasing treatment of the sacraments as *disciplina arcani*.[178] For Cyril of Jerusalem, mystagogical catechesis consisted in lectures on the significance of baptism and the eucharist and took place during Easter Week. Other preachers adopted slightly different practices with respect to what was included as catechesis and what as mystagogy.[179] Two things are notable for present purposes. First, with the introduction

---

[174] See Roten, *Baptême et mystagogie*, pp. 210–216, among others.

[175] See Cyril of Jerusalem *Procat.* 17; see also Gavrilyuk, *Histoire*, pp. 198–205.

[176] See the helpful comparative charts in Harmless, *Augustine*, pp. 75–78, 106, and note the chart of Cappadocian catechetical teaching in Saxer, *Les rites*, pp. 314–315.

[177] See esp. now T. J. Lang, *Mystery and the Making of a Christian Historical Consciousness: From Paul to the Second Century*, BZNW 219 (Berlin: De Gruyter, 2015), for a discussion of "mystery" in the first two centuries.

[178] See the comments of Gavrilyuk, *Histoire*, pp. 159–160; Yarnold, "The fourth and fifth centuries," pp. 109–110; Edward J. Yarnold, "Baptism and the pagan mysteries in the fourth century," *Heythrop Journal* 13 (1972), 258–259. Knupp's discussion of mystagogical teaching in Cyril of Jerusalem (associated rather with his successor, John) and Ambrose of Milan is particularly full, with a theological focus: Knupp, *Mystagogieverständnis*, pp. 241–263.

[179] See n. 176 above. J. N. D. Kelly, *Golden Mouth: The Story of John Chrysostom – Ascetic, Preacher, Bishop* (Ithaca: Cornell University Press, 1995), p. 89, argues that Chrysostom's extant catechetical homilies do not include mystagogical catechesis but that mystagogy was probably performed by another church leader. However, Chrysostom's discussion of baptism could well qualify and Knupp, *Mystagogieverständnis*, pp. 67–68 and *passim*, argues that it was generally absorbed within his normal catechetical lectures rather than constituting a distinct set.

of mystagogical catechesis, a new stage of Christian initiation was formalized in which the neophytes, though technically initiated, were not yet through with their particular instruction, which was considered foundational to their Christian life.[180] Second, this new facet of the catechetical institution provided a new and specific reference point for the language of mystery initiation. Where mystagogy and mystagogues were associated with so-called "gnostic" groups by writers such as Irenaeus and even Clement of Alexandria, in the fourth and fifth centuries mystagogy as initiation into the mysteries of baptism and the eucharist became normal within the church.[181]

2.5 CONCLUSION

Much more could be said in developing any particular point raised above, but even as it is this sketch of the catechumenate stands complete for now. In the exploration of Paul's association with the catechumenate among early Christian interpreters, the present outline suffices to establish some basic issues and trajectories that persisted through the first four centuries. One of the main recurrent themes is the concern for moral formation among catechumens.[182] While certain theological doctrines or formulations were passed on in association with baptism, almost necessarily, it is also the case that, from the earliest hints in the *Didache* and the *Shepherd of Hermas* through the catechetical lectures of Cyril of Jerusalem and John Chrysostom, moral issues were a central concern. The catechumenate as an institution – comprising a group of people inhabiting a liminal space in the church with recognized roles, status, and responsibilities – first comes into view at the end of the second century or beginning of the third, and blossoms fully in the fourth. In subsequent chapters, although this general outline will supply the framework for my treatment of various Pauline interpreters, each will be carefully assessed on their own terms, identifying their particular vocabulary of initiation and ways in which they fit with or diverge from the above sketch.

---

[180] Note that this order of events varied from church leader to church leader.

[181] Clement uses the language of mystagogy positively in relation to Christian knowledge of divine mysteries (e.g., *Strom.* 4.25.162.3; 5.11.74.1; 5.12.79), though the mysteries are not related to baptism or the eucharist. He also uses it in relation to Greek (pagan) mysteries (*Prot.* 2.21.1; *Strom.* 5.14.130.3 [citing Menander]; 7.17.106.3). See also the discussion of mystagogy in John Chrysostom's work in Chapter 6 below.

[182] Wyrwa, "Religiöses Lernen," p. 271 and *passim*, notes the close link between early Christian education and shaping one's way of life.

The modest goals identified at the beginning of the chapter have, then, been met: the "simple outline" has been traced, trends and continuities have been noted, and famously intractable problems addressed. I will now follow the development of catechetical readings of Paul from the late second century through the end of the fourth century, roughly from the time when catechetical practices converge into the catechumenate until the catechumenate reaches its zenith. Chapter 3 will address the earliest association of Paul with emerging catechetical practices in the *Acts of Paul*. In Chapters 4 and 5 I will address the image and interpretation of Paul in Clement and Origen at the time when the catechumenate was first established. This will also entail a consideration of Clement's "gnostic" opponents (among others) and greater attention to Origen's institutional context than the brief account above provides. Following that I turn to John Chrysostom and the fourth century (Chapter 6). In Chapter 7 I will bring the insights of these early interpreters into conversation with contemporary critical scholarship on Paul's letters and profile, before concluding with broader hermeneutical reflections arising from this project (Chapter 8).

3

Narrating the Catechist in the *Acts of Paul*

And Thecla said, "Just give me the seal in Christ and a trial will not touch me." And Paul said, "Thecla, endure and you will receive the water."[1]

Having illuminated the endpoint of the present study in Chapter 1 and surveyed the development of the catechumenate in Chapter 2, we are now in a position to begin the trek through Pauline interpretations in a roughly chronological fashion. The narrative presentation of Paul's activities in the *Acta Pauli* (*APl*) supplies the first treatment of Paul in which he is assimilated to an emerging catechetical process, common at least to Asia Minor and North Africa, though broader commonalities are also evident.[2]

The question that will occupy the present chapter is this: How is Paul portrayed in the *Acts of Paul*?[3] The short answer, to be developed further below, is that Paul is presented as the archetypal teacher who compellingly spreads the gospel, characterized particularly by resurrection and self-control, and whose pattern other teachers follow. He converts and baptizes multiple people across the Roman empire, with enthralling teaching and miraculous healings. While the general portrayal of Paul

---

[1] *APl* 3.25: καὶ εἶπεν Θέκλα Μόνον δός μοι τὴν ἐν Χριστῷ σφραγῖδα, καὶ οὐχ ἅψεταί μοι πειρασμός. καὶ εἶπεν Παῦλος Θέκλα μακροθύμησον, καὶ λήψῃ τὸ ὕδωρ; text in R. A. Lipsius (ed.), *Acta Apostolorum Apocrypha: Acta Petri, Acta Pauli, Acta Petri et Pauli, Acta Pauli et Theclae, Acta Thaddaei* (Hildesheim and New York: Georg Olms, 1972).

[2] For a discussion of Irenaeus' relationship to a catechetical reading of Paul, see the discussion in relation to Clement of Alexandria in Chapter 4 below.

[3] An initial study of Paul's non-baptism of Thecla can be found in Benjamin A. Edsall, "(Not) baptizing Thecla: early interpretive efforts on 1 Cor 1:17," *Vigiliae Christianae* 71, no. 3 (2017), 235–260.

in the *Acta Pauli* is obviously consonant with widespread hagiographical tendencies in early Christianity, manifest in numerous apocryphal Acts and Gospels, one particular element has been a sticking point for some scholars, which, it is argued, demonstrates a tacit criticism of Paul. The sticking point is the Thecla narrative, perhaps the most well-known and widespread section of the apocryphal collection, in which Paul seems strangely absent, even cowardly, in his refusal to baptize or defend Thecla. In fact, as will become clear, it is exactly this narrative that most clearly illuminates Paul's assimilation to late second-century catechetical practice.[4]

Before addressing this point directly, it is important to briefly clarify the text and transmission of the *Acts of Paul*, insofar as they impinge on the present argument. Following a discussion of these textual matters, I will provide a quick plot summary, before exploring the puzzle of Thecla's baptism and its importance for the catechetical presentation of Paul.

3.1 TEXTUAL MATTERS

3.1.1 Manuscripts and Mentions

The date and authorship of the *Acta Pauli* are difficult to determine and these considerations are complicated, moreover, by the manuscript history. Of the numerous textual problems that attend the study of the *Acts of Paul*, one issue will be particularly relevant: whether the Thecla narrative we have is likely to have "originated" as part of the larger *Acta Pauli* and, if so, what that larger body of stories included. Despite a recent and salutary challenge from Glen Snyder, for the reasons outlined below I think the available evidence still points rather to a single work, the *Acts of Paul*, which was penned in the late second century and was excerpted and expanded in subsequent centuries, coinciding in particular for the Thecla material with the rise of the cult of Saint Thecla in the fourth century.[5]

---

[4] Though not cast in quite these terms, the recent analysis of Thecla and conversion in Niederhofer, *Konversion*, is largely congruent with what follows. Unfortunately, I gained access to Niederhofer's work too late to offer a full engagement, though some points of agreement (and occasional disagreement) are included in the footnotes.

[5] Glenn E. Snyder, *Acts of Paul: The Formation of a Pauline Corpus*, WUNT II/352 (Tübingen: Mohr Siebeck, 2013). On the Thecla cult, see Stephen J. Davis, *The Cult of Saint Thecla: A Tradition of Women's Piety in Late Antiquity*, Oxford Early Christian Studies (Oxford: Oxford University Press, 2001). On the expanded Thecla material, see Gilbert Dagron (ed.), *Vie et miracles de Sainte Thècle. Texte grec, traduction et commentaire*, Subsidia Hagiographica 62 (Brussels: Société des Bollandistes, 1978).

The principle manuscripts for the *Acta Pauli* are a fourth-century Greek codex (P.Hamburg) and a sixth-century Coptic codex (P.Heidelberg), both published by Carl Schmidt in the first part of the twentieth century.[6] These are supported by smaller papyrus contributions and more developed Greek, Latin, Syriac, Armenian, and Arabic textual traditions for different sections of the text.[7] Some parts of what we refer to as the *Acts of Paul* circulated independently – at least including the Thecla narrative (*APl* 3–4), the martyrdom (*APl* 12–14), the Ephesus Act (*APl* 9), and the embedded letter *3 Corinthians* (*APl* 3), which even received a commentary at the hands of Ephrem in the fourth century as part of his collection of Pauline letters.[8] Furthermore, the two principle witnesses are too fragmentary to be completely certain of their contents or order. Even where we are more certain, they fail to overlap at two notable junctures: P.Hamburg begins partway through the Ephesus Act (*APl* 9, with the beginning supplemented by the fourth-century Coptic P.Bod. 41[9]) but lacks the Philippi narrative (with 3 Corinthians; *APl* 10), while

---

[6] Carl Schmidt (ed.), *Acta Pauli. Übersetzung, Untersuchungen und Koptischer Text,* 2nd edn (Leipzig: J. C. Hinrichs, 1905) (supplemented by Carl Schmidt, "Ein Berliner Fragment der alten Πράξεις Παύλου," *Sitzungsberichte der Preussischen Akademie der Wissenschaften,* no. 1 (1931), 37–40), and Carl Schmidt and Wilhelm Schubart, *ΠΡΑΞΕΙΣ ΠΑΥΛΟΥ. Acta Pauli nach dem Papyrus der Hamburger Staats- und Universitäts-bibliothek unter Mitarbeit von Wilhelm Schubart* (Hamburg: J. J. Augustin, 1936).

[7] Lipsius notes these textual traditions in his apparatus. For Latin, see Oscar von Gebhardt (ed.), *Passio S. Theclae virginis. Die lateinischen Übersetzungen der Acta Pauli et Theclae nebst Fragmenten Auszügen und Beilagen herausgegeben,* TUGAL 7 (Leipzig: J. C. Hinrichs, 1902); for Syriac, see William Wright (ed.), *Apocryphal Acts of the Apostles,* vol. 1: *The Syriac Texts* (London: Williams and Norgate, 1871), pp. 127–169. The Mekhitarist Armenian editions are noted and discussed in Valentina Calzolari, "The editing of Christian apocrypha in Armenian: should we turn over a new leaf?" in Valentina Calzolari (ed.), *Armenian Philology in the Modern Era: From Manuscript to Digital Text* (Leiden: Brill, 2014), pp. 274–275, with selected translations in F. C. Conybeare (ed.), *The Armenian Apology and Acts of Apollonius and Other Monuments of Early Christianity,* 2nd edn (London: Swan Sonnenschein, 1896). Some Arabic manuscripts of the martyrdom narrative were edited and translated in Agnes Smith Lewis (ed.), *Acta Mythologica Apostolorum: Transcribed from an Arabic MS. in the Convent of Deyr-Es-Suriani, Egypt, and from MSS in the Convent of St. Catherine, on Mount Sinai,* Horae Seminicae 3–4 (London: Clay and Sons, 1904), pp. 184–189, 217–222.

[8] For the numbering of *Acta Pauli,* I am following Rordorf *et al.* (in François Bovon and Pierre Geoltrain (eds.), *Écrits apocryphes chrétiens,* vol. 1, Bibliothèque de la Pléiade (Saint Herblain: Gallimard, 1997)), which is generally adopted by others, e.g., Snyder, *Acts of Paul*; Richard I. Pervo (ed.), *The Acts of Paul: A New Translation with Introduction and Commentary* (Eugene: Cascade Books, 2014).

[9] *Editio princeps* in Rodolphe Kasser and Philippe Luisier, "Le Papyrus Bodmer XLI en édition princeps: l'épisode d'Éphèses des *Acta Pauli* en copte et en traduction," *Le Muséon* 117, no. 3 (2004), 281–384.

P.Heidelberg contains a full narrative including the Philippi material but is evidently missing the Ephesus Act.

In considering the manuscript difficulties in relation to the Thecla narrative, one also has to address the historical notices to the *Acta Pauli* that begin around the turn of the third century. The earliest explicit notice is provided by Tertullian, in his homily on baptism. In a hypothetical aside during his criticism of a local Cainite female teacher who was, we are told, rejecting baptism,[10] Tertullian notes that if such a woman were to claim the example of Thecla as precedent for female teaching and baptism, he would tell them that "certain Acts of Paul, which are falsely so named" were "compiled" by an Asian presbyter as a misguided show of his love for Paul and, further, that he abdicated his post as a result.[11] Tertullian does not say when this happened nor does he elaborate on what he means by the phrase *eam scripturam construxit* – did he *compose* the text or did he *compile* it?

Less directly, in the first decade of the third century, Tertullian made use of the Pauline martyrdom tradition included in the Martyrdom of Paul (*APl* 14), indicating that he accepted the account (*Scorp.* 15).[12]

---

[10] *Bapt.* 1.2: "And in fact a certain woman from the Cainite heresy who recently stayed here, a most poisonous viper, dragged away many with her doctrine, especially destroying baptism" (atque, adeo nuper conversata istic quaedam de caina haeresi vipera venenatissima doctrina sua plerosque rapuit, imprimis baptismum destruens).

[11] *Bapt.* 17.5: "But if a certain falsely named *Acta Pauli* should defend the example of Thecla for the license of women to teach and baptize, let them know that the presbyter, who composed this work in Asia, as though he could add to Paul's reputation by his own skill, was exposed and although he confessed that he did it out of a love for Paul, he abdicated his position" (quod si quae Acta Pauli, quae perperam scripta sunt, exemplum Theclae ad licentiam mulierum docendi tinguendique defendant, sciant in Asia presbyterum qui eam scripturam construxit, quasi titulo Pauli de suo cumulans, convictum atque confessum id se amore Pauli fecisse loco decessisse). See Willy Rordorf, "Tertullien et les *Actes de Paul* (à propos *de bapt.* 17,5)," in *Lex Orandi – Lex Credendi. Gesammelte Aufsätze zum 60. Geburtstag*, Paradosis 36 (Freiburg-Neuchâtel: Universitätsverlag Freiburg Schweiz, 1993), pp. 475–484, for a discussion of different editions of *Bapt.* 17.5. The textual difficulties, including the lack of explicit subject for the verb "sciant," are emphasized by A. Hilhorst, "Tertullian on the Acts of Paul," in Jan N. Bremmer (ed.), *The Apocryphal Acts of Paul and Thecla*, Studies on the Apocryphal Acts of the Apostles (Kampen: Kok Pharos, 1996), pp. 150–163, who thinks it is doubtful that the title *Acta Pauli* was present in Tertullian's text. Granted the textual difficulty, the witness of Origen and the title of the material in P.Heidelberg provide at least corroborating external evidence for the plausibility of Tertullian's knowing the work under such a title.

[12] *Pace* Snyder, *Acts of Paul*, pp. 234–235, who argues that Tertullian's rejection of the Thecla narrative and his acceptance of the tradition regarding Paul's execution indicates that he received them separately. This view rests on too strong a reading of Tertullian's rejection of the Thecla material and does not address the rhetorical function of the passage in *Scorp.* 15.

Around the same time, Hippolytus mentioned the story of Paul baptizing a lion which is preserved in the Ephesus Act (*APl* 9) and which shares thematic and stylistic features with the Thecla narrative.[13] However, in both of these cases there is no explicit mention of a text. Roughly thirty to forty years later, Origen refers to material from the narrative leading up to and including Paul's martyrdom as being from the *Acts of Paul* and it is just possible that Clement of Alexandria was aware of Paul's sermon in Corinth from *APl* 12.[14]

These external witnesses, then, suggest that a text called the *Acts of Paul* was in circulation in the late second and early third centuries. It included the Thecla incident; something like the Ephesus Act, whose traditions were known and show a tight literary affinity with the Thecla narrative;[15] a martyrdom narrative; and some preceding narrative leading from Corinth to Rome, comprising *Acta Pauli* 3–4, 9, 12–14. The third-century manuscript of 3 Corinthians (P.Bod. 10) also places it in the same general period[16] – though, of course, it may have been added to the extant *Acta Pauli* later, the insertion either bringing along the Philippi material or generating it out of narrative necessity.[17] Furthermore, the beginning of *APl* 3 suggests previous material which is in fact supplied in the Coptic Heidelberg papyrus, whether or not that specific version of the material was in fact "original" to the work.[18]

---

[13] *Comm. in Dan* 3.29.4 (M. Lefèvre (ed.), *Hippolyte. Commentaire sur Daniel*, SC 14 (Paris: Cerf, 1947)); see the discussion of this passage and the others noted here in Snyder, *Acts of Paul*, pp. 222–223, 227, who also notes that Jerome treated the "lion-cycle" as a united narrative.

[14] Origen, *Comm. in Iohan.* 20.12 (Cécile Blanc (ed.), *Origène. Commentaire sur saint Jean*, 5 vols., SC 120, 157, 222, 290, 385 (Paris: Cerf, 1966–1992)); Ronald E. Heine (ed.), *Origen: Commentary on the Gospel of John, Books 13–32*, Fathers of the Church 89 (Washington, D.C.: Catholic University of America Press, 1993), p. 18, argues that books 19–32 were composed around 241; Clement *Strom.* 6.5 mentions a κηρύγμα of Paul but the following citation does not overlap with *Acta Pauli* and Snyder, *Acts of Paul*, p. 223, admits that the connection "is not very likely."

[15] See p. 74 n. 30 below.

[16] See Michel Testuz, *Papyrus Bodmer X–XII* (Cologny-Genève: Bibliotheca Bodmeriana, 1959), *ad loc.*

[17] See White, *Remembering Paul*, pp. 109–110.

[18] The goal of reconstructing an original text is fraught with conceptual difficulties and in many ways is being abandoned in favor of focusing on the effect of the different readings; see particularly Eldon Jay Epp, "The multivalence of the term 'original text' in New Testament textual criticism," *Harvard Theological Review* 92, no. 3 (1999), 245–281, and D. C. Parker, *The Living Text of the Gospels* (Cambridge: Cambridge University Press, 1997) on the New Testament text. The difficulty is of course exacerbated with the small number of manuscripts available for the *Acts of Paul*. The point here, however, is not to discover the original text in any detail. Rather, it is

The implication for the present argument is simply this: the Thecla narrative in the form available to us was part of a larger hagiographical work circulating at the end of the second century that focused on the preaching and miracles of the Apostle Paul. This is important for evaluating alternative scholarly positions below, though a few further comments in relation to oral and literary sources are pertinent here.

3.1.2 Oral and Literary Relationships

Several scholars, most notably Dennis MacDonald and Virginia Burrus, have argued that the Thecla narrative originated as an orally transmitted folktale and was later written down, perhaps by the Asian presbyter.[19] While this remains possible in principle, it is difficult to move beyond the bare statement of the possibility. First, as MacDonald himself notes, it is extremely difficult to separate out oral traditions that have been integrated into the narrative whole.[20] A corollary to this observation is that reading such proposed selections out of, or even against, the context in which they are currently found is methodologically and conceptually problematic; in other words, that approach creates the condition for arbitrary readings without historical or textual grounding. In the form that we currently have the Thecla narrative, integrated as it is within the *Acts of Paul* more broadly, it bears marked similarities with ancient novels,

---

simply that, as far back as the evidence goes, it appears that the Thecla narrative was integrated with at least *APl* 9 and 12–14. My hesitance to accept Glen Snyder's entire argument for the fragmentary nature of the *Acts of Paul* has recently been corroborated by Jan N. Bremmer, "The onomastics and provenance of the *Acts of Paul*," in Francesca P. Barone, Caroline Macé, and Pablo A. Ubierna (eds.), *Philologie, herméneutique et histoire des textes entre orient et occident*, Instrumenta Patristica et Mediaevalia 73 (Turnhout: Brepols, 2017), pp. 528–529, though his appeal to the *Acts of Titus* is perhaps too far afield for the present argument. Bremmer is also followed by Niederhofer, *Konversion*, pp. 23–24.

[19] Dennis R. MacDonald, *The Legend and the Apostle: The Battle for Paul in Story and Canon* (Philadelphia: Westminster, 1983); Virginia Burrus, *Chastity as Autonomy: Women in the Stories of the Apocryphal Acts*, Studies in Women and Religion 23 (Lewiston, ME: E. Mellen Press, 1987); and earlier Stevan L. Davies, *The Revolt of the Widows: The Social World of the Apocryphal Acts* (Carbondale, IL: Southern Illinois University Press; London: Feffer & Simons, 1980), who differs from MacDonald and Burrus in arguing for female *authorship* of the Thecla narrative rather than appealing for origins in oral folklore among circles of early Christian women. Anne Jensen, who is sympathetic to both views, nevertheless finds the marginalization of Tertullian's notice and appeals to otherwise unknown female storytellers to be problematic (Anne Jensen, *Thekla, die Apostolin. Ein apokrypher Text neu entdeckt*, Kaiser Taschenbücher 172 (Gütersloh: Chr. Kaiser, 1999), pp. 76, 79–80).

[20] MacDonald, *The Legend*, p. 18.

which is to say that it appears as a complete compositional whole.[21] Whether or not folktales or some other oral tradition underlie the work circulating in the late second century, we cannot see them now.[22]

Apart from questions of oral sources, there remains the problem of assessing the literary relationship between the *Acts of Paul* and the emerging scriptural profile of Paul. On the one hand, the Thecla narrative in particular shows a remarkable connection with figures otherwise most associated with 2 Timothy, but also from elsewhere in the Pauline corpus.[23] Further, there are clear allusions to Paul's teaching on sexual renunciation in 1 Corinthians 7 (*APl* 3.5) and the Ephesus narrative appears to develop out of Paul's comments in 1 Corinthians 15:32. On the other hand, whether and/or how the author of the *Acta Pauli* knew the canonical Acts is a more difficult issue. While some argue that there is no clear knowledge of Acts,[24] others offer various models of interaction, including imitation, completion, and competition.[25] Addressing all the

---

[21] The connection between *Acta Pauli* and ancient romances was first proposed by Ernst von Dobschütz, "Der Roman in der altchristlichen Literatur," *Deutsche Rundschau* 111 (1902), 96–97; see also Rosa Söder, *Die apokryphen Apostelgeschichten und die romanhafte Literatur der Antike*, Würzburger Studien zur Altertumswissenschaft 3 (Stuttgart: Kohlhammer, 1932).

[22] The oral folktale solution proposed by MacDonald is attended by other difficulties as well with respect to the relation between the *Acts of Paul*, the Pastoral Epistles, and/ or the canonical Acts. Esther Y. Ng, "*Acts of Paul and Thecla*: women's stories and precedent?," *Journal of Theological Studies* 55, no. 1 (2004), 1–29, has a particularly cogent response to the arguments of Burrus *et al.* See also Monika Betz, "Thekla und die jüngeren Witwen der Pastoralbriefe: ein Beispiel für die Situationsgebundenheit paulinischer Tradition," *Annali di Studi Religiosi* 6 (2005), 335–356; Gerd Häfner, "Die Gegner in den Pastoralbriefen und die Paulusakten," *Zeitschrift für die Neutestamentliche Wissenschaft* 92, no. 1 (2001), 64–77.

[23] See Benjamin A. Edsall, "Hermogenes the smith and narrative characterization in *The Acts of Paul*: a note on the reception of 2 Timothy," *New Testament Studies* 64, no. 1 (2018), 108–121, on narrative characterization and the role of Demas and Hermogenes in the narrative.

[24] E.g. Willy Rordorf, "In welchem Verhältnis stehen die apokryphen Paulusakten zur kanonischen Apostelgeschichte und zu den Pastoralbriefen?," in *Lex Orandi – Lex Credendi. Gesammelte Aufsätze zum 60. Geburtstag*, Paradosis 36 (Freiburg-Neuchâtel: Universitätsverlag Freiburg Schweiz, 1993), pp. 449–465; Peter W. Dunn, "The *Acts of Paul* and the Pauline legacy in the second century," unpublished Ph.D. thesis, University of Cambridge (1996), pp. 43–44; Jeremy W. Barrier, *The Acts of Paul and Thecla: A Critical Introduction and Commentary*, WUNT II/270 (Tübingen: Mohr Siebeck, 2009), p. 32; Snyder, *Acts of Paul*, pp. 13–14.

[25] See Dassmann, *Der Stachel*, p. 273; Richard Bauckham, "The Acts of Paul as a sequel to Acts," in Bruce W. Winter and Andrew D. Clarke (eds.), *The Book of Acts in its First Century Setting*, vol. 1: *Ancient Literary Setting* (Grand Rapids: Eerdmans; Carlisle: Paternoster, 1993), pp. 105–152; Claudia Büllesbach, "Das Verhältnis der Acta Pauli zur Apostelgeschichte des Lukas: Darstellung und Kritik der Forschungsgeschichte," in F. W.

relevant passages would well exceed the limits of this chapter, but suffice it to say that I find the position of Wilhelm Schneemelcher, suitably qualified, to be generally persuasive. He writes:

The AP [in its known form] comes from a time in which the NT canon surely existed and was known. The speech of the Acts of Paul displays considerable affinity with the speech of Acts, but of course also with that of other New Testament texts. One can only assume that the author had known Acts. But his work is not dependent on Acts but rather on the circulating tradition about Paul and his works. The AP belongs to a different epoch of church history and every comparison with Acts must keep this fact in view.[26]

Two qualification need to be added to Schneemelcher's view, however. The first is that in the period that the *Acts of Paul* was written, the New Testament *canon* certainly did not exist. However, the texts that would later be included in the canon *did* exist and were in circulation.[27] Second, the notion of a "different epoch" should not be pressed too far. Although it is true that early Christians were aware of a distinction between the apostolic generation and their own, it is not clear that this shift constituted a recognized discontinuity in textual production.[28] The *Acta Pauli*, then, are a sort of free parallel account of Paul's activities that modeled itself on Acts to some extent but did not feel bound by it. For centuries it

---

Horn (ed.), *Das Ende des Paulus. Historische, theologische und literaturgeschichtliche Aspekte*, BZNW 106 (Berlin: De Gruyter, 2001), pp. 215–237; Pervo, *Making of Paul*, pp. 157–158; and Niederhofer, *Konversion*, pp. 24–25.

[26] "Die AP stammen aus einer Zeit, in der der Kanon des NT sicher existierte und bekannt war. Die Sprach der AP zeigt beachtliche Verwandtschaft mit der Sprach der Apg., aber natürlich auch anderer neutestamentlicher Schriften. Man wird annehmen dürfen, daß der Verfasser die Apg. gekannt hat. Aber sein Werk ist nicht von der Apg. abhängig, sondern von der umlaufenden Tradition über Paulus und sein Wirken. Die AP gehören einer anderen Epoche der Kirchengeschichte an, und jeder Vergleich mit der Apg. muß diese Tatsache im Auge behalten"; cited and critiqued in Rordorf, "Verhältnis," p. 453, and see the response in Wilhelm Schneemelcher, "Acts of Paul," in Wilhelm Schneemelcher (ed.), *New Testament Apocrypha*, vol. 2, trans. R. M. Wilson (Cambridge: James Clarke & Co Ltd.; Louisville: Westminster/John Knox, 1992), pp. 232–233. See also Daniel Marguerat, "Les 'Actes de Paul': une relecture des Actes canoniques," in *La première histoire du christianisme. Les Actes des apôtres*, LD 180 (Paris: Cerf; Geneva: Labor et Fides, 1999), pp. 369–391.

[27] This can be thought of perhaps usefully as an "emerging canon" of widely revered scriptures – including Pauline letters and Gospels; see the discussion of the canon in relation to early Christian institutions in Markschies, *Christian Theology*, pp. 191–299.

[28] A similar point has been made by Francis Watson in relation to early gospels. He makes a strong case for continuity of textual production throughout the first two centuries; Francis Watson, *Gospel Writing: A Canonical Perspective* (Grand Rapids: Eerdmans, 2013).

sat comfortably beside the (by then) canonical book of Acts, evidently without either one being seen as a challenge to the other.[29]

The approach of the present chapter, then, will build on this account. Rather than Snyder's fragmentary view of the *Acts of Paul* in the second century, we will proceed on the view that the Thecla narrative circulated in the company of a larger narrative that runs through the martyrdom of Paul. And rather than treating pre-textual oral traditions, the analysis will focus on the novelistic hagiographical form that appropriated the emerging profile of Paul.

3.2 *ACTA PAULI*: A PLOT SUMMARY

I turn now to a brief review of the *Acts of Paul* in order to identify the main contours of the narrative and its presentation of Paul. More space will be devoted to the Thecla portion of the story owing to its evidently anomalous portrayal of Paul. Although order and contents of the *Acta Pauli* at the time of its composition or compilation are not entirely clear, the present overview will follow the traditional order while restricting itself to the sections identified above as most likely present at the end of the second century: the Thecla narrative, the Ephesus Act, and the martyrdom (*APl* 3–4, 9, 12–14).[30]

The story of Paul and Thecla begins with Paul's arrival in Iconium to stay with Onesiphorus, in whose house he teaches about self-control (ἐγκράτεια) and resurrection, with great results. Many people come to hear him and the betrothed virgin Thecla becomes enthralled by his message,

---

[29] There is some parallel here with both infancy gospels and post-resurrection dialogue gospels. All these texts exploit lacunae in the widely known scriptural texts as vehicles for their own stories and teachings while not feeling entirely restricted to the plot of their "base" texts; see the discussion of this dynamic in Markus N. A. Bockmuehl, *Ancient Apocryphal Gospels*, Interpretation: Resources for the Use of Scripture in the Church (Louisville: Westminster John Knox, 2017). Note also that Frances M. Young, *Biblical Exegesis and the Formation of Christian Culture* (Cambridge: Cambridge University Press, 1997), p. 240, suggests that the resonances with Pauline letters and Acts is part of a broader mimetic tendency within the early Christian reception of scripture: "Christian narrative was mimetic of scripture, and intended to inspire mimesis."

[30] The common ordering of the Thecla narrative and the Ephesus Act has been challenged by Snyder, *Acts of Paul*, p. 230 and *passim*. He argues that, although they probably originated together, the placement of the Ephesus Act *after* the Thecla narrative by Rordorf and others (by harmonizing P.Heid. and P.Hamb) is unjustified. Snyder suggests that it may have been the other way around. This is part of his larger argument for an explicitly minimalistic approach to the textual integrity of the *Acta Pauli*; see the discussion of the textual difficulties and origins above.

even without the benefit of seeing Paul personally (*APl* 3.1–7).[31] Thecla is so captivated by Paul's teaching that her fiancé, Thamyris, becomes concerned and attempts to intervene.[32] After a series of imprisonments and trials, during which Thecla remains a silent presence, the governor of Iconium exiles Paul for "corrupting the women" (3.15, 21). For her refusal to marry Thamyris, thereby transgressing the law, Thecla is sentenced to the fire (3.20–21).[33] While standing on the pyre, Thecla has a vision of Christ, appearing in the form of Paul, who is praying for her in a grave near the city, before she is saved from the fire by a divinely appointed hailstorm (3:22). Thecla finds Paul again after this ordeal and offers to cut her hair and follow him, though he appears to put her off. Undeterred, she then asks for "the sign in Christ" (i.e., baptism), and Paul admonishes endurance because "you will receive the water."[34]

Paul then goes to Antioch along with Thecla, where a certain Alexander attempts to buy Thecla from Paul with "goods and gifts (4.1).[35] After

---

[31] The emphasis on Paul's teaching in this episode (and elsewhere in the *Acts of Paul*) stands out somewhat from the central importance of miracles for conversion presented in the other early Apocryphal Acts; see Jan N. Bremmer, "Conversion in the oldest *Apocryphal Acts*," in *Maidens, Magic and Martyrs in Early Christianity: Collected Essays I*, WUNT I/379 (Tübingen: Mohr Siebeck, 2017), p. 190.

[32] Bremmer suggests that the efficacy of Paul's teaching is further emphasized by the fact that his ungainliness could not have contributed to Thecla's attraction; see Jan N. Bremmer, "The portrait of the Apostle Paul in the apocryphal *Acts of Paul*," in T. Greub and M. Roussel (eds.), *Figurationen des Porträts* (Munich: Wilhelm Fink, 2018), pp. 425–426, 432, and *passim*. It should be remembered, though, that his appearance could not have swayed her either way initially, since she had not yet seen Paul.

[33] 3.20: "And when he assembled the council, he addressed Thecla, 'Why don't you marry Thamyris in accordance with the law of the Iconians?'…Theocleia, her mother cried out, 'Burn the lawless woman, burn the unmarried woman in the middle of the theater so that all the women under this instruction may be afraid'" (καὶ συμβούλιον ποιήσας ἐκάλεσεν τὴν Θέκλαν λέγων Διὰ τί οὐ γαμεῖ κατὰ τὸν Ἰκονιέων νόμον τῷ Θαμύριδι;…Θεοκλεία ἡ μήτηρ αὐτῆς ἀνέκραγεν λέγουσα Κατάκαιε τὴν ἄνομον, κατάκαιε τὴν ἄνυμφον ἐν μέσῳ θεάτρου, ἵνα πᾶσαι αἱ ὑπὸ τούτου διδαχθεῖσαι γυναῖκες φοβηθῶσιν).

[34] 3.25: καὶ εἶπεν Θέκλα Μόνον δός μοι τὴν ἐν Χριστῷ σφραγῖδα, καὶ οὐχ ἅψεταί μοι πειρασμός. καὶ εἶπεν Παῦλος Θέκλα μακροθύμησον, καὶ λήψῃ τὸ ὕδωρ.

[35] It is unclear whether this is Pisidian or Syrian Antioch. The decision hinges on how one is to read the description of Alexander (συριάρχη or σύρος), which varies between manuscripts. The Greek manuscript favored by Lipsius, *Acta Apostolorum Apocrypha*, *ad loc.* reads συριάρχη, while other Greek manuscripts and the Coptic read σύρος/ ογϲγр[οϲ], and the Syriac lacks either. As Bremmer notes, naming Alexander as a "Syrian" would be superfluous in Syria (Jan N. Bremmer, "Magic, martyrdom and women's liberation in the *Acts of Paul and Thecla*," in *Maidens, Magic and Martyrs in Early Christianity: Collected Essays I*, WUNT I/379 (Tübingen: Mohr Siebeck, 2017), pp. 158–159), and several scholars have argued that the description is a later addition to be omitted from critical editions (see W. M. Ramsay, *The Church in the Roman Empire before a.d. 170* (London: Putnam, 1893), p. 381; MacDonald, *The Legend*, pp. 40–42;

Paul denies his relationship with Thecla, promptly disappearing from the scene, Alexander accosts Thecla, who rejects his advances. The jilted Alexander then has Thecla arrested and brought to trial,[36] where she is condemned *ad bestias*. In the arena, Thecla is delivered yet again, baptizing herself in a pool full of deadly seals and being freed from ropes by a miraculous fire.

Finally, the governor declares Thecla innocent and sets her free. Her witness in the arena has converted "all the women," who proclaim "it is the one God who saved Thecla" (4.13). Tryphanea invites Thecla back to her home for eight days, where Thecla instructs her in the word of God before setting out to find Paul, with her "loins" girded and her chiton arranged in a manly fashion. Upon finding Paul, she explains what happened and is commissioned by Paul to "teach the word of God" (4.16). Thecla then returns to Iconium to preach and sets off for a life of ministry. We are finally told that, "after bearing witness to these things, she went into Seleucia and, illuminating many with the word of God, she slept in a noble repose."[37]

Paul next arrives in Ephesus from Smyrna, according to P.Bod. 41, and is received with joy by the community there. His preaching in Ephesus, including the story about his baptizing a lion, creates such a rush to "the faith" (ⲁⲩ[ⲟⲩ]ⲛⲁ6 ⲙ̄ⲙⲟ9ⲉ ⲟⲅⲱ9 ⲁⲧⲡⲓⲥⲧⲓⲥ) that the ruler of Asia is upset and wants to kill Paul.[38] Procla, a local benefactress, is converted and baptized with her household. Local "jealousy" leads to Paul's arrest, trial before the governor, and imprisonment.[39] While Paul is in prison, the governor Hieronymus and his freedman Diophanes become jealous of Paul's influence over their wives, Artemilla and Eboula, and make an effort to

---

and Dunn, "The *Acts of Paul*," pp. 21–22). On the other hand, if Lipsius is correct, the description ⲥⲩⲣⲓⲁⲣⲭⲏⲥ does more than simply indicate Alexander's origin; it indicates his social standing. (Note that Lipsius' decision was rejected by von Gebhardt, *Passio S. Theclae*, p. xcviii, and Léon Vouaux (ed.), *Les actes de Paul et ses lettres apocryphes*, Les apocryphes du nouveau testament (Paris: Librairie Letouzey er Ané, 1913), p. 195.) I tentatively follow Lipsius here, though the interpretive difference is not great for present purposes.

[36] Presumably on the grounds of her (implicit) mistreatment of the imperial honors associated with Alexander's position; see the comments in MacDonald, *The Legend*, p. 41.

[37] 4.18: καὶ ταῦτα διαμαρτυραμένη ἀπῆλθεν εἰς Σελεύκειαν, καὶ πολλοὺς φωτίσασα τῷ λόγῳ τοῦ θεοῦ μετὰ καλοῦ ὕπνου ἐκοιμήθη.

[38] Reading ⲛ̄ⲧⲁⲥⲓⲁ with Kasser and Luisier for the manuscript's ⲛ̄ⲧⲁⲙⲓⲁ; Kasser and Luisier, "Le Papyrus Bodmer," p. 325 n. 12.

[39] So far the material has been preserved only in P.Bod. 41; P.Hamburg picks up the narrative while Paul is offering his defense before the governor (p. 7 of P.Bod. 41).

speed up his death in the arena.[40] Eboula, who had been a student of Paul "night and day,"[41] brings Artemilla to him, where he convinces her to give up her lavish ways and she begs to be baptized.[42] Being miraculously freed from his chains, Paul leads the women to the river, where he baptizes Artemilla. Paul is then sent to the arena, only to be delivered again from martyrdom.

Finally, Paul goes to Rome, where he converts a great multitude from Caesar's household. The wine bearer Patroclus, whom Paul raises from the dead, in the fashion of Eutychus in Acts 20, becomes the particular sticking point.[43] When Patroclus is questioned by Nero about his resurrection and Paul, it comes out that Paul is recruiting soldiers for the kingdom of heaven. Paul is therefore brought before Nero, who condemns him to be decapitated (*APl* 14.2–4). Longinus and Cescus, the two soldiers assigned to the task, are intrigued by Paul's teaching and want to know more about the kingdom about which he teaches, eventually begging for salvation (14.5). He defers their baptism until after his death, however, in favor of martyrdom. He leaves the baptism to the agency of Luke and Titus, who are at Paul's grave the day after his burial. When Luke and Titus hear that Paul had promised baptism to Longinus and Cescus, they give them the "seal in the Lord" (ἔδωκαν αὐτοῖς τὴν ἐν κυρίῳ σφραγῖδα; 14.7).

---

[40] The first part of this scene is presumed to be present in the lost three pages of P.Bod. 41 and is otherwise supplied by P.Hamburg. I find Pervo's argument that this episode is a later interpolation unconvincing; Pervo, *Making of Paul*, pp. 234–236. As it stands, the baptism of Artemilla provides further thematic links with the Thecla narrative. Like Thecla, Artemilla and Euboula are so taken with Paul's teaching that they visit him in prison, thus angering their husbands as Thecla angered Thamyris. Further, the characters are integrated with the full lion narrative such that a simple interpolation would be difficult to explain, even if a fuller source-critical explanation were possible. This is suggested but not pursued by Snyder, *Acts of Paul*, p. 71.

[41] 9.16: ἡ γυνὴ μαθήτρια ἦν Παύλου καὶ νυκτὸς καὶ ἡμέρης παρεκάθητο αὐτῷ.

[42] καὶ ταῦτα Ἀρτεμύλλα ἀκούσασα μετὰ Εὐβούλας ἐδεήθη Παύλου, ἵνα λούσῃ ἤδη ἐν θεῷ. καὶ εἰς αὔριον ἦν τὰ θηριομαχῖα; P.Hamb. 2, lines 34–36. Kasser and Luisier, "Le Papyrus Bodmer," p. 330, claim that both women demand baptism, though according to P.Hamburg Eboula is already a disciple of Paul and only Artemilla asks to be baptized. Further, in both the Greek and the Coptic versions, only Artemilla is baptized by Paul.

[43] *APl* 14.4. The similarities and tensions between the story in the *Acta Pauli* and that of Acts 20 have led some to argue that the Patroclus version could in fact be the older of the two (Snyder, *Acts of Paul*, pp. 57–58) or that the two draw on a common oral tradition (MacDonald, *The Legend*, pp. 25–26). In its current form, however, the story post-dates Acts, perhaps by as much as a century, and it is highly unlikely that the author/editor was not aware of the Eutychus account; see the discussion in 3.1.2 above.

The picture of Paul that arises from these three narratives is that of the persuasive teacher. His divinely inspired messages cause betrothed virgins to reject their suitors, benefactors to devote themselves to a new Lord, married women to forsake their marriage bed, and executioners to convert and be baptized. On the other side, his effective teaching causes jealous fiancés to condemn their brides-to-be, husbands to plot his destruction, and rulers to sentence him to death. Moreover, his own ministry is the pattern for others who follow him. Thecla is commissioned by Paul to "go and teach the word of God," while Luke and Titus are shown to continue Paul's ministry by completing the initiation of the executioners. In most cases, Paul not only teaches, but his teaching appears to lead inexorably toward baptism. Indeed, he baptizes most of his named converts himself.

It is in this light, however, that his refusal to baptize Thecla appears most strange. If Paul is the archetypical early Christian teacher, whose instruction on the way to baptism includes a marked emphasis on sexual morality, how does his behavior in the Thecla narrative fit this profile?[44] Are there any interpretive guides supplied in the narrative? How might one understand this refusal of baptism within the wider context of second- and third-century Christianity? In fact, the oddity of the presentation of Paul vis-à-vis Thecla makes more clear what is involved in this vision of Paul's ministry. In short, Paul is presented not only as a persuasive teacher but also as the wise catechist, who is able to discern the necessary timing of baptism for his converts. To clarify matters, I begin with a survey of two principle alternatives to this reading of the Thecla narrative before developing it in some more detail below.

3.3 NOT BAPTIZING THECLA: TWO ALTERNATIVES

Probably the most common way to explain Paul's deferral of Thecla's baptism is to read it as indicating a critical stance toward Paul, perhaps as a cipher for male Christian leaders, which reflects a *Sitz im Leben* in a female Christian group.[45] On this reading, Paul is mistaken to think

---

[44] As noted in Chapter 2, a concern for sexual morality accompanied the process of initiation from the very earliest stages; see Hermas *Vis.* 3.2–7; *Did.* 3.3; 1 Cor. 6:7–9; see also the comments on the apparent difficulties here in Niederhofer, *Konversion*, p. 146.

[45] For a fuller discussion and critique of this reading, see Edsall, "(Not) baptizing Thecla," pp. 239–242. Reading Paul as a cipher is put forward in a particularly strong form by Luise Schottroff, ""Ich kenne die Frau nicht…, sie ist auch nicht mein": die zwei Gesichter des Paulus," in Renate Jost and Ursula Kubera (eds.), *Wie Theologen Frauen*

Thecla weak and therefore he is wrong to see a need to delay her baptism. As Beate Wehn puts it, "Paul's picture of women in ActThecl 25 turns out to be false, therefore, in the case of Thecla. This fact signifies a fundamental criticism against the person of Paul in the Acts of Thecla."[46] Paul's absence from Antioch, leaving Thecla to face Alexander and the subsequent trials alone, only makes this criticism more clear.[47] But, although it is true that Paul's conduct in Antioch is unusual, to say the least, to read his refusal to baptize Thecla as a veiled criticism leads to more difficulties than it solves.

In the first place, at no point either in the Thecla narrative or in the wider *Acta Pauli*, as we know it, does any positive character – much less Thecla – express any disappointment or frustration with Paul. Rulers, husbands, fiancés, and dubious companions might object to his teaching, but throughout Paul remains a remarkably positive, persuasive, and powerful figure. Thecla herself only ever wants Paul's approval, first in baptism and then in commissioning. Glenn Snyder is therefore right to refer to the Thecla narrative as "hagiography."[48] A Pauline-critical reading would also stand in tension with the wider positive reception of Paul in the early Church: he is the apostle for the (proto-)orthodox and (proto-)heterodox alike.[49] Further, an appeal to the originally oral form of the Thecla narrative will not support the reading. The great difficulties faced in attempting to reconstruct the oral form mean that any *Sitz im Leben*

---

sehen. Von der Macht der Bilder, Frauenforum (Freiburg: Herder, 1993), p. 12; but see also Davies, *Revolt*, p. 107, and Burrus, *Chastity, passim*.

[46] Beate Wehn, "'Selig die Körper der Jungfräulichen': Überlegungen zum Paulusbild der Thekla-Akten," in C. Janssen, L. Schottroff, and B. Wehn (eds.), *Paulus. Umstrittene Tradition – lebendige Theologie. Eine feministische Lektüre* (Gütersloh: Kaiser, 2001), p. 189: "Paulus' Frauenbild in ActThecl 25 erweist sich also in bezug auf Thekla als falsch. Dieser Erweis bedeutet fundamentale Kritik an der Person des Paulus in den ActThecl." Elisabeth Esch-Wermeling, *Thekla–Paulusschülerin wider Willen? Strategien der Leserlenkung in den Theklaakten*, NAbh 53 (Münster: Aschendorff, 2008), pp. 84–85, argues in a similar vein, though without claiming that the text criticizes Paul; on her argument, see further below.

[47] Similar readings to Wehn's can be found in B. Diane Lipsett, *Desiring Conversion: Hermas, Thecla, Aseneth* (New York: Oxford University Press, 2011), pp. 74–75; Barrier, *Acts of Paul*, p. 136; and Pervo, *Acts of Paul*, p. 87; and more mutedly in Peter-Ben Smit, "St. Thecla: remembering Paul and being remembered through Paul," *Vigiliae Christianae* 68, no. 5 (2014), p. 562.

[48] Snyder, *Acts of Paul*, pp. 120–137.

[49] Dunn, "The *Acts of Paul*," p. 64, argues that Tertullian was alone in his rejection of the Thecla narrative. It is not clear that Tertullian rejects the Thecla narrative *tout court*, but Dunn's observations stand on either reading.

posited for the story must be conjectural at best.[50] The ancient redactor, being literate enough to gather stories and stitch them into a novelistic hagiography, evidently did not interpret this presentation as critical of Paul. If the story were originally critical, one wonders why it would have been included in the collection at all, particularly if Tertullian is correct to claim "love of Paul" as the motivating factor.

The recent and incisive source and redactional reading of the *Acts of Paul* by Elisabeth Esch-Wermeling provides a better alternative to the Pauline-critical readings, even if it is not itself ultimately satisfactory. Esch-Wermeling's principal goal is to understand the compositional history of the Thecla narrative, as an independent narrative, and to illuminate the *Leserlenkungen* (reading cues) provided by the final redactor. According to her reading, the Antioch episode is the seed from which the rest grew, originally not featuring Paul at all. The key redactional strategy noted by Esch-Wermeling is the use of framing. For instance, Paul's absence during Thecla's troubles in Antioch is framed by his prayerful support in the previous Iconium episode and the joyful reunion with Paul afterwards. The reader, then, is able to read as though Paul is present, perhaps again praying from a distance.[51]

This redactional framework provides Esch-Wermeling with her solution to Paul's non-baptism of Thecla. The Antioch material in its original form did not portray Thecla baptizing herself but rather, she argues, it was an act of voluntary martyrdom, from which she was rescued and vindicated by God.[52] The redactor turned this martyrdom and rescue into a baptismal scene by inserting an explanatory statement, "And she cast herself, saying 'In the name of Jesus Christ, on my last day, I am baptized'," thus producing Thecla's double "casting" of herself.[53] This insertion is framed by the foreshadowing in *APl* 3.25, when Thecla requests the "sign," and the *denouement* in 4.15, when she tells Paul she has been baptized. Therefore, Paul *must* defer Thecla's baptism in Iconium because that event is already present in the Antioch episode.

---

[50] Notably, the source-critical reading in Esch-Wermeling, *Thekla* (followed by Lipsett, *Desiring Conversion*, p. 64), argues that the original form of the Thecla story did not include Paul at all. Even Esch-Wermeling, though, is not sanguine about reconstructing a pre-*textual* form of the story (p. 145).

[51] Esch-Wermeling, *Thekla*, pp. 205–211; see pp. 189–205 for her discussion of framing.

[52] Ibid., p. 176.

[53] *APl* 4.9: καὶ ἔβαλεν ἑαυτὴν λέγουσα Ἐν τῷ ὀνόματι Ἰησοῦ Χριστοῦ ὑστέρᾳ ἡμέρᾳ βαπτίζομαι. Esch-Wermeling argues that this ἔβαλεν ἑαυτὴν is evident as an insertion because it stands in tension with the later statement that ἡ μὲν οὖν ἔβαλεν ἑαυτήν, as well as with the intervening cry from the crowd, Μὴ βάλῃς ἑαυτὴν εἰς τὸ ὕδωρ.

There is no space here to engage Esch-Wermeling's arguments in full. Even so, while she offers incisive observations throughout the study – her discussion of the complex relationship with the Pastoral Epistles is particularly valuable[54] – there is a fundamental tension between her source-critical and redaction-critical programs: she wants to highlight various tensions within the narrative while at the same time demonstrating cogently how the redactor competently integrated the old Antioch story with the new surrounding material. If, however, the tensions have been resolved by a competent redactor, how does one differentiate between that and something that was, from the start, a coherent composition? The better the redactor, the fewer the awkward narrative seams, and the less evidence for a redactor in the first place. In relation to the baptism of Thecla, the tensions highlighted by Esch-Wermeling can be accounted for either by cues internal to the narrative or though understanding the broader early Christian context of its composition. Three brief examples must suffice.[55]

In the first place, the proposed double casting of Thecla (*APl* 4.9) is not a redundancy but rather part of building narrative momentum. The second statement recapitulates the first in the context of a comparison between the fate of Thecla and that of the seals.[56] Second, Esch-Wermeling argues that Paul's refusal to baptize Thecla makes little sense after she had just proved herself in her Iconium trial. Further, she suggests that Paul's evident knowledge of her forthcoming trials should have provided further motivation for him to baptize her.[57] Within the context of second-century baptismal theology, however, forthcoming trials to one's purity would have been a grave concern; post-baptismal sin was not easily dealt with. In the *Acts of Paul*, Paul himself has already signaled the importance of this issue: "Blessed are those who guard their baptism" (*APl* 3.6).[58] Third,

---

[54] Esch-Wermeling, *Thekla*, pp. 27–70. Her thematic approach, rather than one that focuses on biographical features, is illuminating. On the issues of biographical approaches to the relationship between the Thecla narrative and the Pastoral Epistles, see Edsall, "Hermogenes," pp. 108–121.

[55] A fuller version of these points can be found in Edsall, "(Not) baptizing Thecla," pp. 235–260.

[56] I am thankful to Dr. Catherine Playoust for this observation. Note also that Snyder, *Acts of Paul*, p. 143 n. 154, refers to this as an "*apparent* duplication" (emphasis original), though his narrative solution differs slightly from my own.

[57] Esch-Wermeling, *Thekla*, p. 84: "Diese Reaktion des Apostels auf die Bitte seiner Schülerin ist unverständlich, denn Theklas Vorbildlichkeit wird innerhalb des gesamten Zyklus bezeugt und steht außer Frage. Gerade wenn Paulus eine weitere Prüfungssituation für seine junge Schülerin erwartet, müsste dies eher ein Argument für die Spendung der Taufe sein, da sie Stärkung für kommende Aufgraben verleihen kann."

[58] See further the discussion in the next section.

Esch-Wermeling argues that Thecla's continued search for baptism after her trial in Iconium was redundant, since her first endurance of (quasi-) martyrdom would have sufficed as a kind of baptism.[59] Even if blood baptism by martyrdom were viewed by the author as a substitute for regular baptism, however, Thecla's survival in Iconium means that she cannot have experienced one.[60]

Without Esch-Wermeling's proposed tensions, whether internal doublets or narrative inconsistencies, her explanation for why Paul refuses to baptize Thecla no longer answers the question. Rather, her broader analysis of reading cues and framing highlights the tight integration of Thecla's baptismal theme within narrative as a whole. Moreover, her objections to the narrative logic of Paul's refusal point toward the importance of taking the late second-century context of baptismal thought and practice into account. It is within that context that the solution to Paul's non-baptism of Thecla can be understood, even in relation to the *Acts of Paul* as a whole.

3.4 THECLA, INITIATION, AND SELF-CONTROL

That Thecla is presented as an initiate into Christianity has been suggested before, in passing by Jeremy Barrier and more fully by David Dunn.[61] This observation, however, has not previously been integrated with the broader picture of Paul in the *Acts of Paul* or the development of the catechumenate in the late second century.[62]

---

[59] Esch-Wermeling, *Thekla*, pp. 87–88; see also the similar comments in Jensen, *Thekla*, p. 96.

[60] Her appeal to the martyrdom of Saturus in the *Passion of Perpetua*, which is described as a second baptism (*Pas. Perp.* 21.1), falls short of showing that blood and water baptism were interchangeable because Saturus himself was already baptized. He was the catechist for Perpetua *et al.* See the discussion in Chapter 2.3.2 above and see further below.

[61] Barrier, *Acts of Paul*, and David J. Dunn, "'Her that is no bride': St. Thecla and the relationship between sex, gender, and office," *St Vladimir's Theological Quarterly* 53, no. 4 (2010), 37–68. Willy Rordorf, "Quelques jalons pour une interprétation sympolique des *Actes de Paul*," in David H. Warren, Ann Graham Brock, and David H. Pao (eds.), *Early Christian Voices in Texts, Traditions, and Symbols: Essays in Honor of François Bovon*, BIS 66 (Leiden and Boston: Brill, 2003), p. 252, states, "le presbytre qui...a rédigé les *Actes de Paul*, a eu un projet en tête: il voulu écrire un texte *initiatique*," though his principle concern is the symbolic presentation of overcoming sexual passion. Jensen, *Thekla*, p. 93, notes the importance of appreciating "die frühchristliche Taufpraxis," though she does not pursue the insight. On Thecla's conversion, see now esp. Niederhofer, *Konversion*.

[62] For instance, Barrier, *Acts of Paul*, p. 163, relies on later parallels in the *Didasc. apost.* 16 and *TA* 21, and even then the proposed overlaps are not as clear as one might like. Dunn, "Her that is no bride," p. 54 n. 37, appeals to Cyril of Jerusalem for the anti-demonic

To begin, it is helpful to recall that the image of Paul in the *Acta Pauli* is principally focused on his activities as a teacher.[63] In the Thecla narrative Paul arrives in Iconium and immediately makes an impact with his teaching on self-control and resurrection.

Blessed are the pure in heart...the chaste in flesh...the self-controlled...those who put off this world...who have wives as though they do not[64]...who fear God... who revere the scriptures[65]...who receive the wisdom of Jesus Christ...who guard their baptism...who have grasped the understanding of Jesus Christ...who have left the worldly form[66] because of their love of God...the merciful...the bodies of virgins...[67]

While the emphasis on self-control, particularly oriented around sexual renunciation, is clear, the importance of the resurrection and future judgment appears in the rewards for each of the blessed groups. Some of these will "become God's angels," "rest with the Father and the Son," judge angels, and be blessed "at the right hand of the Father."[68] The virgins, in particular, "will not lose their reward for chastity" (τὸν μισθὸν τῆς ἁγνείας). They will be saved on the "day of the Son" for an eternal rest.[69] Concern for sexual self-control also appears in Paul's sermon in Ephesus (*APl* 9), in which the baptized lion becomes a celibate, ignoring the advances of a lioness.

understanding of post-baptismal anointing. Further, his argument that Thecla becomes a confessor prior to her being baptized, thus reversing the *ordo salutis* (p. 51 n. 31), is not rooted in any data from the period of the composition of the *Acta Pauli*.

[63] This is particularly true in the three sections most likely to have been part of the initial version: the Thecla narrative, the Ephesus episode, and the martyrdom. While miracles do feature, it would be more accurate to say that they happen *to* Paul rather than are done *by* Paul.

[64] Cf. 1 Cor. 7:29.

[65] Literally "the oracles of God" (τὰ λόγια τοῦ θεοῦ) but a clear reference to scripture after the pattern of Rom. 3:2.

[66] ἐξελθόντες τοῦ σχήματος τοῦ κοσμικοῦ appears to be an allusion to τὸ σχῆμα τοῦ κόσμου τούτου in 1 Cor. 7:13.

[67] *APl* 3.5–6: Μακάριοι οἱ καθαροὶ τῇ καρδίᾳ...οἱ ἁγνὴν τὴν σάρκα τηρήσαντες...οἱ ἐγκρατεῖς... οἱ ἀποταξάμενοι τῷ κόσμῳ τούτῳ...οἱ ἔχοντες γυναῖκας ὡς μὴ ἔχοντες...οἱ φόβον ἔχοντες θεοῦ...οἱ τρέμοντες τὰ λόγια τοῦ θεοῦ...οἱ σοφίαν λαβόντες Ἰησοῦ Χριστοῦ...οἱ τὸ βάπτισμα τηρήσαντες...οἱ σύνεσιν Ἰησοῦ Χριστοῦ χωρήσαντες...οἱ δι᾽ ἀγάπην θεοῦ ἐξελθόντες τοῦ σχήματος τοῦ κοσμικοῦ...οἱ ἐλεήμονες...τὰ σώματα τῶν παρθένων...

[68] Cf. 1 Cor. 6:3.

[69] Demas and Hermogenes, Paul's crooked companions, also indicate an emphasis on resurrection (*APl* 3.12), though they are not an authoritative narrative voice. An emphasis on the coming Day of the Lord was typical of Paul's missionary teaching: see Rom. 2:5, 16; 1 Cor. 1:8, 5:5; Phil. 1:10, 2:16; 1 Thess. 5:2–5; Edsall, *Paul's Witness*, pp. 170–173, 200–202.

Thecla is evidently able to hear Paul's message from her neighboring window, but she cannot see him (*APl* 3.7). Rather, she sees other women and virgins going into Onesiphorus' home to hear Paul and she feels unworthy to go herself. Even so, she is enthralled with Paul's teaching and focuses on it to the neglect of human interaction and personal care.[70] She is persuaded, then, by Paul's teaching and yet remains geographically and figuratively marginal in relation to the Christian community in Iconium.[71]

Once Paul is imprisoned, Thecla's fixation on his teaching remains and she seeks him out in his cell to sit at his feet (*APl* 3.18) until she is dragged before the governor with him (3.20). Thecla is silent throughout her ordeal; she is not reported as speaking anything until after she is delivered from her first trial. When she does, her first word is "Paul."[72] She does, however, follow Paul's teaching on self-control – that they are blessed who leave "the worldly form" because of a love for God and who maintain a virginal purity. Thecla both abandons the "worldly" institution of marriage for chastity and is willing to abandon the "worldly form" entirely through martyrdom, from which she is ultimately rescued. In other words, she takes the first steps to become a follower of Paul, a part of the Christian community, by her ascetic denial of self and adoption of self-control.

Throughout this episode, Paul's teaching and its implications for believers in their civic/social context drives the narrative forward. If we did not have the subsequent Antioch episode, Thecla would not likely have commanded the attention she did in late antiquity on the basis of her role in Iconium.

When Thecla finds Paul again after being delivered from the arena, it is then that she first requests baptism. The order of events is important. Thecla's initial request is not for baptism; she simply wants to cut her hair and follow Paul wherever he goes. The cutting of the hair is part of a process of masculinization that runs throughout the narrative, which

[70] Barrier, *Acts of Paul*, pp. 87–88, argues that "Thecla desires to go in to Paul to experience a more intimate (i.e. sexual) relationship to Paul" (p. 88). This reading, however, fails to appreciate how Thecla's desire functions within a text that explicitly rejects such sexual impulses in favor of ἐγκράτεια. The point, rather, seems to be that Thecla's non-sexual desire for Paul and his teaching overcomes any desire for normal familial or sexual intercourse, which is what leads to the confrontation with her spurned fiancé.

[71] See Niederhofer, *Konversion*, p. 59: "Die räumliche Trennung der Orte entspricht der Trennung der Figuren…Die Orte zeigen, dass sich die Figur Thekla an diesem Punkt der Erzählung lokal gesehen an einem anderen Ort als Paulus und Onesiphorus befindet."

[72] See Esch-Wermeling, *Thekla*, p. 38.

Glenn Snyder rightly links with the theme of ἐγκρατεία.[73] Paul, however, does not see that Thecla is prepared for such a commitment.[74] What looks at first like a rejection of Thecla's offer in 3.25 turns out in 4.1 not to be so since he takes her with him to Antioch. Indeed, there is no explicit answer to Thecla's question. Paul's initial comments are more lament than answer: "The time is shameful and you are beautiful. Would that another trial not overtake you worse than the first, and you not endure but rather act cowardly." It is only then that Thecla requests baptism as an apotropaic measure: if she is baptized, then a temptation will not touch her. This exploits the range of the term πειρασμός, bringing in both the trial to come and the importance of sexual renunciation, even in the face of temptation. Baptism, however, is not apotropaic; it is for those already proved continent and pure who are capable of guarding it. So Paul exhorts Thecla, "endure and you will receive the water."[75]

Elements of Thecla's martyr-baptism itself may be symbolically linked with various elements of late second-century baptismal practice. For instance, Barrier argues that Thecla's nudity in the Antioch theater mimics pre-baptismal stripping of candidates.[76] The cloud which covers her after baptism is sometimes taken to be equated with the donning of clean robes after baptism, and the deluge of aromatic oils from the women in the crowd with the post-baptismal unction.[77] These links are more difficult, however, since each element also has a clear narrative function: the stripping in relation to execution, the cloud to protect Thecla's purity,

---

[73] Snyder, *Acts of Paul*, pp. 139–141. See also Ross Kraemer, "The conversion of women to ascetic forms of Christianity," *Signs* 6, no. 2 (1980), 298–307; Elizabeth A. Castelli, "'I will make Mary male': pieties of the body and gender transformation of Christian women in late antiquity," in J. Epstein and K. Straub (eds.), *Body Guards: The Cultural Politics of Gender Ambiguity* (New York: Routledge, 1991), pp. 29–49; Jensen, *Thekla*, pp. 113–116; Betz, "Thekla," pp. 352–356; Esch-Wermeling, *Thekla*, p. 267; Lipsett, *Desiring Conversion*, p. 85; and Niederhofer, *Konversion*, pp. 148–149. Note similar (though not identical) themes in *GThom* 114; *GMary* 9.9; *Pass. Perp.* 10.7. Snyder notes that, with the themes of ἐγκρατεία and masculinization together, "the *Acts of Paul and Thekla* may therefore be providing a narrative representation of Gal 3:28's thesis that there is no 'male and female in baptism'"; Snyder, *Acts of Paul*, p. 143. See also Smit, "St. Thecla," pp. 551–563; Betz, "Thekla," pp. 335–356; and the general discussion of ἐγκρατεία in Dunn, "The *Acts of Paul*," pp. 78–88.

[74] Niederhofer, *Konversion*, pp. 147, 149, suggests that Thecla's commitment to external changes (cutting her hair) indicates that, while her conversion was in process, it was not yet complete.

[75] See Niederhofer, *Konversion*, pp. 149–150.

[76] In context, this nudity is related to her martyrdom in the arena; note the stripping of martyrs in *Pass. Perp.* 20.2; see also Bremmer, "Magic, martyrdom," p. 161.

[77] Barrier, *Acts of Paul*, pp. 163–164; See also Dunn, "Her that is no bride," p. 54.

and the oils to defeat the attacking beasts. It is the concern with endurance and purity-maintenance before baptism that most clearly highlights Thecla as an initiate.[78]

As outlined in Chapter 2 above, from its earliest hints in the *Didache*, the *Shepherd of Hermas*, and Justin Martyr, the process that would become the catechumenate focused particularly on moral evaluation during the liminal phase between conversion and baptism. Hermas' stones that fell near but not in the water (i.e., baptism) are those who could not cope with the "true purity" (ἡ ἁγνότης τῆς ἀληθείας) required by baptism (*Vis.* 3.2–7). Justin Martyr indicates a period of evaluation between being persuaded by the gospel and baptism itself, during which time the baptismal candidates are taught to pray for forgiveness of previous sins while fasting (*Apol.* 1.61.1–3).[79] By the time that Clement of Alexandria and Tertullian were writing, the catechumenate in Carthage and Alexandria was a period that concerned itself principally with moral teaching and evaluation, though of course not to the exclusion of confessional instruction.[80] In fact, the presentation of baptism in the *Acts of Paul* is remarkably consonant with the view of Tertullian, despite his reservations about Thecla.

First, the author of the *Acta Pauli* indicates his familiarity with the catechumenate and specified times for baptism in the Ephesus episode. Tertullian famously discusses the link between baptism and Pentecost, as well as the expected behavior during the period between Easter and Pentecost. According to him, during that period, the *spatium pentecostes*, one is not to kneel during prayer or do anything else that is associated with anxiety because it is devoted to joyful celebration.[81] Moreover, in his treatise on baptism, Tertullian notes that while any day can be suitable for baptism, without any loss in effect, Easter is the most solemn day and the *spatium pentecostes* is only slightly less auspicious.[82] Although

---

[78] Niederhofer, *Konversion*, pp. 195, 209, suggests that the use of ἐπιστρέφω in 4.34 may allude to the completion of Thecla's conversion (*Umkehr*), partly with reference to 1 Thess. 1:9–10.

[79] Note that fasting before baptism is also indicated in *Did.* 7.4.

[80] E.g., Clement, *Strom.* 6.1.1.3; *Paed.* 1.1.1.4, 1.1.2.1; Tertullian, *Paen.* 6.2–4; *Bapt.* 18–19 and *passim*. See Chapter 2 above, and Chapter 4 below on Clement.

[81] *Or.* 23.2: "Tantundem et [*viz.* in addition to the Lord's day] spatio Pentecostes quae eadem exultationis sollemnitate dispungitur"; text in G. F. Diercks (ed.), "De Oratione," in E. Dekkers (ed.), *Corpus Christianorum*, Series Latina 1 (Turnhout: Brepols, 1954), pp. 255–274.

[82] *Bapt.* 19.1–3: "Diem baptismo sollemniorem pascha praestat, cum et passio domini in qua tinguimur adimpleta est....exinde pentecoste ordinandis lavacris laetissimum

Tertullian provides the first clear discussions of Pentecost in the early Church, the reference to it in *APl* 9 and a mention by Hippolytus indicate that its practice was not unique to Carthage.[83] Indeed, he himself suggests that he "received" his Pentecost practice and does not feel the need to defend it.[84] In *APl* 9, after Paul is notified by an angelic visitor about coming trouble for the Antiochene Christians, we are told that he could not be sad on account of Pentecost, "which was a kind of feast for those who believed in Christ, catechumens with believers."[85] The reason for Paul's inability is not provided but the link with Tertullian fits well. Rather than mourning, they celebrated a joyful agape meal (9.4). Later we are told that Paul's teaching, which takes place during the period of Pentecost, leads to the baptism of Procla and her household in that same period (9.11), to whom we will return below.

Second, developing a point already noted, the catechumenate in the late second century was concerned above all with establishing the baptizand's aptitude for the Christian life. There was not a fixed length for the catechumenate, but rather the length of time spent as a catechumen depended on the age and character of the person. As Tertullian writes, "according to each person's nature and disposition, even age, delaying baptism is more useful, particularly in the case of children."[86] It is well within Paul's prerogative as a teacher to evaluate his charges on a case-by-case basis and to delay the baptism of those deemed unready. Thecla is a young virgin, effectively a female child still under her father's legal

---

spatium est…ceterum omnis dies domini est: omnis hora, omne tempus habile baptismo. si de sollemnitate interest, de gratia nihil refert."

[83] See the discussion in Rouwhorst, "Origins," pp. 312–314, who argues that Pentecost began in the west and only later was adopted by the eastern churches. Beckwith, *Calendar and Chronology*, p. 61, notes that Tertullian is the first to mention a specific *day* of Pentecost, rather than a period of time (*spatium*).

[84] In *Or.* 23.2, Tertullian explicitly states that "we have received" the practice concerning the Lord's day, and his subsequent linked discussion suggests that he received that practice as well; see also *Ieun.* 14.2–3, which uses a common practice of exultation during the period of Pentecost as part of the common ground on which to base his argument in favor of Montanist celebrations.

[85] 9.4: ⲡⲁⲩⲗⲟⲥ ⲇⲉ ⲙ̄ⲡϥϭⲙ ϭⲁⲙ ⲁϣⲕⲙ̄ ⲉⲧⲃⲉ ⲧⲡⲉⲛⲧⲏⲕⲟⲥⲧⲏ· ϫⲉ ⲛⲉⲥϣⲟⲟⲡ ⲛ̄ⲥⲙⲁⲧ ⲛ̄ϣⲁⲉⲓⲉ· ⲛ̄ⲛⲉⲛⲧⲁⲟⲩⲣ̄ ⲡⲓⲥⲧⲉⲩⲉ ⲁⲡⲉⲭⲣ̄ⲥ ⲁⲩⲱ ⲛ̄ⲕⲁⲑⲏⲕⲟⲩⲙⲉⲛⲟⲥ· ⲙⲛ̄ ⲛⲉⲧⲛ̄ ⲡⲓⲥⲧⲉⲩⲉ. It is possible that the actual term ⲕⲁⲑⲏⲕⲟⲩⲙⲉⲛⲟⲥ is not present in the Greek *Vorlage* and that the fourth-century Coptic translator is glossing a less explicit term or phrase. For example, the sixth-century P.Heidelberg has a tendency to make baptismal language more explicit than its Greek counterpart – e.g., from "washing" to "baptism" in 4.15. Given that P.Hamburg is missing this section of the narrative, however, we are in the dark on this point.

[86] *Bapt.* 18.4, cited in Chapter 2.3.3 above.

authority.[87] The challenges to her purity, which are certainly going to arise, provide motivation for Paul's deferral.

The hesitation evidenced by Paul and described by Tertullian reflects the widespread conviction that, while pre-baptismal sin was cleansed in baptism, post-baptismal sin was a potentially disastrous issue. As early as the *Shepherd of Hermas*, there was discussion among Christian groups about whether one was granted the possibility of repentance from post-baptismal sin. While Hermas' answer is "yes, but only one" (*Man.* 4.3.3), Tertullian's view was more strict: post-baptismal repentance was a severely restricted possibility.[88]

Moreover, post-baptismal sin is not only a danger to the sinner, but could also implicate the baptismal sponsors. One of the reasons why Tertullian argues for delaying baptism for children and the unprepared is to eliminate the (unspecified) danger that the later failure of the baptized poses to their sponsors in the community.[89] Contrary to Esch-Wermeling's assertion, therefore, that Paul's premonition of Thecla's further testing should encourage him to baptize her, the opposite is the case: Paul's fore-knowledge that testing is on the horizon leads directly to his deferral on the grounds that there remains a possibility that she will "act the coward" (δειλανδρήσῃς). As he says in his opening sermon, it is the bodies of virgins and those who "guard their baptism" that are blessed.[90]

The picture of Paul that emerges, then, is not one of an inconsistent coward, but rather a responsible catechist. Thecla's request in 3.25 effectively acts as her enrollment for baptism and accordingly Paul indicates

---

[87] Betz, "Thekla," pp. 350–352, notes the relationship between Thecla and the "blessings" pronounced in Paul's initial sermon in Iconium: "Dabei ist der Körper der Thekla, der repräsentativ für die 'Körper der Jungfräulichen' steht" (p. 352); see also Niederhofer, *Konversion*, pp. 64–65.

[88] *Bapt.* 8.5 (trans. modified from Evans, *Baptism*): "'But the world sinned once more [after the flood], so that this equating of baptism with the flood is not valid.' [Yes, the world sinned], and so is appointed for the fire, as also a person is when he renews his sins after baptism: so that this also needs to be accepted as a sign and a warning to us" ('sed mundus rursus deliquit, quo male comparetur baptismus diluvio.' itaque igni destinatur, sicut et homo cum post baptismum delicta restaurat: ut hoc quoque in signum admonitionis nostrae debeat accipi). See the discussion of Hermas in Grundeken, "Baptism," pp. 130–131, 135; see also Gavrilyuk, *Histoire*, pp. 106–108, and the earlier comments in Dekkers, *Tertullianus*, pp. 164–165.

[89] *Bapt.* 18.4 cited in Chapter 2.3.3 above.

[90] Cyprian also draws on Paul's authority to emphasize the importance that those "illuminated by the light of Christ" (inluminati christi lumine), that is the baptized, should continue to avoid vices like jealousy; *De zelo* 10 (Manlio Simonetti (ed.), "Ad Donatum, De mortalitate; Ad Demetrianum; De opere et eleemosynis; De zelo et livore," in *Sancti Cypriani Episcopi Opera*, CCSL IIIA.2 (Turnhout: Brepols, 1976), pp. v–86).

that if she endures – that is to say, if she proves her moral fortitude in the face of the impending πειρασμός – she will in fact be baptized.[91] Once she has "received the washing" in Antioch (4.15), she again seeks out Paul. Her experience of initiation – from conversion to instruction to "enrollment" to endurance to baptism – is now complete and is affirmed by Paul.[92]

As in the case of his teaching in Ephesus and Rome, Paul's message in Iconium leads to baptism. The actual act of baptizing his converts, however, is not his main task. He is happy to leave the baptism of Thecla for another to complete and the baptism of Longus and Cestus to the agency of Titus and Luke.

An underlying exegetical resource for this presentation of Paul, which accentuates his teaching role while downplaying his role in baptism, is found in the statement in 1 Corinthians 1:17: "For Christ did not send me to baptize but to preach the gospel."[93] Paul's teaching, preparing his listeners for the ἐγκράτεια required by the Christian life, leads almost inexorably to baptism for those who hear it, whether one is a young virgin or an imperial guard. Paul's relationship to the actual act of baptism is ambivalent, however, both in 1 Corinthians 1:14–17 and in the *Acts of Paul*. Further, just as Paul identifies himself as a "co-worker" of God in his teaching activities (1 Cor. 3:5–9) – "what is Apollos and what is Paul...I planted, Apollos watered, but God caused the growth...we are God's co-workers..." – so also does Thecla note that Paul's teaching worked in concert with God: "I have received the washing, Paul. For the one who worked with you for the gospel worked also with me for the washing."[94] Remarkably, in the place of Apollos' watering, Thecla has become God's co-worker for her own baptism. This places Paul's work of pre-baptismal teaching implicitly in the role of planting, which is here

---

[91] The term μακροθυμέω in *APl* 3.25 implies a stronger notion of endurance, beyond mere waiting.

[92] A similar suggestion is made by Dunn, "The *Acts of Paul*," p. 79 n. 18, where he identifies Paul's motivation for leaving Thecla as wanting "to give Thecla a decisive trial of her Christian character and her vow of Chastity." It interesting to note that, even before being commissioned by Paul, Thecla imitates the Apostle by instructing people in "God's word" (κατηχήσασα...τὸν λόγον τοῦ θεοῦ), which leads in turn to their own "belief" and joy (*APl* 4.39; see Niederhofer, *Konversion*, pp. 217–218). Note, however that baptism is not mentioned explicitly here and so it is not clear that the term κατηχίζειν itself is being used in a technical sense for pre-baptismal instruction.

[93] I develop the connection with 1 Cor. 1:17 in Edsall, "(Not) baptizing Thecla," pp. 235–260; it is absent from the list of Pauline passages in Niederhofer, *Konversion*, p. 232.

[94] *APl* 4.15: Ἔλαβον τὸ λουτρόν, Παῦλε· ὁ γὰρ σοὶ συνεργήσας εἰς τὸ εὐαγγέλιον κἀμοὶ συνήργησεν εἰς τὸ λούσασθαι.

equated with "the gospel." The activities of Paul, then, as presented in 1 Corinthians 1:17 and 3:5–9, supply an underlying logic for his actions during Thecla's initiation, as well as the broader image of Paul as the archetypal early Christian teacher, as we shall see.

3.5 PAUL BAPTIZING OTHERS

Paul's reticence to baptize Thecla appears to stand in tension with his quick and evidently unproblematic baptism of Procla and Artemilla.[95] Two points, however, mitigate the tension significantly.[96] The first is that, where Thecla is a young virgin, both Procla and Artemilla are mature women. We are told in *APl* 9.11 that Procla was baptized with those of her household (ⲙⲛ ⲛⲉⲧⲉ ⲛⲟⲩⲥ ⲧⲏⲣⲟⲩ). Her place at the head of her household indicates that Procla is married, though the fact that no husband is mentioned may suggest that she is a widow. Artemilla is also married and it is her attention to Paul that creates dissonance with her husband. After all, Paul is the one who teaches those married to forego sexual contact, in 3.6. The impending challenges to Thecla's purity, then, simply do not apply to the married women in the same way.

This is related to the second point, namely that in both cases there are indications that the baptizands underwent a period of pre-baptismal instruction and evaluation. As was noted earlier, Procla is baptized as a result of Paul's teaching in Ephesus during the *spatium pentecostes*. The preceding notice that Pentecost was a festival celebrated by "catechumens with believers" suggests that the author is positioning Procla as a catechumen (along with her household), already partially integrated with the Ephesian Christian community.[97] Further, Paul's time teaching in Ephesus was long enough to occasion opposition from the Asian leaders (9.11) and, perhaps, also to note Procla's "good works" (ⲛ̄ϩⲁⲅ ⲛ̄ϩⲱⲃ) for her Ephesian neighbors. In the late second century, baptizing a married (or widowed) woman already involved in the Christian community and

---

[95] For the sake of economy, I am omitting a full discussion of Paul's baptism of the lion in *APl* 9. Suffice it to note here that Snyder has noted the evidence that a previous "catechetical process" has led to the lion's immersion; Snyder, *Acts of Paul*, p. 87.

[96] Although it is unclear whether Paul's work in Myra (*APl* 5) was part of the *Acta Pauli* in the late second century, it is worth noting that the considerations aired below apply *mutatis mutandis* to the baptism of Hermocrates and his wife.

[97] The baptism of a named person along with the rest of their household appears to be related also to several notices in Acts, such as the baptism of Lydia in Acts 16:15 or the jailer in 16:31–34; see also the baptism of Crispus in 18:8 and Stephanas in 1 Cor. 1:16.

known for her good works is an entirely different prospect than baptizing a young virgin whose future commitment is unclear.

The case of Artemilla is similar. Despite some chronological difficulties,[98] the text in P.Hamburg states that Paul's instruction of Artemilla and Eboula took place across multiple days (νυκτὸς καὶ ἡμέραις, 9.18). Artemilla's close relationship with her freedwoman, Eboula, who was already a disciple of Paul (μαθήτρια ἦν Παύλου, 9.16), indicates that her encounter with Paul in prison was not the first time she had heard (about) his message. Indeed, the fact that she changes into "darker clothing" (σκυθροπότερα ἱμάτια) rather than wearing something bright or ostentatious suggests that she was already familiar with his ascetic emphases. Paul's rebuke of Artemilla is met with her continued desire for baptism. While it may seem that her evaluation is short by comparison with Procla's or Thecla's, it is notable that Artemilla had a distinct advantage over Thecla aside from her status as a married woman: she had a sponsor in Eboula. Eboula's function is not emphasized within the narrative, of course, but it would have been readily recognizable to those readers who had themselves entered the church through a catechetical process, such as it was in the late second century. Moreover, if Artemilla, Procla, and Thecla did not have exactly the same process of initiation, this is only in keeping with Tertullian's observation that the deferral of a person's baptism was up to the baptizer's judgment on their character and preparation.

3.6 CONCLUSION

The presentation of Paul in the *Acta Pauli*, then, emphasizes his role as teacher and casts that in ways that are consonant with the catechetical process of initiation emerging at the time of its composition.[99] Paul is the perennially persuasive preacher, concerned with the self-control and sexual morality of his fellow believers, whose teaching leads converts

---

[98] Pervo, *Acts of Paul*, pp. 234–236, notes these and argues that they indicate that the scene was a later interpolation. Somewhat more simply, Schmidt and Schubart, ΠΡΑΞΙΣ ΠΑΥΛΟΥ, p. 90, solved the difficulty by arguing that just P.Hamb 3.1–5 was an interpolation; see the discussion in Gérard Poupon, "L'accusation de magie dans les Actes apocryphes," in *Les Actes apocryphes des apôtres*, Publications de la faculté de théologie de l'université de Genève 4 (Geneva: Labor et Fides, 1981), p. 86.

[99] See now the comments in Bremmer, "Conversion," p. 195: "It is interesting to note that our texts repeatedly stress the fact that the newly converts [*sic*] still have to be further educated in the faith. In other words, they depict conversion as a process. This process will have been an obvious fact for many of the fresh Christian converts as the Christians had instituted the catechumenate to instruct in the faith those who wanted to join them."

to baptism even where the act of baptism is left to the agency of others. Rather than posing a difficulty to this picture, Paul's deferral of Thecla's baptism highlights his sensitivity to the preparedness of the baptismal candidate in relation to moral (sexual) purity and endurance. With this perspective in mind, it is interesting to note that later retellings of the Thecla narrative – whether in a full narrative expansion as in the *Life and Miracles of Saint Thecla* or in brief liturgical outline as in the tenth-century Constantinopolitan *Synaxarium* – explicitly name what the second-century author narrated: Paul's relation to Thecla was as one engaged in catechesis.[100]

Narrating Paul's teaching role in a way that fits with catechetical practice at the end of the second century is the first step in the path that culminates at the end of the fourth century with the Paul of the *Constitutiones apostolorum* and Euthalian traditions, the apostle of catechesis and initiation. The following chapters will turn from narrative representations to the pedagogical, philosophical, and exegetical appropriation of Paul among Alexandrian thinkers. There, too, we shall see that Paul's image is presented in terms consonant with their models of instruction and initiation.

---

[100] See *Vit. et mir. s. Theclae* 1.1.23–30 (Paul engaged in catechesis, calling, and salvation of the Gentiles, "instructing the word concerning faith" (τὸν περὶ τῆς πίστεως κατηχοῦντα λόγον); Dagron, *Vie et miracles*) and the *Synaxarium ecclesiae Constantinopolitanae*, Sept. 24.1 ("She was catechized in the word of faith by Paul the divine Apostle" (Κατηχήθη δὲ τὸν λόγον τῆς πίστεως παρὰ Παύλου τοῦ θείου ἀποστόλου); text in H. Delehaye (ed.), "Synaxarium ecclesiae Constantinopolitanae (e codice Sirmondiano nunc Berolinensi)," *Acta Sanctorum* 62 (1902), 1–94). See also the catechetical reading of the *Acta Pauli* by John Chrysostom in Chapter 6.2 below.

4

Clement's Pedagogical Interpretation: Milk and Meat

If, then, the "milk" is nourishment for children and the "solid food" is for the mature, as is said by the apostle, catechesis shall be considered "milk" as the first nourishment of the soul and mystical contemplation shall be considered "solid food."[1]

As we saw in Chapter 2, Clement of Alexandria stands at the beginning of the period when the catechumenate became increasingly widespread, consciously formulated, and visible to contemporary scholars. Where the *Acta Pauli* narrate Paul (and Thecla) in terms of emerging catechetical practice, Clement interprets Paul's writings and ministry activities in explicitly catechetical language.

Moreover, Clement's catechetical treatment of Paul is inextricably related to his larger pedagogical goal of developing a proper account of Gnostic progression, beginning from conversion and extending through one's Christian life.[2] The language with which Clement discusses catechetical emphases is shaped by a two-sided struggle for a *via media* between a rejection of philosophy on the one hand and an intra-Christian

---

[1] Clement *Strom.* 5.10.66.2: εἰ τοίνυν τὸ μὲν γάλα τῶν νηπίων, τὸ βρῶμα δὲ τῶν τελείων τροφὴ πρὸς τοῦ ἀποστόλου εἴρηται, γάλα μὲν ἡ κατήχησις οἱονεὶ πρώτη ψυχῆς τροφὴ νοηθήσεται, βρῶμα δὲ ἡ ἐποπτικὴ θεωρία·

[2] Note that due to Clement's penchant for the term Gnostic, it becomes easily confused with the continuing contemporary practice to group Valentinians, Basilideans, and others under the gnostic moniker. For the purposes of clarity, then, when speaking of Clement's ideal Christian I will capitalize the word Gnostic. The others will be referred to as "gnostics," to indicate both the constructive element of the label and the fact that Clement views their knowledge as illegitimate; see 4.2.1 below.

anthropological division of believers on the other.[3] Within this struggle, Paul provides both a personal model of the true Gnostic, who guides those less advanced in their spiritual knowledge, and textual support for Clement's pedagogical framework. Clement's catechetical reading of Paul, then, like his construal of the catechumenate itself, is embedded within this larger pedagogical vision. In other words, a catechetical Paul is, for the Alexandrian philosopher, fundamentally a pedagogical Paul.

In order to better appreciate Clement's catechetical framing of Paul, this chapter will first review the structure of the catechumenate in Alexandria, as it appears in Clement's writings, and the language he uses to refer to it. I will examine the problems that the catechumenate poses for Clement and his interlocutors, and highlight the ways in which he frames Paul's activities as a teacher to integrate the catechumenate within Clement's broader ecclesiological and pedagogical vision. Finally, I will look more broadly at the way in which Clement reads Paul's activities and letters in catechetical/pedagogical terms. These broader uses reveal the more subtle ways that Clement's institutional context shaded his presentation of Paul beyond explicit exegesis of contested passages.

4.1 CLEMENT'S CATECHUMENATE: STRUCTURE AND TERMINOLOGY

In Clement's writings an institutional catechumenate appears for the first time, not described directly but rather showing "through his work in filigree."[4] And yet, while important elements of catechetical practice are absent or only allusively present, he nevertheless demonstrates great concern over the place of catechetical instruction in the Christian life. Put briefly, Clement wanted to provide a pedagogical-theological framework that could include everyone from the neophyte to the Gnostic, without dismissing either the sufficiency of the first or the legitimacy of the second.[5]

---

[3] See *Strom.* 1.1.18 for the former and *Paed.* 1.6 for the latter. This dynamic, which also touches on the important relation of faith and knowledge in Clement, is addressed further below.

[4] Saxer, *Les rites*, p. 101, quoted in Chapter 2.3.1 above.

[5] See further the discussion in Chapter 4.2 below. The balancing act highlighted here has been noted since Eugène de Faye, *Clément d'Alexandrie. Étude sur les rapports du christianisme et de la philosophie grecque au IIe siècle* (Paris: Minerva, 1906), pp. 137–139 and *passim*; see also Walther Völker, *Der wahre Gnostiker nach Clemens Alexandrinus*, TU 57 (Berlin: Akademie Verlag, 1952), pp. 5–7; S. R. C. Lilla, *Clement of Alexandria: A Study in Christian Platonism and Gnosticism* (Oxford: Oxford University Press, 1971), pp. 34, 141; and H. Strutwolf, "Theologische Gnosis bei Clemens Alexandrinus und

4.1.1 Structure

The most general parameters of Clement's catechumenate appear to be enrollment on one end and baptism on the other. He appears to allude to the practice of enrolling one's name to declare interest in baptism in *Strom.* 6.1.1.3, where he describes the *Paedagogus* as relating the "way of life" that grows out of catechesis "for those enrolled to be men."[6] Although elsewhere Clement can also speak of the Gnostic as having enrolled (ἐγγεγραφότι) among the "friends" of God or enrolling (ἐγγραφῆναι) among the apostles,[7] the facts that catechetical instruction is for those "who have enrolled" and that such enrollment is closely linked with a way of life suggests an initial formal enrollment, though further details are unavailable.[8] That baptism is the endpoint of catechesis is clear, however. "Catechesis leads to faith and faith is taught at baptism by the Holy Spirit."[9] This brings about the "first transition" (πρώτη μεταβολή), from faithlessness to faith.[10] Baptism, for Clement, is also the

Origenes," in Christoph Markschies and J. van Oort (eds.), *Zugänge zur Gnosis*, Patristic Studies 12 (Leuven: Peeters, 2013), pp. 94–95.

[6] See *Strom.* 1.1.9.3 and the comments in Van den Hoek, "'Catechetical' school," p. 69 n. 47.

[7] *Strom.* 6.9.73.6–74.1; 6.13.106.1–2. Note that ἐγγράφειν was later the standard term for baptismal enrollment; for John Chrystostom see Chapter 6.1 below.

[8] Clement also makes no mention of sponsors or specific communal and/or liturgical practices associated with the catechumenate (such as sponsorship or prayer); see the comments in Saxer, *Les rites*, pp. 74–75.

[9] *Paed.* 1.6.30, cited in Chapter 2.3.1.

[10] Clement speaks of a πρώτη and δευτέρα μεταβολή in *Strom.* 7.10.57.4. Recently, Andrew Itter has argued that Clement in fact has a ten-stage soteriological progression that involves multiple stages of baptism (or even multiple "gnostic baptisms") and purification on the way to mystical contemplation, though his arguments are unconvincing; Andrew C. Itter, *Esoteric Teaching the Stromateis of Clement of Alexandria*, VC Sup 97 (Leiden: Brill, 2009), pp. 37–51, 128–132. His position involves misreading the *Paedagogus* as signaling a transition from faith to knowledge (p. 51), misunderstanding *Paed.* 1.6.26.2–3 as referring to "stages" of baptism where Clement is expressly rejecting such an understanding of perfection, as well as numerous other difficulties. The mention of ἡ πρώτη μεταβολή σωτήριος ἡ ἐξ ἐθνῶν εἰς πίστιν and ἡ δευτέρα ἡ ἐκ πίστεως εἰς γνῶσιν which penetrates εἰς ἀγάπην περαιουμένη (*Strom* 7.10.57.3) cannot be read as does Itter (pp. 37–38) to signal three soteriological "stages," part of "the order in which the initiate ascends to God and is saved," since being πιστός is itself sufficient knowledge and perfection in Clement's mind (see further below and see also T. Camelot, *Foi et gnose. Introduction a l'étude de la connaissance mystique chez Clément d'Alexandrie*, Études de théologie et d'histoire de la spiritualité 3 (Paris: Librarie philosophique J. Vrin, 1945), pp. 23–29). For a critique of Itter on these and other points, see particularly the reviews in Matyáš Havrda, "Review: Andrew C. Itter. *Esoteric Teaching in the Stromateis of Clement of Alexandria* (Supplements to *Vigiliae Christianae*, 97), Brill, Leiden – Boston 2009, pp. xix+233," *Adamantius* 18 (2012), 573–579, and S. R. C. Lilla,

"illumination" and "perfection" of the neophyte, who is now God's child. Here Clement turns inherited Christian baptismal vocabulary to his own particular use: baptism is illumination because the new Christian "knows God."[11] As faith is imparted by the Holy Spirit at "illumination," so also are sonship and perfection because the believer shares in Christ's own baptism, which was marked by these characteristics.[12]

In the interim between enrollment and baptism, catechetical instruction was concerned with two tasks: imparting the Christian way of life and the fundamentals of belief.[13] In the first case, adopting the proper way of life involves more than simply learning a few Christian practices for Clement; it is a matter of removing sins and healing the passions.[14] The divine Pedagogue, whom the Christian Gnostic is to imitate,[15] works progressively with the goal "to improve the soul, not to teach, to guide in a life of self-control, not a knowledgeable one."[16] The reason for this

---

"Review: *Esoteric Teaching in the Stromateis of Clement of Alexandria*," *Augustinianum* 50, no. 2 (2010), 577–591.

[11] Illumination as baptism is signaled explicitly in Justin Martyr *Apol.* 1.61.10–12 (cited in Chapter 2.2.3) and may well be present in the extended ending of the Thecla narrative in *Acta Pauli* 4.18 (cited in Chapter 3.2).

[12] *Paed.* 1.6.25.1–26.2: "For we have been illuminated, which means to know God. The one who knows the perfect is not then imperfect.…And the same applies to us, for whom Christ is the paradigm. Being baptized, we are illuminated; being illuminated we are adopted; being adopted we are perfected; being perfected we are made immortal. He says 'I said you are all gods and sons of the most high' " (Ἐφωτίσθημεν γάρ· τὸ δὲ ἔστιν ἐπιγνῶναι τὸν θεόν. Οὔκουν ἀτελὴς ὁ ἐγνωκὼς τὸ τέλειον.…Τὸ δὲ αὐτὸ συμβαίνει τοῦτο καὶ περὶ ἡμᾶς, ὧν γέγονεν ὑπογραφὴ ὁ κύριος· βαπτιζόμενοι φωτιζόμεθα, φωτιζόμενοι υἱοποιούμεθα, υἱοποιούμενοι τελειούμεθα, τελειούμενοι ἀπαθανατιζόμεθα· 'ἐγώ', φησίν, 'εἶπα, θεοί ἐστε καὶ υἱοὶ ὑψίστου πάντες.').

[13] Clement does not specify a setting for this catechetical instruction. If Le Boulluec and other are correct, however, that Clement was ordained as a preacher in Alexandria (Le Boulluec, "Clément," pp. 67–69), then that could have provided an occasion for him to engage in catechesis apart from a "school" setting.

[14] See the comments of Le Boulluec, "Clément," p. 96, on the purpose of the *Paedagogus*.

[15] Speaking to those engaging in teaching, Clement states, δεῖ δὲ ὡς οἷόν τε τὸν κύριον μιμεῖσθαι (*Strom.* 1.1.9.3); see also *Strom.* 2.19.97.1 and the comments in Judith L. Kovacs, "Divine pedagogy and the Gnostic teacher according to Clement of Alexandria," *Journal of Early Christian Studies* 9, no. 1 (2001), 5–6, who is following the lead of Méhat, *Étude*, pp. 60–61.

[16] *Paed.* 1.1.1.4–1.1.2.1: Κεκλήσθω δ' ἡμῖν ἐνὶ προσφυῶς οὗτος ὀνόματι παιδαγωγός, προακτικός, οὐ μεθοδικὸς ὢν ὁ παιδαγωγός, ᾗ καὶ τὸ τέλος αὐτοῦ βελτιῶσαι τὴν ψυχήν ἐστιν, οὐ διδάξαι, σώφρονός τε, οὐκ ἐπιστημονικοῦ καθηγήσασθαι βίου. Strutwolf, "Theologische Gnosis," p. 101, notes that Clement's theological and pedagogical program is rooted in the notion that the divine relation to the world is fundamentally pedagogical. This point is also related to Clement's view of scripture itself as pedagogically oriented; see also Benno A. Zuiddam, "Early orthodoxy: the scriptures in Clement of Alexandria," *Acta Patristica et Byzantina* 21, no. 2 (2010), 307–319.

distinction is that Gnostic teaching is only for those whose three human aspects – habits, actions, and passions (τὰ ἤθη, αἱ πράξεις, τὰ πάθη) – are brought under the tutelage of the "heavenly guide."[17] This work is completed, in a way, only at baptism, when sins have been "washed" away from the eyes of the soul so that it is free to contemplate the divine.[18] This moral groundwork is required for all subsequent Christian life since, once one is "washed from all sins," moral rectitude is required: "the one who has received forgiveness for sins must sin no longer."[19] Only the divine Logos, the Pedagogue, can heal one's passions, however; for Clement, the passions are an irrational disease of the soul only curable by divine intervention.[20] This is why one who teaches others, who "sows in the Spirit," brings to the listener only "the *beginning* of faith, *eagerness for the way of life*, an *impulse* toward truth, an inquiring *initiative*, a *trace* of knowledge."[21] These are the "basic resources of salvation" (ἀφορμαὶ σωτηρίας), which are actualized, or perfected, at baptism, where the Spirit imparts faith and illumination. In light of the prior need for moral formation, the divine Pedagogue "first exhorts, then guides, then teaches."[22]

---

[17] *Paed.* 1.1.1.2–3; *pace* John Ferguson, *Clement of Alexandria*, YWAS 289 (New York: Twayne Publishers, 1974), p. 69, the three human qualities noted here correspond with preparation for faith and baptism, rather than three stages of Clement's pedagogical framework, as is indicated at the end of *Paed.* 1.1.1.2.

[18] *Paed.* 1.6.28.1–2; *pace* Itter, *Esoteric Teaching*, p. 131, Clement is not speaking here of a quasi-Platonic anamnesis where believers "remember themselves as beings of light." As Saxer, *Les rites*, p. 78, notes, and as does Itter elsewhere, "Clément prend...position contre la préexistence platonicienne des âmes" (see also Strutwolf, "Theologische Gnosis," p. 99). Rather, the eye full of light is simply a healthy eye, from the perspective of ancient physiology, which is able to behold that which is outside itself, the flowing of the Holy Spirit. Clement appears to be drawing on Matt. 6:22–23 (the healthy eye makes the body φωτεινόν) and the narrative of Paul's conversion in Acts 9, where his eyes were healed so that he would be filled with the Holy Spirit.

[19] Respectively, *Paed.* 1.6.28.1–2; *Strom.* 2.13.56.1: Τὸν οὖν εἰληφότα τὴν ἄφεσιν τῶν ἁμαρτιῶν οὐκέτι ἁμαρτάνειν χρή.

[20] See *Paed.* 1.1.1.2 and Lilla, *Clement of Alexandria*, pp. 96–97, with other examples cited there. The discussion in Völker, *Der wahre Gnostiker*, pp. 98–109 ("Das Werk des Logos"), remains valuable. On the unity of the Logos in Clement's pedagogical vision, see Rizzi, "Literary problem," pp. 154–163, who maintains this view while rejecting a commonly proposed tripartite structure to Clement's literary project.

[21] *Strom.* 1.1.4.3: συμβάλλεται [*viz.* ὁ σπείρων εἰς τὸ πνεῦμα] γοῦν τὰ μέγιστα τῷ περιτυχόντι κατὰ τὴν θείαν πρόνοιαν, ἀρχὴν πίστεως, πολιτείας προθυμίαν, ὁρμὴν τὴν ἐπὶ τὴν ἀλήθειαν, κίνησιν ζητητικήν, ἴχνος γνώσεως, συνελόντι εἰπεῖν ἀφορμὰς δίδωσι σωτηρίας. On the role of the Holy Spirit in giving faith at baptism, see above, p. 96. The use of ἴχνος seems to invoke a hunting metaphor in which the Gnostic teacher has provided the student with the first footprint of knowledge, to be used in tracking it down in the course of the hunt.

[22] *Paed.* 1.1.3.3: ὁ πάντα φιλάνθρωπος λόγος, προτρέπων ἄνωθεν, ἔπειτα παιδαγωγῶν, ἐπὶ πᾶσιν ἐκδιδάσκων. Knauber, "Ein frühchristliches Handbuch," p. 327, among others, notes the distinction that Clement draws between παιδαγωγία and διδασκαλία. It is

The true Gnostic, who is "the Lord's image," follows in this pattern, instructing those less advanced in the Christian life and "renewing them for salvation."[23]

The second aspect of catechesis – imparting the fundamentals of Christian belief – is also evident in Clement's list of the "basic resources of salvation," namely, the "beginning of faith...an inquiring initiative, a trace of knowledge." In Clement's view, "believing is not possible without catechesis."[24] Moreover, there are certain "things said in faith" (perhaps including baptismal confessions, prayers, etc.) which the believer (ὁ πιστός) is able to repeat even if they are an unlettered neophyte.[25] "Bare faith" (ψιλὴ πίστις) is sufficient for a basic Christian commitment – we have already noted that baptism is a perfecting illumination – and as such it already carries a compressed or abbreviated knowledge of the essential things.[26] The righteous person (ὁ δίκαιος) is one who can "chew the cud": the word having first been ingested "from outside...through catechesis," it can "be sent back from the stomach of the mind, so to speak, to the faculty for rational recollection."[27] The "word" therefore first enters a person during catechesis and that instruction can later be recalled in an ordered fashion.[28]

---

important for Clement, however, that it is the *same* Logos that exhorts, guides, and teaches; see Rizzi, "Literary problem," p. 157.

[23] *Strom* 7.9.52.2–3: ...τὸν κύριον, οὗ κατ' εἰκόνα παιδεύων ὁ τῷ ὄντι ἄνθρωπος δημιουργεῖ καὶ μεταρρυθμίζει καινίζων εἰς σωτηρίαν τὸν κατηχούμενον ἄνθρωπον; see also Strutwolf, "Theologische Gnosis," pp. 94–95. Völker, *Der wahre Gnostiker*, p. 75, rightly notes that the defeat of sin, acquiring the proper way of life, is the first step toward salvation.

[24] *Ecl. proph.* 28.3: "For as believing is not possible without catechesis, so comprehension is not possible without knowledge" (ὡς γὰρ οὐκ ἔστι πιστεῦσαι ἄνευ κατηχήσεως, οὕτως οὐδὲ καταλαβέσθαι ἄνευ γνώσεως).

[25] *Strom.* 1.6.35.2: ...ἄνευ γραμμάτων πιστὸν εἶναι δυνατόν φαμεν. On "the things said in faith," see Matyáš Havrda, *The So-Called Eighth Stromateus by Clement of Alexandria: Early Christian Reception of Greek Scientific Methodology*, Philosophia Antiqua (Leiden: Brill, 2016), pp. 139–140, and see further below, p. 99.

[26] *Strom.* 7.10.57.3: ἡ μὲν οὖν πίστις σύντομός ἐστιν, ὡς εἰπεῖν, τῶν κατεπειγόντων γνῶσις... In *Strom.* 5.1.2.5 Clement compares those with "common faith" to those who are moved in faith to ask for healing, to whom Jesus says "your faith has healed [or 'saved'] you" (ἡ μὲν γὰρ κοινὴ πίστις καθάπερ θεμέλιος ὑπόκειται (τοῖς γοῦν θεραπευθῆναι ποθοῦσιν ὁ κύριος πιστῶς κινουμένοις ἐπέλεγεν· 'ἡ πίστις σου σέσωκέν σε·')).

[27] *Paed.* 3.11.76.1: Πᾶν γὰρ "διχηλοῦν καὶ μαρυκώμενον" καθαρόν ἐστιν, ὅτι τὸ διχηλοῦν δικαιοσύνην ἐμφαίνει τὴν ἰσοστάσιον μηρυκάζουσαν τὴν οἰκείαν δικαιοσύνης τροφήν, τὸν λόγον ἔκτοσθεν μὲν εἰσιόντα κατὰ ταὐτὰ τῇ τροφῇ διὰ κατηχήσεως, ἔνδοθεν δὲ ἀναπεμπόμενον ὥσπερ ἐκ κοιλίας τῆς διανοίας εἰς ἀνάμνησιν λογικήν.

[28] This model – learning basics for later recollection – was a widespread pedagogical strategy among philosophical schools, as seen in the *Enchiridion* of Epictetus or Epicurus' *Kyriai Doxai*. See the comments in Hadot, *Philosophy*, pp. 71–72; *pace* Itter, *Esoteric Teaching*, p. 113.

In all cases, however, catechetical instruction is only the first step, the foundation upon which further moral development and learning should be built.[29] As already noted, the Christian way of life "grows out of catechesis," from controlling the passions to eliminating them entirely.[30] Moreover, while faith is already an abbreviated knowledge, related to instruction and the illumination that occurs at baptism, Clement also maintains that "knowledge is the proof of the things received through faith."[31] Understanding "the things said in faith" requires further learning.[32] Baptism, faith, and the instruction leading to them, then, provide the first step, where moral perfection and knowledge are yet inchoate, rather than the final one.[33] This larger vision for Gnostic progress is, for Clement, integrated with his pedagogical approach to the catechumenate and it is precisely that pedagogical framing of initiation and the Christian life that factors into his reading of Paul.

An important characteristic of Clement's catechumenate is its inherited nature. As we saw in Chapter 2, the two widespread purposes of catechesis were moral evaluation and the imparting of basic doctrine. Teaching precedes baptism in the *Didache*, the *Shepherd of Hermas*, Justin Martyr, and Tertullian. Even more prominent in these writers is the concern for moral evaluation: candidates had to prove that they were suitable before they were allowed access to community worship and support.[34] As Piotr Ashwin-Siejkowski rightly notes, during this period persecution was

---

[29] See Völker, *Der wahre Gnostiker*, pp. 221–222, on the connection between faith and baptism, faith being "der Zugang zum Christentum."

[30] On the move from μετριοπάθεια to ἀπάθεια in Clement, see Lilla, *Clement of Alexandria*, pp. 103–106.

[31] *Strom.* 7.10.57.3: ...ἡ γνῶσις δὲ ἀπόδειξις τῶν διὰ πίστεως παρειλημμένων; see also n. 26 above.

[32] *Strom.* 1.6.35.2: "But just as even without literacy we say it is possible to be a believer, in the same way we confess that there is no understanding the things said in faith without learning" (ἀλλὰ καθάπερ καὶ ἄνευ γραμμάτων πιστὸν εἶναι δυνατόν φαμεν, οὕτως συνιέναι τὰ ἐν τῇ πίστει λεγόμενα οὐχ οἷόν τε μὴ μαθόντα ὁμολογοῦμεν.) Clement continues: "It is not simply faith that produces approval of things well said and non-approval of alien things but faith in company with learning" (τὰ μὲν γὰρ εὖ λεγόμενα προσίεσθαι, τὰ δὲ ἀλλότρια μὴ προσίεσθαι οὐχ ἁπλῶς ἡ πίστις, ἀλλ' ἡ περὶ τὴν μάθησιν πίστις ἐμποιεῖ. 1.6.35.2–3). See also *Strom.* 1.1.8.2 (with a citation of Isa. 7:9), 2.4.17.4; and Völker, *Der wahre Gnostiker*, pp. 281–282.

[33] See *Strom.* 5.1.5.2; 6.13.105.1; 7.10.55.1–3. See also Piotr Ashwin-Siejkowski, *Clement of Alexandria: A Project of Christian Perfection* (London: T. & T. Clark, 2008), pp. 152–164, and Völker, *Der wahre Gnostiker*, pp. 150–152, among others.

[34] Resources could include care for the poor, widows, or other groups in need (1 Tim. 5:3–16; Ignatius *Poly.* 4.1; Justin Martyr *Apol.* 1.67), and note the provisions for traveling and immigrating Christians in *Did.* 11–13.

continually on the horizon, a point reinforced by Eusebius' account of the Severan persecution during Clement's life.[35] Regulating this community access was important for practical theological as well as moral reasons. Such, then, was the shape of the catechumenate that Clement inherited and which he acknowledged as valid. It was this inherited construal of the catechumenate that led to further problems for him, explored below.

4.1.2 Terminology

While André Méhat was correct in observing that Clement's use of κατηχήσις extended to cover "elementary instruction common to catechumens, neophytes, and all ordinary Christians," it is not clear on that basis that such terminology in Clement never refers specifically to pre-baptismal instruction.[36] We have already seen that, in Clement's pedagogical framework, the formation of πίστις in the Christian is inextricably related to baptism and is not possible without catechesis. It is unsurprising then that Clement's κατηχήσις language is closely related to both baptism and faith in the passages discussed above.[37]

Even so, Clement also appears to speak of "instruction" in relation to neophytes and as the common first stage of the Christian life, as Méhat maintained. For instance, he states early in the *Stromateis* that "discourses are the offspring of the soul; therefore we call those who instruct 'fathers.'"[38] In this case a baptismal connection is not evident. There remains, however, a link with the language of pedagogy and an emphasis on memory (*Strom.* 1.1.2.1–2) which, when combined with the imagery of begetting, points toward early phases of Christian instruction. For Clement, instruction is intrinsically related to the formation, the spiritual birth, of the Christian. This process is necessarily not restricted

---

[35] Ashwin-Siejkowski, *Clement*, p. 154; Eusebius *Hist. eccl.* 6.1–3, 6 (Clement as head of the school, who (evidently) left Alexandria owing to Severus' persecution, making the position available to Origen). Others question Eusebius' identification of the persecution with Septimus Severus: see Gemeinhardt, "Glaube, Bildung, Theologie," p. 451.

[36] Méhat, *Étude*, p. 302: "On met généralement la catéchèse en relation avec le baptême; on se représente l'enseignement du minimum nécessaire pour donner un contenu à la foi du candidat. Rien dans Clément ne permet de l'entendre en ce sens....il n'y a pas d'enseignement spécial pour les catéchumènes, mais un enseignement élémentaire, commun aux catéchumènes, aux néophytes, et à tous les chrétiens ordinaires."

[37] See the material covered in Turck, "Catéchein," pp. 367–369; Knauber, "Ein frühchristliches Handbuch," pp. 311–334; Saxer, *Les rites*, pp. 73–74; Neymeyr, *Die christlichen Lehrer*, pp. 52–58; and Van den Hoek, "'Catechetical' school," pp. 67–71.

[38] *Strom* 1.1.1.2–3: ...ψυχῆς δὲ ἔγγονοι οἱ λόγοι. αὐτίκα πατέρας τοὺς κατηχήσαντάς φαμεν...

to the pre-baptismal phase, since the believer is supposed to progress toward Gnostic perfection.

In *Strom.* 1.2.19.4 Clement defends the study of philosophy by arguing that many things can confer honor on the artist that do not directly contribute to the end product, since "erudition is a credit to one who adduces chief doctrines for the persuasion of the hearers, engendering amazement among those instructed."[39] Here too a connection with initial instruction appears operative. In the first place, the things presented are τὰ κυριώτατα τῶν δογμάτων, the foundational doctrines of the Christian community.[40] Further, they are presented to οἱ ἀκροώμενοι, the hearers, a term that was possibly associated with the emerging catechumenate prior to Clement.[41] The lack of explicit baptismal context may be mitigated by Clement's appeal to persuasion: the person still unreformed in habits, actions, and passions is the person who needs to be persuaded. Beyond that, however, "teaching" displaces such a need.[42] In *Strom.* 6.11.89.2 Clement speaks of culling the necessary elements from philosophy for the benefit of οἱ κατηχούμενοι, used there in parallel with ἐπαΐοντες ("listeners").[43] The close connections of κατήχησις, baptism, and initial teaching elsewhere in Clement's writing may appear to weight judgment in favor of a pre-baptismal reference in these passages as well.[44] The difficulty is that, for Clement, one need not progress beyond the "common faith" to be a Christian, and in this sense one could remain at the same level of instruction as the neophyte throughout one's life. In this way, catechesis as "initial instruction" could, therefore, extend beyond the pre-baptismal phase.

---

[39] *Strom.* 1.2.19.4: πολλὰ δ᾽ οὖν καὶ μὴ συμβαλλόμενα εἰς τέλος συγκοσμεῖ τὸν τεχνίτην, καὶ ἄλλως ἡ πολυμαθία διασυστατικὴ τυγχάνει τοῦ παρατιθεμένου τὰ κυριώτατα τῶν δογμάτων πρὸς πειθὼ τῶν ἀκροωμένων, θαυμασμὸν ἐγγεννῶσα τοῖς κατηχουμένοις, καὶ πρὸς τὴν ἀλήθειαν συνίστησιν. Dietmar Wyrwa, *Die christliche Platonaneignung in den Stromateis des Clemens von Alexandrien*, AzKG 53 (Berlin: De Gruyter, 1983), p. 135, argues that this passage, along with 1.1.16.1, indicates a denigration of knowledge for knowledge's sake; see also Méhat, *Étude*, p. 186.

[40] One could draw an analogy with the Epicurean *Kyriai Doxai* or the Aristotelian epistemic importance of πίστις, which Clement elsewhere (mis)appropriates. See Elizabeth A. Clark, *Clement's Use of Aristotle: The Aristotelian Contribution to Clement of Alexandria's Refutation of Gnosticism*, TSR 1 (New York: Edwin Mellen, 1977), pp. 16–26.

[41] Notably, Méhat, *Étude*, p. 67, translates τοῖς κατηχουμένοις as "des catéchumènes" and later does not note the prior Christian appropriation of the terminology (pp. 286–287).

[42] This is the context for his statements in *Paed.* 1.1.1.3–1.1.2.1, noted above, p. 97.

[43] See the comments in Méhat, *Étude*, p. 287.

[44] Völker, *Der wahre Gnostiker*, p. 337, reads the phrase εἰς ὠφέλειαν τῶν κατηχουμένων καὶ μάλιστα Ἑλλήνων ὄντων in terms of Clement's concern to win over educated Greeks to Christianity, in line with his catechetical language elsewhere.

From this perspective, however, "catechesis" remains only *the first step* of Clement's pedagogical vision of the Christian life; it is something elementary that should be "perfected" at baptism so that the believer can move on in the pursuit of true Gnostic knowledge of God.[45]

Language of initiation in Clement, then, includes κατήχησις terminology, which is linked with that of faith, knowledge, illumination, perfection, the Christian πολιτεία, and the control or healing of the passions.[46] It is in connection with these ideas that Clement's catechetical Paul appears. These elements, though, function also within his broader epistemological, theological, and pedagogical framework, where they take on differentiated significance, with space for development within each one. Clement develops a carefully nuanced account of faith, knowledge, and perfection (among other things) in order to find the middle ground that allows for both the uneducated and Gnostics to be constructive members of the same ecclesial body.[47]

4.2 PEDAGOGICAL PROBLEMS AND PAULINE SOLUTIONS

4.2.1 Pedagogical Problems

To the extent that the emerging catechumenate provided the Alexandrian Christian community with a recognizable framework for basic confessional instruction and moral evaluation, it left untouched the issue of how one attained further knowledge of God. Indeed, when Clement was writing there was no widespread pedagogical framework that took one from neophyte to Gnostic within his proto-orthodox church. This absence was noted by both insiders and outsiders, by critics such as

---

[45] Clement also makes more extended use of κατήχησις language, which nevertheless retains the quality of foundational instruction: it is that which provides the basic grammar for life in whatever tradition he has in view. Jews can, therefore, be "instructed in the Law" (*Strom.* 1.2.174.1; 6.15.124.1); and Greeks and Romans "instructed" in their own traditions (*Prot.* 10.96.2). He even finds analogies for the link between instruction and illumination (read: catechesis and baptism) in Greek philosophy: *Strom.* 5.2.15.3, drawing an analogy with Plato in particular.

[46] This is also related to Clement's use of mystery initiation terminology (e.g., μύησις, ἀμύητος) in relation to preparation for more advanced knowledge; see Strutwolf, "Theologische Gnosis," p. 94.

[47] See *Strom.* 1.10.46.3–4 (my emphasis): "Neither, then, let the one who acts well be slandered by the one who is able to speak well nor the one who speaks well be reproached by the one who is suited for acting well. *But in acting each one brings forth that which is appropriate to each*" (οὔτ' οὖν βλασφημητέος ὁ εὐποιητικὸς πρὸς τοῦ εὖ λέγειν δυναμένου οὐδὲ μὴν κακιστέος ὁ οἷός τε εὖ λέγειν πρὸς τοῦ εὖ ποιεῖν ἐπιτηδείου· πρὸς δὲ ὃ ἑκάτερος πέφυκεν ἐνεργούντων).

Galen and Celsus, and by philosophically oriented Christians such as Valentinus and Basilides, as well as by anti-philosophical Christians. The former two groups denigrated foundational Christian confessions as simple and ignorant, while the latter rejected any attempt to build a more advanced philosophical theology on the foundations of baptismal faith.[48] In other words, Clement was forced to navigate a complex spectrum of opponents. At one extreme are those who denigrate the Christian emphasis on πίστις in favor of γνῶσις (e.g., Galen and Celsus) and at the other extreme are those who reject γνῶσις in favor of πίστις (non-philosophical Christians). In between these two extremes were the so-called "gnostic" groups associated with Valentinus and Basilides, who affirmed πίστις in principle but configured its relation to γνῶσις in ways that Clement found problematic. These disagreements, moreover, carried implications for how each group valued the catechumenate and its role in supplying foundational moral and doctrinal teaching.

It is debatable the extent to which Clement viewed his work, particularly in the *Stromateis*, as a response to the challenge posed by Celsus. On the one hand, Celsus' emphasis on the badly derivative nature of Christianity appears to be countered by Clement's continual refrain that true barbarian philosophy is present in Christianity, with Moses being the source of the later Greek wisdom. Such is the view of Salvatore Lilla.[49] On the other hand, as Lilla himself notes, Clement borrowed that apologetic move from Jewish predecessors such as Philo and Aristobulus, as well as the Platonist Numenius of Apamea, all of whom were writing prior to Celsus' challenge.[50] What is clear, however, is that Clement knew that some "Greeks" viewed the Christian emphasis on πίστις with intellectual derision.[51] Galen uses Christian and Jewish credulity as the benchmark

---

[48] For a recent account of Clement's interpretation of Paul in relation to these interlocutors, along with the *simpliciores*, see Kovacs, "Reading," pp. 325–343.

[49] Lilla, *Clement of Alexandria*, pp. 34–37.

[50] On Clement's debt to Philo regarding Moses, see esp. Annewies van den Hoek, *Clement of Alexandria and His Use of Philo in the Stromateis: An Early Christian Reshaping of a Jewish Model*, VC Sup 3 (Leiden: Brill, 1988), pp. 48–68; see also Lilla, *Clement of Alexandria*, p. 32. Alain Le Boulluec, *La notion d'hérésie dans la littérature grecque, IIe–IIIe siècles* (Paris: Études augustiniennes, 1985), pp. 364–365, argues that, if Clement was responding directly to Celsus, it is the end of *Strom.* 7 that has "le plus de chances de correspondre à ce projet." There Clement addresses the multiplicity of identifiably Christian groups.

[51] *Strom.* 2.2.8.4: πίστις δέ, ἣν διαβάλλουσι κενὴν καὶ βάρβαρον νομίζοντες Ἕλληνες... The irony here is that the equation between πίστις and πρόληψις which Clement goes on to make comes from Epicurus (as he notes in 2.4.16.3) and was present within his middle Platonic context; see further below, p. 105. On πίστις/*fides*, see now Teresa Morgan, *Roman Faith and Christian Faith* (Oxford: Oxford University Press, 2015), who

for unthinking faith. "If I had in mind people who taught their pupils in the same way as the followers of Moses and Christ teach theirs – for they order them to accept everything on faith – I should not have given you a definition."[52] Clement's response to such criticism is closely integrated with his response to other early Christians who were working under similar conditions but who arrived at answers that Clement found lacking.

Before Galen was writing, Basilides and Valentinus were working out their own way to understand and build upon the developing framework and theology of Christian initiation. By all accounts, faith was crucial for salvation but these thinkers differed in their understanding of πίστις and in the philosophical and exegetical resources deployed in the service of that understanding.[53] According to Clement, the Basilideans consider faith to be "natural," a mental comprehension of learned notions without need for proof, while also being a choice.[54] The consonance of "choice" and "nature" works, in their view, because the "worldly" faith of each different nature is a consequence of a supra-worldly "choice" while also being a "gift…appropriate to the hope of each person."[55] For

emphasizes the constant theme that the object of trust must be proven worthy of it. Expecting "faith" without providing sufficient grounds was, from that perspective, nonsensical (see pp. 39–45, 65–74, 457–458, and *passim*).

[52] From the lost treatise Εἰς τὸ πρῶτον κινοῦν ἀκίνητον (*On the Primary Unmoved Mover*), preserved in an Arabic life of Galen; see Richard Walzer, *Galen on Jews and Christians*, Oxford Classical and Philosophical Monographs (London: Oxford University Press, 1949), reference 5 for translation and discussion. See also Galen *Puls. diff.* 2.4 (text in C. G. Kühn, *Claudii Galeni Opera Omnia*, vol. 8 (Leipzig: Knobloch, 1824), p. 579.13–17) and 3.3 (Kühn, p. 657.1–3), also discussed by Walzer.

[53] This is related to broader disagreements relating to the quality of creation, its perfectibility, and the witness of scripture to salvation within history; see the discussion in Strutwolf, "Theologische Gnosis," pp. 97–101.

[54] *Strom.* 2.3.10.1–2: "Those in Basilides' circle consider faith to be natural, insofar as they attribute it to choice [election?], discovering [their] teachings by mental comprehension without demonstration" (Ἐνταῦθα φυσικὴν ἡγοῦνται τὴν πίστιν οἱ ἀμφὶ τὸν Βασιλείδην, καθὸ καὶ ἐπὶ τῆς ἐκλογῆς τάττουσιν αὐτήν, τὰ μαθήματα ἀναποδείκτως εὑρίσκουσαν καταλήψει νοητικῇ).

[55] *Strom.* 2.3.10.3–11.1: "Basilides' followers say, further, that faith together with choice are fitting [personal?] at each level; on the other hand, [they say] that the worldly faith of each nature follows from the consequence of a supra-worldly choice [election?] and that even the gift of faith is appropriate to the hope of each person" (ἔτι φασὶν οἱ ἀπὸ Βασιλείδου πίστιν ἅμα καὶ ἐκλογὴν οἰκείαν εἶναι καθ' ἕκαστον διάστημα, κατ' ἐπακολούθημα δ' αὖ τῆς ἐκλογῆς τῆς ὑπερκοσμίου τὴν κοσμικὴν ἁπάσης φύσεως συνέπεσθαι πίστιν κατάλληλόν τε εἶναι τῇ ἑκάστου ἐλπίδι καὶ τῆς πίστεως τὴν δωρεάν). This passage is very difficult and I am grateful to Edward Jeremiah for his criticisms of an earlier translation. It is unclear whose choice is at stake here (and in 2.3.10.1), whether the "gift of faith" signifies that the choice is that of divine election or, rather, whether Clement objects to a view that a

Clement, this is having one's cake and eating it too: if faith is assigned to natural choice (ἐκλογή), then it is no longer by "free will" (προαίρεσις) and humans can no longer be held responsible for their belief or unbelief (*Strom.* 2.3.11.1).

To the definition of faith as cataleptic, involving actual knowledge, Clement rather defines it as proleptic, remaining at the level of a preconception that can, with learning, *become* cataleptic.[56] In other words, for Clement the Basilidean position effectively reduces to a natural determinism that does not allow sufficient room for progress in understanding.

Yet, as we have seen, Clement does not want to say that "faith" is distinct from knowledge in an absolute sense. That is his problem with the Valentinian position. "Now the Valentinians, assigning faith to us, the simpletons, want knowledge to be inherent in them who are saved by nature according to their greater share of the superior seed, saying it [knowledge] is separated as far from faith as is the spiritual is from the physical."[57] Linked with his response to the Basilideans, Clement rejects "salvation by nature." Such determinism makes repentance, baptism, and the rest of theology irrational; it lacks the "voluntary faith" that is the "foundation of salvation."[58] What becomes clear elsewhere is that

preexistent soul's choice determines the faith of an earthly human person. The contrast between ἐκλογή here and προαίρεσις in 2.3.11.1, may suggest that the former is Clement's principal objection. Further, the phrase καθ' ἕκαστον διάστημα is ambiguous; I take it to refer to different levels ("intervals") of reality, including the worldly and supra-worldly noted in the subsequent clause (note the Platonic parallels adduced in Matyáš Havrda, "Some observations on Clement of Alexandria, *Stromata*, book five," *Vigiliae Christianae* 64, no. 1 (2010), 8 n. 20). Even so, Löhr admits that the significance of an "interval" in Clement's argument here is unclear (Winrich Alfried Löhr, *Basilides und seine Schule. Eine Studie zur Theologie- und Kirchengeschichte des zweiten Jahrhunderts*, WUNT 83 (Tübingen: Mohr Siebeck, 1996), p. 55 n. 22).

56 *Strom.* 2.4.17.1; see also the comments in Lilla, *Clement of Alexandria*, pp. 129–130, and now Kovacs, "Reading," p. 338, and Havrda, *Eighth Stromateus*, p. 136. Löhr, *Basilides*, p. 53, notes the Stoic epistemological background of the term κατάληψις, as well as the evident difference in the use that Clement attributes to Basilides' school.

57 *Strom.* 2.3.10.2–3: οἱ δὲ ἀπὸ Οὐαλεντίνου τὴν μὲν πίστιν τοῖς ἁπλοῖς ἀπονείμαντες ἡμῖν, αὐτοῖς δὲ τὴν γνῶσιν τοῖς φύσει σωζομένοις κατὰ τὴν τοῦ διαφέροντος πλεονεξίαν σπέρματος ἐνυπάρχειν βούλονται, μακρῷ δὴ κεχωρισμένην πίστεως, ᾗ τὸ πνευματικὸν τοῦ ψυχικοῦ, λέγοντες. See also the analysis of Clement's rejection of "gnostic" determinism in Strutwolf, "Theologische Gnosis," pp. 96–99, who relates it to a broader disagreement about their views about creation.

58 *Strom.* 2.3.11.2: "As a result, neither then is baptism reasonable, nor the blessed seal, nor the Son, nor the Father. But, I think, [on their view] God is found to be the distribution of natures to them, which does not have the foundation of salvation: voluntary faith" (ὥστε οὐδὲ βάπτισμα ἔτι εὔλογον οὐδὲ μακαρία σφραγὶς οὐδὲ ὁ υἱὸς οὐδὲ ὁ πατήρ· ἀλλὰ θεός, οἶμαι, ἡ τῶν φύσεων αὐτοῖς εὑρίσκεται διανομή, τὸν θεμέλιον τῆς σωτηρίας, τὴν ἑκούσιον πίστιν, οὐκ ἔχουσα).

Clement also rejects the distinction between "spiritual" and "physical" people who are allotted either knowledge or faith.[59] In the *Paedagogus*, Clement alludes to the Valentinian position, that there are some who are (naturally) spiritual γνωστικοί while others are merely ψυχικοί, but he maintains that "faith is the one universal human salvation" and that "all who put off fleshly desires are equally πνευματικοί with the Lord."[60]

Clement's description of the Valentinian position suggests a particular scriptural basis for their view. The confluence of γνῶσις, ψυχικός, and πνευματικός language is only found in the New Testament in 1 Corinthians.[61] In 1 Corinthians 2:6–7, 13–14, we read that Paul "speaks wisdom to the wise," that he "interprets spiritual things for spiritual people," and that "the ψυχικός person does not receive things from God's spirit."[62] In 3:1–3 Paul tells the Corinthians that they were not yet πνευματικοί thanks to their internal divisions that render them "fleshly."[63] In 8:7 Paul states that not all have knowledge, and in 12:8 that the Spirit gives it. That this language is not simply Clement's importation onto the Valentinians is indicated by its presence in the *Tripartite Tractate* (NHC I,5), *Excerpta ex Theodoto*, Irenaeus, Hippolytus (if he is the author of the *Refutatio*), and Tertullian.[64] Tertullian in particular, though treating

---

[59] There is the further Valentinian distinction of the "material" people who are destined for destruction (see *Trip. tract.* 119.9–20), which Clement does not discuss. On Clement's disagreement here, see Ashwin-Siejkowski, *Clement*, pp. 122–125.

[60] *Paed.* 1.6.30.2–1.6.31.2: μία καθολικὴ τῆς ἀνθρωπότητος σωτηρία ἡ πίστις…Οὐκ ἄρα οἱ μὲν γνωστικοί, οἱ δὲ ψυχικοὶ ἐν αὐτῷ τῷ λόγῳ, ἀλλ᾽ οἱ πάντες ἀποθέμενοι τὰς σαρκικὰς ἐπιθυμίας ἴσοι καὶ πνευματικοὶ παρὰ τῷ κυρίῳ.

[61] See the collection of "gnostic" readings of the following passages in Pagels, *Gnostic Paul*, pp. 57–78, though she strangely offers no "gnostic" readings of 1 Cor. 3:1–3, nor does she cite Tertullian *Praes. haer.* 27.

[62] 1 Cor. 2:13–14: "And we speak these things not in human teachings with wise words but in spiritual teachings, interpreting spiritual things for spiritual people. But the *psychikos* person does not receive things from God's spirit" (ἃ καὶ λαλοῦμεν οὐκ ἐν διδακτοῖς ἀνθρωπίνης σοφίας λόγοις ἀλλ᾽ ἐν διδακτοῖς πνεύματος, πνευματικοῖς πνευματικὰ συγκρίνοντες. ψυχικὸς δὲ ἄνθρωπος οὐ δέχεται τὰ τοῦ πνεύματος τοῦ θεοῦ·).

[63] 1 Cor. 3:1, 3: "And I, brothers and sisters, was not able to speak to you as spiritual people but as fleshly ones, as infants in Christ…For you are still fleshly. For wherever there is jealousy and strife among you, are you not fleshly and behaving in accordance with human standards?" (Κἀγώ, ἀδελφοί, οὐκ ἠδυνήθην λαλῆσαι ὑμῖν ὡς πνευματικοῖς ἀλλ᾽ ὡς σαρκίνοις, ὡς νηπίοις ἐν Χριστῷ….ἔτι γὰρ σαρκικοί ἐστε. ὅπου γὰρ ἐν ὑμῖν ζῆλος καὶ ἔρις, οὐχὶ σαρκικοί ἐστε καὶ κατὰ ἄνθρωπον περιπατεῖτε).

[64] *Trip. Tract.* 118–119; *Exc.* 58–62; Irenaeus *Haer.* 1.6.1; [Hippolytus] *Haer.* 34–36 (text in M. David Litwa (ed. and trans.), *Refutation of All Heresies*, Writings from the Greco-Roman World 40 (Atlanta: SBL Press, 2015)); Tertullian *Praes. haer.* 27. For a full discussion of these passages (*sans* Tertullian), see Thomassen, *Spiritual Seed*, pp. 46–82, who divides them into "eastern" and "western" streams of Valentinianism. Thomassen argues that the stream represented by Clement, "Theodotus," Irenaeus, and [Hippolytus]

specific groups rather loosely, claims that "heretics" make use of 1 Corinthians 3:1 (among other passages) to make space for their own claims to knowledge, to prove that, while the apostles carried out their teaching function "simply and fully," the churches "accepted something different than what the apostles produced by their own fault."[65] It would appear on that basis, then, that Clement's problem with the Valentinians was not simply philosophical but was oriented around the treatment of specific scriptural passages.

There remains a serious question about whether Clement accurately represents the views of the Basilideans here, particularly in connection with natural determinism, or those of the Valentinians in respect to their anthropologically determined, soteriological dualism.[66] As Alain Le Boulluec notes, Clement often resorts to "heresiological reduction," producing an "amalgam" as a way to highlight common problems which he can then address synthetically.[67] This appears to be the case in *Strom.* 2.3.10.[68] What is important for present purposes, however, is the fact that Clement constructs his own argument about the relation of faith and knowledge – as they relate to the relative roles of catechesis and further study – in response to his portrayal of these other positions.

The third group in Clement's three-front struggle comprises those who reject philosophy entirely.[69] Probably aware of external criticisms and almost certainly aware of internal philosophical developments in theology among various "gnostic" groups, these Christians consider

---

is distinctively western in the authors' concern for the salvation of the ψυχικός and the automatic redemption (by nature) of the πνευματικοί.

[65] *Praes. haer.* 27.1–4: "uideamus ne forte apostoli quidem simpliciter et plene, ecclesiae autem suo uitio aliter acceperint quam apostoli proferebant....Tenent correptas ab apostolo ecclesias...item ad Corinthios scriptum quod essent adhuc carnales qui lacte educarentur, nondum idonei ad pabulum, qui putarent se scire aliquid quando nondum scirent quemadmodum scire oporteret"; see also 1 Cor. 8:2.

[66] See p. 107 n. 64 on Valentinian soteriology and Chapter 2.3.6 above.

[67] Le Boulluec, *La notion*, pp. 332–354; the discussion of "la réduction hérésiologique" is on pp. 343–344.

[68] Löhr, *Basilides*, pp. 52, 57, explicitly follows Le Boulluec's lead on this point. In his extended discussion of the matter ("Exkurs III," pp. 186–190), he concludes that it is highly questionable whether Basilides ever used the phrase φύσει σωζόμενος or advanced its theological implications. Christoph Markschies, *Valentinus Gnosticus? Untersuchungen zur valentinianischen Gnosis mit einem Kommentar zu den Fragmenten Valentins*, WUNT 65 (Tübingen: Mohr Siebeck, 1992), p. 13 and n. 15, notes a similar dynamic in passing.

[69] De Faye, *Clément*, pp. 137–139, notes the conflict with the *simpliciores*. See also Völker, *Der wahre Gnostiker*, pp. 5–6; Méhat, *Étude*, pp. 294–336; Lilla, *Clement of Alexandria*, p. 141; Kovacs, "Reading," pp. 333–336.

philosophy either as an extraneous and distracting affair or as an intrinsically evil pursuit that only leads to wickedness.[70] Moreover, the Apostle Paul himself had warned against those who "take captive through philosophy and vain deceit according to human tradition."[71] In contrast with the Valentinians (or external Greeks) who relativize faith, these believers reject appeals to knowledge beyond the "bare faith" in which they were baptized.[72] Clement answers their various objections – Paul was only concerned with criticizing Epicureans – but such minor details did not supply an alternative, pro-philosophy framework. In order to address their concerns while not ignoring those of the "gnostics," Clement needed to find space within the concept of faith and in its liturgical expression in catechesis and baptism, a space to incorporate the scriptural language of faith and knowledge, a means to address the criticisms represented by Celsus and Galen, as well as the challenge of the Valentinians.

The final point to make here about Clement's pedagogical problem is that, in addition to philosophical and exegetical issues, there was a concrete institutional edge involved. As he put it in responding to the natural determinism of the Basilideans (and Valentinians), such a position renders all efforts at moral or philosophical development useless. If they are correct, the catechumenate and baptism do not lead to faith and salvation, then, and the masses of "unlettered" Christians are marginalized as liminal community members, πιστοί who are qualitatively distinct from the γνωστικοί and inhabit a soteriologically ambivalent space. Moreover, for all their denigration of (elementary) faith, it appears that Clement faced a situation in which his opponents' actual catechetical/baptismal practice looked very much like his own community's practice.[73] He could not simply reject the importance of γνῶσις, however, perhaps by

---

[70] *Strom.* 1.1.18.3–4: "The chattering of those ignorantly timid ones has not escaped me, saying that the faith must concern itself with the most essential and important matters but that we should pass over external and superfluous things, which delay and occupy us pointlessly concerning things that do not contribute to the goal. Others even think that philosophy entered life from an evil source, some evil inventor, for the purpose of human suffering" (οὐ λέληθεν δέ με καὶ τὰ θρυλούμενα πρός τινων ἀμαθῶς ψοφοδεῶν χρῆναι λεγόντων περὶ τὰ ἀναγκαιότατα καὶ συνέχοντα τὴν πίστιν καταγίνεσθαι, τὰ δὲ ἔξωθεν καὶ περιττὰ ὑπερβαίνειν μάτην ἡμᾶς τρίβοντα καὶ κατέχοντα περὶ τοῖς οὐδὲν συμβαλλομένοις πρὸς τὸ τέλος. οἳ δὲ καὶ πρὸς κακοῦ ἂν τὴν φιλοσοφίαν εἰσδεδυκέναι τὸν βίον νομίζουσιν ἐπὶ λύμῃ τῶν ἀνθρώπων πρός τινος εὑρετοῦ πονηροῦ).

[71] Col. 2:8, addressed by Clement in *Strom.* 1.11.50.3–6, and see his treatment of 2 Tim. 2:16 in 1.10.49.3.

[72] Note the criticism of this ψιλὴ πίστις in *Strom.* 1.9.43.1, despite the fact that Clement elsewhere speaks positively of it.

[73] See the discussion of Valentinian initiation in Chapter 2.3.6 above.

finding different terminology to accomplish similar goals. This is because there was another faction within the church who reacted strongly to the philosophical speculations of Valentinus and company by rejecting philosophy as a whole in favor of πίστις. Such a reduction will not do for Clement, though, who is himself a philosophical teacher and who values the scripturally rooted language of γνῶσις. Clement wanted to preserve philosophy in the service of the church while rejecting the "heretics" for having illegitimate philosophy rather than true philosophy, paganism rather than piety, for their treason to the ecclesial canon.[74]

4.2.2 Clement's Pauline Solution

Clement's response to these pedagogical problems was to develop a differentiated account of faith that was philosophically justified and exegetically grounded, incorporating the scriptural language and concerns aired by all sides. While the structure of "faith" is articulated at various points throughout his work, Clement's use of πίστις to respond to his opponents is particularly evident in three places: *Paed.* 1.6, *Strom.* 2.2–4, and *Strom.* 5.1.[75] These passages accomplish three things: they draw an essential connection between faith and knowledge, they argue for a dual function of πίστις in its relation to knowledge, and they ground Clement's discussion exegetically in two Pauline passages. In this way they tie together his concern for catechesis and Gnostic progression while answering the challenges posed by "gnostics" and anti-philosophical factions alike.

In *Paed.* 1.6, Clement directly addresses the charges of those "puffed up in knowledge" who claim Christians are "children" with respect to the "childish and well-despised quality" of their education.[76] No doubt

---

[74] See esp. the discussion of Clement's construal and response to "heresies" in Le Boulluec, *La notion*, pp. 263–438, from whom these descriptions are drawn.

[75] The philosophical account of πίστις in *Strom.* 8.3 is fragmentary and, while its structure coheres with Clement's discussions elsewhere, his Christian intellectual commitments (clearly laid out in the *prooemium*) are not the principal concern in that section. See Matyáš Havrda, "Galenus Christianus? the doctrine of demonstration in *Stromata* VIII and the question of its source," *Vigiliae Christianae* 65, no. 3 (2011), 345–346, and his extended discussion of the passage with its Greek philosophical antecedents in Havrda, *Eighth Stromateus*, pp. 145–174.

[76] *Paed.* 1.6.25.1: "Now it is more than possible for us to strip down and combat those given to finding fault. For we are not designated 'children' and 'infants' in relation to the childish and contemptible quality of our education, as those puffed up in knowledge have slanderously alleged." (Ἔξεστι δὲ ἡμῖν ἐκ περιουσίας πρὸς τοὺς φιλεγκλήμονας ἐπαποδύσασθαι· οὐ γὰρ παῖδες ἡμεῖς καὶ νήπιοι πρὸς τὸ παιδαριῶδες καὶ εὐκαταφρόνητον τῆς μαθήσεως προσηγορεύμεθα, καθὼς οἱ εἰς γνῶσιν πεφυσιωμένοι διαβεβλήκασιν); see also 1 Cor. 4:6, 18–19; 8:1.

this description could include external critics such as Celsus or Galen, but Clement's principal aim appears to be the Valentinian distinction between γνωστικοί (or πνευματικοί) and ψυχικοί within the church. His initial argument emphasizes the perfection and illumination of the believer at baptism because, as Paul says, "you are all one in Christ Jesus."[77] The center of his response, however, consists in an extended discussion of 1 Corinthians 3:1–3, providing a counter-reading of what appears to have been an important text for his Valentinian interlocutors.[78] Paul's comments in this passage point *prima facie* toward different levels of maturity and teaching within the Corinthian community: only the spiritual are able to receive the spiritual teaching while the rest are left with "milk."[79]

Clement resists this implication by means of a dense and twisting argument through which he seeks to establish that milk and meat share the same essence, fundamental to the Christian life, though in different states.[80] That is to say, Clement argues that milk and meat are merely quantitatively, rather than qualitatively, distinct. In the first place, he argues that the promise of milk as part of an eschatological hope indicates that it is not simply the food of infants but the also the mature hope of the believer.[81] Milk, therefore, represents something perfectly nourishing for the Christian. Paul is presented as saying

I instructed you in Christ with simple, true, and natural spiritual nourishment. For such is the life-giving nourishment of milk, welling up in affectionate breasts...

---

[77] Gal. 3:28, cited in *Paed.* 1.6.31.1.

[78] Of course, Clement's discussion of 1 Cor. 3:1–3 is also related to his various treatments of 1 Cor. 2:6–16 in relation to the development of the Christian; see Strawbridge, *Pauline Effect*, p. 53, and see further in Chapter 7. Le Boulluec, "Aux origines," pp. 34, 40, also notes in passing the importance of this passage for Clement's view of catechesis.

[79] See the discussion in Kovacs, "Reading," pp. 328–331 and *passim*, who emphasizes the importance of 1 Cor. 2–3 for Clement's refutation of the Valentinians.

[80] The analysis that follows is largely in agreement with that offered in Annewies van de Bunt, "Milk and honey in the theology of Clement of Alexandria," in *Fides Sacramenti – Sacramentum Fidei: Studies in Honour of Pieter Smulders* (Assen: Van Gorcum, 1981), pp. 27–39. Penniman comments, "Clement does not hide his struggle to bring coherence to the different possible senses of the Pauline text"; Penniman, *Raised on Christian Milk*, p. 97. On the ancient discourse of breastfeeding and *paidea*, see Denise Kimber Buell, *Making Christians: Clement of Alexandria and the Rhetoric of Legitimacy* (Princeton: Princeton University Press, 1999), pp. 121–130, and Dawn LaValle, "Divine Breastfeeding: Milk, Blood, and *Pneuma* in Clement of Alexandria's *Paedagogus*," *Journal of Late Antiquity* 8, no. 2 (2015), 322–336.

[81] Citing Exod. 3:8 as indicating a future hope for Christians (see also Heb. 4:7–11); *Paed.* 1.6.34.3–36.1.

Just as nurses nourish newborn children with milk so also am I, by the word which is the milk of Christ, instilling spiritual nourishment in you.[82]

The emphasis, according to Clement, is not on the fact that the Corinthians were like children but that Paul's teaching was as unimpeachably nourishing as mother's milk because its content was the Word of Christ himself.[83] On this reading, it is those who have ingested the milk that are spiritual, while the "fleshly" remain those who are recently instructed and unbaptized.[84] The "spiritual" Christian – which is to say, every baptized believer – remains a mature milk drinker until after death, when they achieve a proximity to God previously unattained.[85]

Still, Clement is not yet satisfied with this one angle of interpretation.[86] He continues in the rest of *Paed.* 1.6 to illustrate various ways in which milk and meat are to be construed as different states of the same substance. He argues that solid food is simply a condensed accumulation of

[82] *Paed.* 1.6.35.3–36.1: κατήχησα ὑμᾶς ἐν Χριστῷ ἁπλῇ καὶ ἀληθεῖ καὶ αὐτοφυεῖ τροφῇ τῇ πνευματικῇ· τοιαύτη γὰρ ἡ τοῦ γάλακτος ζωοτρόφος οὐσία, φιλοστόργοις πηγάζουσα μαστοῖς· ὡς νοεῖσθαι τὸ πᾶν τῇδε· ὥσπερ τῷ γάλακτι αἱ τίτθαι τοὺς παῖδας τοὺς νεογνοὺς ἐκτρέφουσιν, κἀγὼ δὲ οὕτω τῷ Χριστοῦ γάλακτι λόγῳ πνευματικὴν ὑμῖν ἐνστάζων τροφήν.

[83] See the comments on this passage in Buell, *Making Christians*, pp. 138–139, and the catalogue of "logos/milk" passages in Van de Bunt, "Milk and honey," pp. 32–36.

[84] *Paed.* 1.6.36.3–4: "For, on the one hand, he [*viz.* Paul] called those 'spiritual' who have already believed in the Holy Spirit, and 'fleshly' those who are newly catechized and not yet purified; he fairly calls them 'still fleshly' who think fleshly thoughts in the same matter as the Gentiles" (Πνευματικοὺς μὲν γὰρ τοὺς πεπιστευκότας ἤδη τῷ ἁγίῳ πνεύματι προσεῖπεν, σαρκικοὺς δὲ τοὺς νεοκατηχήτους καὶ μηδέπω κεκαθαρμένους, οὓς 'ἔτι σαρκικοὺς' εἰκότως λέγει ἐπ' ἴσης τοῖς ἐθνικοῖς τὰ σαρκὸς ἔτι φρονοῦντας); see also οἱ νεωστὶ κατηχούμενοι in 1.6.36.2.

[85] *Paed.* 1.6.36.6–37.1: "For with it [*viz.* the transformed body in 'coming age'], having a face equal to the angels, we shall see the promise 'face to face'…the promise after our departure from here" (σὺν αὐτῇ γὰρ τὸ πρόσωπον ἰσάγγελον ἔχοντες πρόσωπον πρὸς πρόσωπον τὴν ἐπαγγελίαν ὀψόμεθα.…ἡ ἐπαγγελία μετὰ τὴν ἐνθένδε ἀπαλλαγήν). This interpretation is also in keeping with Clement's description elsewhere of mystical contemplation and divine proximity as achieved after death; see *Strom* 7.10.57.1–5, where one enters the presence of God μετά…τὴν ἐν σαρκὶ τελευταίαν ὑπεροχήν, and see also the comments on this passage in Jean Daniélou, *Gospel Message and Hellenistic Culture*, trans. John A. Baker, A History of Early Christian Doctrine Before the Council of Nicaea 2 (London: Darton, Longman & Todd, 1973), p. 451; Völker, *Der wahre Gnostiker*, p. 388; Lilla, *Clement of Alexandria*, pp. 181–184; *pace* Itter, *Esoteric Teaching*, pp. 37–38.

[86] *Pace* Buell, *Making Christians*, pp. 138–142, who argues that *Paed.* 1.6.34.3–36.1 and 1.6.36.2–37.2 constitute two different interpretations of 1 Cor. 3:1–3. The continuity in Clement's emphasis on milk being the continuing diet of the mature points rather to two stages in the same argument; see also the comments in Penniman, *Raised on Christian Milk*, pp. 97–98, and LaValle, "Divine Breastfeeding," p. 325. Clement signals his shift in approach, as Buell rightly notes, in 1.6.37.3.

milk. "They have the same essence, for just so the same word is mild and gentle like milk and firm and hardened like solid food."[87] This is evident, according to Clement, based on the fact that milk is simply aspirated blood, infused with the spirit, transformed for the nourishment of infants.[88] This secures a connection with the eucharistic flesh and blood which, like all human flesh and blood, are essential for life and inextricably linked with the cycle of producing and rearing children.[89]

So the milk, though it is formulated for "infants" and suitable for their easy digestion, cannot *simply* be equated with preliminary instruction. Paul's "milk" has an ongoing fundamental importance for the believer; it continues to course through them and give life.[90] Given Clement's concern to integrate catechetical instruction and basic faith within the broader process of Gnostic Christian maturation, this is hardly surprising. Even so, his interpretation of 1 Corinthians 3:1–3 in this section retains a close connection between pre-baptismal catechesis and milk. Building on the eschatological imagery of "milk and honey" from Exodus 3:8, Clement later expands the connection between milk and honey to include an affinity with water, thereby linking it with baptism.[91] Milk, water, and honey combine in the purification of sins and the healing of passions brought about by the Word.[92] His rebuttal to the Valentinian challenge,

---

[87] *Paed.* 1.6.37.3–38.1: ...ταὐτὸν δὲ τῇ οὐσίᾳ· ὡσαύτως γὰρ καὶ ὁ λόγος ὁ αὐτὸς ἢ ἀνειμένος καὶ ἤπιος ὡς γάλα ἢ πεπηγὼς καὶ συνεστραμμένος ὡς βρῶμα.

[88] *Paed* 1.6.44.3: "It was shown by us...that blood turns into milk for pregnant women by a transformation, but not one in essence (Ἀποδέδεικται δὲ ἡμῖν...τὸ αἷμα εἰς γάλα ταῖς κυούσαις κατὰ μεταβολήν, οὐ κατ' οὐσίαν χωρεῖν). On the medical background of this argument, see esp. LaValle, "Divine Breastfeeding," pp. 322–336, who is followed by Penniman, *Raised on Christian Milk*, p. 99 with n. 71.

[89] The eucharistic overtones are noted by Van de Bunt, "Milk and honey," p. 36; *pace* Buell, *Making Christians*, pp. 145–146, who argues against their presence. This relates to similar begetting/instructing connections drawn elsewhere; see *Strom.* 3.15.98.4: τῷ γὰρ κατὰ λόγον τεκνοποιησαμένῳ καὶ ἀναθρεψαμένῳ καὶ παιδεύσαντι ἐν κυρίῳ καθάπερ καὶ τῷ διὰ τῆς ἀληθοῦς κατηχήσεως γεννήσαντι κεῖταί τις μισθὸς ὥσπερ καὶ τῷ ἐκλεκτῷ σπέρματι. In context, Clement is arguing for the place of both married and celibate people within the community of faith and his emphasis is rather on the validity of the biological procreation. The assumed importance of "true instruction" supplies the basis for his argument. See the comments of Buell, *Making Christians*, pp. 81–82, on this passage.

[90] *Paed.* 1.6.39.1–4; see also the discussion in Buell, *Making Christians*, pp. 154–159, who situates Clement's discussion in the context of ancient reproductive discourse.

[91] See Van de Bunt, "Milk and honey," p. 36: "Baptism anticipates rest in eternity."

[92] See *Paed.* 1.6.50.3–51.1, where a kinship (συγγένεια) between water and milk is posited like that between the λόγος and baptism, such that the spiritual food (λόγος, milk) is linked with the spiritual washing at baptism (water) for the forgiveness of sins. The λόγος is also mixed with honey for its sweetness in φιλανθρωπία in the healing of passions and cleansing of sins.

then, is that "milk" is not *only* suitable for catechumens and uneducated believers but for all πιστοί because it contains *in nuce* the perfect spiritual nourishment which will, by repeated ingestion, become the Apostle's "solid food."[93] Catechesis remains the first spiritual meal, so to speak.

Clement's argument that "milk" is a continuous element of the mature Christian diet, that it is both the first and last food of the soul, is closely related to his discussion of faith, which like milk is first appropriated at baptism and remains fundamental throughout one's life. As he puts it at the beginning of *Paed.* 1.6, "faith is, so to speak, an impulse born in time and also the *telos* which actualizes the promise established forever."[94] This differentiated faith is argued carefully in response to "gnostic" and philosophical interlocutors in *Strom.* 2.2–4. It is a well-known feature of Clement's epistemology that πίστις functions both as the non-demonstrable foundation of knowledge and as the consummation of knowledge.[95] Faith is both preconception (πρόληψις) – a mental assent to invisible matters which is the foundation for all willing and acting – and the judgment that follows after knowledge, acting as its deciding criterion.[96] In contrast

---

93 See the comments in LaValle, "Divine Breastfeeding," pp. 332–333 and *passim*, who emphasizes the continual need for instruction and growth after baptism, as well as Clement's overriding concern to establish a unified account of the Christian life, from beginning to end.

94 *Paed.* 1.6.28.5: "Ἔστι γοῦν, ὡς εἰπεῖν, ὁρμὴ μὲν ἡ πίστις ἐν χρόνῳ γεννωμένη, τέλος δὲ τὸ τυχεῖν τῆς ἐπαγγελίας εἰς αἰῶνας βεβαιούμενον. Clement's language of a "promise established forever" may relate to his cryptic comments in *Prot.* 1.6.4 that believers are "begotten in God before the foundation of the world," which Itter, *Esoteric Teaching*, p. 114, reads problematically as "pre-existent life in the Word of God." Given that Clement expressly rejects the pre-existent life of individual souls, as Itter acknowledges elsewhere, it is hard to take such poetic language in the *Protrepticus* at face value when categories such as election (as suggested by Havrda, "Review," p. 578) or promise can account for it in terms that Clement does not elsewhere reject.

95 See the classic treatment in Camelot, *Foi et gnose*, pp. 26–48, 64–67, whose general position is echoed in Alfredo Brontesi, *La soteria in Clemente Alessandrino* (Rome: Università Gregoriana, 1972), pp. 537–540; Daniélou, *Gospel Message*, pp. 312–313, 320–321; Peter Karavites, *Evil, Freedom, and the Road to Perfection in Clement of Alexandria*, VC Sup 43 (Leiden: Brill, 1998), p. 142; Osborn, *Clement*, pp. 161–165; and Ashwin-Siejkowski, *Clement*, pp. 165–168; see also earlier de Faye, *Clément*, pp. 201–216. The philosophical presentation of πίστις is noted variously in Havrda, *Eighth Stromateus*, pp. 134–145 and *passim*.

96 *Strom.* 2.2.8.4–9.1: "Now faith…is a voluntary preconception, a pious assent…But others assign faith to be the mental assent to something that is not evident [to the senses]" (πίστις δέ…πρόληψις ἑκούσιός ἐστι, θεοσεβείας συγκατάθεσις…ἄλλοι δ' ἀφανοῦς πράγματος ἐννοητικὴν συγκατάθεσιν ἀπέδωκαν εἶναι τὴν πίστιν); *Strom.* 2.4.15.5 (drawing on the view of Aristotle): "Now Aristotle says that 'faith' is a judgment, following from knowledge, that a particular thing is true. Therefore, faith is more important than knowledge and is its criterion (Ἀριστοτέλης δὲ τὸ ἑπόμενον τῇ ἐπιστήμῃ κρῖμα, ὡς ἀληθὲς

with Clement's presentation of the Basilidean and Valentinian positions, his view of faith is consonant with free will (προαίρεσις) involved in the movement from preconception to judgment. It is this differentiated character that links faith and knowledge. "Knowledge, then, is characterized by faith and faith is characterized by knowledge by some divine reciprocal relationship."[97]

The themes of "milk" and faith in Clement's response come together in *Strom* 5.1. It is also at this point that the double-edged quality of his pedagogical vision becomes clear. Basing his arguments on Paul's letters allows him to rebut both groups on grounds they recognize as authoritative. At the outset he notes that one cannot have faith without knowledge just as there is no Father without the Son.[98] The two cohere because there is space within πίστις itself, a point Clement finds in Romans 1:17, where Paul states that God's righteousness is revealed "from faith to faith" (ἐκ πίστεως εἰς πίστιν).

The apostle manifestly announces a double faith, or rather a single faith which allows for growth and perfection. For the common faith lies underneath, like a foundation…while the special [faith][99] that is built on it is perfected with the believer and the [faith] that results from learning is brought to completion along with it [*viz.* the special faith]…[100]

τόδε τι, πίστιν εἶναί φησι. κυριώτερον οὖν τῆς ἐπιστήμης ἡ πίστις καὶ ἔστιν αὐτῆς κριτήριον). See Havrda, *Eighth Stromateus*, p. 136; and Lilla, *Clement of Alexandria*, pp. 131–135.

[97] *Strom.* 2.4.16.2–3: πιστὴ τοίνυν ἡ γνῶσις, γνωστὴ δὲ ἡ πίστις θείᾳ τινὶ ἀκολουθίᾳ τε καὶ ἀντακολουθίᾳ γίνεται.

[98] *Strom.* 5.1.1.3: ἤδη δὲ οὔτε ἡ γνῶσις ἄνευ πίστεως οὔθ᾽ ἡ πίστις ἄνευ γνώσεως, οὐ μὴν οὐδὲ ὁ πατὴρ ἄνευ υἱοῦ·; see the comments in Völker, *Der wahre Gnostiker*, p. 330, on this passage.

[99] "Special" (ἡ ἐξαίρετος) is taken, in the contrast with "common" (ἡ κοινή), in the etymological sense of the word: that which applies or is accessible to particular groups or people rather than something in general possession. It is not "special" in the sense of qualitatively superior, since Clement maintains an emphasis on there being "one faith," but only in the sense of restricted membership for those who have made the effort to build upon the common faith. De Faye, *Clément*, pp. 209–210: "C'est la même foi chez l'un et chez l'autre à des degrés différents d'épanouissement"; see also Völker, *Der wahre Gnostiker*, p. 228; *pace* Lilla, *Clement of Alexandria*, pp. 139, 155, who overplays the difference between common faith and gnostic learning.

[100] *Strom.* 5.1.2.3–6: "δικαιοσύνη δὲ θεοῦ ἐν αὐτῷ ἀποκαλύπτεται ἐκ πίστεως εἰς πίστιν." φαίνεται οὖν ὁ ἀπόστολος διττὴν καταγγέλλων πίστιν, μᾶλλον δὲ μίαν, αὔξησιν καὶ τελείωσιν ἐπιδεχομένην· ἡ μὲν γὰρ κοινὴ πίστις καθάπερ θεμέλιος ὑπόκειται…ἡ δὲ ἐξαίρετος ἐποικοδομουμένη συντελειοῦται τῷ πιστῷ καὶ συναπαρτίζεται αὐτῇ ἡ ἐκ μαθήσεως περιγινομένη… On this passage, see Havrda, "Some observations," pp. 4–5, and Clark, *Clement's Use*, p. 24; see also *Strom.* 2.12.53.1. In 2.20.126.1–4, Clement uses the language of "from faith to faith" in the context of the moral advancement of the believer by fleeing the "passions" (τὰ πασχητιῶντα). Elsewhere (2.6.29.2–4), he takes the phrase ἐκ πίστεως εἰς πίστιν in relation to a movement from the prophets to the

The double character of the single faith answers Basilides and Valentinus, whom Clement brings back to dispute his understanding of their natural determinism.[101] A faith that admits growth and is inextricably linked with knowledge can thereby be the foundation *and* that which is built upon it.[102] As he says elsewhere, knowledge is the "perfection of faith" which happens "beyond catechesis" and is worked out in line with the "ecclesiastical canon."[103]

On the other hand, the concerns of the anti-philosophical traditionalists are also addressed here, if implicitly. In response to their rejection of philosophical theological development, Clement finds a space within faith itself for further learning. Similar to his discussion of milk and meat, his reading of Romans 1:17 argues that "bare faith" is only the first stage of faith in the Christian life. Subsequent Gnostic development is to be understood as an organic growth rather than a foreign intrusion onto a pure baptismal faith. Clement has already gestured in this direction earlier in the *Stromateis*. "But just as we say that it is possible to be an unlearned believer, so also do we confess that it is not possible for one who has not learned to understand the things said in faith" (*Strom.*

---

gospel, a development overseen by the same Lord: "faith...which is one perfected from the prophets to the gospel by one and the same Lord teaching salvation" (εἰς πίστιν...τὴν μίαν τὴν ἐκ προφητείας εἰς εὐαγγέλιον τετελειωμένην δι' ἑνὸς καὶ τοῦ αὐτοῦ κυρίου διδάσκων σωτηρίαν).

[101] *Strom.* 5.1.3.2–3: "Indeed, the commandments which are in accordance with the old and with the new covenant are redundant if one is saved by nature, as Valentinus wishes, and if someone is a believer and elect by nature, as Basilides believes" (παρέλκουσι τοίνυν αἱ ἐντολαὶ αἵ τε κατὰ τὴν παλαιὰν αἵ τε κατὰ τὴν νέαν διαθήκην, φύσει σωζομένου, ὡς Οὐαλεντῖνος βούλεται, τινὸς καὶ φύσει πιστοῦ καὶ ἐκλεκτοῦ ὄντος, ὡς Βασιλείδης νομίζει).

[102] *Strom.* 5.1.5.2–3: "For we know to be the best that inquiry which is in conjunction with faith, which builds upon the foundation of faith, that magnificent knowledge of truth" (τὴν μὲν γὰρ μετὰ πίστεως συνιοῦσαν ζήτησιν, ἐποικοδομοῦσαν τῷ θεμελίῳ τῆς πίστεως τὴν μεγαλοπρεπῆ τῆς ἀληθείας γνῶσιν, ἀρίστην ἴσμεν).

[103] *Strom.* 6.18.165.1: "But he [*viz.* Paul] teaches that knowledge, which is the perfection of faith, goes above and beyond catechesis in accord with the majesty of the Lord's teaching and the ecclesiastical canon" (ἀλλὰ τὴν γνῶσιν διδάσκει, τελείωσιν οὖσαν τῆς πίστεως, ἐπέκεινα περισσεύειν τῆς κατηχήσεως κατὰ τὸ μεγαλεῖον τῆς τοῦ κυρίου διδασκαλίας καὶ τὸν ἐκκλησιαστικὸν κανόνα). Méhat, *Étude*, p. 303, argues that this passage cannot refer to pre-baptismal catechesis because "Le 'canon ecclésiastique' règle donc la gnose, non la catéchèse. Il a son domaine *au-delà* de l'enseignement...Le 'canon ecclésiastique'...est dirigé contre les hérétiques; il n'est pas catéchétique" (emphasis original). But Clement is simply saying that the gnosis that moves *beyond* catechesis is still in keeping with the Lord's teaching and the ecclesial rule. Reading a concern for pre-baptismal instruction here does not change that point but rather is in keeping with Clement's concern for continuity between basic catechesis and further teaching, between "faith" and "knowledge." See also the comments in Osborn, *Clement*, pp. 174–175.

1.6.35.2–3). He affirms both the sufficiency of "bare faith" and the value of working to understand confessional or liturgical formulae – what is "said in faith."

It is Clement's view of faith as unified but internally differentiated that enables him to argue for a hidden knowledge, on the basis of scriptural and philosophical precedent, without concern that he is replicating the dualistic anthropology he rejects. Later, in *Strom.* 5, he returns to the material of 1 Corinthians 2–3, the site of his disagreement with the Valentinians in *Paed.* 1.6. Now when Paul says "we speak wisdom to the perfect" (1 Cor. 2:6), Clement understands him to refer to that which is beyond catechesis while remaining in fundamental continuity with it.[104] Milk and meat can also take on different roles, as in the citation that opens this chapter.

> If, then, the "milk" is nourishment for children and the "solid food" is for the mature, as is said by the apostle, catechesis shall be considered "milk" as the first nourishment of the soul and mystical contemplation shall be considered "solid food."[105]

On the one hand this quote stands in tension with Clement's comments in *Paed.* 1.6, where he argues against restricting "milk" to catechetical instruction.[106] It builds on Clement's interpretation of similar language in Hebrews 5:12–6:2 earlier in *Strom.* 5.10.[107] On the other hand, Clement

[104] See *Strom.* 5.10.65.4–66.2, which begins with a citation of 1 Cor. 2:6 and links it with the "milk"/"meat" distinction in 1 Cor. 3:1–3; see also the comments in Völker, *Der wahre Gnostiker*, pp. 370–371.

[105] *Strom.* 5.10.66.2, text cited above, p. 93 n. 1.

[106] This tension is highlighted by Buell, *Making Christians*, pp. 128–129. Kovacs offers a more nuanced account in her recent discussion; Kovacs, "Reading," pp. 325–343. Noting Kovacs' comments, Penniman, *Raised on Christian Milk*, pp. 104–105, nevertheless argues that the treatments in *Paed.* 1.6 and *Strom.* 5.10.66 represent "two different frameworks for understanding spiritual development written with two distinct audiences in mind" and that "Clement does not explicitly articulate a progressive, stage-by-stage paradigm for Christian growth from milk to solid food. This must be inferred from the text." However, Penniman notes in the same place that "the *Stromateis* can be read as an elaborate explanation of Clement's earlier claim [*viz.* in the *Paedagogus*] that the formation of a Christian begins with the milk of preaching, and then gradually solid food is introduced through guided instruction." For (further) evidence of Clement's "explicit articulation" of this connection, see further below.

[107] *Strom.* 5.10.62.2–4: "And again to the Hebrews [he says], 'For even you who ought to be teachers by this time,' referring to those growing old in the old covenant, 'again need someone to teach you what the basic fundamentals of God's discourses are, and you have become again those who need milk and not solid food. For everyone who partakes of milk is an infant, ignorant of the milk of righteousness,' having been entrusted (only) with the first teachings." (αὐτίκα τοῖς Ἑβραίοις 'καὶ γὰρ ὀφείλοντες εἶναι διδάσκαλοι διὰ τὸν χρόνον' φησίν, ὡς ἂν ἐγγηράσαντες τῇ διαθήκῃ τῇ παλαιᾷ, 'πάλιν χρείαν ἔχετε τοῦ διδάσκειν

is not simply being inconsistent. He has already established a continuity between milk and meat, a point reiterated earlier in *Strom.* 5.8,[108] and the fact that faith grows from its beginning at baptism.[109] So, absent Clement's polemical need to undermine Valentinian anthropology, the "milk" of catechetical instruction can be distinguished from the goal of a solid food. But these are integrated within his spectrum of spiritual progress.

In the course of his argument for the simultaneous perfection and immaturity of the faith and knowledge imparted during catechesis, Clement establishes a scriptural basis in 1 Corinthians 3:1–3 (with Hebrews 5:12) and Romans 1:17.[110] Further, as Paul's writings were the foundation for his construal of πίστις, Paul himself is cast in the role of catechist and Gnostic instructor.[111] It is Paul who catechized the Corinthians in the perfectly nourishing milk and it is Paul who makes manifest the need for growth in faith while modeling the practice of hiding γνῶσις from the unprepared. It may also have been a Pauline influence from 1 Corinthians that induces Clement to place love as that to which faith and knowledge lead: "the beginning and the end, I say they are faith and love."[112] As Paul states in 1 Corinthians 13, knowledge and faith are nothing without love, which remains supreme when one is face to face with God (vv. 2, 8, 13). Foundational instruction leading to faith, growth in knowledge, mystical contemplation in the presence of love – these Pauline themes work with Clement's various philosophical influences and provide resources for the

---

ὑμᾶς, τίνα τὰ στοιχεῖα τῆς ἀρχῆς τῶν λογίων τοῦ θεοῦ, καὶ γεγόνατε χρείαν ἔχοντες γάλακτος καὶ οὐ στερεᾶς τροφῆς· πᾶς γὰρ ὁ μετέχων γάλακτος ἄπειρος λόγου δικαιοσύνης, νήπιος γάρ ἐστι,' τὰ πρῶτα μαθήματα πεπιστευμένος·).

[108] See also *Strom.* 5.8.48.8–9, where the evidence of "milk" as "first instruction" that hardens into "meat" is found among Greek writers.

[109] See the observations in Van de Bunt, "Milk and honey," p. 38.

[110] The emphasis on exegetical foundations should not be taken to the exclusion of Greek philosophical influence on Clement, as in the view of Völker, *Der wahre Gnostiker*, and thoroughly criticized in Lilla, *Clement of Alexandria*. Nevertheless it helpfully captures something of Clement's explicit theological priorities – the truth of scripture and the rule of truth as the foundation for all *gnosis*, philosophy as merely propaedeutic. See e.g., Strom. 1.5.28.2–3; 1.5.29.3–4: εἶεν δ' ἂν καὶ αἱ ἐντολαὶ καὶ αἱ προπαιδεῖαι ὁδοὶ καὶ ἀφορμαὶ τοῦ βίου – that is they are the means rather than the *telos*, along with the "commandments"; 1.5.30.1–2; 1.5.32.4; 1.20.99.4).

[111] It may be that the narrative of Paul's blinding and baptism in Acts 9 influenced Clement's own language of baptism and illumination in subtle ways; see p. 97 n. 18 above.

[112] *Strom.* 7.10.55.5–6: ἥ τε ἀρχὴ καὶ τὸ τέλος, πίστις λέγω καὶ ἡ ἀγάπη; cf. 7.10.57.5. The importance of love is noted by Völker, *Der wahre Gnostiker*, p. 447 and *passim*; Osborn, *Clement*, p. 255; Ashwin-Siejkowski, *Clement*, pp. 154–155; and others.

integration of his inherited catechumenate within his larger pedagogical vision.[113]

4.3 PAUL'S CATECHETICAL ACTIVITY IN CLEMENT'S WRITINGS

Clement's presentation and reading of Paul in catechetical terms is not exhausted by his appropriation of 1 Corinthians 3:1–3 and Romans 1:17 for his integration of catechesis with further learning. It is of course the case that, for Clement, Christ is the divine Pedagogue, the Gnostic teacher who descended from heaven.[114] Even so, Paul provides Clement with the personal example of the true Gnostic, the image of the Lord whose actions and writings are eminently useful for Clement's project.[115] We have already seen how Paul's discussions of "milk" and "meat," of speaking "wisdom to the perfect," supplied Clement with the resources to respond to challenges from both "gnostic" and obscurantist opponents. One could also point to Clement's reading of Colossians 1:25–27 in which Paul speaks of esoteric knowledge revealed by Christ and transmitted by Paul.[116]

The true Gnostic imitates their Lord and, in doing so, "assembles and refurbishes" the one being instructed working toward their salvation.[117] It is in teaching others according to their needs that the Gnostic proves their worth and demonstrates their participation and union with the divine.[118] This Gnostic pedagogical approach is exemplified in Paul's

---

[113] See Osborn, *Clement*, and Ashwin-Siejkowski, *Clement*, for helpfully nuanced views of the relation between Clement as Christian exegete and Clement as philosopher. Earlier work by Lilla, *Clement of Alexandria*, effectively demonstrated Clement's debt to his middle Platonist context as a counterbalance to those like Walther Völker who saw Clement's philosophy "nur das Äußere, gleichsam die Schale sei, die das Christentum... als Nußkern in sich birgt" (Völker, *Der wahre Gnostiker*, p. 9).

[114] E.g., *Paed.* 1.1.1.3–4; *Strom.* 5.1.12.3; *Hyp.* fr. 14. See Lilla, *Clement of Alexandria*, pp. 158–159.

[115] See the comments in Kovacs, "Divine pedagogy," pp. 8, 19–20, and Völker, *Der wahre Gnostiker*, p. 388.

[116] See *Strom.* 5.10.60.1–61.2; this passage, among others, is noted in Lilla, *Clement of Alexandria*, p. 147, and Völker, *Der wahre Gnostiker*, p. 388.

[117] *Strom* 7.9.52.2–3 (cited above); see the discussion in Buell, *Making Christians*, p. 52, who speaks of Clement's Gnostic "producing another Christian," and Kovacs, "Divine pedagogy," pp. 14–15, 17, and *passim*. See also Clement's discussion of the "man of God" in *Prot.* 10.104.2.

[118] *Strom.* 7.9.52.1–2: "Now one who takes on the care of teaching others greatly increases their Gnostic worthiness, undertaking the stewardship of the greatest good on earth in word and deed, through which one mediates connection and fellowship with the divine" (Πλεῖον δέ τι καὶ μᾶλλον ἐπιτείνει τὸ γνωστικὸν ἀξίωμα ὁ τὴν προστασίαν τῆς τῶν ἑτέρων

treatment of Timothy and relation to Judaism. Paul circumcises Timothy, according to Clement, because he judged that a sudden departure from the Law would set the Jews in opposition rather than win them over, which is his stated aim in 1 Corinthians 9:20. "I became to the Jews like a Jew so that I may win Jews, to those under the Law like one under the Law – not being in fact under the Law – so that I might win those under the Law."[119] Clement refers to this as the example of "condescension," in which the true Gnostic teacher will engage "for the sake of the salvation of those near."[120] Within Clement's broader pedagogical schema, a concern for salvation is found especially in connection with the initial phases of Christian life. It is catechesis that leads to faith and baptism, which is the universal salvation for all. When Clement depicts Paul speaking to the Corinthians, it is in the capacity of the Gnostic teacher: "I instructed [catechized] you in Christ with simple, true, and natural spiritual nourishment" (*Paed.* 1.6.35.3).

Elsewhere, Clement's portrayal of Paul is similarly colored by his association with catechesis and initiation. For instance, he situates Paul among "barbarian philosophers," identifying him with the group of sages from whom Greek philosophers derived their wisdom.[121] It is this

---

διδασκαλίας ἀναλαβών, τοῦ μεγίστου ἐπὶ γῆς ἀγαθοῦ τὴν οἰκονομίαν λόγῳ τε καὶ ἔργῳ ἀναδεξάμενος, δι' ἧς πρὸς τὸ θεῖον συνάφειάν τε καὶ κοινωνίαν ἐμμεσιτεύει).

[119] *Strom.* 7.9.53.3–4: "Then the noble apostle circumcised Timothy, proclaiming and writing that a circumcision made by hands benefits no one. But lest he force those Hebrew listeners who still resisted his reins to break from the Synagogue, by dragging them suddenly from the law to the circumcision of the heart by faith, accommodating himself, he became a Jew to Jews, so that he might win many" (αὐτίκα Τιμόθεον ὁ γενναῖος περιέτεμεν ἀπόστολος, κεκραγὼς καὶ γράφων περιτομὴν τὴν χειροποίητον οὐδὲν ὠφελεῖν· ἀλλ' ἵνα μή, ἀθρόως ἀποσπῶν τοῦ νόμου πρὸς τὴν ἐκ πίστεως τῆς καρδίας περιτομήν, ἀφηνιάζοντας ἔτι τοὺς ἀκροωμένους τῶν Ἑβραίων ἀπορρῆξαι τῆς συναγωγῆς ἀναγκάσῃ, συμπεριφερόμενος Ἰουδαίοις Ἰουδαῖος ἐγένετο, ἵνα πάντας κερδήσῃ').

[120] *Strom.* 7.9.53.4: "The one who, for the sake of their neighbors' salvation, condescends so far as to accommodate himself [to them]…" (ὁ τοίνυν μέχρι τῆς συμπεριφορᾶς διὰ τὴν τῶν πέλας σωτηρίαν συγκαταβαίνων); see the discussion of this in Kovacs, "Divine pedagogy," pp. 18–19, and Margaret M. Mitchell, "Pauline accommodation and 'condescension' (συγκατάβασις): 1 Cor 9:19–23 and the history of influence," in *Paul and the Emergence of Christian Textuality: Early Christian Literary Culture in Context*, WUNT I/393 (Tübingen: Mohr Siebeck, 2017), pp. 202–209.

[121] This was a common view in this period, held to different effect by Posidonius, Numenius, Celsus, Philo, and others while reaching back to Plato's own. See Arthur J. Droge, *Homer or Moses? Early Christian Interpretations of the History of Culture*, HUT 26 (Tübingen: Mohr Siebeck, 1989), pp. 89–91; the discussion of Celsus in Lilla, *Clement of Alexandria*, pp. 36–39; and Tatian in Matthew R. Crawford, "Tatian, Celsus, and Christianity as 'barbarian philosophy' in the late second century," in Lewis O. Ayres and Clifton Ward (eds.), *Rise of the Christian Intellectual*, AZK (Berlin: De Gruyter, forthcoming).

group, according to Clement, who "refer to catechesis and illumination as rebirth: 'I gave birth to you in Christ Jesus,' as the noble apostle says somewhere."[122] In 1 Corinthians 4:15 Paul tells the Corinthians "I gave birth to you in Jesus Christ *through the gospel*." Clement has dropped the phrase διὰ τοῦ εὐαγγελίου and replaced its instrumental function with his own catechetical/initiatory framework: "to instruct and to illuminate" (τὸ κατηχῆσαί τε καὶ φωτίσαι).[123] Paul, then, speaks in the language of the barbarian sages, which corresponds also with the teaching function of Clement's true Gnostic as well as with the language of his catechumenate.

The full scope and plan of Paul's teaching is also treated by Clement in terms exemplary for his own work. Paul "clearly demonstrates the guiding principle of knowledge" when writing to the Corinthians. The Apostle writes in 2 Corinthians 10:15–16 that, as the faith of the Corinthians grows, he hopes to be "made abundantly great among you in accordance with our *canon*" so that he might preach the gospel εἰς τὰ ὑπερέκεινα ὑμῶν. Clement sees this phrase not as a reference to a further geographical spread of Paul's gospel, since he had already preached throughout Achaea and Athens, but rather to a teaching of γνῶσις, that which abounds beyond catechesis. Moreover, Paul's teaching of this further knowledge is κατὰ τὸν κανόνα ἡμῶν, which Clement reads as the "ecclesiastical canon," that which supplies the continuity between the catechesis Paul had already imparted to the Corinthians and the knowledge to which he would lead them.[124]

---

[122] *Strom.* 5.2.15.3: ἐπεὶ καὶ παρὰ τοῖς βαρβάροις φιλοσόφοις τὸ κατηχῆσαί τε καὶ φωτίσαι ἀναγεννῆσαι λέγεται, καὶ 'ἐγὼ ὑμᾶς ἐγέννησα ἐν Χριστῷ Ἰησοῦ' ὁ καλός που λέγει ἀπόστολος. Though she does not emphasize the place of catechesis, Buell, *Making Christians*, p. 62, rightly notes that in this passage "[p]rocreation, the production of likeness, education, and perfection all converge."

[123] See the discussion of *Paed.* 1.6.25.1–26.1 above, pp. 109–110.

[124] *Strom.* 6.18.164.4–165.2: "The apostle clearly demonstrates the guiding principle of knowledge for those able to discern it, writing to those Corinthian Greeks here: 'We have hope that as faith grows in you we will be held in much higher esteem in accordance with our *canon*, so that we may proclaim the gospel beyond you,' not meaning the extension of the proclamation in spatial terms...but he teaches that knowledge, which is the perfection of faith, goes above and beyond catechesis in accord with the majesty of the Lord's teaching and the ecclesiastical canon." (τὸ δὲ ἡγεμονικὸν τῆς γνώσεως σαφῶς ὁ ἀπόστολος τοῖς διαθρεῖν δυναμένοις ἐνδείκνυται, τοῖς Ἑλλαδικοῖς ἐκείνοις γράφων Κορινθίοις ὧδέ πως· 'ἐλπίδα δὲ ἔχοντες αὐξανομένης τῆς πίστεως ὑμῶν ἐν ὑμῖν μεγαλυνθῆναι κατὰ τὸν κανόνα ἡμῶν εἰς περισσείαν, εἰς τὰ ὑπερέκεινα ὑμῶν εὐαγγελίσασθαι,' οὐ τὴν ἐπέκτασιν τοῦ κηρύγματος τὴν κατὰ τὸν τόπον λέγων...ἀλλὰ τὴν γνῶσιν διδάσκει, τελείωσιν οὖσαν τῆς πίστεως, ἐπέκεινα περισσεύειν τῆς κατηχήσεως κατὰ τὸ μεγαλεῖον τῆς τοῦ κυρίου διδασκαλίας καὶ τὸν ἐκκλησιαστικὸν κανόνα.)

Finally, alongside casting Paul in the role of catechist and Gnostic teacher, Clement takes Paul's metaphor of "engrafting" the Gentiles onto the holy root (Rom. 11:17–24) and follows it through with four different modes of engrafting. Each different mode follows according to the preparation of the branch to be grafted into the tree. Those who have undergone the propaedeutic training of philosophy or the Law[125] are grafted in deeply, while the heretics and wild ones must themselves be stripped of errant spurs before being fitted to the tree. In an ideal situation Gnostic teaching can bring about the graft of an entire "eye" (that is, a bud), representing the ability to look deeply into the truth of matters.[126] In the case of the majority of Gentiles, however, the graft is simply a shallow link, between bark and trunk. "The untrained from the Gentiles are instructed, receiving the word superficially."[127] Paul's botanical language of grafting, then, supplies a rich metaphor for various types of Christian conversion which is teased out in line with Clement's larger pedagogical vision: Catechesis is sufficient, if elementary – one is grafted in after all – while other types of preparatory teaching can take one beyond such elementary learning toward a more perfected faith. Clement's Paul, as the true Gnostic, is a model to philosophers, a universal and consistently canonical teacher to correct the "gnostics," and a gentle gardener for the simple. The whole plant, however, from root to fruit, receives nourishment in common. It is the "milk" of the Word that brings faith and allows for growth within faith.

Excursus: Paul's Catechesis in Irenaeus?

At this point it is helpful to pause momentarily and return to Irenaeus, whose witness to converging catechetical practice was examined in Chapter 2. There we noted that, while Irenaeus appears to use catechesis language in relation to baptismal instruction, he does not provide clear evidence for an institutional catechumenate. Nevertheless, his description of Paul's activities in those terms raises the question of whether Clement might have been preceded or encouraged in this explicit connection by Irenaeus.[128]

---

[125] *Strom.* 1.5.29.3–4; and see also C. Broc-Schmezer, "La philosophie grecque comme propédeutique à l'Évangile: Clément d'Alexandrie," *Foi et Vie* 47, no. 4 (2008), 83–86, among others, on the propaedeutic function of philosophy in Clement's work.

[126] See the extended discussion of the metaphor in *Strom.* 6.15.119.2–4.

[127] *Strom.* 6.15.119.1–2: κατηχοῦνται οἱ ἐξ ἐθνῶν ἰδιῶται ἐξ ἐπιπολῆς δεχόμενοι τὸν λόγον·

[128] On Clement's knowledge of Irenaeus, see esp. L. G. Patterson, "The divine became human: Irenaean themes in Clement of Alexandria," *Studia Patristica* 31 (1997), 497–516, and also Osborn, *Clement*, pp. 282–292.

Irenaeus' use of Paul has received numerous treatments in recent years. Beginning with the brief assessment by Ernst Dassmann in 1979, the long influential view that Paul was a problematic figure for Irenaeus owing to his use by "gnostics" has been largely overturned: Paul's letters were in fact authoritative for Irenaeus and used without hint of hesitation.[129] For Irenaeus, Paul is unproblematically *the* Apostle, who speaks harmoniously with the rule of truth, and provides the ground for Irenaeus' understanding of the divine economy of salvation.[130] In narrower terms and more to the point for the present study, though, Irenaeus spends little time portraying Paul's teaching activities; it is his letters that Irenaeus uses so frequently. Certainly, he relates that Paul "was a preacher of truth" who taught in accordance with the rule of truth, but even here this claim is not attended by any further portrayal.[131] The exception to this trend is found in *Haer.* 4.24.1–2.

In this section of book 4, Irenaeus is concerned to demonstrate from scripture that the Law and Prophets prefigured the Christian faith, as part of his overarching argument for the unity of the Old and New covenants.[132] In *Haer.* 4.23, Irenaeus draws on John 4:35–38 to argue that the "fields white for the harvest" had been made so by the preparation of the "patriarchs and the prophets" (4.23.1). Philip and the Ethiopian eunuch provide a clinching argument for this point, when considered within late second-century catechetical practice: although Philip spent

---

[129] Dassmann, *Der Stachel*, pp. 292–315. The older view is set out in J. Werner, *Der Paulinismus des Irenaeus*, TU 6.2 (Leipzig: Hinrichs, 1889). See also the responses in Rensberger, "Apostle," pp. 316–329; Richard A. Norris, Jr., "Irenaeus' use of Paul in his polemic against the gnostics," in William S. Babcock (ed.), *Paul and the Legacies of Paul* (Dallas: Southern Methodist University Press, 1990), pp. 79–98, and the very full treatment in Noormann, *Irenäus als Paulusinterpret*. This view remains dominant: see Jason M. Scarborough, "The making of an apostle: second and third century interpretations of the writings of Paul," unpublished Ph.D. thesis, Union Theological Seminary, New York (2007), pp. 202–208; Pervo, *Making of Paul*, pp. 220–228; Blackwell, "Paul and Irenaeus," pp. 190–206; White, *Remembering Paul*, pp. 136–139.

[130] On Paul as *the* Apostle, see Noormann, *Irenäus als Paulusinterpret*, p. 517, and Blackwell, "Paul and Irenaeus," pp. 195–196. On the use of Paul in relation to the divine economy of salvation, see Norris, "Irenaeus' use," pp. 90–92; Noormann, *Irenäus als Paulusinterpret*, pp. 379–426; and Blackwell, "Paul and Irenaeus," pp. 200–202.

[131] *Haer.* 4.41.4: "Apostolum vero praedicatorem esse veritatis et omnia consonantia veritatis praeconio docuisse"; on Paul as consonant with other apostles in Irenaeus, see Dassmann, *Der Stachel*, pp. 313–315; Noormann, *Irenäus als Paulusinterpret*, pp. 39–52; White, *Remembering Paul*, pp. 139–142.

[132] See the general account in Mary Ann Donovan, *One Right Reading? A Guide to Irenaeus* (Collegeville, MN: Liturgical Press, 1997), pp. 115–123, though she does not explicitly discuss chapters 23–24, which interest us here.

little time with the eunuch, the latter was easily persuaded about Christ and baptized on the spot. Philip was justified in doing so because the eunuch "had been pre-instructed by the prophets."[133] This preparatory instruction included both an emphasis on monotheism ("God the Father") and ethical requirements ("rules for the moral life"[134]). All that remained at that point was letting him know about the *adventus Filii Dei*, the coming of the Son of God.

Paul's ministry, then, is contrasted with this easy conversion and baptism in 4.24.1–2. As Paul himself had said, "I labored more than all of them."[135] This is, Irenaeus explains, because of Paul's role as Apostle of the Gentiles (*gentium Apostolus*). The other apostles had an easy task of teaching because they could make use of scriptural proofs and the Jewish listeners had at least received instruction against adultery, fornication, anger, etc. (4.24.1). Paul, on the other hand, had to start from the ground up. The Gentiles benefited not at all from the harmony of the truth between the Prophets and the apostles because they were entirely ignorant of the former group (4.24.2). Therefore, Paul had to begin his instruction (*primo catechizabat*) with a rejection of idolatry and the worship of a single creator God and his Son (4.24.1). Paul's labor at bringing the Gentiles into the Church, then, involves handing on material consonant with the rule of faith and efforts at moral formation. In other words, it appears as though Irenaeus has subtly painted Paul's ministry with late second-century colors.

If Irenaeus' comments look similar to Clement's catechetical Paul, however, that is unfortunately where the similarities end, in this respect. Perhaps more marked than this similarity is the difference in their treatment of similar passages. The phrase in Romans 1:17a, so crucial for Clement's pedagogical scheme, is not cited at all by Irenaeus, according to the survey of Rolf Noormann.[136] Further, as we have seen above, for Clement, Paul's discussion of milk and solid food is centrally important to his incorporation of catechetical instruction within his broader pedagogical vision. Irenaeus, in contrast, shows little concern for such a

---

[133] *Haer.* 4.23.2: "facile suasit ei credere eum esse Jesum Christum...Nihil enim aliud deerat ei qui prophetis fuerat praecatechizatus"; see also 3.12.7 (on Cornelius) and 3.12.15 (on Peter's instruction of Cornelius).

[134] Translation from Rousseau, Hemmerdinger, and Doutreleau, *Contre les Hérésies IV, ad loc.*: "les règles de la vie morale."

[135] 1 Cor. 15:10: περισσότερον αὐτῶν πάντων ἐκοπίασα, cited at the beginning of *Haer.* 4.24.1.

[136] Noormann, *Irenäus als Paulusinterpret.*

project. His reading of 1 Corinthians 3:1–3 (perhaps also with reference to Hebrews 5:14)[137] owes much more to his concerns for the economy of salvation.[138] Near the end of book 4, Irenaeus picks up the "milk and meat" language. His famous argument, that the history of humanity is also the history of progression toward perfection,[139] raises the objection in *Haer.* 4.38.1, why did God not make humanity perfect from the beginning? Irenaeus answers that, while God certainly could have brought his full perfection to humans from the start, they would not have been able to handle it. "And *because of this* Paul says to the Corinthians, 'I gave you milk to drink, not food, for you were not able to bear it.'"[140] Irenaeus does note that Paul's statement addresses the spiritual state of the Corinthians, but this is absorbed by his larger point: that God's perfection cannot be given to beings that have not yet themselves matured.[141]

Does Irenaeus, then, provide Clement with any precedent for an explicit connection between Paul and catechesis? It would appear that the answer to this question may be "yes, but only barely so." We have already seen that the presentation of Paul in the *Acts of Paul* is colored by emerging catechetical practices so it is, in one sense, unsurprising to find hints of the same thing in Irenaeus. But, as Irenaeus falls just short in showing evidence of an institutional catechumenate, so also does his portrayal of Paul at best *suggest* a direct connection with catechesis. Irenaeus' use of κατηχίζω does not qualify as a technical term, if only for its rarity in his discussions of the rule of faith and baptism. Nevertheless, his suggestive account of Paul's catechetical ministry may represent a certain interpretive impulse carried through more fully by Clement in shaping his own portrayal of the apostle.

---

[137] This possible allusion is noted in Rousseau, Hemmerdinger, and Doutreleau, *Contre les Hérésies IV*, pp. 950–951, who are followed by Noormann, *Irenäus als Paulusinterpret*, p. 262 n. 506.

[138] Penniman, *Raised on Christian Milk*, p. 107: "Irenaeus...sought to overcome the negative connotations associated with the Corinthian infants by making infancy the inescapable and universal fact of human nature's material existence."

[139] See Patterson, "Irenaean themes," pp. 500–503, and Eric F. Osborn, *Irenaeus of Lyons* (Cambridge: Cambridge University Press, 2001), pp. 85–86.

[140] *Haer.* 4.38.2 (Greek frag. 23): καὶ διὰ τοῦτο Παῦλος Κορινθίοις φησίν· Γάλα κτλ.

[141] Note the comments in Noormann, *Irenäus als Paulusinterpret*, p. 262, who notes that Irenaeus' emphasis is "neu" since "Paulus wird eher die Anfangsgründe der christlichen Lehre im Blick haben"; see also Norris, "Irenaeus' use," p. 91. Another Pauline text, which will be cast in catechetical terms in the fourth century, 1 Cor. 3:6–7, is similarly absorbed into Irenaeus' divine economy concerns; see *Haer.* 4.25.3.

4.4 CONCLUSION

We have seen in this chapter the reciprocal relationship of Clement's inherited catechetical commitments with his reading of Paul and his broader pedagogical and apologetic concerns. Facing division in the Alexandrian churches over the value of the catechumenate, the status of faith, and the value of knowledge, Clement drew heavily on Paul to craft a middle way between the Scylla of philosophical elitism – even as far as what he perceived as a natural determinism related to knowledge – and the Charybdis of anti-philosophical obscurantism. Paul's imagery of "milk" and "meat" in 1 Corinthians 3:1–3 allowed Clement to argue for an ultimate sufficiency and value for catechesis (and therefore the catechumenate), while also arguing for its essential relation with Gnostic knowledge. Reflecting to such an extent on this passage further enabled Clement to argue that the alternative (Valentinian) appeal to a "milk" and "meat" distinction was untenable on scriptural, biological, and liturgical grounds.[142] Moreover, Paul's statement in Romans 1:17 that God's righteousness is revealed "from faith to faith" supplied Clement with "clear" support for his development of a differentiated faith, one that "allows growth and development."

Paul's teaching activity also afforded Clement the opportunity to cast the apostle in the role of the true Gnostic teacher whose work included catechesis and baptism (illumination), as well as taking his congregations "beyond catechesis" into knowledge, but always in line with the "ecclesiastical canon" that protected him from falling prey to "gnostic" heresy.[143] Paul's condescension and concern for appropriately hidden wisdom supplied scriptural precedent and justification for Clement's own esoteric proclivities, as well as a suitable response to those who complained that further Gnostic teaching fell afoul of Paul's own criticism of philosophy. In short, Paul's texts and personal example supplied Clement's solution to all sides of his struggle for the integration of the catechumenate within a broader pedagogical framework.

---

[142] See Buell's discussion of Clement's motivation for relying so extensively on 1 Cor. 3:1–3; Buell, *Making Christians*, pp. 146–148.

[143] The inclusion of baptism within Paul's apostolic remit potentially stands in contrast with the presentation of Paul in the *Acts of Paul*, which sets Paul's relationship to baptism in a more ambivalent light.

5

Cultivating the Soul: Origen's Catechetical Paul

Paul, the farmer, plows the soul of the catechumen, making prepared fallow land in their soul in accordance with the divine Jeremiah who declares to them, "Prepare fallow lands for yourselves…"[1]

Origen of Alexandria (and later Caesarea) was an enigmatic and controversial figure even during his own life, to say nothing of the later Origenist controversies that arose in the fourth century.[2] Evidently born into a Christian family, he showed enormous intellectual and moral passion even as a young man, which translated into a life of literary productivity unprecedented in early Christianity.[3] Unfortunately, only a small fraction of what Origen produced comes down to us in its original Greek. Thanks to the industrious work of Rufinus and Jerome, a significant number of

---

[1] Origen, *Frag. in 1 Cor.* 41: ἀροτριᾷ Παῦλος ὁ γεωργὸς κατηχουμένου ψυχήν, νεώματα ποιῶν ἐν τῇ ψυχῇ αὐτοῦ κατὰ τὸν θεῖον Ἰερεμίαν τὸν φάσκοντα αὐτοῖς Νεώσατε ἑαυτοῖς νεώματα…; text in Claude Jenkins, "Origen on 1 Corinthians," *Journal of Theological Studies* 9–10 (1908), 231–247, 353–372, 500–514, 29–51.

[2] On this, see esp. Elizabeth A. Clark, *The Origenist Controversy: The Cultural Construction of an Early Christian Debate* (Princeton: Princeton University Press, 1992); see also the brief discussions in Joseph W. Trigg, *Origen*, The Early Church Fathers (London: New York: Routledge, 1998), pp. 62–66; Jon F. Dechow, "Pseudo-Jerome's anti-Origenist anathemas (*ACO* 1:5:4–5)," in Sylwia Kaczmarek and Henryk Pietras (eds.), *Origeniana Decima: Origen as Writer*, BETL 244 (Leuven: Peeters, 2011), pp. 955–965; and Fürst, *Origenes*, pp. 154–165. The first half of *Adamantius* 19 is devoted to a variety of angles on the Origenist controversy; see the introductory essay of Roberto Alciati and Federico Fatti, "La controversia origenista: un affare mediterraneo; The Origenist controversy: a Mediterranean affair," *Adamantius* 19 (2013), 7–9.

[3] On his early education, see Eusebius *Hist. eccl.* 6.2.1–16. Crouzel even suggests that Origen may have been the "most prolific writer of the ancient world"; Crouzel, *Origen*, p. 37. See the overview of Origen's literary output in Fürst, *Origenes*, pp. 15–28.

Origen's homilies, several commentaries, and a few treatises have been preserved in Latin.[4] There are, additionally, various fragments preserved in the works of others and in catenae.[5]

Despite the sad state of his works, however, Origen still manages to appear as a brilliant and important interpreter of Paul's letters, whose work made a deep impact on the generations of interpreters who followed.[6] Unlike the state of scholarship on Paul in Clement of Alexandria, there has been a long and steady recognition of the importance of the Apostle to the Gentiles for Origen's thought and particularly for his biblical interpretation.[7] Like Clement, Origen explicitly links Paul's letters and

---

[4] See the discussion of the textual transmission in Crouzel, *Origen*, pp. 37–49; Karen Jo Torjesen, *Hermeneutical Procedure and Theological Structure in Origen's Exegesis*, PTS 28 (Berlin: De Gruyter, 1985), pp. 14–18; and also the brief discussion in Christoph Markschies, "Origenes: Leben – Werk – Theologie – Wirking," in *Origenes und sein Erbe. Gesammelte Studien*, TU 160 (Berlin: De Gruyter, 2007), pp. 1–13.

[5] For example, the catenae traditions on the Psalms contain a wealth of material from Origen and also demonstrate the complicated nature of catenae witnesses; see Cordula Bandt, "Origen in the *Catenae* on Psalms II: The Rather Complicated Case of Psalms 51 to 76," *Adamantius* 20 (2014), 14–27. The fragments from Origen's 1 Corinthians Commentary (see Francesco Pieri, "Origen on 1 Corinthians: homilies or commentary?," *Studia Patristica* 56, no. 4 (2013), 143–156) are similarly found in the catena tradition, notably in the Paris manuscript on which Cramer's edition was based (John Anthony Cramer, *Catenae graecorum patrum in Novum Testamentum* (Oxford: Oxford University Press, 1838–1844)), which was evidently copied from the tenth-century Vat. gr.762 (Gregory-Aland no. 1915; see Jenkins, "Origen," p. 231), and in the shorter eleventh-century Vat.gr.692 (Gregory-Aland no. 1993).

[6] This impact is also related to Origen's broader importance for the beginnings of biblical commentary in the Early Church; see Alfons Fürst, "Origen: exegesis and philosophy in early Christian Alexandria," in Josef Lössl and J. W. Watt (eds.), *Interpreting the Bible and Aristotle in Late Antiquity: The Alexandrian Commentary Tradition Between Rome and Baghdad* (Farnham: Ashgate, 2011), pp. 13–32.

[7] According to Henri de Lubac, *History and Spirit: The Understanding of Scripture According to Origen* (San Francisco: Ignatius Press, 2007), p. 82 n. 198, recognizing the importance of Paul for Origen's interpretation of the Old Testament reaches back at least to A. Salmeron in 1602. More recently, see Völker, "Paulus," pp. 258–279; Aleith, *Paulusverständnis*, pp. 98–110; Marguerite Harl, *Origène et la fonction révélatrice du verbe incarné*, Patristica Sorbonensia 2 (Paris: Éditions du Seuil, 1958), p. 262; Henri Crouzel, *Origène et la "connaissance mystique,"* Museum Lessianum section théologique 56 (Paris: Desclée de Brouwer, 1961), p. 48; Crouzel, *Origen*, pp. 67–68; Theresia Heither, *Translatio religionis. Die Paulusdeutung des Origenes in seinem Kommentar zum Römerbrief*, BBK 16 (Berlin: De Gruyter, 1990); Cocchini, *Il Paolo*, *passim*; B. Studer, "Die doppelte Exegese bei Origenes," in G. Dorival and A. Le Boulluec (eds.), *Origeniana Sexta*, BETL 118 (Leuven: Peeters, 1995), p. 321; Trigg, p. *Origen*, p. 49; Scarborough, "Making," pp. 209–245; Mitchell, *Paul, the Corinthians*, pp. 11, 35–37, 48–57; Sylwia Kaczmarek, "L'*Exemplum* di Paolo nel *Commento alla lettera ai Romani*," in Sylwia Kaczmarek and Henryk Pietras (eds.), *Origeniana Decima: Origen as Writer*, BETL 244 (Leuven: Peeters, 2011), pp. 445–456; Heiser, *Paulusinszenierung*, pp. 127–155; and

activities to his catechetical framework, though he differs from his predecessor in significant ways, related to their differing institutional and
intellectual contexts.

As is always the case when interpreting early Christian writers, although
Origen clearly values Paul's letters, he is by no means exclusively interested
in Paul. As Walther Völker perceptively noted, "Paulinism forms here [*viz.*
in Origen's writings] only one impact, only one factor alongside all other
factors."[8] For Origen, Paul spoke and wrote *the* gospel, the same gospel
proclaimed by all the other apostles and hidden in the Old Testament.[9] To
that extent, Paul was simply one more apostolic voice teaching the same
true doctrine. Furthermore, Origen's vision for the Church extended well
beyond a concern for catechumens. Indeed, he was eager for his students
and the congregation to move past the beginning stages of their faith
and progress in knowledge, improving toward perfection in action, belief,
and knowledge.[10] As Peter Martens has demonstrated, for Origen this

---

Christoph Markschies, "Origenes und Paulus: Das Beispiel der Anthropologie," in Jörg
Frey, Benjamin Schliesser, and Veronika Niederhofer (eds.), *Der Philipperbrief des Paulus
in der hellenistisch-römischen Welt*, WUNT I/353 (Tübingen: Mohr Siebeck, 2015),
p. 361.

[8] Völker, "Paulus," p. 258: "Der Paulinismus bildet hier nur einen Einschlag, nur einen
Faktor neben ganz anderen Faktoren"; see also Crouzel, *Origen*, p. 79: "On minds as
encyclopedic as those of Clement and Origen a great many influences have had an effect."

[9] See *Comm. in Iohan.* 1.4.25–26 (text from Blanc, *Origène. Commentaire sur saint
Jean*): "It is possible to adduce [evidence] for the fact that the whole New Testament is
'gospel' from what Paul says, when he writes somewhere, 'According to my gospel.' For we
do not have in writing any book by Paul normally called a gospel, but everything – what
he preached and said, was gospel…And if Paul's statements were gospel, it follows to say
that Peter's sayings were also gospel and generally that which presents Christ's sojourn
and prepares for his arrival and produces it in the souls of those who desire to receive the
one standing at the door" (Ἔστι δὲ προσαχθῆναι ἀπὸ τῶν ὑπὸ Παύλου λεγομένων περὶ τοῦ
πᾶσαν τὴν καινὴν εἶναι τὰ εὐαγγέλια, ὅταν που γράφῃ· Ἀατὰ τὸ εὐαγγέλιόν μου'· ἐν γράμμασι
γὰρ Παύλου οὐκ ἔχομεν βιβλίον εὐαγγέλιον συνήθως καλούμενον, ἀλλὰ πᾶν, ὃ ἐκήρυσσε καὶ
ἔλεγε, τὸ εὐαγγέλιον ἦν…. Εἰ δὲ τὰ Παύλου εὐαγγέλιον ἦν, ἀκόλουθον λέγειν ὅτι καὶ τὰ Πέτρου
εὐαγγέλιον ἦν καὶ ἁπαξαπλῶς τὰ συνιστάντα τὴν Χριστοῦ ἐπιδημίαν καὶ κατασκευάζοντα
τὴν παρουσίαν αὐτοῦ ἐμποιοῦντά τε αὐτὴν ταῖς ψυχαῖς τῶν βουλομένων παραδέξασθαι τὸν
ἑστῶτα ἐπὶ τὴν θύραν); see also the comments in Heiser, *Paulusinszenierung*, p. 139. It is
worth noting, however, that Origen could also subordinate Paul's letters to the Gospels,
though not so as to place their fundamental congruence in question; see *Comm. in Iohan.*
1.5.27–31.

[10] On the concern for perfection, see the still valuable study of Walther Völker,
*Das Vollkommenheitsideal des Origenes. Eine Untersuchung zur Geschichte der
Frömmigkeit und zu den Anfängen christlicher Mystik*, BHT 7 (Tübingen: Mohr
Siebeck, 1931), supplemented now by the discussion of the progress of the soul in
Torjesen, *Hermeneutical Procedure*, pp. 70–85. See also Theresia Heither, "Glaube in
der Theologie des Origenes," *Erbe und Auftrag* 67 (1991), 255–265; Gaetano Lettieri,
"Progresso," in Adele Monaci Castagno (ed.), *Origene dizionario. La cultura, il pensiero,*

movement toward perfection was closely linked with a life of progressive scriptural interpretation.[11]

Origen's reading of Paul, then, takes place within his broader canonical and ecclesial vision. It remains the case, nevertheless, that Paul *was* important for Origen's thought, and this importance extends his use of Pauline statements for hermeneutical leverage. If Paul is one among other apostles, this indicates that the Apostle's teaching was fundamentally ecclesiastical, which is to say that not only was it in harmony with scriptures and the other apostles,[12] but it was also pedagogically deployed with the moral and doctrinal perfection of Christians in view.[13] As will become clear throughout this chapter, Paul's letters and personal example provided Origen with a model for his own teaching and interpretive activities, extending from the rebuttal of critics to the guidance of catechumens to mystical interpretation among the mature believers.[14] When one takes his institutional context into consideration, moreover, one can see better how Origen's Pauline model functioned within the social and ecclesial structures that shaped Origen's own life, and how Paul supplies both textual warrant and personal paradigm for Origen's work. To this end, and as above, the present chapter begins with a discussion of the catechumenate during Origen's ministry. I will then discuss his Caesarean institutional context more broadly, in which the bulk of his homilies and writings were completed, before turning to his complex presentation and appropriation of Paul. There I argue that Origen's hermeneutical use of Paul – that is,

---

le opere (Roma: Città Nuova, 2000), pp. 379–392; Manlio Simonetti, *Origene esegeta e la sua tradizione* (Brescia: Morcelliana, 2004), pp. 37–43; Peter W. Martens, *Origen and Scripture: The Contours of the Exegetical Life*, Oxford Early Christian Studies (Oxford: Oxford University Press, 2012), pp. 101–106. For Origen's treatment of the *simpliciores*, see below, pp. 165–168.

[11] Martens, *Origen and Scripture*, pp. 89–106 and *passim*.

[12] See *Comm. in Iohan.* 6.6.39; *Comm. in Matt.* 15.7 (text in Ernst Benz and E. Klostermann (eds.), *Origenes Werke. Origenes Matthäuserklärung, 1. Die griechisch erhaltenen Tomoi*, vol. X, GCS 40 (Leipzig: Hinrichs, 1935)); *Hom. in Gen.* 6.1; *Hom. in Ex.* 5.1; *Hom. in Lev.* 7.4.1–2 (all three in W. A. Baehrens (ed.), *Origenes Werke. Homilien zum Hexateuch in Rufins Übersetzung*, vol. VI, GCS 29 (Leipzig: Hinrichs, 1920)), etc. See also Cocchini, *Il Paolo*, pp. 128–129; Kaczmarek, "L'*Exemplum* di Paolo," pp. 448–450, who notes Origen's treatment of Paul as an example to the *doctores ecclesiae* in his teaching; and Christoph Markschies, "Paul the Apostle," in John Anthony McGuckin (ed.), *The Westminster Handbook to Origen*, ed. John Anthony McGuckin (Louisville: Westminster John Knox, 2004), p. 168, who notes the larger canonical context in which Origen understands Paul.

[13] E.g., *Comm. in Iohan.* 10.15.86. This is an important point to which I will return below.

[14] So also Cocchini, *Il Paolo*, p. 61; Markschies, "Paul," p. 167; and Tloka, *Griechische Christen*, p. 101.

his appeal to interpretive guidelines provided by Paul's letters – is closely related to his institutionally situated pedagogical appeals to Paul, and that the two together provide the context in which Paul, the one who cultivates the soul of the catechumen, can be appreciated.

5.1 ORIGEN'S CATECHUMENATE

Origen's vision of the catechumenate is inextricably bound up with his larger pedagogical concern for the gradual perfection of the believer. This process begins with moral purification and extends throughout the life of the believer as they pass through multiple stages of moral and intellectual purification until they are able to encounter God, even in the present through inspired mystical interpretation of scripture. Perhaps the most well-known description of this journey of the soul is Origen's twenty-seventh homily on Numbers.[15] This homily contains a framework for Origen's entire pedagogical vision of the Christian life, from initial conversion, through catechesis, to baptism and the continuing moral and intellectual development that follows in the soul's journey to God.[16]

As we saw earlier in the discussion of *Cels.* 3.51.7–19 (Chapter 2.3.7), Origen viewed catechumens as a "particular class" of community members (ἰδίᾳ…ποιήσαντες τάγμα), who received introductory teaching (εἰσαγωγή) concerning both the pure life and basic doctrine. This phase begins with a decision to pursue the pure life and an initial belief in Christ, and it ends with baptism. In the terms of his twenty-seventh homily on Numbers, the catechetical phase begins with the exodus from Egypt – when one believes "that Christ was born of the Virgin and the Holy Spirit, and that the Word made flesh came into this world"[17] – and ends with crossing the Red Sea,

---

[15] A focus on the journey of the soul is made explicit in *Hom. in Num.* 27.2.2–3; 4.1–2; 5.2, etc.; and note the similar discussion in *Hom. in Ex.* 5. See also Torjesen, *Hermeneutical Procedure*, pp. 76–77; Young, *Biblical Exegesis*, p. 242; Oleksandra Vakula, "Spiritual progress and a disciple of Christ as a model of the perfect Christian in Origen," *Studia Patristica* 51 (2011), 45–59; and Anders-Christian Jacobsen, *Christ – the Teacher of Salvation: A Study on Origen's Christology and Soteriology*, Adamantiana 6 (Münster: Aschendorff, 2015), pp. 312–315 and *passim*, among others.

[16] A difficult feature of Origen's treatments of the soul's journey is the lack of obvious correlation among the smaller stages between different homilies, even within the series on Numbers itself. Nevertheless, the general movement remains the same, even if Origen is "always scaling knowledge in terms of higher and lower levels" (Torjesen, *Hermeneutical Procedure*, p. 76). See also the more recent account of Origen's "pedagogical soteriology" as it is related to his Christology in Jacobsen, *Teacher of Salvation*, pp. 312–326.

[17] *Hom. in Num.* 27.3.2 (translation from Thomas P. Scheck (trans.), *Origen. Homilies on Numbers*, ed. Christopher A. Hall, Ancient Christian Texts (Downers Grove: IVP Academic,

passing through the water while confessing one's belief in the "one true God and his son Jesus Christ whom he sent."[18] While Origen does not explicitly call the Red Sea crossing a "baptism" in *Hom. in Num.* 27, it is nevertheless a common image for baptism throughout his writings[19] and its implicit function becomes clear in 27.11.2 when he explains that the Israelites later camped "near" the Red Sea because "it is enough to have entered it only once."[20] Between Egypt and the Red Sea, however, are other intermediate stages of development as the soul progresses through various temptations in acquiring virtue, and during this time teaching "is ordinarily about moral instruction," that is, "milk."[21]

Origen does not paint an idealized picture of the initiation process, noting among the scriptural types both "confused commotion" in Rameses and a struggle against the devil in Buthan.[22] But during one's

2009)): "credimus Christum natum ex virgine et Spiritu sancto et 'Verbum carnem factum' venisse in hunc mundum" (text from W. A. Baehrens (ed.), *Origenes Werke. Homilien zum Hexateuch in Rufins Übersetzung*, vol. VII, GCS 30 (Leipzig: Hinrichs, 1921)).

[18] *Hom. in Num.* 27.10.2: "Credamus tantum in 'unum verum Deum et quem misit filium suum Iesum Christum.'"

[19] See *Hom. in Ex.* 5.1; *Hom. in Jesu* 26.2 ("post digressionem rubri maris, id est post gratiam baptismi"; text in Annie Jaubert (ed.), *Origène. Homélies sur Josué*, SC 71 (Paris: Cerf, 1960)); *Comm. in Iohan.* 6.44.227; Saxer, *Les rites*, pp. 158–159; Crouzel, *Origen*, p. 223; F. Ledegang, *Mysterium Ecclesiae: Images of the Church and Its Members in Origen*, BETL 156 (Leuven: Peeters, 2001), pp. 420–423; Gunnar Hällström, "More Than Initiation? Baptism According to Origen of Alexandria," in David Hellholm, Tor Vegge, Øyvind Norderval, and Christer Hellholm (eds.), *Ablution, Initiation, and Baptism: Late Antiquity, Early Judaism, and Early Christianity*, vol. 2 BZNW 176 (Berlin: De Gruyter, 2011), pp. 993–994, and see further below (p. 161) on the role of Paul in this interpretive move.

[20] Origen also equates the crossing of the Jordan with baptism, even in the same passage, where he notes that the Red Sea also stands for baptism as in *Hom. in Jesu* 5.1; see also *Hom. in Jesu* 4.1, *Hom. in Num.* 26.4.1; *Hom. in Luc.* 21.4.

[21] Quote from *Hom. in Num.* 27.1.2: "Unde ad similitudinem corporalis exempli est aliqui etiam in verbo Dei cibus 'lactis,' apertior scilicet simpliciorque doctrina, ut de moralibus esse solet." See also 27.5.2 (trans. Scheck): "And when it [*viz.* the soul] has conquered one temptation and its faith has been proved by it, from there it goes to another one; and it passes as it were from one stage to another; and then, when it prevails over the things that have happened and endures them faithfully, it moves on to another stage. And, thus, the progress through each of the temptations of life and faith will be said to have stages in which increases in virtues are acquired one by one..." ("Ubi cum vicerit unam tentationem et fides eius in ea fuerit probata, inde venit ad aliam et quasi de una mansione ad alteram transit et ibi cum obtinuerit, quae acciderint, et fideliter tulerit, pergit ad aliam; et ita per singula quaeque tentamenta vitae ac fidei profectus 'mansiones' habere dicetur, in quibus per singula virtutum quaeruntur augmenta..."). See also *Hom. in Iud.* 5.6 (text in Baehrens, *Homilien zum Hexateuch*); *Hom. in Jer.* 5.13.2–3 (text in Pierre Nautin (ed.), *Origène. Homélies sur Jérémie*, SC 232, 238 (Paris: Cerf, 1976–1977)).

[22] *Hom. in Num.* 27.9.1–2; see also *Hom. in Ex.* 5.3 (which reflects on the same travel itinerary) and *Hom. in Jer.* 4.3 (which discusses the presence of catechumens at martyrdoms).

sojourn in the catechumenate there remain small stages of progress, indicated by Iroth, a small village whose entrance signifies "association [with the Christian community?] and modest abstinence."[23] Even after passing through baptism, one faces the "bitterness" of continuing discipline during the initial stages of spiritual progress (27.10.2).

During this phase between initial conversion and baptism, the catechumen passes through a liminal space in the Church.[24] On the one hand, catechumens are a part of the community, regularly addressed in homilies and included in discussions of ecclesial benefits and activities.[25] On the other hand, they have not yet "put on Jesus"[26] or "received the symbol of purification"[27] in baptism because they have not yet "died to sin," which is the prerequisite for burial with Christ in baptism.[28] Moreover, until catechumens

---

[23] *Hom. in Num.* 27.9.3: "quod est indicium conversationis et abstinentiae mediocris."

[24] In fact, Origen's construal of the moral and doctrinal development *before* baptism raises difficult questions for his view of infant baptism, in which no previous moral development or even failure appears possible. Hällström, "Initiation," pp. 1000–1004, argues that Origen solved this difficulty by appealing to the soul's inherent uncleanliness acquired by inhabiting a body, which he differentiates from intentional sin, such that baptized children are being cleansed of the former rather than the latter. How this fits with his scheme of the progress of the soul is not clear and one wonders whether, perhaps, baptized children are among those who Origen thinks are "born prematurely" into the Christian faith, on which see further below (*Comm. in Rom.* 8.9.690; text in C. P. Hammond Bammel (ed.), *Der Römerbriefkommentar des Origenes. Kritische Ausgabe der Übersetzung Rufins*, 3 vols., AGBL 16, 33, 34 (Freiburg im Breisgau: Herder, 1990–1998); 8.10.7, in Thomas P. Scheck, *Origen: Commentary on the Epistle to the Romans, Books 6–10*, Fathers of the Church 104 (Washington, D.C.: Catholic University of America Press, 2002)). Note that citations of Origen's *Comm. in Rom.* are according to Hammond Bammel's edition – with book, chapter, and edition page number – with Scheck's differing divisions noted alongside for ease of cross-reference.

[25] *Hom. in Jesu* 4.1 (catechumens as part of the ecclesial community); *Comm. in Matt.* 11.18 (catechumens listed as those being healed in the church); *En. in Job* 21.11 (MPG 17: 77, lines 49–53; catechumens as imitating Christ). Christoph Markschies, "'...für die Gemeinde im Grossen und Ganzen nicht geeignet...'? Erwägungen zu Absicht und Wirkung des Predigten des Origenes," in *Origenes und sein Erbe. Gesammelte Studien*, TU 160 (Berlin: De Gruyter, 2007), p. 60, notes Jerome's later judgment that Origen's homilies should be understood "als Texte für Anfänger, die sich erst noch reinigen müssen (also doch wohl mindestens auch Katechumenen)."

[26] *Adnot. in Deut.* 27.19 (MPG 17: 33, lines 52–53): μηδέπω δὲ τὸν Ἰησοῦν ἐνδυσάμενοι, ἀλλ' ἔτι καὶ κατηχουμένοις ἐνάριθμοι.

[27] *Cels.* 3.51.7–14, cited in Chapter 2.3.7 above.

[28] *Comm. in Rom.* 5.8.422 (Scheck, 5.8.4): "Teaching through this that if someone previously died to sin, that person is necessarily buried with Christ in baptism. If one has not truly died to sin, it is not possible to be buried with Christ" ("docens per haec quia si qui prius mortuus est peccato is necessario in baptismo consepultus est Christo; si uero non ante quis moritur peccato non potest sepelliri cum Christo"); see also 5.8.10 and the comments in Gramaglia, "Battesimo," p. 45.

are baptized they remain condemned, members of the community who are not yet morally pure and do not celebrate the eucharist, undertaking the initial stages of the soul's progress, which is a "time of dangers."[29] Even so, this dangerous liminal period is only temporary: the trajectory of the desert journey leads to and through the baptismal sea. It is to this end that Origen exhorts the catechumens to take the crucial step of baptism in faith so that they may eventually progress to true knowledge of God.[30] As for Clement of Alexandria, it is a journey that is for all believers in principle, though we shall see later that Origen does not think that all will desire or be able to continue beyond the foundations of the baptismal faith.[31]

Alongside the Red Sea imagery, an emphasis on moral preparation for knowledge was highlighted by Origen with cultivation imagery.[32] Before a teacher is able to sow the "holy seeds" – that is "the word concerning the Father, concerning the Son and Holy Spirit, the word concerning the Resurrection, the word concerning the punishment, the word concerning the final rest, concerning the Law, the Prophets and in general each of the Scriptures"[33] – they are to tear out the thorns and plow to make the ground fallow. The field, in this analogy, is the soul of the believer, for whom teachers in particular are responsible.[34]

"This," then, "the Lord says to the men of Judah and those dwelling in Jerusalem: prepare fallow lands for yourselves and do not sow among the thorns." This word is principally addressed to the teachers lest they prematurely

---

[29] See *Hom. in Iud.* 9.2.519 ("Therefore, these are thus condemned"; "illi ergo sic reprobati sunt") and *Hom. in Num.* 27.10.1 ("We said that the time of progress is a time of dangers"; "Diximus tempus profectuum tempus esse periculorum") respectively.

[30] For Origen's exhortations, see *Hom. in Luc.* 21.4 (cited in Chapter 2.3.7 above); *Hom. in Iud.* 5.6; *Hom. in Jesu* 9.9; etc.

[31] More will be said about these *simpliciores* below, pp. 165–168. See also the full treatment in Gunnar Hällström, *Fides Simpliciorum According to Origen of Alexandria*, Commentationes Humanarum Litterarum 76 (Ekenäs, Finland: Societas Scientarium Fennica, 1984).

[32] See *Comm. in Cant.* 3.8–9 (text in W. A. Baehrens (ed.), *Origenes Werke. Homilien zu Samuel I, zum Hohelied und zu den Propheten. Kommentar zum Hohelied, in Rufins und Hieronymus' Übersetzung*, vol. VIII, GCS 33 (Leipzig: Hinrichs, 1925)), where catechumens are likened to trees that are not yet fruitful but can be made so by the careful cultivation of God. Note also the comments on "purification as a precondition for salvation" in Jacobsen, *Teacher of Salvation*, pp. 318–320.

[33] *Hom. in Jer.* 5.13.2: ...τὰ σπέρματα τὰ ἅγια, τὸν περὶ τοῦ πατρὸς λόγον, τὸν περὶ τοῦ υἱοῦ, τὸν περὶ τοῦ ἁγίου πνεύματος, τὸν λόγον τὸν περὶ ἀναστάσεως, τὸν λόγον τὸν περὶ κολάσεως, τὸν λόγον τὸν περὶ ἀναπαύσεως, τὸν περὶ νόμου, τὸν περὶ προφητῶν, καὶ ἀπαξαπλῶς ἑκάστου τῶν γεγραμμένων...

[34] See comments in Monaci Castagno, *Origene predicatore*, p. 68: "The preacher has the responsibility for the salvation of the soul for those who listen to him."

sow their teachings among thorns in their hearers, before making fallow lands in their souls. For whenever they, "putting their hand to the plow," make fallow lands in souls, according to the "beautiful" and "good land" of those hearers, then when they sow they do not sow "among thorns."[35]

Even those who are not teachers, moreover, are exhorted to "become" their "own farmer," preparing the fallow land that God has given to them.[36]

Two points arise from this passage that are particularly relevant here. The first is that all "hearers" – a term increasingly associated with the catechumenate and Christian initiation in the late second and early third centuries – require moral cultivation, which is a teacher's initial task.[37] The second is that the initial moral concerns are preparatory for elementary doctrinal teaching. The "holy seeds" noted by Origen are not the arcane mysteries he is so interested in at other times; they are basic doctrines associated with fundamental apostolic teaching and baptismal confessions elsewhere in his writings, from both the Alexandrian and the Caesarean periods of his life.[38] In the preface to his *De principiis*, unfortunately only preserved in Rufinus' Latin translation, Origen notes that

---

[35] *Hom. in Jer.* 5.13.2: "Τάδε" οὖν "λέγει κύριος τοῖς ἀνδράσιν Ἰούδα καὶ τοῖς κατοικοῦσιν Ἰερουσαλήμ· νεώσατε ἑαυτοῖς νεώματα, καὶ μὴ σπείρετε ἐπ' ἀκάνθαις." Ὁ λόγος οὗτος μάλιστα τοῖς διδάσκουσι λέγεται, ἵνα μὴ πρότερον ἐμπιστεύσωσιν τὰ λεγόμενα τοῖς ἀκροαταῖς πρὸ τοῦ νεώματα ποιῆσαι ἐν ταῖς ψυχαῖς αὐτῶν. Ὅταν γὰρ "ἀρότρῳ ἐπιβαλόντες τὴν χεῖρα" νεώματα ποιήσωσιν ἐν ταῖς ψυχαῖς, κατὰ "τὴν γῆν τὴν καλὴν" καὶ "ἀγαθὴν" τούτων ἀκουόντων, τότε σπείροντες οὐ σπείρουσιν "ἐπ'" ἀκάνθαις."

[36] *Hom. in Jer.* 5.13.3: Ἀλλὰ ἐρεῖ τις τῶν ἀκουόντων· ἐγὼ οὐ διδάσκω, οὐχ ὑπόκειμαι ταύτῃ τῇ ἐντολῇ. Καὶ σὺ γεωργὸς γενοῦ σεαυτοῦ, καὶ μὴ σπείρῃς ἐπ' ἀκάνθαις, ἀλλὰ νέωμα ποίησόν μοι τὸ χωρίον, ὃ πεπίστευκέν σοι ὁ θεὸς τῶν ὅλων·

[37] This point confirms again the concern about moral preparation for the Christian life that is ubiquitous in early Christian discussions of initiation. In addition to the works cited in Chapter 2 above, see also the comments in Harl, *Fonction révélatrice*, pp. 318–319; Jean Daniélou, *Origen*, trans. Walter Mitchell (London: Sheed and Ward, 1955), p. 54; Karen Jo Torjesen, "Pedagogical soteriology from Clement to Origen," in Lothar Lies (ed.), *Origeniana Quarta. Die Referate des 4. Internationalen Origenskongresses*, Innsbrucker theologische Studien 19 (Innsbruck: Tyrolia, 1987), pp. 375–376; and Hällström, "Initiation," pp. 996–997.

[38] How the "holy seeds" in *Hom in Jer.* 5.13.2 are related to the "spiritual seeds" at the end of 5.13.3 is difficult to say. Erwin Schadel, *Origenes. Die griechisch erhaltenen Jeremiahomilien*, Bibliothek der Griechischen Literatur 10 (Stuttgart: Hiersemann, 1980), pp. 264–265 (followed by Esther Abbattista, *Origene legge Geremia. Analisi, commento e riflessioni di un biblista di oggi*, Tesi Gregoriana. Serie Teologia 159 (Rome: Editrice Pontificia Università Gregoriana, 2008), pp. 72–73 n. 41), argues that they were to be identified, which is seen in the resumptive quality of the comments in 5.13.3, restating the previous emphasis on preparation for teaching in different terms. This appears more satisfying than the reading of John Clark Smith (ed.), *Origen: Homilies on Jeremiah, Homily on 1 Kings 28*, Fathers of the Church 97 (Washington, D.C.: Catholic University of America Press, 1998), p. 56 n. 148, in which the "spiritual seeds" are taken as a distinct, more advanced, and presumably later set of teachings.

even those "who seemed somewhat dull in the investigation of divine knowledge" believe the bare necessities: about the one creator God (who is good and just), his Son (who was born of the Father and was the agent of creation before assuming human form in the incarnation), the Holy Spirit, the post-mortem fate and freedom of the soul, the spiritual realm of the devil and angels, the temporally limited quality of the world, and the scriptures as the product of the Holy Spirit.[39] The confessions of the one God and his Son are associated with baptism in *Hom. in Num.* 27.4–10, noted above, and a knowledge of the devil is explicitly linked with a baptismal renunciation in *Hom. in Num.* 12.4.5.[40] The sowing of "spiritual seeds" that feature in the baptismal rite, then, is predicated on moral formation and teaching during the catechumenate.

Origen does not explicitly state when such foundational teaching takes place; he certainly never speaks directly of special sessions for catechesis. He does indicate that catechumens were expected to be present alongside the baptized at his daily homilies on the Old Testament, though he does not tell us whether this was a requirement or simply usual practice, or whether the relative composition of the audience differed greatly between days.[41] Pierre Nautin argued suggestively that the daily reading

---

[39] *Princ.* praef. 3 (text in Henri Crouzel and Manlio Simonetti (eds.), *Origène. Traité des Principes*, 4 vols., SC 252, 253, 268, 269 (Paris: Cerf, 1978–1980); trans. in John Behr (trans. ed.), *Origen: On First Principles*, Oxford Early Christian Texts (Oxford: Oxford University Press, 2017)): "Now it ought to be known that the holy apostles, in preaching the faith of Christ, delivered with utmost clarity to all believers, even to those who seemed somewhat dull in the investigation of divine knowledge, certain points that they believed to be necessary..." ("Illud autem scire oportet, quoniam sancti apostoli fidem Christi praedicantes de quibusdam quidem, quaecumque necessaria crediderunt, omnibus credentibus, etiam his, qui pigriores erga inquisitionem divinae scientiae videbantur, manifestissime tradiderunt"). The list of topics continues in §§4–8. On the authorship of scripture by the Spirit, see Francesca Cocchini, *Origene. Teologo esegeta per una identità cristiana* (Bologna: EDB, 2006), pp. 40–41.

[40] "Well, then, let us see when we made these promises, when we declared these words to the devil. Let each believer remember – when they first came to the baptismal waters, received the first seals of the faith and approached the font of salvation – what words they used at that time and in that place and what they declared to the devil: that they would not make use of his pomp or indulge in his works or submit in any way to any of his services and pleasures" (trans. modified from Scheck; "Videamus ergo, quando nos ista promisimus, quando haec verba diabolo denuntiavimus. Recordetur unusquisque fidelium, cum primum venit ad aquas baptismi, cum signacula fidei prima suscepit et ad fontem salutaris accessit, quibus ibi tunc usus sit verbis et quid denuntiaverit diabolo: non se usurum pompis eius neque operibus eius neque ullis omnino servitiis eius ac voluptatibus pariturum"). See further Ledegang, *Mysterium Ecclesiae*, pp. 430–431.

[41] See *Hom. in Jesu* 4.1.308 (catechumens hearing the Law "cotidie"); see also the discussion in Nautin, *Origène*, pp. 391–395.

and sermon schedule would cover the entire Old Testament in three years
and that this can be correlated with the three-year catechumenate in
the *Traditio apostolica*.[42] On this reading, then, Origen's Old Testament
sermons were directed principally at the needs of the catechumens,
thereby supplying a concrete institutional form for Caesarean catechetical
instruction. Unfortunately, Origen himself does not indicate the expected
length of the catechumenate, nor can one confidently extrapolate directly from the *Traditio apostolica* to wider church practice in the early
third century.[43] Even so, his sermons provided the occasion for Origen
to teach at least some catechumens the elementary doctrines that he felt
were important in preparation for baptism.[44]

Of course, as noted earlier, for Origen moral progress is not confined
to the catechumenate; if catechumens need to progress, believers must
also "stretch toward what is ahead" of them in a process of continual
growth.[45] Doctrinal foundations are important but they are meant to
be built upon rather than left bare.[46] Nevertheless, like Clement, Origen
viewed foundational moral and doctrinal preparation as ideally situated
prior to baptism. Although within the church there would inevitably be
believers at different stages of spiritual growth, Origen considers some
to be "born prematurely" – baptized prior to being fully prepared for
the Christian life – who thereby force the teacher to return to a state of
maternal birth pains, "until Christ is formed in them."[47]

---

[42] Nautin, *Origène*, p. 395; followed by Schadel, *Jeremiahomilien*, pp. 20–21; Joseph
W. Trigg, *Origen: The Bible and Philosophy in the Third-Century Church* (Atlanta: John
Knox, 1983), p. 177; and Heine, *Origen*, pp. 179–180.

[43] See the discussion of the relation of the *Traditio apostolica* and broader catechetical
practice in Chapter 2 above. Note that Nautin's reliance on his postulated "reading
cycle" is also rejected by Markschies, "Erwägungen," p. 59.

[44] This also fits with the view of Simonetti, "Origene," pp. 299–308, that Origen's catechetical teaching is represented by his homiletical approach to texts such as the Song
of Songs, rather than the more precise and detailed work of his commentaries. In this
case, it is not a matter of differing methods between the two, but rather similar methods
worked out with varying audiences in view. See also the arguments for Origen's pedagogical interpretive strategies in Torjesen, *Hermeneutical Procedure, passim*.

[45] *Hom. in Jer.* 18.8: "And in the case of those who hear these things, then, whether
catechumens who are in the process of leaving the Gentile life or believers who have
already progressed in 'stretching toward what is ahead'…" (Καὶ τῶν ἀκουόντων οὖν ταῦτα,
εἴτε κατηχουμένων καταλιπόντων τὸν ἐθνικὸν βίον εἴτε πιστῶν ἤδη προκεκοφότων ἐν τῷ "τοῖς
ἔμπροσθεν ἐπεκτείνεσθαι"…).

[46] See Gramaglia, "Battesimo," p. 45.

[47] *Comm. in Rom.* 8.9.690 (Scheck, 8.10.7): "errantes et in fide titubantes ac uelut in
aborsum quoddam redactos materno affectu rursum parturiendo donec Christus
formaretur in eis." In context, Origen is referring to Paul's own ministry practice with the

This brief discussion, along with the material surveyed in Chapter 2 above, is sufficient to show that Origen knew of and engaged with a catechumenate that held a firm place within the Christian community. The presence of catechumens is presumed in many places, and in others catechumens are discussed and explicitly addressed.[48] Catechumens constituted a particular "order" of church members with a recognized status in relation to the believers responsible for them. They were supplied with moral and doctrinal teaching in preparation for baptism, which stood as the doorway between the pagan life, which catechumens were in the process of leaving, and the Christian life.[49] Like Clement before him, Origen views the catechumenate as only the first stage in a long process of maturation and learning, one which contains *in nuce* the sorts of moral and spiritual progress that will continue throughout the Christian life. The journey of the soul from "Egypt" continues through "stages" even after passing through the Red Sea, and those who hear the exhortations of scripture should apply them to themselves "in whatever position they stand."[50] The elementary faith and basic doctrine imparted during the catechumenate is sufficient for the Christian masses because baptism brings purification and remission of sins, but it is not the final goal in Origen's vision of the Christian life. As we shall see further below, the baptismal doctrine of "Christ crucified" is for the simple and imma-ture, while greater mysteries await the believer who is not "dull in the investigation of divine knowledge."[51]

---

baptized Galatians who wanted to follow the Law, drawing particularly on the cluster of images in Rom. 14:2, 1 Cor. 3:2, and Heb. 5:12–14, to which we will return below.

[48] Other places where catechumens are discussed (rather than addressed) are *Hom. in Num.* 3.1; *Comm. in Cant.* 3.8–9; *Comm. in Rom.* 2.9.150 (Scheck 2.13.2); *Hom. in Ex.* 10.4, etc.

[49] The catechumenate as a process of leaving pagan life is seen in a number of ways, per-haps most succinctly in *Hom. in Jer.* 18.8, cited on p. 138 n. 45 above.

[50] *Comm. in Rom.* 8.9.690 (Scheck 8.10.7): "Haec eadem et unusquisque in ecclesia positus apud semet ipsum reputet ut in quocumque loco stat..." In the immediate con-text, Origen is speaking about different ministries in the church, though, as a general hermeneutical principle, it applies broadly to his interpretive approach.

[51] On the sufficiency of even "bare faith" (ψιλὴ πίστις), see *Cels.* 1.9 and Hällström, *Fides Simpliciorum*, pp. 11, 27. See also the comments on faith in Harl, *Fonction révélatrice*, p. 261; Werner Schütz, *Der christliche Gottesdienst bei Origenes*, Calwer theologische Monographien 8 (Stuttgart: Calwer, 1984), p. 126; Crouzel, *Origen*, p. 113; Heither, *Translatio religionis*, p. 68; and the earlier work of Völker, *Vollkommenheitsideal*, p. 80. On Origen's reading of 1 Cor. 2:2, see further below (p. 163) and Riemer Roukema, "La prédication du Christ crucifié (1 Corinthiens 2,2) selon Origène," in G. Dorival and A. Le Boulluec (eds.), *Origeniana Sexta*, BETL 118 (Leuven: Peeters, 1995), pp. 523–529.

5.1.1 Some Comments on Origen's Catechetical Terminology

Before leaving the discussion of Origen's catechumenate and moving on
to a fuller account of his institutional contexts, it is helpful to note briefly
the variety of terminology and images with which Origen refers to the
initial stages of Christian initiation. When he uses the language of catechesis, and certainly in the cases where his Latin translators do, he is normally referring to Christian catechumens.[52] However, he regularly refers
to various stages of the Christian life as part of a continuum. As we have
already seen, he makes use of scriptural images to describe the Christian
life which incorporate the first steps of initiation, say, between Egypt and
the Red Sea, within a broader context. The language of "milk" and "solid
food" is also a staple of Origen's discussions of Christian progress.[53] In
these ways, then, his language and imagery of the catechumenate is largely
traditional, drawn either from scripture or from previous Christian use.[54]

It appears that Origen himself is much more interested in spurring
believers to higher forms of knowledge, the "solid food," investigating
spiritual mysteries hidden in scripture and the world. As Henri Crouzel
put it, "The only kind of knowledge that really interests Origen is the
kind that he calls 'mystical.'"[55] Although, as will become clear below,
Crouzel's comment does not exactly reflect Origen's concern to accommodate himself to his hearers at varying levels of progress, it does
nevertheless suggest why Origen does not spend much time discussing

---

[52] Potential exceptions occur when he cites biblical texts such as Luke 1:4, though I think
it is likely that Origen would have read that as a reference to his contemporary Christian
practice, or when he refers to others being instructed in a particular way of life, as in his
discussion of the Jews in *Comm. in Rom.* 3.2.204–205 (Scheck 3.2.3), where the abridged
Latin text reads "Iudaeos uero cum dicit: 'si autem tu Iudaeus cognominaris et requiescis
in lege,' et reliqua, quibus addit: 'qui ergo doces alium te ipsum non doces qui praedicas
non furandum furaris,' et cetera," and the longer Greek text reads Ἴδε σὺ Ἰουδαῖος ἐπονομάζῃ
καὶ ἐπαναπαύῃ νόμῳ καὶ καυχᾶσαι ἐν θεῷ καὶ γινώσκεις τὸ θέλημα καὶ δοκιμάζεις τὰ διαφέροντα
κατηχούμενος ἐκ τοῦ νόμου, πέποιθάς τε σεαυτὸν ὁδηγὸν εἶναι τυφλῶν, φῶς τῶν ἐν σκότει,
παιδευτὴν ἀφρόνων, διδάσκαλον νηπίων, ἔχοντα τὴν μόρφωσιν τῆς γνώσεως καὶ τῆς ἀληθείας ἐν
τῷ νόμῳ· ὁ οὖν διδάσκων ἕτερον σεαυτὸν οὐ διδάσκεις; (2.17–21 in codex Athon. Laura 184
B64; text in Otto Bauernfeind (ed.), *Der Römerbrieftext des Origenes nach dem codex von
der Goltz (cod. 184, B64 des Athosklosters Lawra)*, TU 44.3 (Leipzig: Hinrichs, 1923)).

[53] This will be addressed more fully below (pp. 165–169) in relation to Origen's Pauline
influence.

[54] This is similar, therefore, to his baptismal terminology; see Hällström, "Initiation,"
pp. 990–991.

[55] Crouzel, *Origen*, p. 99; note also his emphasis on spiritual interpretation in Henri
Crouzel, "Le contexte spirituel de l'exégèse dite spirituelle," in G. Dorival and a. Le
Boulluec (eds.), *Origeniana Sexta*, BETL 118 (Leuven: Peeters, 1995), pp. 333–342.

the catechumenate as such. The moral and doctrinal preparation of catechesis, the foundation of "bare" baptismal faith, is for Origen *primarily* a prerequisite to encountering the Logos of God in scripture. Unlike Clement, he does not focus on legitimating the catechumenate within a larger vision of Christian progress; that is taken for granted. Clement's pedagogical model – with the Logos acting first as pedagogue and then as teacher – becomes for Origen "a kind of forecourt or entry way" to his own account of the journey of the soul.[56] The way in which Origen frames his intellectual and pastoral concerns is related to two further institutional contexts in which he worked, to which we now turn.

5.2 HOMILIST AND THEOLOGIAN: ORIGEN'S INSTITUTIONAL CONTEXTS

5.2.1 Origen's Caesarean School

Clarifying the institutional contexts in which Origen worked is difficult and remains debated. As Christoph Markschies noted, "During his life, Origen taught in two very different cities in extremely different contexts, and it is not so simple to reconstruct them exactly."[57] We have already seen in Chapter 2 above that there remains a case in favor of Origen taking on a "catechetical school" in Alexandria, which he later expanded to include more advanced philosophical studies.[58] When he went to Caesarea, however, he established his own philosophical school, a place for advanced study whose highest goals were oriented toward the Christian life.[59] Even while engaged in this work, Origen was also responsible for preaching daily sermons on Old Testament books which were accommodated to fit catechumens and simple believers alike. Given that the bulk of his writings were composed in Caesarea, including nearly all his extant homilies and

---

[56] Torjesen, "Pedagogical soteriology," p. 375.

[57] Markschies, *Christian Theology*, p. 76.

[58] As Simonetti, "Origene," p. 300, notes, "Origen was convinced that it was not possible to impart one and the same teaching, in which were certain particularly nuanced and profound notions, to all his students indifferently...therefore they should be reserved only for those who had attained a more elevated level of instruction."

[59] See in particular Ilinca Tanaseanu-Döbler, "Philosophie in Alexandria: der Kreis um Ammonios Sakkas," in Tobias Georges, Felix Albrecht, and Reinhard Feldmeier (eds.), *Alexandria*, COMES 1 (Tübingen: Mohr Siebeck, 2013), pp. 109–126, and Rizzi, "La scuola di Origene," pp. 105–119, who emphasize the continuity between Origen's Caesarean school and other philosophical schools, even while noting his distinctively Christian orientation.

commentaries, it is there that I will focus our attention here.[60] Though the discussion in this section must be kept brief, I begin with Origen the schoolmaster before turning to Origen the homilist.

The principal witness for Origen's new, or at least further developed, school context in Caesarea is the *Oratio panegyrica* of Gregory Thaumaturgus, a member of Origen's first cohort in Caesarea,[61] which can be correlated with the earlier developments in Alexandria reflected in Origen's letter to Alexander of Jerusalem and the description of his activities by Eusebius.[62] Gregory's rather ornate account of his time with Origen does not lend itself to a clear step-by-step reconstruction of Origen's curriculum, though a few important elements emerge.[63] According to Gregory, Origen began his philosophical program by preparing the

[60] Works from his Alexandrian period include *De principiis*, the first five books of his John commentary, the first six books of his commentary on Genesis, commentaries on Psalms 1–25 and Lamentations, *De resurrectione*, and the *Stromateis*; see Nautin, *Origène*, pp. 368–371; Crouzel, *Origen*, p. 39; and Fürst, *Origenes*, pp. 22–28. Of those, only the first two survive in anything more than fragments. For recent scholarship on Caesarea Maritima and the Christian community there, see the collection of essays in Osvalda Andrei (ed.), *Caesarea Maritima e la scuola origeniana. Multiculturalità, forme di competizione culturale e identità christiana* (Brescia: Morcelliana, 2013).

[61] On the authorship of this, see Henri Crouzel, "Faut-il voir trois personnages en Grégoire le Thaumaturge?," *Gregorianum* 60 (1979), 289–300, whose arguments are followed by Markschies, "Erwägungen," p. 59 n. 11, and developed further by Michael Slusser, "Saint Gregory Thaumaturgus," *Expository Times* 120, no. 12 (2009), 573–580, and Francesco Celia, "Gregory of Neocaesarea: a re-examination of the biographical issue," *Adamantius* 22 (2016), 172–173 and *passim*, with further bibliography there. Crouzel was arguing against Nautin, *Origène*, pp. 81–86. Note also the detailed discussion of this debate in Peter Guyot and Richard Klein (eds.), *Gregor der Wundertäter. Oratio prosphonetica ac panegyrica in Origenem = Dankrede an Origenes*, Fontes Christiani 24 (Freiburg: Herder, 1996), pp. 45–63, which concludes generally in favor of the traditional view. As will become clear below, however, Crouzel's ancillary argument about the conversion of Gregory is less satisfactory.

[62] *Hist. eccl.* 6.18–19, which contains both Eusebius' description of Origen's expanded teaching activities (6.18) and Origen's letter to Alexander (6.19). On the pedagogical vision in Gregory's *Oratio*, see now David Satran, *In the Image of Origen: Eros, Virtue and Constraint in the Early Christian Academy*, Transformation of the Classical Heritage 58 (Oakland: University of California Press, 2018), which unfortunately appeared too late for me to be able to engage with it here.

[63] See the discussion in Blossom Stefaniw, "Exegetical curricula in Origen, Didymus, and Evagrius: pedagogical agenda and the case for Neoplatonic influence," *Studia Patristica* 44 (2010), 283–284; see also Henri Crouzel (ed.), *Grégoire le Thaumaturge. Remerciement a Origène suivi de La lettre d'Origène a Grégoire. Texte grec, introduction, traduction et notes*, SC 148 (Paris: Cerf, 1969), pp. 68–70; Jacobsen, "Conversion," pp. 148–149; Markschies, *Christian Theology*, pp. 57–58; Gemeinhardt, "Glaube, Bildung, Theologie," pp. 456–460 (drawing on Gregory's account but with an emphasis on Origen's Alexandrian teaching); and Rizzi, "La scuola di Origene," pp. 113–118.

souls of his students, removing wild and random outgrowths, tearing up brambles and weeds, plowing the soil. That is, through reproach, prohibition, and Socratic dialectic, Origen prepared his students for further stages of learning.[64] After this initial stage, he passed on the "true words" (οἱ τῆς ἀληθείας λογοί), "sowing the seeds at a good time" and attending to the conditions of their souls' "soil" (*Or. pan.* 7.97–102). "In this way, then, that part of our soul that evaluates expressions and discourses was trained with reason."[65]

Origen, whose spiritual understanding of the world is well known,[66] then taught his students about the natural world, beginning with physics and the study of things in terms of their "primary elements" (τὰ πρώτιστα στοιχεῖα), before moving to geometry as the "firm foundation" (κρηπῖδα τινὰ ἀσφαλῆ) for the subsequent knowledge of astronomy (*Or. pan.* 8.109–114). These studies, along with the previous dialectic, all serve a propaedeutic purpose, leading to the most important aspect of philosophical study, a soul at equilibrium with virtuous habits.[67] Even this step, however, is not the end goal of Origen's teaching, as it is, according to Gregory, among certain philosophers. The capstone of Origen's course was discourse about God, theology proper, and the religious life.[68] He

---

[64] *Or. pan.* 7.93: "Thorns and thistles and the whole family of wild weeds or plants which our arrogant and overgrown souls sent up and put out...everything he cut out and uprooted by reproofs and restriction; his upbraiding of us is even quite Socratic..." (ἀκάνθας μὲν καὶ τριβόλους καὶ πᾶν τὸ τῶν ἀγρίων γένος βοτανῶν ἢ φυτῶν, ὅσον ὑλομανοῦσα ἀνέπεμπε καὶ ἀνεδίδου σεσοβημένη ἡ ψυχὴ ἡμῶν...πᾶν ἐκκόπτων καὶ ἐξαίρων τοῖς ἐλέγχοις καὶ τῷ κωλύειν· καθαπτόμενος ἡμῶν καὶ μάλα Σωκρατικῶς ἔστιν...); text from Crouzel, *Remerciement*.

[65] *Or. pan.* 9.106: Οὕτως μὲν τὸ περὶ τὰς λέξεις καὶ τοὺς λόγους κριτικὸν ἡμῶν τῆς ψυχῆς μέρος λογικῶς ἐξεπαιδεύετο·

[66] See, among others, Studer, "Exegese," *passim*, and Simonetti, *Origene esegeta*, pp. 29–33. Origen's view that all physical objects signify a spiritual reality has recently been interpreted as a "sacramental" view of the world in Hans Boersma, *Scripture as Real Presence: Sacramental Exegesis in the Early Church* (Grand Rapids: Baker Academic, 2017), p. 124 and *passim*.

[67] *Or. pan.* 9.115. Notably, Eusebius speaks directly of this propaedeutic character in *Hist. eccl.* 6.18.3: "For he introduced everyone he saw had talent to philosophical subjects as well, instructing [them] in geometry and mathematics and the other preparatory studies (εἰσῆγέν τε γὰρ ὅσους εὐφυῶς ἔχοντας ἑώρα, καὶ ἐπὶ τὰ φιλόσοφα μαθήματα, γεωμετρίαν καὶ ἀριθμητικὴν καὶ τἄλλα προπαιδεύματα παραδιδούς); see also Wyrwa, "Religiöses Lernen," p. 286, and Gemeinhardt, "In Search," pp. 96–97. Note the recent discussion of Origen's tensive relationship with Greek philosophy – criticism of philosophers while noting the propaedeutic use of philosophy – in Fürst, *Origenes*, pp. 73–95.

[68] *Or. pan.* 13.150: "How could I put in words his teaching about theology and piety in addition to all the rest of his hard work and passion?" (Ἐπὶ τῇ ἄλλῃ πάσῃ φιλοπονίᾳ καὶ σπουδῇ τὴν περὶ θεολογίας διδασκαλίαν καὶ εὐλάβειαν πῶς ἂν ἐξέλθοιμι τῷ λόγῳ). Similarly, Origen's letter to Gregory famously subsumes philosophy as a servant to theology,

encouraged his students to study the breadth of available literature –
from philosophy to poetry – to acquaint them with the variety of human
arguments about God and to identify the useful things for the students.[69]
His goal, however, was to impress upon them the superiority of God's
witness and that of his prophets to that of the philosophers.[70] Origen
served as the paradigmatic interpreter of scriptures for his students.[71]
"He expounded and clarified whatever was obscure and enigmatic, as are
many things in the holy utterances."[72] According to Gregory, Origen was
successful in his interpretation not only because of his extensive study,

advocating a philosophical "spoiling of the Egyptians"; *Ep. Greg.* 1–2. See also Martens, *Origen and Scripture*, pp. 29–31; Tanaseanu-Döbler, "Philosophie in Alexandria," pp. 115–117; and Gemeinhardt, "Glaube, Bildung, Theologie," p. 455.

[69] *Or. pan.* 13–14; see also the comments in Mark Edwards, "Origen's Platonism: questions and caveats," *Zeitschrift für Antikes Christentum* 12, no. 1 (2008), 25–26. This position resonates with similar complaints against credulous philosophers (who simply accept and defend the first thing they come across) in Galen; see *Ord. lib. prop.* 1.5 (in Ioannes Marquardt, Iwanus Mueller, and Georgius Helmreich (eds.), *Claudii Galeni Pergameni scripta minora*, vol. II (Leipzig: Teubner, 1891)). Concern for intellectual independence appears relatively widespread in second- and third-century philosophical discourse; see Matyáš Havrda, "Intellectual independence in Christian and medical discourse of the 2nd–3rd centuries," in Lewis O. Ayres and Clifton Ward (eds.), *Rise of the Christian Intellectual*, AZK (Berlin: De Gruyter, forthcoming).

[70] See Young, *Biblical Exegesis*, p. 95 and *passim*; Miyako Demura, "Origen and the exegetical tradition of the Sarah–Hagar motif in Alexandria," *Studia Patristica* 56, no. 4 (2013), 73–81; Tanaseanu-Döbler, "Philosophie in Alexandria," p. 117; Rizzi, "La scuola di Origene," pp. 116–117. The common corollary that Origen wanted to *replace* Greco-Roman instruction with scripture, however, is perhaps to go to far: see the discussions in Tloka, *Griechische Christen*, pp. 51–85; Martens, *Origen and Scripture*, pp. 38–40; and Gemeinhardt, "Glaube, Bildung, Theologie," pp. 452–453. Giancarlo Rinaldi, "Pagani e christiani a Caesarea Maritima," in Osvalda Andrei (ed.), *Caesarea Maritima e la scuola origeniana: Multiculturalità, forme di competizione culturale e identità christiana* (Brescia: Morcelliana, 2013), pp. 69–72, notes Origen's ambivalence about Greek *paedeia*, which is dangerous and yet also a fundamental part of Origen's own theological work.

[71] Gregory also hints that he came into close contact with scriptures only after beginning studies with Origen in *Or. pan.* 6.85, where he cites Jonathan's love for David, noting, "although reading these things after the fact [ὕστερον] in the holy scriptures, at the time [πρότερον] I experienced it no less clearly than it was written." See also the comments in Rizzi, "La scuola di Origene," pp. 116–117: "ethics is transformed into morality, such that the catalogue of virtue can be enriched by wisdom, patience and, above all, piety, εὐσέβεια, which becomes the culminating and summative virtue of all...the knowledge of God and the true religiosity which are evoked must be considered in Christian terms... and only the bible can offer the proper point of departure for a similar investigation [*viz.* similar to that of contemporary philosophical schools into the platonic themes περὶ τὸν θεῖον καὶ εὐσέβεια]."

[72] *Or. pan.* 15.174: αὐτὸς ὑποφητεύων καὶ σαφηνίζων ὅ τί ποτε σκοτεινὸν καὶ αἰνιγματῶδες ἦ, οἷα πολλὰ ἐν ταῖς ἱεραῖς ἐστι φωναῖς.

but also because he was imbued with the same spirit that inspired the scriptural authors, and this enabled him to lead his students into a present paradise of the soul.[73]

The question remains: What kind of "school" is this of which Gregory was a part? Was it an intra-Christian school of higher theological education, an independent philosophical school directed only at philosophical education with no direct link to the Church, or something in between? In 1968, Adolf Knauber influentially argued that the lack of clear evidence for Christian theology or practice in Gregory's *Oratio*, along with the explicitly philosophical content, indicated that Origen's Caesarean school was a sort of mission through philosophy.[74] In his view, the data point toward

an undertaking, that – at least in its fundamental conception and in its internal objective – was oriented around pagan (or also hellenist-syncretist) students, who were searching for "wisdom" and who had so far sought it in vain, perhaps in the advanced schools of the time. Origen's school sees its goal (which develops from an entirely internal tendency) as the winning of such a circle (of "philosophical" youths in the sense of contemporary philosophy) for Christianity.[75]

Gregory, Knauber argues, "had come to Origen unbaptized" and at no point in his *Oriatio* does he mention his baptism. If he had wanted to be

---

[73] *Or. pan.* 15.179: "He says these things, I think, in no other way than by sharing in the divine spirit. For the same spirit is needed by those who prophesy and those who listen to the prophets" (Λέγει τε ταῦτα οὐκ ἄλλως οἶμαι ἢ κοινωνίᾳ τοῦ θείου πνεύματος· τῆς γὰρ αὐτῆς δυνάμεως δεῖ προφητεύουσί τε καὶ ἀκροωμένοις προφητῶν·); 15.183–16.184: "That man was truly paradise for us...That one [is] truly a paradise of luxury, he [is] true joy and luxury" (παράδεισος ἡμῖν ὄντως οὗτος ἦν...Οὗτος παράδεισος ἀληθῶς τρυφῆς, αὕτη ἀληθὴς εὐφροσύνη καὶ τρυφή). On the tradition of the inspired interpreter of scripture, see Karen Jo Torjesen, "The Alexandrian tradition of the inspired interpreter," in L. Perrone (ed.), *Origeniana Octava: Origen and the Alexandrian Tradition/Origene e la Tradizione Alessantrina*, vol. I, BETL 166 (Leuven: Leuven University Press, 2003), pp. 287–299, who focuses on Alexandria though the broadly Platonic view that "like can know like."

[74] Adolf Knauber, "Das Anliegen der Schule des Origenes zu Cäsarea," *Münchener Theologische Zeitschrift* 19 (1968), 182–203. He is followed by Crouzel, *Origen*, pp. 27–28, and by Jacobsen, "Conversion," pp. 145–157, who alters Knauber's views somewhat (see below).

[75] Knauber, "Anliegen," p. 196: "Es handelt sich also bei der Origenesschule von Cäsarea um ein Unternehmen, das – wenigstens seiner Grundkonzeption und seiner innersten Zielsetzung nach – auf pagane (oder auch hellenistisch-synkretistische) Studenten ausgerichtet ist, die auf der Suche nach 'Weisheit' sind und die sie vielleicht anderswo – auf den Hohen Schulen der Zeit – bisher vergebens gesucht haben. Ihr Endziel sieht die Schule des Origenes (das geht aus der ganzen immanenten Tendenz hervor) in der Gewinnung solcher Kreise (von 'Philosophie'-Jüngern im Sinne der Zeitphilosophen) für das Christentum."

baptized, he would have needed to go to the church and enroll as a catechumen, a process wholly distinct from Origen's school.[76] It was, then,
effectively unconnected from the ecclesial community, though, of course,
the fact that Origen's teaching aimed at winning students for Christianity
indicates that the disconnect was not complete. In fact, the reworking of
Knauber's arguments by Anders-Christian Jacobsen shifts principally on
this point: contrary to Knauber's view, there may have been some overlap
between the Caesarean congregation and Origen's school.[77]

While there are certain strengths to this position, in my view it falls
down on at least three important points. First, Knauber and his followers
underestimate the debt to explicitly Christian (and, specifically, Origenist)
material in the *Oratio*. On the one hand, the genre of panegyric does
not allow for or encourage a comprehensive recounting of what Gregory
learned under Origen. He is speaking directly to fellow students and
the master himself, all of whom are well aware of the full extent of the
teaching.[78] On the other hand, even a cursory comparison with the above
discussion of catechesis and the journey of the soul highlights obvious
similarities: a movement from physical to spiritual knowledge through the
soul's progress; moral preparation as a crucial prerequisite for receiving
true teaching; an end goal of knowing God through spiritual exegesis
of scriptures.[79] As we noted, Gregory himself highlights the *telos* of theology in the school as well as the central importance of inspired spiritual
interpretation. Spiritual interpretation of scripture is a profoundly and
specifically Christian practice for Origen, which leads to the next point.

Second, Knauber's reading suggests that Origen was willing to pass
on esoteric theological ideas and to model spiritual interpretation to the
uninitiated. Certainly, Gregory highlights the emphasis on the moral life
of the soul in Origen's instruction, as Knauber and others note. But it is
difficult to imagine how Origen would have conceived of this apart from
baptism and the indwelling of the Spirit. In his rejoinder to Celsus, Origen
claims that, while philosophers may hawk their wares to just anyone,
Christians do not do so.[80] Christians restrict even initiation itself, in addition to the "mysteries," to the morally pure, a category Origen reserves

[76] Ibid., pp. 198, 196: "Gregor war vielmehr als Ungetaufter zu Origenes gekommen...Von
einer Aufnahme in die Kirche, von einer Taufe und von einer Teilnahme an den heiligen
Mysterien erfahren wir nichts"; "Begreiflicherweise brauchte in einer solchen 'Schule'
vorderhand von Katechumenat und Taufe noch nicht die Rede zu sein..."
[77] Jacobsen, "Conversion," pp. 150–151, 155.
[78] So Markschies, *Christian Theology*, p. 88.
[79] See Stefaniw, "Exegetical curricula," p. 284; Markschies, *Christian Theology*, p. 89.
[80] *Cels.* 3.50–51, cited and discussed in Chapter 2.3.7 above.

for those properly prepared and cleansed in baptism.[81] In his homilies on Jeremiah, discussed above, Origen extolls the importance of moral preparation before even elementary, pre-baptismal doctrinal instruction.[82] While he occasionally emphasizes that the gift of the Spirit is not inextricably linked with the act of baptism – since some like Simon Magus were baptized without really converting and did not receive the Spirit[83] – he reserves spiritual understanding of scripture for advanced believers.[84]

Third, Knauber's argument that Gregory came to Origen "unbaptized" appears to run against the indications of the *Oratio* itself. In the fifth section of his *Oratio*, Gregory recounts his biography up to the time of meeting Origen, beginning with his birth into an evidently pagan family with its inherited "superstition" (ὑπὸ πατρὶ δὲ δεισιδαίμονι; 5.48). After his father died and he became an orphan, however, Gregory made a beginning with the "true knowledge" (5.49). "For then," he says, "I was first converted to the saving and true word – how I don't know – more by compulsion than willingly. For what judgment did I have when I was fourteen?"[85] In his edition of the *Oratio*, Henri Crouzel considers this a reference merely to Gregory's first encounter with Christianity, and his translation maintains a vague quality with reference to the word μετετέθην.[86] In saying that he was converted, or "transferred," to the true Logos, however, Gregory appears to indicate that he had

---

[81] *Cels.* 3.59–61 and on pre-baptismal condemnation *Hom. in Iud.* 9.2.519, cited above (p. 133). See also A. Usacheva, "The exegetical requirements in Origen's late works: mystical and intellectual aspects of perfection according to Origen and his followers," in Anders-Christian Jacobsen (ed.), *Origeniana Undecima: Origen and Origenism in the History of Western Thought. Papers of the 11th International Origen Congress, Aarhus University*, BETL 279 (Leuven: Peeters, 2016), pp. 877–880; and Simonetti, *Origene esegeta*, p. 77–78, who notes the restriction of advanced teaching for the mature.

[82] *Hom. in Jer.* 5.13.2, discussed above (pp. 133–134), and see the surrounding material.

[83] *Hom. in Ezek.* 6.5 (text in Marcel Borret (ed.), *Origène. Homélies sur Ezéchiel*, SC 352 (Paris: Cerf, 1989)); see als Hällström, "Initiation," pp. 1004–1005. The example of Cornelius in Acts 10 serves as Origen's positive example of the distinction between baptism and receiving the Spirit; see *Hom. in Num.* 3.1.

[84] On this, see generally Torjesen, *Hermeneutical Procedure*, among others, and the extension of her work in Elizabeth Ann Dively Lauro, *The Soul and Spirit of Scripture within Origen's Exegesis* (Boston: Brill, 2005).

[85] *Or. pan.* 5.50: τότε γὰρ πρῶτον ἐπὶ τὸν σωτήριον καὶ ἀληθῆ μετετέθην λόγον, οὐκ οἶδ᾽ ὅπως, κατηναγκασμένος μᾶλλον ἤπερ ἑκών. Τίς γὰρ ἐμοὶ κρίσις ἦν, ὄντι τεσσαρεσκαιδεκαετεῖ;

[86] Crouzel, *Remerciement*, pp. 50–51, 117: "...la première rencontre de Grégoire avec le Christianisme..."; "Je passais du côté du Verbe." The translation in Michael Slusser (ed. and trans.), *St. Gregory Thaumaturgus. Life and Works*, Fathers of the Church 98 (Washington, D.C.: Catholic University of America Press, 1998), p. 99, is "I was turned over to the saving and true Word" though Slusser does not resolve the question of whether or not Gregory was baptized prior to meeting Origen.

become a Christian.[87] Gregory highlights the force of the passive form here, rendered actively in Crouzel's translation ("je passais"),[88] when he vacillates about his agency in conversion: looking back from the vantage point of maturity and further study he is able to wonder whether he had the intellectual and moral fortitude to make such a judgment on his own and, as he does a bit later, to attribute his good fortune to divine providence, which allowed him to become a Christian just at the age when youthful ignorance and indiscretion become culpable moral deficiencies (5.52). In the early third century, a conversion to the "salvific and true word" – a conversion to Christianity in the complete sense – was normally attended by baptism; it was not until completing that ritual that one could rightly say they had been "transferred." If my reading of Gregory's biographical account is correct, then, he came to Origen as a baptized though immature and undereducated Christian. In other words, Gregory came to Origen as one of the *simpliciores* and Origen convinced him that a philosophical approach to the Christian life is superior. As in all his work, Origen here too was principally concerned with guiding simple believers in their souls' journeys to God by means of philosophy and spiritual interpretation of scripture.[89]

This still leaves Origen's school in a somewhat ambiguous relationship with the Church. On the one hand, Gregory's account suggests that Origen's students were philosophically inclined Christians, though Gregory's own biography does not necessitate that *every* student was a Christian, any more than one can be sure that every student had equal access to the advanced spiritual interpretation. If there were non-Christian students, then no doubt Knauber and Jacobsen would be right that Origen saw his teaching in those cases as somehow directed toward that person's

---

[87] See the brief comments in Gemeinhardt, "In Search," p. 96. A similar argument has been made by Konstantinos M. Fouskas, Γρηγόριος ὁ Νεοκαεσαρείας Επίσκοπος ὁ Θαυματυργός *(ca. 211/3–270/5)* (Athens: University of Athens Press, 1969), pp. 69–70, though I have not had access to the work. It is cited in Slusser, *Gregory*, p. 2 n. 6.

[88] A similarly active rendering is given by Peter Guyot; see Guyot and Klein, *Oratio*, p. 141: "Damals trat ich nämlich zum ersten Mal zu dem heilbringenden und wahren Wort über."

[89] See the comments on this point in Markschies, *Christian Theology*, p. 89. The moral and exegetical emphasis in Origen's pedagogical vision is in keeping with broader exegetical trends in second- and third-century philosophical circles, particularly among the Neoplatonists: see Scholten, "Katechetenschule," pp. 22–29; Markschies, *Christian Theology*, p. 70; Stefaniw, "Exegetical curricula," pp. 281–294; Fürst, "Exegesis and philosophy," pp. 16–17; and the now classic work of Hadot, *Philosophy*, pp. 71–72, 82–89, 100–101, and *passim*.

conversion.[90] Moreover, it appears that the school itself was not funded by the Caesarean church and so was in that sense "independent."[91] For present purposes, then, the most important element of Origen's academic context is that it provided the occasion for him to offer advanced spiritual teachings. It may be that the interpretations in his commentaries reflect his teaching among the philosophically advanced students, as has sometimes been argued.[92]

5.2.2 Origen's Caesarean Homilies

Alongside his work with philosophically inclined students in his school, we noted earlier that Origen offered daily sermons on the Old and New Testaments to the church in Caesarea.[93] The level of moral, intellectual, and spiritual progress varied among the parishioners addressed, ranging from church officials to new catechumens and including all levels of the faithful in between.[94] In his sermons we find the full range of Origen's care for his fellow Christians, accommodating himself to the ignorant

---

[90] As Knauber points out, Eusebius' account of Origen's activities in Alexandria does not involve restricting his philosophy instruction to a Christian audience; Knauber, "Anliegen," p. 201.

[91] See the discussion in Markschies, *Christian Theology*, pp. 76–91.

[92] See Heine, *Origen*, p. 190; Jacobsen, "Conversion," pp. 154–156; and the earlier proposals in Simonetti, "Origene," p. 299–308. Christoph Markschies, "Origenes und die Kommentierung des paulinischen Römerbriefs: einige Bermerkingen zur Rezeption von antiken Kommentartechniken im Christentum des dritten Jahrhunderts und ihrer Vorgeschichte," in *Origenes und sein Erbe: Gesammelte Studien*, TU 160 (Berlin: De Gruyter, 2007), pp. 63–90, notes that Origen's commentary on Romans is oriented toward the pedagogical growth of the reader – even the advanced reader, it evidently presumes – which fits with the concerns outlined by Gregory Thaumaturgus above.

[93] See the discussion in 5.1 above. On this aspect of Origen's work, see generally Monaci Castagno, *Origene predicatore*; Markschies, "Erwägungen," pp. 35–62; Heine, *Origen*, pp. 171–187; and Morwenna Ludlow, "Origen as Preacher and Teacher: A Comparison of Exegetical Methods in His Writings on Genesis and The Song of Songs," in William John Lyons and Isabella Sandwell (eds.), *Delivering the Word: Preaching and Exegesis in the Western Christian Tradition* (Sheffield: Equinox, 2012), pp. 45–61. Origen's devotion to the wellbeing and progress of the church is emphasized by Stefan C. Alexe, "Origène et l'Église visible," in R. J. Daly (ed.), *Origeniana Quinta*, BETL 105 (Leuven: Peeters, 1992), pp. 467–473.

[94] See Monaci Castagno, *Origene predicatore*, pp. 68, 83; Young, *Biblical Exegesis*, pp. 242–243; and R. P. C. Hanson, *Allegory and Event: A Study of the Sources and Significance of Origen's Interpretation of Scripture* (Louisville: Westminster John Knox, 2002), p. 213, who speaks of Origen's accommodation to "the average man in the pew."

and morally flaccid, applying scripture for the progress of their souls, exhorting catechumens and believers alike, and alluding to higher planes of spiritual meaning to which all should aspire.[95]

As Karen Torjesen has demonstrated, Origen's exegetical method in his homilies followed a general pattern, adjusted somewhat in response to the specifics of the text being interpreted, which took the hearer from the letter of the text to the spiritual meaning for the believer.[96] According to Torjesen, the three levels of meaning in biblical texts corresponding with the human body, soul, and spirit, famously expounded in book 4 of *De principiis*, are primarily oriented around the stages of the soul's development. That is, these are not, strictly speaking, three levels of meaning inherent in every text but rather three modes of interpretation which are keyed for different purposes.[97] In practice, Origen often moves very quickly from a literal to a spiritual interpretation of a text, and the specific focus of the spiritual content is shaped by who is listening. It is in this larger homiletical/hermeneutical context that we can better understand Origen's regular appeal to catechumens in his homilies.[98] They are in need of an interpretation that speaks to their specific point of progress so

---

[95] This comes out particularly clearly in the discussion of different songs in *Hom. in Cant.* 1.1 (in Baehrens, *Samuel, Hohelied und Propheten*); note the comments on this point in Monaci Castagno, *Origene predicatore*, pp. 66–67, and Ludlow, "Origen as Preacher," pp. 48–58. The entire discussion in Markschies, "Erwägungen," pp. 35–62, constitutes a defense of this against previous evaluations of Origen's homilies as both unsuitable for uneducated Christians and unrepresentative of Origen's full intellectual prowess: e.g., in Hanson, *Allegory and Event*, pp. 185–186, and Schadel, *Jeremiahomilien*, pp. 22–23, among others.

[96] Torjesen, *Hermeneutical Procedure*, pp. 22–48 and *passim*; see also the outline of Origen's homiletic structures in Markschies, "Erwägungen," pp. 43–44, and the detailed discussion in Monaci Castagno, *Origene predicatore*, pp. 95–127. Abbattista, *Origene legge Geremia*, pp. 280–288, gives examples of different modes of scriptural interpretation – anagogical, spiritual, figural – and considerations of textual obscurity and spiritual progress from Origen's homilies on Jeremiah.

[97] Torjesen, *Hermeneutical Procedure*, p. 41. Part of the strength of Torjesen's argument is that it neatly sidesteps the fact that in practice Origen normally only discusses two meanings, the literal and the spiritual, ignoring the "soul" reading. Dively Lauro, *The Soul and Spirit of Scripture within Origen's Exegesis*, whose view bears similarities with the earlier work of Schadel, *Jeremiahomilien*, pp. 46–50, has argued against Torjesen that Origen should be read as indicating three levels of meaning and that all three are normally present in his exegesis, though I remain unconvinced by this refinement. Mitchell, *Paul, the Corinthians*, p. 48 argues similarly to Torjesen, but approaches Origen's discussion from the perspective of rhetorical composition.

[98] Of course, the dialogical structure of Origen's homilies means that he appeals to other groups as well, alongside the catechumens, as he adapts himself to their abilities; see Markschies, "Erwägungen," pp. 46–47, and Cocchini, *Il Paolo*, p. 128.

he exhorts them to come forward in penance,[99] to make haste and follow through with baptism,[100] to let Christ enter them,[101] etc. On the other hand, and occasionally in the same homily, Origen addresses the believers at a different level of development with another level of meaning.[102] Whether or not Pierre Nautin is correct that Origen's Old Testament homilies were primarily directed at catechumens and functioned as official catechetical instruction, they nevertheless highlight his constant contact with and concern for catechumens. Although Origen was certainly most interested in spiritual knowledge, he accommodated himself to the *simipliciores*, whether catechumens or baptized believers.[103]

These two institutional frameworks – the school and the Church – are also reflected in Origen's account of the Christian community. Like Clement of Alexandria before him, Origen viewed the Christian life as one of constant progress toward perfection.[104] In principle, he desires that all believers will strain to progress in the journey of the soul, through the stages of increasing perfection revealed in Israel's journey to the promised land. On the other hand, he is at times quite blunt about the fact that some simply will not, or cannot, ascend to the higher stages of spiritual learning.[105] From the beginning of his career to the end, Origen was in contact with those "who seemed somewhat dull in the investigation of divine knowledge" because, in his view, "it is possible that not every mind is capable of being renewed so as to be broadened by the understanding of knowledge."[106] As in the case of different levels of

---

[99] *Hom. in Luc.* 21.4.

[100] *Hom. in Jesu* 9.9.355.

[101] *Hom. in Cant.* 2.7.

[102] E.g., *Hom. in Jesu* 9.9; *Hom. in Cant.* 2.7. See also the comments on Origen's construal of the *simpliciores* and the relationship between that category and other groups within the church in Monaci Castagno, *Origene predicatore*, p. 91 (restated more recently in Adele Monaci Castagno, "Semplici," in Adele Monaci Castagno (ed.), *Origene dizionario. La cultura, il pensiero, le opere* (Roma: Città Nuova, 2000), p. 442).

[103] Of course, Origen's interest in the spiritual sense was not opposed to the literal, as Torjesen's model discussion makes clear; see also Markschies, "Erwägungen," pp. 48–49.

[104] At the end of his classic work, Walther Völker highlighted the fact that for Origen even the perfect are described as "followers" (*Nachfolgern*) because final perfection is not attained in this life; Völker, *Vollkommenheitsideal*, pp. 215–228; see also Vakula, "Spiritual progress," pp. 45–59.

[105] See *Comm. in Matt.* 15.6: "...The many in the church are infants and nurslings in Christ..." (...οἱ πολλοὶ τῆς ἐκκλησίας ἐν Χριστῷ νήπιοι καὶ θηλάζοντες...).

[106] Citations from *Princ.* praef. 3 (cited above) and *Comm. in Rom.* 9.1.717 (trans. from Scheck 9.1.13: "Potest tamen fieri ut non omnis sensus in hoc possit renouari ut agnitione scientiae dilatetur." See further the discussion of "milk" and "meat" in 5.3.2 below.

scriptural interpretation, despite the fact that he can speak of three or four levels of believers within the church, in practice he often reverts to two groups, the simple and the advancing, a two-tier image of the church into which his more differentiated pictures easily fit.[107] It is important for Origen that these spiritual levels are permeable, especially in the direction of spiritual progress; they remain a constant concern for the teacher who must accommodate himself to the listeners.[108] As we have already noted, Origen himself was engaged with people across the spectrum of spiritual progress, bringing basic instruction to the basic and esoteric mysteries to the advanced.

But, while there would always be those beginning their Christian life in the Church, there was evidently a group of Christians who rejected Origen's account of spiritual progress, evidently preferring a less philosophically elaborated faith.[109] For Origen, while basic faith is certainly sufficient for entry into the Christian life – being associated with baptismal confessions and basic doctrinal affirmations – it serves as the foundation from which knowledge is to be sought, a stage to be superseded.[110]

---

[107] Compare the three levels of believers in *Princ.* 4.2.4 (11) (the fleshly simple believers, those who have made considerable progress, and the "perfect" person), the four levels in *Hom. in Jesu* 9.9 ("women, infants, and proselytes" as stages of initial growth before attaining manhood) and the comments in Simonetti, "Origene," p. 300 with n. 5, and Hällström, *Fides Simpliciorum*, p. 20.

[108] See the comments in Markschies, "Erwägungen," pp. 52–54, on the theme of "repentance" (Umkehr) and "conversion" (Bekehrung) in Origen's homilies, urging his listeners toward spiritual growth; see also Monaci Castagno, *Origene predicatore*, pp. 214–220, on Origen's exhortations to penitence. Hanson, *Allegory and Event*, p. 214, argues against this permeability on the basis of Origen's "rationalism," which knows that "the intellectual will outstrip the uneducated believer in his spiritual progress, and, as far as I can see, outstrip him, at least in this world, permanently." This, however, is to confuse Origen's pragmatic realization of the limits of human capacities, on which I agree with Hanson, with the *principle* of spiritual growth that undergirds his exhortations toward growth and understanding.

[109] Hällström, *Fides Simpliciorum*, pp. 8, 94, notes that these *simplices* are "treated by Origen as theological opponents, as critics of this exegesis and challenges of his speculations," and that "[t]he doctrines held by the simplices coincide remarkably well with the Rule of the Faith…In fact Origen explicitly confirms the relation between the teaching of the Church and the belief of the multitudes." Note, however, that Markschies, "Erwägungen," p. 58, has suggested that such a rejection of Origen's hermeneutic does not necessarily indicate that the *simpliciores* were in fact uneducated; rather, it may only indicate that they held to a different hermeneutical theory that devalued the kind of speculative theology in which he engaged.

[110] The high value of basic faith is noted in *Frag. 1 Cor.* 8: "We received power from believing in Jesus 'Christ crucified.' And insofar as we lack this faith, we are left wanting in the ability to have the things from God in ourselves" (Δύναμιν ἐλάβομεν ἀπὸ τοῦ πιστεύειν εἰς Ἰησοῦν Χριστὸν ἐσταυρωμένον· καὶ ὅσον λείπομεν ἐν τῇ πίστει <ταύτῃ>, τοσοῦτον λειπόμεθα

The elementary doctrines available to all, which he enumerates in the preface to *De principiis*, remain unexamined at this level, the journey of the soul barely begun.[111] Origen considers these *simpliciores* to be intellectually deficient, possessing only "bare faith" (ψιλὴ πίστις) and reading scripture with an unhelpful literalism.[112] For him, however, philosophical scriptural interpretation is a *sine qua non* for being a mature believer. "[T]he all engrossing activity that demarcates mature Christians from the simpler is their unreserved commitment to scriptural scholarship."[113]

The theme of literalism here is important and will be addressed further below. For now, the discussion of Origen's institutional contexts is sufficient for setting up what follows. While in Caesarea, he was engaged in both elementary homiletical instruction and advanced philosophical teaching and spiritual interpretation of scriptures. Different levels of meaning in the scriptures correspond for him to different levels of spiritual progress among believers, for whom or by whom the text is being interpreted. Catechumens featured clearly as part of Origen's homiletical context and perhaps filtered into some of his philosophical teaching, though, if so, likely only at its initial stages. As will become clear below, his view of Paul is shaped by his institutional commitments and needs, even as the Apostle's writings shape Origen's own approach to scripture and the Christian life.

5.3 ORIGEN'S PAUL

Origen's Paulinism was, as Francesca Cocchini put it, "particularly complex."[114] On the one hand, Paul holds a privileged hermeneutical place

ἐν τῇ δυνάμει τοῦ ἔχειν ἐν ἑαυτοῖς τὰ ἀπὸ τοῦ θεοῦ). See Harl, *Fonction révélatrice*, pp. 261–262, 300; Crouzel, *Origen*, p. 113; Heither, *Translatio religionis*, p. 68.

[111] Origen also makes room for a more developed faith at the end of spiritual progress, a faith which believes only what is true; see *Comm. in Iohan.* 32.15.175–179 and the succinct account in Martens, *Origen and Scripture*, pp. 101–106.

[112] See *Hom. in Gen.* 6.1 and the account of the *simpliciores* in Hällström, *Fides Simpliciorum*, pp. 11, 25–26, 41–43, etc. for the themes here. See also the more recent and largely congruent summary in Monaci Castagno, "Semplici," pp. 440–443, building on her earlier arguments in Monaci Castagno, *Origene predicatore*.

[113] Martens, *Origen and Scripture*, p. 91, who is commenting on the opening of Origen's John commentary; see also Mitchell, *Paul, the Corinthians*, p. 57, who argues that Origen sees "human life" in "exegetical terms" involving a need to develop the ability to see knowledge which is "veiled."

[114] She goes on to note that it is also "at least in certain respects, contradictory"; Cocchini, *Il Paolo*, p. 27. Markschies, "Origenes und Paulus," p. 371 and *passim*, accounts for these tensions and inconsistencies with a "model of a fluid network of ordered-knowledge," as opposed to a strictly consistent knowledge hierarchy. Cocchini's study remains the

within Origen's system of thought, the principal warrant for and example of spiritual interpretation of scripture, which we have already seen is only available to the mature believer.[115] Paul spoke wisdom to the perfect, just as Origen endeavored to do in his school with students such as Gregory. On the other hand, Paul was the apostle of Christian pedagogy, exemplifying pastoral condescension, accommodation to those still in need of "milk," himself stooping to engage in that most fundamental work of preparing catechumens' souls for true doctrine and baptism.[116] He was "empowered to be the minister of the new covenant" who "fulfilled the gospel" across the Mediterranean in the churches he "taught."[117] Although his was a vocation better than that of a "baptizer," nevertheless he did not refrain from such a task when necessary for those in his care.[118] In other words, Origen's Paul engaged in a ministry that looked remarkably like Origen's own.[119] In what follows, I will first illuminate the way in which Origen cast Paul and read his letters within a catechetical framework linked with his broader vision of pedagogical progress. I will then examine his "milk" and "meat" imagery in more detail to highlight the way in which Origen's two-tier vision of the Church shaped his appropriation of this imagery in a way that differs from his predecessor, Clement of Alexandria.

---

most full and insightful treatment of Origen's understanding of Paul, though she does not note the connection with the catechumenate nor does she provide any sustained discussion of Origen's institutional context as a contributing factor.

[115] On the hermeneutical priority of Paul, see Cocchini, *Il Paolo*, pp. 117–118, the works cited at p. 127 n. 7 above, and see further below.

[116] See the discussion in Mitchell, "Pauline accommodation," pp. 209–212, and Monaci Castagno, *Origene predicatore*, p. 67, who notes Origen's appeal to Moses and Christ as paradigmatic interpreters alongside Paul.

[117] *Comm. in Iohan.* 5.3.1: "Now, the one who was empowered to be the minister of the new covenant – not of the letter but the Spirit – Paul, who fulfilled the gospel from Jerusalem and around as far as Illyricum, did not write to every church he taught" ('Ὁ δὲ ἱκανωθεὶς διάκονος γενέσθαι τῆς καινῆς διαθήκης, οὐ γράμματος, ἀλλὰ πνεύματος, Παῦλος, ὁ πεπληρωκὼς τὸ εὐαγγέλιον 'ἀπὸ Ἱερουσαλὴμ καὶ κύκλῳ μέχρι τοῦ Ἰλλυρικοῦ', οὐδὲ πάσαις ἔγραψεν αἷς ἐδίδαξεν ἐκκλησίαις). In context, Origen is setting up a contrast between his long discourse on John and the greater apostle's brevity in writing. For Pauline epithets in Origen more broadly, see Heiser, *Paulusinszenierung*, pp. 127–155; see also Cocchini, *Il Paolo*, pp. 54–65.

[118] *Frag. in 1 Cor.* 5 (cited below); see also the description of Paul's baptism of John's disciples in Acts 17; *Comm. in Iohan.* 6.33.168. On the tradition of privileging preaching over baptism and interpretations of 1 Cor. 1:17, see Edsall, "(Not) baptizing Thecla," pp. 235–260.

[119] See the comments in Cocchini, *Il Paolo*, p. 61, and now Strawbridge, *Pauline Effect*, pp. 50–51.

5.3.1 A Catechetical Paul: Cultivating the Soul

As we saw above, the first steps of the Christian journey of the soul consist in an initial conversion – belief in the incarnation, for instance, in *Hom. in Num.* 27.3.2 – which is a response to the preaching of the gospel. As Origen states at the beginning of his commentary on John, Paul preached the gospel, a message that "presents Christ's sojourn and prepares for his *parousia* and imparts it [*viz.* his *parousia*] into the souls of those who desire to receive the one standing at the door."[120] In other words, for Origen Paul's preaching involved a change in the souls of his listeners. Moreover, as Origen notes in commenting on 1 Corinthians 1:17, this preaching was specifically his "lot" as Apostle to the Gentiles, a superior calling, over and above other related tasks such as baptism. "To preach the gospel is better than baptizing. And since Paul knew that some were set apart for baptizing, he was thankful to have a better lot than baptizing."[121] This gospel preaching was not necessarily limited to the initial conversion, however, since Origen notes that "the things he proclaimed and said are also the things he wrote" to churches of baptized believers.[122]

According to Origen, Paul's ministry also included specifically *catechetical* work: preparing the souls of catechumens for learning true doctrine and baptism. Commenting on Paul's defense of his apostolic right to material support in 1 Corinthians 9:9–11, Origen highlights the catechetical labor that Paul undertook on behalf of the Corinthians, building on Paul's statement that Deuteronomy's injunctions about muzzling oxen are written for the believers.

Surely, then, these things have been said for us who have received the new covenant, and have been written about people, if the statement is understood spiritually according to the divine apostle. But what is the meaning of "that the one who plows should plow in hope and the one who threshes does so in hope of sharing?" Paul, the farmer, plows the soul of the catechumen, making prepared

---

[120] *Comm. in Iohan.* 1.4.25–26, cited above (p. 128 n. 9).

[121] *Frag. in 1 Cor.* 5: Μεῖζον τὸ εὐαγγελίζεσθαι τοῦ βαπτίζειν· καὶ ἐπειδὴ ᾔδει ὁ Παῦλος ἀφωρισμένους τινὰς πρὸς τὸ βαπτίζειν, εὐχαριστεῖ ἐπὶ τῷ κρείττονα κλῆρον ἔχειν τοῦ βαπτίζειν. *Comm in Matt.* 15.6 interprets bringing children to Jesus (Matt. 19:14–15) as a reference to bringing the immature to Christ, who then remain "infants" in him until they grow into maturity. Paul's ministry in Corinth is taken as the model of this practice. For the frequency statistics and discussion of Origen's philological reading of ἀπόστολος/ ἀποστέλλειν in *Comm. in Iohan.* 32.17.205–208, see Heiser, *Paulusinszenierung*, pp. 135–136.

[122] *Comm. in Iohan.* 1.4.25, quoted above, p. 128.

fallow land in their soul in accordance with the divine Jeremiah who declares to them, "Prepare fallow lands for yourselves" for the reception of seeds, obviously, about which it is written, "A sower went out to sow." And after sowing the new things he [*viz.* Paul] says, "I keep an eye on the seeds lest the 'birds of heaven' come and take the planted seed. And whenever it bears fruit and produces fruits of righteousness and when it is already 'white for the harvest,' it is permitted for me to take the rest. For he will not be offended whenever he remembers how much I toiled so that I might plow his soul, so that I could sow, how much I persisted until his matured seed came the threshing floor. And that is why it is permitted for me to take food from him. But I will not at all make use of this power, but I do this thing 'in hope' of offering the produce to the master. For I am a farmer, not so that I might take the things owed to God into my own storehouses."[123]

This small fragment from Origen's work on 1 Corinthians contains nearly the whole of his view of Paul *in nuce*.[124] Paul serves here as a model for an ecclesial reading of scripture, understanding the spiritual meaning of the old covenant for those in the new covenant.[125] As Origen puts it elsewhere, Paul teaches believers how to read scriptures in a way befitting Christians.[126] In the present passage, 1 Corinthians 9:9–11 does not receive a spiritual interpretation but rather a straightforward rhetorical expansion. Origen first supplies the meaning of the passage: Paul is the one who plows in hope in his preparation of catechumens' souls. This is followed by two scriptural passages that help interpret Paul's statement, followed by a short statement in the voice of Paul incorporating the broader scriptural resonances within his own comments on plowing in hope. Given Origen's link elsewhere between agricultural imagery and

---

[123] *Frag. in 1 Cor.* 41 (text in Jenkins, "Origen," pp. 511–512): Οὐκοῦν δι' ἡμᾶς τοὺς τὴν καινὴν διαθήκην παρειληφότας εἴρηται ταῦτα, καὶ περὶ ἀνθρώπων γέγραπται, πνευματικῶς τοῦ ῥητοῦ νοουμένου κατὰ τὸν θεῖον ἀπόστολον. τίς δὲ ὁ νοῦς; Ὅτι ὀφείλει ἐπ' ἐλπίδι ὁ ἀροτριῶν ἀροτριᾶν καὶ ὁ ἀλοῶν ἐπ' ἐλπίδι μετέχειν. ἀροτριᾷ Παῦλος ὁ γεωργὸς κατηχουμένου ψυχήν, νεώματα ποιῶν ἐν τῇ ψυχῇ αὐτοῦ κατὰ τὸν θεῖον Ἰερεμίαν τὸν φάσκοντα αὐτοῖς Νεώσατε ἑαυτοῖς νεώματα, πρὸς ὑποδοχὴν δηλονότι σπερμάτων, περὶ ὧν γέγραπται Ἐξῆλθεν ὁ σπείρων τοῦ σπεῖραι. καὶ μετὰ τοῦ σπεῖραι τὰ νεωθέντα Ἐπιτηρῶ, φησί, τὰ σπέρματα, μήποτε ἐλθόντα τὰ πετεινὰ τοῦ οὐρανοῦ ἄρῃ τὸν σπόρον· καὶ ὅταν καρποφορήσῃ καὶ ποιήσῃ καρποὺς δικαιοσύνης καὶ ὅτ<ε> λευκή ἐστιν ἤδη πρὸς θερισμόν, ἔξεστί μοι λοιπὸν λαβεῖν. οὐ γὰρ σκανδαλισθήσεται ἐπὰν μνησθῇ ὅσα κέκμηκα, ἵνα αὐτοῦ τὴν ψυχὴν ἀροτριάσω, ἵνα σπείρω, πῶς ἐπέμεινα μέχρις οὗ ἔλθῃ ὁ σπόρος αὐτοῦ τελειωθεὶς ἐπὶ τὴν ἅλω. καὶ διὰ τοῦτο λαμβάνειν μοι ἔξεστιν ἀπ' αὐτοῦ τροφάς. ἀλλ' οὐ πάντως κέχρημαι τῇ ἐξουσίᾳ, ἀλλ' ἐπ' ἐλπίδι τοῦτο ποιῶ, παραστῆσαι τὸ γέννημα τῷ οἰκοδεσπότῃ· γεωργὸς γάρ εἰμι· οὐχ ἵνα τὰ ὀφειλόμενα ἀποδοθῆναι τῷ θεῷ εἰς τὰς ἐμὰς λάβω ἀποθήκας.

[124] This passage is unfortunately not discussed by Cocchini.

[125] Origen also appears to allude to Rom. 7:14 here – οἴδαμεν γὰρ ὅτι ὁ νόμος πνευματικός ἐστιν – which is an important passage for justifying his spiritual approach to scripture; see Cocchini, *Il Paolo*, pp. 125–126.

[126] *Hom. in Gen.* 6.1, and see further below.

the early stages of the Christian life, it is not surprising that he carries this into Paul's mention of plowing and threshing. The connection is not simply with new Christians in general; Origen specifically makes the link here between Paul and the catechumenate.

In the first place, he portrays Paul as one who "cultivates" the catechumen's soul. As Origen goes on to speak in Paul's voice, it appears that he is portraying Paul himself as engaging in catechesis, in this way acting as a model for Origen's own contemporary practices.[127] On the other hand, Paul continues to cultivate catechumens' souls for Origen because Paul's gospel is contained in his letters. Second, Origen explicitly links Paul's work among the Corinthians with moral preparation for elementary doctrines outlined in *Hom. in Jer.* 5.13, discussed earlier.[128] Paul "plows, making prepared fallow land in their soul in accordance with the divine Jeremiah who declares to them, 'Prepare fallow lands for yourselves.'" As we saw above, this preparation involves tearing out vice and sin in order to make one's soul a hospitable environment for the "holy seeds." Paul, as voiced by Origen, explains that he maintains surveillance over the seeds he has planted, toiling until they are mature and harvested. In other words, he takes part in all parts of Christian development: he prepares the soul in catechesis, implants the teachings, and continues to watch them until the believer is mature.[129]

This link between Paul and initiatory agricultural imagery also appears in Origen's interpretation of 1 Corinthians 3:6, "I planted, Apollos watered but it is God who caused the growth." In both *Hom. in Jer.* 5.13.3 and *Frag. in 1 Cor.* 14, Origen interprets this passage by emphasizing the role of God in the work. "If Paul planted, he co-planted with the principal planter, God. If Apollos watered, he co-watered with the principal waterer, Christ. For God plants."[130] This is not taken by

---

[127] See Heiser, *Paulusinszenierung*, p. 141: "The gardener, Paul, is no longer a community founder [i.e. being presented as a missionary attempting to convert Gentiles], but rather he is an instructor for the newly converted." The link between "cultivation" and Jeremiah for Origen is related to his broader view of the prophet as concerned fundamentally with conversion and moral preparation (in Cocchini's terms, "denuncia di peccato e intivo alla conversione"; see Cocchini, *Origene*, p. 209).

[128] This connection is also noted in Heiser, *Paulusinszenierung*, p. 141.

[129] This point is related to Origen's theology of the Logos, whose cultivation in the soul through exegesis and reflection bridges Origen's views of reason and revelation; see Fürst, *Origenes*, pp. 96–97.

[130] *Frag. in 1 Cor.* 14: Εἰ ἐφύτευσεν ὁ Παῦλος, συνεφύτευσε τῷ φυτεύοντι προηγουμένως θεῷ· εἰ ἐπότισεν Ἀπολλώς, συνεπότισε τῷ προηγουμένως ποτίσαντι Χριστῷ· φυτεύει γὰρ ὁ θεός· In *Hom. in Jer.* 5.13.3, Origen states that the seeds planted by teachers do not grow on their own but are caused to grow by God.

Origen, however, to minimize the work of Paul and other teachers. In the context of *Hom. in Jer.* 5.13, he has just spoken of the work of teachers in uprooting sin and vice from the souls of those in their charge, and in *Princ.* 3.1.19 he uses 1 Corinthians 3:6 to credit Paul and Apollos with real work.[131] While later writers will explicitly interpret "planting" as preaching and "watering" as baptism, the way in which Origen relates it to Christian initiation remains largely implicit, only visible once situated within a broader understanding of how his agricultural images – plowing, sowing, watering, reaping – work within his catechetical context. Just as Paul plows, so he also plants the "good seeds" in the catechumens and oversees their growth.

The final point that arises from *Frag. in 1 Cor.* 41 is that Paul's model of spiritual interpretation relates to differentiated abilities to hear the word. Paul teaches a spiritual reading of the scriptures, moving from the bare letter of the text about oxen to a truth about the Church. Later in the same work, Origen spells out an epistemological distinction between catechumens and believers more strictly. Paul's "five words" that he would rather speak to instruct the Corinthians (ἵνα καὶ ἄλλους κατηχήσω; 1 Cor. 14:19) become words directed at the five senses when "speaking spiritually" (τὸ πνευματικῶς λαλεῖν), that is, "the catechetical word which comes through the five senses is prescribed for those who listen in church, as they are also being instructed by the five words."[132] While "catechumens" can only attend to the "bare instruction of the scriptures," the believers have an epistemological advantage such that they can rightly understand the explanations.[133] Origen knows, of course, that in practice some believers

---

[131] *Princ.* 3.1.19 (following a citation of 1 Cor. 3:6 and a brief emphasis on God's role): "And in this way our perfection does not come about from our own actions, nor indeed is it prepared without us, but God effects the majority of it" (οὕτω καὶ ἡ ἡμετέρα τελείωσις οὐχὶ μηδὲν ἡμῶν πραξάντων γίνεται, οὐ μὴν ἀφ' ἡμῶν ἀπαρτίζεται, ἀλλὰ θεὸς τὸ πολὺ ταύτης ἐνεργεῖ).

[132] *Frag. in 1 Cor.* 63: ὁ δὲ τῆς κατηχήσεως λόγος ὁ διὰ τῶν πέντε αἰσθήσεων ἐπὶ τῶν ἀκουόντων ἐν ἐκκλησίᾳ τέτακται, ὡς καὶ αὐτῶν ὑπὸ τῶν πέντε λόγων κατηχουμένων.

[133] Ibid.: "For those not knowing the clarity of what is said, but attending only to the bare instruction of the scriptures, are called catechumens. But those who hear the 'interval of the sounds' from scripture, they are not catechumens but believers" (οἱ γὰρ μὴ εἰδότες τὴν τῶν λεγομένων τρανότητα, ἀλλὰ μόνῃ τῇ ψιλῇ τῶν γραφῶν περιηχήσει προσέχοντες, κατηχούμενοι χρηματίζουσιν· οἱ δὲ τῆς τῶν φθόγγων διαστολῆς ἀκούοντες ἀπὸ τῆς γραφῆς οὗτοι οὐ κατηχούμενοι ἀλλὰ πιστοί). The phrase τῆς τῶν φθόγγων διαστολῆς is also borrowed from the context in 1 Cor. 14. The twofold structure of hearing – those who hear the bare words and those who can understand the explanations (drawing on a musical metaphor of distinguishing intervals) – is reflected in *Hom. in Jesu* 9.9.354–355, which refers to a two-step liturgical process which begins with a scriptural reading that is followed by an explanation. On Origen's distinction between the "flesh" of

are obtuse to the deeper meanings of scripture and some catechumens are already very receptive to the Spirit.[134] As we already noted, he thinks that some believers were "born prematurely."[135] What is important here is that Origen has again cast Paul into the mold of his catechetical and pedagogical framework, with particular reference to the epistemological distinction afforded believers. In his sixth homily on Genesis, Origen differentiates a literal "Jewish" understanding of scripture in contradistinction from a "Christian" understanding.[136] He famously writes, "If one wants to be a Christian and disciple of Paul, let him hear him saying that 'the Law is spiritual.'"[137] Paul's own ministry among the churches, as represented by his "five words," includes then both the spiritual interpretation of scripture and catechetical teaching directed toward the masses in the Church. This description of instructing catechumens fits neatly with Origen's experience of daily sermons on Old Testament books.

Elsewhere in his writings, Origen relates Paul to the catechumenate in a more indirect fashion, appropriating his letters in relation to his catechetical concerns, though not clearly depicting Paul's own ministry as such. Some of these passages have already been touched on above in the discussion of Origen's catechumenate. In his commentary on Song of Songs, he muses over the meaning of the rare term ἀμόρα, referring it to a certain kind of tree which can support the weak or wounded (here the bride, "wounded with love").[138] Origen contrasts the *amora* trees with the

---

scripture and the spiritual meaning reserved for the advanced, see Francesca Cocchini, "L'intelligenza spirituale della Scrittura come principio di teologia: la prospettiva dei Padri e in particolare di Origene," *Lateranum* 74, no. 1 (2008), 69–79, and Simonetti, *Origene esegeta*, pp. 19–20, among others noted above.

[134] See his discussion of Cornelius as an advanced catechumen in *Hom. in Num.* 3.1.

[135] *Comm. in Rom.* 8.9.690 (cited above, p. 136 n. 47).

[136] The distinction between Jewish and Christian interpreters for Origen reflects hermeneutical categories more than social or religious groups, not only because Origen is happy to draw on Philo for his interpretive approach but also because he recognizes that Paul was educated as a Jew under Gamaliel. This, he argues, actually gives Paul the academic pedigree that strengthens his importance as a hermeneutical guide; see esp. *Hom. in Lev.* 7.4.1–2. See the discussion in Monaci Castagno, *Origene predicatore*, pp. 97–100, and also Martens, *Origen and Scripture*, pp. 135–160, who emphasizes that Origen's critique of Jewish literalism focuses on specific instances of literal reading rather than the use of it across the board.

[137] *Hom. in Gen.* 6.1: "Si autem vult Christianus esse et Pauli discipulus, audiat eum dicentem quia 'lex spiritualis est.'"

[138] *Comm. in Cant.* 3.8. There is an insertion from Rufinus here, explaining the difference between the Greek and Latin texts of Song 2:5, though the subsequent discussion follows a typical trajectory for Origen, moving from the literal to the spiritual sense. The latter sense is only accessible if one is imbued with the same grace from God as was bestowed upon Solomon, the author.

following fruitful apple trees that cover the wounded bride, arguing that the former represent unfruitful trees (*arbores infructuosae*) which are as yet only fragrant. To identify the ecclesial referent for these fruitless, fragrant trees he turns to 1 Corinthians 1:2; they are "those who invoke the name of our Lord Jesus Christ in every place, theirs and ours."[139] Origen explains that they are those who invoke the name of Christ and are thereby fragrant without having yet produced fruit by coming to "faith" with "all confidence and freedom." According to Origen, with the help of Paul's description, "In this passage we can understand catechumens in the church, by whom in some way the church is 'strengthened.' "[140] Paul's letter, therefore, supplies the hermeneutical key that unlocks the mysterious reference to the *amora* trees. It does so, for Origen, because Paul himself has already spoken about the two groups within the church who "invoke the name" of Christ but yet remain in a place distinct from that of the believers: "their" place is not identical with "ours."

A particularly common combination, which will be explored in more detail below, is the link between Paul's milk and meat imagery and catechetical and pedagogical concerns. In his commentary on Matthew, Origen takes the opportunity afforded by the story of Jesus blessing the children (Matt. 19:13–15) to reflect on what this means for the church. "On one level, the story recorded happened back then: the children were brought to Jesus because the ones bringing them wanted him to lay hands on them and pray. On another level, one must know that there is not a time when children, that is, with respect to the soul, are not being brought to Jesus."[141] These souls are received by Christ as children in his care, some as "infants" (νήπια) and others as "nurslings" (θηλάζοντα), depending on their relative levels of maturity. The character of this group, even after their initial acceptance by Jesus, is identified with the help of Paul in 1 Corinthians 3:1: he was not able to speak to them as spiritual but rather as fleshly people, "as infants in Christ." Origen continues, "Such children as these are brought to Jesus both then and always," in a

---

[139] *Comm. in Cant.* 3.8, citing 1 Cor. 1:2: "qui invocant nomen Domini nostri Iesu Christi in omni loco ipsorum et nostrum."

[140] Ibid.: "In quo loco possumus nos catechumenos ecclesiae intelligere, super quos ex parte aliqua 'confirmatur' ecclesia." The phrase "super quos" points toward the supportive role of the catechumen-"trees" on top of which the bride leans. These are the ones who "non cum omni fiducia et libertate accedunt ad fidem."

[141] *Comm. in Matt.* 15.6: Τότε μὲν ἡ ἀναγεγραμμένη ἱστορία γέγονε τοῦ καὶ προσενηνέχθαι παιδία τῷ Ἰησοῦ, βουλομένων τῶν προσφερόντων ἐπιθεῖναι αὐτὸν τὰς χεῖρας αὐτοῖς καὶ προσεύξασθαι. ἰστέον δὲ ὅτι οὐκ ἔστιν ὅτε οὐ προσφέρεται παιδία τὴν ψυχὴν τῷ Ἰησοῦ.

process later referred to as "ecclesiastical catechesis," and are only able to drink "milk" rather than the solid food of the mature.[142] Paul's work with the Corinthian believers first required that he bring their infant souls to Christ, that he feed them on milk, and that he take care over their development. In other words, Paul's milk and meat imagery is leveraged by Origen here to explain the conversion and maturation process of believers as the spiritual sense of Jesus' engagement with the children in Matthew 19. Origen's catechetical Paul therefore also touches on his larger pedagogical vision in moving believers from milk to meat.

Alongside the focus of Origen's Romans commentary on the transferal of the true *religio* from Israel to the Church and from the physical to the spiritual plane, the text contains several catechetical readings of Paul's letter. Indeed, for Origen the Christian life itself is caught up in the dynamic of this transition from the physical to the spiritual.[143] Perhaps unsurprisingly, Paul's discussion of baptism in Romans 6 is one of the passages that elicits a connection with the catechumenate, here by way of pre-baptismal moral formation. Commenting on Paul's statement that all those "baptized into Christ Jesus were baptized into his death," Origen brings out the "more lofty understanding" ("per altiorem intellegentiam") which shows that, just as baptism with Christ symbolizes being buried with him in death, so one must first die to sin before undergoing such a burial. "Just as no living person is able to be buried with a dead person, so also no one who yet lives to sin is able to be buried in baptism with Christ who is dead to sin."[144] Baptism does not itself confer moral purity, as Origen shows with reference to Simon Magus elsewhere, but rather it presupposes a certain moral purity.[145] We have already seen that moral preparation of the soul is a crucial part of the catechetical process, for Origen, and here he finds further apostolic precedent for this in Paul's discussion of death and resurrection in baptism. Shortly after this, Origen again brings out the agricultural metaphor of being "planted together"

---

[142] Ibid.: "τὰ τοιαῦτα δὴ παιδία προσηνέχθη <καὶ> τότε καὶ ἀεὶ προσάγεται τῷ Ἰησοῦ"; see 15.7 for the κατήχησις ἐκκλησιαστικὴ καὶ διδασκαλία.

[143] On this dynamic in his Romans commentary, see Heither, *Translatio religionis*, pp. 63–64. On p. 259, she states: "Die Dynamik christlichen Lebens ist für Origenes eingebettet in den großen heilsgeschichtlichen Prozeß der *translatio religionis*. In jedem einzelnen muß die Herrschaft der Sünde und des Todes gebrochen werden, muß das Fleisch sterben, damit der Geist alles erfüllen kann. Origenes zeigt, was das konkret bedeutet."

[144] *Comm. in Rom.* 5.8.428 (Scheck 5.8.10): "sicut nemo uiuus potest sepelliri cum mortuo ita nemo qui adhuc uiuit peccato potest in baptismo consepelliri Christo qui mortuus est peccato…"

[145] See the comments of Heither, *Translatio religionis*, pp. 260–261.

with Christ in his death.[146] This reinforces the connection with catechetical moral preparation, which we have already seen is regularly associated with plowing and then planting the "holy seeds."

One particularly interesting passage on catechetical instruction arises from Rufinus' Latin translation of Origen's Romans commentary. Slightly before the discussion of death to sin, the text reads as follows.

> Indeed, it seems to me that the apostle did not begin this chapter idly when he said, "or are you ignorant?" Through it he showed that then, that is in the time of the apostles, it was not just the form of the mysteries that was taught to those who were baptized, as we see happening now, but also their power and rationale, and on the grounds that they knew and had learnt that those baptized are baptized into Christ's death…[147]

The cryptic phrase "not as we see happening now" reveals something of the peri-baptismal teaching advocated by the writer, as well as a criticism of some contemporary practice. What is particularly unclear here is whether the author of the aside was Origen or Rufinus.[148] If the sentiment originated with Origen, then this passage suggests two interesting things. First, it suggests that Origen advocated restricting the meaning of the mysteries, including baptism, until after the candidate had been baptized. His complaint is that proper theological instruction in the mysteries was not always adequately provided for neophytes, who did not receive the *virtus et ratio* for what had happened. This would be the earliest example of a practice common from the middle of the fourth century, in the form of post-baptismal mystagogical catechesis.[149] Second, and more to the

---

[146] *Comm. in Rom.* 5.9.431–432 (Scheck 5.9.1–2) following the citation of Rom. 6:5–6: "nunc complantatos nos ad mortis eius similitudinem…" See also the comments in Schelkle, *Paulus*, pp. 211–212, who notes the subsequent influence of Origen's agricultural reading of Paul's statements in connection with Christian initiation.

[147] *Comm. in Rom.* 5.8.426 (Scheck 5.8.8): "Mihi uero ne illud quidem otiose praemisisse in hoc capitulo uidetur apostolus quod dicit: 'aut nescitis?' Per quod ostendit quia tunc, hoc est apostolorum temporibus, non ut nunc fieri uidemus typus tantummodo mysteriorum his qui baptizabantur sed et uirtus eorum ac ratio tradebatur et tamquam scientibus et edoctis quia qui baptizantur in morte Christi baptizantur…"

[148] Of course, in its current form – written in Latin in the condensed version of Origen's much longer Greek commentary – the phrase is certainly from Rufinus. It remains possible in principle, though, that the sentiment underlying Rufinus' comment originated in the Greek text that he was translating.

[149] This is perhaps a reason to find more of Rufinus than Origen in this particular passage. The use of *mysterium* here evidently to refer to baptism (and affiliated rituals?) also fits well with a fourth-century context. It is possible that Origen is one of the first to shift the language of mystery in this way, though Rufinus' translation obscures and contracts the underlying Greek and makes such investigations notoriously difficult.

point for the present argument, the passage subtly implies that Paul's practice of peri-baptismal instruction corresponds with that of the mid-third century (or late fourth century, if it comes from Rufinus). Taken in the context of Origen's wider discussion of Romans 6, this completes the image of Paul as catechist: he emphasizes the importance of pre-baptismal moral purification, baptism itself as an initial "planting" with Christ, and contemporaneous or at least closely related teaching on the meaning of baptism itself.

The catechetical institution of Origen's day is therefore fully manifest in Paul's own ministry.[150] His favorite catechetical and baptismal imagery from the Old Testament, moreover, is also drawn from Paul's letters. We have seen repeatedly the presence of agricultural imagery in Origen's depiction of Paul's catechetical activity, an interpretive move warranted by Paul's own imagery in 1 Corinthians 3 and Romans 6. The interconnection with Jeremiah's injunction to "prepare the fallow lands" runs in both directions, both as something which prophetically supports Paul's descriptions of moral preparation and as that which already contains, on a spiritual level, the ecclesial exhortations that Paul later makes explicit.[151] Origen's other common image of Christian initiation, passing though the desert and the Red Sea (or Jordan river), is also given warrant in Paul's letters. Paul's comments in 1 Corinthians 10:1–4 – Israel in the desert was "baptized into Moses" in the Red Sea, after which they had spiritual food and drink even from "the rock" that was Christ – supplied the foundation for Origen's much more thorough allegory of the Exodus narrative. Origen explicitly grounds his catechetical or initiatory reading of Israel in the desert in Paul in several places and even extends this same theme to other river crossings.[152] Even Elijah's crossing of the Jordan river is read, through a Pauline lens, to signify the baptism into Christ the rock that was to come.[153] Origen's catechetical reading of Paul, then, not only

---

[150] See the comments of Kaczmarek, "L'*Exemplum* di Paulo," pp. 448–450, 454–455. On p. 450, she states "Per Origene ciò che Paolo fa e come lo fa, diventano, allora, *ipso facto, exemplum*, anche in casi meno evidenti."

[151] The presence of Paul's ecclesial interpretation is already noted in *Hom in Jer.* 5.132–133. Origen's view that the spiritual christological or ecclesial meaning is already present mystically in the prophetic utterance is well articulated in Boersma, *Sacramental Exegesis*, pp. 219–248.

[152] Origen appeals to Paul as the key for this interpretation in *Comm. in Iohan.* 6.44.227; *Hom. in Jesu* 5.1; *Hom. in Ex.* 5, etc. See the comments in Theresia Heither, *Predigten des Origenes zum Buch Exodus. Lateinisch-deutsch* (Münster: Aschendorff, 2008), pp. 14–15.

[153] *Comm. in Iohan.* 6.46.239–240: "... taking his cloak and rolling it he struck the water, which was divided at that very place and they both passed through, that is he and

involved depicting Paul's ministry in catechetical terms but also finding hermeneutical warrant in Paul's letters for ecclesial interpretations of the Old Testament which focused on initiation.[154]

Even so, as noted earlier, for Origen Paul was more than a catechetical figure; he was the apostle of spiritual progress. Paul desired that all move from "the shadow to the truth" ("ab hac umbra ad veritatem debemus adscendere") and modeled the way of progress in his spiritual interpretation of scripture.[155] Paul even demonstrated this journey of the soul in his own life, moving from persecutor of the Church to perfect apostle in a gradual progression.[156] In one of his homilies on Luke, Origen praises efforts toward spiritual progress to his listeners, and demonstrates his point with an appeal to Paul. "In this age, as I said, progress which entails growth of the soul is within our power. If, though, this is not sufficient testimony, then let us take another example from Paul."[157]

It is within this framework of spiritual progress that Origen most often deploys the milk and meat imagery from Paul. As a responsible teacher,

---

Elisha. For he became better suited to be taken up when he had been baptized in the Jordan, since Paul named the more incredible passing through water "baptism," as we said before...And if anyone takes offense at "he struck the water" because of the things we taught about the Jordan, namely that it is a figure of the Word who descended to our world [lit. descended our descent], let them read that for the apostle the 'rock' was Christ" (...λαβὼν τὴν μηλωτὴν αὐτοῦ καὶ εἰλήσας ἐπάταξεν τὸ ὕδωρ, ὅπερ διηρέθη ἔνθα καὶ ἔνθα, καὶ διέβησαν ἀμφότεροι, δηλονότι αὐτὸς καὶ ὁ Ἐλισαῖος. Ἐπιτηδειότερος γὰρ πρὸς τὸ ἀναληφθῆναι γεγένηται ἐν τῷ Ἰορδάνῃ βαπτισάμενος, ἐπεὶ τὴν δι' ὕδατος παραδοξοτέραν διάβασιν βάπτισμα, ὡς προπαρεθέμεθα, ὠνόμασεν ὁ Παῦλος....Ἐὰν δέ τις προσκόπτῃ τῷ "Ἐπάταξεν τὸ ὕδωρ" διὰ τὰ παραδεδομένα ἡμῖν περὶ τοῦ Ἰορδάνου, ὃς τύπος ἦν τοῦ τὴν κατάβασιν ἡμῶν καταβάντος λόγου, λεκτέον ὅτι παρὰ τῷ ἀποστόλῳ σαφῶς ἡ πέτρα Χριστὸς ἦν).

[154] See also the discussion in *Comm. in Cant.* 2.8, which draws on a now familiar range of Pauline texts.

[155] The quote is from *Hom. in Lev.* 7.4.1–2, which emphasizes Paul's concern for spiritual progress; *Hom. in Lev.* 8.5.3 introduces a spiritual interpretation with the exhortation "let us follow the path of understanding opened for us by the Apostle Paul" ("exsequemur, Apostolo nobis Paulo pandente intelligentiae viam").

[156] See *Comm. in Iohan.* 20.17.136–143 (and elsewhere in that commentary); *Hom. in Jer.* 1.16. See also the discussion in Cocchini, *Il Paolo*, pp. 36–37, who notes that Origen uses this Pauline biography to undermine "gnostic" arguments for the fixed nature of the soul; and comments in Heither, *Translatio religionis*, p. 32, and Heiser, *Paulusinzenierung*, p. 137.

[157] *Hom. in Luc.* 20.7 (followed by a compressed citation of Eph. 4:13; translation modified from Joseph T. Lienhard (ed. and trans.), *Origen: Homilies on Luke; Fragments on Luke*, Fathers of the Church 94 (Washington, D.C.: Catholic University of America Press, 1996)): "Huius, ut dixi, aetatis profectus, qui incrementum habet animae, in nostra est potestate. Si autem hoc non sufficit testimonium, etiam aliud de Paulo sumamus exemplum."

Paul did not simply deliver injunctions about spiritual progress from the heights of spiritual knowledge but he accommodated himself to different groups, the fleshly infants and the mature spiritual people. On the model of the high priest serving in the temple, "Paul knew to change robes, to use one with the people and another in service of holy matters."[158] According to Origen, Paul's actions in circumcising Timothy or observing the Law in Jerusalem in the book of Acts should be understood in this way. Paul, as one "who worships in spirit and in truth," nevertheless performs symbolically to accommodate himself to those enslaved to the symbol (or type) rather than the truth it signifies.[159] He can do this because he is guided by the goal of "elevating" the thoughts of his listeners beyond the "earthly teachings about the Law" to the spiritual meaning contained therein.[160] And, of course, Origen's depiction of Paul in this respect is also based in Paul's own self-presentation as a variable teacher (1 Cor. 9:19–21).[161]

Paul's gospel preaching – to know nothing but Christ crucified (1 Cor. 2:2) – is also situated within this framework of accommodation and spiritual development. Rather than taking Paul's claim as an indication of the singular and rhetorically sparse proclamation of the cross as the most profound gospel truth, Origen emphasizes Paul's statement that he was speaking to the Corinthians as infants, not capable of ingesting the solid food of the mysteries that he imparts to the mature (1 Cor. 2:6; 3:1–2).[162] Paul, as a paradigmatic teacher, worked with the symbolic and the physical in order to reach those for whom more elevated knowledge was inaccessible. The fact that the masses are ignorant is a crucial motivation for the accommodating teacher.

This is why we must live as a Christian in a spiritual and in a physical manner. And where it is necessary to preach the gospel "physically," claiming "to know

---

[158] *Hom. in Lev.* 4.6.4 (translation modified from Gary Wayne Barkley (ed. and trans.), *Origen: Homilies on Leviticus 1–16*, Fathers of the Church 83 (Washington, D.C.: Catholic University of America Press, 1990)): "Sic sciebat Paulus mutare stolas et alia uti ad populum, alia in ministerio sanctorum."

[159] *Comm. in Iohan.* 13.18.111: Τάχα <δὲ> δέδοταί ποτε εὐλόγως καὶ τὸν ἀληθινὸν προσκυνητὴν ἐν τῷ πνεύματι καὶ ἀληθείᾳ προσκυνοῦντα τυπικά τινα ποιεῖν, ἵνα τοὺς τῷ τύπῳ δεδουλωμένους οἰκονομικώτατα ἐλευθερώσας τῶν τύπων προσαγάγῃ τῇ ἀληθείᾳ, ὥσπερ φαίνεται Παῦλος ἐπὶ Τιμοθέου πεποιηκώς, τάχα δὲ καὶ ἐν Κεγχρεαῖς καὶ Ἱεροσολύμοις, ὡς ἐν ταῖς Πράξεσι τῶν ἀποστόλων γέγραπται. See also *Hom. in Num.* 6.1, noted by Völker, *Vollkommenheitsideal*, p. 278.

[160] *Comm. in Iohan.* 10.15.86: ἐπᾶραι μὲν ἡμῶν τὸ φρόνημα βουληθέντι ἀπὸ τῶν γηΐνων περὶ τοῦ νόμου δογμάτων οὐ πάνυ δὲ παραστήσαντι πῶς ταῦτα μέλλει γίνεσθαι.

[161] This connection is made by Origen in *Comm. in Iohan.* 10.7.28–31.

[162] On this see esp. Roukema, "La prédication," pp. 523–529, and the comments on perfection and interpretation in Usacheva, "Exegetical requirements," pp. 876–877.

nothing" among the fleshly except "Jesus Christ and him crucified," one must do so. But whenever they are found to be prepared in the spirit and bearing fruit in it, loving heavenly wisdom, one should share with them the word who returned from having been made flesh to what "he was in the beginning with God."[163]

Everything – from gospel preaching to moral formation to instruction in the mysteries – is done with a view to the spiritual progress of the listener or reader.[164] In this way, Origen's portrayal of Paul as a catechist is part and parcel of his concern for leading believers from the letter that kills to the Spirit that gives life.[165] Paul cultivates the soul of catechumens, plants holy seeds, baptizes (occasionally), and guides the neophytes in a growing spiritual understanding of scripture by supplying both a general hermen-eutical structure – the Law is spiritual and written "for our sake" – and warrant for specific spiritual readings.[166]

---

[163] *Comm. in Iohan.* 1.7.43: Διόπερ ἀναγκαῖον πνευματικῶς καὶ σωματικῶς χριστιανίζειν· καὶ ὅπου μὲν χρὴ τὸ σωματικὸν κηρύσσειν εὐαγγέλιον, φάσκοντα "μηδὲν εἰδέναι" <ἐν> τοῖς σαρκίνοις "ἢ Ἰησοῦν Χριστὸν καὶ τοῦτον ἐσταυρωμένον," τοῦτο ποιητέον· ἐπὰν δὲ εὑρεθῶσι κατηρτισμένοι τῷ πνεύματι καὶ καρποφοροῦντες ἐν αὐτῷ ἐρῶντές τε τῆς οὐρανίου σοφίας, μεταδοτέον αὐτοῖς τοῦ λόγου ἐπανελθόντος ἀπὸ τοῦ σεσαρκῶσθαι ἐφ' ὃ "ἦν ἐν ἀρχῇ πρὸς τὸν θεόν"; see also *Comm. in Iohan.* 1.9.58; 1.31.217.

[164] This applies to Origen's exegetical and rhetorical approach – as seen in Torjesen, *Hermeneutical Procedure*, and Mitchell, *Paul, the Corinthians*, pp. 48–49 – as well as to Origen's treatment of the literal meaning as pedagogically intended to lead to deeper knowledge, as noted by L. Lies, "Die 'Gottes würdige' Schriftauslegung nach Origenes," in G. Dorival and A. Le Boulluec (eds.), *Origeniana Sexta*, BETL 118 (Leuven: Peeters, 1995), pp. 367–369.

[165] See *Hom. in Lev.* 7.5.4–5 (Barkley trans.): "Know that they are figures written in the divine volumes and, for that reason, examine and understand what is said as spiritual and not as carnal. For if you receive those things as carnal, they wound you and do not sustain you. For even in the Gospels, it is 'the letter' that 'kills.'" ("Agnoscite quia figurae sunt, quae in divinis voluminibus scripta sunt, et ideo tamquam spiritales et non tamquam carnales examinate et intelligite quae dicuntur. Si enim quasi carnales ista suscipitis, laedunt vos et non alunt. Est enim et in evangeliis "littera," quae "occidit.") Origen explicitly applies his Pauline hermeneutic, movement from letter to spirit, to the Gospel text in *Hom. in Luc.* 14.84.

[166] Paul as exemplar of accommodation is seen also in *Comm. in Iohan.* 1.9.58, 1.31.217; and *Hom. in Ex.* 8.5 (Greek fragment, which corresponds only loosely with the Latin translation in that place). Origen appeals to Paul as a hermeneutical key in, e.g., *Princ.* 4.2.4–6 (note esp. 4.2.6 (13) and the appeal to 1 Cor. 10:11); *Hom. in Lev.* 1.4.3–4, 4.6.4, 7.4.1–2, 8.5.3; *Comm. in Cant.* prologue.3, etc. In addition to the specific exeget-ical warrant provided by Paul with reference to the Exodus narrative noted above, see also Origen's appeals to Paul for specific spiritual readings in, e.g., *Hom. in Cant.* 2.1; *Hom. in Lev.* 4.9.1, 7.1.8, 9.2.1, 15.2.3 See also Cocchini, *Il Paolo*, pp. 117–118, and Mitchell, *Paul, the Corinthians*, p. 57, among others.

5.3.2 "The many are infants…"

This point brings us to one of the more interesting elements of Origen's reading of Paul, which demonstrates both affinities and differences with that of Clement of Alexandria. We already noted above that Origen's Paul is tightly connected with his pedagogical vision for the progress of the soul and deeper scriptural understanding. In that context Origen regularly makes use of Paul's "milk" and "meat" imagery to designate the shifting "diet" of the maturing believer. Often he brings a cluster of passages into play which he uses to describe different dietary steps along the way to ingesting truly solid food: 1 Corinthians 2:1–5 and 3:1–3; Hebrews 5:12–14 (sometimes with 6:1); and Romans 14:2. His ninth homily on Joshua is a parade example of this reading, which also surfaces in numerous other places.[167]

Toward the end of that homily, Origen explains Joshua 8:34–35 – "Jesus read all the words of the Law…to the ears of the whole church of the sons of Israel and to the women and infants and proselytes"[168] – as referring to different groups within the Church. The "sons of Israel" are those who are "perfect" and can defend against the devil. To these "strong men" goes the "strong [or solid] food" (1 Cor. 3:2; Heb. 5:12–14).[169] Women, on the other hand, are those who are not yet able to produce useful things on their own but rather are limited to imitating the men.[170] These women are the ones who eat vegetables because they are weak (Rom. 14:2).[171] Infants are neophytes who yet require the "milk" of the

---

[167] Unsurprisingly, the cluster is found in his comments on 1 Cor. 3:1–2 in *Frag. 1 Cor.* 12 and in his discussion of Rom. 14:3–4 in *Comm. in Rom.* 9.36.763 (Scheck 9.36.1); see also *Comm. in Rom.* 2.10.183 (Scheck 2.14.14), 4.6.313 (Scheck 4.6.4); *Hom. in Gen.* 14.4; *Hom. in Lev.* 1.4; *Or.* 27.5 (text in Paul Koetschau (ed.), *Origenes Werke. Buch V–VIII Gegen Celsus, Die Schrift von Gebet*, vol. 2, GCS 3 (Leipzig: Hinrichs, 1899)); *Cels.* 3.54. See esp. the careful discussion in Francesca Cocchini, "La questione dei cibi (Rm 14) nel Commento di Origene alla Lettera ai Romani," *Adamantius* 18 (2012), 218–225, who focuses on Rom. 14:2 and Origen's careful exposition of each element of food by means of other scriptural passages.

[168] The translation reflects the Latin of Rufinus' translation: "non erat ullum verbum ex omnibus, quae mandavit Moyses, quod non legerit Iesus in auribus totius ecclesiae filiorum Israhel. Et addit etiam: mulieribus et infantibus et proselytis."

[169] *Hom. in Jesu.* 9.9.354: "dicimus viris quidem fortibus fortem tradi cibum, illis videlicet, de quibus Apostolus dicit: perfectorum autem est cibus solidus…'viri' quidem intelliguntur illi, qui 'in omnibus perfecti stare norunt armati adversus astutias diaboli'" (citing Eph. 6:11). This passage is discussed in Monaci Castagno, *Origene predicatore*, pp. 83–86, 90.

[170] *Hom. in Jesu.* 9.9.354: "'mulieres' vero illi, qui nondum ex semet ipsis, quae utilia sunt, gerunt, sed imitando viros et eorum exempla sectando."

[171] Ibid.: "etiam velut 'infirmi,' ut sunt 'mulieres,' 'oleribus vescuntur.'"

gospel for their growth.[172] Proselytes, on the other hand, are catechumens or those who want to be affiliated with the Church but have not yet registered as a catechumen.[173]

These stages are meant to be temporary, however, since legal status and even gender noted in Joshua have only to do with spiritual growth and not with a fixed anthropological status.[174] Therefore Origen exhorts the "proselytes," "infants," and "women" to hasten toward spiritual growth, all growing within the boundaries of the church community and toward the example set by the "men."[175] Thus far Origen's presentation of "milk" and "meat" has a great deal in common with Clement's description of the Christian life, in which milk drinkers eventually mature into those who can stomach solid food.[176] A subtle difference, however, is in place even at this level: where Clement works hard to demonstrate that "milk" and "meat" are made up of the same material, this is evidently not a concern for Origen. Rather, he is happy to speak of milk, vegetables, and meat (or solid food) in such a way that Clement's biological description of the maturation process breaks down. There is no sense in which milk can coagulate into a vegetable, no matter how much is accumulated.[177]

---

[172] Ibid.: "Infantes vero erunt, qui nuper fide suscepta 'lacte' evangelico nutriuntur."

[173] Ibid.: "Proselyti autem catechumeni videbuntur vel hi, qui iam sociari fidelibus student."

[174] Ibid.: (translation from Barbara J. Bruce (trans.), *Origen: Homilies on Joshua*, ed. Cynthia White, Fathers of the Church 105 (Washington, D.C.: Catholic University of America Press, 2002)): "For divine Scripture does not know how to make a separation of men and women according to sex. For indeed sex is no distinction in the presence of God, but a person is designated either a man or woman according to the diversity of spirit" (Non enim novit scriptura divina secundum sexum separationem virorum ac mulierum facere. Etenim sexus apud Deum nulla discretio est, sed pro animi diversitate vel vir vel mulier designatur). See also the comments in Cocchini, "La questione," p. 223.

[175] Ibid. (Bruce trans.): Nevertheless, you "proselytes," that is, catechumens, should not remain catechumens indefinitely…But make haste to lay hold of the grace of God so that you too may be numbered with the church of the sons of Israel. And you "infants, do not be made children in perceptions, but be little ones in malice, and be perfect in perceptions," just as even the Apostle says to the Hebrews, "Leaving behind the discussion of the first principles of Christ, let us hasten onward to perfection." But you also who under the name "women" are weak, slack, and sluggish, may you be warned so that "you may raise up the slack hands and loose knees," that is, that you may stir up neglectful and idle spirits and assume a bold firmness in accomplishing legal and gospel precepts and hasten swiftly to the perfection of strong men." A lack of attention to these calls for progress dogs the otherwise excellent discussion in Penniman, *Raised on Christian Milk*, pp. 122–134.

[176] Cocchini, "La questione," pp. 224–225, also notes Clement's precedent for Origen's use of these passages.

[177] See the discussion in Chapter 4.2.2 above and see also the comments in Penniman, *Raised on Christian Milk*, p. 111.

This difference is related to a further distinction between Origen and Clement's configuration of milk and meat as stages of maturation: Origen considers it a matter of fact that some simply will not be able or willing to make progress. As he says in his commentary on Matthew, "the many are infants" who are consistently being brought to Christ.[178] They are the ones who receive the "sensible words" keyed to their five senses because they are not capable of more. Significantly, Origen notes that he encounters this group specifically "in the church" (ἐν ἐκκλησίᾳ).[179] The daily homilies preached by him supply an institutional framework for elementary teaching directed at catechumens as well as those who are not yet capable of attaining to spiritual understandings. In that context, difficult theological disputes should be avoided for the sake of those who cannot understand them.

If someone is weaker in understanding and so does not have perfect faith, such that they could not grasp the word by means of more hidden mysteries, disputes about such ideas should not be stirred up with them on account of the things they cannot understand.[180]

The philosophical approach of Origen's school curriculum and spiritual understanding is, in principle, open to any who are willing to apply themselves. Those encountered in his homilies, however, are dominated by a different group: the *simpliciores*.

Clement's anxiety over Valentinian anthropological divisions is not particularly prominent here.[181] In its place is a recognition that the way of spiritual progress is such that the majority of baptized believers will not undertake it. Clement and Origen shared a similar philosophical and theological context, at the very least while Origen was still in Alexandria. The school context depicted by Gregory Thaumaturgus did not include space for the non-philosophical fideist, who would reject Origen's spiritual reading of scripture, nor for the intellectually

---

[178] *Comm. in Matt.* 15.6 (cited above, p. 149 n. 105).

[179] *Frag. in 1 Cor.* 63 (cited above, p. 156); see also the comments in Monaci Castagno, "Semplici," pp. 440–441 (and earlier in Monaci Castagno, *Origene predicatore*, p. 92).

[180] *Comm. in Rom.* 9.36.763 (Scheck 9.36.1): "...si qui infirmior est sensibus et non est ita perfectae fidei ut de secretioribus mysteriis capiat uerbum non debere ei per ea quae intellegere non potest disceptationes cogitationum moueri."

[181] Origen addresses Valentinian views of the "fixed" soul elsewhere, often by means of an appeal to Paul's biography. In fact, his entire construal of the journey of the soul is at odds with a view that one's soul cannot progress from material to spiritual realities. See p. 162 n. 156 above; Strutwolf, "Theologische Gnosis," p. 102, on Origen's arguments against distinct natures; and Fürst, *Origenes*, pp. 37–44, on Origen's ambivalence in relation to "gnostic" thought.

"dull," like those mentioned in the preface to *De principiis*. That context encouraged and even fostered the view that the progress of the soul was a movement from "virtue to virtue" toward perfect faith.[182] This notion bears marked similarity with Clement's interpretation of Romans 1:17 ("from faith to faith") discussed earlier. The two thinkers did not, however, share the experience of daily homilies delivered to a congregation including catechumens, neophytes, and the slack.[183] Although the distinction between the philosophically adept and the "dull" runs throughout Origen's thought, no doubt his daily engagement with the *simpliciores* helped cement the thought that "the many are infants."

5.4 CONCLUSION

Origen's catechetical interpretation of Paul, rich and nuanced, made a deep impact on subsequent writers. Certainly, John Chrysostom shows clear affinities with Origen's work, even appropriating the epithet "farmer of souls" for his own portrayal of Paul.[184] As we have seen, Origen's interpretation of Paul mirrors his own ministry and institutional contexts in a variety of ways. Perhaps at the most abstract level, just as Origen was negotiating inherited traditions of Pauline interpretation and his own interpretive impulses, so also was he negotiating between inherited catechetical and homiletical institutions on one side and his newly developed philosophical school on the other. Origen saw that, while catechesis was foundational to baptismal faith, preparing the "fallow" soul for the "good seeds" of doctrine, it was only a bare foundation, something to be built upon with subsequent spiritual development. Those who underwent catechesis could, in his view, be "born prematurely" into the Christian community and in any case all neophytes remained in need of milk until they could mature through vegetables to attain the "solid food" of the mysteries. In this way Origen also inherits Clement's discussion of milk and meat, while modifying it such that milk and meat are no longer equated with catechesis and further instruction. Rather milk principally covers the elementary instruction of neophytes and the

---

[182] See *Hom. in Gen.* 10.4 on the phrase "from virtue to virtue," and *Comm. in Iohan.* 20.32.285, 32.15.177, and elsewhere for Origen's discussion of a mature or perfected faith.

[183] That is to say, we know nothing of any such practice for Clement while he was in Alexandria.

[184] See Chapter 6.2 below and see also the comments on Origen's impact in the east in Simonetti, *Origene esegeta*, pp. 83–84.

simpliciores, an epistemological division maintained within the baptized community itself.

This pedagogical concern, with its specific institutional inflection in Caesarea, factors directly into Origen's depiction of Paul's work and his interpretation of Paul's letters. Paul is himself a catechist, "cultivating" catechumens' souls, imparting doctrine, and, where necessary, baptizing them. But Origen's Paul is also the teacher who takes the believer from neophyte to spiritual mystic, supplying both general warrant and specific examples of spiritual interpretation of scripture. Catechumens can hear only the bare word of scripture, but if they become a "disciple of Paul" they can learn to read scripture like a Christian. Most believers, however, are incapable (or unwilling) to put the work in for spiritual progress, leaving them only suited for the basics. Origen knows that this latter group are those whom he meets in church when he delivers the homilies. Those attaining to advanced knowledge, on the other hand, Origen instructs in his school. Likewise Paul accommodates himself to the "infants" but he also speaks "wisdom to the perfect." While others have noted that Origen saw himself in Paul's ministry,[185] it is now clear that this carried specific institutional freight which shaped the way in which Origen portrayed Paul and exegetically deployed his writings.

---

[185] See the comments in Cocchini, *Il Paolo*, p. 61: "It is evident that Origen had found in the diverse apostolic activity of Paul the mirror in which to recognize the complex articulation of his own work, both that carried out as a presbyter who preached publicly in church and that exercised as a commentator on scripture..."

6

Paul the Catechist, Chrysostom, and the Fourth Century

One may see Paul even in prison, instructing amid his very chains, guiding in mysteries, and in the court doing the same thing again, and in a shipwreck, and in a storm, and among a myriad of dangers.[1]

Around the same time that the editor of the *Constitutiones apostolorum* was compiling his work, John Chrysostom was working his way up in the ecclesial hierarchy in Antioch, being ordained a deacon in 380/381 CE and priest in 386 CE, at the age of thirty-seven.[2] A little over a decade after his ordination as a priest, John was unexpectedly promoted to the role of Bishop of Constantinople, the most important city of the Roman east.[3]

As is well known, John Chrysostom was particularly devoted to Paul and was long revered – indeed, still is revered in Orthodox circles – as

---

[1] John Chrystostom *Stat.* 1.11: Καὶ ἔστιν ἰδεῖν Παῦλον ἐν αὐτῷ τῷ δεσμωτηρίῳ, ἐν αὐταῖς ταῖς ἁλύσεσι κατηχοῦντα, μυσταγωγοῦντα, καὶ ἐν δικαστηρίῳ πάλιν τὸ αὐτὸ τοῦτο ποιοῦντα, καὶ ἐν ναυαγίῳ, καὶ ἐν χειμῶνι, καὶ ἐν μυρίοις κινδύνοις. Except where otherwise indicated, texts for John Chrysostom are from MPG vols. 47–64. I have corrected the Migné text of his homilies on Pauline letters in light of the better text in F. Field (ed.), *Sancti patris nostri Joannis Chrysostomi archiepiscopi Constantinopolitani Interpretatio omnium Epistolarum Paulinarum per homilias facta*, 7 vols., Bibliotheca patrum ecclesiae Catholicae (Oxford: J.H. Parker, 1849–1862).

[2] See the biographical details in Kelly, *Golden Mouth* (birth, pp. 296–298; diaconate, p. 36; priesthood, p. 55).

[3] Ibid., pp. 104–109. Kelley's chronology of these major events is substantially in line with the still standard work of Chrysostomus Baur, *John Chrysostom and His Time*, trans. M. Gonzaga (Westminster, MD: Newman Press, 1959–1960), and see also the biographical account in Rudolf Brändle, *John Chrysostom: Bishop, Reformer, Martyr*, ed. Wendy Mayer, trans. John Cawte and Silke Trzcionka, Early Christian Studies 8 (Strathfield: St Pauls, 2004).

his premier interpreter.[4] Moreover, from his upbringing by a Christian mother through his time as a monk and his subsequent ordinations and promotions, Chrysostom gained an intimate and long-term familiarity with the catechumenate.[5] In fact, in his extensive corpus of homilies, treatises, and letters John uses κατήχησις/κατηχεῖν language more than any other Greek writer from antiquity.[6] Remarkably, twelve of his catechetical homilies delivered during Lent and Easter Week have been preserved, in which we are able to catch a clear view of the kinds of instruction that Chrysostom gave to those who had enrolled for baptism.[7] In this context of a flourishing catechumenate and a deep love for Paul, the connection between the two becomes very clear.

Of course, as with the writers discussed earlier, it is true that the catechumenate is only one stage of the Christian life for Chrysostom. His pastoral vision extended well beyond initiation to encompass moral growth throughout the whole of the life of the believer. John Chrysostom consciously adopted the role of psychagogue for his congregations, caring for their souls and leading them to virtue. This involved a careful attention to the rhetorical needs of his listeners, adapting himself to the variety of their needs and addressing his audience directly at their different levels of development.[8] Chrysostom's broader concern for his

---

[4] On Chrysostom as a Pauline interpreter, see esp. Mitchell, *Heavenly Trumpet*; Heiser, *Paulusinzenierung*; and Courtney Wilson Vanveller, "Paul's therapy of the soul: a new approach to John Chrysostom and anti-Judaism," unpublished Ph.D. thesis, Boston University (2015).

[5] In addition to the biographical information in Kelly, *Golden Mouth*, see also Chrysostom's *Sac.* 1 for his own sketch of his early life.

[6] Based on a search for those terms (with all their inflected forms) in *TLG*.

[7] These appear to comprise homilies from two or three different years, with the first set originating from around 388 CE. See Antoine Wenger (ed.), *Jean Chrysostome. Huit catéchèses baptismales inédites*, SC 50 (Paris: Cerf, 1957), pp. 63–65; Paul W. Harkins (ed. and trans.), *John Chrysostom: Baptismal Instructions*, ACW 31 (Westminster, MD: Newman Press, 1963), pp. 15–18; Finn, *Liturgy of Baptism*, pp. 8–9; Auguste Piédagnel and Louis Doutreleau (eds.), *Jean Chrysostome. Trois catéchèses baptismales*, SC 366 (Paris: Cerf, 1990), pp. 31–39; Domenico Sartore, "Aspetti cristologici delle catechesi battesimali del Crisostomo," in Magnus Löhrer and Elmar Salmann (eds.), *Mysterium Christi. Symbolgegenwart und theologische Bedeutung*, Studia Anselmiana 116 (Rome: Pontificio Ateneo S. Anselmo, 1995), pp. 132–133; and Knupp, *Mystagogieverständnis*, pp. 55–65. See Appendix for list and abbreviations.

[8] This theme has been recently emphasized in relation to the theme of divine pedagogy and rhetoric as a therapy of the soul by David Rylaarsdam and Courtney Vanveller, respectively: see Rylaarsdam, *Divine Pedagogy*, pp. 55–98 and *passim*; Vanveller, "Paul's Therapy of the Soul," pp. 47–50 and *passim*. See also Wendy Mayer, "The persistence in late antiquity of medico-philosophical psychic therapy," *Journal of Late Antiquity* 8, no. 2 (2015), 345–351. John Chrysostom discusses the responsibilities of priests for their

congregants' progress in virtue, in the direction of divine perfection, frames his approach to the catechumenate, his use of catechetical and teaching terminology, and his presentation of Paul.[9] Like Origen before him, Chrysostom finds in Paul the perfect example for his own life and ministry.[10] This fact is reflected both in his use of catechetical terminology and in his presentation of Paul.

In order to appreciate Chrysostom's use of catechetical language in relation to Paul it will be helpful first to situate his own catechetical practices in relation to the general outline of the fourth-century catechumenate traced in Chapter 2. Furthermore, sketching his view of the catechumenate and the language he uses to denote it will lay the appropriate foundation for understanding his depiction of Paul as *the* catechist for the Church.

6.1 CHRYSOSTOM'S CATECHUMENATE

6.1.1 Shape and Significance

During Chrysostom's tenure as priest and bishop, the catechumenate was a firm institution within his church, entailing a recognized status, expected roles and responsibilities, and a clear relationship to the larger group.[11] Chrysostom maintained the two-level process of catechesis,

---

congregation (including treating Paul as a paradigm for proper priestly actions) in book 6 of *De sacerdotis*. On the audience for John's sermons, see particularly the work of Wendy Mayer: "John Chrysostom: extraordinary preacher, ordinary audience," in Mary Cunningham and Pauline Allen (eds.), *Preacher and Audience: Studies in Early Christian and Byzantine Homilies* (Leiden: Brill, 1998), pp. 105–137; "Female participation and the late fourth-century preacher's audience," *Augustinianum* 39 (1999), 139–147; "Who came to hear John Chrysostom Preach? Recovering a late fourth-century preacher's audience," *Ephemerides Theologicae Lovanienses* 76 (2000), 73–87.

[9] The use of Paul as an exemplar for the process of Christian deification is highlighted in particular by Pak-Wah Lai, "John Chrysostom and the hermeneutics of exemplar portraits," unpublished Ph.D. thesis, Durham University (2010), pp. 153–172. See also Rylaarsdam, *Divine Pedagogy*, pp. 157–193; Vanveller, "Paul's Therapy of the Soul," pp. 50–62.

[10] See the comments in Mitchell, *Heavenly Trumpet*, pp. 322, 377.

[11] See the general outlines of Chrysostom's catechumenate in Gavrilyuk, *Histoire*, pp. 220–230; Saxer, *Les rites*, pp. 241–250; Roten, *Baptême et mystagogie*, pp. 137–216. Also useful are Knupp, *Mystagogieverständnis*, pp. 35–65; Finn, pp. *Liturgy of Baptism*, 31–42; and the earlier account in Baur, *John Chrysostom*, pp. 79–88. Isabella Sandwell, *Religious Identity in Late Antiquity: Greeks, Jews, and Christians in Antioch* (Cambridge: Cambridge University Press, 2007), pp. 198–204, is significant for highlighting the variegated quality of Christian commitment in fourth-century Antioch. Notably, Chrysostom assumes such institutional stability in the catechumenate that he

discussed earlier, in which the first stage lasted for an indefinite period of time and the second stage was a shorter period of intense instruction, normally associated with Lent.[12] Given the tendency for delaying baptism in the fourth century, it is possible that catechumens outnumbered the πιστοί on certain occasions.[13]

A catechumen in the first stage inhabited a carefully defined liminal space within the church. Catechumens were present for homilies and participated generally in festivals, though they were not privy to the celebration of the eucharist and did not participate in Easter. As Chrysostom notes in one place, the catechumen "does not celebrate Pascha, though fasting each year, because he does not share the offering."[14] This not only highlights a distinction in participation, but it also signals the multi-year duration ("each year") of the catechumenate. Within the weekly liturgy itself, the catechumens were recognized during the prayer for them, offered by the deacon between the homily and the celebration of the eucharist.[15] Occasionally their presence militated against an explicit discussion of the eucharist.[16] Moreover, they were included in consideration of church discipline: penalties for infractions differed depending on whether one was a catechumen or one of the faithful.[17] The catechumen, in short, "knows

can recount a supposed Marcionite practice of hiding a catechumen under a dead body before baptizing them (in an effort to enact a "baptism for the dead"); see *Hom. 1 Cor.* 40.1. Whether or not this was current Marcionite practice, the anecdote demonstrates that John and his audience could take the existence of the catechumenate for granted even among groups they considered heretical.

[12] See Roten, *Baptême et mystagogie*, pp. 11–27, 163–164, 188–190, 200, on deferment of baptism, the Lenten catechumenate, enrollment in it, and distinctions between different levels of catechumens.

[13] This is articulated in sociologically nuanced terms in Sandwell, *Religious Identity*, p. 199; see also the scholars listed at p. 60 n. 166 above.

[14] *Adv. Jud.* 3.5.1: Ὁ γοῦν κατηχούμενος οὐδέποτε πάσχα ἐπιτελεῖ, καίτοι νηστεύων κατ' ἐνιαυτόν, ἐπειδὴ προσφορᾶς οὐ κοινωνεῖ.

[15] Chrysostom gives an extensive interpretation of this prayer during one homily, see *Hom. 2 Cor.* 2.5. On the exclusion from the eucharist, see *Hom. Eph.* 3.5; see the discussion of the prayer for and dismissal of catechumens and sinners in Frans van de Paverd, *Zur Geschichte der Messliturgie in Antiocheia und Konstantinopel gegen Ende des vierten Jahrhunderts. Analyse der Quellen bei Johannes Chrysostomos*, OCA 187 (Rome: Pontifical Institution for Oriental Studies, 1970), pp. 447–460; see also Maxwell, *Christianization*, p. 120. There were also evidently limits to what catechumens were allowed to pray (or knew how to pray): see *Proph. obscurit.* 2.5.

[16] See *Hom. 1 Cor.* 36.5, noted in the discussion of this fact by Maxwell, *Christianization*, p. 85 and n. 105.

[17] See, e.g., *Adv. Jud.* 2.3.6 (how to treat different groups "infected" with Judaism); *Hom. Matt.* 75.5 (different punishments for those of different status). Similar concern for how to deal with erring catechumens is found in some earlier Church canons, e.g., Nicene canon §14 and the Synod of Elvira §§4, 10.

Christ, understands the faith, attends to the divine oracles, is not far from divine knowledge, knows the will of their master."[18]

Nevertheless, although catechumens were members of the community in one sense, theirs was a marginal membership and Chrysostom regularly contrasts the κατηχούμενοι with the πιστοί. In his view, ultimately there are two groups of people, the initiated and the uninitiated.[19] As he says, "The catechumen is a stranger to a believer. He does not have the same head, nor does he have the same father nor the same city...For one, Christ is king but, for the other, sin and the devil."[20] In another passage he states bluntly, "One who is a monk, should he be a catechumen, is not a brother. The believer, even if a layman, is a brother."[21] The catechumen in this first level of initiation could still be exhorted by John to heed the message that Jesus takes away sins and, therefore, that they should put off their baptism no longer.[22]

Those in the second stage of the catechumenate, referred to by Chrysostom as φωτιζόμενοι ("those being illuminated") as well as κατηχούμενοι,[23] were women and men who had heeded the call and enrolled their name (ἐγγράφεσθαι) in the baptismal registry.[24] After the enrollment

---

[18] *Hom. Heb.* 13.5: Κἂν γὰρ κατηχούμενός τις ᾖ, ἀλλὰ τὸν Χριστὸν οἶδεν, ἀλλὰ τὴν πίστιν ἔγνω, ἀλλὰ τῶν θείων ἐπακούει λόγων, ἀλλ᾽ οὐ πόρρω ἐστὶ τῆς θείας γνώσεως, οἶδε τὸ θέλημα τοῦ Δεσπότου αὐτοῦ.

[19] See *Adv. Jud.* 2.3.6 where the title of "initiated" is reserved for the faithful, to the exclusion of all others, including catechumens; see also *Cat.* 3.8, which refers to οἱ ἀμύητοι κατηχούμενοι. See the comments in Sandwell, *Religious Identity*, p. 195; *pace* Finn, *Liturgy of Baptism*, p. 33.

[20] *Hom. Jo.* 25.3: Ἀλλότριος γὰρ ὁ κατηχούμενος τοῦ πιστοῦ. Οὐ γὰρ ἔχει κεφαλὴν τὴν αὐτήν, οὐκ ἔχει πατέρα τὸν αὐτόν, οὐκ ἔχει πόλιν...βασιλεὺς τούτῳ ὁ Χριστός, ἐκείνῳ δὲ ἡ ἁμαρτία καὶ ὁ διάβολος.

[21] *Hom. Heb.* 25.3: ὁ μὲν μοναχὸς ὤν, ἂν κατηχούμενος ᾖ, οὐκ ἀδελφός· ὁ δὲ πιστός, κἂν κοσμικὸς ᾖ, ἀδελφός ἐστιν; note also the differing treatments concerning liturgical participation and church discipline in the previous notes.

[22] *Hom. Jo.* 18.1: "Let the catechumens hear, and those who put off their own salvation to their final breaths" (Ἀκουέτωσαν οἱ κατηχούμενοι, καὶ πρὸς ἐσχάτας ἀναπνοὰς τὴν οἰκείαν ἀναβαλλόμενοι σωτηρίαν).

[23] A detailed account of the Lenten catechumenate represented in Chrysostom's catechetical homilies is provided in Finn, *Liturgy of Baptism*, pp. 43–85; see also Kaczynski, *Catecheses*, pp. 73–82.

[24] *Cat.* 7.9: "You all, now, such as have been deemed worthy to enroll in this heavenly book" (Πάντες τοίνυν ὅσοι κατηξιώθητε ἐγγραφῆναι τῇ ἐπουρανίῳ ταύτῃ βίβλῳ); *Pent.* 2.3: "Those who have enrolled for adoption today" (οἱ σήμερον εἰς τὴν υἱοθεσίαν ἐγγραφέντες). See also P. van der Aalst, "De initiatie in het christelijk leven te Antiochië op het einde van de vierde eeuw," *Christelijk Oosten en Hereniging* 12, no. 1–2 (1959), 6–7; Finn, *Liturgy of Baptism*, pp. 50–52; Saxer, *Les rites*, p. 245; and Kaczynski, *Catecheses*, p. 75. Josef Knupp has a detailed discussion of enrollment, with attention to the attendant status shift and communal expectations involved; Knupp, *Mystagogieverständnis*, pp. 72–80.

and questioning the baptizand's sponsors, the φωτιζόμενοι listened to daily catechetical lectures, in addition to the regular daily homilies, which were attended by prayer and exorcism.[25] While the full content of the teaching is not clear, given the fact that other teachers contributed to the Lenten instruction,[26] Chrysostom's catechetical lectures covered a number of topics, including doctrinal and creedal instruction with explanations of the baptismal and eucharistic rites (i.e., mystagogical instruction), though the theme to which they returned consistently was moral instruction.[27] Because the faithful were to be on a recognizably superior moral plane to that of the uninitiated masses, catechumens were therefore to be striving fearlessly toward moral rectitude since "God does not command impossible things."[28] As much as this striving is related to Chrysostom's concern for continual growth in virtue throughout believers' lives, it is also related to the dangers of post-baptismal sin.[29] The catechumenate was, for Chrysostom, a time of moral formation and evaluation which

[25] See the discussion of prayer, sponsors, and exorcism in Finn, *Liturgy of Baptism*, pp. 54–58, 73–85; Saxer, *Les rites*, pp. 244–253; Piédagnel and Doutreleau, *Trois catéchèses*, pp. 44–46; Knupp, *Mystagogieverständnis*, pp. 90–98.

[26] *Cat.* 12.1: "Your noble teachers in these recent days have feasted you sufficiently and you have enjoyed their continuous spiritual exhortation" (Ἱκανῶς ὑμᾶς εἱστίασαν ἐν ταῖς παρελθούσαις ἡμέραις οἱ καλοὶ διδάσκαλοι καὶ συνεχοῦς ἀπελαύσατε τῆς πνευματικῆς αὐτῶν παραινέσεως); see also *Cat.* 7.19; 3.30.

[27] This point is well known. See similar comments in E. P. Jackson, *The Holy Spirit in the Catechesis and Mystagogy of Cyril of Jerusalem, Ambrose, and John Chrysostom* (New Haven: Yale University Press, 1987), p. 112; Saxer, *Les rites*, p. 246; Sartore, "Aspetti cristologici," p. 133; Roten, *Baptême et mystagogie*, p. 34; Maxwell, *Christianization*, p. 121; Gavrilyuk, *Histoire*, p. 167; and Everett Ferguson, *Baptism in the Early Church: History, Theology, and Liturgy in the First Five Centuries* (Grand Rapids: Eerdmans, 2009), p. 537. On the content of Chrysostom's instructions and its relation to mystagogical themes, see esp. Knupp, *Mystagogieverständnis*, and also Finn, *Liturgy of Baptism*, pp. 37–39.

[28] *Hom. Act.* 23.3: "What, do you flee? 'Yes,' he says, 'but I am not able to keep his commands.' God does not command impossible things, does he?" (Τί φεύγεις; Ναί, φησίν, ἀλλ' οὐ δύναμαι φυλάξαι. Οὐκοῦν τὰ ἀδύνατα ἐπέταξεν ὁ Θεός;); see also the requirement of moral progress for baptism in *Cat.* 1.2. Of course, often both believers and catechumens fell short of Chrysostom's moral ideals; following the above citation, Chrysostom goes on to criticize catechumens, as well as those baptized as children or while sick or under compulsion, for failing to live up to the zeal for living in accordance with God's desires. See also *Hom. Jo.* 25.3; *Hom. Matt.* 4.7; *Hom. Heb.* 9.2, 13.5 (on the content of the "good life"); and the comments in Knupp, *Mystagogieverständnis*, pp. 75–76.

[29] See *Hom. Act.* 1.6: "For there is nothing, neither sin or impiety, such that it does not yield or make way for the gift. For grace is divine...But we pay a penalty for those sins committed after baptism as great as we would have if those earlier ones [*viz.* the sins before baptism] were recalled, indeed, much worse. For the sinful action is no longer single, but doubled, even trebled" (Οὐ γὰρ ἔστιν, οὐκ ἔστιν οὐδὲν ἁμάρτημα, καὶ ἀσέβημα, ὅπερ οὐκ εἴκει καὶ παραχωρεῖ τῇ δωρεᾷ· θεία γάρ ἐστιν ἡ χάρις...ὑπὲρ δὲ τῶν μετὰ τὸ

culminated with a break from one's former life of sin, as it had been for Christians reaching back to the second century.

Never far from an apt metaphor, John Chrysostom likened the process of catechesis to that of elementary instruction:

For, just as a person learning how to read first has to hear the elementary syllables, so also does the Christian need to know these things firmly, and not vacillate concerning them. Now, if one should need teaching again, that person does not yet have the foundation. For it is necessary for a well-established person to be fixed, to stand and not shift. But if one who has been catechized and baptized should be likely to hear about the faith again after ten years – even that it is necessary to believe in the resurrection of the dead – that person does not yet have the foundation. They are seeking again the beginning of Christianity.[30]

Two points are worth noting here. First, Christian catechesis, for John, constitutes foundational teaching upon which all later, presumably more advanced, teaching will build. He appears to have in mind here particular doctrinal points, indicated by the reference to belief in the resurrection. Elsewhere he indicates that even before enrolling for baptism one must already be convinced that Christ is fully God.[31] Because catechesis is the equivalent of elementary grammar, it is properly learned at the outset of one's Christian life. However, Chrysostom acknowledges, and no doubt knows from experience, that "the elements" (τὰ στοιχεῖα) are not always fully appropriated by students. There are those who are baptized and still lacking in basic theological and moral grammar even a decade later. This discrepancy between the pedagogical ideal and reality accounts partially for the slippage between Chrysostom's use of catechesis language to refer specifically to pre-baptismal instruction and his occasional use of it for foundational instruction more broadly.[32] Still, in an ideal situation, the overlap between the formal catechumenate and "elementary" catechesis was total.

βάπτισμα τοσαύτην διδόαμεν δίκην, ὅσην ἂν εἰ καὶ ἐκεῖνα ἀνεκλήθη, καὶ πολλῷ χείρονα. Οὐκέτι γὰρ ἁπλοῦν ἐστι τὸ ἁμάρτημα, ἀλλὰ διπλοῦν, καὶ τριπλοῦν).

[30] *Hom. Heb.* 9.1: Καθάπερ γὰρ τὸν εἰς τὴν μάθησιν τῶν γραμμάτων εἰσερχόμενον, τὰ στοιχεῖα δεῖ πρῶτον ἀκοῦσαι· οὕτω καὶ τὸν Χριστιανὸν ταῦτα εἰδέναι ἀκριβῶς, καὶ μηδὲν ἀμφιβάλλειν περὶ αὐτῶν. Εἰ δὲ δέοιτο πάλιν διδασκαλίας, οὔπω τὸν θεμέλιον ἔχει· τὸν γὰρ ἑδραῖον πεπηγέναι χρὴ καὶ ἑστάναι, καὶ μὴ μετακινεῖσθαι. Εἰ δὲ μέλλοι τις κατηχηθείς, καὶ βαπτισθεὶς μετὰ ἔτη δέκα περὶ πίστεως πάλιν ἀκούειν, καὶ ὅτι πιστεῦσαι χρὴ εἰς ἀνάστασιν νεκρῶν· οὔπω τὸν θεμέλιον ἔχει, πάλιν τὴν ἀρχὴν τοῦ Χριστιανισμοῦ ζητεῖ.

[31] See *Hom. Act.* 1.6. This may have been a means to weed out Arians; see the comments in Sartore, "Aspetti cristologici," p. 134, who focuses on the christological content of Chrysostom's catechesis.

[32] See further below (pp. 180–182) on the flexibility of Chrysostom's catechetical terminology.

Second, the analogy with "grammar school" suggests a standardized setting in which students and teachers inhabit mutually recognized roles. The importance of teachers for imparting this foundational instruction is alluded to in the passage by Chrysostom's use of the term διδασκαλία. Speaking to "those about to be illuminated," he calls catechumens "unmarked sheep" in a dangerous wilderness. Teachers and exorcists have therefore been sent by the king to prepare a safe place for the sheep and strengthen shaky walls.[33] When commenting on the leadership qualifications listed in Titus, he states that a teacher should be someone able to "fight enemies and take captive every thought," as well as having "the character of a teacher, that is to say, one who is able to instruct the word."[34]

It appears, however, that instructing catechumens was not at all limited to those who were ordained (deacons, priests, and bishops) but extended in some way to all of the faithful.[35] There seems to have been a generalized responsibility for teaching the catechumens, at least in the first stage of the catechumenate, prior to enrollment for baptism.[36]

[33] *Cat.* 3.7: "For the catechumen is an unbranded sheep, a desolate inn, a doorless shelter lying open to absolutely everyone, a den for robbers, a refuge for beasts, a dwelling-place for demons. Since, then, it seemed right to the King on account of his great love for humanity that this desolate inn…become a royal court, he sent us who teach and even exorcise to prepare our shelter. And we who teach make unsound walls firm through teaching" (καὶ γὰρ πρόβατον ἀσφράγιστον ὁ κατηχούμενός ἐστι καὶ πανδοχεῖον ἔρημον καὶ ἀθύρωτον καταγώγιον πᾶσι προκείμενον ἁπλῶς, λῃστῶν καταδρομή, θηρίων καταφυγή, δαιμόνων οἴκησις. ἐπεὶ οὖν ἔδοξε τῷ βασιλεῖ διὰ πολλὴν φιλανθρωπίαν τὸ πανδοχεῖον τοῦτο τὸ ἔρημον…βασιλικὰς αὐλὰς γενέσθαι, διὰ τοῦτο ἔπεμψε προετοιμάζοντας τὸ καταγώγιον ἡμᾶς τοὺς διδάσκοντας κἀκείνους τοὺς ἐξορκίζοντας. καὶ ἡμεῖς μὲν οἱ διδάσκοντες τοὺς τοίχους σαθροὺς ὄντας ποιοῦμεν ὀχυροὺς διὰ τῆς διδασκαλίας·). An analogy with a shepherd appears again in *Sac.* 2.2–3, though there he notes also the differences between shepherds and priests – the one can coerce his flock and the other cannot. Note also the pairing of "teachers" and "catechesis" in *Adfu.* 13.1.

[34] *Hom. Tit.* 2.2: Ὁ γὰρ οὐκ εἰδὼς μάχεσθαι τοῖς ἐχθροῖς, καὶ αἰχμαλωτίζειν πᾶν νόημα…πόρρω ἔστω θρόνου διδασκαλικοῦ…ὃ δὲ μάλιστα χαρακτηρίζει τὸν διδάσκαλον, τοῦτό ἐστι, τὸ δύνασθαι κατηχεῖν τὸν λόγον, οὗ πρόνοια οὐδεμία νῦν.

[35] So Maxwell, *Christianization*, p. 113: "Chrysostom ultimately wished for laypeople to learn enough to instruct others."

[36] This may have extended even to post-enrollment catechesis, if anything is to be gained by comparison with *CA* 8.32.17 ("if the teacher [*viz.* of catechumens] is a lay person, but experienced in the word [ἔμπειρος δὲ τοῦ λόγου] and virtuous in life, let him teach. For they are all taught by God"). The phrase ἔμπειρος τοῦ λόγου exactly parallels earlier instructions regarding illiterate candidates for bishop (Ἔστω οὖν, εἰ δυνατόν, πεπαιδευμένος· εἰ δὲ καὶ ἀγράμματος, ἀλλ᾿ οὖν ἔμπειρος τοῦ λόγου, καθήκων τῇ ἡλικίᾳ; *CA* 2.1.2), which is itself derived from its source in *Didac. apost.* 4 ("If he cannot read, he should be capable and wise in the word and advanced in years" [ܪ. ܐ ܟ ܐܢ ܗܘ ܩܪܐ ܕܠܐ ܡܨܐ ܘܚܟܝܡ ܘܣܟܘܠܬܢ ܢܗܘܐ ܒܡܠܬܐ ܘܩܫܝܫ ܒܫܢܘ̈ܗܝ]"); text in Vööbus, *Didascalia*, 52, lines 17–18).

Those who have been believers for a long time should instruct others, in Chrysostom's view, and he even gives advice on how to go about doing so.[37] Echoing Origen, he explains that, although one's neighbor cultivates the earth, the believer is to "cultivate" their *neighbors'* souls such that lay Christians become "the cause for catechumens."[38] A wife, for instance, is to "introduce" her unbelieving husband to the faith through "teaching and catechesis."[39] Given the importance of sponsors for the introduction of catechumens, it may be that this generalized responsibility is related to sponsorship.[40] The teaching activity of every believer even holds eschatological importance, according to Chrysostom: in the final judgment believers are supported by those they have taught and instructed while alive.[41]

For both Chrysostom and his parishioners, as is to be expected in the late fourth century, the catechumenate was a fact of everyday life. Not only were many of the Christians in Antioch and Constantinople catechumens in one stage or another, but those who were already initiated heard a deacon pray for the catechumens before every eucharist, saw their priest speak to catechumens during his homilies, and were themselves tasked with participating in the initiation of catechumens through instruction and sponsorship. All parties were aware of the status differential between catechumens and believers (even if the occasional monk-catechumen was

---

[37] See *Hom. Heb.* 8.2 for the obligation and *Hom. Col.* 11 for the advice (speak to the issue at hand and do not ramble).

[38] *Hom. Act.* 18.5: "They cultivate the earth – you, cultivate their souls. They bring you crops – you, lead them up to heaven. Whoever supplies the start is the cause of everything else to follow. Therefore, you should be the 'cause' for catechumens among those who live near you" (γεωργοῦσιν ἐκεῖνοι τὴν γῆν, σὺ γεώργησον αὐτῶν τὰς ψυχάς· φέρουσί σοι καρποὺς ἐκεῖνοι, σὺ εἰς τὸν οὐρανὸν αὐτοὺς ἀνάγαγε. Ὁ τὴν ἀρχὴν δούς, οὗτος καὶ τῶν ἄλλων αἴτιος πάντων. Ἄρα καὶ σὺ αἴτιος ἔσῃ τῶν κατηχουμένων ἐκεῖ, τῶν ἐν τοῖς χωρίοις τοῖς πλησίον).

[39] *Hom. Gen.* 5: "'And how,' he says, 'is a wife able to save her husband?' By teaching, catechizing, leading him toward the message of piety" (Καὶ πῶς, φησί, δύναται σῶσαι γυνή; Διδάσκουσα, κατηχοῦσα, ἐνάγουσα πρὸς τὸν τῆς εὐσεβείας λόγον), commenting here on 1 Cor. 7:16.

[40] Chrysostom addresses sponsors in *Cat.* 7.15–16; see also Wenger, *Huit catéchèses baptismales inédites*, pp. 75–76; Finn, *Liturgy of Baptism*, p. 56; Piédagnel and Doutreleau, *Trois catéchèses*, pp. 41–42. Knupp, *Mystagogieverständnis*, pp. 78–79, following Finn, emphasizes the involvement of the sponsors during the Lenten catechumenate, though he does not speculate about any prior engagement.

[41] *Adv. Jud.* 7.5: "In this way those who live and teach and catechize, when they see those who were led to salvation by them pleading their case for them, they will be filled with great confidence" (οὕτως οἱ ζῶντες καὶ διδάσκοντες καὶ κατηχοῦντες, ἰδόντες τοὺς ὑπ᾽ αὐτῶν διασωθέντας συνηγοροῦντας αὐτοῖς ἐκεῖ, πολλῆς ἐμπλησθήσονται τῆς παρρησίας).

a difficult category for some).[42] Moreover, all were aware that the liminal status of the catechumen was also inherently teleological: to be a catechumen was to be one who would be baptized in the future, however distant.[43] Catechesis was expected to lead to baptism as a matter of course and, therefore, was closely related to it conceptually.

As noted, however, for Chrysostom initiation only constituted the first stage in the Christian life. Like Clement and Origen before him, he desired continual moral progress for the believer throughout one's life, modeled on God's divine example. David Rylaarsdam has recently emphasized that Chrysostom's vision of "divine pedagogy" is a unifying theme that runs throughout his thought.[44] Drawing on late antique pedagogical practice, Chrysostom describes the Christian experience of God's condescension (συγκατάβασις) by which he addresses humans at the level of their ability to spur them on to moral and intellectual perfection.[45] Not unlike Clement of Alexandria's true Gnostic, for Chrysostom ecclesial leaders are to imitate God's practice of condescension in their own pastoral work, a task modeled most perfectly by Paul.[46] Therefore, just as Chrysostom's pastoral concerns are more varied than the present focus on the catechumenate might otherwise indicate, so also are his images of Paul.[47] In this light it is unsurprising that his concerns for the catechumenate overlap with his pedagogical concern for believers more broadly.

---

[42] See *Hom. Heb.* 25.3, cited above, p. 174.

[43] Van de Paverd, *Geschichte der Messliturgie*, p. 447: "Nach den Aussagen des Kirchenvaters ist das Katechumenat eine Übergangszeit, die man möglichst bald mit der Taufe abschließen soll."

[44] Rylaarsdam, *Divine Pedagogy*; see also the earlier comments in Young, *Biblical Exegesis*, p. 249. The arguments of Vanveller, "Paul's Therapy of the Soul," complement this understanding of Chrysostom's thought from the perspective of rhetoric as therapy of the soul.

[45] In addition to Rylaarsdam's extensive discussion, see also Mitchell, "Pauline accommodation," pp. 205–214, who discusses Clement and Origen in addition to Chrysostom, and Vanveller, "Paul's Therapy of the Soul," pp. 50–62.

[46] On his discussion of Paul, see Rylaarsdam, *Divine Pedagogy*, pp. 157–193, and Tloka, *Griechische Christen*, pp. 130–133.

[47] There are, for instance, the images of Paul the herald (Heiser, *Paulusinszenierung*, pp. 257–261) Paul the philosopher and rhetorician (Rylaarsdam, *Divine Pedagogy*, p. 192), or Paul the priest (Mitchell, *Heavenly Trumpet*, p. 322; Manfred Lochbrunner, *Über das Priestertum. Historische und systematische Untersuchung zum Priesterbild des Johannes Chrysostomus*, Hereditas: Studien zur Alten Kirchengeschichte 5 (Bonn: Borengässer, 1993), pp. 169–172). Mitchell, *Heavenly Trumpet*, and Heiser, *Paulusinszenierung*, in particular, offer valuable catalogues of Chrysostom's Pauline images.

6.1.2 Chrysostom's Catechetical Terminology

As already illustrated, John Chrysostom readily uses the words κατηχεῖν and κατήχησις as technical terms in relation to activities and persons associated with the catechumenate. In that context, catechesis is foundational instruction that (ideally) occurs at the start of one's Christian life. It is also closely related to the language of "teaching," such that "teaching and instruction" are often paired together. The wife who is introducing her husband to the Church goes about her task with "teaching and instructing" (διδάσκουσα, κατηχοῦσα).[48] In contradistinction from outsiders who benefit from signs, the Church needs only "teaching and instruction."[49] Examples proliferate. Also linked with the language of catechesis, as already indicated, is that of "initiation." The faithful are "the initiated" (οἱ μεμυημένοι), while the catechumens are still "uninitiated" (οἱ ἀμύητοι).[50] The dividing line between the two is baptism.[51]

Still, Chrysostom at times uses catechesis language that is not connected clearly with the catechumenate itself. In some cases he can describe a person as being "instructed" in a way of life or a tradition of thought. For instance, he describes Israel's time in the desert as one of continual "oral instruction" (ἡ κατήχησις ἡ ἀπὸ τῶν ῥημάτων).[52] The whole earth will be "instructed by the word of God" (πᾶσα ἡ γῆ τῷ λόγῳ τοῦ Θεοῦ κατηχεῖσθαι).[53] Jews are "instructed in the Law," while others can be "instructed" in Greek thought.[54] Furthermore, he extends the righteous person's ability to instruct others, drawing on Psalm 111:6, by claiming that the righteous continue to instruct after their death by means of their memory.[55] In these cases, the importance of catechesis as somehow foundational remains in place. The people of Israel in the desert receive their instruction at Sinai, prior to "inheriting" the land. Jews and Greeks are

---

[48] As in *Hom. Gen.* 5, cited above, p. 178.
[49] *Hom. 1 Cor.* 36.1: Οὐδὲ γὰρ χρείαν ἔχει ὁ πιστὸς σημεῖον ἰδεῖν, ἀλλὰ διδασκαλίας δεῖται μόνον καὶ κατηχήσεως; see also *Hom. Heb.* 9.1; *Hom. Tit.* 2.2; *Adv. Jud.* 7.5 (all cited above, pp. 176–178).
[50] See *Cat.* 3.8 and *Adv. Jud.* 2.3.6 cited above (p. 174).
[51] Lochbrunner, *Priestertum*, p. 284, notes that the phrase ἴσασιν οἱ μεμυημένοι (also paralleled by ἴσασιν οἱ μυσταγωγούμενοι) refers to the result of "Grundeinweihung in das christliche Leben" (basic initiation into the Christian life.) The point of initiation is specifically the reception of baptism and the eucharist.
[52] *Laed.* 13.18.
[53] *Exp. Ps.* 147.4.
[54] Jews and the Law: see *Hom. Rom.* 6.1 and *Comm. Is.* 1.5; Greek instruction: see *Hom. 1 Cor.* 7.7.
[55] *Exp. Ps.* 111.4.

"instructed" in their respective laws and traditions as a means of providing an elementary grammar for their lives and conduct.[56]

Given that John is also bound to use catechesis language loosely in his citations of statements from the New Testament, one particular passage helpfully illuminates the overtones that he wants to evoke with catechesis language. In his discussion of Paul's arrival in Jerusalem, Chrysostom explains the phrase "they have been told about you" (κατηχήθησαν περὶ σοῦ; Acts 20:21) quite specifically: "I did not say 'they heard' but 'they were instructed' – that is, they were taught and they believed."[57] This explanation illustrates that catechetical language had distinct implications for him. Catechesis, in whatever context, is closely linked with both "teaching" and "belief" and it forms a foundation for further action. Regularly, in describing the missionary activities of the early Church, he couches his discussions in terms of "catechesis" – the prophet Isaiah "instructed" the Ethiopian eunuch in preparation for baptism (as in Irenaeus' account noted earlier);[58] Apollos' previous "instruction" provided the opportunity to receive the Spirit (having already received the baptism of John); the church addressed in Hebrews is urged to recall the time of their "catechesis"; Jesus "instructs" the Samaritan woman in a pattern like that of fourth-century pedagogical practices; Thomas is catechized by his fellow disciples to make him "more faithful" (πιστότερον).[59] This apparent looseness in terminology is indicative of Chrysostom's effort to articulate at least two things: the meaning of these passages for his listeners in terms they can understand and his view of the scriptural and historical precedent for catechesis. A third element will be added to this in the discussion of Paul below. Suffice it here simply to highlight the fact that catechetical language for Chrysostom is dominantly related to the catechumenate and, where a clear institutional

---

[56] Note also *Hom. 1 Cor.* 36.3 on "catechizing" Nebuchadnezzar (πῶς τὸν ἄγριον ἐκεῖνον μετέβαλε καὶ κατήχησε καὶ εἰς πίστιν ἤγαγε). The movement of turning, instruction, and introduction is closely paralleled by Chrysostom's discussions of Christian initiation.

[57] *Hom. Act.* 46.1: Οὐκ εἶπον, Ἤκουσαν· ἀλλὰ, *Κατηχήθησαν*, τουτέστιν, ἐδιδάχθησαν καὶ ἐπίστευσαν; see also the link between "instruction" and "believing" in *Hom. Phil.* 2.2 (Chrysostom paraphrasing Paul's comments in Philippians on his defense): Ἐὰν γὰρ εὑρεθῶσι πολλοὶ οἱ κατηχηθέντες πιστεύσαντες, εὔκολός μοι ἡ ἀπολογία ἔσται.

[58] The preparatory function of the prophets is linked with a view of history as a long, slow pedagogical process directed by God. This occurs in other writers than Chrysostom (see above and also Gavrilyuk, *Histoire*, pp. 84–85) but was also part of Chrysostom's view of God's συγκατάβασις (see Rylaarsdam, *Divine Pedagogy*, pp. 29–30 and *passim*).

[59] Respectively, *Hom. Act.* 19.5 (see also *Hom. Matt.* 9.37 and generally *Hom. Jo.* 34.2 on being "instructed" by the prophets in preparation for Jesus); *Hom. Act.* 40.2 (see also *Hom. Rom.* 31.1; *Hom. Rom.* 16.3); *Hom. 2 Cor.* 4:13; *Hom. Jo.* 32.2; *Hom. Jo.* 87.1.

connection is lacking, he primarily has in view foundational teaching that prepares one for encountering Christ (normally in baptism). This remains the case in his treatment of Paul.

6.2 CHRYSOSTOM AND PAUL THE CATECHIST

Of all of Chrysostom's epithets for the Apostle Paul, "teacher of the world" was perhaps his favorite.[60] The scope of this phrase, the whole world, is for Chrysostom neither hyperbolic nor aspirational. After the death of the emperor Julian (363 CE) and the establishment of Nicene orthodoxy under Theodosius, John lived in a world in which Christianity had (evidently) triumphed.

> For when the impious emperor piteously fell, and another, a pious man, succeeded him, all these horrible things immediately came undone...Who would not find these incidents a sufficient inducement to piety?...Is not the cross preached, and the world runs toward it? Is not death proclaimed to be a matter of reproach, and all leap to it?[61]

When the (Gentile) world has become Christian, Paul the Apostle to the Gentiles becomes the teacher of the world.[62] For Chrysostom, however, this description would not quite capture the significance of Paul. It is not a matter of a simple historical development; Paul himself converted the world (*in nuce*) during his own ministry.[63] To articulate the importance

---

[60] The phrase ὁ τῆς οἰκουμένης διδάσκαλος or some variant thereof occurs nearly sixty times in Chrysostom's corpus (see *Cat.* 8.7) and is even picked up in various spuriously attributed texts; see the comments in Mitchell, *Heavenly Trumpet*, p. 383, and the discussion in Rylaarsdam, *Divine Pedagogy*, pp. 159–166. Heiser, *Paulusinszenierung*, p. 267, notes additionally the connection with the tendency in Stoic philosophy to attribute universal significance to their teachers. See also his discussion of this epithet in the context of *Cat.* 8.9 on pp. 411–412, where Heiser notes the combination of teaching and action in Chrysostom's presentation of Paul the teacher.

[61] *Laud.* 4.6–7 (trans. from Mitchell, *Heavenly Trumpet*): Ἐπειδὴ γὰρ ὁ μὲν ἀσεβὴς βασιλεὺς ἔπεσεν ἐλεεινῶς, ἕτερος δὲ εὐσεβὴς διεδέξατο, πάντα εὐθέως ἐλύετο τὰ δεινά·...Ταῦτα τίνα οὐχ ἱκανὰ ἐφελκύσασθαι πρὸς τὴν εὐσέβειαν;...οὐ σταυρὸς κηρύττεται, καὶ ἡ οἰκουμένη προστρέχει; οὐ θάνατος καταγγέλλεται ἐπονείδιστος, καὶ πάντες ἐπιπηδῶσι;

[62] See the comments in Mitchell, *Heavenly Trumpet*, p. 362. Heiser, *Paulusinszenierung*, p. 267, connects Chrysostom's conviction about the universality of Christianity with the *cunctos populos* edict under Theodosius II.

[63] *Laud.* 4.10: "...a man standing in the marketplace, having a trade in skins, became so powerful that he led the entire human race – Romans, Persians, Indians, Scythians, Ethiopians, Sauromatians, Parthians, Medes and Saracenes – singly to the truth; and in less than thirty years at that!" (Ἄνθρωπος γὰρ ἐπ' ἀγορᾶς ἑστηκώς, περὶ δέρματα τὴν τέχνην ἔχων, τοσοῦτον ἴσχυεν, ὡς καὶ Ῥωμαίους, καὶ Πέρσας, καὶ Ἰνδούς, καὶ Σκύθας, καὶ Αἰθίοπας, καὶ Σαυρομάτας, καὶ Πάρθους, καὶ Μήδους, καὶ Σαρακηνούς, καὶ ἅπαν ἁπλῶς τὸ τῶν ἀνθρώπων γένος πρὸς τὴν ἀλήθειαν ἐπαναγαγεῖν ἐν ἔτεσιν οὐδὲ ὅλοις τριάκοντα; trans. from Mitchell,

of Paul's teaching activity – both in its own context and for his late fourth-century congregation[64] – Chrysostom appropriates catechetical terminology and imagery in his interpretations of the Apostle's letters and actions.[65]

Certain passages of Paul's letters tend to elicit discussions of his teaching role. Unsurprisingly by this point in the study, the opening chapters of 1 Corinthians hold a clear importance for Chrysostom in this regard.[66] In his commentary on Isaiah, he turns to 1 Corinthians 3:6 to resolve a tension arising from the fact that Isaiah 3:4 treats young men in leadership as a threat and 1 Timothy 3:6 warns against appointing a neophyte (νεόφυτος), even while being addressed to a young leader, Timothy.[67] John explains,

Indeed, it [*viz.* scripture] says these things not to reprove youth, since even Paul himself, when he says "not the neophyte…," speaks not of the young man, but of the newly planted, that is, one who has been [recently] catechized. For "to plant" is to catechize and to teach, as when he says, "I planted, Apollos watered."[68]

This interpretive move accomplishes three things for Chrysostom. The first, and most obvious, is that he is able to resolve the tension (ostensibly) posed by the leadership of Timothy as a young man. Second, he subtly identifies Paul's ministry with the processes of initiation in place during Chrysostom's day; Paul's teaching in Corinth is specifically correlated with pre-baptismal instruction. Third, following from the previous point,

---

Heavenly Trumpet). See the comments in Vanveller, "Paul's Therapy of the Soul," pp. 39–44, on Chrysostom's construal of Paul's rhetorical superiority.

[64] Heiser, *Paulusinszenierung*, p. 268: "Das zentrale Kennzeichen der Inszenierung des Paulus als Lehrer besteht in der universalen Relevanz seiner Worte und Taten."

[65] The catechetical presentation of Paul traced below is related also to the image of Paul as the ideal ascetic, prevalent in philosophical and monastic circles (so Heiser, *Paulusinszenierung*, pp. 527–554), and both should be read within the broader relationship between catechesis and psychagogy noted above (p. 238), explored particularly by Vanveller, "Paul's Therapy of the Soul," pp. 47–60.

[66] Undoubtedly, this is related to the fact that Paul's ministry – and more specifically his *activities* in Corinth – is a central concern in 1 Cor. 1–4.

[67] 1 Tim. 3:6 is also brought up in restrictions against ordaining the newly initiated in *CA* 2.2.1 (see also *Didasc. apost.* 4; Vööbus, *Didascalia*, pp. 52–53) and Nicene canon §2.

[68] *Comm. Isa.* 3.3: Οὐ τοίνυν τὴν ἡλικίαν διαβάλλων ταῦτά φησιν· ἐπεὶ καὶ ὁ Παῦλος, ὅταν λέγῃ· Μὴ νεόφυτον…οὐ τὸν νέον τὴν ἡλικίαν φησίν, ἀλλὰ τὸν νεωστὶ φυτευθέντα, τουτέστι, κατηχηθέντα· φυτεῦσαι γὰρ τὸ κατηχῆσαί φησι καὶ διδάξαι, ὥσπερ ὅταν λέγῃ· Ἐγὼ ἐφύτευσα, Ἀπολλῶς ἐπότισε. As Dumortier notes, Chrysostom is playing on the etymology of νεόφυτος, which was not normally active in its regular reference to a new convert; Jean Dumortier, *Jean Chrysostome. Commentaire sur Isaïe*, trans. Arthur Liefooghe, SC 304 (Paris: Cerf, 1983), p. 161 n. 2.

this interpretation both clarifies for his listener what kind of instruction is at stake in 1 Corinthians 3:6, according to Chrysostom's reading, and reinforces Paul's work and writings as authoritatively setting precedent for contemporary Christian practice.[69]

Despite the facts that baptism is a crucial initiatory step for John Chrysostom, and that for him Paul is the perfect exemplar of priesthood,[70] nevertheless he sees Paul's vocation as being primarily devoted to preaching and teaching.[71] Discussing Paul's claim that he was sent to preach rather than baptize (despite the fact that he did baptize some of his converts) in 1 Corinthians 1:16–17, Chrysostom elucidates what he sees to be the difference between the two roles.

"Why did he baptize if he was not sent to baptize? He was not fighting against the one who sent him, but going above and beyond in doing this...For preaching the gospel is the province of only one or two people, but baptizing is open to all who have the priesthood. To baptize a person who has received instruction and been convinced is for anyone; for the free choice of the one who approaches accomplishes everything else, along with the grace of God. But whenever it is necessary to instruct unbelievers, this requires great labor and wisdom...For just as teaching wrestlers is the province of a noble man and wise trainer, but even one who cannot wrestle may bestow the crown upon the victor, even though the crown makes the victor more illustrious. So also it is with baptism. For it is impossible to be saved apart from it, but one who baptizes does nothing great, receiving a free choice that is already prepared."[72]

---

[69] See the comments in Tloka, *Griechische Christen*, pp. 132, 167, and *passim*.

[70] The priest, of course, playing an important role in baptism; see his treatment of Paul as the ideal priest in *Sac.* 6.5 and *passim*. See also Lochbrunner, *Priestertum*, pp. 169–172. Mitchell's analysis highlights the way in which John Chrysostom saw his own vocation in Paul's life; Mitchell, *Heavenly Trumpet*, p. 382.

[71] Heiser, *Paulusinszenierung*, addresses the epithets concerning Paul as preacher (Verkündigung) on pp. 253–266 and Paul as teacher (Lehre) on pp. 265–268. He concludes that the presentation of Paul as preaching and teaching to the whole world "stages the universal relevance of their scriptural tradition for the community" (p. 559).

[72] *Hom. in 1 Cor.* 3.3: Καὶ τίνος ἕνεκεν μὴ ἀποσταλεὶς βαπτίζειν, ἐβάπτιζεν; Οὐ μαχόμενος τῷ ἀποστείλαντι, ἀλλ' ἐκ περιουσίας τοῦτο ποιῶν....τὸ μὲν γὰρ εὐαγγελίζεσθαι ἑνός που καὶ δευτέρου, τὸ δὲ βαπτίζειν παντὸς ἂν εἴη τοῦ τὴν ἱερωσύνην ἔχοντος. Ἄνθρωπον μὲν γὰρ κατηχούμενον λαβόντας καὶ πεπεισμένον βαπτίσαι, παντὸς οὑτινοσοῦν ἐστιν· ἡ γὰρ προαίρεσις τοῦ προσιόντος λοιπὸν ἐργάζεται τὸ πᾶν, καὶ ἡ τοῦ Θεοῦ χάρις· ὅταν δὲ ἀπίστους δέῃ κατηχῆσαι, πολλοῦ δεῖ πόνου, πολλῆς τῆς σοφίας...Ὥσπερ γὰρ τὸ μὲν διδάξαι τοὺς παλαίοντας, ἀνδρός ἐστι γενναίου καὶ παιδοτρίβου σοφοῦ, τὸ δὲ ἐπιθεῖναι τὸν στέφανον τῷ νικήσαντι καὶ τοῦ μὴ δυναμένου παλαίειν ἐστί, καίτοιγε ὁ στέφανος λαμπρότερον ποιεῖ τὸν νικήσαντα· οὕτω καὶ ἐπὶ τοῦ βαπτίσματος· ἀδύνατον μὲν γὰρ χωρὶς αὐτοῦ σωθῆναι, οὐδὲν δὲ μέγα ὁ βαπτίζων ποιεῖ, προαίρεσιν παρεσκευασμένην λαβών. On Paul's labor and wisdom in teaching, see also Vanveller, "Paul's Therapy of the Soul," pp. 56–57 and *passim*.

Here, again, Paul's teaching is correlated with pre-baptismal instruction. Notably, John reads Paul's explicit language of preaching the gospel (εὐαγγελίζεσθαι) in terms of catechesis, describing the person taught as ἄνθρωπον...κατηχούμενον λαβόντας. While there seems to be no clearly demarcated boundary between "preaching" and "teaching" (or "instructing") in Chrysostom's initiation vocabulary here,[73] his catechetical reading of 1 Corinthians 1:17 is supported by the fact that, for him, preaching, catechesis, and baptism are all part of a single initiatory process.[74] The teacher, like the wrestling coach, is teaching for a purpose: both are guiding their charges toward the "crown" (ὁ στέφανος).[75] Moreover, as we have already seen, Chrysostom situates the catechumenate within his broader view of the soul's growth toward divine virtue, which influences his framing of Paul's link with the catechumenate as well. Paul's catechetical work here – exhorting, teaching, and catechizing the Corinthians prior to baptism – shares with his post-baptismal ministry the same goal.[76]

This picture of "Paul the catechist" was not only leveraged by Chrysostom for exegetical purposes; it also featured as part of his encomiastic portraits of Paul.[77] On multiple occasions, John's description of Paul dwelt on his imprisonments and sufferings in order to demonstrate that, far from being hindered by his external circumstances, he triumphed through them.[78] "They sent him with the prisoners so that he might not escape, but he catechized those prisoners."[79] Paul, even while in prison,

---

[73] The combination of "instruction/catechesis" with "teaching" in many settings, along with Chrysostom's occasional use of catechesis for foundational instruction (not specifically linked with the catechumenate), illustrates his flexible and associative language of initiation; see above, pp. 180–182.

[74] See Paul's shift from "preaching" to "instructing" in *Hom. 1 Cor.* 21.1. Heiser, *Paulusinszenierung*, pp. 264–265, notes that Chrysostom's epithet "Paul the one who enlightened the world" draws together aspects of teaching with firmly established baptismal imagery of enlightening, further emphasizing the united quality of initiation in Chrysostom's view. Elevation of teaching over baptism is part of the interpretive tradition that precedes Chrysostom: see Edsall, "(Not) baptizing Thecla," pp. 235–260.

[75] This is also relatively common "Pauline" imagery: see 1 Cor. 9:25; Phil 4:1; 2 Tim 2:5 and 4:8.

[76] See the comments in Vanveller, "Paul's Therapy of the Soul," p. 51: "all of Paul's words... serve the unitary goal of meeting the needs of his hearers, of guiding their souls to virtue and health."

[77] On this, the excellent treatment of Mitchell, *Heavenly Trumpet*, remains the standard.

[78] "Chrysostom delightedly exclaims that opposition to the gospel, rather than hindering it, actually worked toward its success"; Mitchell, *Heavenly Trumpet*, p. 307, and note her treatment of Chrysostom's various encomia on Paul's chains (pp. 176–185).

[79] *Laud.* 7.12 (translation modified from Mitchell, *Heavenly Trumpet*, p. 487): Μετὰ δεσμωτῶν ἔπεμψαν, ἵνα μὴ φύγῃ· ὁ δὲ τοὺς δεσμώτας κατήχησε.

before the courts, on a sea voyage, and amid countless dangers is seen "catechizing amid his chains, guiding in mysteries."[80] In both passages, the activity highlighted by Paul is catechesis and in the second passage this is paired with the language of mystagogy, an important feature related to the catechumenate.[81] Further, in both the encomium of *De laudibus Pauli* and the oration of *De statuis,* the picture of Paul is designed for emulation: the Antiochene Christians are to take courage in their own lives and struggles, knowing, by Paul's example, that endurance is possible.[82] Paul not only "instructs" during his life but, as an exemplar of the righteous man, his memory continues to instruct people even after his death.[83]

Moreover, just as we noted above that believers are to "cultivate" their neighbors' souls, elsewhere Chrysostom describes Paul in similar terms: "that blessed man, the amazing teacher of the world, the noble instructor, who cultivates our souls."[84] Andreas Heiser has argued that Chrysostom's use of this epithet differs from Origen's since "he is in fact no longer portrayed as the community founder but rather as a teacher for all Christians."[85] While it is true that Chrysostom does not specifically name catechumens here, two points are worth noting. First, this epithet occurs in the context of one of John's catechetical homilies, and we have already noted that soul-cultivation was elsewhere linked with catechetical preparation by Chrysostom. Second, it will not do to separate the image of Paul as "a teacher for all Christians" from that of Paul as a catechist, for Chrysostom, because the latter role is part and parcel with the former, just as the catechumenate is the initial stage of a Christian life united by constant progress in virtue.[86]

Notably, Chrysostom's appropriation of catechetical language for Paul posed a potential difficulty for his congregation on at least one occasion: understanding Paul's comment that "no one is able to say

---

[80] *Stat.* 1.11, text cited above (p. 170); see the similar picture in *Hom. Col.* 10.3.

[81] See further in 6.2.2 below.

[82] See the analysis in Mitchell, *Heavenly Trumpet*, pp. 401–404, and Lai, "Exemplar portraits," pp. 153–712, who frames Chrysostom's appeals to Paul within his theology of deification. Note that the use of Paul as the ideal catechumen also features in the encomia as well as the baptismal catecheses; see 6.2.1 below.

[83] See the description of the righteous man in *Exp. Ps.* 111.4, noted above (p. 180).

[84] *Cat.* 11.16: ...τοῦ μακαρίου τούτου τοῦ θαυμαστοῦ τῆς οἰκουμένης διδασκάλου, τοῦ καλοῦ παιδοτρίβου, τοῦ γεωργοῦ τῶν ἡμετέρων ψυχῶν...

[85] Heiser, *Paulusinzenierung*, p. 274: "Wie Origenes inszeniert Chrysostomus einen Bauern Paulus, der nicht mehr als Gemeindegründer, sondern als Lehrer aller Christen tätig ist."

[86] Elsewhere, Heiser notes a similar point in relation to Paul's status as νυμφαγωγός (Heiser, *Paulusinzenierung*, p. 422).

'Jesus is Lord' except by the Holy Spirit" (1 Cor. 12:3). As seen above, according to Chrysostom, the catechumen "knows Christ, understands the faith, hears the divine words, is not far from divine knowledge, knows the will of his master."[87]

One says, "What then should we say about catechumens? For if no one is able to say that Jesus is Lord except by the Holy Spirit, what should we say concerning them who name his name but are lacking the Spirit?" But the present discussion is not about them. For there were no catechumens then; rather he is only speaking about believers and unbelievers.[88]

This illuminating passage raises at least two important issues. In the first place, Chrysostom here explicitly notes the historical difference between his own congregation and the Corinthian church in question.[89] Second, the need for such a clarification, even if it is a rhetorical one, demonstrates that Chrysostom thought it possible that such an objection on behalf of catechumens could be present among his listeners. This is doubly important: it shows that his catechetical reading/portrayal of Paul was a deliberate interpretive move (rather than a naïve anachronism) and it shows that this catechetical reading/portrayal of Paul was successful. At least some parishioners, it seems, took Chrysostom's catechetical image of Paul quite seriously.[90]

The picture of Paul as catechist in Chrysostom's work could be greatly extended, thanks to the size of his corpus and his love of Paul. Rather than follow it exhaustively, however, I will simply highlight a few of the more striking places in which John's catechetical reading appears.

Integral to portraying Paul as the catechist for his congregations (and, indeed, all congregations, according to Chrysostom) is the treatment of the Apostle's initial teaching as catechesis. We have already noted

---

[87] *Hom. Heb.* 13.5, cited above (p. 174).

[88] *Hom. 1 Cor.* 29.2: Τί οὖν, φησί, περὶ τῶν κατηχουμένων ἂν εἴποιμεν; εἰ γὰρ οὐδεὶς δύναται εἰπεῖν Κύριον Ἰησοῦν, εἰ μὴ ἐν Πνεύματι ἁγίῳ, τί ἂν εἴποιμεν περὶ τούτων, ὀνομαζόντων μὲν αὐτοῦ τὸ ὄνομα, Πνεύματος δὲ ἀπεστερημένων; Ἀλλ' οὐ περὶ τούτων ὁ λόγος αὐτῷ νῦν· οὐ γὰρ ἦσαν κατηχούμενοι τότε· ἀλλὰ περὶ πιστῶν καὶ ἀπίστων.

[89] See the comments in Young, *Biblical Exegesis*, p. 253, who notes that, though Chrysostom typically engaged in "ancient literary criticism" which "had no sense of anachronism or historical distance," he was "not unaware that the text belongs to another 'narrative' from that to which he and his congregation belong."

[90] It is worth noting that Chrysostom's explanation that "there were no catechumens" in view does not actually solve the difficulty presented by reading this passage within the framework of the institutional catechumenate. If there were no catechumens at that point, there were certainly catechumens listening to the sermon in which scripture is read that says that there is no way to declare "Jesus is Lord" without the Spirit.

Chrysostom's approach to this above, though his exegetical efforts there were focused on resolving tensions raised by the passages in question. For instance, we find Chrysostom portraying Paul as reminding his readers of their own catechesis. When Paul speaks of his work among the Corinthian believers in 1 Corinthians 9:12, John assumes the persona of Paul, stating that he ("Paul") was at pains to avoid "'any hinderance to the gospel,' that is, your catechesis."[91] Paul's teaching, correlated with pre-baptismal "planting" elsewhere, is again explained here in catechetical terms intelligible to his audience. Further, this account of the Apostle fits with John Chrysostom's broader understanding of Christian psychagogy: Paul provides a prime example (ὑπόδειγμα) of a teacher who is able to adapt to the weakness of his listeners in accomplishing his catechetical task.[92]

In his third homily on 1 Corinthians, Chrysostom draws on the practice of baptismal enrollment to explain what is at stake in the Corinthian factions, with each person claiming allegiance to Paul, Apollos, etc. "If it was not fitting to apply to themselves the names of Paul, Apollos, and Cephas, how much less so for others? If it was not fitting to register the teacher and chief of apostles as their patron, even one who catechized so many people, how much more so for those who are of no account?"[93] The term for registering used here (ἐπιγράφεσθαι) is similar to the term commonly used for baptismal enrollment (ἐγγράφεσθαι) but was also used in the context of choosing an official patron or teacher.[94] Chrysostom highlights the extent to which the Corinthians were misguided by playing on the concept of inscription. Paul "catechized" the Corinthians, which should lead – according to initiatory practice in Chrysostom's church – to their enrollment for baptism. But now, instead of undertaking baptismal registration, they "register" themselves as *Paul's* students. And if it is illegitimate to treat the Apostle in such a manner, with all his

[91] *Hom. 1 Cor.* 21.3: ἢ ἐγκοπήν τινα δοῦναι τῷ εὐαγγελίῳ, τουτέστι, τῇ κατηχήσει ὑμῶν. See also *Hom. 1 Cor.* 21.2; *Hom. 1 Tim.* 17.2 (of Paul's reminder to Timothy); *Hom. 2 Cor.* 4:13 3.4 (reminding the recipients of Hebrews).

[92] The weak state of the Corinthians is given as the motivation for Paul's concern to avoid certain hindrances (ἐπειδὴ γὰρ ἀσθενέστερον Κορίνθιοι διέκειντο), which is subsequently highlighted as an "example" (*Hom. 1 Cor.* 21.3). This adaptability is related to the themes of divine concession and care for the soul, noted above (pp. 61, 238).

[93] *Hom. 1 Cor.* 3.1: Εἰ γὰρ Παύλου καὶ Ἀπολλὼ καὶ Κηφᾶ οὐκ ἐχρῆν ἐπιφημίζειν ἑαυτοῖς τὰ ὀνόματα, πολλῷ μᾶλλον ἑτέρων. Εἰ τὸν διδάσκαλον, καὶ πρῶτον τῶν ἀποστόλων, καὶ τοσοῦτον κατηχήσαντα δῆμον, οὐκ ἐχρῆν ἐπιγράφεσθαι, πολλῷ μᾶλλον τοὺς οὐδὲν ὄντας.

[94] For ἐπιγράφειν, see *Hom. 1 Cor.* 1.1 (Ὁ διδάσκαλος ὑμῶν Χριστός· καὶ ὑμεῖς ἀνθρώπους ἐπιγράφεσθε τῆς διδασκαλίας προστάτας); *Hom. Phil.* 1.3 (καὶ ἐκεῖνον ἐπιγραφόμεθα διδάσκαλον); Lucian *Herm.* 14 (οἱ τὸν Πλάτωνα ἐπιγραφόμενοι); and the other examples listed in LSJ *s.v.* ἐπιγράφω III.5.

qualifications, how much more foolish is it to enroll under others? Even the "first of the apostles" (πρῶτος τῶν ἀποστόλων) cannot claim such allegiance.

The final example comes from Chrysostom's homilies on 2 Timothy and is notable not only for its catechesis language, but also for the fact that it draws on apocryphal material. Commenting on 2 Timothy 4:16, he asks "what sort of 'first defense' is he [*viz.* Paul] speaking about? He had already stood before Nero and escaped, but when he catechized his wine bearer he then beheaded him."[95] As noted in Chapter 3, the story of Paul and Nero's wine bearer comes from the martyrdom of Paul preserved in *APl* 14. In that story Patroclus, the wine bearer, came to listen to Paul "teaching the word of God," before becoming sleepy, falling from the window, and being revived by Paul.[96] While no baptism is specified as a result of Paul's teaching in *APl* 14, Patroclus later boldly claims to be a Christian, leading to his imprisonment. As Chrysostom reads this story, however, Paul's διδασκαλία becomes explicitly κατήχησις, suggesting that Paul's teaching of Patroclus is what led to his being a Christian.[97] In fact, as I argued in Chapter 3 above, a catechetical reading of Paul's activity in (at least some parts of) the *Acts of Paul* is justified apart from and prior to Chrysostom's particular interpretive commitments. On his telling of Paul's martyrdom, though, it was part of Paul's greatest task that led ultimately to his death: instructing Nero's favored servant.

The catechumenate was not only a personal experience common to John Chrysostom and his parishioners; it was also an institution that pervaded fourth-century church life in Antioch and Constantinople. Catechumens, though excluded from full participation, particularly with respect to the celebration of the eucharist, were recognized community members with a weekly liturgical element, institutional parameters, trajectory, and integration with the body of the "faithful." This institutional context provided both the resources and the occasion for Chrysostom's depiction of Paul as the catechist. His catechetical reading of Paul allowed him to communicate the significance of Paul's teaching – in relation to its initial recipients as well as for his own listeners – and suggest a continuity

---

[95] *Hom. 2 Tim.* 10.2: Ποίαν δὲ πρώτην ἀπολογίαν λέγει; Παρέστη ἤδη τῷ Νέρωνι, καὶ διέφυγεν· ἐπειδὴ δὲ τὸν οἰνοχόον αὐτοῦ κατήχησε, τότε αὐτὸν ἀπέτεμεν.

[96] *APl* 14.1: ἤκουσεν αὐτοῦ διδάσκοντος τὸν λόγον τοῦ θεοῦ. The parallels with Acts 20:29 have long been noted.

[97] Chrysostom may have found support for this interpretation in the statement that it was at Paul's teaching that "many souls were converted to the Lord" (πολλαὶ ψυχαὶ προσετίθεντο τῷ κυρίῳ; *APl* 14.1).

of praxis between the Apostle and the fourth-century catechumenate. The success of both of these elements is thrown into sharp relief by Chrysostom's acknowledgment of historical difference for the sake of assuaging his listeners' concerns about the status of catechumens. Moreover, his depiction of Paul as the most virtuous Christian, whom everyone should imitate, and his casting of Paul as the ideal figure of the psychagogue and priest are closely related to Paul's role as the catechist: these were necessary qualities for a teacher.[98] The injunctions to imitate Paul extended from his virtue to his teaching activities, serving as an example for all Christians, who were to act on their general responsibility to participate in catechetical instruction through sponsorship and (at least unofficial) teaching.

6.2.1 Paul the Catechumen

This picture of Paul as a model of virtue and practice was regularly presented by John Chrysostom. Even while praising the Apostle's great achievements and superior (even supra-angelic) virtue, he emphasizes strongly the human side of Paul so as not to put such moral heights out of reach for his listeners.[99] This kind of appeal to Paul, noted above in Chrysostom's depiction of the Apostle's teaching activities, is also present in his account of Paul's conversion. Chrysostom portrays Paul as an ideal catechumen whose conversion and initiation process provide an example not only for the numerous catechumens in the congregation, but also for those who had already been baptized but had not yet begun to be actively engaged in their new community.[100]

Chrysostom's depiction of Paul's conversion appears in different contexts in which the general contours are the same, despite differing emphases. According to his presentation, Paul was a catechumen without need of a human catechist. Paul's conversion/initiation experience follows the framework familiar to a late fourth-century congregation, though in

---

[98] See *Hom. Tit.* 2.2, cited in 6.1.1 above.

[99] See Mitchell, *Heavenly Trumpet*, *passim*; Lai, "Exemplar portraits," pp. 130–172; see also *Laud.* 2.10.

[100] Chrysostom's construal of Paul's conversion is also closely aligned with his concern for depicting the conversion to non-Jewish orthodox Christianity as part of the healing of the soul; see Vanveller, "Paul's Therapy of the Soul," p. 64: "John's psychagogic framing of Paul, first as patient and then as physician, simultaneously appropriates and repudiates Paul's Jewishness in a way that serves to bolster his construct of Paul as an exemplar of non-Jewish Christian orthodoxy."

a compressed and intensified way. In his discussion of the conversion narrative in Acts 9, Chrysostom begins with a question, "Why then did he [*viz.* Christ] not call up one of the chief apostles, and send him to catechize Paul?"[101] Such an effort was unnecessary because Paul "needed to be inducted not by humans, but rather by Christ himself."[102] Chrysostom is clear on this point: "that man" Ananias (οὗτος) taught Paul nothing, but merely baptized him. As we have already noted, Chrysostom considers the act of dispensing baptism to be less significant than the effort of catechetical instruction. The former is an act that works with the willingness of the baptizand, while the latter works against the unreformed nature of the catechumen to form them into something worth baptizing.[103] Ananias has had the physical element of the sacrament outsourced to him, but that is the limit of his contribution.[104]

Despite this lack of catechetical instruction, at the moment of his baptism Paul "absorbed much grace from the Spirit by his zeal and great enthusiasm."[105] As the author of Acts says, "immediately he began to preach about Christ in the synagogues, that he is the son of God" (Acts 9:20). Chrysostom repeats the point for emphasis, "Look! Immediately he was a teacher in the synagogues."[106] How is such a change possible in the absence of any sort of instruction? In what way was he "inducted" by Christ during this experience? Chrysostom's answer is that, although he needed no teaching, "the experience itself became his instruction."[107] This rather vague explanation will have been more intelligible for those listeners who had been paying close attention earlier in that series of homilies. In his opening homily on Acts, Chrysostom dedicates part of his

---

[101] *Hom. Act.* 20.1: Τί δήποτε οὐδένα τῶν κορυφαίων ἀποστόλων οὔτε ἐκάλεσεν, οὔτε ἀπέστειλε πρὸς τὴν τοῦ Παύλου κατήχησιν;

[102] *Hom. Act.* 20.1: Ὅτι οὐκ ἐχρῆν δι' ἀνθρώπων ἐνάγεσθαι, ἀλλὰ δι' αὐτοῦ τοῦ Χριστοῦ·; see the comments on the guidance of the divine psychagogue in Vanveller, "Paul's Therapy of the Soul," pp. 67–70.

[103] See the discussion of *Hom. 1 Cor.* 3 above (pp. 184–185).

[104] This account stands in tension with the version of Paul's conversion given in *Ep. apost.* 31 (extant only in Ethiopic; edition and French translation in L. Guerrier and S. Grébaut (eds. and trans.), *Le Testament en Galilée de Notre-Seigneur Jésus-Christ*, Patrologia Orientalis 9 (Paris: Firmin-Didot, 1913), pp. 212–214; English in Julian V. Hills (ed. and trans.), *The Epistle of the Apostles* (Santa Rosa, CA: Polebridge Press, 2009)). There Jesus tells the other apostles (rather than Ananias) to instruct Paul after his conversion, prior to his taking up the mission to the Gentiles; see also the general discussion of the text's portrayal of Paul in Dassmann, *Der Stachel*, pp. 261–266.

[105] *Hom. Act.* 20.1: Ἅμα γοῦν τῷ βαπτισθῆναι ἐπεσπάσατο πολλὴν τοῦ Πνεύματος τὴν χάριν ἀπὸ τοῦ ζήλου καὶ τῆς προθυμίας τῆς πολλῆς.

[106] Ibid.: Ὅρα, εὐθέως διδάσκαλος ἦν ἐν ταῖς συναγωγαῖς·

[107] Ibid.: Ἆρα οὐκ ἐδεήθη διδασκαλίας ἑτέρας, ἀλλὰ τὸ συμβὰν γέγονε διδασκαλία.

time to explaining the timing of baptism and exhorting the catechumens present not to delay their own baptism. He argues that one cannot have the benefit of baptismal grace unless one is suitably vigilant and sober in mind,[108] which requires time for such preparation. As he does so often, Chrysostom presents Paul as a clear example of this. "Grace did not come immediately, but three days passed in between, during which he was blind, while he was being cleansed and prepared by fear."[109] Paul's circumstances, through which Christ instructed him for baptism, took him from unprepared erstwhile opponent of the Church to being a prepared cloth ready to receive the dye of the Spirit.[110]

Paul's portrait as ideal catechumen also occurs during Chrysostom's catechetical lectures. In a homily delivered to neophytes sometime during Easter Week, he directs the attention of his newly baptized listeners to Paul. Although Paul was a violent persecutor of the Church,

> when he enjoyed the benefit of the benevolence from the master, and having been illuminated by the light that is [only] apprehended by the mind, he set aside the darkness of his error and was led to the truth. And through baptism he cleansed himself of all his previous sins. Suddenly, without a single intervening moment, the one who had formerly acted for the sake of Jews in everything and attacked the church immediately began to confound those living in Damascus, preaching that the crucified one is the Son of God.[111]

Paul's biography is ideal for Chrysostom's purposes here because, when it is read within the catechetical framework of the fourth century, the Apostle can be shown to embody all of Chrysostom's goals for his own listeners. Even with a remarkably short period of preparation, Paul demonstrated

---

[108] *Hom. Act.* 1.5: Οὐ γὰρ ἔστιν, οὐκ ἔστι χάριτος ἀπολαῦσαι μὴ νήφοντα; see also the comments in Roten, *Baptême et mystagogie*, pp. 33–34.

[109] *Hom. Act.* 1.6: Οὕτω καὶ ἐπὶ Παύλου· οὐκ εὐθέως ἡ χάρις ἦλθεν, ἀλλὰ τρεῖς ἡμέραι ἐγένοντο μεταξύ, ἐν αἷς ἦν τυφλός, ὑπὸ τοῦ φόβου σμηχόμενος καὶ προπαρασκευαζόμενος; see also Mitchell, *Heavenly Trumpet*, p. 257 n. 269.

[110] This analogy is Chrysostom's own: Καθάπερ γὰρ οἱ τὴν ἁλουργίδα βάπτοντες, πρότερον ἑτέροις τισὶ τὸ δεχόμενον τὴν βαφὴν προπαρασκευάζουσιν, ἵνα μὴ ἐξίτηλον γένηται τὸ ἄνθος (*Hom. Act.* 1.6). This is not to exclude the importance of Paul's own will in the process of conversion (so Vanveller, "Paul's Therapy of the Soul," p. 70), just as it factored in Chrysostom's discussion of Paul's instruction of others for baptism; see the comments on *Hom. in 1 Cor.* 3.3 above (p. 185).

[111] *Cat.* 8.7: ἐπειδὴ φιλανθρωπίας ἀπέλαυσε παρὰ τοῦ δεσπότου καὶ καταυγασθεὶς τῷ φωτὶ τῷ νοητῷ ἀπέθετο τὸ σκότος τῆς πλάνης καὶ πρὸς τὴν ἀλήθειαν ἐχειραγωγήθη καὶ διὰ τοῦ βαπτίσματος ἀπελούσατο τὰ προλαβόντα ἅπαντα ἁμαρτήματα, ἀθρόον οὐδὲ τὸ τυχὸν ἀναβαλλόμενος, ὁ πρὸ τούτου ὑπὲρ Ἰουδαίων ἅπαντα πράττων καὶ πορθῶν τὴν ἐκκλησίαν, εὐθέως συνέχυνε τοὺς Ἰουδαίους τοὺς κατοικοῦντας ἐν Δαμασκῷ, κηρύσσων ὅτι ὁ ἐσταυρωμένος αὐτός ἐστιν ὁ υἱὸς τοῦ Θεοῦ; see the comments in Mitchell, *Heavenly Trumpet*, p. 251 n. 235.

immediate moral and doctrinal transformation. As Chrysostom hopes for his catechumens, Paul "set aside the darkness of his error" and was led willingly to baptism. Further, as Chrysostom hopes for his neophytes, and for all the πιστοί, Paul's initiation led to his energetic preaching about Christ as the Son of God. The generalized responsibility for teaching, noted above, is here shown to be taken up by Paul, not after many years in the Church, but immediately and powerfully.

6.2.2 Paul the Mystagogue

The final element of Chrysostom's appropriation of catechetical language for Paul pertains also to the final stage of instruction: mystagogy. As we noted earlier (Chapter 2.4), the language of mystagogy, which had long been closely associated with Greek mysteries and so-called "gnostic" groups in early Christianity, became widespread in the fourth century in relation to catechetical instruction.[112] The anxieties of Irenaeus over the gnostic μυσταγωγοί and their varying systems of μυσταγωγία are no longer in play when Cyril of Jerusalem states, "The daily mystagogical lectures are beneficial to you."[113] During this period, mystagogical catechesis consisted primarily in the explanation of baptism and the eucharist for the benefit of those already baptized (so Cyril of Jerusalem and Ambrose) or those enrolled for baptism during Lent (so Theodore of Mopsuestia).[114] John Chrysostom included mystagogical instruction in the course of the Lenten homilies so that the baptizands might understand beforehand the rites in which they were about to participate.[115]

Chrysostom uses the terms μυσταγωγεῖν and μυσταγωγία to refer to teaching and events surrounding initiation in three ways. First, and most

[112] Although a positive appropriation of mystagogical language begins with Clement of Alexandria and Origen, even there it is used primarily in analogy with the better-known Greek (pagan) mysteries; e.g., Clement *Strom.* 4.25.162.3; Origen *Cels.* 3.60.

[113] Cyril of Jerusalem *Myst.* 2.1 (in Reischl and Rupp, *Opera*). He goes on to say that they are "new teachings" and "new accounts of practices" given to those renewed from the old to the new: Χρήσιμαι ὑμῖν αἱ καθ᾽ ἡμέραν μυσταγωγίαι, καὶ διδασκαλίαι καινότεραι, καινοτέρων οὖσαι πραγμάτων ἀπαγγελτικαί, καὶ μάλιστα ὑμῖν, τοῖς ἀνακαινισθεῖσιν ἀπὸ παλαιότητος εἰς καινότητα. For μυσταγωγοί and μυσταγωγία in Irenaeus, see respectively *Haer.* 1.14.1, 1.8.17; see also Roten, *Baptême et mystagogie*, pp. 51–52.

[114] The timing of Ambrose's mystagogical instruction is provided in *Myst.* 1.2 – explaining the mysteries before baptism would be thought a betrayal (*prodo*) rather than an explanation (*edo*).

[115] See *Cat.* 7.12; Gavrilyuk, *Histoire*, p. 255. Chrysostom limits the "mysteries" to the baptismal rite itself – beginning with the renunciation of Satan and ending with eucharist; *Cat.* 7.17–27.

generally, he often uses mystagogy language to refer to the event of initiation itself, including both the baptism and the celebration of the first eucharist. The faithful are at times referred to simply as οἱ μυσταγωγούμενοι, those who have been initiated, while those who guided them are οἱ μυσταγωγοῦντες.[116] The event of initiation is the point at which one transitions from sickness to health, after which point sins take on a new, insidious significance.[117] Examples of this general use could be multiplied.[118] Alongside the general use, the terminology could also apply to particular elements of the initiation process. It is at baptism that the Spirit is received, ἐν τῇ μυσταγωγίᾳ.[119] In explaining the significance of the Pauline baptismal motif of being "watered with the Spirit," and "sharing one body" (1 Cor. 12:13–14), Chrysostom states, "that is, we all came to the same initiation, we enjoy the same table."[120] That is, they came previously to baptism and they are consequently still free to enjoy the eucharist.[121]

Mystagogy is also the teaching that prepares one for the event of baptismal initiation. The mysteries, according to Chrysostom, are to be received in physical and mental health (rather than *in extremis*), for otherwise "how can one who is beside themselves be prepared carefully for initiation?"[122] When speaking to his congregation, he often makes

---

[116] See respectively *Hom. Jo.* 85.3 and *Hom. 1 Cor.* 40.1.

[117] For the transition from sickness to health, see *Hom. Act.* 1.8 (a wife watching ἑτέρου μυσταγωγουμένου, though Migne notes a textual difficulty here); and for the dangers of post-initiation sin, see *Hom. Jo.* 28.1: "For we do not pay these same penalties for those same sins but much harsher ones when we err after mystagogy" (Τῶν γὰρ αὐτῶν ἁμαρτημάτων οὐ τὰς αὐτὰς τίννυμεν δίκας, ἀλλὰ πολλῷ χαλεπωτέρας, ὅταν μετὰ μυσταγωγίαν πλημμελήσωμεν).

[118] See *Cat.* 1.49 and 3.3; *Hom. 1 Cor.* 3.3; Knupp, *Mystagogieverständnis*, p. 67 and *passim*; Roten, *Baptême et mystagogie*, pp. 55–57.

[119] *Hom. Jo.* 78.3. It is significant for Chrysostom's baptismal theology of the Spirit that his rite evidently lacked a post-baptismal anointing (so Cyril and Ambrose) or signing (so Theodore). See the synopsis of post-baptismal rites in Hugh M. Riley, *Christian Initiation: A Comparative Study of the Interpretation of the Baptismal Liturgy in the Mystagogical Writings of Cyril of Jerusalem, John Chrysostom, Theodore of Mopsuestia, and Ambrose of Milan*, The Catholic University of America Studies in Christian Antiquity 17 (Washington, D.C.: Catholic University of America Press, 1974), pp. 349–363; and the synopsis of the Cappadocians in Saxer, *Les rites*, pp. 314–315.

[120] *Hom. 1 Cor.* 30.2: Τουτέστι, πρὸς τὴν αὐτὴν ἤλθομεν μυσταγωγίαν, τῆς αὐτῆς ἀπολαύομεν τραπέζης. Kohlgraf, *Ekklesiologie*, pp. 307–309, notes that, for Chrysostom, the Church-as-body image in Ephesians is important for expanding the account from 1 Corinthians.

[121] See Roten, *Baptême et mystagogie*, p. 53. At times (e.g., *Natal.* 7), Chrysostom refers to the eucharist as μυσταγωγία, but not in the immediate context of initiation. Both the eucharist and baptism are often referred to by him with the plural μυστήρια, as noted by Roten, *Baptême et mystagogie*, pp. 83, 93.

[122] *Hom. Act.* 1.7: μυστηρίων δὲ καιρός, ὑγεία φρενῶν, καὶ σωφροσύνη ψυχῆς...πῶς ἄν τις ἐξεστηκὼς δυνηθείη μετὰ ἀκριβείας μυσταγωγεῖσθαι;

veiled reference to mystagogical instruction, claiming that the "initiates" know or that they have been "instructed in the mysteries with care."[123] While this instruction included discussions of the baptismal rites and the first eucharist, though with far less theological development than one finds in similar accounts from Ambrose or Theodore of Mopsuestia, John Chrysostom's characteristic concern for moral development is present there as well.[124] His use of mystagogical terminology reflects the close connection between mystagogical instruction and mystagogical initiation; the one implies the other.[125]

We already saw above that Chrysostom associated Paul with mystagogy in his depiction of Paul in chains, "instructing amid his very chains, initiating" those around him.[126] While these kinds of encomiastic treatments of Paul were designed by Chrysostom for imitation, the image presented here can only be imitated to an extent: a lay person may participate in "instructing" but they do not participate in the mystagogy itself. It was the prerogative of priests to preside over baptism and the eucharist. Importantly, Paul is not described explicitly as a μυσταγωγός, but rather his activities are identified with mystagogy. As the catechumenate is the preparation for the marriage in baptism, Paul is the νυμφαγωγός who leads the bride to the bridegroom.[127] For Chrysostom, though, the *true*

---

[123] *Hom. 1 Cor.* 24.5: οὐδὲν ἀγνοεῖς τῶν δι' αὐτοῦ τελεσθέντων, μετὰ ἀκριβείας μυσταγωγηθεὶς ἅπαντα (in reference to the eucharist); *Hom. Rom.* 2.6: ἴστε δὲ οἱ μύσται τὸ λεγόμενον (in relation to the "enlightenment" of believers); *Hom. 1 Tim.* 5.3: Ἴστε οἱ μύσται τὸ εἰρημένον (in reference to the "mystery" of *Pascha* and the Spirit); etc.

[124] In the first two homilies in the Papadopoulos-Kerameus series (*Cat.* 2–5), for instance, mystagogical discussions are interspersed with the pressing issue of swearing that Chrysostom saw as rife among in his congregations. On the theological development in Ambrose and Theodore, see Enrico Mazza, *Mystagogy: A Theology of Liturgy in the Patristic Age*, trans. Matthew J. O'Connell (New York: Pueblo, 1989), pp. 14–104.

[125] So also Knupp, *Mystagogieverständnis*, p. 289: "Somit bedeutet Mystagogie für Chrysostomus einen ganzheitlichen Prozeß, der mit der Einschreibung in die Taufbewerberliste beginnt und in der Initiationsfeier seine Vollendung findet."

[126] *Stat.* 1.11 (cited on p. 170 n. 1); see also *Hom. Act.* 9:1 4.3: "As for Onesimus, who had become a runaway slave and thief and had stolen some of his master's goods, Paul received and converted him, and thus guided him to the holy mystagogy..." (Τὸν γοῦν Ὀνήσιμον δραπέτην καὶ κλέπτην γενόμενον, καὶ τῶν δεσποτικῶν ὑφελόμενόν τι χρημάτων, ὑποδεξάμενος ὁ Παῦλος καὶ μεταβαλών, καὶ οὕτω πρὸς τὴν ἱερὰν χειραγωγήσας μυσταγωγίαν...).

[127] *Cat.* 4.9: πλὴν ἀλλ' ἐπιλαβώμεθα τῆς χειρὸς τοῦ νυμφαγωγοῦ Παύλου, ὃς τὸ πλῆθος διατεμὼν εἰσαγαγεῖν ἡμᾶς πρὸς αὐτὴν δυνήσεται. The bridal imagery is dominant in Chrysostom's catechetical instructions; see Sartore, "Aspetti cristologici," pp. 143–146; Mazza, *Mystagogy*, p. 126; Riley, *Christian Initiation*, p. 100. Heiser, *Paulusinzenierung*, pp. 269–270, notes that Chrysostom uses this epithet in relation to Paul's election as the one specially appointed to present the Church as the bride of Christ; Heiser therefore includes it among Chrysostom's "ecclesiological" epithets for Paul. See also the

mystagogue is God himself, because the human agent of mystagogy "introduces nothing" to the process. "Every work is by the power of God, and that one is your mystagogue."[128] This activity is only able to be generalized to a limited extent.

Paul's mystagogy, however, also includes lessons in virtue. The image of Paul in prison, carrying out his ministry, is turned by Chrysostom to highlight the fact that Paul's virtue is achievable for his parishioners. Paul's flesh did not hinder his virtue and, moreover, even his stints in prison and chains "were no hindrance" in that respect, "at least, so Paul taught."[129] The mystagogy in view here does not correlate easily with teaching about the mysteries of baptism and the eucharist, though it is in keeping with Chrysostom's dominantly moral concerns in his catechetical homilies.[130] Paul's mystagogy is part of his ministry that stands as an exemplar for all elements of Christian initiation. Depending on his pastoral needs, Chrysostom portrays Paul as catechist, catechumen, and mystagogue.

6.3 CHRYSOSTOM'S CATECHIST IN THE FOURTH CENTURY

While Chrysostom's work allows us to trace his reading in some detail, elements of his catechetical reading are present in other fourth-century writers in a variety of locales.[131] Writing in the West around the time that Chrysostom was writing in the East, the commentator Ambrosiaster developed a reading of 1 Corinthians 1:17 similar to Chrysostom's explored above. He states bluntly, "it is better to preach the gospel than to baptize; for that reason he said that he was not sent to baptize but to preach the

---

extended discussion of Chrysostom's marriage imagery in relation to the reception of Ephesians in Kohlgraf, *Ekklesiologie*, pp. 310–352.

[128] *Hom 1 Cor.* 8.1: Οὐδὲν γὰρ ἄνθρωπος εἰς τὰ προκείμενα εἰσάγει, ἀλλὰ τὸ πᾶν τῆς τοῦ Θεοῦ δυνάμεως ἔργον ἐστί, κἀκεῖνός ἐστιν ὑμᾶς ὁ μυσταγωγῶν. Roten, *Baptême et mystagogie*, p. 58, connects this specifically with the eucharist, despite the context in which Chrysostom is discussing baptism.

[129] *Hom. Jo.* 75.5: Τὸν γοῦν Παῦλον οὐκ ἐκώλυσε τῆς σαρκὸς ἡ φύσις γενέσθαι τοιοῦτον, οἷος ἐγένετο…Πρόσθες καὶ δεσμωτήριον καὶ κλεῖθρα, καὶ οὐδὲ οὕτω κώλυμα γίνεται ταῦτα τῇ ἀρετῇ. Οὕτω γοῦν ἐμυσταγώγησεν ὁ Παῦλος. See esp. Mitchell, *Heavenly Trumpet*, pp. 176–186, for an account of Chrysostom's encomiastic treatment of Paul's chains.

[130] As Enrico Mazza, *Mystagogy*, p. 109, puts it, "his mystagogy stresses an element not present like anything to the same extent in the mystagogy of the other Fathers of the Church: the continual emphasis on moral behavior."

[131] The work of Heiser, *Paulusinzenierung*, in particular emphasizes the inherited quality of most of Chrysostom's epithets and "staging" for Paul.

gospel."[132] Ambrosiaster goes on to explain this elevation of teaching by noting that "not all who baptize are qualified to preach the gospel. For the words spoken during baptism are formulaic."[133] Although he does not include explicit language of catechism, Ambrosiaster interestingly may conflate the words (*verba*) spoken during baptism with the preaching of the gospel (*evangelizare*). Though brief, this could point toward a similarly unified view of initiation in which "preaching" leads toward baptism and, in this case, even features *during* the baptismal rite itself.[134]

More directly, as Chrysostom read Paul's letters in light of the catechumenate, couching Paul's discussions of teaching in terms of cat-echetical instruction, so also did other fourth-century writers in both the West and the East. According to the Armenian translation of Ephrem the Syrian's commentary on Paul's letters, he read the greeting "to the holy and faithful" in Ephesians 1:1 and Colossians 1:1 as speaking to two distinct groups. "'To the holy and faithful,' that is 'to the baptized and the catechumens.'"[135] The faithful, πιστοί, are those already baptized for Chrysostom as well. Marius Victorinus wrote in Rome in the midst of the influx of catechumens noted earlier.[136] His reading of Galatians 6:6 reflects this even as he explains the Greek etymology of the term κατηχίζειν. "This is the meaning: κατηχίζειν is 'to surround with sound' or even 'to make a sound to someone,' which happens when a certain

[132] *Comm. in 1 Cor.* 1:17 (MPL 17: 187–188): "'Non enim misit me Christus baptizare, sed evangelizare' Quoniam majus est evangelizare, quam baptizare; ideo non se missum baptizare dicit, sed evangelizare."

[133] *Comm. in 1 Cor.* 1:17: "non magnum esse baptizare, quia non omnis qui baptizat, idoneus est et evangelizare. Verba enim sollemnia sunt, quae dicuntur in baptismate."

[134] Note also that Ambrose of Milan reads 1 Cor. 1:17 in relation to Paul's vocation as a *stabularius* (innkeeper) who cares for the Church, along with the other apostles (*Exp. Luc.* 7, lines 792–808; in Marc Adriaen (ed.), "Expositio evangelii secundum Lucam," in *Sancti Ambrosii Mediolanensis Opera*, vol. 4, CCSL 14 (Turnhout: Brepols, 1957), pp. 1–400). Notably, while the focus of care for the apostolic *stabularii* is on preaching and baptism, Paul himself is singled out in relation to teaching.

[135] *Comm. Eph.* 1:1: "սրբոց և հաւատացելոց, այս ինքն վկրատորաց և երախայից"; on Col 1:1: "Սրբոց, ասէ, և հաւատացելոց: Սուրբս զկնրատորսն կոչէ, և հաւատացելոց զերախայսն անուանէ" ("'To the holy,' he said, 'and to the faithful': 'Holy' refers to the baptized and 'faithful' names the catechumens"); text in Ephrem, *Srboyn Ep'remi Matenagrut'iwnk'*, vol. 3 (Venice: Monastery of St. Lazarus, 1836), p. 139 lines 3–4, p. 165 lines 19–21; Latin translation in Ephrem, *S. Ephræm Syri Commentarii in Epistolas d. S. Pauli* (Venice: Monastery of St. Lazarus, 1895), pp. 141, 169.

[136] See *Comm. Eph.* 2.6.18 (in F. Gori (ed.), *Marius Victorinus. In epistulam Pauli ad Ephesios, In epistulam Pauli ad Galatas, In epistulam Pauli ad Philippenses*, CSEL 83/2 (Salzburg: Österreichischen Akademie der Wissenschaften, 1986)), where he lists various groups from saints and bishops to catechumens.

person begins to be a Christian by initiation, and the sound of God and Christ is made to him, and spoken in his ears, and is fixed in his soul."[137] Here, Victorinus' focus on verbal communication is partly shaped by the fact that the text he is commenting on has such communication in view. However, it is also consonant with fourth-century catechetical practice, which may well have encouraged him to connect Paul's term κατηχίζειν with the beginning of Christian instruction.

Notably, Chrysostom's reading of 1 Corinthians 3:6 is preceded by a similar reading from Gregory of Nyssa: "It says, 'Guiding those who approach the mystery.' This comment fits Apollos beautifully, who watered Paul's planting. For the apostle planted through catechesis, but Apollos watered, when he baptized, leading those whom Paul had instructed to the mystery through mystical regeneration."[138] More explicitly than did Chrysostom, Gregory identifies the planting with catechesis and the watering with baptism. Gregory himself was deeply concerned about proper catechetical instruction, composing the extensive *Oratio catechetica* which focused, in contrast with much prior catechetical writing, almost entirely on doctrinal and mystagogical issues, leaving only the very end of the final chapter for a discussion of moral formation.[139]

Retrospectively, then, one can see a line of catechetical interpretations of 1 Corinthians 3:6 extending from the *Acts of Paul*, through Origen, into the fourth century. Even more broadly, the connection between milk and catechesis so prevalent in Clement and Origen's writings may also appear in passing in the *Didascalia apostolorum*. Originating perhaps as early as the late third century, but whose extant Syriac version is from the fourth,[140] that church order document

---

[137] *Comm. Gal.* 2.6.6 (in Gori, *Marius Victorinus*): "Sensus iste: κατηχεῖν est circumsonare vel iuxta adsonare, quod contingit cum aliqui initio Christianus incipit esse et illi deus et Christus adsonatur et dicitur in aures eius atque in animum inmittitur..."

[138] *Ref. conf. Eunom.* 218–219 (in Werner Jaeger (ed.), *Gregorii Nysseni opera*, vol. 2.2 (Leiden: Brill, 1960)): μυσταγωγῶν, φησί, τοὺς προσιόντας τῷ μυστηρίῳ. τοῦτο καλῶς ἔχει λέγειν περὶ Ἀπολλῶ τοῦ τὴν φυτείαν Παύλου ποτίζοντος. φυτεύει μὲν γὰρ διὰ τῆς κατηχήσεως ὁ ἀπόστολος, ποτίζει δὲ βαπτίζων ὁ Ἀπολλῶς διὰ τῆς μυστικῆς ἀναγεννήσεως προσάγων τοὺς παρὰ Παύλου κατηχουμένους τῷ μυστηρίῳ.

[139] See the plan of the work outlined in Raymond Winling, *Grégoire de Nysse. Discours catéchétique*, SC 453 (Paris: Cerf, 2000), p. 25, and see the discussion of moral formation in *Or. Cat.* 40.4 (Winling, *Discours*, pp. 332–337). Gregory of Nyssa also composed the oration on those who delay their baptism (*De iis qui baptismum differunt*; MPG 46: 416–432).

[140] See the discussion in Vööbus' introduction to his translation; Vööbus, *Didascalia*, vol. 1, pp. 25*–28*.

refers to the instruction passed on by bishops in relation to baptism as "milk."[141]

Chrysostom's less common portrayal of Paul the mystagogue can also be seen in passing in Gregory Nyssen's *Oratio catechetica*. In moving from the contemplation of visible to invisible realities, Gregory states that Paul himself follows this pedagogical method with the Ephesians. "And the great Paul, having begun [*viz.* from the visible], initiates the people in Ephesus, implanting in them through teaching an ability to know 'what is the depth and the height, the breadth and length.'"[142] Gregory goes on to relate each of Paul's points to parts of the cross, though the image of Paul the mystagogue is not developed further there.[143] The easy reference to mystagogy here reflects the approach to such mystery language in the fourth century, absent any anxiety of contamination with Greek mysteries that plagued earlier writers.

As we have seen in previous chapters, images of Paul as "catechist" and catechetical interpretations of his letters hardly originated in the fourth century. Their proliferation during that period, however, is no doubt due in part to the increasingly widespread standardization of the catechumenate, the increased number of catechumens, and the increased number of extant works from the period. These early Christian teachers and writers are developing an interpretive tradition that preceded them. The texts that activate Chrysostom's catechetical reading, along with some of the other readings noted here, are in many cases the same texts that elicited similar readings in earlier writers. For Chrysostom, Paul as catechist provides the model for contemporary catechetical practices, even where institutional differences persist. The concern for moral formation is related to Paul's own virtue and his teaching. The way in which catechesis leads to baptism is rooted in Paul's ministry.

---

[141] *Didasc. apost.* 9 (ed. Vööbus, *Didascalia*, vol. I, p. 109 line 19–p. 110 line 4). Bishops are described as "those who, begat you anew through the water…who reared you with the word, like 'milk'" etc. (ܩܘܩܘܝܢ ܪܟܠܝܘܢ ܐܝܟ ܪܚܠܒܐ ܐܢܘܢ…ܡܢ ܡܝܐ ܐܘܠܕܘܟܘܢ ܪܚܕ ܒܢܝܐ ܐܢܘܢ).

[142] Gregory Nyssen *Or. cat.* 32.75: ἀλλὰ καὶ τὴν ὄψιν γενέσθαι τῶν ὑψηλοτέρων νοημάτων διδάσκαλον, ὅθεν καὶ ὁ μέγας ὁρμηθεὶς Παῦλος μυσταγωγεῖ τὸν ἐν Ἐφέσῳ λαόν, δύναμιν αὐτοῖς ἐντιθεὶς διὰ τῆς διδασκαλίας πρὸς τὸ γνῶναι Τί ἐστι τὸ βάθος καὶ τὸ ὕψος, τό τε πλάτος καὶ τὸ μῆκος·

[143] See the Euthalian *Epitome* 701A–705A (noted in Chapter 1 above), in which Ephesians marks the end of the catechetical progression (mystagogy?) of the beginning of Paul's letter collection. Later, in the ὑπόθεσις section (761C–764A), Ephesians is also referred to as a "catechetical" letter.

Arriving at the end or the fourth century, then, we find both the golden age of the catechumenate and the culmination of the association between Paul and the catechumenate that began toward the end of the second century. In terms of the questions posed in Chapter 1, we have now surveyed "what happened" when these early writers read about Paul in their catechetical contexts. What remains now is to begin to answer the second question: "What, if anything, do these early readings mean for interpreters of Paul today?" In order to answer this question, the next chapter will begin with a synthetic analysis of the previous historical material to identify key recurring themes and the textual resources on which a catechetical reading of Paul is built. I will then situate the ancient interpretations of particular passages within contemporary New Testament Studies, before turning to the broader images of Paul at stake in contemporary scholarship and the catechetical Paul of Chrysostom and his predecessors. The final chapter will then reflect on the hermeneutical framework within which ancient readings can act as constructive dialogue partners with contemporary modes of interpretation.

7

Textual Resources and a Catechetical Paul

> Everyone knows that Paul was misunderstood very soon in the early Church. As yet, however, much less investigated is the question "how was Paul misunderstood?"[1]

This epigraph, as noted in the Introduction, reflects a common view of early Christian interpretation of Paul that dominated the first half of the twentieth century. If Seesemann's language of "misunderstanding" is problematic, the question he poses nevertheless remains helpful here. The interrogative "how" can of course be taken in more than one sense. For his part, Seesemann generally limits himself to discussing the ways in which Clement of Alexandria's theology differs from his own view of Paul's thought. But the question points beyond this to a more fruitful inquiry if we understand "how" to signify a question about the factors that led the early readers of Paul to make the interpretive decisions that they did. To that end, in Chapters 3 to 6 we have now analyzed in some detail the way in which one factor shaped how writers from the late second century to the late fourth century portrayed Paul and interpreted his letters. What began as a subtle narrative presentation in the *Acts of Paul* culminates in a view of Paul as the apostle of initiation, writing "catechetical" letters in the Euthalian Apparatus, and declaring apostolic canons about the catechumenate in the *Constitutiones apostolorum*.

---

[1] Seesemann, "Paulusverständnis," p. 312: "Daß Paulus in der Alten Kirche sehr bald mißverstanden wurde, ist allbekannt. Viel weniger ist man jedoch bisher der Frage nachgegangen, wie Paulus mißverstanden wurde…"

Having now traversed the development of these catechetical presentations individually, the time has come for a more synthetic analysis. In the present chapter I will explore the textual resources that were deployed by these interpreters in the service of their various projects and bring these into conversation with contemporary scholarly approaches to the Apostle. In this way, this chapter acts as a sort of threshold between the historical account of Pauline reception and the hermeneutical question about the meaning or value of these early readers for contemporary scholarship. To begin, we will draw together the various interpretations of Paul surveyed above, highlighting particularly the recurring textual resources and the implications for the view of Paul more broadly present among these early readers. These elements will then be brought into dialogue with contemporary scholarship on Paul and its critical forebears, both at the detailed exegetical level and at the level of a more general Pauline image.

The extensive, diverse, even fragmentary, state of New Testament scholarship means that these conversations will be brief and selective. The exegetical discussion will focus primarily on exegesis of passages in 1 Corinthians 1–3 which recurred in the previous chapters, with some reference also to Hebrews and Romans. Differing interpretive strategies between ancient and contemporary readers suggest different underlying images of Paul, in the present case particularly with reference to Paul's relationship to ecclesial structures and authorities. This leads to the discussion of broader Pauline images, which is here limited to the contrast between the catechetical image of Paul (and its implications) and the image of Paul as a controversial and independent figure. Allowing for differences in the details, I suggest that such an image of Paul is prevalent today, and I trace a brief genealogy through F. C. Baur back to the debate between Erasmus and Luther. Notably, in the genealogy of this Pauline image, interpretations of 1 Corinthians 1–3, and its relative priority over other Pauline passages, find an important place again. In other words, the textual basis for the catechetical Paul, drawn from 1 Corinthians 1–3, runs throughout this chapter as it moves from detailed exegetical discussion to exploring the role that those passages play in constructing a broader image of Paul.

Although the chapter covers much ground, it also remains somewhat too brief. This is not least because in the archaeological and genealogical assessment of one's own field of study, and so in a sense of one's own academic formation, there is always more to be uncovered. For instance, while I mention it in passing in Chapter 1.1, more could be said about the debated place of institutional structures among Pauline communities which was so influentially exemplified in the debate between Rudolph Sohm and Adolf von Harnack.[2] The impact of contemporary institutions on exegetical discussion would also be a very useful, if difficult, area of further research. A fruitful place to begin might be a study of Ernst Käsemann's explicit engagement with the ecumenical movement, the World Council of Churches, in the course of his Pauline or broader New Testament exegesis.[3] To do so here, though, would exceed the bounds of what is already a long chapter.

Nonetheless, even with the limited scope of the present argument, the analysis below will, I hope, illuminate how early Christian interpretation can be situated within contemporary exegetical debates, and offer insights into the contours and resources of the texts in question. We begin now with the summary analysis of the catechetical Paul.

7.1 A CATECHETICAL PAUL: RESOURCES AND IMPLICATIONS

7.1.1 Summary

Beginning perhaps as early as Irenaeus but more clearly in the *Acts of Paul*, the image of the Apostle was being subtly influenced by the emerging catechetical institution. We saw earlier that the author of the *Acts of Paul* portrayed Paul as the premier example of persuasive preaching and teaching.[4] His sermons enthralled listeners, particularly Thecla, and called all to a life of chastity, whether or not one was already married. Being baptized after conversion required the demonstration of previous moral transformation, and Paul exercised his prerogative as instructor to delay Thecla's baptism until she had proved to be able to maintain

---

[2] On this debate, its legacy, and its exegetical foundations, see White, "Traditional and ecclesiastical," pp. 651–669.

[3] For Käsemann, his ecumenical institutional commitments worked dialectically with his early exegetical investigations on the Church as the body of Christ. On the one hand, his exegesis provided foundational resources for his theological engagement (Ernst Käsemann, "Aspekte der Kirche," in *Kirchliche Konflicte*, vol. 1 (Göttingen: Vandenhoeck & Ruprecht, 1982), p. 12), while on the other hand his contemporary commitments – from a rejection of nationalist churches to a constructive ecumenical impulse and engagement – shaped his exegetical questions and decisions (see Käsemann, "Theological problem," p. 110). A clear picture of Käsemann's theological method is evident in his famous 1963 address to the World Council of Churches: Ernst Käsemann, "Unity and diversity in New Testament ecclesiology," *Novum Testamentum* 6, no. 4 (1963), 290–297.

[4] For a more complete argument for what follows, see Chapter 3 above.

the faith under trials. Her request for baptism to ward off a coming trial (πειρασμός) suggested a misunderstanding of baptism as an apotropaic act. Paul, on the other hand, exhorts "endurance" in trials before baptism (*APl* 3.25). As elsewhere in early Christianity, the possibility of Thecla becoming unfaithful after baptism was too great a danger to risk on a young, untested postulant.[5]

This portrayal of Paul was constructed, we saw, from a variety of sources. On the one hand, we should not discount the possibility of oral or other local traditions available to the writer which are otherwise lost to contemporary scholars.[6] More important for present purposes are the textual resources that underpin this presentation of the Apostle. In Paul's opening sermon in Iconium, we noted a conflation of Pauline material, particularly regarding virginity from 1 Corinthians 7, with Jesus traditions preserved particularly in the Matthean beatitudes. Paul's teaching, then, is portrayed as being in harmony with Jesus' own message. Furthermore, the narrative mode is shaped by impulses traceable to Paul's self-presentation in his letters, particularly in 1 Corinthians. In addition to the emphasis on virginity (or chastity, for those already married) in 1 Corinthians 7, we noted that Paul's primary role as "teacher" and his deferral of Thecla's baptism reflected his statement in 1 Corinthians 1:17 that he was sent to preach the gospel rather than baptize. As is the case across Christian communities in the late second century, baptism remains a crucial step for initiation, and Paul's teaching leads people in that direction. The act of baptism, however, was not itself an integral part of his ministry. Similarly, the image of Paul and Apollos as a "co-workers" for the planting and watering of new believers (1 Cor. 3:6) recurs in relation to Thecla's own baptism: while Paul has planted the gospel, now she has become God's co-worker for her own baptism.

The image of Paul, then, is not simply that of a rogue apostle preaching his own gospel, contrary to the criticisms of Demas and Hermogenes (*APl* 3.12–14). Rather he is one who both works within the parameters of Jesus' teaching and acknowledges other teachers such as Thecla who are baptized independently of him. Paul's commissioning of Thecla indicates that they are both treated as proclaiming the same gospel, which Luke

---

[5] See the above discussion in Chapter 3.4 (citing Tertullian *Bapt.* 8.5 and 18.4; Cyprian *De zelo* 10) and Chapter 6.1.1 (citing Chrysostom *Hom. Act.* 1.6); note also *Didasc. apost.* 5 (in Vööbus, *Didascalia*, vol. 1, p. 60): "everyone who does evil after baptism is already condemned to the fiery Gehena."

[6] So the argument in Marguerat, "Paul after Paul," pp. 5–6, 9, and see the discussion of oral traditions in Chapter 3 above.

and Titus continue to serve after Paul's death. Paul, then, is a divine teacher and a careful catechist who is closely aligned with Jesus and the work of other Christian teachers.

This image of Paul and his connection with the catechumenate we found even more explicit in the work of Clement of Alexandria.[7] Clement displays a deep concern for the place of the catechumenate within his broader pedagogical vision for the Christian life. He portrays Paul as the true Gnostic, who models the work of the Logos, the true pedagogue for humanity. In this role Paul imparts esoteric knowledge, wisdom, and mysteries to those who are able to receive them, but for others he condescends to address them where they are.[8] To defend this view of Christian progression – stretching continuously from conversion, through catechesis and baptism, to the end of life and ascension to God – Clement leaned heavily on two Pauline texts and on the image of Paul's ministry. The mention of "milk" and "solid food" in 1 Corinthians 3:1–3 offered Clement both the challenge of refuting his interlocutors, evidently on their own terms, and the basis for his argument in favor of a fundamental continuity between initial catechetical instruction and subsequent advanced teaching. The first stage was one of improving the soul and controlling passions, while the later stages added further teaching on the basis of the moral groundwork. Teaching that went "beyond catechesis" simply expanded what was present already in the catechesis itself and was guided by the same "ecclesiastical canon," just as "milk" and "meat" have the same essence but in a different form.[9] Further, to counter both the Valentinians and those Christians who rejected philosophy, Clement took Paul's phrase "from faith to faith" in Romans 1:17 to show that the same faith encompasses the whole of Christian life. Philosophically developed theology and elementary catechesis are both within the framework of his pedagogically differentiated faith.[10] Milk, then, is catechesis and solid food is the later theological instruction.[11] Paul is shown to have supplied the framework for Christian initiation in addition to his concern for the mysteries. Furthermore, as the true Gnostic, Paul condescended to *act* pedagogically by circumcising Timothy (Acts 16:3), because he

---

[7] For a more complete argument for what follows, see Chapter 4 above.

[8] See Clement's treatment of Paul and his interpretation of Col. 1:25–17 in *Strom.* 5.10.60.1–61.2.

[9] *Strom.* 6.18.165.1 and *Paed.* 1.6.37.3–38.1.

[10] *Strom.* 5.1.2.3–6.

[11] *Strom.* 5.10.66.2.

endeavored to be "a Jew to Jews" so that he might "win" them (1 Cor. 9:20).[12]

From this discussion, two points concerning Clement's portrayal of Paul emerge clearly. The first is that 1 Corinthians 3:1–3 and Romans 1:17 supply a basic framework for Clement's construal of progress in Christian life and teaching. These passages secure the sufficiency and ongoing validity of catechetical teaching while also allowing him to emphasize the importance of further theological and philosophical learning. The second point is that, as in the case of the *Acts of Paul*, Clement's Paul is one who teaches in harmony within the wider Church tradition. Clement links Paul's ministry and teaching directly with the activity of the divine Logos and, as is expected, displays no qualms at interpreting Paul and Acts together in light of one another, in addition to harmonized readings with numerous other scriptural texts. Paul, then, is a pedagogue – working with catechesis to form the souls of new converts – and a teacher – imparting Gnostic knowledge to the prepared. He works within the canon of the Church and provides a theological framework and a paradigmatic example of Clement's vision for the Church.

A similar vision of Paul is present in Origen, who leans on several of the same Pauline images for his own portrait of the Apostle. For Origen, Paul appears as a mature Christian teacher who is able to accommodate himself to the beginner while also leading believers to the spiritual interpretation of scripture and the mysteries. Drawing from Paul's self-presentation in 1 Corinthians 1:17, Origen's Apostle is called to the "greater" task of preaching.[13] Origen's engagement with the catechumenate is a consistent part of his ministry, made clear particularly in relation to his homilies delivered in Caesarea. His dual vocation there as a philosophical teacher in his school and as a homilist in the church relates to his bipartite view of the Church which maps directly onto the two institutional structures: the "many" are infants who cannot (or will not) pursue the mysteries of spiritual interpretation. They are those whom Origen instructs during his daily sermons, addressing catechumens among other *simpliciores*. In addition to 1 Corinthians 3:1–3, which he puts to regular use along with Hebrews 5:14 and Romans 14:2 to describe the basic instruction of catechumens and *simpliciores*, Origen emphasizes the material surrounding it from 1 Corinthians 2:1–3:6. Paul speaks mysteries to the mature, but for the immature he speaks only

---

[12] Both cited in *Strom.* 7.9.53.3–4.
[13] *Frag. 1 Cor.* 5.

"Christ crucified" as he cultivates the soil of their souls to uproot vice and prepare them for the holy seeds of Christian doctrine. Paul, then, "cultivates the souls of catechumens" (1 Cor. 3:6),[14] who are eventually planted with Christ in baptism (Rom. 6:5). Just as Jesus receives children from his disciples in Matthew, so also Paul brings his "infant" converts to Christ, as do Origen and others in his own day. Like Clement, and in continuity with the pedagogically sensitive Paul in the *Acts of Paul*, Origen reads Paul's circumcision of Timothy in Acts as further demonstrating his willingness to condescend to his audience for the purpose of taking them from the truths of the material world to the spiritual mysteries to which they point. Origen's Paul is ecclesial and pedagogical, from the catechetical stage to deeper exegetical and theological training. The former is only the beginning of many stations of the Christian life in a progress toward spiritual perfection.

In the fourth century, John Chrysostom displays the fullest example of catechetical readings of Paul, while evidence of similar images of Paul emerges across the Roman empire and beyond, from Marius Victorinus in the West to Ephrem in the East. Notably, John Chrysostom does not normally attempt to justify his catechetical reading of Paul on exegetical or historical grounds. Rather, he presumes the image of Paul in that role and then deploys it in a variety of exegetical, encomiastic, and pastoral contexts. Similarly, as seen in Chapter 1, Paul's role as apostle of initiation in the *Constitutiones apostolorum*, declaring ecclesial canons about the catechumenate and baptism, is simply taken for granted. The author of the Euthalian Apparatus, moreover, not only supplied an explicit pedagogical development in Paul's letters from catechesis to spiritual mysteries but also arranged the text of the letters themselves to aid in this progressive development.

For John Chrysostom, as for every author surveyed above, 1 Corinthians 1–4 forms an important basis for his catechetical portrait of the Apostle. Paul's principal task is that of teaching – a teaching that leads to baptism – while the actual ritual act normally falls to others. Hence, Paul "planted" while Apollos is the one who "watered" the Corinthians (1 Cor. 3:6). Like Ambrosiaster, and building on a longer interpretive trajectory, Chrysostom sees 1 Corinthians 1:17 as supplying scriptural warrant for this emphasis on Paul's teaching activities, and particularly on the early catechetical stages of instruction. Drawing also on the image

---

[14] See *Frag. 1 Cor.* 41.

of Paul in the Pastoral Epistles and Acts, he argues that Paul supplies
the criteria for who can teach catechumens while also demonstrating the
ministry himself.[15] Just as God and Christ condescend to humanity in
history and scripture, so Paul condescended to teach the ignorant, and
thereby supplied a model of virtue and the Christian life for all who come
after. Paul teaches in harmony with the other apostles and with Christ
while he engages in catechesis and mystagogy for neophytes.

7.1.2 Implications

Across all these authors, despite their variations in exegetical focus, there are
a few notable recurring Pauline resources to which they return again and
again. The first three chapters of 1 Corinthians supply a crucial foundation
for a pedagogical and adaptive image of Paul from the *Acts of Paul* through
the late fourth century, possibly even including the Valentinian interlocutors
faced by Clement of Alexandria, which undergirds the close association
forged between the Apostle and the catechumenate.[16] Interestingly, as noted
in Chapter 2, early twentieth-century scholarly reconstructions of catechetical materials in the New Testament also regularly drew on 1 Corinthians 1–3
to support the idea of a fixed catechesis shared by the broader early Christian
movement. Romans also supplied resources for catechetical readings by
Clement and Origen, though in both cases they brought in the passages from
Romans as further support for an aspect of Paul's ministry identified in 1
Corinthians. In addition, early writers ubiquitously borrowed from Acts and
the Gospel traditions to fill out their image of Paul's ministry, though again
these are often interpreted in relation to passages from 1 Corinthians.[17]

Apart from the dominance of 1 Corinthians in these portrayals of Paul,
three further points arise from the survey above. First, it may be obvious,
but is worth noting, that these writers are not concerned with producing historical accounts of Paul's life and ministry as such. Rather, they
recognized themselves as being among those addressed by Paul – through

---

[15] The importance of the Pastoral Epistles for the early Pauline reception is emphasized well
in Aageson, *Paul*; see also White, *Remembering Paul*, pp. 116–121, 142–158. Notably,
however, the Pastoral Epistles play a relatively minor role in providing explicit resources
for a catechetical image of Paul.

[16] It is worth mentioning here that Margaret Mitchell has already noted and described
in fascinating detail the way in which Paul's Corinthian correspondence served as the
diolkos for early Christian hermeneutical reflection: "the road to early Christian hermeneutics [runs] through Corinth"; Mitchell, *Paul, the Corinthians*, p. 4.

[17] E.g., the circumcision of Timothy and Paul's self-proclaimed variability in 1 Cor. 9:20, or
the image of Jesus and the children in Origen's *Comm. in Matt.* 15.6.

his ministry activity and his letters – and therefore being implicated in his ministry; they produce their Pauline images from that perspective.[18] Even the *Acts of Paul*, which purports to present a narrative account of Paul's ministry, was allegedly written out of "love for Paul."[19] This is not to say that they did not occasionally recognize the historical distance between their own time and that of Paul. We noted in Chapter 6 how Chrysostom could acknowledge the lack of a catechumenate in Paul's Corinth to solve an interpretive issue arising from his catechetical presentation of the Apostle. Further, although Origen appears to take the historical veracity of scriptural accounts of Paul as given, his scriptural hermeneutic did not require that all details relate to actual historical events, nor was that his interest.[20] Scripture, after all, uses material language and images to speak about spiritual realities, and it is the latter that are the truly important goal. The authors were reading Paul with the assumption that he would speak to them and provide answers to their questions.

The second point is that Paul is a thoroughly ecclesial figure for these authors. This is clear and overt in Origen, Chrysostom, and the *Constitutiones apostolorum*, and is evident more subtly in the *Acts of Paul* and Clement of Alexandria. In these latter two, Paul is depicted as being closely aligned with the figure and work of Christ. Further, for both writers, Paul works within a larger context that includes other teachers and ministers, even if he serves as the paradigmatic example of the (Gnostic) teacher. By the late fourth century, Paul stands among the other apostles and imparts ecclesial canons. While he is certainly *the* Apostle for all writers explored in Chapters 2–6, there are nevertheless others, including other apostles, among whom Paul works. If the emerging ecclesial institutions are only subtly present in the *Acts of Paul*, for the writers from Clement onward, Paul works within and even helps to establish the ecclesial vision and structures inhabited by the interpreters. His letters and personal example demonstrate, for these readers, a concern for proper baptismal preparation and execution, for the subsequent

---

[18] See the similar comments on Reformation interpreters in Chester, *Reading Paul*, p. 59.

[19] That is to say, the author had no interest in pursuing a historical account "wie es eigentlich gewesen," in the (now infamous) words of Ranke.

[20] See the comments in Cocchini, *Origene*, p. 211: "Origen was well aware that history was essentially limited, dealing with times and places in any case 'other' and 'distant' from those which constituted the immediate context that he was invited to know." While Cocchini is commenting on Origen's reading of Jeremiah, he could make similar distinctions in New Testament interpretation, between what a story literally conveyed about Jesus and its spiritual meaning for believers, as in *Comm. in Matt.* 15.6 (discussed on p. 158).

progress of the Christian life, and for the institutional framework that makes such progress possible.

This leads to the third point: the Paul of these authors is fundamentally a pedagogical figure. For Clement, Origen, and John Chrysostom, and in a more subtle way for the author of the *Acts of Paul*, Paul's ministry and message is marked by his willingness to condescend to his listeners. We saw in the *Acts of Paul* that the Apostle was careful to assess Thecla's preparation for baptism, displaying initial concern over her ability to "guard her baptism" (*APl* 3.6) under duress. On Clement's and Origen's readings, the milk/meat framework of 1 Corinthians 3:1–3 is not merely a polemic of the moment but reflects Paul's deeper conviction that there is more than one level of teaching and his concern for the maturation of believers, that they should in fact move from "milk" to "meat."[21] John Chrysostom, too, treated Paul as the human exemplar of divine condescension.[22]

In all cases, this pedagogical image of Paul was linked with catechetical instruction. Such initial teaching was not the end of Paul's task as Apostle to the Gentiles, but it was nevertheless a crucial part of his ministry: in preaching and training believers for baptism, Paul provided precedent for Clement's pedagogical framework, as well as for Origen's and John Chrysostom's ministries. For the author/compiler of the Euthalian traditions, Paul's letters, properly construed, continue to catechize and lead believers in spiritual development.[23] In other words, *Paul's pedagogical quality was ecclesiologically inflected in specific, institutionally linked ways*. The consistency with which the pedagogical image of Paul was associated with the catechumenate by the fourth century suggests that it had become an interpretive tradition, one that functioned within the broader set of ecclesial traditions in that period.

It is important to emphasize that these readings and re-presentations of Paul cannot be reduced to roughshod misreadings or ignored as the product of blithe anachronism. Rather, they are the product of an interpretive dynamic at play in the encounter between the horizon of the interpreters and the Pauline texts.[24] These writers' horizons were shaped by their particular historical contexts and their negotiation of various institutional and intellectual traditions, and their horizons in turn provided the vantage point from which they could come to an understanding of Paul's

---

[21] I return to the distinction between these two ways of reading Paul below, pp. 230–250.
[22] In addition to Chapter 6 above, see also Rylaarsdam, *Divine Pedagogy*, pp. 157–193.
[23] Chrysostom also views Paul's letters as continuing his ministry after his death; see Chapter 6.2 above.
[24] This anticipates the fuller discussion in Chapter 8 below.

letters. Origen in Caesarea, for instance, negotiated two institutional contexts – as schoolmaster and homilist – for which he found resources in scripture and the interpretive tradition received from Clement regarding milk and solid food. The catechumenate featured as an important part of Origen's vision for Christian progress, then, precisely because it features as the first "milky" step in the process of learning to ingest the "solid food" of the mysteries. The figure and writings of Paul helped Origen to understand his own role in this process of negotiation.

These observations prepare the way for bringing the ancient interpreters explored here into dialogue with twentieth- and twenty-first-century historical-critical New Testament scholarship. Further hermeneutical reflections on the relationship between old and new interpretations, as they emerge from this work, will follow in Chapter 8. At present, all that is needed is the practical observation that the work of early Pauline interpreters impinges upon contemporary Pauline interpretation at the levels of individual exegetical points, broader images of Paul, and the general interpretive dynamic. At each level these early interpretations can become fruitful dialogue partners not despite their historical and potential philosophical or hermeneutical distance from modern interpreters but because of it. Differing historical situations that encourage, even require, particular sets of questions and differing concerns force interested interpreters to engage with textual resources perhaps otherwise overlooked or suppressed.

7.2 READING THE OLD WITH THE NEW

In what follows, I will explore the ways in which the early presentations of Paul examined here can be brought into conversation with more recent Pauline scholarship, at the level of exegetical detail and at the broader level of constructed Pauline images. The interpretive dynamic just noted will also come to light here. Three caveats are warranted at the start, however.

First, and as noted earlier, the field of New Testament Studies is wide and varied; not all interpretive paradigms or scholars are engaged to the same extent by these ancient interpreters. For instance, in the case of the so-called New Perspective and its detractors, the theological questions and interpretive anxieties about the relationship of Judaism and Christianity are entirely lacking in the interpreters surveyed above or, perhaps in some cases, not lacking but actually reversed.[25] The textual resources from 1

---

[25] John Chrysostom's treatment of Christians who also attend the synagogue or observe the Jewish festival calendar is well known; see Robert Louis Wilken, *John Chrysostom*

Corinthians, which Clement, Origen, and John Chrysostom relied on to shape their image of Paul, are largely bypassed in many recent major Pauline studies, which focus rather on the meaning and implications of theological terminology such as justification, righteousness, and grace.[26] The question of a catechetical or pedagogical Paul is simply not on the

---

and the Jews: Rhetoric and Reality in the Late 4th Century (Berkeley: University of California Press, 1983). This stands in sharp contrast with, for instance, James D. G. Dunn's overt concern for Jewish–Christian rapprochement in his various works; see his recent work, Dunn, *Neither Jew nor Greek*. This is not to say, however, that there is no overlap between patristic writers and other aspects of the New Perspective, as argued by Athanasios Despotis and Matthew Thomas: see Athanasios Despotis, *Die "New Perspective on Paul" und die griechisch-orthodoxe Paulusinterpretation*, Veröffentlichungen des Instituts für Orthodoxe Theologie 11 (St. Ottilien: EOS, 2014); Matthew J. Thomas, *Early Perspectives on Works of the Law: A Patristic Study*, WUNT II (Tübingen: Mohr Siebeck, 2018).

[26] For example, Douglas A. Campbell, *The Deliverance of God: An Apocalyptic Rereading of Justification in Paul* (Grand Rapids: Eerdmans, 2009), never cites 1 Cor. 3:1–3 and only cites 1 Cor. 1:17b and 1 Cor. 2:6 once in relation to Paul's claim for rhetorical simplicity (p. 161). Similarly, N. T. Wright, *Paul and the Faithfulness of God*, 2 vols., Christian Origins and the Question of God 4 (Minneapolis: Fortress Press; London: SPCK, 2013), evidently never cites 1 Cor. 3:1–3 directly. (The apparent citation of 1 Cor. 3:1 on p. 432 listed in his index is in fact an error: the citation in question is a reference to 2 Cor. 3:1.) His discussions of 2:6–8 focus on the "apocalyptic" elements of Paul's vision for the victory of Christ over the powers and so, understandably, he gives no space to a pedagogical image of Paul in the book. In line with the central debate in Pauline scholarship for the last century or more, Wright's discussions of Romans 1:17 also focus principally on the meaning of δικαιοσύνη, with the exception of a brief comment on p. 502 n. 126. James D. G. Dunn, *The Theology of Paul the Apostle* (Grand Rapids: Eerdmans, 1998), is slightly more balanced in his treatment of these passages, owing at least in part to his attempt at a comprehensive account of Paul's theology. Even so, he explicitly privileges Romans as "a kind of template" of Paul's mature thought (pp. 25–26) and the best basis for our own views of Paul. The work of Johan Christiaan Beker, *Paul the Apostle: The Triumph of God in Life and Thought* (Philadelphia: Fortress, 1980), though differing from many New Perspective concerns, cites 1 Cor. 3 only once and finds these a sarcastic rather than pedagogical Paul (p. 218), on which see further below (pp. 218–225). This privileging of Romans as the center or clearest statement of Paul's thought reaches back at least to the Reformers (Melanchthon referred to Romans as a "doctrinae christianae compendium" (*Loci communes* 0.17; text in Philipp Melanchthon, *Loci communes 1521. Lateinisch – Deutsch*, trans. Horst Georg Pöhlmann (Gütersloh: Gütersloher Verlagshaus, 1993), p. 24), a view also taken by later Lutheran New Testament scholars such as Rudolf Bultmann, *Theology of the New Testament*, 2 vols. (London: SCM, 1952), vol. 1, p. 190, and Günther Bornkamm, "The Letter to the Romans as Paul's last will and testament," in Karl P. Donfried (ed.), *The Romans Debate* (Edinburgh: T. & T. Clark, 1991), pp. 16–28. John Barclay's recent contribution (John M. G. Barclay, *Paul and the Gift* (Grand Rapids: Eerdmans, 2015)) explicitly follows the theological lead of post-Reformation, protestant discussions of grace, and focuses within the Pauline corpus primarily on Galatians and Romans.

radar for these scholars.[27] On the other hand, feminist or post-colonial writers may perhaps feel that a pedagogical image of Paul needs to be rejected on ethical grounds, as that which reproduces (or at least risks the reproduction of) unhealthy authoritarian power structures.[28] I will return to the question of differing or competing images of Paul below, but it is precisely this lack of overlap, even contradiction, between the catechetical image of Paul and contemporary scholarly readings that leads to my next caveat.

The discussion here is not intended to be a comprehensive engagement with the possible interpretations or reception history of these key passages. Indeed, this is not even a comprehensive engagement with the interpretations of these passages in each of the early authors discussed in the previous chapters. The guiding (and therefore constraining) theme in Chapters 3–6, the importance of the catechumenate for interpreting and presenting Paul, entailed that only those interpretations of 1 Corinthians 1–3 (and related passages) that were related to the catechetical presentation of Paul were covered in any detail. It remains the case, though, that Clement, Origen, and John Chrysostom were not opposed to finding multiple meanings in the same passage and putting them to different use, depending on the context. A few of these will in fact be highlighted below. This point is part of the reason why the present argument will not claim that we should (or could) simply adopt one of these early readings. Rather, the purpose here is simply to situate the early readers of Paul within contemporary exegetical discussions in order to show that these "pre-critical" readers can act as valuable dialogue partners for contemporary scholars.

The third caveat relates to the role of institutions in interpretation. It is true today, as it was in antiquity, that institutions factor differently into

---

[27] I will return briefly to early twentieth-century treatments of catechetical materials in the New Testament briefly in Chapter 7.2.2 below.

[28] E.g., the problematizing of "imitation" themes in Paul by Elizabeth A. Castelli, *Imitating Paul: A Discourse of Power*, Literary Currents in Biblical Interpretation (Louisville: Westminster/John Knox Press, 1991), or the attempt to recover silenced female prophetic figures in Corinth by Antoinette Clark Wire, *The Corinthian Women Prophets: A Reconstruction Through Paul's Rhetoric* (Minneapolis: Fortress Press, 1990). Note also the efforts of Neil Elliot to liberate Paul from possible hierarchical and oppressive readings of his letters, including relatively gentle versions of social hierarchy such as Gerd Theissen's category of "love patriarchalism"; see Neil Elliott, *Liberating Paul: The Justice of God and the Politics of the Apostle* (Minneapolis: Fortress Press, 2006), pp. 64–65 and *passim*, which critiques Gerd Theissen, *The Social Setting of Pauline Christianity: Essays on Corinth*, trans. John H. Schütz (Philadelphia: Fortress Press, 1982).

the work of different interpreters, some more so than others. So, while institutional concerns do not always appear in contemporary exegetical arguments, they begin to operate more clearly at the level of one's larger image of Paul. Nevertheless, in the remainder of this chapter the institutional influences on contemporary interpreters recede somewhat from view. It is still worth noting, however, that modern New Testament scholarship writes, for the most part, from a Western academic context for an audience of other Western academics.

7.2.1 Scriptural Resources

As we have seen, the principal textual basis for the image of the "catechetical" Paul is found in 1 Corinthians 1–3. The other passages that played an important role – Romans 1:17 for Clement, Hebrews 5:14 and Romans 14:2 for Origen – were read in connection with the self-presentation of Paul that is grounded in the opening chapters of 1 Corinthians. It is these key passages, then, which will be the focus of the discussion here.

7.2.1.1 *1 Corinthians 1:17 and 3:6*
In the face of a factious Corinthian community, with various groups rallying behind different teachers, including at least Paul and Apollos, the Apostle Paul evidently felt compelled to justify his message and ministry in Corinth.[29] The indications that some Corinthians were rallying around Paul and Apollos are often related by scholars to Paul's attempt to distance himself from the role of baptizer in 1 Corinthians 1:17.[30]

Despite the fact that the catechetical framework, which provided solutions for Paul's potentially puzzling statements, is absent from contemporary discussions of 1 Corinthians 1:17 and 3:6, contemporary interpretations nevertheless sound remarkably similar to those provided by the early readers, including some evident anxiety that Paul might

---

[29] The literature on the Corinthian factions is enormous and ever-growing. The bibliography provided in Wolfgang Schrage, *Der erste Brief an die Korinther*, 4 vols., EKK 7 (Neukirchen-Vluyn: Neukirchener, 1991–2001), is representative, though the debate has continued since then with a notable increase in studies focused on educational parallels, on which see below, pp. 222–223. For my part, I still find Benjamin Fiore's reading compelling, in which 1 Cor. 4:6 indicates that the issue at stake is not two, three, or four actual parties but rather a broader spirit of factionalism, addressed by Paul through figured speech "applied" to Paul and Apollos; Benjamin Fiore, "'Covert allusion' in 1 Corinthians 1–4," *Catholic Biblical Quarterly* 47, no. 1 (1985), 85–102.

[30] The connection is drawn with 1 Cor. 1:12 and 3:4, which themselves frame the key passages for the catechetical image of Paul.

denigrate baptism. Scholars as different as Hans Conzelmann and Gordon Fee, for instance, both state baldly that Paul's comments do not "devalue" or "minimize" baptism.[31] Johannes Weiss, linking 1:17 with 3:6, suggested that Paul's elevation of his teaching role related to the fact that he had actually left baptizing the Corinthians (apart from the very first converts) to Apollos.[32] More recently, Wolfgang Schrage has adopted a modified version of this view, though he notes that "one cannot say who carried out baptism among the mission community in place of the Apostle."[33] Schrage argues, however, that this historical fact is related to Paul's awareness of his own limits as an apostle: not every person has every gift and even "an apostle is no ecclesial jack of all trades."[34] Another solution emphasizes a distinction between what Paul was *sent* to do and what he may have been *allowed* to do. The purpose of his apostolic commission was preaching, while baptism "can be administered by anyone."[35] Perhaps the most common reading of 1 Corinthians 1:17 today, however, relates it not principally to 3:6 but rather emphasizes verse 17b ("not in wise words lest the cross of Christ be in vain") in relation to Paul's characterization of his message in 1:18–2:16.[36] Such an

---

[31] Hans Conzelmann, *1 Corinthians: A Commentary on the First Epistle to the Corinthians*, ed. James Waterson Leitch, George W. MacRae, and James W. Dunkly, Hermeneia (Philadelphia: Fortress Press, 1975), pp. 36–37; and Gordon D. Fee, *The First Epistle to the Corinthians*, NICNT (Grand Rapids: Eerdmans, 1987), p. 63, respectively. See also Schrage, *Korinther*, vol. I, p. 157, and Joseph A. Fitzmyer, *First Corinthians: A New Translation with Introduction and Commentary*, AB 32 (London: Yale University Press, 2008), p. 147.

[32] Johannes Weiss, *Der erste Korintherbrief*, 9th rev. edn, KEK 5 (Göttingen: Vandenhoeck & Ruprecht, 1910), pp. 19–20, who is explicitly following Theodor Zahn on this point, without evident reference to the similar interpretations in antiquity. Note also the brief comments in Johan Albrecht Bengel, *Gnomon Novi Testamenti*, 3rd edn, ed. Ernst Bengel and Johann Christian F. Steudel, 2 vols. (Tübingen: Ludov. Frid. Fues, 1835), vol. II, p. 103: "Quo quis mititur, id agere debet...Operosa baptismi actio, saepe suscepta, impedisset praedicationem: ceteroqui apostoli baptizarunt, Matth. 28, 19. primos praesertim discipulos."

[33] Schrage, *Korinther*, vol. I, p. 157: "Wer anstelle des Apostels die Taufe in den Missionsgemeinden vollzogen hat, läßt sich nicht sagen."

[34] Ibid.: "ein Apostel ist kein kirchlicher Allroundman."

[35] Conzelmann, *1 Corinthians*, pp. 36–37, though his comments on what constitutes "a non-historic mode of existence" ("eine ungeschichtliche Existenzweise") are unclear to me. See also Heinrich A. W. Meyer, *Kritisch exegetisches Handbuch über den ersten Brief an die Korinther*, KEK 5 (Göttingen: Vandenhoeck und Ruprecht, 1870), pp. 33–34; C. F. Georg Heinrici, *Der erste Brief an die Korinther*, 8th edn, KEK 5 (Göttingen: Vandenhoeck und Ruprecht, 1896), p. 65.

[36] This is related to the "rhetorical" focus of many studies of Corinthian factionalism: e.g., Timothy H. Lim, "'Not in persuasive words of wisdom, but in the demonstration of the spirit and power'," *Novum Testamentum* 29, no. 2 (1987), 137–149; Stephen

emphasis tends to glide over potential theological difficulties posed by Paul's comment on baptism in favor of emphasizing the rhetorical simplicity of the gospel.[37] Paul's apparent denigration of baptism here, then, is merely a shock tactic aimed at unsettling any factional lines built upon loyalty to the one who administered baptism.

It is notable how easily the early Christian interpretations of 1 Corinthians 1:17 and 3:5–9 can be situated within the contemporary exegetical debate; potential difficulties posed by Paul's elevation of preaching over baptism had already been recognized and addressed in antiquity.[38] Whether or not the writer of the *Acts of Paul* saw 1:17 as presenting a problem, the narrative of Thecla nevertheless gives a view of Paul in which the preaching and the baptizing are unified by early Christian initiatory practice, leading from catechetical instruction and moral evaluation to baptism. Origen's and Chrysostom's interpretations also work within their larger catechetical and pedagogical frameworks to obviate any possible rejection of baptism. Both writers found precedent in 1:17 for the priorities of their own ministry, locating teaching at the front and center. Baptism is not, itself, thereby denigrated – Chrysostom notes explicitly that "it is impossible to be saved" apart from it and Origen refers to it as "putting on Christ"[39] – but is rather put in a particular relationship with the extended process of catechetical instruction. In fact, this framework, which was rooted in their ecclesial experience, supplied a robust connection between preaching, teaching, and baptism that contemporary scholars must derive from Pauline theology more generally.

M. Pogoloff, *Logos and Sophia: The Rhetorical Situation of 1 Corinthians*, SBLDS 134 (Atlanta: Scholars Press, 1992); A. Duane Litfin, *St. Paul's Theology of Proclamation: 1 Corinthians 1–4 and Greco-Roman Rhetoric*, SNTSMS 79 (Cambridge: Cambridge University Press, 1994); R. Dean Anderson Jr., *Ancient Rhetorical Theory and Paul*, CBET 17 (Kampen: Kok Pharos, 1996), pp. 221–248; Johan S. Vos, *Die Kunst der Argumentation bei Paulus. Studien zur antiken Rhetorik*, WUNT 149 (Tübingen: Mohr Siebeck, 2002); Bruce W. Winter, *Philo and Paul Among the Sophists*, SNTSMS 96 (Cambridge: Cambridge University Press, 1997).

[37] So in Anthony C. Thiselton, *The First Epistle to the Corinthians: A Commentary on the Greek Text*, NIGTC (Grand Rapids: Eerdmans, 2000), pp. 142–143; Roy E. Ciampa and Brian S. Rosner, *The First Letter to the Corinthians*, PNTC (Grand Rapids: Eerdmans; Nottingham: Apollos, 2010), pp. 85–86; Dieter Zeller, *Der erste Brief an die Korinther*, KEK 5 (Göttingen: Vandenhoeck & Ruprecht, 2010), p. 95.

[38] In addition to the discussions of the *Acts of Paul*, Origen, and John Chrysostom above, see the more extensive treatment of early interpretations of 1 Cor. 1:17 in Edsall, "(Not) baptizing Thecla," pp. 235–260.

[39] Chrysostom *Hom. in 1 Cor.* 3.3: ἀδύνατον μὲν γὰρ χωρὶς αὐτοῦ σωθῆναι; Origen *Adnot. in Deut.* 27.19. Tertullian's response to the Cainite preacher in *De Baptismo* makes this anxiety even more clear; see Edsall, "(Not) baptizing Thecla," pp. 249–250.

Gordon Fee, for instance, argues against those who would see baptism purely as a "secondary matter" by claiming that Paul did not see it that way. "For him baptism comes *after* the hearing of the gospel, but it does so as the God-ordained mode of faith's response to the gospel."[40] The continuing debate about *why* Paul emphasizes his call to preach over baptizing – whether he was simply admitting his own limits, attempting to startle his listeners to attention, or referring to the fact that his ministry did not, in fact, include baptism to any great extent – includes within its range of possible interpretations the readings suggested by the *Acts of Paul*, Origen, and John Chrysostom.

If one primary difference remains between early and contemporary interpretations, it is the connection made between "planting" and teaching and between "watering" and baptism in 1 Corinthians 3:6. Most scholars today reject such a one-to-one correspondence between these terms, arguing that both "planting" and "watering" are fundamentally about instructing the community.[41] Indeed, Johannes Weiss explicitly rejected what he saw as the early Christian impulse ("so die Väter") to link Paul's agricultural metaphor with preaching and baptizing.[42] Nevertheless, a connection between Paul and initial preaching and teaching remains strong both in antiquity and today. Paul's establishment of the Corinthian community remains the first stage of teaching – planting – which is complemented by the work of Apollos, even for those who reject the watering/baptism parallel.[43] In fact, in the experience of the Corinthian community, Paul's teaching evidently constituted their first introduction to the Christian faith and it is important to note that he clearly expects that his Corinthian readers have been baptized (e.g., 1 Cor. 1:14 and 6:9–11), even if he did not undertake all the baptisms himself. Preaching followed by baptism, therefore, were fundamental parts of the Corinthian conversion experience.[44] So it is hard to dismiss entirely a connection between "watering" and baptism, given how naturally the

---

[40] Fee, *Corinthians*, p. 64. Thiselton, *Corinthians*, p. 142, simply asserts that dividing between "a sacramental ministry and a preaching ministry" is "a mistake."

[41] Schrage, *Korinther*, vol. I, p. 291; Ciampa and Rosner, *First Letter*, p. 146. See also C. K. Barrett, *A Commentary on the First Epistle to the Corinthians*, BNTC (London: Adam & Charles Black, 1968), p. 85; Conzelmann, *1 Corinthians*, p. 73 n. 44.

[42] Weiss, *Korintherbrief*, p. 76.

[43] The comments in Ciampa and Rosner, *First Letter*, p. 146, are representative on this point: "the 'planter,' the one who establishes the church, and the 'waterer,' the one who pastorally leads it, are both equally indispensable to its growth."

[44] See 1 Cor. 6:9–11 and 12:13, in addition to 1:13–16. On Paul's treatment of baptism during his ministry in Corinth, see Edsall, *Paul's Witness*, pp. 78–82.

experience of the Corinthians can be mapped onto the early Christian readings. At the very least, it is easy to understand how early Christians – reading Paul's letter to discover resources meaningful within their own (institutional) context – could have made the association without much trouble, even if one ultimately decides against such a view.

7.2.1.2 *1 Corinthians 2:6–3:3*

Between these two passages, 1 Corinthians 1:17 and 3:6, lies the bedrock of the catechetical and pedagogical presentations of Paul, particularly those seen in Clement and Origen, and here again we find that the scope of contemporary exegetical debates includes the interpretive options put forward by the early catechetical readers of Paul examined here.[45] Not only that, but the differences between Clement, Origen, and John Chrysostom in interpreting 1 Corinthians 3:1–3 mirror the differences among interpreters today, all of which find some basis in the contours of Paul's argument, a brief look at which will be helpful here.

Beginning in 1 Corinthians 1:17 and extending through the end of chapter 4, Paul engages in a series of challenges to the self-proclaimed "wise" or "spiritual" members of the Corinthian community who are involved in the problem of the community's factions. In 1:17–18, he opposes his gospel message with "wise speech" (οὐκ ἐν σοφίᾳ λόγου) that would enervate the "cross of Christ"; his "word of the Cross" (ὁ λόγος…ὁ τοῦ σταυροῦ) appears as foolishness to all who are not in the process of being saved. What at first seems to be a difference of style appears also to include the different content of worldly and divine wisdom in verse 21: by God's wisdom the world did not know *God* through its own wisdom. In contrast to "Jews" and "Greeks," Paul's message is "Christ crucified," which proves its divine wisdom by the fact that those who are not being saved ("Jews" and "Gentiles") can only see it as foolishness, while those being saved ("Jews" and "Greeks") experience it as power (vv. 22–24).

Paul returns again to the opposition between the simplicity of his message and the wisdom of the world in 2:1–5. There he claims that his preaching was without "superiority of message or wisdom," lacking "persuasive words of wisdom" and relying on "divine power" rather than

---

[45] For a more comprehensive discussion of the early reception of 1 Cor. 2:6–16 – under the categories of (1) rhetorical maneuvers and apologetics, (2) exegetical evidence for particular interpretations or theological concepts, and (3) the foundation for accounts of different types of Christian wisdom and related formation – see Strawbridge, *Pauline Effect*, pp. 24–56.

"human wisdom." This generally consistent, if somewhat vague, contrast between his message and "wisdom" shifts in 2:6, however, when Paul claims that he *does* teach wisdom, but only to the mature. This is not human wisdom, of course, which Paul has just denounced, but "divine wisdom" that is either spoken or hidden "in a mystery."[46] Rather than being generally available to all, this wisdom is revealed "through the Spirit," which believers ("we") have "received from God" (2:10–12). Paul's teaching, therefore, is given in "spiritual teachings, interpreting spiritual things for spiritual people" (v. 13). Whatever such spiritual teaching entailed, however, he claims that he could not engage in it among the Corinthians because they were "fleshly" rather than spiritual, "infants in Christ" who required "milk" (3:1–2). This was demonstrated by their divisiveness, not recognizing that the different teachers such as Paul and Apollos were in fact both working together with God (3:3–9).

Though brief, this general overview highlights the number of important interpretive decisions involved in discerning the meaning of Paul's argument. What is Paul's wisdom and who are the "mature" who are able to receive it? What is the relationship between Paul's wisdom and his "word of the cross"? In what way are the Corinthians still "fleshly" rather than "spiritual" in 1 Corinthians 3:1–3 when Paul has indicated in 2:12 that the Corinthian readers had in fact received the Spirit? Does Paul's argument suggest a kind of two-tier Christianity? As demonstrated earlier, Clement's and Origen's answers to these questions share a deep similarity, worked out within a broad pedagogical vision of the Christian life stretching from conversion and catechesis to the post-mortem life with God. According to Clement, Paul's wisdom, the solid food that is reserved for the mature, is the ever-solidifying milk of Christ that culminates in "mystical contemplation."[47] Paul's advanced instruction in the mysteries is not qualitatively distinct from the catechetical milk imparted to new believers but it is distinct nevertheless. We saw in Chapter 4 that Clement clearly advocates for pedagogical secrecy, withholding the "solid food" from infants, despite its fundamental continuity with the milk from which it is composed. Both the milk and the meat stem from Christ himself and are in accordance with the "ecclesiastical canon."[48] The "infants" can and should grow to

---

[46] The syntax of 1 Cor. 2:7 has sparked much debate from antiquity to the present. See the discussion in T. J. Lang, "We speak in a mystery: neglected Greek evidence for the syntax and sense of 1 Corinthians 2:7," *Catholic Biblical Quarterly* 78, no. 1 (2016), 68–89, who argues for taking ἐν μυστηρίῳ with the finite verb λαλοῦμεν.

[47] *Strom.* 5.1.2.3–6; see Chapter 4.2.2 above.

[48] See *Strom.* 6.18.165.1.

be "mature" and able to receive the solid food, eliminating the possibility he saw for a two-tier Church among the Valentinians. In support of this, Clement also appeals to Romans 1:17, arguing that the Christian life is a movement "from faith to faith," in which deeper knowledge perfects one's initial faith while retaining its fundamental essence. The Corinthians, however, were not yet ready for the advanced wisdom. Their factions betrayed their lack of moral preparation that is supplied by the divine "Pedagogue," particularly for baptismal candidates within the catechetical structure, but occasionally still required for immature baptized Christians.[49]

Origen's treatment differs from this in only a few ways. The first is that while the spiritual life of the believer is characterized by a constant spiritual journey, nevertheless some cannot or will not progress along the path to maturity. They are the "infants" whom he addressed each day in his homilies.[50] Moreover, those prepared for more advanced study received different food that is not presented, by Origen, simply as a greater accumulation of basic instruction. Rather than appealing to Romans 1:17 to establish a continuum of faith, he tends to make use of Hebrews 5:14f and Romans 14:2, with which he was able to maintain a distinction between initial and more advanced instruction. For both Clement and Origen, however, the catechumenate is important for their construal of Paul's interpretation of the "milk"/"meat" contrast. The Christian community comprises differing levels of believers, from the convert to the catechumen to the neophyte and on up to Clement's "true Gnostic." When Paul says, then, that he speaks wisdom to the mature, he is referring to a more advanced teaching than what is offered to new converts, though it is related to the same Christ and the same gospel as that imparted to those not yet morally prepared for deeper wisdom.

Contemporary readers of these passages are divided in their interpretations, principally between those who identify Paul's "wisdom," and therefore the solid food, with the "word of the cross" and those who identify it with more advanced teaching. The majority of interpreters, especially since the middle of the twentieth century, have argued for the former. As Udo Schnelle put it,

The "mystery of God" (see 1 Cor. 2:1, 7; 4:1; μυστήριον τοῦ θεοῦ) was understood differently by Paul and the Corinthians. As the "Lord of glory" (1 Cor. 2:8: κύριος τῆς δόξης), Christ was clearly regarded by the Corinthians as the archetypal image

---

[49] See Chapter 4.1.2 and 4.2.2 above.
[50] *Comm. in Matt.* 15.6; *Frag. in 1 Cor.* 63; see the discussion in Chapter 5.3.2 above for this and what follows.

of the "divine human," who transformed the spiritual ones into the next age already in this age through baptism in faith. *Over against this, Paul links the "mystery of God" exclusively to the cross* because the "wisdom of God" (σοφία θεοῦ), in the form of the crucified one as the "Lord of glory," sets itself against "human wisdom" (σοφία ἀνθρώπων).[51]

But identifying the "word of the cross" with Paul's "wisdom" in 1 Corinthians 2:6 does not yet answer the question about the identity of the "mature" or about the distinction that Paul draws between how he *did* teach the Corinthians versus how he *wanted* to teach them. One solution is to read Paul's comments in 2:6–3:3 as sarcastic: his apparent approval of wisdom in 2:6–15 is drastically undercut in 3:1–3, challenging the Corinthian quest for higher status with the reality that there is only the word of the cross, all while borrowing and redefining the Corinthians' own vocabulary.[52] On this reading, when Paul claims that he could not speak to the Corinthians ὡς πνευματικοῖς, the phrase should be read to indicate that, although the Corinthians are spiritual, insofar as they received the Spirit at baptism, Paul was not able to speak to them in that fashion because of their factional behavior.[53] Gordon Fee, for instance, argues that, despite the developmental implications of the infant/mature and milk/solid food imagery, Paul is not suggesting that such spiritual progress is at stake (or even possible) because he is at pains to avoid any suggestion of "classes of Christians or grades of spirituality."[54]

Yet, for some who link Paul's "wisdom" directly with the "word of the cross," the pressure of the developmental imagery pushes their interpretation of 3:1–3 in a different direction. This reading interprets Paul's reference to milk and solid food as indicating a certain limited development, a later elaboration on the same message. As early as 1896, Heinrici rejected any essential distinction between Paul's gospel and his "wisdom" in 2:6, even while allowing for a difference in the "form and framing" ("Form und Fassung") of the teaching based on the moral progress of the listeners.[55] More recently, scholars such as Florian Voss, Sigurd

---

[51] Schnelle, *Paulus*, p. 209, my emphasis.

[52] So Richard A. Horsley, *1 Corinthians*, ANTC (Nashville: Abingdon Press, 1998), p. 61; see also Fitzmyer, *First Corinthians*, p. 187, and Lang, *Mystery*, p. 53, who refers to the "insurrectionary character of Paul's argumentative strategy" in 2:6–3:1.

[53] See Fee, *Corinthians*, p. 123; Schrage, *Korinther*, vol. 1, p. 249; Sigurd Grindheim, "Wisdom for the perfect: Paul's challenge to the Corinthian church (1 Corinthians 2:6–16)," *Journal of Biblical Literature* 121, no. 4 (2002), 704.

[54] Fee, *Corinthians*, pp. 122–123.

[55] Heinrici, *Korinther*, p. 116. In this way, Heinrici's interpretation prepares the way for the later profusion of "rhetorical" readings of 1 Corinthians 1–4; see Pogoloff, *Logos and Sophia*; Litfin, *St. Paul's Theology*.

Grindheim, and T. J. Lang have taken a similar line of argumentation.[56] Notably, once a distinction or development is admitted between the milk and the solid food, between the infants and the mature, specifying the limits of that development becomes quite difficult.[57]

However strong the theological continuity between the milk and the solid food, for Paul to reserve some teaching for certain mature believers nevertheless continues to suggest difference, even if it is a difference construed as progress. This leads other scholars away from the image of a rhetorically focused Paul – a combatant who turns his opponents' terms against them and undercuts the Corinthians' claim to spiritual progress – toward a more pedagogically oriented Paul, one concerned precisely with spiritual progress. This view has at times emphasized a connection between Paul's language and that of the mystery religions, as in the case of Hans Conzelmann, though that connection has generally fallen out of favor.[58] In fact, the language of "milk" and "solid food," "infants" and "mature," is widespread in antiquity, occurring in discussions of philosophical learning, religious progress, and elementary education.[59] The links with education are so strong that Devin White has

---

[56] Florian Voss, *Das Wort vom Kreuz und die menschliche Vernunft. Eine Untersuchung zur Soteriologie des 1. Korintherbriefes*, FRLANT 199 (Göttingen: Vandenhoeck & Ruprecht, 2002), p. 190; Grindheim, "Wisdom," p. 708; Lang, *Mystery*, p. 65. See also William Baird, "Among the mature: the idea of wisdom in I Corinthians 2:6," *Interpretation* 13, no. 3 (1959), 425–432; Barrett, *First Epistle*, p. 81; Wilhelm Thüsing, "'Milch' und 'feste Speise' (1Kor 3,1f und Hebr 5,11–6,3): Elementarkatechese und theologische Vertiefung in neutestamentlicher Sicht," in Thomas Söding (ed.), *Studien zur neutestamentlichen Theologie*, WUNT I/82 (Tübingen: Mohr Siebeck, 1995), p. 27; Matthias Konradt, "Die korinthische Weisheit und das Wort vom Kreuz: Erwägungen zur korinthischen Problemkonstellation und paulinischen Intention in 1 Kor 1–4," *Zeitschrift für die Neutestamentliche Wissenschaft* 94 (2003), 209–210; and Ciampa and Rosner, *First Letter*, pp. 122–123.

[57] See the comments in Weiss, *Korintherbrief*, p. 72: "Eine nähere Ausdeutung der Metaphern (inwiefern nämlich das Evangelium vom Kreuze der leichtverkaulichen Milch, die verwirrenden Mitteilungen höherer Weisheit der schwereren festen Speise gleichen) ist ästhetisch unstatthaft."

[58] Conzelmann, *1 Corinthians*, p. 60. See also Meyer, *Korinther*, p. 57; Jean Héring, *La première épître de Saint Paul aux Corinthiens*, 2nd edn (Neuchâtel: Delaschaux & Niestlé, 1959), p. 25; Christophe Senft, *La première épitre de Saint-Paul aux Corinthiens*, CNT 2:7 (Neuchâtel: Delachaux & Niestlé, 1979), p. 48. See the criticism in, e.g., Thüsing, "'Milch' und 'feste Speise,'" pp. 23–24, and Zeller, *Der erste Brief*, p. 132.

[59] E.g., Epictetus *Diss.* 2.16.24–31; Philo *Congr.* 14–19; Quintillian *Inst.* 2.4.1–5. See also the discussions of these passages in, e.g., Robert S. Dutch, *The Educated Elite in 1 Corinthians: Education and Community Conflict in Graeco-Roman Context*, JSNT Sup 271 (London: T. & T. Clark, 2005), pp. 249–252; Zeller, *Der erste Brief*, p. 152 and n. 385; Adam G. White, *Where is the Wise Man? Graeco-Roman Education as a Background to the Divisions in 1 Corinthians 1–4*, LNTS 356 (London: Bloomsbury,

recently argued that the only relevant resonance at play in Paul's developmental language here is that of "ancient Mediterranean education."[60] On his reading, "the 'milk and solid food' may depict two tiers of early Christian instruction...the Corinthians have received and understood the most basic Christian instruction but have not advanced to more weighty knowledge."[61] These levels of "curricular attainment" are both distinct and related; the later "wisdom" will build upon what came before but it is not merely a further explanation of the same thing.[62] The development from one level to another involves not only intellectual progress but also moral formation, which is the point truly at issue for Paul in his interactions with the fractious Corinthians.[63] While this reading accounts for Paul's developmental images in a straightforward fashion, what is not as clear is the nature or extent of the continuity between the "wisdom" that Paul speaks to the "mature" and the milk that he gives to the infants. If Paul's reserved teaching is not simply another form of the "word of the cross," then it leaves open the possibility that the former entirely supersedes the latter.

An anxiety over the implications of Paul's comments, then, stretches from Clement of Alexandria and his interlocutors all the way to the present and appears to be established in the text itself. The evident variation between mutually exclusive ways of being (spiritual versus fleshly) and stages of maturity (infants versus mature) leaves interpreters with difficult decisions to make.[64] Thankfully, the goal here is not to solve this difficulty

---

2015), pp. 138–139; and Devin L. White, *Teacher of the Nations: Ancient Educational Traditions and Paul's Argument in 1 Corinthians 1–4*, BZNW 227 (Berlin: De Gruyter, 2017), pp. 61–65. Markus N. A. Bockmuehl, *Revelation and Mystery in Ancient Judaism and Pauline Christianity*, WUNT II/36 (Tübingen: Mohr Siebeck, 1990), p. 159 (cited by Devin White at p. 107) notes in passing that 1 Cor. 2:6–3:3 "remains consistent with a commonplace of both pagan and Jewish religion in antiquity: secret divine wisdom is properly reserved for those who are qualified...I am inclined to see this disposition in Paul as a pedagogical measure and as a matter of straightforward common sense."

[60] White, *Teacher of the Nations*, p. 59.

[61] Ibid., pp. 61–62; he notes his predecessors in Dutch, Zeller, and Adam White, cited in n. 59 above.

[62] White, *Teacher of the Nations*, p. 108.

[63] Ibid., pp. 34–35, 83–85, and *passim*. See also Max J. Lee, "Ancient Mentors and Moral Progress According to Galen and Paul," in Rebekah Ecklund and Jay Phelan (eds.), *Doing Theology for the Church: Essays in Honor of Klyne R. Snodgrass* (Eugene: Wipf & Stock, 2014), pp. 55–70. The earlier work on psychagogy in Paul remains relevant for this discussion; see esp. Abraham J. Malherbe, *Paul and the Thessalonians: The Philosophic Tradition of Pastoral Care* (Philadelphia: Fortress, 1987), and Glad, *Paul and Philodemus*.

[64] The tension in Paul's differing contrasts is noted in Zeller, *Der erste Brief*, p. 155, and Schrage, *Korinther*, vol. I, p. 279, among others.

but to highlight it in the course of situating the early interpreters surveyed above among contemporary exegetical debates.

In his 2010 commentary, Dieter Zeller tries to bring together a pedagogical reading of 1 Corinthians 2:6–3:3 and an identification of "wisdom" in 2:6 with the "word of the cross," with the former acting as a sort of "Meta-Theorie" of the latter.[65] This move is part of his attempt to rule out any interpretation that produces a "two-class Christianity."[66] In the process, Zeller rejects the value of the commonly noted parallel in Hebrews 5:11–6:3 and also argues that Paul did not want to distinguish "two types of Christians from one another" as did "the Gnostics and Clement of Alexandria."[67] We have seen, however, that this is not an accurate characterization of Clement's treatment of Paul's imagery in 1 Corinthians 3:1–3. The Alexandrian philosopher does not distinguish between two types of Christians but rather distinguishes between developmental stages on the single continuum of faith, a view that Zeller is otherwise open to. Moreover, while the language of Hebrews 5:14f is useful for Clement occasionally, it is Romans 1:17 that ties together catechetical instruction and further learning. Clement is able to distinguish between "milk" and "solid food" only insofar as both are the same substance in different forms; the spiritual life moves from faith to faith, which is to say, it develops without ever surpassing faith for something like knowledge. If Origen displays less anxiety about the relation between milk and meat, it is only because the unity of the two had already been established and was part of his own ministerial practice, as he urges the *simpliciores* on to greater learning in his sermons and guides those willing to undertake the effort in his school of philosophy.

As we have seen, however, while Clement and Origen's readings emphasize certain of the resources in 1 Corinthians 1–3 and interlock suggestively with other Pauline and New Testament material, they do not quite address themselves to the rhetorical flow of 1 Corinthians 1–3 in particular. This is a sticking point for those scholars who think that any distinctions between Paul's "wisdom" and his "word of the cross" would amount to an unstable argument on his part. Notably, though, even here the early readers can be found. Although 1 Corinthians 2:6–3:1–3 does not feature in his catechetical image of Paul, John Chrysostom does discuss the passages in his seventh and eighth homilies on 1 Corinthians.

---

[65] Zeller, *Der erste Brief*, p. 154.
[66] Ibid., p. 153.
[67] Ibid., p. 155.

While he certainly recognizes the difficulties of the passage, Chrysostom takes a simple line of interpretation: the "wisdom" that Paul speaks in 1 Corinthians 2:6 is nothing other than his preaching (τὸ κήρυγμα), the way of salvation by the cross, and the "mature" are those who believe.[68] As in the work of contemporary scholars, this interpretation produces some tension when Paul then goes on to call the mature and Spirit-filled Corinthian believers "fleshly."[69] Chrysostom's solution is to note that even those who have worked miracles can be "carnal" if they fail to live up to Christ's moral standards.[70] Within his broader pedagogical image of the Christian life and Paul's ministry, Chrysostom's interpretation of 1 Corinthians 2:6–3:3 can be seen to bring together certain catechetical and pedagogical implications – particularly the concern with moral preparation for spiritual development – with the rhetorical considerations that seek to link Paul's wisdom in 2:6 with the preceding argument. When one includes Chrysostom's interpretation, it becomes evident that the contemporary exegetical discussions of 1 Corinthians 2:6–3:3 continue to run along the lines of observations and concerns that were already in play from the late second century to the late fourth century.

7.2.1.3 *Hebrews 5:14 and Romans 1:17*

Before closing the discussion of exegetical details, it will be useful to consider very briefly two further passages that featured in the early Christian catechetical readings of Paul: Hebrews 5:14–6:1 and Romans 1:17. While the language of Hebrews 5:14f appeared in Clement's discussion of "milk" and "meat," it was Origen who drew most heavily on the passage, linking it regularly with 1 Corinthians 3:1–3 as another witness to Paul's pedagogical practice.[71] For contemporary scholars, the

---

[68] *Hom. in 1 Cor.* 7.1: "Now by 'wisdom' he means the preaching and the manner of salvation, namely, being saved by the cross; and by 'the perfect' he means those who have believed" (Σοφίαν δὲ λέγει τὸ κήρυγμα καὶ τὸν τρόπον τῆς σωτηρίας, τὸ διὰ σταυροῦ σωθῆναι· τελείους δὲ τοὺς πεπιστευκότας). This passage is cited and dismissed in Meyer, *Korinther*, p. 58.

[69] *Hom. in 1 Cor.* 8.1: "And how does he call those who have attained the Spirit to such an extent 'fleshly,' even having passed through such praise at the beginning?" (Καὶ πῶς τοὺς Πνεύματος ἐπιτυχόντας τοσούτου, σαρκικοὺς καλεῖ, καὶ ὧν ἀρχόμενος τοσαῦτα διῆλθεν ἐγκώμια;)

[70] *Hom. in 1 Cor.* 8.1: "As a result it is possible for one who has done signs to be fleshly" (Ὥστε ἔστι καὶ σημεῖα ποιήσαντα εἶναι σαρκικόν). Chrysostom comes back to this point again at 8.2.

[71] Rom. 14:2, a passage related to Heb. 5:14 in Origen's exegesis of 1 Cor. 3:1–3, offers a less interesting comparison with contemporary exegesis, largely because modern interpreters only ever read Paul's references to eating "vegetables" literally, or, in the case of Robert Jewett, as rhetorical exaggeration in reference to actual food consumed

language in Hebrews is at best an independent analogue for Paul's use in 1 Corinthians 3 and few indeed would follow the patristic commentators who take Paul as its author.[72] Nevertheless, a recognition that Hebrews 5:11–6:1 bears similarities with Greek and Roman pedagogical concerns could be taken to indicate a closer conceptual relationship with 1 Corinthians 3:1–3.[73] In fact, Harold Attridge's principle concern about linking the milk/meat imagery in Hebrews with that of 1 Corinthians is that "Paul is more sarcastically pointed and…ultimately…undermines the idea of a separate 'solid food' apart from Christ crucified."[74] As we have seen, though, Attridge's brief interpretation of 1 Corinthians 1–3 is far from the only reading, and his own observations about the use of "commonplace" material from "classical education theory" in Hebrews 5 could lay the groundwork for the connection he rejects.[75]

Turning finally to Romans 1:17, the meaning of the phrase ἐκ πίστεως εἰς πίστιν is famously obscure, with no consensus among scholars on the horizon. It is generally acknowledged that the phrase on its own is ambiguous and so some consideration of Romans as a whole and even Pauline thought more generally is necessary to understand it.[76] The well-known double-sided meaning of πίστις, denoting both faith and faithfulness,[77] only adds a layer of ambiguity about whose πίστις is at stake here. Does, then, the phrase denote a movement from God's faith(fulness) to

by Roman Christians; see Robert Jewett, *Romans: A Commentary*, ed. Eldon Jay Epp, Hermeneia (Minneapolis: Fortress, 2007), p. 71, for his discussion of interpretive options and arguments for his own rhetorical reading.

[72] Harold W. Attridge, *The Epistle to the Hebrews: A Commentary on the Epistle to the Hebrews*, ed. Helmut Koester, Hermeneia (Philadelphia: Fortress, 1989), p. 159, argues for a "purely formal" relationship in which both authors draw "on the same commonplace imagery"; see also Otto Michel, *Der Brief an die Hebräer*, 14th edn, KEK 13 (Göttingen: Vandenhoeck und Ruprecht, 1984), p. 233.

[73] Heb. 5:11–14 is discussed in relation to 1 Cor. 3 in White, *Teacher of the Nations*, pp. 64–65 (see also White, *Wise Man*, p. 139); and note the connection with "griechisch-hellenistischer Pädagogik" suggested in Hans-Friedrich Weiss, *Der Brief an die Hebräer*, 15th edn, KEK 13 (Göttingen: Vandenhoeck & Ruprecht, 1991), pp. 332–333, among others.

[74] Attridge, *Hebrews*, p. 159.

[75] Quotes from ibid.

[76] See the comments in Morna D. Hooker, "Another look at πίστις Χριστοῦ," *Scottish Journal of Theology* 69, no. 1 (2016), 46–47, which focuses on the phrase πίστις Χριστοῦ but applies to Rom. 1:17a as well; see also Douglas A. Campbell, "Romans 1:17: A *crux interpretum* for the πίστις Χριστοῦ debate," *Journal of Biblical Literature* 113, no. 2 (1994), 270–271.

[77] See now esp. Morgan, *Roman Faith*, who emphasizes the close relationship between trust and the presumed trustworthiness of the one in whom trust is placed.

that of the believer,[78] from Christ's faithfulness to our faith in him,[79] from the faith of the old covenant to the faith of the new,[80] from the faith of one believer to others in the growing church,[81] from a beginning faith to a more mature faith for the believer;[82] or is it merely an emphatic construction?[83]

Among these contemporary exegetical options, the readings of Clement and Origen can easily be situated. It was seen briefly in Chapter 5 that Origen's reading emphasized the transition from old to new covenant, the *translatio religionis*.[84] This was not entirely to the exclusion of spiritual progress, though such was not Origen's emphasis. As is familiar by now, Clement's reading of "from faith to faith" was a crucial part of his argument for a unified vision of the Christian life from neophyte to Gnostic.[85] What is notable here, however, is not simply the fact that

[78] Hooker, "Another look," pp. 46–62; Wright, *Paul*, p. 502 n. 126; James D. G. Dunn, *Romans*, 2 vols., WBC 38ab (Waco, TX: Word Books, 1988), vol. 1, pp. 43–44. Cranfield assigns this view to Ambrosiaster and Karl Barth (C. E. B. Cranfield, *A Critical and Exegetical Commentary on the Epistle to the Romans*, 2 vols. (London: T. & T. Clark, 1975–1979), vol. 1, pp. 99–100), and see also Charles Raith, II, "Theology and interpretation: the case of Aquinas and Calvin on Romans," *International Journal of Systematic Theology* 14, no. 3 (2012), 314, for this reading in Thomas Aquinas.

[79] Campbell, "Romans 1:17," pp. 265–285.

[80] Charles L. Quarles, "From faith to faith: a fresh examination of the prepositional series in Romans 1:17," *Novum Testamentum* 45, no. 2 (2003), 1–21; Origen *Comm. in Rom.* 1.18.79 (Scheck 1.15.1).

[81] Jewett, *Romans*, pp. 346–347. Also open to this reading are William Sanday and Arthur C. Headlam, *A Critical and Exegetical Commentary on the Epistle to the Romans*, 5th edn, ICC (Edinburgh: T. & T. Clark, 1902), pp. 26–28, though it is not their preferred interpretation. It bears some similarity with Augustine's interpretation (*Spir. et lit.* 11.18; text in Carolus F. Vrba and Josephus Zycha (eds.), *Sancti Aureli Augustini. De peccatorum meritis et remissione et de baptismo parvulorum, De spiritu et littera, De natura et gratia, De natura et origine animae, Contra duas epistulas Pelagianorum*, CSEL 60 (Vienna: F. Tempsky, 1913)) in terms of movement from the faith of the preacher to that of the hearers; see the discussion in John W. Taylor, "From Faith to Faith: Romans 1.17 in the Light of Greek Idiom," *New Testament Studies* 50, no. 4 (2004), 340–341, who also ultimately opts for the missionary expansion interpretation.

[82] In addition to Clement of Alexandria, see also Sanday and Headlam, *Romans*, pp. 26–28; Calvin *Comm. in Rom. ad loc.* (on whom see Raith, "Theology and interpretation," p. 317).

[83] So Michael Wolter, *Der Brief an die Römer*, EKK 6,1 (Neukirchen-Vluyn: Neukirchener Theologie; Ostfildern: Patmos Verlag, 2014), pp. 125–126, who argues that it means "Glaube und nichts als Glaube überall, vom Anfang bis zum Ende," despite the fact that he does note that εἰς πίστιν is not a straightforward rhetorical intensification of ἐκ πίστεως.

[84] See the discussion and bibliography above, esp. the discussions of this theme in Heither, *Translatio religionis*.

[85] Remarkably, the treatment of Clement in Taylor, "Faith to Faith," p. 343, entirely overlooks these large-scale discussions of Rom. 1:17 in Clement's work, mentioning only

Clement's reading happens to bear some similarity with current exegetical options, but that his reading of Romans 1:17 is justified with reference to a broader approach to Paul in which he is seen as a good pedagogue, a true imitator of the divine pedagogy in the Logos. As Origen's differing interpretive emphasis shows, their shared approach did not itself directly *determine* Clement's reading, but rather enabled and grounded his interpretation. As in the case of 1 Corinthians 1–3 above, the compressed and ambiguous quality of Romans 1:17 admits multiple readings, which draw on one's construal of the larger text (including scripture as a whole or broader historical considerations from the first century). Furthermore, the fact that the character of faith itself is being addressed in the passage means that definitions elucidated elsewhere can – even must – be potentially valid factors for the interpretation of Romans 1:17. The underdetermined quality of Paul's statement, with its inevitable reliance on larger construals of πίστις, suggests that its meaning cannot be read definitively. In the process of our contemporary exegetical discussions, though, the voices of Clement and Origen remain valuable for their attention to the text as much as for their occasional strangeness to modern ears.

Engaging with these early interpreters does not, of course, absolve contemporary exegetes of their interpretive task, nor could one simply adopt the view of one reader without engaging with the interpretive issues raised by the others. Indeed, it would be disingenuous if I were to claim that I was simply adopting the view of, say, Origen on 1 Corinthians 3:1–3. This is because the justification for such a decision already necessarily lies outside of Origen's own reasoning and it must include, at least implicitly, an argument for the failure of other interpretive options available today. So, though I might arrive at a similar conclusion, the path to that point must look very different. Such an argument is less a recovery of Origen's reading than it is a new interpretive construction built partially with recycled material.[86]

---

his brief treatment in *Qui div. sal.* 8.5.1, in which Clement reads the passage as a shift from old to new covenants. It is worth noting also that Taylor follows Quarles, "From faith to faith," pp. 1–21, in his interpretation of John Chrysostom, which has since been thoroughly countered in Robert Matthew Calhoun, "John Chrysostom on ἐκ πίστεως εἰς πίστιν in Rom. 1:17: a reply to Charles L. Quarles," *Novum Testamentum* 48, no. 2 (2006), 131–146.

[86] Note Stephen Chester's similar comments on the value of Reformation readings of Paul: "We are interpreting for different times and to simply repristinate the exegesis of the Reformers would represent an unhelpful nostalgia that evades present challenges rather than meets them"; Chester, *Reading Paul*, p. 1.

The astute critic of the present argument may point out that there is a disparity between my own implicitly historical approach to interpretation here – for Paul, the early interpreters, and contemporary exegetes alike – and the (Neo)platonic hermeneutical stance of Clement, Origen, and John Chrysostom. This discrepancy is certainly present, though I think that it is less significant than it may at first seem, largely for the reason articulated above about new interpretive constructions, which will be expanded in the following chapter. Even so, if early Christian methods and interpretative assumptions are no longer our own, these writers have repeatedly proven to be attentive and careful readers from whom one can learn and with whom one can reflect on one's own underlying commitments and questions. Moreover, in practical terms, their larger catechetical framework and pedagogical vision of the Christian life supplies a remarkably similar picture of Paul's argument and ministry to those scholars who highlight the links between 1 Corinthians 1–3 and ancient education. I submit that this similarity is not accidental. Rather, it reflects a genuine interpretive possibility for 1 Corinthians 1–3, illuminated for the author of the *Acts of Paul*, Clement, Origen, and Chrysostom by the light of their catechetical institutional contexts.

The different interpretive strategies employed by ancient and contemporary readers to address the tensions and contours of the Pauline texts point not only toward differences in historical location or methodological assumptions – both of which are of course at play – but also toward differences in scholars' underlying image of Paul. The emphasis on Paul's critique of rhetoric and worldly wisdom, in particular, presents a Paul focused on persuasion and working with oppositional categories, not one who is pedagogically focused and working within a framework of gradual development and differentiated teaching. The dominant contemporary reading of Paul's argument in 1 Corinthians 1–3 presents a writer who "reverses his rhetoric in 2:6" to oppose directly the Corinthians' reliance on "cultural wisdom," thereby eliminating any possibility for claims to spiritual maturity over another believer.[87] As we shall see, this oppositional reading of Paul has broader ground and deeper roots than the argument of 1 Corinthians, and stands in deep tension with the catechetical or pedagogical image of the Apostle.

---

[87] The quotes are from Pogoloff, *Logos and Sophia*, p. 142, but are indicative of the majority on this point, as seen above.

7.2.2 Images of Paul Then and Now

Despite the recently renewed interest in the educational background of Paul's argument in 1 Corinthians 1–4, it hardly needs to be said that an association between Paul and the catechumenate is not often proposed in scholarly discussion today. Even so, the implications of the catechetical image of Paul presented by these ancient writers extend beyond the exegetical minutiae and touch also on broader questions of Pauline image formation. As noted above, a catechetical Paul is fundamentally a pedagogical and ecclesial Paul, an image of the Apostle as one standing among other apostles, working within an ecclesial canon and speaking harmoniously with the early Church leaders. Further, this Paul does not impart his greatest mysteries to his converts at first: he guides them in spiritual growth, with basic physical matters leading to spiritual truths (Clement, Origen), and early moral struggles leading to a life of perfect virtue (*Acts of Paul*, Chrysostom).

In attempting to bring this image of Paul together with contemporary images, one immediately faces the problem that there is no single image of Paul prevalent in contemporary scholarship. In the (mildly acerbic) assessment of one recent writer: "The 'real' Paul, as he is normally described [in contemporary Pauline discourse]...was Protestant, liberal, dialogical, feminist, and/or anti-imperial. The Paul of 'tradition' was and is Catholic, conservative, rigid, homophobic, and fixated on power."[88] One might add to this list the debates about the Jewishness of Paul (his indebtedness to halakhah or otherwise),[89] his indebtedness to Stoicism,[90] an apocalyptic versus a *heilsgeschichtliche* Paul, etc.[91] Even a cursory

---

[88] White, *Remembering Paul*, p. 3.

[89] E.g., Peter J. Tomson, *Paul and the Jewish Law: Halakha in the Letters of the Apostle to the Gentiles*, CRINT 3:1 (Assen: Van Gorcum; Minneapolis: Fortress Press, 1990); Karin Finsterbusch, *Die Thora als Lebensweisung für Heidenchristen. Studien zur Bedeutung der Thora für die paulinische Ethik*, SUNT 20 (Göttingen: Vandenhoeck & Ruprecht, 1996); Markus N. A. Bockmuehl, *Jewish Law in Gentile Churches: Halakhah and the Beginning of Christian Public Ethics* (Edinburgh: T. & T. Clark, 2000); David J. Rudolph, *A Jew to the Jews: Jewish Contours of Pauline Flexibility in 1 Corinthians 9:19–23*, WUNT II/304 (Tübingen: Mohr Siebeck, 2011). See also Paula Fredricksen, "Judaizing the nations: the ritual demands of Paul's gospel," *New Testament Studies* 56, no. 2 (2010), 232–252. A rejection of this presentation of a halakhic Paul has recently been put forward by Wright, *Paul*, p. 1434 and *passim*; see also John M. G. Barclay, "'Do we undermine the Law?' A study of Romans 14.1–15.6," in James D. G. Dunn (ed.), *Paul and the Mosaic Law*, WUNT 89 (Tübingen: Mohr Siebeck, 1996), pp. 287–308.

[90] See esp. Troels Engberg-Pedersen, *Paul and the Stoics* (Edinburgh: T. & T. Clark, 2000), and his many other contributions.

[91] Apocalyptic Paul: Ernst Käsemann, "The beginning of Christian theology," in *New Testament Questions of Today*, trans. W. J. Montague (London: SCM Press, 1969),

glance at the field of Pauline studies would appear to justify the comment of Eckart Reinmuth, "There are many images of Paul; there is no original Paul."[92] Nevertheless, there is one line of interpretation, one particular and pervasive dichotomy in Pauline images, that helps to shed light on the relationship between images of the Apostle now and then. This is the division between images of Paul as a pedagogically ecclesial figure and those of Paul as a confrontational and independent figure.

Before moving forward, however, I should note here that, while this latter image of Paul was and remains prevalent among New Testament scholars, a kind of catechetical reading of Paul was at one time put forward as an alternative. As noted in Chapter 2, the interest in discovering catechetical materials in Paul's letters was quite prevalent in the first half of the twentieth century, but has since been heavily criticized and is generally ignored today.[93] In these works, the image of Paul does not feature prominently in their textual archaeology nor does the implicit image share particularly close affinities with the catechetical Paul of the early readers discussed here. In the works of Alfred Seeberg, Philip Carrington, and Edward Selwyn, for instance, the discussion of catechetical material is primarily a formal consideration, an effort to find a common substratum of instruction underlying the New Testament texts.[94] Still, this view of Paul and the early Church did presume a sort of early ecclesial

---

pp. 82–107; J. Louis Martyn, *Theological Issues in the Letters of Paul* (Edinburgh: T. & T. Clark, 1997); Campbell, *Deliverance of God*; see also the discussion in R. Barry Matlock, *Unveiling the Apocalyptic Paul: Paul's Interpreters and the Rhetoric of Criticism*, JSNT Sup (Sheffield: Sheffield Academic Press, 1996). *Heilsgeschichtliche* Paul: Oscar Cullmann, *Salvation in History* (London: SCM, 1967); Michael Wolter, *Paulus. Ein Grundriss seiner Theologie* (Neukirchen-Vluyn: Neukirchener, 2011); Wright, *Paul*.

[92] Eckart Reinmuth, *Paulus. Gott neu denken*, Biblische Gestalten 9 (Leipzig: Evangelische Verlagsanstalt, 2004), p. 8: "Paulusbilder gibt es viele; einen originalen Paulus gibt es nicht."

[93] See the history of scholarship and criticisms in Edsall, "*Kerygma*, catechesis," pp. 410–441.

[94] Seeberg, *Der Katechismus*; Carrington, *The Primitive Christian Catechism*; Selwyn, *The First Epistle of St. Peter*. Also important for this line of inquiry, though he distinguished between the *didache* and the *kerygma*, focusing primarily on the latter, is C. H. Dodd, *The Apostolic Preaching and Its Developments: Three Lectures with an Appendix on Eschatology and History* (London: Hodder and Stoughton, 1936) (and later C. H. Dodd, "The Primitive Catechism and the Sayings of Jesus," in A. J. B. Higgins (ed.), *New Testament Essays: Studies in Memory of Thomas Walter Manson* (Manchester: Manchester University Press, 1959), pp. 11–29). In the 1966 reprint of Seeberg's work, the introduction by Ferdinand Hahn traces several lines of Seeberg's influence in subsequent scholarship, including in the formulation of form-criticism as a method; Alfred Seeberg, *Der Katechismus der Urchristenheit*, Theologische Bücherei: Neudrucke und Berichte aus dem 20. Jahrhundert 26 (Munich: Kaiser, 1966), pp. x–xxxii.

unity, at least insofar as it was a requirement for the harmonizing tendencies of these reconstructions.[95] Furthermore, scholars such as Erich
Dinkler argued that initial catechetical instruction formed the foundation
of Pauline ethical teaching.[96] In a limited way, then, one might argue that
this line of interpretation resembles the catechetical reading offered by
Chrysostom and others. The similarities end here, however, and, in terms
of the image of Paul at work in interpretation, the educational/peda-
gogical focus of those scholars discussed earlier offers a closer analogue.

7.2.2.1 F. C. Baur and a Paul of Oppositions

The image of Paul as a confrontational and independent figure seems on the
surface to have much to commend it. As he himself records in Galatians 2,
Paul confronted Peter and the Judaizers at Antioch, stood as a minority of
one against a tide of contrary opinion, and did not deviate from his gospel
even a whit. The established authorities of the early Church, the pillars
in Jerusalem, agreed with him and his mission on his own terms and yet
he was still left to wrestle his churches away from Judaizers in Galatia,
Corinth, and Philippi, bringing them back to his law-free gospel. Any other
picture, such as that presented by Acts, is a later attempt to domesticate the
radical Apostle to the Gentiles. From this perspective, it is easy to see how
Heinrich Seesemann, among others, could read the early interpretations so
easily as *mis*interpretations.

Indeed, this view of Paul is widespread still within contemporary
Pauline scholarship. Of course, most scholars would not accept every
tenet of this image of Paul, and certainly not when put so briefly. Still,
examples of a confrontational Paul who holds fast to his gospel are not
difficult to find. On the one hand, entire studies and collected volumes
are dedicated to investigating Paul's arguments with his "opponents."[97]

---

[95] The criticisms in James E. Crouch, *The Origin and Intention of the Colossian Haustafel*,
FRLANT 109 (Göttingen: Vandenhoeck & Ruprecht, 1972), pp. 14–17; Erhardt
Güttgemanns, *Candid Questions Concerning Gospel Form Criticism: A Methodological
Sketch of the Fundamental Problematics of Form and Redaction Criticism*, trans.
William G. Doty, PTMS 26 (Pittsburgh: Pickwick Press, 1979), p. 311; James D. G.
Dunn, *Unity and Diversity in the New Testament: An Inquiry into the Character of
Earliest Christianity* (London: SCM, 1977), p. 34, and others remain relevant.

[96] Erich Dinkler, "Zum Problem der Ethik bei Paulus," in *Signum Crucis. Aufsätze zum
Neuen Testament und zur Christlichen Archäologie* (Tübingen: Mohr Siebeck, 1967),
pp. 234–235. Note that Dinkler is building explicitly on the work of Seeberg and
Selwyn (among others) but he is nevertheless less optimistic about scholars' ability to
reconstruct the oral catechesis underlying Paul's letters.

[97] E.g, Dieter Georgi, *The Opponents of Paul in Second Corinthians* (Edinburgh: T. &
T. Clark, 1987); Gerd Lüdemann, *Opposition to Paul in Jewish Christianity*, trans.

Some, such as Michael Goulder, maintain the well-worn division between Paul (and Paulinism more generally) and early Jewish Christianity.[98] Even among those who want to reject such binary divisions, a pugnacious view of Paul often remains present. For example, in his seminal article on "The incident at Antioch," James Dunn reproduces a familiar image of Paul.

> It was at this point that Paul intervened and confronted Peter. The vividness with which he recalls the scene indicates the importance of the stand which he felt he must make…The significance of Paul's stand should not be underestimated. For the first time, probably, he had come to see that the principle of "justification through faith" applied not simply to the acceptance of the gospel in conversion, but also to the whole of the believer's life.[99]

Paul stands (alone?) to confront Peter, pushing back against the pressure of common Jewish practice, which is even being followed by the other apostles (established in detail in the preceding thirty pages of Dunn's article), to defend his gospel. The definitive Pauline gospel is formulated by himself in the heat of the conflict, and certainly not held in common with the other apostles, at least at that early stage.

In the case of Goulder and Dunn, among others, the basic contours of this image of Paul can be traced back to Ferdinand Christian Baur, the parade example of such a view, whose arguments continue to influence the practice of New Testament scholarship and whose work is undergoing something of a minor renaissance at present.[100] At the beginning

M. Eugene Boring (Minneapolis: Fortress, 1989); Stanley E. Porter (ed.), *Paul and His Opponents*, Pauline Studies 2 (Leiden: Brill, 2005).

[98] Michael D. Goulder, *A Tale of Two Missions* (London: SCM, 1994), in addition to Lüdemann in the previous note; see also the arguments in Ian J. Elmer, *Paul, Jerusalem and the Judaisers: The Galatian Crisis in Its Broadest Historical Context*, WUNT II/258 (Tübingen: Mohr Siebeck, 2009).

[99] James D. G. Dunn, "The incident at Antioch (Gal. 2:11–18)," *Journal for the Study of the New Testament* 18 (1983), 36. It is perhaps also worth noting that Dunn's famous insistence on Paul's rejection of certain Jewish laws as "identity markers" for the purpose of Gentile inclusion reproduces something like F. C. Baur's national/universal dichotomy, though attended by a notable concern for Jewish and Christian dialogue and without Baur's idealist-dialectical baggage. See further below.

[100] On Goulder's and Dunn's links with Baur, see esp. James Carleton Paget, "The Reception of Baur in Britain," in Martin Bauspiess, Christof Landmesser, and David Lincicum (eds.), *Ferdinand Christian Baur und die Geschichte des frühen Christentums*, WUNT I/333 (Tübingen: Mohr Siebeck, 2014), pp. 379–380, who also singles out Francis Watson in this respect. Broader treatments of Baur can be found in an increasing number of places: see Peter C. Hodgson, *The Formation of Historical Theology: A Study of Ferdinand Christian Baur* (New York: Harper & Row, 1966); Horton Harris, *The Tübingen School* (Oxford: Clarendon, 1975); William Baird, *History of New Testament Research*, vol. 1: *From Deism to Tübingen* (Minneapolis: Fortress, 1992), pp. 258–278 (including a discussion of his Tübingen school); Bauspiess, Landmesser, and Lincicum,

of his work on Paul, Baur states unequivocally, "That Christianity, in the universal historical importance which it achieved, was the work of the Apostle Paul is undeniably a matter of historical fact."[101] This is true, as he makes clear elsewhere, because it is Paul who supplied the definitive universal interpretation for the death of Jesus, stripping it of Jewish and nationalist limitations and transforming it "into a free, universal, purely spiritual sphere."[102] In this way, Paul did not work in harmony with those who advocated a gospel still entangled with the Jewish Law.

> Not even for an instant, says the Apostle, did I give way to them for the purpose of the subjugation required of me, in order that the truth of the Gospel, the principles of true Christianity, freed from Judaism, might be upheld and carried on in the churches founded by me.[103]

Paul here stands in opposition to the other apostles and it is only a later "catholicizing orientation" in the Church that attempts to bridge the gap between what are in fact two entirely distinct gospels.[104]

This distinction, then, requires a careful stratigraphy of Pauline traditions, identifying what is early and authentic to filter out what is later and pseudonymous.[105] For Baur, a touchstone for authentically

---

Ferdinand Christian Baur; Werner Georg Kümmel, *Das Neue Testament. Geschichte der Erforschung seiner Probleme*, Orbis Academicis (Freiburg: Karl Alber, 1970), pp. 156–176; and Johannes Zachhuber, *Theology as Science in Nineteenth-Century Germany: From F. C. Baur to Ernst Troeltsch*, Changing Paradigms in Historical and Systematic Theology (Oxford: Oxford University Press, 2013), pp. 21–72.

[101] Ferdinand Christian Baur, *Paul the Apostle of Jesus Christ: His Life and Work, His Epistles and His Doctrine*, 2nd edn, trans. Eduard Zeller, 2 vols. (London: Williams and Norgate, 1875), vol. I, p. 3 (= Ferdinand Christian Baur, *Paulus, der Apostel Jesu Christi. Sein Leben und Wirken, seine Briefe und Seine Lehre. Ein Beitrag zu einer kritischen Geschichte des Urchristentums*, 2nd edn, 2 vols. (Leipzig: Fues, 1866), vol. I, p. 6). Citations of Baur are generally taken from available English translations, which have been checked against (and occasionally altered in light of) the German.

[102] Ferdinand Christian Baur, *Lectures on New Testament Theology*, ed. Peter C. Hodgson, trans. Robert F. Brown (New York: Oxford University Press, 2016), pp. 155–156 (= Ferdinand Christian Baur, *Vorlesungen über neutestamentliche Theologie*, ed. Ferdinand Friedrich Baur (Leipzig: Fues, 1864), p. 131.) (This is repeated nearly verbatim from his earlier treatment in Baur, *Paul*, vol. II, p. 125 = Baur, *Paulus*, vol. II, p. 135.) He goes on to say on the same page that "All particularities of Judaism disappeared for him in the universalism of Christianity."

[103] Baur, *Paul*, vol. I, p. 122 (slightly altered); see his earlier comments on pp. 119–120.

[104] Quote from Ferdinand Christian Baur, *History of Christian Dogma*, ed. Peter C. Hodgson, trans. Robert F. Brown and Peter C. Hodgson (New York: Oxford University Press, 2014), p. 108, and see also the comments on Paul's gospel as "against" Peter's in Baur, *Paul*, vol. I, p. 124.

[105] On Baur's "canon criticism" and its theological entailments, see David Lincicum, "Ferdinand Christian Baur and the theological task of New Testament introduction," in Bauspiess, Landmesser, and Lincicum, *Ferdinand Christian Baur*, pp. 91–105.

Pauline material is Galatians, which offers unparalleled access to the place of Paul's mission in relation to others in the early Church.[106] It is Galatians that illuminates the harmonizing bias of Acts, and Galatians that "gives us what knowledge we have of the original relation in which our Apostle stood to the other Apostles, and thus shows us the process of development by which the struggle with Judaism led to a more distinct perception and appreciation of the essential principle of Christianity."[107] If one tries to harmonize Galatians and Acts, a figure of Paul emerges who is of a dubiously vacillating character.[108] On the contrary, Baur argues, Paul stands in sharp contrast with Peter, whose "irresolution" leads to the Antiochene conflict.[109] Paul himself would never compromise his "essential principles" in that way, despite some interpretations of 1 Corinthians 9:20.[110]

Baur's is a Paul of oppositions: Paul versus Peter, universal versus national, Gentile Christian versus Jewish Christian, and unflinching gospel fidelity versus irresolute vacillation.[111] The primacy that he gives to Galatians and his concern for a resolute Paul shapes his treatment of 1 Corinthians 1–3, the primary textual resource for a catechetical or pedagogical Paul. In his earliest foray into Pauline interpretation, and still maintained fourteen years later in his full work on Paul, Baur argued that to understand the factions in Corinth one had to read it through the "well-known relationship in which Peter and Paul…actually stood to one another," which Baur finds most clearly in Galatians.[112] It is primarily this

---

[106] See the comments in Christof Landmesser, "Ferdinand Christian Baur als Paulusinterpret: die Geschichte, das Absolute und die Freiheit," in Bauspiess, Landmesser, and Lincicum, *Ferdinand Christian Baur*, pp. 174–177.

[107] Baur, *Paul*, vol. 1, p. 257; see also the similar comments on p. 105, and Baur, *Lectures*, p. 156, where opposition to Judaism is identified as "the essential element of his theological framework."

[108] Baur, *Paul*, vol. 1, p. 4.

[109] Ibid., vol. 1, p. 129.

[110] Ibid., vol. 1, p. 131.

[111] Stephen Chester has recently argued strongly that, although this particular opposition is often attributed to the Reformers, in fact its intellectual forerunner is Desiderius Erasmus; Chester, *Reading Paul*, pp. 142–143. Fittingly, in the analysis of Erasmus and Luther below, this opposition does not factor into their differing presentations of Paul in relation to pedagogical and spiritual progress.

[112] Ferdinand Christian Baur, "Die Christuspartei in der korinthischen Gemeinde, der Gegensatz des petrinischen und paulinischen Christenthums in der ältesten Kirche, der Apostel Petrus in Rom," *Tübinger Zeitschrift für Theologie* 3, no. 4 (1831), 76–78: "Nach dem bekannten Verhältnis, in welchem Paulus und Petrus, jener als Heidenapostel, dieser als Judenapostel, theils wirklich zu einander stunden [*viz.* represented esp. in Galatians], theils wenigstens von den Hauptparteien der ältesten christlichen Kirche zu einander stehend gedacht wurden, kann es keinem Zweifel unterworfen seyn, daß die beiden

that authorizes Baur to read the factionalism in Corinth as being fundamentally a division between a Paul group and a Peter group and that shapes his reading of Paul's opponents in 2 Corinthians 10–12, which in turn filters back into his reading of 1 Corinthians.[113]

Given this fundamental opposition, it is hardly surprising to find binary oppositional categories in Baur's reading of 1 Corinthians 1–3. Drawing on Paul's contrast between human and divine wisdom, he writes that

through this [*viz.* the opposition between baptism and preaching in 1 Cor. 1:17] he was led to his principal theme, to set out what is the principal matter for Christianity, which is the same in the preaching and the subject, namely, not human wisdom and rhetorical polish…but rather only the simple doctrine of specific historical facts and, above all, of the great fact of the crucifixion of Jesus.[114]

God's wisdom, in this passage, Paul's "mystery" hidden from previous ages, is identified as "specific historical facts." There can be, then, no growth from being ψυχικός into being πνευματικός because the latter is epistemologically distinct and the former cannot think their way in. What is needed is not growth but "an entirely new, higher consciousness" of the "one principle of all spiritual life," which is Christ himself.[115] In terms of the exegetical discussion above, Baur appears to conclude with many contemporary scholars that Paul's "wisdom" is nothing other than his gospel

Secten, sie sich nach Paulus und Kephas nannte, den Hauptgegensatz bildeten"; see also p. 136. The logic presented in the quote, strictly speaking, refers to J. E. C. Schmidt's argument, but Baur quotes it here uncritically and repeats it in his later, more comprehensive work on Paul; Baur, *Paul*, vol. I, p. 264. Harris, *Tübingen School*, p. 183, notes that "Most of all it was the letter to the Galatians which provided the confirmation which Baur required for his views" (though he also treats it as a secondary confirmation of what is already established in 1 Cor. 1:11–12); and see Hodgson, *Formation*, p. 205. See also the discussion of Baur's reading of Gal. 2:11 in Andreas Wechsler, *Geschichtsbild und Apostelstreit. Eine forschungsgeschichtliche und exegetische Studie über den antiochenischen Zwischenfall (Gal 2, 11–14)*, BZNW 62 (Berlin: De Gruyter, 1991), pp. 31–33, 45–51.

[113] In addition to the above note, see also Baur, *Paul*, vol. I, p. 291, and Baur, "Die Christuspartei," pp. 82–89 (the polemics of 2 Corinthians are explored in more detail from p. 89 of Baur's article). In this sense, Kümmel's argument that Baur's article established the Petrine/Pauline opposition "on the ground of the two Corinthian letters" is not entirely accurate; Kümmel, *Das Neue Testament*, p. 158.

[114] Baur, "Die Christuspartei," p. 69: "Dadurch war er auf sein Hauptthema geführt, auseinander zu setzen, was beim εὐαγγελίζεσθαι und dem Gegenstande desselben, dem Christenthum, die Hauptsache sey, nemlich nicht menschliche Weisheit und Kunst… sondern nur die einfache Lehre von gewißen historischen Thatsachen und vor allem von der großen Thatsache des Kreuzestodes Jesu."

[115] Ibid., pp. 70, 71; see also his comments on Christ as the "principle of the Christian consciousness" in Baur, *Paul*, vol. II, pp. 123–127.

message, and certainly not some reserved higher instruction for more mature believers.[116] The tacit image of Paul at work for Baur, then, is not a pedagogical Paul who accommodates his message and behavior to his audience in a flexible way, but a pugnacious Paul who stands unwaveringly for the truth of his gospel and opposes those who would taint it.[117]

Even without a full treatment of Baur's legacy in New Testament scholarship, his image of Paul is, I think, easily recognizable and tacitly at work in much contemporary historical-critical writing on Paul's letters.[118] This is the case despite the fact that many details of Baur's account have been questioned, criticized, and outright rejected.[119] Indeed, the fact that scholars still find themselves under pressure to counter Baur's arguments is some indication of his continued importance.[120] There are of course exceptions to this, inevitably, in view of the diversity of New Testament Studies at present. What is important to note here, though, is that Baur's presentation of Paul is opposed to the catechetical/pedagogical Paul of the early Church at nearly every point. In the first place, Baur's historical commitments would never have allowed him to associate Paul with an institution that developed slowly over the centuries after his death. Moreover, where the *Acts of Paul*, Clement, Origen, and John Chrysostom relied on 1 Corinthians as the foundation for their image

---

[116] Even Baur's view that the Corinthians could "still not" penetrate "into the depths of the genuine Christian life" does not necessarily indicate that he is willing to admit some distinction in Pauline teaching; Baur, *Paulus*, vol. 1, p. 295, my translation (= Baur, *Paul*, vol. 1, p. 264). His view that the principle of Christian consciousness is nothing but Christ and his identification of preaching and its object suggests that Paul's teaching was simple and consistent, whatever the failures of his listeners may have been.

[117] This is somewhat ironic, in that Baur does explicitly state that the Corinthian letters illuminate Paul's "educating care" ("pädagogischen Sorgfalt"), though it is not a point he develops; Baur, *Paul*, vol. 1, p. 258 (=Baur, *Paulus*, vol. 1, p. 288).

[118] On the legacy of F. C. Baur's work, see David Lincicum, "Ferdinand Christian Baur and biblical theology," *Annali di Storia dell'Esegesi* 30, no. 1 (2013), 79–92; Carleton Paget, "Reception of Baur," pp. 335–386 (esp. pp. 374–382); White, *Remembering Paul*, pp. 20–41; along with the short treatment in Bockmuehl, *Seeing the Word*, pp. 125–130.

[119] See the comments on Baur's dichotomy of Jewish Christianity and Gentile Christianity and his historical-critical project more broadly respectively in Robert Morgan, "Baur's New Testament theology," in Bauspiess, Landmesser, and Lincicum, *Ferdinand Christian Baur*, p. 273; and Lincicum, "Theological task," p. 102. Baird reflects, "In assessing Baur's contribution to NT research, one wonders how a scholar of such importance could have committed so many historical errors"; Baird, *From Deism*, p. 268.

[120] E.g., the attack on Baur's views in Tomson, *Paul and the Jewish Law*, and the criticism of his reading of the Pseudo-Clementines in Markus N. A. Bockmuehl, *The Remembered Peter: In Ancient Reception and Modern Debate*, WUNT 262 (Tübingen: Mohr Siebeck, 2010), pp. 94–96. Other examples are detailed in Carleton Paget, "Reception of Baur," p. 381.

of Paul, Baur opted for Galatians. Where early readers found harmony between Paul and the apostles (no doubt influenced, Baur would say, by the presentation in Acts), Baur found opposition. Finally, where Paul was seen approaching his preaching and catechesis pedagogically, varying his delivery according to his audience, Baur's Paul proclaimed a simple and unwavering truth.

The image of Paul proposed by Baur is not without its supporting textual resources, as we have seen; he was nothing if not an intelligent and creative reader. Even so, the exploration of early Christian presentations of Paul in Chapters 3–6 and the juxtaposition of early readers among contemporary exegetical discussions in this chapter at the very least demonstrate that Baur's preferred resources are not the only ones available for use in constructing a Pauline image. In other words, to produce an image of Paul as an independent and pugnacious apostle, divided from other early Christian leaders, is to emphasize some resources at the expense of others. The same is true, on the other hand, for reading Paul as an ecclesially united pedagogue engaged in catechesis. Furthermore, Baur's creativity functioned within his own intellectual and religious context:[121] adopting the historical-critical method encountered in scholars like Semler, drawing deeply on Hegel's construal of historical development, debating with catholics and protestants within the Tübingen faculty (notably Johann Adam Möhler and Heinrich Ewald), and inheriting a protestant Lutheran religious tradition.[122] Further, Baur's institutional setting in the university worked with his historical-critical commitments to produce a context in which the driving questions concerned academic debates about history and meaning, shaping his definition of theological competence to revolve around historical-critical competence.[123] This, combined with impulses within Baur's Lutheran tradition, shaped his

---

[121] The comment of Gadamer regarding Theodor Mommsen applies to Baur as well: "For example, when you read a classic essay by Mommsen [read: Baur] you immediately know its era, the only era when it could have been written. Even a master of the historical method is not able to keep himself entirely free from the prejudices of his time his social environment, and his national situation etc."; Hans-Georg Gadamer, *Truth and Method*, 2nd rev. edn, trans. William Glen-Doepel, Joel Weinscheimer, and Donald G. Marshall (New York: Continuum, 2002), p. 512.

[122] See the comments in Hodgson, *Formation*, pp. 22–29, 37–39; Kümmel, *Das Neue Testament*, p. 162; Harris, *Tübingen School*, pp. 11–54, 137–158; and White, *Remembering Paul*, pp. 22–24.

[123] See Birgit Weyel, "Ferdinand Christian Baur und die praktische Theologie," in Martin Bauspiess, Christof Landmesser, and David Lincicum (eds.), *Ferdinand Christian Baur und die Geschichte des frühen Christentums*, WUNT I/333 (Tübingen: Mohr Siebeck, 2014), pp. 414–416.

understanding of Paul;[124] Baur himself saw the Reformation as the beginning of a critical approach to scriptures.[125] In fact, to better understand the opposition of an ecclesial/pedagogical Paul against an independent/pugnacious Paul we must push this genealogy further back to the debate between Erasmus and Luther, ostensibly on the freedom or bondage of the will, in which the conflict between these two views of Paul comes clearly to the fore.[126]

7.2.2.2 *Erasmus and Luther's Opposing Pauls*

When Desiderius Erasmus wrote *De libero arbitrio* in 1524, the famous humanist had already contributed decisively to the history of New Testament Studies with the publication of his annotated *Novum Instrumentum* in 1516, giving rise to four further editions. Luther himself had made use of Erasmus' observations in his first commentary on Galatians (1519), though even then not all was to his liking.[127] Five years later, Luther's initial hopes for support from Erasmus had faded and he resigned himself to requesting by letter that Erasmus not oppose him in writing.[128] This, of course, was not to be.

[124] On Baur's project of "scientific" theology, see esp. Zachhuber, *Theology as Science*, who discusses university institutional context on pp. 2–4, 13–14.

[125] See Ferdinand Christian Baur, "Die Einleitung in das Neue Testament als theologische Wissenschaft: ihr Begriff und ihre Aufgabe, ihr Entwicklungsgang und ihr innerer Organismus," *Theologische Jahrbücher* 9–10 (1850–1851), 488 ("Mit der Reformation war erst der Boden gegeben, auf welchem eine Wissenschaft entstehen und gedeihen konnte, deren wesentliche Aufgabe die Kritik sein sollte"). This is a point also noted in Ernst Käsemann, "Einführung," in *Ausgewählte Werke in Einzelausgaben*, vol. I: *Historisch-kritische Untersuchungen zum Neuen Testament*, ed. Klaus Scholder (Stuttgart: Friedrich Frommann, 1963), pp. xv–xvi; and see the brief comments in David Lincicum, "Martin Luther in modern New Testament scholarship," *Oxford Research Encyclopedia of Religion* (2017), http://religion.oxfordre.com. This is not to say, however, that Baur was not critical of elements within the Lutheran tradition; see Baur, *Lectures*, pp. 169, 195.

[126] I am indebted in what follows to the discussion of this debate in Chester, *Reading Paul*, which first alerted me to its significance for the present question. Note that, where possible, I refer the reader to the Latin text of Erasmus provided in the Amsterdam edition (ASD), *Opera Omnia Desiderii Erasmi* (1969–), which is still being produced. Different editions are cited below as otherwise necessary. References to Luther are from the Weimar edition (WA), *D. Martin Luthers Werke* (1883–1929).

[127] See the discussion in Cornelis Augustijn, *Erasmus. Der Humanist als Theologe und Kirchenreformer*, Studies in Medieval and Reformation Thought 59 (Leiden: Brill, 1996), pp. 53–60, and the criticisms noted in Brian Cummings, *The Literary Culture of the Reformation: Grammar and Grace* (New York: Oxford University Press, 2002), pp. 144–145.

[128] WA, *BR* 3, no. 729.

When Erasmus' book appeared, however, it was not the attack that some hoped for but was rather presented in the title as διατριβὴ *sive collatio*, a diatribe or comparison, that is, as an opportunity for Erasmus and Luther to have a civil discussion about matters *adiaphora* (non-essential) rather than *fundamenta*.[129] Rather than engage in dogmatic opposition to Luther's recently published "assertion" on the bondage of the human will,[130] Erasmus wanted to demonstrate what he thought was a more appropriate mode of theological discourse, one in which such discourse is measured.[131] He positions himself as a debater rather than judge, "ready to learn from anyone if something more correct or learned be presented. Yet I would willingly persuade those of average talent not to undertake to contend unyieldingly in such questions which will sooner harm Christian unity than advance piety."[132] In Erasmus' view, the "harm" of Luther's approach comes not only from the combative quality of assertions, especially those which are not established by the Church, but also from the public probing of deep scriptural mysteries which the believer is not equipped to handle.

For there are some restricted holy places in the Holy Scriptures into which God did not wish us to penetrate more deeply and, if we try to do so, then the deeper we go, the more and more blind we become…Many things are reserved for that time when we shall no longer see through a glass darkly or in a riddle, but in which we shall contemplate the glory of the Lord when his face shall be revealed.[133]

[129] See esp. the discussion in Marjorie O'Rourke Boyle, *Rhetoric and Reform: Erasmus' Civil Dispute with Luther*, HHM 71 (Cambridge, MA: Harvard University Press, 1983), pp. 5–45 and *passim*; Cummings, *Literary Culture*, pp. 145–156; and Chester, *Reading Paul*, pp. 13–20.

[130] *Assertio omnium articulorum* 36; WA, *A* VII, p. 142 lines 23–24; see also comments in Volker Stolle, *Luther und Paulus. Die exegetischen und hermeneutischen Grundlagen der lutherischen Rechtfertigungslehre im Paulinismus Luthers*, ABiG 10 (Leipzig: Evangelische Verlagsanstalt, 2002), p. 269.

[131] *De lib.* Ia2–3 (text in Johannes von Walter (ed.), *De libero arbitrio* Διατριβη *sive collatio per Desiderium Erasmum Roterdamum*, Quellenschriften zur Geschichte des Protestantismus 8 (Leipzig: A. Diechertsche, 1935); translations of this text are from E. Gordon Rupp and Philip S. Watson (eds.), *Luther and Erasmus: Free Will and Salvation* (Philadelphia: Westminster Press, 1969), unless otherwise noted (here p. 36)).

[132] *De lib.* Ia6 (translation modified from Rupp and Watson): "…paratus a quocumque discere, si quid afferatur rectius aut compertius, quamquam illud libenter persuaserim mediocribus ingeniis, in huius generis quaestionibus non adeo pertinaciter contendere, quae citius laedant Christianam concordiam, quam adiuvent pietatem."

[133] *De lib.* Ia7 (translation modified from Rupp and Watson): "Sunt enim in divinis litteris adyta quaedam, in quae deus noluit nos altius penetrare, et si penetrare conemur, quo fuerimus altius ingressi, hoc magis ac magis caligamus…Multa servantur ei tempori, cum iam non videbimus per speculum et in aenigmate, sed revelata facie domini gloriam conteplabimur." The term "adyta" here alludes to the Vulgate translation for the inner recesses of the Temple; cf. 1 Chr 28.11.

In addition to the genuine mysteries, which are out of reach for all Christians until the eschaton, there is also the matter of determining what is appropriate for the masses, such things that, "even if they were true and might be known," it would be improper "to prostitute them before common ears."[134] This, Erasmus argues, is precisely the problem with Luther's assertion. Even if it were true that human will is entirely bound either to God or to Satan, publishing such a view could only have a negative effect on those who find in it a cheap determinism.[135] Establishing this more tempered mode of theological discourse is the purpose of the preface to Erasmus' *Diatribe* and he observes in closing that it is "almost more relevant to the main issue than the disputation itself."[136]

In support of his view, Erasmus relies on the example of the Apostle Paul in 1 Corinthians. "Paul knew the difference between what things are lawful and what are expedient. It is lawful to speak the truth; it is not expedient to speak to the truth to everybody at every time and in every way."[137] Even more familiar to us at this point is perhaps Erasmus' appeal to 1 Corinthians 2:1–6.

And so Paul, as a wise dispenser of the Divine word, often brings charity to bear, and prefers to follow that which is fitting for one's neighbors rather than the letter of the law: and possesses a wisdom that he speaks among the perfect, but among the weak he judges himself to know nothing, save Jesus Christ and him crucified.[138]

---

[134] *De lib.* Ia9: "Iam sunt quaedam eius generis, ut etiamsi vera essent et sciri possent, non expediret tamen ea prostituere promiscuis auribus."

[135] *De lib.* Ia10.

[136] *De lib.* Ia11: "Haec verbosius praefatus merito videar, nisi pene magis ad rem pertinerent, quam ipsa disputatio." The rhetorical force of Erasmus' use of diatribe and the significance of Luther's rejection of it is eloquently demonstrated in O'Rourke Boyle, *Rhetoric and Reform*, pp. 5–42.

[137] *De lib.* Ia9: "Paulus novit discrimen inter ea, quae licent, et ea, quae expediunt," alluding to 1 Cor. 6:12 and 10:23.

[138] *De lib.* Ia11 (translation modified from Rupp and Watson): "Itaque Paulus tamquam prudens dispensator sermonis divini frequenter adhibita in consilium caritate mavult id sequi, quod expedit proximo, quam quod ex sese licet, et habet sapientiam quam loquitur inter perfectos, inter infirmos nihil iudicat se scire, nisi Jesum Christum, et hunc crucifixum," perhaps alluding also to 1 Cor. 6:12 and 2 Cor. 3:6 (see also Rom. 7:6). His *Annotation* on 1 Cor. 2:6 also explicitly highlights Paul's pedagogical concern not to give the impression that theology was only available in simple terms (text in ASD, VI-8, p. 60). Erasmus' translation of δε in 1 Cor. 2:6 with *porro* rather than *autem* may further signal that he saw the wisdom for the mature as standing in continuity with the word of the cross, part of a pedagogical development rather than a rhetorical opposition; see the text and comments in ASD VI-3, pp. 198–199, where the editor refers to his comments on Erasmus' translation of John 8:16, ASD VI-2, p. 101.

The strong resonance with Origen's reading of 1 Corinthians 2:1–6 is not accidental;[139] Erasmus had encountered the Alexandrian around the turn of the century and he remained a fundamentally important influence ever after.[140] In his early work the *Enchiridion militis Christiani* (1503), penned shortly after his discovery of Origen's writings, Erasmus extolled Paul as the primary guide for "the interpretation of divine scripture," followed by Origen, Ambrose, Jerome, and Augustine.[141] He argues, following Origen, that scripture itself, like the Apostle who expounds it, conceals and reveals according to the ability and maturity of the reader. Paul's comments on milk, solid food, and eating only vegetables fulfill a similar function for Erasmus here as they did for Origen.[142] As he says in his conflict with Luther, "Holy Scripture has its own language, adapting itself to our understanding."[143]

Pedagogical dissimulation played an important role in Erasmus' reading of Paul and Peter's disagreement recorded in Galatians 2. Where readers from Augustine to Aquinas had seen in this account a true conflict arising from Peter's actions, Erasmus followed Jerome in seeing Peter's actions as *dissimulatio* for the purpose of educating the Antiochene believers.[144]

---

[139] See the discussion of Origen's *Comm. in Rom.* 9.36.763 (Scheck 9.36.1) on p. 167 above.

[140] See esp. André Godin, *Érasme. Lecteur d'Origène* (Geneva: Librairie Droz, 1982), who dates Erasmus encounter with Origen to 1501; see also the brief comments on the role of Origen in the Erasmus/Luther debate in Fürst, *Origenes*, pp. 179–181. For an account of the various editions of Origen available in the sixteenth century, see the brief treatment in Giancarlo Pani, "'In toto Origene non est verbum de Christo': Lutero e Origene," *Adamantius* 15 (2009), 140–143.

[141] *Enchir.* 324–326 (ASD V-8, 118): "Ex interpretibus diuinae scripturae eos potissimum delige, qui a littera quammaxime recedunt. Cuiusmodi sunt imprimis post Paulum Origenes, Ambrosius, Hieronymus, Augustinus"; see also the comments in James D. Tracy, *Erasmus of the Low Countries* (Berkeley: University of California Press, 1996), pp. 32–33.

[142] See *Enchir.* 339–344 (ASD V-8, p. 120), which draws on 1 Cor. 3:2 and Heb. 5:13–14; and see further *Enchir.* 366–371 (ASD V-8, p. 122) where Erasmus brings in Rom. 14:3 as another food-related analogy for those who cannot look beyond the letter to the Spirit. It is worth noting here also that Erasmus' interpretation of 1 Cor. 1:17 in his *Paraphrases* of 1 Corinthians (Joannes Clericus (ed.), *Desiderii Erasmi Roterodami Opera Omnia*, vol. VII: *Paraphrases in N. Testamentum* (Hildesheim: G. Olms, 1962), pp. 861–862) is strikingly similar to that of Origen and John Chrysostom, in which the rite of baptism is presented as an easy task while the preceding moral formation is the superior and more difficult work.

[143] *De lib.* Ia11 (translation modified from Rupp and Watson): "Habet scriptura sacra linguam suam semet ad nostrum sensum attemperans." For a more complete presentation of Erasmus' hermeneutics, including his negotiation of the letter/Spirit dichotomy and the bridging role of allegory, see esp. Manfred Hoffmann, *Rhetoric and Theology: The Hermeneutic of Erasmus* (Toronto: University of Toronto Press, 1994).

[144] Chester's dismissal of Jerome's reading is perhaps too hasty (Chester, *Reading Paul*, p. 14 n. 3) and it does not do justice to the difficulty faced in pairing Gal. 2:11 with

Peter and Paul were not truly in conflict but were engaged in a staged exercise to demonstrate the truth of the gospel in relation to the Law without giving unnecessary offense to the observant Jewish believers.[145] Just as Paul adapts his teaching according to his audience, so also should Luther and Erasmus refrain from airing theological disputes that are not constructive for the lay person.

If Erasmus' Paul stands in fundamental and intentional continuity with Origen's Paul and supports a similar hermeneutic of scriptural mystery, dissimulation, and progress, Luther rejects this view in no uncertain terms.[146] In Luther's letter to Erasmus noted above, he alludes to Galatians 2:11 in a way that signals both his disagreement with Jerome's interpretation of the Antioch incident and his own appropriation of a particular Pauline persona. If Erasmus publishes a critique of Luther's *dogmata*, the Reformer states, "necessity will compel us to oppose you to your face."[147] The phrase "in faciem resistere" recalls the Vulgate rendering of Galatians 2:11 as "in faciem ei resisti."[148] Luther views the

---

other parts of Paul's letters, such as 1 Cor. 9:20. Tertullian, for instance, posits a development in Pauline thought between Gal. 2:11 and 1 Cor. 9:20 (*Marc.* 1.20.3), while others such as Clement (and Eusebius) solve the problem by identifying Κηφᾶς with one of the seventy disciples rather than Peter (Clement *apud* Eusebius *Hist. eccl.* 1.12.2). However strained Jerome's reading may appear to many today, it is nevertheless a relatively elegant attempt to make Paul's comments in Galatians consistent with his words elsewhere, as well as with the New Testament more broadly. See further the survey of interpretations from Origen to the present in John Kenneth Riches, *Galatians Through the Centuries*, Blackwell Bible Commentaries (Oxford: Blackwell, 2008), pp. 106–113; see also Alfons Fürst, "Origenes und Ephräm über Paulus' Konflikt mit Petrus (Gal. 2, 11–14)," in *Von Origenes und Hieronymus zu Augustinus. Studien zur antiken Theologiegeschichte*, AZK (Berlin: De Gruyter, 2011), pp. 195–208, on the links between Ephrem and Origen on this passage.

[145] See his *Annotationes* on Gal. 2:11 in ASD VI-9, 78–92 (esp. pp. 84–88); see also the comments in Tracy, *Erasmus*, p. 117, who is followed by Chester, *Reading Paul*, p. 14. On the controversy between Jerome and Augustine, see the recent discussion in Jason A. Myers, "Law, lies and letter writing: an analysis of Jerome and Augustine on the Antioch incident (Galatians 2:11–14)," *Scottish Journal of Thelogy* 66, no. 2 (2013), 127–139, with reference also to the debate over the so-called New Perspective on Paul.

[146] In fact, as Chester, *Reading Paul*, p. 19, notes, Luther had already published his disagreement with the Erasmus/Jerome interpretation of Gal. 2:11 in his first commentary on Galatians; see also Fürst, *Origenes*, p. 180. Pani, "Lutero e Origene," pp. 135–149, notes Luther's longstanding dislike of Origen and characterizes the debate between Erasmus and Luther as a conflict between the former's "origenismo" and the latter's rejection of knowledge, his "agnostinismo" (p. 144), despite the fact that Luther likely had not read anything by Origen directly.

[147] WA, *BR* 3, no. 729: "Hoc solum timebatur, ne quando per adversarios adducereris editis libellis in dogmata nostra grassari, et tum nos necessitas urgeret, tibi in faciem resistere."

[148] See the discussion of this allusion in Chester, *Reading Paul*, pp. 13–14.

conflict between Peter and Paul not as one of pedagogical dissimulation but rather as reflecting a genuine error on the part of Peter that had to be corrected by Paul. Luther, here, casts himself in the role of Paul.[149] The error to be corrected in the case of the *De servo arbitrio*, however, is not one of legal praxis but of dogma and its supporting hermeneutical approach. As Brian Cummings has recently noted, "Luther and Erasmus are not only arguing about texts, they are also arguing about how to argue about texts."[150] On the one hand, not only does Luther argue that the freedom of the will is not among the *adiaphora*,[151] but even more fundamentally he rejects the notion that scripture speaks obscurely, only intelligible to the spiritually mature.

> That in God there are many things hidden, of which we are ignorant, no one doubts…But that in Scripture there are some things abstruse, and everything is not plain – this is an idea put about by the ungodly Sophists, with whose mouth even you speak here, Erasmus…I admit, of course, that there are many texts in the Scriptures that are obscure and abstruse, not because of the majesty of their subject matter, but because of our ignorance of their vocabulary and grammar. But none of these impede the knowledge of all things in Scripture.[152]

This hermeneutical stance eliminates the possibility of accepting Erasmus' incentives for spiritual interpretation provided by divine anthropomorphism in scripture, for example. Where Erasmus wants to show the dangers of a literal interpretation, Luther refers these matters to "grammar and the figurative use of words (*grammatica…et figuris verborum*), which even children understand."[153] Therefore, Luther

---

[149] "Im Widerstand des Paulus gegen Petrus in Antiochien fand er das Paradigma für sein eigenes Rollenverständnis. Und erst dadurch entwickelte er seinen eigentlichen Paulinismus" (Stolle, *Luther und Paulus*, p. 95).This is, in fact, a broad tendency in Luther's writings; see esp. ibid., pp. 73–107. He discusses the Antioch incident on pp. 94–97.

[150] Cummings, *Literary Culture*, p. 150.

[151] *De serv.* 1 (WA 18, p. 609; translations of this work are from Rupp and Watson, *Luther and Erasmus*, unless otherwise noted).

[152] *De serv.* 1 (WA 18, p. 606; translation modified from Rupp and Watson): "In deo esse multa abscondita, quae ignoremus, nemo dubitat…Sed esse in scriptura quaedam abstrusa et non omnia exposita, invulgatum est quidem per impios Sophistas, quorum ore et tu loqueris hic Erasme…Hoc sane fateor, esse multa loca in scripturis obscura et abstrusa, non ob maiestatem rerum, sed ob ignorantiam vocabulorum et grammaticae, sed quae nihil impediant scientiam omnium rerum in scripturis." See also the comments in Chester, *Reading Paul*, p. 30.

[153] *De serv.* 1 (WA 18, p. 639; translation modified from Rupp and Watson): "Grammatica enim ista sunt et figuris verborum composita, quae etiam pueri norunt." This is related to Luther's overarching rejection of allegorical interpretation, which he linked

counters Erasmus' pedagogical reading of 1 Corinthians 2–3 with his own. As Erasmus had advocated, Luther claims that he is in fact only preaching "Jesus crucified" and speaking "wisdom among the perfect." The difference is, though, that "'Christ crucified' brings all these things with him, even including that 'wisdom among the perfect.'"[154] For Luther, all believers, who are by definition inhabited by the Spirit of God, qualify as the mature. "For there is no other wisdom to be taught among Christians than that which is hidden in a mystery and pertains to the perfect."[155] In other words, there is no graduated increase in scriptural interpretation or understanding with spiritual maturity. Scripture speaks the same truth clearly to all believers. This filters further into Luther's reading of 1 Corinthians 3:1–3. Where Erasmus understands the "carnal" status of the Corinthians in terms of weakness (*infirmitas*), Luther sees it simply as an error (*vitium*): "for he accuses them of forming sects and parties, which is not a matter of weakness or lack of capacity for more solid doctrine, but malice and the old leaven, which he commands them to clean out."[156] This is not a question of maturity or progressive teaching but of errors that need to be opposed and corrected. Indeed, in a sermon nearly twenty years later, Luther characterizes Paul's demeanor in 1 Corinthians as unpleasant and angry ("unlustig und zornig"), in sharp contrast with the pedagogically careful Paul of Erasmus and his patristic models.[157]

This hermeneutical stance can also be situated within Luther's broader construal of the relationship between moral formation and faith or piety. Erasmus, in continuity with the interpretive tradition prevalent in the early Church and exemplified in the catechetical interpretation of Paul,

---

particularly with the work of Origen; see also the comments in Pani, "Lutero e Origene," pp. 144–145.

[154] *De serv.* 1 (WA 18, p. 639): "At Christus crucifixus haec omnia secum affert, ipsamque adeo sapientiam inter perfectos…"

[155] *De serv.* 1 (WA 18, p. 639): "…cum nulla sit alia sapientia inter Christianos docenda, quam ea quae abscondita est in mysterio et ad perfectos pertinet…"

[156] *De serv.* v (WA 18, p. 734; translation modified from Rupp and Watson): "Nam quod Corinthios Paulus carnales appellat, non certe infirmitatem, sed vitium significat, cum arguat eos sectis et partibus laborare, quod non est infirmitas aut incapacitas solidioris doctrinae, sed malicia et fermentum vetus, quod expurgare iubet." This passage is related to the larger debate between Erasmus and Luther over the interpretation of Isa. 40 and Gen. 6:3, in which Luther felt that he had the upper hand with the dictum of interpreting scripture by scripture; see the comments in Augustijn, *Erasmus*, pp. 252–253. Of course, Erasmus and Jerome also appealed to the same interpretive rule, though with results that differed from those of Luther; see O'Rourke Boyle, *Rhetoric and Reform*, p. 46.

[157] *Sermo* 30, "Predigt am 9. Sonntag nach Trinitatis" (WA 49, p. 534), preserved in both the German manuscript S and the Latin/German manuscript R.

considered one's ability to understand the spiritual meaning of scripture to follow *from* moral preparation.[158] As we saw above, the average Christian is too morally corrupt in Erasmus' view to be able to understand the mysteries of scripture. Further, according to the *Acts of Paul*, Clement, Origen, and John Chrysostom, moral preparation precedes faith (and baptism). This is a crucial point for the catechetical reading of Paul that influenced Erasmus.

For Luther, however, moral development proceeds *from* faith or piety.[159] In his popular and influential *Von der Freiheit eines Christenmenschen*, he wrote that it is "through faith" that one "becomes holy, righteous, true, peaceful, free, and full of all good things, a true child of God."[160] That is to say, these virtues are not part of one's *preparation* for the Christian life but rather stand already possessed (and yet, of course, never fully so) at the beginning. Faith in Christ, by its very nature, "fulfills every commandment and without all other works makes one righteous."[161] In addressing the issue of moral behavior later in the same work, Luther states, "Therefore, the person must always be good and righteous first [*gut und frum sein*; *viz.* remembering that faith alone makes one righteous], before all of his good works, and good works *follow and proceed* (*folgen und außgahn*) from the righteous, good person."[162] This righteous and good person, the

---

[158] See the recent discussion of rhetoric, moral formation, and spiritual progress in Erasmus in Jennifer A. Herdt, *Putting on Virtue: The Legacy of the Splendid Vices* (Chicago: University of Chicago Press, 2008), pp. 109–122 and *passim*.

[159] See the comments in ibid., p. 178: "Union with Christ is not the culmination but the precondition for any process of sanctification." For a balance to Herdt's analysis, which places more emphasis on the experiential or empirical basis for Luther's rejection of mimetic virtue and so on his argument that moral development proceeds from faith, see Simeon Zahl, "Non-competitive agency and Luther's experiential argument against virtue," *Modern Theology* 34 (2018), 1–24 (accessed via "Early View" at https://doi.org/10.1111/moth.12410).

[160] *Freiheit* 10 (WA 7, p. 24; trans. modified from Tryntje Helfferich, *Martin Luther: On the Freedom of a Christian, with Related Texts* (Indianapolis: Hackett, 2013), pp. 24–25): "Und alßo durch den glauben die seele von dem gottis wort heylig, gerecht, warhafftig, fridsam, frey, und alle gutte voll, eyn warhafftig kind gottis wirt." The analogous Latin text (WA 7, p. 53) treats "God's word" more specifically as "God's promises" ("haec promissa dei"), to which one holds by "firm faith" ("firma fide").

[161] *Freiheit* 13 (WA 7, p. 26, my translation): "... das er [*viz.* der Glaube] alle gepott erfullet und on alle andere werck frum macht." The phrase "frum macht" is Luther's translation of his Latin "iustificet" (WA 7, p. 55).

[162] *Freiheit* 23 (WA 7, p. 32, translation modified from Helfferich, emphasis added): "... alßo das allweg die person zuvor muß gut und frum sein vor allen gutten wercken, und gutte werck folgen und außgahn von der frumen gutten person." The analogous Latin phrase only includes "bonus" ("gut") here while "iustus" ("frum") appears later (WA 7, p. 61). It is worth noting that Luther's target here is the question of whether certain works are required for salvation (as he makes clear again further down in §23

person already "perfect" and imbued with the Spirit, in the terms of *De servo arbitrio*, is enabled to read and understand scripture rightly and to will the good and do it. This understanding of the relation between moral formation and spiritual understanding is crucial to the hermeneutical disagreement between the Reformer and the Humanist. Erasmus reads a mysterious scripture, which requires reliable guides to spiritual understanding through the overcoming of moral turpitude. Luther's scripture is clear, however, to all and sundry, to whomever has simply believed in Christ and received the Spirit. Accordingly, Erasmus' Paul is a pedagogue, necessary for his hermeneutic, while Luther's Paul is an opposer of error, paradigmatic for Luther's own theological program.

More, of course, can be and has been said about the image and use of Paul in Luther and Erasmus.[163] It is enough for the present inquiry to note that the contrast between Erasmus and Luther in their approach to Paul mirrors the contrast between ancient and contemporary readings of Paul. The decisive ground for Luther's image of Paul is not 1 Corinthians but rather Galatians and Romans.[164] Luther's Paul, like that of Baur later, is a man of oppositions: law versus gospel, Paul versus Peter, scripture versus tradition, etc. This is not to say that Luther did not find pastoral resources in Pauline letters; that he certainly did. But I want to suggest that it is of fundamental importance for subsequent Pauline scholarship, formed as it was and is by nineteenth-century German protestant scholars, that Luther's Paul rejects the ancient pedagogical reading strategy that was so central to the catechetical Pauline images in Clement, Origen, and John Chrysostom. It is true, of course, that Luther's Paul was not entirely original to him, as he drew in particular on Augustine's reading of the Apostle.[165] But his interpretation took place at a crucial time in

---

and which comes out in the Latin "opera enim up non faciunt fidelem, ita nec iustum"; WA 7, p. 62), which is distinct from the question of spiritual progress addressed by Clement, Origen, and Chrysostom. For them, the right mode of living is bound up with the Christian life and spiritual progress but they are not concerned with the question of the relation between works and salvation since moral preparation, faith, and baptism are part of the spectrum or journey of the spiritual life as a whole.

[163] In comparison with studies on Luther, however, the topic of Erasmus' interpretation of Paul is remarkably under-researched and ripe for a full investigation.

[164] It is no accident that in Stolle's expansive discussion of the exegetical and hermeneutical foundations of Luther's Paulinism (with reference particularly to the doctrine of justification) there are no citations of 1 Cor. 3:1–3 listed in the index and only two which include 1 Cor. 2:1–6, 1 Cor. 1:17–2:16 (Stolle, *Luther und Paulus*, p. 90), and 1 Cor. 2:6–16 (ibid., p. 92). These passages evidently do little constructive work for Luther's image of Paul.

[165] Note the analysis of Augustine's reading of 1 Cor. 3:1–3 in Penniman, *Raised on Christian Milk*, pp. 165–200, which is suggestive for the present argument. Penniman

the history of scriptural interpretation, which continues to shape theological and exegetical discussions today. And in his debate with Erasmus, the exegetical resources deployed throughout both their arguments demonstrates that Luther's view of an oppositional Paul had to provide counter-readings of the key exegetical passages for the opposing view. That Luther's Paul came to dominate for so long should not make us lose sight of the fact that the alternative pedagogical image of Paul, in which the insights of the early readers explored here are not so out of place, is not the sheer error that Seesemann and others supposed.

7.3 CONCLUSION

This chapter has covered much ground. In brief, what began as a summary of the previous chapters' findings turned to a short synthetic analysis of the continuities and discontinuities between early Christian catechetical images of Paul and the interpretive dynamic within which these exegetical and theological decisions were made. The catechetical Paul highlighted in Chapters 3–6 is more than simply the juxtaposition of Paul and the catechumenate in bare terms. It was based on the illumination of certain Pauline resources, particularly in 1 Corinthians 1–3, and arose from the needs posed by early Christian debates about the place of catechetical instruction in a believer's spiritual development. This image of Paul was, therefore, shaped also by the broader pedagogical needs or assumptions being circulated and debated in the early Church.

The chapter then brought these early interpreters into dialogue with contemporary Pauline studies, first at the level of exegetical detail and then in relation to a broader image of Paul. Notably, in both cases, although the relation between Paul and the catechumenate was absent among modern scholars, similar exegetical decisions were noted among scholars who have emphasized the relevance of ancient education for understanding Paul's letters. Furthermore, in light of the diversity of Pauline images among contemporary scholars, I focused on one particular image – that

argues that Augustine saw "growth from milk to solid food...not simply [as] a conceptual problem" but that he "came to view the weaning of Christians as too risky a practice to implement as a catechetical program in the church at large" (p. 200). Chester, *Reading Paul*, pp. 63–103, discusses "the medieval context of the Reformers," beginning with Augustine and tracing the influence of his "exegetical grammar." See also the contributions in Part II of Robert Kolb, Irene Dingel, and Lubomir Batka (eds.), *The Oxford Handbook of Martin Luther's Theology* (Oxford: Oxford University Press, 2014).

of the pugnacious and independent Paul – and its relation with the cat-echetical, pedagogical Paul seen in the *Acts of Paul*, Clement, Origen, and John Chrysostom. This pugnacious Paul was identified first in F. C. Baur and his legacy before being traced back to the debate between Erasmus and Luther in the 1520s, where it appears with particular clarity as a rejection of Erasmus' pedagogical view of the Apostle.[166]

It needs to be pointed out again here, as it was in passing above, that the hermeneutical dynamic seen among the early Christian writers – reception as the encounter between the reader and the text, shaped by a particular horizon which is itself shaped by social, intellectual, and insti-tutional concerns – is also at play among these Reformation and contem-porary writers. Luther's and Erasmus' engagement with their received interpretive traditions – their rejection of medieval scholasticism, their evaluation of the Church fathers, their related but distinct emphases on the text and content of scripture – are themselves established areas of research.[167] Baur's reception of a critical approach to the New Testament and Christian history, his debt to the Reformation, and his negotiation of his historical context were illuminated briefly above and have been explored more fully by others, if not in terms of the language adopted here. This fundamental interpretive similarity helps to illuminate the way in which early, Reformation, and contemporary interpreters of Paul can be brought together into a fruitful dialogue. This remains so even though the resulting images of Paul – from Baur and Origen, for instance – are so divergent. The present chapter has endeavored to show that the construc-tion of Pauline images is closely related to the emphasis and deemphasis of various textual resources available to the interpreter, bounded as one is by one's historical context.

---

[166] That some of Luther's arguments are anticipated by Augustine and that Erasmus was intentionally imitating Origen highlights the fact that this debate is not original to the Reformation period.

[167] See the bibliography noted above, esp. Cummings, *Literary Culture*, on Luther and Erasmus' intellectual context and conflict; Augustijn, *Erasmus*, pp. 261–262, on Luther's view of the Church Fathers ("...nur die Schrift hat Authorität, sie ist 'sui ipsius interpres, omnium omnia probans, iudicans et illuminans'; die Väter haben keine. Augustin und Hieronyus waren beide in den großen Irrtümern befangen. Der Grund der Haltung Luthers gegenüber den Vätern liegt auf der Hand: er wurde mit der Waffe von Väteraussprüchen angegriffen. An der ersten Stelle aus *De servo arbitrio* haben wir das gleiche festestellt. Später haben wir gesehen, daß Luther konsequen auch den Bibelforsher Hieronymus zurückweist"; p. 262); and Hoffmann, *Rhetoric and Theology*, on Erasmus' hermeneutic and its debt to preceding interpretive tradition.

This chapter has, I hope, served its purpose to bring the ancient and modern interpreters of Paul together in a meaningful way. The contingency and strangeness of patristic interpretation – early readers' tendencies and interpretive freedom which often appear anachronistic from a contemporary vantage point – have been presented as something intelligible on their own terms and also in relation to contemporary exegetical debates. Now that the possibility of a dialogue of sorts between ancient and modern readers has been demonstrated in practice, it remains to reflect on how it might work in theory: that is to say, how we might more confidently hold together the catechetical Paul of the early readers with the pugnacious Paul of contemporary Pauline scholarship.

8

Conclusion: Reception as Iteration – A Sketch

> Every actualization in understanding can be regarded as a historical potential
> of what is understood. It is part of the historical finitude of our being that we
> are aware that others after us will understand in a different way. And yet it is
> equally indubitable that it remains the same work whose fullness of meaning
> is realized in the changing process of understanding, just as it is the same his-
> tory whose meaning is constantly in the process of being defined.[1]

My argument in the previous chapters – laying out the contemporary
context of studies of Pauline reception; tracing the development of a
particular, institutionally shaped interpretation of Paul; bringing ancient
and contemporary interpretations of Paul into a kind of dialogue –
has, I hope, demonstrated one primary thing: that ancient interpreters'
approaches to Paul within their own historical and institutional contexts
are intelligible and valuable for both historical and exegetical debates
about Paul today. *That* this is the case is, for an increasing number of
scholars, thankfully not a novel conclusion. Nevertheless, in my experience, reception-historical studies still face widespread incomprehension
in relation to their value for understanding the New Testament texts
themselves. Even as studies of reception history gain more traction in the
publishing world of New Testament scholarship, with dedicated commentaries, encyclopedia, journals, and monograph series, the very fact of
these separate dedicated outlets can be seen to frame reception as a marginal curiosity: studying the afterlife of a work as something distinct from
the meaning of the text, which is properly accessed by historical-critical

---

[1] Gadamer, *Truth and Method*, p. 373.

(or narratological or sociological) means.[2] This separation of meaning and reception is precisely what I want to reframe here. My argument is that the meaning of the text is inextricably bound up with its reception and that our current historically oriented interpretive paradigm is no less an aspect of "reception" than the readings of the early Christians or the Reformers.

The question for reflection here, then, is *how* is this the case? How can contemporary interpreters understand our relationship with both the New Testament and its early interpreters in such a way that the "dialogue" between interpreters from different historical contexts becomes intelligible?[3] An answer to the question of "how?" can only be sketched in a preliminary way. Even in the face of such an intricate problem, perhaps masked somewhat by the rhetorical simplicity of the question, what I offer here are still *concluding* reflections for the above study, not a study on its own. This is why, although there have been an increasing number of proposals regarding the value of reception history in relation to New Testament interpretation in recent years, my limited engagement with them must be largely relegated to footnotes.[4]

---

[2] See the similar comments in William John Lyons, "Hope for a troubled discipline? Contributions to New Testament Studies from reception history," *Journal for the Study of the New Testament* 33, no. 2 (2010), 208. Dedicated outlets for reception-historical studies include the *Journal of the Bible and its Reception*; De Gruyter's monograph series Studies of the Bible and its Reception; the *Encyclopedia of the Bible and Its Reception*; and Blackwell's Bible Commentary Series. See also the documentation of similar views in James G. Crossley, "The end of reception history: a grand narrative for biblical studies and the neoliberal Bible," in Emma England and William John Lyons (eds.), *Reception History and Biblical Studies: Theory and Practice*, Scriptural Traces 6/Library of Hebrew Bible 615 (London: Bloomsbury, 2015), pp. 45–46.

[3] The term "dialogue" here is in scare quotes because of the qualified way in which the encounter between readers and texts can be said to be a dialogue. See more on this below.

[4] Chief among these proposals, in terms of both its size and its impact on the field, is that of Ulrich Luz, especially the recent distillation of his views in Luz, *Theologische Hermeneutik*. Also noteworthy in this respect are the proposals in a 2010 special issue of the *Journal for the Study of the New Testament* (see Jonathan Roberts and Christopher Rowland, "Introduction," *Journal for the Study of the New Testament* 33, no. 2 (2010), 131–136, and particularly Lyons, "Hope," pp. 207–220), the edited volume by Emma England and William John Lyons, *Reception History and Biblical Studies*; and Chester, *Reading Paul*, esp. pp. 13–59. Note too the proposals of James G. Crossley, "An immodest proposal for biblical studies," *Relegere* 12, no. 1 (2012), 153–177, and Brennan W. Breed, *Nomadic Text: A Theory of Biblical Reception History* (Bloomington: Indiana University Press, 2014) (both of whom reiterate their position in the volume edited by England and Lyons). The survey of Robert Evans, *Reception History, Tradition and Biblical Interpretation: Gadamer and Jauss in Current Practice*, vol. 4, LNTS 510 (Bloomsbury, 2014), and the Jauss-inspired discussion of David Paul Parris, *Reception Theory and Biblical Hermeneutics* (Eugene: Pickwick, 2008), are also helpful. The limits of the

The conceptual framework I propose here, then, is that of iteration. From this perspective, readings of Paul's letters emerge as iterations of Pauline interpretation, actualizations of textual potentialities in the encounter between interpreter and text in a particular context.[5] Any given reading contains possible but not necessary configurations of (Pauline) textual resources and illuminates certain contours of the texts being interpreted. Each iteration, because it is a product of an encounter between text and reader, tells us something both about the text *and* about the reader. As new contexts arise, new questions are posed to the text by readers (and *by* the text *to* readers, in a sense qualified below), which occasions new interpretations. Or, as Ulrich Luz put it, "new contexts activate new meaning-potential in texts."[6] In line with the epigraph at the beginning of this chapter, then, the process of interpretation is perennially open to new insight.

Fundamental to the analogy of iteration is the idea that iterative readings take place over time, for individual re-readings as well as between different readers in different periods.[7] Understanding one's own reading as (only) one iteration of a particular work, even as our own particular interpretations shift over time, offers two benefits for framing New Testament Studies. The first is that an "iterative" view upsets the still popular, if often tacit, search for *the* meaning of a work as the result of historical, literary, or exegetical approaches. This comes out still, for instance, in the arguments noted above about which scholarly view represents the "real" Paul.[8] From the perspective of interpretation as iteration, the category of the "real" Paul loses its analytic *cachet*. The second benefit is related to the

---

current discussion also exclude the possibility of a wider-ranging debate on canon and interpretation, the role of the implied or hypothetical reader, the place of psychology, etc.

[5] After arriving at this terminology, I was pleased and distressed in equal measure to find it already used in Evans, *Reception History*, pp. 50–51, 54, 275. (It is also used in passing by Penniman, *Raised on Christian Milk*, p. 203, who speaks of "the iterable nature of milk and solid food as a structuring paradigm.") Evans generally follows H.-G. Gadamer's hermeneutic, including an emphasis on the compatibility with historical-critical work and Gadamer's hermeneutic. Where H. R. Jauss and Gadamer come into conflict – particularly in the attempt to turn the latter's *wirkungsgeschichtliche Bewusstsein* into a literary method – Evans follows Gadamer.

[6] Luz, *Theologische Hermeneutik*, pp. 521–522: "Neue Kontexte aktivieren in den Texten neue Sinnpotentiale."

[7] There is also a possible non-linear aspect to iterative reading, such that two readings which occur simultaneously, but in two different places by interpreters who are unaffected by one another, also qualify as particular iterations of that text. This highlights the heuristic quality, rather than a presumed ontological quality, of the imagery of iteration adopted here.

[8] See the comments in Chapter 7.2.2 above.

first: absent a quest for *the* meaning of a work, this framework highlights the value of engaging with iterations produced by others, even (or perhaps especially) "others" who stand at a great distance from us, to learn more about what the work in question can and does mean. This is the iterative framework I will briefly attempt to justify below.

At this point, some readers may wonder why broader reflections on reception and hermeneutics have been left to the Conclusion rather than being placed in the Introduction. The principal reason for this is that I see these reflections as arising *from* the previous historical and exegetical discussions, emerging in my own mind in the course of my research, rather than guiding it clearly from the outset. In other words, this chapter is not about a "method" of interpretation; there are no rules to guide readers in their respective reading endeavors here. In fact, this lack of "method" is not merely a passive feature, omitted for lack of space, but is fundamentally constructive, enabling interpretive links between early and contemporary readers to be formed more easily.[9]

In viewing interpretation (and so reception) as iteration, the present sketch builds upon the trend, noted in the Introduction, away from evaluating the adequacy of previous interpretations and toward attempting to appreciate them for their own creative appropriation of Paul's letters.[10] Bringing together the early and contemporary readers of Paul in the previous chapter has, moreover, signaled a hermeneutical shift that I explore

---

[9] On this point, Gadamer rightly questions the existence of a method for understanding a text which transcends its own historical conditions: "One might wonder whether there is such an art or technique of understanding"; Gadamer, *Truth and Method*, pp. 265–266. This is not to say that one cannot or should not articulate guidelines for interpretation in particular instances or with particular goals in mind (historical, theological, etc.). I am sympathetic, for instance, to Luz's emphasis on the ethical respect for the text as "other," sincerity (*Wahrhaftigkeit*) in interpretation, and his "Kriterium der Folgen"; Luz, *Theologische Hermeneutik*, pp. 523–524, 544–545. Nor do I think that Gadamer is simply being naive in his rejection of "art or technique" (as argued in Werner G. Jeanrond, "After Hermeneutics: The Relationship Between Theology and Biblical Studies," in Francis Watson (ed.), *The Open Text: New Directions for Biblical Studies?* (London: SCM, 1993), pp. 93–94) or that his arguments represent "a full-scale attack on the role of method in hermeneutics" (so Anthony C. Thiselton, *New Horizons in Hermeneutics: The Theory and Practice of Transforming Biblical Reading* (Grand Rapids: Zondervan, 1992), p. 313). Rather, Gadamer's point is that methodological suspicion and interpretive guidelines are just as related to a particular interpretive horizon as are the readers who employ them. Gadamer is not against *methods* in understanding in specific instances, but against the articulation of a historically transcendent method (singular) that supplies the proper rules for reading and will thereby produce the proper outcome and secure the "scientific" status of interpretive disciplines.

[10] See the earlier discussion in Chapter 1.2.1.

further here, namely, placing ancient readers on the same footing as their modern and postmodern counterparts.

8.1 ITERATIVE READING: A SKETCH

There are four crucial elements which undergird this iterative account of Pauline interpretation: (1) a series of interpretations that are fundamentally shaped by shifting interpretive paradigms or other contextual factors; (2) a text that is "iterable," that is, subject to multiple readings while plausibly constituting a sufficient continuity across time; (3) a distancing of the interpretation from an ideal of duplication, from mere repetition or replication. These will lead in turn (4) to the language of "questions and answers" to describe the process of iteration. In elucidating these elements further below, a link between general observations and the previous historical or exegetical material will help to give the broader hermeneutical comments a specific point of reference. I turn now to the matter of shifting interpretive paradigms.

8.1.1 Horizons and "Tradition"

As we have seen in the course of the present study, the interpretive contexts, intellectual paradigms, and institutional commitments of Pauline interpreters have shifted in identifiable ways from antiquity to the present. Moreover, these shifts have shaped the language and images used by Pauline interpreters. By focusing on the development of the catechumenate, shifts that might otherwise appear to be amorphous or mercurial have been given a concrete focal point. On the one hand, the interpretive tradition of reading Paul within a catechetical/pedagogical framework stands in some contrast with dominant, oppositional modes of reading his letters discussed earlier, shaped in turn by interpretive impulses that have arisen within Reformational and early critical contexts.[11] On the other hand, even within each interpretive tradition, differences arise between readers of Paul as their particular commitments (as varied as may be) and exegetical questions come into play. This much is, I think, uncontroversial: there has been a series of interpretations and contextual factors that shift over time and, moreover, this will remain the situation as long as there are readers of the Pauline corpus.[12]

---

[11] See Chapter 7.2.2 for discussions of these points.
[12] Not incidentally, a similar observation underlies the influential arguments by Han Robert Jauss in favor of recognizing "literary history" as a challenge (and key) to interpretation;

The question remains, though, as to how we should conceptualize these contextual elements and their impact on interpreters. For this purpose, the language of "tradition" and interpretive "horizons" remains useful. In adopting this language, I mean to evoke the work of Hans-Georg Gadamer (1900–2002), though my own appropriation of it differs slightly from his account.[13] Tradition, according to Gadamer, is characterized by a dialectic of activity and passivity, or subjectivity and objectivity. Every individual interpreter inhabits a tradition, transmitted to them by means of language itself, broadly construed, which provides the grounds for all understanding.[14] Gadamer calls an awareness of being so situated *wirkungsgeschichtliche Bewusstsein*, one's consciousness of being affected by history.[15] In Gadamer's hands, then, *Wirkungsgeschichte* is explicitly *not* an appeal for extended histories of interpretation but rather an appeal for scholars to recognize their own historicity and embedded position within a tradition.[16] If an interpreter cannot simply

see esp. Hans Robert Jauss, "Literary history as a challenge to literary theory," in *Toward an Aesthetic of Reception History*, trans. Timothy Bahti, Theory and History of Literature 2 (Minneapolis: University of Minnesota Press, 1982), pp. 3–45 (originally published as Hans Robert Jauss, *Literaturgeschichte als Provokation* (Frankfurt-am-Main: Suhrkamp, 1970)). In the categories of contemporary New Testament Studies, however, his initial proposal is more suited as a description of a historically situated, narrative-critical or rhetorical approach than it is to the kind of reception history that came to characterize his work; see his comments on the "one-sidedness" of his initial proposal in Hans Robert Jauss, *Question and Answer: Forms of Dialogic Understanding*, trans. Michael Hays, Theory and History of Literature 68 (Minneapolis: University of Minnesota Press, 1989), pp. 224–225. Similar observations are made by recent interpreters, such as Chester, *Reading Paul*, p. 50 (who links historical distance with "divine wisdom") and Luz, *Theologische Hermeneutik*, *passim*. In relation to the Hebrew Bible, this point has been made very forcefully, by Breed, "Reception history as an ethology," pp. 95–110, developing arguments from his earlier discussion in Breed, *Nomadic Text*.

[13] Gadamer's defense of "tradition" and appropriation of Husserl's metaphor of "horizon" was set out in the 1960 publication of *Wahrheit und Methode* (now in its seventh German edition; Hans-Georg Gadamer, *Wahrheit und Methode. Grundzüge einer philosophischen Hermeneutik* (Tübingen: Mohr, 2010)). In what follows, I rely on the English edition in Gadamer, *Truth and Method*.

[14] Gadamer, *Truth and Method*, p. 441: "Verbal form and traditionary content cannot be separated in the hermeneutic experience. If every language is a view of the world [*viz*. as it is for Humboldt], it is so not primarily because it is a particular type of language (in the way that linguists view language) but because of what is said or handed down in this language."

[15] Ibid., p. 301 (emphasis original): it is "primarily consciousness of the hermeneutical *situation*." In other words, it is an awareness of the affected state of one's own consciousness.

[16] See ibid., p. 341: "I have already pointed out above that historically effected consciousness is something other than inquiry in to the history of a particular work's effect – as it were, the trace a work leaves behind. It is, rather, a consciousness of the work itself, and hence itself has an effect." Notably, Luz acknowledges this point while maintaining

withdraw from such a tradition, to observe phenomena from a critically neutral space, neither are they simply determined by it. One's tradition, in Gadamer's broad sense, is not an abstract, pre-existent object
that imposes itself on interpreters, but is only extant insofar as people
participate in the process of transmission.[17] The tradition provides the
grounds that enable interpreters to understand, while not determining
their specific interpretation or mode of participation in the tradition.[18]
"To be situated within a tradition does not limit the freedom of knowledge but makes it possible."[19]

And yet, in a way, one's tradition does limit one's freedom of knowledge in exactly the same moment that it enables understanding in the
first place. For this, Gadamer's language of "horizon" is useful. Just as
a person cannot see beyond the horizon from their own vantage point,
so also an interpreter's view is bounded in important ways by their
own horizon. In keeping with the metaphor, though, one's horizon is
never a fixed entity, closed to other vantage points, because within "the

---

that the term can be usefully used to describe "ein bestimmtes Forschungsgebiet, d.h.
als Bezeichnung für eine exegetisch-historische Subdisziplin"; Luz, *Theologische
Hermeneutik*, p. 361.

[17] This is developed usefully on the analogy of "play"; Gadamer, *Truth and Method*,
pp. 101–134. Each instantiation of a game, a piece of music, or a production of a play is
part of the meaning of that object and through multiple successive instantiations "a tradition is formed with which every new attempt must come to terms" (p. 119). Reading,
like play, also involves understanding that "is always a kind of reproduction, performance, and interpretation" (p. 160). Note, however, the possibility of non-contiguous
iterations of the same text, which are nevertheless still not produced by readers apart
from their particular tradition, as noted on p. 253 n. 7 above.

[18] Gadamer, *Truth and Method*, p. 290 (emphasis original): "*Understanding is to be
thought of less as a subjective act than as participating in an event of tradition*, a process
of transmission in which past and present are constantly mediated."

[19] Ibid., p. 361. See also the comments regarding the constructive role of "prejudice"
and historical distance of tradition in Anthony C. Thiselton, *The Two Horizons: New
Testament Hermeneutics and Philosophical Description with Special Reference to
Heidegger, Bultmann, Gadamer, and Wittgenstein* (Exeter: The Paternoster Press,
1980), pp. 305–306. Gadamer's account of tradition and the inheritance of a language
that precedes and exceeds individual speakers bears a certain resemblance to other
descriptions of attempts to particularize individual interpretive contexts. Recently, Rita
Felski, *The Limits of Critique* (Chicago: University of Chicago Press, 2015), pp. 20–22,
borrowed Heidegger's notion of "moods" to describe this dynamic, while Gadamer's
student Hans Robert Jauss adopted and developed Gadamer's language of "horizon."
As part of the "linguistic turn," Derrida spoke of the "exorbitance" of language as
that which encompasses all communication as a sort of proto-writing, undergirding
and subverting all acts of communication; see Jacques Derrida, *Of Grammatology*,
trans. Gayatri Chakravorty Spivak (Baltimore: Johns Hopkins University Press, 1998),
pp. 157–164.

historical movement of human life...[h]orizons change for a person who is moving."[20] In coming to an understanding with another, either a person or a text, one's horizon is not left behind but is in fact brought directly into play.[21] It can be challenged or extended by our engagement with the other, but it remains an inescapable feature of our ability to understand.[22] One can, moreover, speak of a collective horizon, shared among multiple people who inhabit similar cultural, philosophical, or social contexts, though to do so is to point toward an abstraction, produced from overlapping (but never identical) viewpoints.[23] In this way, one can imagine a collective horizon in quasi-objective terms of this overlap, extending the metaphor of "horizon" insofar as no two people can inhabit exactly the same space and so share exactly the same horizon.

Two things follow from these observations which are relevant for the present argument. First, while Gadamer tends to treat "tradition" in relation to one's "horizon" in relatively monolithic terms – perhaps best signified with a capital-"T" Tradition – in practice a person can and does inhabit multiple different (lower-case) "traditions"[24] insofar as one's "horizon" is formed by a variety of intellectual, personal, historical, cultural, and institutional factors whose relationships may fall anywhere on a spectrum from harmonious to tensive. The interpreter, in other words, stands in the center of a figurative Venn diagram of interlocking and overlapping "traditions" and commitments of which they are only partially

---

[20] Gadamer, *Truth and Method*, p. 304.

[21] See ibid., p. 305.

[22] For Gadamer, understanding is characterized by a "fusion of horizons," though this remains a difficult concept to illuminate adequately. On the one hand, the necessity of such a fusion follows from his open and dynamic account of one's horizon, which is always developing and coming into contact with others while remaining inescapably one's own. On the other hand, especially in the engagement between readers and texts, it is a fusion in which the decisive horizon is that of the reader; see p. 259 n. 30 below.

[23] This is perhaps what Gadamer is pointing toward when he states that, in addition to moving with us, it is "something into which we move"; Gadamer, *Truth and Method*, p. 304.

[24] In my view, Gadamer's singular Tradition is best read as a marker for otherwise undefined historical, social, and cultural factors which shape interpretation. In speaking of multiple "traditions" here, I mean to highlight the multifaceted contexts of life which shape a particular person and which, for Gadamer, all constitute one's Tradition. In Paul Ricoeur's analysis of tradition, following Gadamer, he distinguishes between tradition as a "formal concept of traditionality" and tradition in its "material content," otherwise described with the plural, "traditions"; Paul Ricoeur, *Time and Narrative*, trans. Kathleen McLaughlin and David Pellauer, 3 vols. (Chicago: University of Chicago Press, 1984–1988), vol. III, p. 221.

aware.[25] And not only the interpreter but also the author of a text inhabits a similarly complex horizon which can manifest in a work in a variety of ways and is related to the excessiveness of language, a quality which has been articulated in different ways since antiquity.[26] In the encounter between a reader and a text, the interpreter must negotiate the complex issues raised by countervailing tendencies in different traditions (or even within the same tradition).[27] For Gadamer, this is where one's horizon is brought into play explicitly as an object of reflection, to be risked in the dialogue between reader and text. And yet, even in such a dialogical engagement, "the interpreter's own horizon is decisive."[28] It is only a dialogue in an extended sense of the word.[29]

The second point to make here relates to the danger of understanding Gadamer, or interpretation more broadly, in a strictly deterministic logic of cause and effect. The fact that one cannot extricate oneself from Tradition, in its broad sense, does not mean that one always submits "to every tradition," in the narrower sense.[30] Precisely because one's horizon is

---

[25] This image is also used in Margaret B. Adam, "'This is my story, this is my song…': a feminist claim on scripture, ideology and interpretation," in Harold C. Washington, Susan Lochrie Graham, and Pamela Lee Thimmes (eds.), *Escaping Eden: New Feminist Perspectives on the Bible* (Sheffield: Sheffield Academic Press, 1998), p. 226, to illustrate the varied nature of one's "community involvements."

[26] This applies whether it is construed as a metaphysical excessiveness – in which language participates in or strives toward an ideal or divine realm of meaning only available to speakers in a partial or particular way – or in the more Derridian sense of the infinite play of signs and signifiers and the unending deferral of meaning. Gadamer himself later recognized an affinity between his account of language and the "linguistic turn"; Gadamer, *Truth and Method*, p. 417 n. 39. See also Umberto Eco's sketch of symbols and hermeneutics from Stoic and Platonic roots, through the early Church, medieval period, and Renaissance in relation to modern theories of "unlimited semiosis"; Umberto Eco, *The Limits of Interpretation* (Bloomington: Indiana University Press, 1997), pp. 8–22.

[27] Clement of Alexandria's negotiation of a *via media* between "gnostic" and anti-philosophical tendencies, both of which were found within the Alexandrian Christian community, may serve to illustrate this point.

[28] Gadamer, *Truth and Method*, p. 388. See also the comments in Jauss, *Question and Answer*, p. 206: "The meaning that a historically distant text can recapture for us does not emerge solely from the folds of the original horizon. It stems to an equal degree from the later horizon of experience belonging to the interpreter."

[29] So Jauss, *Question and Answer*, p. 213: "I should add that the expression 'begin a conversation with the text' remains necessarily metaphorical, since the interpreter must himself first stage the role of the other so that the text can speak, respond to a question, and be understood in the end as a 'question posed to me.'" This observation also speaks to Ulrich Luz's dialogical hermeneutic, in which he explicitly rejects Gadamer's "fusion of horizons" in favor of a "meeting of horizons" in order to preserve the text in its otherness; Luz, *Theologische Hermeneutik*, p. 386.

[30] See Paul Ricoeur, "Hermeneutical logic," in *Writings and Lectures*, vol. II: *Hermeneutics*, trans. David Pellauer (Cambridge: Polity, 2013), p. 76: "The rehabilitation of prejudice

so multifaceted, a particular "tradition" – in the narrower sense – does not function as a necessary determinant for one's interpretation. This opens up space for criticizing aspects of one's Tradition, of deciding between contrasting impulses, of having one's horizon reshaped and reorganized by an encounter with a text.[31] So, too, the participatory and non-formal nature of the relationship between interpreter and horizon should not be treated as a strict logic – in which case it saws off the hermeneutical branch it is sitting on[32] – but is rather to be construed dialectically.[33] In concrete terms, while the catechetical inflection of the horizons of the *Acts of Paul*, Clement, Origen, and John Chrysostom lends these writers a certain continuity in their Pauline interpretations, their differences show that this common inflection does not lead to a crass determinism. It is rather one part of their horizon which must be balanced against other concerns – parishioners, opponents, institutional developments, philosophical questions – all of which supply the basis on which they are able to come to an understanding of Paul's letters. In the case of contemporary scholarship, a collective horizon influenced by post-Reformational and academic concerns supplies a different basis for understanding, which carries with it different criteria of validity. We will return to this again momentarily. For now, it is enough to say that shifting interpretive paradigms which shaped the series of interpretations traced in Chapters 2–7 are usefully

---

[*viz.* by Gadamer] does not signify submission to every tradition, but only to the impossibility of removing oneself from the condition for historical transmission." See also his comments in Ricoeur, *Time and Narrative*, vol. III, pp. 222–223.

[31] The difficulty of finding space for critique of tradition in Gadamer's theory was classically articulated in Jurgen Habermas, "Zu Gadamers 'Wahrheit und Methode'," in *Hermeneutik und Ideologiekritik*, ed. Karl-Otto Apel (Frankfurt: Suhrkamp, 1971), pp. 52–53. See also the comments in Ricoeur, *Time and Narrative*, vol. III, pp. 223–224 and *passim* (reiterated in Ricoeur, "Logic," pp. 94–95), and note that Luz also picks up on Habermas' critique in Luz, *Theologische Hermeneutik*, pp. 387–388.

[32] As articulated well in Ricoeur, "Logic," 110: "The same alternative redoubles itself: if all understanding is historically mediated, must we say that hermeneutic reflection of hermeneutics is too? Or should we say that we understand the contextual relativity of interpretation only in light of a regulative idea of 'rational' discourse or of 'unlimited, unhindered communication?' In the first case, hermeneutics confesses its own finitude, at the heart of its universal claim...In the second case, hermeneutics transcends itself in reflection and reinscribes itself in the tradition of transcendental philosophy. In the first case, the hermeneutics of hermeneutics remains faithful to its basic thesis, but excludes all scientificity. In the second case, it pleads for a concept of scientificity distinct from the concept (at least in English) of science, but it denies its thesis about the priority of pre-understanding over reflection."

[33] Gadamer, *Truth and Method*, p. 293, speaks to the non-formal quality of the hermeneutical circle (see also pp. 281–282).

conceptualized in terms of an interpreter's Tradition and horizon, which are both dynamic and require the participation of the reader.

8.1.2 The Iterable Text

The second element of my proposal for an iterative framework for interpretation turns from one's interpretive horizon to the specific object under investigation, the text "itself." The suggestion here is simply this: the limited materiality of the text being interpreted supplies a sufficient, objective continuity that extends across time to include all readers of that text. In Gadamer's terms, cited in the epigraph above, amid differing interpretations of the Pauline corpus, it is "indubitable that it remains the same work" that is being encountered. This continuity is important for the simple fact that, in order for a "dialogue" about reading Paul's letters to be possible between myself and, say, John Chrysostom, we must both be reading the same thing. A dialogue in which the two parties are speaking about two different objects is an exercise in talking past one another, even in a staged dialogue like that which takes place in interpretation of a written work.

When I speak of the iterability of the text "itself," I am appealing in the first instance to the material limits of a given textual object, in their most banal sense.[34] That is to say, a text only includes a limited number of words, sentences, statements, etc. These lexical and syntactic features provide the *resources* upon which every interpretation of that text is based.[35] From the perspective of interpretive activity, these are the textual resources that are being reiterated by readers in light of the latter's horizon.[36]

---

[34] The philosophical problems raised by the digitization of such material texts and their continuing status as material objects cannot, of course, be addressed here.

[35] This view differs somewhat from the arguments of Brennan Breed and others who critique the notion of an "original" text which is being received; see Breed, *Nomadic Text*, pp. 75–92. If one has difficulty speaking of an "original" text of Daniel or Job, even conceptually, this is not the case for a letter of Paul which, on Breeds terms (p. 90), is indeed a type of "utterance" of an "individual." Moreover, even where one might speak of the "text" itself as entirely caught up in the movement of reception and interpretation, without an "original" to be transmitted, one can still speak of an objectivity to the text or tradition being received in the moment it is being encountered by the reader, even if its contents are not entirely stable across time. It is true, nevertheless, that the continuity of a text involves a certain fuzziness, even to these most banal material limits, as reflected in manuscript variation.

[36] Recently Ben White has described this interpretive activity within the framework of "reputational entrepreneurs." The ambiguities and tensions in Paul's own writings and the subsequent tradition "meant that he could be idealized by a variety of reputational

As we have seen with respect to the Pauline corpus, readers in antiquity and today must make interpretive choices amid the ambiguities of 1 Corinthians 1–3 and between the apparently differing self-presentation of the Apostle in different letters. To make such interpretive decisions, reading some texts in light of others, elevating certain passages while subordinating others, is to produce an iteration of Pauline resources. And an interpretive "iteration" of Paul is always a "reiteration" insofar as the meaning of the text is only ever mediated through interpretive activity. Even if one wants to avoid the more radical phenomenological implications of this observation for the ontology of textual meaning,[37] it nevertheless remains the case that whatever a text means is never accessible apart from the activity and participation of an interpreter.[38]

As noted earlier, though, this account is not intended to strip texts of their ability to surprise, challenge, or disappoint readers. There is no doubt that readers have all these experiences (and more!) when they encounter a text. The text has a certain objectivity, articulated through the textual resources that constitute it, to which interpreters must accommodate themselves. It is this fact that certain anthropomorphizing metaphors are gesturing toward: speaking of a text that "invites," "questions," "pushes back" against, or "rejects" a particular reading.[39] In a qualified way, then, we can speak of a text's "agency," by which I mean the way in which its material limits constrain certain interpretations under certain conditions.[40] The text's "agency" is not simply that of the author, whose own horizon and intentionality are only partially inscribed in the text, and

entrepreneurs"; White, *Remembering Paul*, p. 105 and *passim*; building in particular on the work of Barry Schwartz, *Abraham Lincoln and the Forge of National Memory* (Chicago: University of Chicago Press, 2000).

[37] That is, if one still wants to maintain that texts do in fact contain meanings in themselves, which are accessed in various ways by interpreters.

[38] These implications are well articulated in Gadamer, *Truth and Method*, p. 462: "There is no being-in-itself that is increasingly revealed when Homer's *Iliad* or Alexander's Indian Campaign speak to us in the new appropriation of tradition; but, as in genuine dialogue, something emerges that is contained in neither of the partners by himself."

[39] This point is also related to the process of reciprocal questioning that arises in the encounter between a reader and a text; see below, p. 267.

[40] To go into more depth here in discussing *which* interpretations and conditions are relevant would greatly exceed the limits of this chapter. Suffice it to say that I think these interpretations and conditions vary between interpretive paradigms, though I am sympathetic with Eco's description of "an artistic text" as that which contains, "among its major analyzable properties, certain structural devices that encourage and elicit interpretive choices"; Eco, *Limits*, p. 50. This functions for Eco within a limited textual openness in which the literal sense grounds the process of "interpretation and use" (pp. 53–58), a division which is more problematic; see below, pp. 264–265.

this to differing degrees depending on the genre of the text in question.[41] Nor is it to be conflated with the interpretive agency of a hypothetical "first reader" who can only be accessed through a historical reconstruction.[42] Historical considerations in relation to both the author and the audience can and do shape a large number of interpretations, even in the case of Origen and John Chrysostom, though they are only part of the textual "object." It is this objective aspect of the text, though, that *affects* readers, that constrains interpretation, and that gives rise to the familiar question about what the text "wants to say."[43] While in principle the limits of a text due to material constraints may be very broad indeed, in practice the variation has appeared rather less broad in the present study. The ease with which the ancient interpretations were slotted into contemporary exegetical debates in Chapter 7 perhaps speaks to certain practical limits set by Paul's letters. And, yet, the variation among interpreters then and now also speaks to the variety of iterations of textual resources that have occurred over time.[44] These arise in the dialectical relationship between the reader and the textual object.[45]

[41] See the comments on this point in Gadamer, *Truth and Method*, pp. 328, 334; Jauss, "Literary history," pp. 22–24; Jauss, *Question and Answer*, pp. 216, 230–231; and more recently Moisés Mayordomo-Marín, "Wirkungsgeschichte als Erinnerung an die Zukunft der Texte (Hinführung)," in Moisés Mayordomo-Marín (ed.), *Die prägende Kraft der Texte. Hermeneutik und Wirkungsgeschichte des Neuen Testaments*, Stuttgarter Bibelstudien 199 (Stuttgart: Verlag Katholisches Bibelwerk, 2005), p. 11. Note also the discussion throughout Evans, *Reception History*, whose argument often returns to the positive role of the originating historical context in the production of meaning within the hermeneutical systems of Gadamer and Jauss. Even in Derrida's radically deconstructive project, the historical considerations produced with "all the instruments of traditional criticism" can reveal, to an extent, what the text or author is *trying* to say, which itself acts as an "indispensable guardrail" in interpretation, without which "critical production would risk developing in any direction at all and authorize itself to say almost anything"; Derrida, *Of Grammatology*, p. 158; see also the comments on Derrida in Eco, *Limits*, pp. 36–37, 54. Of course, a genre is not an entirely closed entity and so a text may be construed in multiple genres over time; see Breed, *Nomadic Text*, p. 87.

[42] As in Jauss, *Question and Answer*, pp. 222–223; see also Evans, *Reception History*, p. 275. Gadamer warned against identifying textual meaning with the "original reader," noting that in its normal use "the idea of the original reader is full of unexamined idealization"; Gadamer, *Truth and Method*, p. 395.

[43] The difference between "reception" and "effect" of a text, signifying the active/passive dialectic in interpretive activity, was raised by Jauss, *Question and Answer*, p. 225, and more recently in Luz, *Theologische Hermeneutik*, p. 361.

[44] The limits of the material examined here, constrained by appeals to catechesis, partially account for this by excluding some of the more radical interpretations of Paul supplied by certain so-called "gnostic" writers. A full exploration of the history of interpretation would no doubt throw up many more iterations of Pauline interpretation.

[45] See Eco, *Limits*, p. 58: "I am trying to keep a dialectical link between *intentio operis* and *intentio lectoris*."

8.1.3 Iteration Without Duplication

Interpretive horizons and iterable texts, then, lead to the next point in the "iterative" interpretive framework: iteration without duplication. By this I mean that interpretation is never mere repetition or reproduction of what a given text says.[46] In the broadest sense, this can be seen as a hermeneutical analogue to Heraclitus' maxim that "one cannot step into the same river twice."[47] From this perspective, pure repetition is philosophically untenable: even to say the same words in a new context is to engage in a new act of communication that necessarily differs from the original.[48] This follows from the inescapably decisive role that the reader's horizon plays in the process of interpretation. As Gadamer put it, "The understanding of something written is not a repetition of something past but the sharing of a present meaning."[49] There is often, in the interpretive process, an attempt at duplication, one in which a reader tries to come to terms with what the text is "trying to say." But even with the most careful attention to the text, it nevertheless remains *my* attention that marks the process, and that mark cannot be erased.[50] Taking this point seriously undermines any easy division between "interpretation" and "application" or "use," since there is no moment in the encounter

---

[46] This view has been applied to engagement with the apostolic fathers by Ulrich Luz and Stephen Chester, though it applies equally to the scriptural texts that the ancient and modern interpreters were reading; Luz, *Theologische Hermeneutik*, p. 511; Chester, *Reading Paul*, pp. 1, 327.

[47] Heraclitus *Frag.* 6 (in Hermann Diels (ed.), *Die Fragmente der Vorsokratiker. Griechisch und Deutsch*, vol. I, 2nd edn (Berlin: Weidmann, 1906), p. 58).

[48] This point, long noted in different ways by philosophers, is made in a radical way in Jacques Derrida, "Economimesis," *Diacritics* 11, no. 2 (1981), 2: "Once inserted into another network, the 'same' philosopheme is no longer the same, and besides it never had an identity external to its functioning. Simultaneously, 'unique and original' philosophemes, if there are any, as soon as they enter into articulated composition with inherited philosophemes, are affected by that composition over the whole of their surface and under every angle."

[49] Gadamer, *Truth and Method*, p. 392; see also p. 473: "Every appropriation of tradition is historically different: which does not mean that each one represents only an imperfect understanding of it. Rather, each is the experience of an 'aspect' of the thing itself... This means that assimilation is no mere reproduction or repetition of the traditionary text; it is a new creation of understanding." In fact this comment stands in tension with Gadamer's phenomenological commitments that appear several pages earlier in a denial of any "being in itself" to be present in its various "aspects."

[50] See Gadamer's comments on the historically marked work of Theodor Mommsen; Gadamer, *Truth and Method*, p. 512.

between text and reader for an interpretation without an application or use already in view.[51]

This point can be illustrated with a brief reflection on the early readers examined here. On the one hand, I made an effort to understand each figure on their own terms: that is to say, in relation to the concerns evident in their writings and the historical contexts in which they worked. Indeed, the whole idea of tracing the impact of the catechumenate on their reading of Paul relies on just such a historicizing move. On the other hand, my reading of these interpreters is shaped decisively by the questions with which I approached the texts and, moreover, the "meaning" of the Pauline interpretations in these writers is not limited to their historical horizon or a reconstructed original reading, but is already caught up in my own hermeneutical goal of placing ancient and modern readers in dialogue, a concern necessarily foreign to the early Christian writers.[52]

The ineradicable particularity of my interpretive horizon, however, is not simply a limit but the basis for my ability to understand these writers at all. I do not claim that my understanding of Clement or Origen or John Chrysostom is intrinsically *better* than the view of previous interpreters, though I have of course diverged from some other readers on certain points, or that I understand them better than they understood themselves (thanks to modern historical tools). The claim is, rather, that I do understand *something* about these writers in a way that is both fair to them and productive for my own ends, that is, as answers to my own questions.[53] Moreover, I am claiming that these writers also understand

---

[51] *Pace* Luz, *Theologische Hermeneutik*, pp. 383–384, who is following the arguments of Klaus Berger, and Eco, *Limits*, pp. 57–58. Such a distinction is maintained also, if somewhat tacitly, by Parris, *Reception Theory*, and Chester, *Reading Paul*. As Thiselton rightly noted, Gadamer's discussion of legal hermeneutics was aimed at undermining this kind of distinction; Thiselton, *Two Horizons*, p. 308.

[52] See also the comments in Simon Lloyd Cuff, "Paul's 'new moment': the reception of Paul in Baidou, Eagleton, and Žižik," unpublished D.Phil. thesis University of Oxford (2014), pp. 249–250, on the non-totalizing implications of a Gadamerian hermeneutic: "Gadamer's fusion of horizons avoids the risk of two kinds of totalising. These are on the one hand the totalising impulse which limits any reading to the solely historical (fixated merely on the past) and, on the other, the totalising impulse which limits any reading to the solely ahistorical (focused merely on the present). Interpretation must inevitably involve both past and present to avoid the short-comings of the totalising of either."

[53] See Gadamer, *Truth and Method*, p. 462: "Understanding is not, in fact, understanding better [i.e. in the old view that we can understand an author better than they understood themselves], either in the sense of superior knowledge of the subject because of clearer ideas or in the sense of fundamental superiority of conscious over unconscious production. It is enough to say that we understand in a different way, if we understand at all."

something about Paul's letters in relation to their own questions, from which we are able to learn.

8.1.4 Questions, Answers, and the Movement of Iteration

The language of question and answer helps to clarify what is at stake in this iterative framework. While human understanding and interpretation have long been cast in terms of questions and answers, I take my point of departure here particularly from the work of R. G. Collingwood.[54] In his autobiography, Collingwood offered two principal insights that are germane to the present discussion. First, with respect to the history of ideas, he argued that historians need to come to terms with the fact that there is no stable problem, P, which extends through time and which various thinkers address with greater and lesser degrees of success. Rather "what is thought to be a permanent problem P is really a number of transitory problems p_1 p_2 p_3...whose individual peculiarities are blurred by the historical myopia of the person who lumps them together under the one name P."[55] In the terms proposed above, then, Collingwood recognizes here the iterative quality of philosophical problems.

What drives each iteration of p, for Collingwood, is nothing other than the movement of questions and answers. From his experience working on archaeological digs with his father, he recognized that the "questioning activity" preceded all understanding.[56] He took this in two distinct directions. First, he argued that one cannot understand any historical artifact, text, or event without first understanding the question to which it is an answer.[57] The second direction focuses not on the author's questions but rather on those of the interpreters.

---

[54] See the more extended discussion of Collingwood's and Gadamer's development of a logic of questions and answers in Parris, *Reception Theory*, ch. 3, and Thiselton, *Two Horizons*, pp. 309–310. In antiquity there developed the genre of "questions and answers" used by many writers, including Philo, Plutarch, and Eusebius.

[55] R. G. Collingwood, *An Autobiography* (Oxford: Oxford University Press, 1939), p. 69. This view was taken up also in John Passmore, "The idea of a history of philosophy," *History and Theory* 5, no. 5 (1965), 1–32, and Quentin Skinner, "Meaning and understanding in the history of ideas," *History and Theory* 8, no. 1 (1969), 3–53, both of whom critique Collingwood's ancillary argument that one can never show that a historical thinker was wrong in working out an answer to their question, because their question is only available to us by means of the answer they provide to it.

[56] Collingwood, *Autobiography*, p. 30 and *passim*.

[57] Ibid., pp. 31–32.

I had learnt by first-hand experience that history is not an affair of scissors and paste, but is much more like Bacon's notion of science. The historian has to decide exactly what it is that he wants to know; and if there is no authority to tell him, as in fact (one learns in time) there never is, he has to find a piece of land or something that has got the answer hidden in it, and get the answer out by fair means or foul.[58]

Elsewhere, he states that in the process of interpretation and understanding, "[e]very step in the argument depends on asking a question."[59] If Collingwood's work as a whole does not fully come to terms with the radical hermeneutical potential of these observations,[60] it does nevertheless illuminate that central features of one's horizon, and of a text, are characterized by the process of questioning. Put differently, he illuminates the fact that all understanding is based on preexisting knowledge which conditions the questioner and enables them to know anything at all.

When Gadamer turned to describe "the logic of the human sciences" twenty-five years later, he did so in terms of "a logic of the question," noting that "[a]lmost the only person I find a link with here is R. G. Collingwood."[61] Whereas Collingwood focused on the questions posed by the author of the text and by the readers of the text, however, Gadamer emphasized the reciprocal quality of the questioning.[62] The activity of the historically affected reader,[63] in questioning the text and in reconstructing the question which occasioned the text, is balanced by a receptivity in the reader, who is "perplexed by the traditionary word" and to whom a question is put *by the text*.[64] The true nature of this questioning, for Gadamer, is that it makes things "indeterminate," it "opens up possibilities of meaning, and thus what is meaningful passes into one's own thinking."[65] This is why, in the dialectic of questioning and

---

[58] Ibid., p. 81.

[59] R. G. Collingwood, *The Idea of History* (Oxford: Oxford University Press, 1956), pp. 269–281; see also the constructive role of "historical imagination," in ibid., pp. 237–247.

[60] For instance, Collingwood's discussion at the end of his posthumous *The Idea of History* vacillates between optimism in the ability of historians to know the past and the realization that "historical inquiry reveals to the historian the powers [*viz.* and limits] of his own mind"; Collingwood, *Idea*, p. 218.

[61] Gadamer, *Truth and Method*, pp. 370.

[62] So Parris, *Reception Theory*, pp. 47–49, and note the comments in Ricoeur, *Time and Narrative*, III, p. 222.

[63] That is, one who reckons "with the fundamental non-definitiveness of the horizon in which [one's] understanding moves"; Gadamer, *Truth and Method*, p. 373.

[64] Ibid. I take this as a metaphorical expression of a reader's experience of trying to accommodate oneself to the limited resources provided in a text – that is, its objectivity.

[65] Ibid., p. 375.

being questioned, "reconstructing the question to which the meaning of a text is understood as an answer merges with our own questioning."[66] The implication of this is that the question "posed" by the text, which already presupposes a questioning reader, *and* the co-determining limited resources of the text, are caught up in the inexorable stream of historical movement. This movement of interpretation across time, shaped by varying questions and answers, constitutes the iterative interpretive process, through which "new aspects of meaning" are brought to light.[67] And these "new aspects of meaning" that emerge over subsequent readings must also be reckoned with by interpreters. As Gadamer states in the epigraph to the present chapter

Every actualization in understanding can be regarded as a historical potential of what is understood. It is part of the historical finitude of our being that we are aware that others after us will understand in a different way.[68]

The continual movement of iterative interpretations, the constant difference of interpretations, raises the question: If all interpretations are different, is there any room left for judgments of misreading or error in interpretation?[69] A full answer to this question is hardly possible here and would entail sketching out methodological guidelines, which would necessarily be of limited value. What matters at present is to note that judging the sufficiency or accuracy of other interpretations (historical or contemporary) is not excluded by the iterative framework described above. To say that every interpretation differs, that none lays claim to a definitive understanding of a text, is not to say that every interpretation will be judged equally satisfying or equally appropriate to the text. When Gadamer says, "It is enough to say that we understand in a different way, if we understand at all,"[70] the final conditional clause is crucial. It acknowledges the possibility of misunderstanding while also pointing toward the conditions in which one must make such judgments. *The interpreter who adjudges a previous interpretation to be inadequate must specify the horizon against which the judgment is made.*

---

[66] Ibid., p. 374; on pp. 377–378. Gadamer connects this with the "fusion of horizons" discussed earlier.

[67] See the comments in ibid., p. 373: "it is the course of events [*viz.* in history] that brings out new aspects of meaning in the historical material."

[68] Ibid., p. 373.

[69] This question is posed explicitly in Luz, *Theologische Hermeneutik*, p. 399.

[70] Gadamer, *Truth and Method*, p. 462.

Put differently, and with reference to the interpreters explored earlier, it is one kind of claim to say that Origen, Chrysostom, or Luther *are* wrong, on this or that interpretation, but an entirely different claim to say that they *were* wrong. This discrepancy emerges more clearly against the movement of questions and answers because that paradigm illuminates that the first claim is a statement about the validity or usefulness of their interpretation in relation to a *present* question, a present horizon, rather than its suitability to the text *simpliciter*. The latter statement is a claim about the suitability of their answer to their *own* questions within their *own* horizon, insofar as we can reconstruct it. In situations where interpreters share similar horizons, in which they agree on certain interpretive guidelines, those guidelines can and will serve as criteria for evaluating respective interpretive possibilities. This is to be expected as part of the movement of individual and collective horizons through time.[71] It only becomes intrinsically mistaken if such a consensus forgets its own conditionality.[72]

Within this account of iterative interpretation, then, historical interpretations of Paul stand on equal footing with contemporary interpretations. As we saw in Chapter 7, interpreters then and now encounter Paul's letters within their own horizons and in that encounter produce iterations of Pauline interpretation, drawing on the same limited set of textual resources, illuminating particular contours of the *corpus Paulinum*. Readings of Paul from within different horizons therefore highlight different aspects of Paul's letters that can be valuable in answering a variety of questions, for a variety of interpretive ends.

8.2 (NON-)FINAL THOUGHTS

Much more could and should be said to defend this interpretive framework, of course. That is the task for another time, however. There remain here only a few more comments in relation to the present study.

---

[71] This movement of collective horizons is similar to what Jauss designated the *Erwartungshorizont* of a work or a period, reconstructed through a general account of literary and social expectations culled from other contemporary material; see Jauss, "Literary history," pp. 22–24. Eco also points to the validity of non-definitive consensus within a community of interpreters; Eco, *Limits*, p. 41.

[72] It is notable that Rita Felski has raised a similar critique of "critique" itself as "a distinctive and describable habit of thought," one possible habit of thought among others in literary studies; Felski, *Limits*, p. 6.

First, my argument has now finally come full circle. As I noted at the start, this is a book about Pauline reception in two senses: tracing a particular line of reception in the early Church and reflecting on how such early interpretations might inform contemporary work on the Pauline corpus. These two aspects have now been explored – probably more briefly than they should be and surely at greater length than readers would have liked. We saw in Chapters 2–6 the development and impact of the catechumenate on the presentation and interpretation of Paul from the late second century to the late fourth century. In the final two chapters, the early interpreters were placed in a (staged) dialogue with contemporary interpreters, along with their post-Reformation and critical heritage, before sketching a framework for interpretation as "iteration."

Second, I have tried to formulate this view of reading as broadly as possible, without reference to a *specific* set of theological commitments. This was in part to enable an explanation that could describe the possibility of a constructive dialogue between ancient and contemporary interpreters whose theological (and philosophical) commitments vary. In other words, it is an attempt to be broadly ecumenical in my interpretive framework. This will, no doubt, be unsatisfying for some and, to a certain degree, already takes a particular theological shape in my deliberate avoidance here of the normative claims of the texts I am reading.[73] This does not mean that one cannot or should not hold a debate about the normative claims in Paul's letters or among his interpreters' arguments, only that I have not attempted to adjudicate such a discussion here. Moving into a discussion of the relation between this hermeneutical framework and specific theological commitments or normative claims, however, would expand the present reflections into a book itself. The catechetical readings of Paul surveyed here, for instance, offer potentially rich resources for discussions of the place of moral formation and its relation to knowledge today. Such a discussion, though, leads to much broader theological, ethical, and pastoral questions which cannot be broached here.

Third, the iterative framework proposed here potentially extends far beyond a question about learning from ancient interpreters. Insofar as all readings of Paul involve a configuration of textual resources, all readings can be included as iterations of Pauline interpretation, whether they are represented in history, art, music, popular culture, or politics. This is not

---

[73] This kind of non-theological, theological stance is well articulated in the introduction to Robert Morgan, *The Nature of New Testament Theology* (London: SCM Press, 1973), pp. 22–23.

to say that one will find all readings equally appropriate or satisfactory. It is to say, however, that even where one judges another reading to be inappropriate or unsatisfactory, one can (genuinely) learn something about the interpretive possibilities of Paul's letters and that, in any case, such judgments need to be made in relation to specific frames of reference, judging suitability in relation to particular questions or horizons. Furthermore, this judgment is itself related to one's own horizon. In this way, every interpretation of Paul is inescapably particular.[74]

Finally, there is a question not always raised but continually on the edge of sight in reception-historical studies. Why is it that the meaning of some texts is deferred and diffused through their reception while others are treated as though they speak more or less univocally? I think the answer to this is in fact relatively simple: some texts *call for* attention to their *Wirkungsgeschichte*, their reception and effects in history, precisely because they *have* one – or, in other words, because they are *effective*.[75] Furthermore, there is more at stake in reading texts whose afterlife has had a great impact on a group or society than there is in reading other texts. For instance, while there have been studies of the impact of Origen or Chrysostom or Luther on later writers – indeed, that is a part of the present argument – the importance of these writers, even within today's secularized Western society, pales in comparison with that of the Bible.[76] Nevertheless, as this study has tried to demonstrate, these early readers of Paul remain valuable dialogue partners for contemporary Pauline interpretation, not despite but because of their catechetical assumptions and images.

---

[74] This pushes back against a subtle suggestion in Chester, *Reading Paul*, p. 59, that we are looking for what is of "lasting value in previous interpretations." It seems to me, though, that what is of lasting value is only intelligible to us by way of what is of *present* value.

[75] See the comments in Luz, *Theologische Hermeneutik*, p. 361, on the relation of *Wirkungsgeschichte* and *Wirkkraft*.

[76] See the discussion in Crossley, "The End," pp. 49–58. This point is also a partial answer to the question posed by William Lyons about why "the Nestle-Aland Greek New Testament is in its 27th edition" (now its 28th), while "Chrysostom's homilies on 1 Corinthians have no critical edition"; Lyons, "Hope," p. 216 n. 13.

Appendix

Chart of Chrysostom's Catecheses

Piédagnel & Doutreleau (PD)[1] – Montfaucon 1; Papadopoulos-
  Kerameus (PK) 1–3
Wenger[2] – Stavronika 1–8, Papadopoulos-Kerameus 4
Migne *PG* 49 (Montfaucon 1–2)

Lecture[3]	Location	Secondary Location	Harkins[4]
1	Migne 2	Mont. 2	12
2	PD 1	Mont./Migne 1, PK 1	9
3	PD 2	PK 2	10
4	PD 3	PK 3	11
5	Wenger 3	Stav. 3, PK 4	3
6	Wenger 1	Stav. 1	1
7	Wenger 2	Stav. 2	2
8	Wenger 4	Stav. 4	4
9	Wenger 5	Stav. 5	5
10	Wenger 6	Stav. 6	6
11	Wenger 7	Stav. 7	7
12	Wenger 8	Stav. 8	8

[1] Piédagnel and Doutreleau, *Trois catéchèses.*
[2] Wenger, *Huit catéchèses baptismales inédites.*
[3] Following the order in Piédagnel and Doutreleau; see also Kaczynski, *Catecheses,*
  pp. 47–48.
[4] Harkins, *Baptismal Instructions.*

Bibliography

PRIMARY SOURCES

Adriaen, Marc (ed.), "Expositio evangelii secundum Lucam," in *Sancti Ambrosii Mediolanensis Opera*, vol. IV, CCSL 14 (Turnhout: Brepols, 1957), pp. 1–400.

Attridge, Harold W., and Elaine H. Pagels. "The Tripartite Tractate: 1,5:51.1–138.27," in Harold W. Attridge (ed.), *Nag Hammadi Codex I (The Jung Codex): Introductions, Texts, Translations, Indices*, 2 vols., Nag Hammadi Studies 22, 23 (Leiden: Brill, 1985), vol. I, pp. 159–337, and vol. II, pp. 217–497.

Audet, Jean-Paul (ed.), *La Didachè. Instructions des apôtres*, Études Bibliques (Paris: Gabalda, 1958).

Baehrens, W. A. (ed.), *Origenes Werke. Homilien zum Hexateuch in Rufins Übersetzung*, vol. VI, GCS 29 (Leipzig: Hinrichs, 1920).

(ed.), *Origenes Werke. Homilien zum Hexateuch in Rufins Übersetzung*, vol. VII, GCS 30 (Leipzig: Hinrichs, 1921).

(ed.), *Origenes Werke. Homilien zu Samuel I, zum Hohelied und zu den Propheten. Kommentar zum Hohelied, in Rufins und Hieronymus' Übersetzung*, vol. VIII, GCS 33 (Leipzig: Hinrichs, 1925).

Bardy, Gustave (ed.), *Eusèbe de Césarée. Histoire ecclésiastique*, 3 vols., SC 31, 41, 55 (Paris: Cerf, 1952–1958).

Barkley, Gary Wayne. (ed. and trans.), *Origen: Homilies on Leviticus 1–16*, Fathers of the Church 83 (Washington, D.C.: Catholic University of America Press, 1990).

Bauernfeind, Otto (ed.), *Der Römerbrieftext des Origenes nach dem codex von der Goltz (cod. 184, B64 des Athosklosters Lawra)*, TU 44.3 (Leipzig: Hinrichs, 1923).

Behr, John (ed. and trans.), *Origen: On First Principles*, 2 vols., Oxford Early Christian Texts (Oxford: Oxford University Press, 2017).

Benz, Ernst, and E. Klostermann (eds.), *Origenes Werke. Origenes Matthäuserklärung, 1. Die Griechisch Erhaltenen Tomoi*, vol. X, GCS 40 (Leipzig: Hinrichs, 1935).

Blanc, Cécile (ed.), *Origène. Commentaire sur saint Jean*, 5 vols., SC 120, 157, 222, 290, 385 (Paris: Cerf, 1966–1992).

Blomkvist, Vemund (ed. and trans.), *Euthalian Traditions: Text, Translation and Commentary*, TU 170 (Berlin: De Gruyter, 2012).

Bobichon, Philippe (ed. and trans.), *Justin Martyr, Dialogue avec Tryphon. Édition critique, traduction, commentaire*, 2 vols., Paradosis 47/1–2 (Fribourg: Éditions universitaires de Fribourg, 2003).

Borret, Marcel (ed.), *Origène. Contre Celse*, 5 vols., SC 132, 136, 147, 150 (Paris: Cerf, 1967–1976).

(ed.), *Origène. Homélies sur Ezéchiel*, SC 352 (Paris: Cerf, 1989).

Botte, Bernard (ed.), *Hippolytus. La tradition apostolique, d'après les anciennes versions*, 2nd edn, SC 11 bis (Paris: Cerf, 1984).

Bovon, François, and Pierre Geoltrain (eds.), *Écrits apocryphes chrétiens*, vol. I, Bibliothèque de la Pléiade (Saint Herblain: Gallimard, 1997).

Bradshaw, Paul F. (ed.), *The Canons of Hippolytus*, trans. Carol Bebawi, Grove Liturgical Study 50. Bramcote, Notts.: Grove Books, 1987.

Bright, William (ed.), *The Canons of the First Four General Councils of Nicaea, Constantinople, Ephesus and Chalcedon: With Notes*, 2nd edn (Oxford: Clarendon, 1892).

Bruce, Barbara J. (trans.), *Origen: Homilies on Joshua*, ed. Cynthia White, Fathers of the Church 105. Washington, D.C.: Catholic University of America Press, 2002.

Clericus, Joannes (ed.), *Desiderii Erasmi Roterodami Opera Omnia*, vol. VII: *Paraphrases in N. Testamentum* (Hildesheim: G. Olms, 1962).

Conybeare, F. C. (ed.), *The Armenian Apology and Acts of Apollonius and other Monuments of Early Christianity*, 2nd edn (London: Swan Sonnenschein, 1896).

Cramer, John Anthony (ed.), *Catenae graecorum patrum in Novum Testamentum*, 8 vols. (Oxford: Oxford University Press, 1838–1844).

Crouzel, Henri (ed.), *Grégoire le Thaumaturge. Remerciement a Origène suivi de La lettre d'Origène a Grégoire. Texte grec, introduction, traduction et notes*, SC 148 (Paris: Cerf, 1969).

Crouzel, Henri, and Manlio Simonetti (eds.), *Origène. Traité des Principes*, 4 vols., SC 252, 253, 268, 269 (Paris: Cerf, 1978–1980).

Crouzel, Henri, François Fournier, and Pierre Périchon (eds.), *Origène. Homélies sur S. Luc*, SC 87 (Paris: Cerf, 1962).

Dagron, Gilbert (eds.), *Vie et miracles de Sainte Thècle. Texte grec, traduction et commentaire*, Subsidia Hagiographica 62 (Brussels: Société des Bolandistes, 1978).

Delehaye, H., "Synaxarium ecclesiae Constantinopolitanae (e codice Sirmondiano nunc Berolinensi)," *Acta Sanctorum* 62 (1902), 1–94.

Diels, Hermann (ed.), *Die Fragmente der Vorsokratiker. Griechisch und Deutsch*, vol. I, 2nd edn (Berlin: Weidmann, 1906).

Diercks, G. F. "De Oratione," in E. Dekkers (ed.), *Corpus Christianorum*, Series Latina I (Turnhout: Brepols, 1954), pp. 255–274.

Dumortier, Jean (ed.), *Jean Chrysostome. Commentaire sur Isaïe*, trans. Arthur Liefooghe, SC 304 (Paris: Cerf, 1983).

Ehrman, Bart D (ed.), *The Apostolic Fathers*, LCL 24–25 (Cambridge, MA: Harvard University Press, 2003).

Ephrem. S. *Ephræm Syri Commentarii in Epistolas d. S. Pauli* (Venice: Monastery of St. Lazarus, 1895).

Srboyn Ep'remi Matenagrut'iwnk', vol. III (Venice: Monastery of St. Lazarus, 1836).

Erasmus, Desiderius. *Opera Omnia Desiderii Erasmi* (Amsterdam: North Holland; Amsterdam and Boston: Elsevier; Leiden and Boston: Brill, 1969–).

Evans, Ernest (ed.), *Tertullian's Homily on Baptism* (London: SPCK, 1964).

Faller, O. (ed.), *Ambrosius. Explanatio symboli, De sacramentis, De mysteriis, De paenitentia, De excessu fratris, De obitu Valentiniani, De obitu Theodosii*, vol. IV, CSEL 73 (Salzburg: Österreichischen Akademie der Wissenschaften, 1955).

Field, F. (ed.), *Sancti patris nostri Joannis Chrysostomi archiepiscopi Constantinopolitani Interpretatio omnium Epistolarum Paulinarum per homilias facta*, 7 vols., Bibliotheca patrum ecclesiae Catholicae (Oxford: J.H. Parker, 1849–1862).

Fredouille, Jean-Claude (ed.), *Tertullien. Contre les valentinians*, 2 vols., SC 280–281 (Paris: Cerf, 1981).

Funk, F. X. (ed.), *Didascalia et constitutiones apostolorum*, 2 vols. (Paderborn: Ferdinand Schönigh, 1905–1906).

Gebhardt, Oscar von (ed.), *Passio S. Theclae virginis. Die lateinischen Übersetzungen der Acta Pauli et Theclae nebst Fragmenten Auszügen und Beilagen herausgegeben*, TUGAL 7 (Leipzig: J. C. Hinrichs, 1902).

Geerlings, Wilhelm (ed.), "Traditio apostolica = Apostolische Überlieferung," in *Zwölf-Apostel-Lehre; apostolische Überlieferung*, Fontes Christiani 1 (Freiburg: Herder, 1991), pp. 141–313.

Gori, F. (ed.), *Marius Victorinus. In epistulam Pauli ad Ephesios, In epistulam Pauli ad Galatas, In epistulam Pauli ad Philippenses*, CSEL 83/2 (Salzburg: Österreichischen Akademie der Wissenschaften, 1986).

Guerrier, L., and S. Grébaut (ed.), *Le Testament en Galilée de Notre-Seigneur Jésus-Christ*, Patrologia Orientalis 9 (Paris: Firmin-Didot, 1913).

Guyot, Peter, and Richard Klein (eds.), *Gregor der Wundertäter. Oratio prosphonetica ac panegyrica in Origenem = Dankrede an Origenes*, Fontes Christiani 24 (Freiburg: Herder, 1996).

Hammond Bammel, C. P. (ed.), *Der Römerbriefkommentar des Origenes. Kritische Ausgabe der Übersetzung Rufins*, 3 vols., AGBL 16, 33, 34 (Freiburg im Breisgau: Herder, 1990–1998).

Harkins, Paul W. (ed. and trans.), *John Chrysostom: Baptismal Instructions*, ACW 31 (Westminster, MD: Newman Press, 1963).

Heffernan, Thomas J. (ed.), *The Passion of Perpetua and Felicity* (New York: Oxford University Press, 2012).

Heine, Ronald E. (ed.), *Origen: Commentary on the Gospel of John, Books 1–10*, Fathers of the Church 80 (Washington, D.C.: Catholic University of America Press, 1989).

(ed.), *Origen: Commentary on the Gospel of John, Books 13–32*, Fathers of the Church 89 (Washington, D.C.: Catholic University of America Press, 1993).

Hills, Julian V. (ed. and trans.), *The Epistle of the Apostles* (Santa Rosa, CA: Polebridge Press, 2009).

Hoek, Annewies van den, and Claude Mondésert (eds.), *Clément d'Alexandrie. Les Stromates, Stromate IV*, SC 463 (Paris: Cerf, 2001).

Irmscher, J., F. Paschke, and B. Rehm (eds.), *Die Pseudoklementinen I. Homilien*, 2nd edn, GCS (Berlin: Akademie, 1969).

Jaeger, Werner (ed.), *Gregorii Nysseni opera*, vol. II.2 (Leiden: Brill, 1960).

Jaubert, Annie (ed.), *Origène. Homélies sur Josué*, SC 71 (Paris: Cerf, 1960).

Jenkins, Claude, "Origen on 1 Corinthians," *Journal of Theological Studies* 9–10 (1908), 231–247; 353–372; 500–514; 29–51.

Kaczynski, Reiner (ed.), *Johannes Chrysostomus. Catecheses Baptismales = Taufkatechesen*, 2 vols., Fontes Christiani 6 (Freiburg: Herder, 1992).

Kasser, Rodolphe, and Philippe Luisier, "Le Papyrus Bodmer XLI en édition princeps: l'épisode d'Éphèses des *Acta Pauli* en copte et en traduction," *Le Muséon* 117, no. 3 (2004), 281–384.

Koetschau, Paul (ed.), *Origenes Werke. Buch V-VIII Gegen Celsus, Die Schrift von Gebet*, vol. II, GCS 3 (Leipzig: Hinrichs, 1899).

Kroymann, E. "De Corona," in E. Dekkers (ed.), *Corpus Christianorum*, Series Latina 1 (Turnhout: Brepols, 1954), pp. 1037–1065.

Kühn, C. G. (ed.), *Claudii Galeni Opera Omnia*, vol. VIII (Leipzig: Knobloch, 1824).

LaGarde, Paul de (ed.), *Aegyptica* (Gottingen: Arnold Hoyer, 1883).

Le Boulluec, Alain, and Pierre Voulet (eds.), *Clément d'Alexandrie. Les Stromates. Stromate V*, 2 vols, SC 278–279 (Paris: Cerf, 1981).

Lefèvre, M. (ed.), *Hippolyte. Commentaire sur Daniel*, SC 14 (Paris: Cerf, 1947).

Lewis, Agnes Smith (ed.), *Acta Mythologica Apostolorum: Transcribed from an Arabic MS. in the Convent of Deyr-Es-Suriani, Egypt, and from MSS in the Convent of St. Catherine, on Mount Sinai*, Horae Seminicae 3–4 (London: Clay and Sons, 1904).

Lienhard, Joseph T. (ed. and trans.), *Origen: Homilies on Luke; Fragments on Luke*, Fathers of the Church 94 (Washington, D.C.: Catholic University of America Press, 1996).

Lindsay, Wallace Martin (ed.), *Isidori Hispalensis episcopi Etymologiarum sive Originvm libri XX*, vol. I (Oxford: Clarendon, 1911).

Lipsius, R. A. (ed.), *Acta Apostolorum Apocrypha. Acta Petri, Acta Pauli, Acta Petri et Pauli, Acta Pauli et Theclae, Acta Thaddaei* (Hildesheim and New York: Georg Olms, 1972).

Litwa, M. David (ed. and trans.), *Hippolytus. Refutation of All Heresies*, Writings from the Greco-Roman World 40 (Atlanta: SBL Press, 2015).

Long, H. S. (ed.), *Diogenis Laertii vitae philosophorum*, 2 vols. (Oxford: Clarendon Press, 1964).

Luther, Martin, *D. Martin Luthers Werke* (Weimar: H. Böhlau, 1883–1929).

Marrou, Henri-Irénée, Marguerite Harl, Claude Mondésert, and Chantal Matray (eds.), *Clément d'Alexandrie. Le pédagogue*, 3 vols., SC 70, 108, 158 (Paris: Cerf, 1960–1970).

Marquardt, Ioannes, Iwanus Mueller, and Georgius Helmreich (eds.), *Claudii Galeni Pergameni scripta minora*, vol. II (Leipzig: Teubner, 1891).

Mau, J. (ed.), *Plutarchi moralia*, vol. 5.2.1 (Leipzig: Teubner, 1971).

Mekerttchian, Karapet Ter, and S. G. Wilson, "S. Irenaeus, Εἰς ἐπίδειξιν τοῦ ἀποστολικοῦ κηρύγματος, The proof of the apostolic preaching with seven fragments, Armenian version," *Patrologia Orientalis* 12 (1919), 655–746.

Melanchthon, Philipp. *Loci communes 1521. Lateinisch – Deutsch*, trans. Horst Georg Pöhlmann (Gütersloh: Gütersloher Verlagshaus, 1993).

Metzger, Marcel (ed.), *Les constitutions apostoliques*, 3 vols., SC 320, 329, 336 (Paris: Cerf, 1985–1987).

Migne, J.-P (ed.), *Patrologia cursus completus (series Graeca)*, 162 vols. (Paris: Migne, 1857–1886).

(ed.), *Patrologia cursus completus (series Latina)*, 221 vols. (Paris: Migne, 1844–1864).

Mondésert, Claude (ed.), *Clément d'Alexandrie. Le protreptique*, 2nd edn, SC 2 (Paris: Cerf, 1949).

Munier, Charles (ed. and trans.), *Justin. Apologie pour les chrétiens. Introduction, texte critique, traduction et notes*. SC 507. Paris: Cerf, 2006.

(ed.), *Tertullien. La pénitence*, SC 316 (Paris: Cerf, 1984).

Musurillo, Herbert (ed.), *The Acts of the Christian Martyrs: Introduction, Texts and Translations*, OECT (Oxford: Clarendon, 1972).

Nautin, Pierre (ed.), *Lettres et écrivains chrétiens des IIe et IIIe siècles*, Patristica 2 (Paris: Cerf, 1961).

(ed.), *Origène. Homélies sur Jérémie*, 2 vols., SC 232, 238 (Paris: Cerf, 1976–1977).

Parisot, D. Ioannes (ed.), *Aphraatis Sapientis Persae Demonstrationes I–XXII*, Patrologia Syriaca 1.1 (Paris: Firmin-Didot, 1894).

Piédagnel, Auguste, and Louis Doutreleau (eds.), *Jean Chrysostome. Trois catéchèses baptismales*, SC 366 (Paris: Cerf, 1990).

Refoule, François (ed.), *Tertullien. Traité de la prescription contre les hérétiques*, SC 46 (Paris: Cerf, 1957).

Reichert, Eckhard (ed.), *Die Canones der Synode von Elvira. Einleitung und Kommentar* (Hamburg: Hamburg University, 1990).

Reischl, W. C., and J. Rupp (eds.), *Cyrilli Hierosolymorum archiepiscopi opera quae supersunt omnia* (Hildesheim: Olms, 1967).

Robinson, J. Armitage (ed. and trans.), *St. Irenaeus: The Demonstration of Apostolic Preaching*, Translations of Christian Literature IV: Oriental Texts (London: SPCK, 1920).

Rousseau, Adelin (ed.), *Irénée de Lyon. Démonstration de la prédication apostolique*, SC 406 (Paris: Cerf, 1995).

Rousseau, Adelin, and Louis Doutreleau (eds.), *Irénée de Lyon. Contre les hérésies I*, 2 vols., SC 263–264 (Paris: Cerf, 1979).

Rousseau, Adelin, B. Hemmerdinger, and Louis Doutreleau (eds.), *Irénée de Lyon. Contre les hérésies IV*, SC 100 (Paris: Cerf, 1965).

Rupp, E. Gordon, and Philip S. Watson (eds.), *Luther and Erasmus: Free Will and Salvation* (Philadelphia: Westminster Press, 1969).

Sagnard, François (ed.), *Clément d'Alexandrie. Extraits de Théodote*, SC 23 (Paris: Cerf, 1970).

Schadel, Erwin (ed.), *Origenes. Die griechisch erhaltenen Jeremiahomilien*, Bibliothek der Griechischen Literatur 10 (Stuttgart: Hiersemann, 1980).

Scheck, Thomas P. (ed.), *Origen: Commentary on the Epistle to the Romans, Books 1–5*, Fathers of the Church 103 (Washington, D.C.: Catholic University of America Press, 2001).

(ed.), *Origen: Commentary on the Epistle to the Romans, Books 6–10*, Fathers of the Church 104 (Washington, D.C.: Catholic University of America Press, 2002).

(trans.), *Origen: Homilies on Numbers*, ed. Christopher A. Hall, Ancient Christian Texts (Downers Grove: IVP Academic, 2009).

Schmidt, Carl, (ed.) *Acta Pauli. Übersetzung, Untersuchungen und Koptischer Text*, 2nd edn (Leipzig: J. C. Hinrichs, 1905).

"Ein neues Fragment der Heidelberger Acta Pauli," *Sitzungsberichte der königlich Preussischen Akademie der Wissenschaften*, no. 8 (1909), 216–220.

Schmidt, Carl, and Wilhelm Schubart (eds.), ΠΡΑΞΕΙΣ ΠΑΥΛΟΥ. *Acta Pauli nach dem Papyrus der Hamburger Staats- und Universitäts-bibliothek unter Mitarbeit von Wilhelm Schubart* (Hamburg: J. J. Augustin, 1936).

Simonetti, Manlio (ed.), "Ad Donatum, De mortalitate; Ad Demetrianum; De opere et eleemosynis; De zelo et livore," in *Sancti Cypriani Episcopi Opera*, CCSL IIIA.2 (Turnhout: Brepols, 1976), pp. v–86.

Slusser, Michael (ed. and trans.), *St. Gregory Thaumaturgus: Life and Works*, Fathers of the Church 98 (Washington, D.C.: Catholic University of America Press, 1998).

Smith, John Clark (ed.), *Origen: Homilies on Jeremiah, Homily on 1 Kings 28*, Fathers of the Church 97 (Washington, D.C.: Catholic University of America Press, 1998).

Testuz, Michel (ed.), *Papyrus Bodmer X–XII* (Cologny-Genève: Bibliotheca Bodmeriana, 1959).

Till, Walter, and Johannes Leipoldt (eds.), *Der koptische Text der Kirchenordnung Hippolyts*, TU 58 (Berlin: Akademie, 1954).

Turcan, Marie (ed.), *Tertullian. Les spectacles (De spectaculis)*, SC 332 (Paris: Cerf, 1986).

Verheijen, L. (ed.), *Augustinus. Confessionum libri XIII*, CCSL 27 (Turnhout: Brepols, 1981).

Vööbus, Arthur (ed.), *The Didascalia Apostolorum in Syriac*, 4 vols., CSCO 401, 402, 407, 408 (Louvain: Secrétariat du Corpus SCO, 1979).

Vouaux, Léon (ed.), *Les actes de Paul et ses lettres apocryphes*, Les apocryphes du nouveau testament (Paris: Librairie Letouzey er Ané, 1913).

Vrba, Carolus F., and Josephus Zycha (eds.), *Sancti Aureli Augustini. De peccatorum meritis et remissione et de baptismo parvulorum, De spiritu et littera, De natura et gratia, De natura et origine animae, Contra duas epistulas Pelagianorum*, CSEL 60 (Vienna: F. Tempsky, 1913).

Walter, Johannes von (ed.), *De libero arbitrio Διατριβη sive collatio per Desiderium Erasmum Roterdamum*, Quellenschriften zur Geschichte des Protestantismus 8 (Leipzig: A. Diechertsche, 1935).

Walzer, Richard (ed.), *Galen on Jews and Christians*, Oxford Classical and Philosophical Monographs (London: Oxford University Press, 1949).

Weber, R. (ed.), "Ad Quirinum; Ad Fortunatum," in *Sancti Cypriani Episcopi Opera*, CCSL iii.1 (Turnhout: Brepols, 1972), pp. li–216.

Wenger, Antoine (ed.), *Jean Chrysostome. Huit catéchèses baptismales inédites*, SC 50 (Paris: Cerf, 1957).

Winling, Raymond (ed.), *Grégoire de Nysse. Discours catéchétique*, SC 453 (Paris: Cerf, 2000).

Wright, William. (ed.), *Apocryphal Acts of the Apostles*, vol. i: *The Syriac Texts* (London: Williams and Norgate, 1871).

SECONDARY SOURCES

Aageson, James W., *Paul, the Pastoral Epistles, and the Early Church* (Peabody, MA: Hendrickson, 2008).

Aalst, P. van der, "De initiatie in het christelijk leven te Antiochië op het einde van de vierde eeuw," *Christelijk Oosten en Hereniging* 12, no. 1–2 (1959), 3–18.

Abbattista, Esther, *Origene legge Geremia. Analisi, commento e riflessioni di un biblista di oggi*, Tesi Gregoriana, Serie Teologia 159 (Rome: Editrice Pontificia Università Gregoriana, 2008).

Adam, Margaret B., "'This is my story, this is my song...': a feminist claim on scripture, ideology and interpretation," in Harold C. Washington, Susan Lochrie Graham, and Pamela Lee Thimmes (eds.), *Escaping Eden: New Feminist Perspectives on the Bible* (Sheffield: Sheffield Academic Press, 1998), pp. 218–232.

Alciati, Roberto, and Federico Fatti, "La controversia origenista: un affare mediterraneo; The Origenist controversy: a Mediterranean affair," *Adamantius* 19 (2013), 7–9.

Aleith, Eva, *Paulusverständnis in der alten Kirche*, BZNW 18 (Berlin: De Gruyter, 1937).

Alès, Adhémar d', *La théologie de Tertullien*, 3rd edn, Bibiotheque de théologie historique (Paris: Beauchesne, 1905).

Alexe, Stefan C., "Origène et l'Église visible," in R. J. Daly (ed.), *Origeniana Quinta*, BETL 105 (Leuven: Peeters, 1992), pp. 467–473.

Anderson, R. Dean, Jr. *Ancient Rhetorical Theory and Paul*, CBET 17 (Kampen: Kok Pharos, 1996).

Andrei, Osvalda (ed.), *Caesarea Maritima e la scuola origeniana. Multiculturalità, forme di competizione culturale e identità christiana* (Brescia: Morcelliana, 2013).

Arnold, Brian J., *Justification in The Second Century*, SBR 9 (Berlin: De Gruyter, 2017).

Ashwin-Siejkowski, Piotr, *Clement of Alexandria: A Project of Christian Perfection* (London: T. & T. Clark, 2008).

Attridge, Harold W., *The Epistle to the Hebrews: A Commentary on the Epistle to the Hebrews*, ed. Helmut Koester, Hermeneia (Philadelphia: Fortress, 1989).

Audet, Jean-Paul, "Literary and doctrinal relationships of the 'Manual of Discipline'," in *The Didache in Modern Research*, trans. Jonathan A. Draper, AGJU 37 (Leiden: Brill, 1996), pp. 129–147.

Augustijn, Cornelis, *Erasmus. Der Humanist als Theologe und Kirchenreformer,* Studies in Medieval and Reformation Thought 59 (Leiden: Brill, 1996).

Bain, Andrew M., "Tertullian: Paul as teacher of the Gentile churches," in Michael F. Bird and Joseph R. Dodson (eds.), *Paul and the Second Century,* LNTS 412 (London: T. & T. Clark, 2011), pp. 207–225.

Baird, William, "Among the mature: the idea of wisdom in I Corinthians 2:6," *Interpretation* 13, no. 3 (1959), 425–432.

  History of New Testament Research, vol. 1: *From Deism to Tübingen* (Minneapolis: Fortress, 1992).

Bandt, Cordula. "Origen in the *Catenae* on Psalms II: the rather complicated case of Psalms 51 to 76," *Adamantius* 20 (2014), 14–27.

Barclay, John M. G., "'Do we undermine the Law?' A study of Romans 14.1–15.6," in James D. G. Dunn (ed.), *Paul and the Mosaic Law,* WUNT 89 (Tübingen: Mohr Siebeck, 1996), pp. 287–308.

  Paul and the Gift (Grand Rapids: Eerdmans, 2015).

Bardy, Gustave, "Aux origines de l'école d'Alexandrie," *Recherches de science religieuse* 27 (1937), 65–90.

Barrett, C. K., *A Commentary on the First Epistle to the Corinthians,* BNTC (London: Adam & Charles Black, 1968).

Barrier, Jeremy W., *The Acts of Paul and Thecla: A Critical Introduction and Commentary,* WUNT II/270 (Tübingen: Mohr Siebeck, 2009).

Bauckham, Richard, "The Acts of Paul as a sequel to Acts," in Bruce W. Winter and Andrew D. Clarke (eds.), *The Book of Acts in its First Century Setting,* vol. 1: *Ancient Literary Setting* (Grand Rapids: Eerdmans; Carlisle: Paternoster, 1993), pp. 105–152.

Baur, Chrysostomus, *John Chrysostom and His Time,* trans. M. Gonzaga, 2 vols. (Westminster, MD: Newman Press, 1959–1960).

Baur, Ferdinand Christian, "Die Christuspartei in der korinthischen Gemeinde, der Gegensatz des petrinischen und paulinischen Christenthums in der ältesten Kirche, der Apostel Petrus in Rom," *Tübinger Zeitschrift für Theologie* 3, no. 4 (1831), 61–206.

  "Die Einleitung in das Neue Testament als theologische Wissenschaft: ihr Begriff und ihre Aufgabe, ihr Entwicklungsgang und ihr innerer Organismus," 463–566, 70–94, 222–253, 291–329 in *Theologische Jahrbücher* 9–10. 1850–1851.

  History of Christian Dogma, ed. Peter C. Hodgson, trans. Robert F. Brown and Peter C. Hodgson (New York: Oxford University Press, 2014).

  Lectures on New Testament Theology, ed. Peter C. Hodgson, trans. Robert F. Brown (New York: Oxford University Press, 2016).

  Paulus, der Apostel Jesu Christi. Sein Leben und Wirken, seine Briefe und seine Lehre. Ein Beitrag zu einer kritischen Geschichte des Urchristentums, 2nd edn, 2 vols. (Leipzig: Fues, 1866–1867).

  Paul the Apostle of Jesus Christ: His Life and Work, His Epistles and His Doctrine, 2nd edn, trans. Eduard Zeller, 2 vols. (London: Williams and Norgate, 1875).

  Vorlesungen über neutestamentliche Theologie, ed. Ferdinand Friedrich Baur (Leipzig: Fues, 1864).

Bauspiess, Martin, Christof Landmesser, and David Lincicum (eds.), *Ferdinand Christian Baur und die Geschichte des frühen Christentums*, WUNT I/333 (Tübingen: Mohr Siebeck, 2014).

Becker, Eve-Marie, "Taufe bei Marcion: eine Spurensuche," in David Hellholm, Tor Vegge, Øyvind Norderval, and Christer Hellholm (eds.), *Ablution, Initiation, and Baptism: Late Antiquity, Early Judaism, and Early Christianity*, 3 vols., BZNW 176 (Berlin: De Gruyter, 2011), vol. ii, pp. 871–894.

Beckwith, Roger T., *Calendar and Chronology, Jewish and Christian: Biblical, Intertestamental and Patristic Studies*, AGAJU 33 (Leiden: Brill, 1996).

Beker, Johan Christiaan, *Paul the Apostle: The Triumph of God in Life and Thought* (Philadelphia: Fortress, 1980).

Bengel, Johan Albrecht, *Gnomon Novi Testamenti*, 3rd edn, ed. Ernst Bengel and Johann Christian F. Steudel, 2 vols. (Tübingen: Ludov. Frid. Fues, 1835).

Betz, Monika. "Thekla und die jüngeren Witwen der Pastoralbriefe: ein Beispiel für die Situationsgebundenheit paulinischer Tradition," *Annali di Studi Religiosi* 6 (2005), 335–356.

Blackwell, Ben C., "Paul and Irenaeus," in Michael F. Bird and Joseph R. Dodson (eds.), *Paul and the Second Century*, LNTS 412 (London: T. & T. Clark, 2011), pp. 190–206.

Bockmuehl, Markus N. A., *Ancient Apocryphal Gospels*, Interpretation: Resouces for the Use of Scripture in the Church (Louisville: Westminster John Knox, 2017).

Jewish Law in Gentile Churches: Halakhah and the Beginning of Christian Public Ethics (Edinburgh: T. & T. Clark, 2000).

The Remembered Peter: In Ancient Reception and Modern Debate, WUNT 262 (Tübingen: Mohr Siebeck, 2010).

Revelation and Mystery in Ancient Judaism and Pauline Christianity, WUNT II/36 (Tübingen: Mohr Siebeck, 1990).

Seeing the Word: Refocusing New Testament Study (Grand Rapids: Baker Academic, 2006).

Boersma, Hans, *Scripture as Real Presence: Sacramental Exegesis in the Early Church* (Grand Rapids: Baker Academic, 2017).

Bornkamm, Günther, "The Letter to the Romans as Paul's last will and testament," in Karl P. Donfried (ed.), *The Romans Debate,* rev. and expanded edn, (Edinburgh: T. & T. Clark, 1991), pp. 16–28.

Bradshaw, Paul F., "Conclusions shaping evidence: an examination of the scholarship surrounding the supposed *Apostolic Tradition* of Hippolytus," in Paul van Geest, Marcel Poorthuis, and Els Rose (eds.), *Sanctifying Texts, Transforming Rituals: Encounters in Liturgical Studies* (Leiden: Brill, 2017), pp. 13–30.

The Search for the Origins of Christian Worship: Sources and Methods for the Study of Early Liturgy, 2nd edn (New York: Oxford University Press, 2002).

Bradshaw, Paul F., Maxwell E. Johnson, L. Edward Phillips, and Harold W. Attridge, *The Apostolic Tradition: A Commentary*, Hermeneia (Minneapolis: Fortress, 2002).

Brändle, Rudolf, *John Chrysostom: Bishop, Reformer, Martyr*, ed. Wendy Mayer, trans. John Cawte and Silke Trzcionka, Early Christian Studies 8 (Strathfield: St Pauls, 2004).

Breed, Brennan W., *Nomadic Text: A Theory of Biblical Reception History* (Bloomington: Indiana University Press, 2014).

"What can a text do? Reception history as an ethology of the biblical text," in Emma England and William John Lyons (eds.), *Reception History and Biblical Studies: Theory and Practice*, The Library of Hebrew Bible 615/ Scriptural Traces 6 (London: Bloomsbury, 2015), pp. 95–110.

Bremmer, Jan N., "Conversion in the oldest *Apocryphal Acts*," in *Maidens, Magic and Martyrs in Early Christianity: Collected Essays I*, WUNT I/379 (Tübingen: Mohr Siebeck, 2017), pp. 181–196.

"Magic, martyrdom and women's liberation in the *Acts of Paul and Thecla*," in *Maidens, Magic and Martyrs in Early Christianity: Collected Essays I*, WUNT I/379 (Tübingen: Mohr Siebeck, 2017), pp. 149–166.

"The onomastics and provenance of the *Acts of Paul*," in *Philologie, herméneutique et histoire des textes entre orient et occident*, ed. Francesca P. Barone, Caroline Macé, and Pablo A. Ubierna, Instrumenta Patristica et Mediaevalia 73 (Turnhout: Brepols, 2017), pp. 527–547.

"The portrait of the Apostle Paul in the apocryphal *Acts of Paul*," in T. Greub and M. Roussel (eds.), *Figurationen des Porträts* (Munich: Wilhelm Fink, 2018), pp. 419–437.

Brent, Allen, *Hippolytus and the Roman Church in the Third Century: Communities in Tension Before the Emergence of a Monarch-Bishop*, VC Sup 31 (Leiden: Brill, 1995).

Broc-Schmezer, C., "La philosophie grecque comme propédeutique à l'Évangile: Clément d'Alexandrie," *Foi et Vie* 47, no. 4 (2008), 77–87.

Broek, Roelof van den, "The Christian 'school' of Alexandria in the second and third centuries," in Jan Willem Drijvers and Alasdair A. MacDonald (eds.), *Centers of Learning: Learning and Location in Pre-Modern Europe and the Near East* (Leiden: Brill, 1995), pp. 39–47.

Brontesi, Alfredo, *La soteria in Clemente Alessandrino* (Rome: Università Gregoriana, 1972).

Brox, Norbert, *Der Hirt des Hermas. Übersetzt und erklärt*, KAV 17 (Göttingen: Vandenhoeck & Ruprecht, 1991).

Buechner, Frederick, *The Alphabet of Grace* (New York: Harper One, 2007).

Buell, Denise Kimber, *Making Christians: Clement of Alexandria and the Rhetoric of Legitimacy* (Princeton: Princeton University Press, 1999).

Büllesbach, Claudia, "Das Verhältnis der Acta Pauli zur Apostelgeschichte des Lukas: Darstellung und Kritik der Forschungsgeschichte," in F. W. Horn (ed.), *Das Ende des Paulus. Historische, theologische und literaturgeschichtliche Aspekte*, BZNW 106 (Berlin: De Gruyter, 2001), pp. 215–237.

Bultmann, Rudolf, *Theology of the New Testament*, 2 vols. (London: SCM, 1952).

Bunt, Annewies van de, "Milk and honey in the theology of Clement of Alexandria," in *Fides Sacramenti – Sacramentum Fidei: Studies in Honour of Pieter Smulders* (Assen: Van Gorcum, 1981), pp. 27–39.

Burrus, Virginia, *Chastity as Autonomy: Women in the Stories of the Apocryphal Acts*, Studies in Women and Religion 23 (Lewiston, ME: E. Mellen Press, 1987).

Cabié, Robert, *La Pentecôte. L'évolution de la Cinquantaine pascale au cours des cinq premiers siècles*, Bibliothèque de liturgie (Tournai: Desclée, 1965).

Calhoun, Robert Matthew, "John Chrysostom on ἐκ πίστεως εἰς πίστιν in Rom. 1:17: a reply to Charles L. Quarles," *Novum Testamentum* 48, no. 2 (2006), 131–146.

Calzolari, Valentina, "The editing of Christian apocrypha in Armenian: should we turn over a new leaf?" in Valentina Calzolari (ed.), *Armenian Philology in the Modern Era: From Manuscript to Digital Text* (Leiden: Brill, 2014), pp. 64–291.

Camelot, T., *Foi et gnose. Introduction a l'étude de la connaissance mystique chez Clément d'Alexandrie*, Études de théologie et d'histoire de la spiritualité 3 (Paris: Librarie philosophique J. Vrin, 1945).

Campbell, Douglas A., *The Deliverance of God: An Apocalyptic Rereading of Justification in Paul* (Grand Rapids: Eerdmans, 2009).

"Romans 1:17: A *crux interpretum* for the πίστις Χριστοῦ debate," *Journal of Biblical Literature* 113, no. 2 (1994), 265–285.

Carleton Paget, James, "The reception of Baur in Britain," in Martin Bauspiess, Christof Landmesser, and David Lincicum (eds.), *Ferdinand Christian Baur und die Geschichte des frühen Christentums*, WUNT I/333 (Tübingen: Mohr Siebeck, 2014), pp. 335–386.

Carrington, Philip, *The Primitive Christian Catechism: A Study in the Epistles* (Cambridge: Cambridge University Press, 1940).

Castelli, Elizabeth A., *Imitating Paul: A Discourse of Power*, Literary Currents in Biblical Interpretation (Louisville: Westminster/John Knox Press, 1991).

"'I will make Mary male': pieties of the body and gender transformation of Christian women in late antiquity," in J. Epstein and K. Straub (eds.), *Body Guards: The Cultural Politics of Gender Ambiguity* (New York: Routledge, 1991), pp. 29–49.

Celia, Francesco, "Gregory of Neocaesarea: a re-examination of the biographical issue," *Adamantius* 22 (2016), 172–173.

Cerrato, J. A., "The association of the name Hippolytus with a church order now known as the *Apostolic Tradition*," *St Vladimir's Theological Quarterly* 48, no. 2 (2004), 181–183.

Chester, Stephen J., *Reading Paul with the Reformers: Reconciling Old and New Perspectives* (Grand Rapids: Eerdmans, 2017).

Childs, Brevard S., *The Church's Guide for Reading Paul: The Canonical Shaping of the Pauline Corpus* (Grand Rapids: Eerdmans, 2008).

Ciampa, Roy E., and Brian S. Rosner, *The First Letter to the Corinthians*, PNTC (Grand Rapids: Eerdmans; Nottingham: Apollos, 2010).

Clark, Elizabeth A., *Clement's Use of Aristotle: The Aristotelian Contribution to Clement of Alexandria's Refutation of Gnosticism*, TSR 1 (New York: Edwin Mellen, 1977).

The Origenist Controversy: The Cultural Construction of an Early Christian Debate (Princeton: Princeton University Press, 1992).

Cocchini, Francesca, "L'intelligenza spirituale della Scrittura come principio di teologia: la prospettiva dei Padri e in particolare di Origene," *Lateranum* 74, no. 1 (2008), 69–79.

Origene. Teologo esegeta per una identità cristiana (Bologna: EDB, 2006).

Il Paolo di Origene. Contributo alla storia della recezione delle Epistole paoline nel III secolo, Verba Seniorum 11 (Rome: Edizioni Studium, 1992).

"La questione dei cibi (Rm 14) nel Commento di Origene alla Lettera ai Romani," *Adamantius* 18 (2012), 218–225.

Collingwood, R. G., *An Autobiography* (Oxford: Oxford University Press, 1939).

The Idea of History (Oxford: Oxford University Press, 1956).

Conzelmann, Hans, *1 Corinthians: A Commentary on the First Epistle to the Corinthians*, ed. James Waterson Leitch, George W. MacRae, and James W. Dunkly, Hermeneia (Philadelphia: Fortress Press, 1975).

Cranfield, C. E. B., *A Critical and Exegetical Commentary on the Epistle to the Romans*, 2 vols. (London: T. & T. Clark, 1975–1979).

Crawford, Matthew R., "Tatian, Celsus, and Christianity as 'barbarian philosophy' in the late second century," in Lewis O. Ayres and Clifton Ward (eds.), *Rise of the Christian Intellectual*, AZK (Berlin: De Gruyter, forthcoming).

Crossley, James G., "The end of reception history: a grand narrative for biblical studies and the neoliberal Bible," in Emma England and William John Lyons (eds.), *Reception History and Biblical Studies: Theory and Practice*, Scriptural Traces 6/Library of Hebrew Bible 615 (London: Bloomsbury, 2015), pp. 45–60.

"An immodest proposal for biblical studies," *Relegere* 12, no. 1 (2012), 153–177.

Crouch, James E., *The Origin and Intention of the Colossian Haustafel*, FRLANT 109 (Göttingen: Vandenhoeck & Ruprecht, 1972).

Crouzel, Henri, "Le contexte spirituel de l'exégèse dite spirituelle," in G. Dorival and A. Le Boulluec (eds.), *Origeniana Sexta*, BETL 118 (Leuven: Peeters, 1995), pp. 333–342.

"Faut-il voir trois personnages en Grégoire le Thaumaturge?" *Gregorianum* 60 (1979), 289–300.

Origen, trans. A. S. Worrall (Edinburgh: T. & T. Clark, 1989).

Origène et la "connaissance mystique," Museum Lessianum section théologique 56 (Paris: Desclée de Brouwer, 1961).

Cuff, Simon Lloyd, "Paul's 'new moment': the reception of Paul in Baidou, Eagleton, and Žižik," unpublished D.Phil. thesis, University of Oxford (2014).

Cullmann, Oscar, *Salvation in History* (London: SCM, 1967).

Cummings, Brian, *The Literary Culture of the Reformation: Grammar and Grace* (New York: Oxford University Press, 2002).

Dale, Alfred W. W., *The Synod of Elvira and Christian Life in the Fourth Century: A Historical Essay* (London: Macmillan, 1882).

Daniélou, Jean, *Gospel Message and Hellenistic Culture*, trans. John A. Baker, A History of Early Christian Doctrine Before the Council of Nicaea 2 (London: Darton, Longman & Todd, 1973).

Origen, trans. Walter Mitchell (London: Sheed and Ward, 1955).

Daniélou, Jean, and Régine du Charlat, *La catéchèse aux premiers siècles*, École de la foi (Paris: Fayard-Mame, 1968).

Dassmann, Ernst, *Der Stachel im Fleisch. Paulus in der frühchristlichen Literatur bis Irenäus* (Münster: Aschendorff, 1979).

Davies, Stevan L., *The Revolt of the Widows: The Social World of the Apocryphal Acts* (Carbondale, IL: Southern Illinois University Press; London: Feffer & Simons, 1980).

Davis, Stephen J., *The Cult of Saint Thecla: A Tradition of Women's Piety in Late Antiquity*, Oxford Early Christian Studies (Oxford: Oxford University Press, 2001).

Dechow, Jon F., "Pseudo-Jerome's anti-Origenist anathemas (*ACO* 1:5:4–5)," in Sylwia Kaczmarek and Henryk Pietras (eds.), *Origeniana Decima: Origen as Writer*, BETL 244 (Leuven: Peeters, 2011), pp. 955–965.

Dekkers, E., *Tertullianus en de geschiedenis der liturgie,* Catholica VI-2 (Brussels: Kinkhoren; Desclée de Brouwer, 1947).

Demura, Miyako, "Origen and the exegetical tradition of the Sarah–Hagar motif in Alexandria," *Studia Patristica* 56, no. 4 (2013), 73–81.

Derrida, Jacques, "Economimesis," *Diacritics* 11, no. 2 (1981), 2–25.

Of Grammatology, trans. Gayatri Chakravorty Spivak (Baltimore: Johns Hopkins University Press, 1998).

Despotis, Athanasios, *Die "New Perspective on Paul" und die griechisch-orthodoxe Paulusinterpretation*, Veröffentlichungen des Instituts für Orthodoxe Theologie 11 (St. Ottilien: EOS, 2014).

Dinkler, Erich, *Signum Crucis. Aufsätze zum Neuen Testament und zur Christlichen Archäologie* (Tübingen: Mohr Siebeck, 1967).

Dively Lauro, Elizabeth Ann, *The Soul and Spirit of Scripture within Origen's Exegesis* (Boston: Brill, 2005).

Dobschütz, Ernst von, "Der Roman in der altchristlichen Literatur," *Deutsche Rundschau* 111 (1902), 87–106.

Dodd, C. H., *The Apostolic Preaching and Its Developments: Three Lectures with an Appendix on Eschatology and History.* (London: Hodder and Stoughton, 1936).

"The Primitive Chatechism and the Sayings of Jesus," in A. J. B. Higgins (ed.), *New Testament Essays: Studies in Memory of Thomas Walter Manson* (Manchester: Manchester University Press, 1959), pp. 11–29.

Donfried, Karl Paul (ed.), *The Romans Debate*, rev. and expanded edn (Edinburgh: T. & T. Clark, 1991).

Donovan, Mary Ann, *One Right Reading? A Guide to Irenaeus* (Collegeville, MN: Liturgical Press, 1997).

Draper, Jonathan A., "Vice catalogues as oral-mnemonic cues: a comparative study of the two ways tradition in the *Didache* and parallels from the perspective of oral tradition," in Tom Thatcher (ed.), *Jesus, the Voice, and the Text: Beyond The Oral and the Written Gospel* (Waco, TX: Baylor University Press, 2008), pp. 111–133.

Drijvers, Jan Willem, *Cyril of Jerusalem: Bishop and City*, VC Sup 72 (Leiden and Boston: Brill, 2004).

Droge, Arthur J., *Homer or Moses? Early Christian Interpretations of the History of Culture*, HUT 26 (Tübingen: Mohr Siebeck, 1989).

Dujarier, Michel, *A History of the Catechumenate: The First Six Centuries*, trans. Edward J. Haasl (New York: Sadlier, 1979).

Dunn, David J., "'Her that is no bride': St. Thecla and the relationship between sex, gender, and office," *St Vladimir's Theological Quarterly* 53, no. 4 (2010), 37–68.

Dunn, Geoffrey D., *Tertullian*, The Early Church Fathers (London and New York: Routledge, 2004).

Dunn, James D. G., "The incident at Antioch (Gal. 2:11–18)," *Journal for the Study of the New Testament* 18 (1983), 3–57.

   Neither Jew nor Greek: A Contested Identity, Christianity in the Making 3, (Grand Rapids: Eerdmans, 2015).

   Romans, 2 vols., WBC 38ab (Waco, TX: Word Books, 1988).

   The Theology of Paul the Apostle (Grand Rapids: Eerdmans, 1998).

   Unity and Diversity in the New Testament: An Inquiry into the Character of Earliest Christianity (London: SCM, 1977).

Dunn, Peter W., "The *Acts of Paul* and the Pauline legacy in the second century," unpublished Ph.D. thesis, University of Cambridge (1996).

Dutch, Robert S., *The Educated Elite in 1 Corinthians: Education and Community Conflict in Graeco-Roman Context*, JSNT Sup 271 (London: T. & T. Clark, 2005).

Eastman, David L., *Paul the Martyr: The Cult of the Apostle in the Latin West* (Atlanta: SBL, 2011).

Eco, Umberto, *The Limits of Interpretation* (Bloomington: Indiana University Press, 1997).

Edsall, Benjamin A., "Clement and the catechumenate in the late second century," in Lewis O. Ayres and Clifton Ward (eds.), *Rise of the Christian Intellectual,* AZK (Berlin: De Gruyter, forthcoming).

   "Hermogenes the smith and narrative characterization in *The Acts of Paul*: a note on the reception of 2 Timothy," *New Testament Studies* 64, no. 1 (2018), 108–121.

   "Kerygma, catechesis and other things we used to find: twentieth-century research on early Christian teaching since Alfred Seeberg (1903)," *Currents in Biblical Research* 10, no. 3 (2012), 410–441.

   "(Not) baptizing Thecla: early interpretive efforts on 1 Cor 1:17," *Vigiliae Christianae* 71, no. 3 (2017), 235–260.

   Paul's Witness to Formative Early Christian Instruction, WUNT II/365 (Tübingen: Mohr Siebeck, 2014).

   "Review: JAMES D. G. DUNN. *Neither Jew nor Greek: A Contested Identity*. Volume 3 of *Christianity in the Making* (Grand Rapids; Cambridge: William B. Eerdmans Publishing Company, 2015) Pp. xiv+946," *Australian Biblical Review* 64 (2016), unpaginated.

Edwards, Mark, "Origen's Platonism: questions and caveats," *Zeitschrift für Antikes Christentum* 12, no. 1 (2008), 20–38.

Ekenberg, Anders, "Initiation in the *Apostolic Tradition*," in David Hellholm, Tor Vegge, Øyvind Norderval, and Christer Hellholm (eds.), *Ablution, Initiation, and Baptism: Late Antiquity, Early Judaism, and Early Christianity*, 3 vols., BZNW 176 (Berlin: De Gruyter, 2011), vol. II, pp. 1011–1050.

Elliott, Neil, *Liberating Paul: The Justice of God and the Politics of the Apostle* (Minneapolis: Fortress Press, 2006).

Elmer, Ian J., *Paul, Jerusalem and the Judaisers: The Galatian Crisis in Its Broadest Historical Context*, WUNT II/258 (Tübingen: Mohr Siebeck, 2009).

Engberg-Pedersen, Troels, *Paul and the Stoics* (Edinburgh: T. & T. Clark, 2000).

England, Emma, and William John Lyons (eds.), *Reception History and Biblical Studies: Theory and Practice*, Library of Hebrew Bible 615/Scriptural Traces 6 (London: Bloomsbury, 2015).

Epp, Eldon Jay, "The multivalence of the term "original text" in New Testament textual criticism," *Harvard Theological Review* 92, no. 3 (1999), 245–281.

Esch-Wermeling, Elisabeth, *Thekla–Paulusschülerin wider Willen? Strategien der Leserlenkung in den Theklaakten*, NAbh 53 (Münster: Aschendorff, 2008).

Evans, Robert, *Reception History, Tradition and Biblical Interpretation: Gadamer and Jauss in Current Practice*, vol. IV, LNTS 510 (London: Bloomsbury, 2014).

Faye, Eugène de, *Clément d'Alexandrie: Étude sur les rapports du christianisme et de la philosophie grecque au IIe siècle*, 2nd edn (Paris: Minerva, 1906).

Fee, Gordon D., *The First Epistle to the Corinthians*, NICNT (Grand Rapids: Eerdmans, 1987).

Felski, Rita, *The Limits of Critique* (Chicago: University of Chicago Press, 2015).

Ferguson, Everett, *Baptism in the Early Church: History, Theology, and Liturgy in the First Five Centuries* (Grand Rapids: Eerdmans, 2009).

Ferguson, John, *Clement of Alexandria*, YWAS 289 (New York: Twayne Publishers, 1974).

Finn, Thomas M., *The Liturgy of Baptism in the Baptismal Instructions of St. John Chrysostom*, The Catholic University of America Studies in Christian Antiquity 15 (Washington, D. C.: Catholic University of America Press, 1967).

Finsterbusch, Karin, *Die Thora als Lebensweisung für Heidenchristen. Studien zur Bedeutung der Thora für die paulinische Ethik*, SUNT 20 (Göttingen: Vandenhoeck & Ruprecht, 1996).

Fiore, Benjamin, "'Covert allusion' in 1 Corinthians 1–4," *Catholic Biblical Quarterly* 47, no. 1 (1985), 85–102.

Fitzmyer, Joseph A., *First Corinthians: A New Translation with Introduction and Commentary*, AB 32 (London: Yale University Press, 2008).

Fouskas, Konstantinos M., Γρηγόριος ὁ Νεοκαισαρείας Ἐπίσκοπος ὁ Θαυματυργός *(Ca. 211/3–270/5)* (Athens: University of Athens Press, 1969).

Fredricksen, Paula, "Judaizing the nations: the ritual demands of Paul's gospel," *New Testament Studies* 56, no. 2 (2010), 232–252.

Frey, Jörg, "Ämter," in Friedrich Wilhelm Horn (ed.), *Paulus Handbuch* (Tübingen: Mohr Siebeck, 2013), pp. 408–412.

Fürst, Alfons, "Origen: exegesis and philosophy in early Christian Alexandria," in Josef Lössl and J. W. Watt (eds.), *Interpreting the Bible and Aristotle in Late Antiquity: The Alexandrian Commentary Tradition Between Rome and Baghdad* (Farnham: Ashgate, 2011), pp. 13–32.

  Origenes. Grieche und Christ in römischer Zeit (Stuttgart: Anton Hiersemann, 2017).

"Origenes und Ephräm über Paulus' Konflikt mit Petrus (Gal. 2, 11–14)," in *Von Origenes und Hieronymus zu Augustinus. Studien zur antiken Theologiegeschichte,* AZK (Berlin: De Gruyter, 2011), pp. 195–208.

Gadamer, Hans-Georg, *Truth and Method,* 2nd rev. edn, trans. William Glen-Doepel, Joel Weinscheimer, and Donald G. Marshall (New York: Continuum, 2002). *Wahrheit und Methode. Grundzüge einer philosophischen Hermeneutik,* 7th edn (Tübingen: Mohr, 2010).

Gavrilyuk, Paul L., *Histoire du catéchuménat dans l'Église ancienne,* trans. Françoise Lhoest, Nina Mojaïsky, and Anne-Marie Gueit, Initiations aux pères de l'Église (Paris: Cerf, 2007).

Gelardini, Gabriella, and Harold W Attridge (eds.), *Hebrews in Contexts,* AJEC 91 (Leiden: Brill, 2016).

Gemeinhardt, Peter, "Glaube, Bildung, Theologie: ein Spannungsfeld im frühchristlichen Alexandria," in Tobias Georges, Felix Albrecht, and Reinhard Feldmeier (eds.), *Alexandria,* COMES 1 (Tübingen: Mohr Siebeck, 2013), pp. 445–473.

"In search of Christian paideia: education and conversion in early Christian biography," *Zeitschrift für Antikes Christentum* 16, no. 1 (2012), 88–98.

Georges, Tobias, "Justin's school in Rome: reflections on early Christian 'schools'," *Zeitschrift für Antikes Christentum* 16, no. 1 (2012), 75–87.

Georgi, Dieter, *The Opponents of Paul in Second Corinthians* (Edinburgh: T. & T. Clark, 1987).

Glad, Clarence E., *Paul and Philodemus: Adaptability in Epicurean and Early Christian Psychagogy,* NovT Sup 81 (Leiden: Brill, 1995).

Godin, André, *Érasme. Lecteur d'Origène* (Geneva: Librairie Droz, 1982).

Goulder, Michael D., *A Tale of Two Missions* (London: SCM, 1994).

Graham, Susan L., "Structure and purpose of Irenaeus' *Epideixis,*" *Studia Patristica* 36 (2001), 210–221.

Gramaglia, Pier Angelo, "Battesimo," in Adele Monaci Castagno (ed.), *Origene dizionario. La cultura, il pensiero, le opere* (Rome: Città Nuova, 2000), pp. 45–48.

Grindheim, Sigurd, "Wisdom for the perfect: Paul's challenge to the Corinthian church (1 Corinthians 2:6–16)," *Journal of Biblical Literature* 121, no. 4 (2002), 689–709.

Grundeken, Mark, "Baptism and Μετάνοια in the *Shepherd of Hermas,*" in Mark Grundeken and Joseph Verheyden (eds.), *Early Christian Communities between Ideal and Reality,* WUNT 1/342 (Tübingen: Mohr Siebeck, 2015), pp. 127–142.

Güttgemanns, Erhardt, *Candid Questions Concerning Gospel Form Criticism: A Methodological Sketch of the Fundamental Problematics of Form and Redaction Criticism,* trans. William G. Doty, PTMS 26 (Pittsburgh: Pickwick Press, 1979).

Habermas, Jurgen, "Zu Gadamers 'Wahrheit und Methode.'" in Karl-Otto Apel (ed.), *Hermeneutik und Ideologiekritik* (Frankfurt: Suhrkamp, 1971), pp. 45–56.

Hadot, Pierre, *Philosophy as a Way of Life: Spiritual Exercises from Socrates to Foucault,* ed. Arnold I. Davidson (Malden, MA: Blackwell, 1995).

Häfner, Gerd, "Die Gegner in den Pastoralbriefen und die Paulusakten," *Zeitschrift für die Neutestamentliche Wissenschaft* 92, no. 1 (2001), 64–77.

Hällström, Gunnar, *Fides Simpliciorum According to Origen of Alexandria*, Commentationes Humanarum Litterarum 76 (Ekenäs: Societas Scientarium Fennica, 1984).

"More than initiation? Baptism according to Origen of Alexandria," in David Hellholm, Tor Vegge, Øyvind Norderval, and Christer Hellholm (eds.), *Ablution, Initiation, and Baptism: Late Antiquity, Early Judaism, and Early Christianity*, 3 vols., BZNW 176 (Berlin: De Gruyter, 2011), vol. II, pp. 989–1009.

Hanson, R. P. C., *Allegory and Event: A Study of the Sources and Significance of Origen's Interpretation of Scripture* (Louisville: Westminster John Knox, 2002).

Harl, Marguerite, *Origène et la fonction révélatrice du verbe incarné*, Patristica Sorbonensia 2 (Paris: Editions du Seuil, 1958).

Harmless, William, *Augustine and the Catechumenate* (Collegeville, MN: Liturgical Press, 1995).

Harnack, Adolf, *History of Dogma*, vol. I, trans. Neil Buchanan (Boston: Roberts Brothers, 1895).

Harris, Horton, *The Tübingen School* (Oxford: Clarendon, 1975).

Havrda, Matyáš, "Galenus Christianus? The doctrine of demonstration in *Stromata* VIII and the question of its source," *Vigiliae Christianae* 65, no. 3 (2011), 343–375.

"Intellectual independence in Christian and medical discourse of the 2nd–3rd centuries," In Lewis O. Ayres and Clifton Ward (eds.), *Rise of the Christian Intellectual*, AZK (Berlin: De Gruyter, forthcoming).

"Review: Andrew C. Itter. *Esoteric Teaching in the Stromateis of Clement of Alexandria* (Supplements to *Vigiliae Christianae*, 97), Brill, Leiden – Boston 2009, pp. xix+233," *Adamantius* 18 (2012), 573–579.

The So-Called Eighth Stromateus by Clement of Alexandria: Early Christian Reception of Greek Scientific Methodology, Philosophia Antiqua. (Leiden: Brill, 2016).

"Some observations on Clement of Alexandria, *Stromata*, book five," *Vigiliae Christianae* 64, no. 1 (2010), 1–30.

Heimola, Minna, *Christian Identity in the Gospel of Philip*, Publications of the Finnish Exegetical Society 102 (Helsinki: The Finnish Exegetical Society, 2011).

Heine, Ronald E., *Origen: Scholarship in the Service of the Church*, Christian Theology in Context (New York: Oxford University Press, 2010).

Heinrici, C. F. Georg, *Der erste Brief an die Korinther*, 8th edn, KEK 5 (Göttingen: Vandenhoeck und Ruprecht, 1896).

Heiser, Andreas, *Paulusinszenierung des Johannes Chrysostomus. Epitheta und ihre Vorgeschichte*, STAC 70 (Tübingen: Mohr Siebeck, 2012).

Heither, Theresia, "Glaube in der Theologie des Origenes," *Erbe und Auftrag* 67 (1991), 255–265.

Predigten des Origenes zum Buch Exodus. Lateinisch–deutsch (Münster: Aschendorff, 2008).

Translatio religionis. Die Paulusdeutung des Origenes in seinem Kommentar zum Römerbrief, BBK 16 (Berlin: De Gruyter, 1990).

Helfferich, Tryntje, *Martin Luther: On the Freedom of a Christian, with Related Texts* (Indianapolis: Hackett, 2013).

Herdt, Jennifer A., *Putting on Virtue: The Legacy of the Splendid Vices* (Chicago: University of Chicago Press, 2008).

Héring, Jean, *La première épitre de Saint Paul aux Corinthiens*, 2nd rev. edn (Neuchâtel: Delaschaux & Niestlé, 1959).

Hess, Hamilton, *The Early Development of Canon Law and the Council of Serdica*, OECS (Oxford: Oxford University Press, 2002).

Hilhorst, A., "Tertullian on the Acts of Paul," in Jan N. Bremmer (ed.), *The Apocryphal Acts of Paul and Thecla*, Studies on the Apocryphal Acts of the Apostles (Kampen: Kok Pharos, 1996), pp. 150–163.

Hodgson, Peter C., *The Formation of Historical Theology: A Study of Ferdinand Christian Baur* (New York: Harper & Row, 1966).

Hoek, Annewies van den, *Clement of Alexandria and His Use of Philo in the Stromateis: An Early Christian Reshaping of a Jewish Model*, VC Sup 3 (Leiden: Brill, 1988).

"The 'catechetical' school of early Christian Alexandria and its Philonic heritage," *Harvard Theological Review* 90, no. 1 (1997), 59–87.

Hoffmann, Manfred, *Rhetoric and Theology: The Hermeneutic of Erasmus* (Toronto: University of Toronto Press, 1994).

Holtzmann, Heinrich Julius, "Die Katechese der alten Kirche," in *Theologische Abhandlungen. Carl von Weizsäcker zu seinem siebzigsten Geburtstag gewidmet* (Freiburg: Mohr, 1892), pp. 58–110.

Hooker, Morna D., "Another look at πίστις Χριστοῦ," *Scottish Journal of Theology* 69, no. 1 (2016), 46–62.

Horrell, David G., *An Introduction to the Study of Paul*, 2nd edn (London and New York: T. & T. Clark, 2006).

Horsley, Richard A., *1 Corinthians*, ANTC (Nashville: Abingdon Press, 1998).

Itter, Andrew C., *Esoteric Teaching the the Stromateis of Clement of Alexandria*, VC Sup 97 (Leiden: Brill, 2009).

Jackson, E. P., *The Holy Spirit in the Catechesis and Mystagogy of Cyril of Jerusalem, Ambrose, and John Chrysostom* (New Haven: Yale University Press, 1987).

Jacobsen, Anders-Christian, *Christ – the Teacher of Salvation: A Study on Origen's Christology and Soteriology*, Adamantiana 6 (Münster: Aschendorff, 2015).

"Conversion to Christian philosophy: the case of Origen's school in Caesarea," *Zeitschrift für Antikes Christentum* 16, no. 1 (2012), 145–157.

Jakab, Attila, "Alexandrie et sa communauté chrétienne à l'époque d'Origène," 93–104 in *Origeniana Octava*. Edited by Lorenzo Perrone. BETL 164. Leuven: Peeters, 2003.

Jauss, Hans Robert, *Literaturgeschichte als Provokation* (Frankfurt-am-Main: Suhrkamp, 1970).

"Literary history as a challenge to literary theory," in *Toward an Aesthetic of Reception History*, trans. Timothy Bahti, Theory and History of Literature 2 (Minneapolis: University of Minnesota Press, 1982), pp. 3–45.

Question and Answer: Forms of Dialogic Understanding, trans. Michael Hays, Theory and History of Literature 68 (Minneapolis: University of Minnesota Press, 1989).

Jeanrond, Werner G., "After hermeneutics: the relationship between theology and biblical studies," in Francis Watson (ed.), *The Open Text: New Directions for Biblical Studies?* (London: SCM, 1993), pp. 85–102.

Jefford, Clayton N., "Social locators as a bridge between the *Didache* and Matthew," in Andrew F. Gregory and Christopher M. Tuckett (eds.), *Trajectories through the New Testament and the Apostolic Fathers* (Oxford: Oxford University Press, 2007), pp. 245–264.

Jensen, Anne, *Thekla, die Apostolin. Ein apokrypher Text neu entdeckt*, Kaiser Taschenbücher 172 (Gütersloh: Chr. Kaiser, 1999).

Jensen, Robin M., *Living Water: Images, Symbols and Settings of Early Christian Baptism*, VC Sup 105 (Leiden: Brill, 2011).

Jewett, Robert, *Romans: A Commentary*, ed. Eldon Jay Epp, Hermeneia (Minneapolis: Fortress, 2007).

Johnson, Aaron P., *Eusebius*, Understanding Classics (London: I. B. Taurus, 2014).

Johnson, Maxwell E., *The Rites of Christian Initiation: Their Evolution and Interpretation*, rev. and expanded edn (Collegeville, MN: Liturgical Press, 2007).

Kaczmarek, Sylwia, "L'*Exemplum* di Paolo nel *Commento alla lettera ai Romani*," in Sylwia Kaczmarek and Henryk Pietras (eds.), *Origeniana Decima: Origen as Writer*, BETL 244 (Leuven: Peeters, 2011), pp. 445–456.

Karavites, Peter, *Evil, Freedom, and the Road to Perfection in Clement of Alexandria*, VC Sup 43. (Leiden: Brill, 1998).

Käsemann, Ernst, "Aspekte der Kirche," in *Kirchliche Konflicte*, vol. 1 (Göttingen: Vandenhoeck & Ruprecht, 1982), pp. 7–36.

"The beginning of Christian theology," in *New Testament Questions of Today*, trans. W. J. Montague (London: SCM Press, 1969), pp. 82–107.

"Einführung," in *Ausgewählte Werke in Einzelausgaben*, vol. 1: *Historisch-kritische Untersuchungen zum Neuen Testament*, ed. Klaus Scholder (Stuttgart: Friedrich Frommann, 1963), pp. viii–xxv.

"The theological problem presented by the motif of the body of Christ," in *Perspectives on Paul*, trans. Margaret Kohl (London: SCM, 1971), pp. 102–121.

"Unity and diversity in New Testament ecclesiology," *Novum Testamentum* 6, no. 4 (1963), 290–297.

Kelly, J. N. D., *Golden Mouth: The Story of John Chrysostom – Ascetic, Preacher, Bishop* (Ithaca: Cornell University Press, 1995).

Kirk, Alexander N., *The Departure of an Apostle: Paul's Death Anticipated and Remembered*, WUNT II/406 (Tübingen: Mohr Siebeck, 2015).

Kitzler, Petr, "*Passio Perpetuae* and *Acta Perpetuae*: between tradition and innovation," *Listy filologické* 130, no. 1–2 (2007), 1–19.

Kloppenborg, John S., "*Didache* 1.1–6.1, James, Matthew, and the Torah," in Andrew F. Gregory and Christopher M. Tuckett (eds.), *Trajectories through the New Testament and the Apostolic Fathers* (Oxford: Oxford University Press, 2007), pp. 193–221.

"Pneumatic democracy and the conflict in *1 Clement*," in Mark Grundeken and Joseph Verheyden (eds.), *Early Christian Communities Between Ideal and Reality,* WUNT I/342 (Tübingen: Mohr Siebeck, 2015), pp. 61–81.

Knauber, Adolf, "Das Anliegen der Schule des Origenes zu Cäsarea," *Münchener Theologische Zeitschrift* 19 (1968), 182–203.

"Ein frühchristliches Handbuch katechumenaler Glaubensinitiation: der Paidagogos des Clemens von Alexandrien," *Münchener Theologische Zeitschrift* 23, no. 4 (1972), 318–320.

Knupp, Josef, *Das Mystagogieverständnis des Johannes Chrysostomus,* ed. Anton Bodem and Alois M. Kothgasser, Benediktbeurer Studien 4 (Munich: Don Bosco, 1995).

Kohlgraf, Peter, *Die Ekklesiologie des Epheserbriefes in der Auslegung durch Johannes Chrysostomus. Eine Untersuchung zur Wirkungsgeschichte paulinischer Theologie,* Hereditas 19 (Bonn: Borengässer, 2001).

Kolb, Robert, Irene Dingel, and Lubomir Batka (eds.), *The Oxford Handbook of Martin Luther's Theology* (Oxford: Oxford University Press, 2014).

Konradt, Matthias, "Die korinthische Weisheit und das Wort vom Kreuz: Erwägungen zur korinthischen Problemkonstellation und paulinischen Intention in 1 Kor 1–4," *Zeitschrift für die Neutestamentliche Wissenschaft* 94 (2003), 181–214.

Kovacs, Judith L., "Divine pedagogy and the Gnostic teacher according to Clement of Alexandria," *Journal of Early Christian Studies* 9, no. 1 (2001), 3–25.

"Reading the 'divinely inspired' Paul: Clement of Alexandria in conversation with 'heterodox' Christians, simple believers, and Greek philosophers," in Veronika Cernuskova, Judith L. Kovacs, and Jana Plátová (eds.), *Clement's Biblical Exegesis: Proceedings of the Second Colloquium on Clement of Alexandria (Olomouc, May 29–31, 2014),* VC Sup 139. (Leiden: Brill, 2017), pp. 325–343.

Kraemer, Ross, "The conversion of women to ascetic forms of Christianity," *Signs* 6, no. 2 (1980), 298–307.

Kümmel, Werner Georg, *Das Neue Testament. Geschichte der Erforschung seiner Probleme,* 2nd reworked and expanded edn, Orbis Academicis (Freiburg: Karl Alber, 1970).

Lai, Pak-Wah. "John Chrysostom and the hermeneutics of exemplar portraits," unpublished Ph.D. thesis, Durham University (2010).

Lampe, G. W. H., *A Patristic Greek Lexicon* (Oxford: Clarendon Press, 1961).

Lampe, Peter, *Christians at Rome in the First Two Centuries: From Paul to Valentinus,* ed. Marshall D. Johnson, trans. Michael Steinhauser (London: Continuum, 2003).

Landmesser, Christof, "Ferdinand Christian Baur als Paulusinterpret: die Geschichte, das Absolute und die Freiheit," in Martin Bauspiess, Christof Landmesser, and David Lincicum (eds.), *Ferdinand Christian Baur und die Geschichte des frühen Christentums,* WUNT I/333 (Tübingen: Mohr Siebeck, 2014), pp. 161–194.

Lang, T. J., *Mystery and the Making of a Christian Historical Consciousness: From Paul to the Second Century,* BZNW 219 (Berlin: De Gruyter, 2015).

"We speak in a mystery: neglected Greek evidence for the syntax and sense of 1 Corinthians 2:7," *Catholic Biblical Quarterly* 78, no. 1 (2016), 68–89.

Lang, T. J., and Matthew R. Crawford. "The origins of Pauline theology: paratexts and Priscillian of Avila's *Canons on the Letters of the Apostle Paul*," *New Testament Studies* 63, no. 1 (2017), 125–145.

LaValle, Dawn, "Divine breastfeeding: milk, blood, and *pneuma* in Clement of Alexandria's *Paedagogus*," *Journal of Late Antiquity* 8, no. 2 (2015), 325.

Le Boulluec, Alain, "Aux origines, encore, de l'"école" d'Alexandrie," in *Alexandrie antique et chrétienne. Clément et Origène*, 2nd edn (Paris: Institut d'Études Augustiniennes, 2012), pp. 27–57.

"Clément d'Alexandrie," in Bernard Pouderon (ed.), *Histoire de la littérature grecque chrétienne des origines à 451*, vol. III: *De Clément d'Alexandrie à Eusèbe de Césarée* (Paris: Les Belles Lettres, 2017), pp. 57–169.

La notion d'hérésie dans la littérature grecque, IIe–IIIe siècles, 2 vols. (Paris: Etudes augustiniennes, 1985).

Ledegang, F., *Mysterium Ecclesiae: Images of the Church and Its Members in Origen*, BETL 156 (Leuven: Peeters, 2001).

Lee, Max J., "Ancient mentors and moral progress according to Galen and Paul," in Rebekah Ecklund and Jay Phelan (eds.), *Doing Theology for the Church: Essays in Honor of Klyne R. Snodgrass* (Eugene: Wipf & Stock, 2014), pp. 55–70.

Lettieri, Gaetano, "Progresso," in Adele Monaci Castagno (ed.), *Origene dizionario. La cultura, il pensiero, le opere* (Rome: Città Nuova, 2000), pp. 379–392.

Lies, L., "Die 'Gottes würdige' Schriftauslegung nach Origenes," in G. Dorival and A. Le Boulluec (eds.), *Origeniana Sexta*, BETL 118 (Leuven: Peeters, 1995), pp. 365–372.

Lilla, S. R. C., *Clement of Alexandria: A Study in Christian Platonism and Gnosticism* (Oxford: Oxford University Press, 1971).

"Review: *Esoteric Teaching in the Stromateis of Clement of Alexandria*," *Augustinianum* 50, no. 2 (2010), 577–591.

Lim, Timothy H., "'Not in persuasive words of wisdom, but in the demonstration of the spirit and power'," *Novum Testamentum* 29, no. 2 (1987), 137–149.

Lincicum, David, "Ferdinand Christian Baur and biblical theology," *Annali di Storia dell'Esegesi* 30, no. 1 (2013), 79–92.

"Ferdinand Christian Baur and the theological task of New Testament introduction," in Martin Bauspiess, Christof Landmesser, and David Lincicum (eds.), *Ferdinand Christian Baur und die Geschichte des frühen Christentums*, WUNT I/333 (Tübingen: Mohr Siebeck, 2014), pp. 91–105.

"Martin Luther in modern New Testament scholarship," *Oxford Research Encyclopedia of Religion* (2017), http://religion.oxfordre.com.

Lindemann, Andreas, *Paulus im ältesten Christentum. Das Bild des Apostels und die Rezeption der paulinischen Theologie in der frühchristlichen Literatur bis Marcion*, BHT 58 (Tübingen: Mohr Siebeck, 1979).

Lipsett, B. Diane, *Desiring Conversion: Hermas, Thecla, Aseneth* (New York: Oxford University Press, 2011).

Litfin, A. Duane, *St. Paul's Theology of Proclamation: 1 Corinthians 1–4 and Greco-Roman Rhetoric*, SNTSMS 79 (Cambridge: Cambridge University Press, 1994).

Lochbrunner, Manfred, *Über das Priestertum. Historische und systematische Untersuchung zum Priesterbild des Johannes Chrysostomus*, Hereditas: Studien zur Alten Kirchengeschichte 5 (Bonn: Borengässer, 1993).

Löhr, Winrich Alfried, *Basilides und seine Schule. Eine Studie zur Theologie- und Kirchengeschichte des zweiten Jahrhunderts*, WUNT 83 (Tübingen: Mohr Siebeck, 1996).

Lubac, Henri de, *History and Spirit: The Understanding of Scripture According to Origen* (San Francisco: Ignatius Press, 2007).

Lüdemann, Gerd, *Opposition to Paul in Jewish Christianity*, trans. M. Eugene Boring (Minneapolis: Fortress, 1989).

Ludlow, Morwenna, "Origen as preacher and teacher: a comparison of exegetical methods in his writings on Genesis and the Song of Songs," in William John Lyons and Isabella Sandwell (eds.), *Delivering the Word: Preaching and Exegesis in the Western Christian Tradition* (Sheffield: Equinox, 2012), pp. 45–61.

Lundhaug, Hugo, "Begotten, not made, to arise in this flesh: the post-Nicene soteriology of the *Gospel of Philip*," in Eduard Iricinschi, Lance Jenott, Nicola Denzey Lewis and Philippa Townsend (eds.), *Beyond the Gnostic Gospels: Studies Building on the Work of Elaine Pagels*, STAC 82 (Tübingen: Mohr Siebeck, 2013), pp. 235–271.

"Evidence of 'Valentinian' ritual practice? The *Liturgical Fragments* of Nag Hammadi Codex XI (NHC XI,2a–e)," in Kevin Corrigan and Tuomas Rasimus (eds.), *Gnosticism, Platonism and the Late Ancient World*, NHMS 82. (Leiden: Brill, 2013), pp. 225–243.

Images of Rebirth: Cognitive Poetics and Transformational Soteriology in the Gospel of Philip and the Exegesis on the Soul, NHMS 73 (Leiden: Brill, 2010).

Luz, Ulrich, *Theologische Hermeneutik des Neuen Testaments* (Neukirchen-Vluyn: Neukirchener, 2014).

Lyons, William John, "Hope for a troubled discipline? Contributions to New Testament Studies from reception history," *Journal for the Study of the New Testament* 33, no. 2 (2010), 207–220.

MacDonald, Dennis R., *The Legend and the Apostle: The Battle for Paul in Story and Canon* (Philadelphia: Westminister, 1983).

Malherbe, Abraham J., *Paul and the Thessalonians: The Philosophic Tradition of Pastoral Care* (Philadelphia: Fortress, 1987).

Marguerat, Daniel, "Les 'Actes de Paul': une relecture des Actes canoniques," in *La première histoire du christianisme. Les Actes des apôtres*, LD 180 (Paris: Cerf; Genève: Labor et Fides, 1999), pp. 369–391.

"Paul after Paul: a (hi)story of reception," in *Paul in Acts and Paul in His Letters*, WUNT 310 (Tübingen: Mohr Siebeck, 2013), pp. 1–21.

"Paul après Paul: une histoire de réception," *New Testament Studies* 54, no. 3 (2008), 317–337.

Marjanen, Antti, "A salvific act of transformation or a symbol of defilement? Baptism in the *Valentinian Liturgical Readings* (NHC XI,2) and in the

Testimony of Truth (NHC IX,3)," in Kevin Corrigan and Tuomas Rasimus (eds.), *Gnosticism, Platonism and the Late Ancient World*, NHMS 82 (Leiden: Brill, 2013), pp. 245–259.

Markschies, Christoph, *Christian Theology and Its Institutions in the Early Roman Empire: Prolegomena to a History of Early Christian Theology*, trans. Wayne Coppins, BMSEC (Waco, TX: Baylor University Press, 2015).

"'…für die Gemeinde im Grossen und Ganzen nicht geeignet…'? Erwägungen zu Absicht und Wirkung des Predigten des Origenes," in *Origenes und sein Erbe: Gesammelte Studien*, TU 160 (Berlin: De Gruyter, 2007), pp. 35–62.

Kaiserzeitliche christliche Theologie und ihre Institutionen. Prolegomena zu einer Geschichte der antiken christlichen Theologie (Tübingen: Mohr Siebeck, 2007).

"Origenes: Leben – Werk – Theologie – Wirking," in *Origenes und sein Erbe. Gesammelte Studien*, TU 160 (Berlin: De Gruyter, 2007), pp. 1–13.

"Origenes und die Kommentierung des paulinischen Römerbriefs: einige Bermerkingen zur Rezeption von antiken Kommentartechniken im Christentum des dritten Jahrhunderts und ihrer Vorgeschichte," in *Origenes und sein Erbe. Gesammelte Studien*, TU 160 (Berlin: De Gruyter, 2007), pp. 63–90.

Origenes und sein Erbe. Gesammelte Studien, TU 160 (Berlin: De Gruyter, 2007).

"Origenes und Paulus: das Beispiel der Anthropologie," in Jörg Frey, Benjamin Schliesser, and Veronika Niederhofer (eds.), *Der Philipperbrief des Paulus in der hellenistisch-römischen Welt*, WUNT I/353 (Tübingen: Mohr Siebeck, 2015), pp. 349–372.

"Paul the Apostle," in John Anthony McGuckin (ed.), *The Westminster Handbook to Origen*, (Louisville: Westminster John Knox, 2004), pp. 167–169.

Valentinus Gnosticus? Untersuchungen zur valentinianischen Gnosis mit einem Kommentar zu den Fragmenten Valentins, WUNT 65 (Tübingen: Mohr Siebeck, 1992).

"Wer schrieb die sogenannte *Traditio apostolica*? Neue Beobachtungen und Hypothesen zu einer kaum lösbaren Frage aus der altkirchlichen Literaturgeschichte," in Wolfram Kinzig, Christoph Markschies, and Markus Vinzent (eds.), *Tauffragen und Bekenntnis. Studien zur sogenannten "Traditio apostolica," zu den "Interrogationes de fide" und zum "Römischen Glaubensbekenntnis,"* AKG 74 (Berlin and New York: De Gruyter, 1998), pp. 1–74.

Martens, Peter W., *Origen and Scripture: The Contours of the Exegetical Life*, Oxford Early Christian Studies (Oxford: Oxford University Press, 2012).

Martyn, J. Louis, *Theological Issues in the Letters of Paul* (Edinburgh: T. & T. Clark, 1997).

Matlock, R. Barry, *Unveiling the Apocalyptic Paul: Paul's Interpreters and the Rhetoric of Criticism*, JSNT Sup127 (Sheffield: Sheffield Academic Press, 1996).

Maxwell, Jaclyn LaRae, *Christianization and Communication in Late Antiquity: John Chrysostom and his Congregation in Antioch* (Cambridge and New York: Cambridge University Press, 2006).

Mayer, Wendy, "Female participation and the late fourth-century preacher's audience," *Augustinianum* 39 (1999), 139–147.

"John Chrysostom: extraordinary preacher, ordinary audience," in Mary Cunningham and Pauline Allen (eds.), *Preacher and Audience: Studies in Early Christian and Byzantine Homilies* (Leiden: Brill, 1998), pp. 105–137.

"The persistence in late antiquity of medico-philosophical psychic therapy," *Journal of Late Antiquity* 8, no. 2 (2015), 337–351.

"Who came to hear John Chrysostom preach? Recovering a late fourth-century preacher's audience," *Ephemerides Theologicae Lovanienses* 76 (2000), 73–87.

Mayordomo-Marín, Moisés, "Wirkungsgeschichte als Erinnerung an die Zukunft der Texte (Hinführung)," in Moisés Mayordomo-Marín (ed.), *Die prägende Kraft der Texte. Hermeneutik und Wirkungsgeschichte des Neuen Testaments*, Stuttgarter Bibelstudien 199 (Stuttgart: Verlag Katholisches Bibelwerk, 2005), pp. 11–14.

Mazza, Enrico, *Mystagogy: A Theology of Liturgy in the Patristic Age*, trans. Matthew J. O'Connell (New York: Pueblo, 1989).

Méhat, André, *Étude sur les "Stromates" de Clément d'Alexandrie*, Patristica Sorbonensia 7 (Paris: Éditions du Seuil, 1966).

Ménard, Jacques-É., "L''évangile selon Philippe' et l''exégèse de l'âme'," in Jacques-É. Ménard (ed.), *Les textes de Nag Hammadi. Colloque du Centre d'Histoire des Religions (Strasbourg, 23–25 octobre 1974)*, NHS 7 (Leiden: Brill, 1975), pp. 56–67.

Meyer, Heinrich A. W., *Kritisch exegetisches Handbuch über den ersten Brief an die Korinther*, 5th edn, KEK 5 (Göttingen: Vandenhoeck und Ruprecht, 1870).

Michel, Otto, *Der Brief an die Hebräer*, 14th edn, KEK 13 (Göttingen: Vandenhoeck und Ruprecht, 1984).

Mitchell, Margaret M., *The Heavenly Trumpet: John Chrysostom and the Art of Pauline Interpretation* (Louisville: Westminster John Knox Press, 2002).

"Pauline accommodation and 'condescension' (συγκατάβασις): 1 Cor 9:19–23 and the history of influence," in *Paul and the Emergence of Christian Textuality: Early Christian Literary Culture in Context*, WUNT I/393 (Tübingen: Mohr Siebeck, 2017), pp. 193–217.

Paul, the Corinthians, and the Birth of Christian Hermeneutics (Cambridge: Cambridge University Press, 2010).

Monaci Castagno, Adele, *Origene predicatore e il suo pubblico* (Milan: Franco Angeli, 1987).

"Semplici," in Adele Monaci Castagno (ed.), *Origene dizionario. La cultura, il pensiero, le opere* (Rome: Città Nuova, 2000), pp. 440–443.

Morgan, Robert, "Baur's New Testament theology," in Martin Bauspiess, Christof Landmesser, and David Lincicum (eds.), *Ferdinand Christian Baur und die Geschichte des frühen Christentums*, WUNT I/333 (Tübingen: Mohr Siebeck, 2014), pp. 259–284.

The Nature of New Testament Theology (London: SCM Press, 1973).

Morgan, Teresa, *Roman Faith and Christian Faith* (Oxford: Oxford University Press, 2015).

Myers, Jason A., "Law, lies and letter writing: an analysis of Jerome and Augustine on the Antioch incident (Galatians 2:11–14)," *Scottish Journal of Theology* 66, no. 2 (2013), 127–139.

Nautin, Pierre, *Origène. Sa vie et son œuvre*, Christianisme antique 1 (Paris: Beauchesne, 1977).

Neymeyr, Ulrich, *Die christlichen Lehrer im zweiten Jahrhundert. Ihre Lehrtätigkeit, ihr Selbstverständnis und ihre Geschichte*, VC Sup 4 (Leiden: Brill, 1989).

Ng, Esther Y., "*Acts of Paul and Thecla*: women's stories and precedent?" *Journal of Theological Studies* 55, no. 1 (2004), 1–29.

Niederhofer, Veronika, *Konversion in den Paulus- und Theklaakten. Eine narrative Form der Paulusrezeption*. WUNT II/459 (Tübingen: Mohr Siebeck, 2017).

Nock, Arthur Darby, *Conversion: The Old and the New in Religion from Alexander the Great to Augustine of Hippo* (Oxford: Oxford University Press, 1933).

Noormann, Rolf, *Irenäus als Paulusinterpret. Zur Rezeption und Wirkung der paulinischen und deuteropaulinischen Briefe im Werk der Irenäus von Lyon*, WUNT II/66 (Tübingen: Mohr Siebeck, 1994).

Norris, Richard A., Jr., "Irenaeus' use of Paul in his polemic against the gnostics," in William S. Babcock (ed.), *Paul and the Legacies of Paul* (Dallas: Southern Methodist University Press, 1990), pp. 79–98.

O'Rourke Boyle, Marjorie, *Rhetoric and Reform: Erasmus' Civil Dispute with Luther*, HHM 71 (Cambridge, MA: Harvard University Press, 1983).

Os, Bas van, "Baptism in the bridal chamber: the Gospel of Philip as a Valentinian baptismal instruction," unpublished Ph.D. thesis, Groningen, 2007.

Osborn, Eric F., *Clement of Alexandria* (Cambridge: Cambridge University Press, 2005).

Irenaeus of Lyons (Cambridge: Cambridge University Press, 2001).

Osiek, Carolyn, "Perpetua's husband," *Journal of Early Christian Studies* 10, no. 2 (2002), 287–290.

Shepherd of Hermas: A Commentary, Hermeneia (Minneapolis: Fortress Press, 1999).

Pagels, Elaine H., *The Gnostic Paul: Gnostic Exegesis of the Pauline Letters* (Philadelphia: Fortress Press, 1975).

"Ritual in the Gospel of Philip," in John D. Turner and Anne McGuire (eds.), *The Nag Hammadi Library After Fifty Years: Proceedings of the 1995 Society of Biblical Literature Commenoration*, NHMS 44 (Leiden: Brill, 1997), pp. 280–291.

Pani, Giancarlo, "'In toto Origene non est verbum de Christo': Lutero e Origene," *Adamantius* 15 (2009), 135–149.

Parker, D. C., *The Living Text of the Gospels* (Cambridge: Cambridge University Press, 1997).

Parris, David Paul, *Reception Theory and Biblical Hermeneutics* (Eugene: Pickwick, 2008).

Passmore, John, "The idea of a history of philosophy," *History and Theory* 5, no. 5 (1965), 1–32.

Patterson, L. G., "The divine became human: Irenaean themes in Clement of Alexandria," *Studia Patristica* 31 (1997), 497–516.

Paul, Eugene, *Geschichte der christlichen Erziehung*, vol. 1: *Antike und Mittelalter* (Freiburg: Herder, 1993).

Paverd, Frans van de, *Zur Geschichte der Messliturgie in Antiocheia und Konstantinopel gegen Ende des vierten Jahrhunderts. Analyse der Quellen bei Johannes Chrysostomos*, OCA 187 (Rome: Pontifical Institution for Oriental Studies, 1970).

Penniman, John David, *Raised on Christian Milk: Food and the Formation of the Soul in Early Christianity*, Synkrisis (New Haven: Yale University Press, 2017).

Pervo, Richard I., *The Acts of Paul: A New Translation with Introduction and Commentary* (Eugene: Cascade Books, 2014).

   The Making of Paul: Constructions of the Apostle in Early Christianity (Minneapolis: Fortress Press, 2010).

Pfleiderer, Otto, *Lectures on the Influence of the Apostle Paul on the Development of Christianity, Delivered in London and Oxford in April and May, 1885*, 3rd edn, trans. J. Frederick Smith (London: Williams and Norgate, 1897).

Pieri, Francesco, "Origen on 1 Corinthians: homilies or commentary?" *Studia Patristica* 56, no. 4 (2013), 143–156.

Pogoloff, Stephen M., *Logos and Sophia: The Rhetorical Situation of 1 Corinthians*, SBLDS 134 (Atlanta: Scholars Press, 1992).

Porter, Stanley E. (ed.), *Paul and His Opponents*, Pauline Studies 2 (Leiden: Brill, 2005).

Poupon, Gérard, "L'accusation de magie dans les Actes apocryphes," in *Les Actes apocryphes des apôtres*, Publications de la faculté de théologie de l'université de Genève 4 (Geneva: Labor et Fides, 1981), pp. 71–93.

Quarles, Charles L., "From faith to faith: a fresh examination of the prepositional series in Romans 1:17," *Novum Testamentum* 45, no. 2 (2003), 1–21.

Raith, Charles, II, "Theology and interpretation: the case of Aquinas and Calvin on Romans," *International Journal of Systematic Theology* 14, no. 3 (2012), 310–326.

Rambo, Lewis R., *Understanding Religious Conversion* (New Haven: Yale University Press, 1993).

Ramsay, W. M., *The Church in the Roman Empire before a.d. 170* (London: Putnam, 1893).

Reinmuth, Eckart, *Paulus. Gott neu denken*, Biblische Gestalten 9 (Leipzig: Evangelische Verlagsanstalt, 2004).

Rensberger, David K., "As the apostle teaches: the development of the use of Paul's letters in second century Christianity," unpublished Ph.D. thesis, Yale University, 1981.

Riches, John Kenneth, *Galatians Through the Centuries*, Blackwell Bible Commentaries (Oxford: Blackwell, 2008).

Ricoeur, Paul, "Hermeneutical logic," in *Writings and Lectures*, vol. II: *Hermeneutics*, trans. David Pellauer (Cambridge: Polity, 2013), pp. 65–110.

Time and Narrative, trans. Kathleen McLaughlin and David Pellauer, 3 vols. (Chicago: University of Chicago Press, 1984–1988).

Riley, Hugh M., *Christian Initiation: A Comparative Study of the Interpretation of the Baptismal Liturgy in the Mystagogical Writings of Cyril of Jerusalem, John Chrysostom, Theodore of Mopsuestia, and Ambrose of Milan*, The Catholic University of America Studies in Christian Antiquity 17 (Washington, D.C.: Catholic University of America Press, 1974).

Rinaldi, Giancarlo, "Pagani e christiani a Caesarea Maritima," in Osvalda Andrei (ed.), *Caesarea Maritima e la scuola origeniana. Multiculturalità, forme di competizione culturale e identità christiana* (Brescia: Morcelliana, 2013), pp. 25–94.

Rizzi, Marco, "The literary problem in Clement of Alexandria: a reconsideration," *Adamantius* 17 (2011), 154–163.

"La scuola di Origene tra le scuole di Caesarea e del mondo tardoantico," in Osvalda Andrei (ed.), *Caesarea Maritima e la scuola origeniana: Multiculturalità, forme di competizione culturale e identità christiana* (Brescia: Morcelliana, 2013), pp. 105–119.

Roberts, Jonathan, and Christopher Rowland, "Introduction," *Journal for the Study of the New Testament* 33, no. 2 (2010), 131–136.

Rochat, Louis-Lucien, *Le catéchuménat au IVme siècle d'après les catéchèses de St. Cyrille de Jérusalem* (Geneva: Taponnier & Studer, 1875).

Rordorf, Willy, "In welchem Verhältnis stehen die apokryphen Paulusakten zur kanonischen Apostelgeschichte und zu den Pastoralbriefen?" in *Lex Orandi – Lex Credendi. Gesammelte Aufsätze zum 60. Geburtstag*, Paradosis 36 (Freiburg-Neuchâtel: Universitätsverlag Freiburg Schweiz, 1993), pp. 449–465.

"Quelques jalons pour une interprétation sympolique des *Actes de Paul*," in David H. Warren, Ann Graham Brock, and David H. Pao (eds.), *Early Christian Voices in Texts, Traditions, and Symbols: Essays in Honor of François Bovon*, BIS 66 (Leiden and Boston: Brill, 2003), pp. 251–265.

"Tertullien et les *Actes de Paul* (à propos de bapt. 17,5)," in *Lex Orandi – Lex Credendi. Gesammelte Aufsätze zum 60. Geburtstag*, Paradosis 36 (Freiburg-Neuchâtel: Universitätsverlag Freiburg Schweiz, 1993), pp. 475–484.

Roten, Philippe de, *Baptême et mystagogie. Enquête sur l'initiation chrètienne selon s. Jean Chrysostome*, Liturgiewissenschaftliche Quellen und Forschungen 91 (Münster: Aschendorff, 2005).

Roukema, Riemer, "La prédication du Christ crucifié (1 Corinthiens 2,2) selon Origène," in G. Dorival and A. Le Boulluec (eds.), *Origeniana Sexta*, BETL 118 (Leuven: Peeters, 1995), pp. 523–529.

Rouwhorst, Gerard, "The origins and evolution of early Christian Pentecost," *Studia Patristica* 35 (2001), 309–322.

Rudolph, David J., *A Jew to the Jews: Jewish Contours of Pauline Flexibility in 1 Corinthians 9:19–23*, WUNT 11/304 (Tübingen: Mohr Siebeck, 2011).

Rylaarsdam, David, *John Chrysostom on Divine Pedagogy: The Coherence of His Theology and Preaching*, Oxford Early Christian Studies (Oxford: Oxford University Press, 2014).

Sanday, William, and Arthur C. Headlam, *A Critical and Exegetical Commentary on the Epistle to the Romans*, 5th edn, ICC (Edinburgh: T. & T. Clark, 1902).

Sandt, Huub van de, "Baptism and holiness: two requirements authorizing participation in the *Didache*'s eucharist," in Jonathan A. Draper and Clayton N. Jefford (eds.), *The Didache: A Missing Piece of the Puzzle in Early Christianity* (Atlanta: SBL, 2015), pp. 139–164.

Sandt, Huub van de, and David Flusser, *The Didache: Its Jewish Sources and Its Place in Early Judaism and Christianity*, CRINT 3:5 (Assen: Royal Van Gorcum; Minneapolis: Fortress Press, 2002).

Sandwell, Isabella, *Religious Identity in Late Antiquity: Greeks, Jews, and Christians in Antioch* (Cambridge: Cambridge University Press, 2007).

Sartore, Domenico, "Aspetti cristologici delle catechesi battesimali del Crisostomo," in Magnus Löhrer and Elmar Salmann (eds.), *Mysterium Christi. Symbolgegenwart und theologische Bedeutung*, Studia Anselmiana 116 (Rome: Pontificio Ateneo S. Anselmo, 1995), pp. 131–154.

Satran, David, *In the Image of Origen: Eros, Virtue and Constraint in the Early Christian Academy*, Transformation of the Classical Heritage 58 (Oakland: University of California Press, 2018).

Saxer, Victor, *Les rites de l'initiation chrétienne du IIe au VIe siècle. Esquisse historique et signification d'après leurs principaux témoins*, Centro italiano di studi sull'alto Medioevo 7 (Spoleto: Centro italiano di studi sull' alto Medioevo, 1988).

Scarborough, Jason M., "The making of an apostle: second and third century interpretations of the writings of Paul," unpublished Ph.D. thesis, Union Theological Seminary, New York (2007).

Schelkle, Karl Hermann, *Paulus, Lehrer der Väter. Die altkirchliche Auslegung von Römer 1–11*, 2nd edn (Düsseldorf: Patmos, 1956).

Schenke, Hans-Martin, "Das Evangelium nach Phillipus (NHC II,3)," in Hans-Martin Schenke, Ursula Ulrike Kaiser, Hans-Gebhard Bethge, Katharina Stifel, and Catherine Gärtner (eds.), *NHC I–XIII, Codex Berolinensis 1 und 4, Codex Tchacos 3 und 4*, 3rd edn, Nag Hammadi Deutsch: Studienausgabe (Berlin: Akademie Verlag, 2013), pp. 140–163.

Scherbenske, Eric W., *Canonizing Paul: Ancient Editorial Practice and the Corpus Paulinum* (New York: Oxford University Press, 2013).

Schneemelcher, Wilhelm, "Acts of Paul," in Wilhelm Schneemelcher (ed.), *New Testament Apocrypha*, vol. II, rev. edn, trans. R. M. Wilson (Cambridge: James Clarke & Co Ltd.; Louisville: Westminster/John Knox, 1992), pp. 213–270.

Schnelle, Udo, *Paulus: Leben und Denken*, 2nd rev. and expanded edn, De Gruyter Studium (Berlin: De Gruyter, 2014).

Scholten, Clemens, "Die alexandrinische Katechetenschule," *Jahrbuch für Antike und Christentum* 38 (1995), 16–37.

Schottroff, Luise, "'Ich kenne die Frau nicht…, sie ist auch nicht mein': die zwei Gesichter des Paulus" in Renate Jost and Ursula Kubera (eds.), *Wie Theologen Frauen sehen. Von der Macht der Bilder*, Frauenforum (Freiburg: Herder, 1993), pp. 9–21.

Schrage, Wolfgang, *Der erste Brief an die Korinther*, 4 vols., EKK 7 (Neukirchen-Vluyn: Neukirchener, 1991–2001).

Schütz, Werner, *Der christliche Gottesdienst bei Origenes*, Calwer theologische Monographien 8 (Stuttgart: Calwer, 1984).

Schwartz, Barry, *Abraham Lincoln and the Forge of National Memory* (Chicago: University of Chicago Press, 2000).

Searle, John R., "What is an institution?," *Journal of Institutional Economics* 1, no. 1 (2005), 1–22.

Seeberg, Alfred, *Die Didache des Judentums und der Urchristenheit* (Leipzig: Deichert, 1908).

Der Katechismus der Urchristenheit (Leipzig: Deichert, 1903).

Der Katechismus der Urchristenheit, Theologische Bücherei: Neudrucke und Berichte aus dem 20. Jahrhundert 26 (Munich: Kaiser, 1966).

Seesemann, H., "Das Paulusverständnis des Clemens Alexandrinus," *Theologische Studien und Kritiken* 107 (1936), 312–346.

Segelberg, Eric, "The Coptic-Gnostic Gospel according to Philip and its sacramental system," *Numen* 7 (1960), 189–200.

Selwyn, Edward Gordon, *The First Epistle of St. Peter: The Greek Text with Introduction, Notes and Essays*, 2nd edn (London: Macmillan and Co., 1958).

Senft, Christophe, *La première épitre de Saint-Paul aux Corinthiens*, CNT 2:7 (Neuchâtel: Delachaux & Niestlé, 1979).

Simonetti, Manlio, "Origene Catecheta," *Salesianum* 41 (1979), 299–308.

Origene esegeta e la sua tradizione (Brescia: Morcelliana, 2004).

Skinner, Quentin, "Meaning and understanding in the history of ideas," *History and Theory* 8, no. 1 (1969), 3–53.

Slusser, Michael, "Saint Gregory Thaumaturgus," *Expository Times* 120, no. 12 (2009), 573–580.

Smit, Peter-Ben, "St. Thecla: remembering Paul and being remembered through Paul," *Vigiliae Christianae* 68, no. 5 (2014), 551–563.

Snyder, Glenn E., *Acts of Paul: The Formation of a Pauline Corpus*, WUNT II/352 (Tübingen: Mohr Siebeck, 2013).

Snyder, H. Gregory, "'Above the Bath of Myrtinus': Justin Martyr's 'school' in the city of Rome," *Harvard Theological Review* 100, no. 3 (2007), 335–362.

"A second-century Christian inscription from the Via Latina," *Journal of Early Christian Studies* 19, no. 2 (2011), 157–195.

Söder, Rosa, *Die apokryphen Apostelgeschichten und die romanhafte Literatur der Antike*, Würzburger Studien zur Altertumswissenschaft 3 (Stuttgart: Kohlhammer, 1932).

Stanton, Graham, "Jewish Christian elements in the pseudo-Clementine writings," in Oskar Skarsaune and Reidar Hvalvik (eds.), *Jewish Believers in Jesus* (Peabody, MA: Hendrikson, 2007), pp. 305–324.

Stefaniw, Blossom, "Exegetical curricula in Origen, Didymus, and Evagrius: pedagogical agenda and the case for Neoplatonic influence," *Studia Patristica* 44 (2010), 281–294.

Stewart, Alistair, "'The rule of truth…which he received through baptism' (*Haer.* I.9.4): catechesis, ritual, and exegesis in Irenaeus's Gaul," in Sara Parvis and Paul Foster (eds.), *Irenaeus: Life, Scripture, Legacy* (Minneapolis: Fortress Press, 2012), pp. 151–158.

Stewart-Sykes, Alistair, "*Traditio apostolica*: the liturgy of third-century Rome and the Hippolytean school or Quomodo historia liturgica conscribenda sit," *St Vladimir's Theological Quarterly* 48, no. 2 (2004), 233–248.

Stolle, Volker, *Luther und Paulus. Die exegetischen und hermeneutischen Grundlagen der lutherischen Rechtfertigungslehre im Paulinismus Luthers*, ABiG 10 (Leipzig: Evangelische Verlagsanstalt, 2002).

Strawbridge, Jennifer R., *The Pauline Effect: The Use of the Pauline Epistles by Early Christian Writers*, SBR 5 (Berlin: De Gruyter, 2015).

Strutwolf, H., "Theologische Gnosis bei Clemens Alexandrinus und Origenes," in Christoph Markschies and J. van Oort (eds.), *Zugänge zur Gnosis*, Patristic Studies 12 (Leuven: Peeters, 2013), pp. 91–112.

Studer, B., "Die doppelte Exegese bei Origenes," in G. Dorival and A. Le Boulluec (eds.), *Origeniana Sexta*, BETL 118 (Leuven: Peeters, 1995), pp. 303–323.

Tanaseanu-Döbler, Ilinca, *Konversion zur Philosophie in der Spätantike. Kaiser Julian und Synesios von Kyrene* (Stuttgart: Franz Steiner, 2008).

"Philosophie in Alexandria: der Kreis um Ammonios Sakkas," in Tobias Georges, Felix Albrecht, and Reinhard Feldmeier (eds.), *Alexandria*, COMES 1 (Tübingen: Mohr Siebeck, 2013), pp. 109–126.

Taylor, John W., "From faith to faith: Romans 1.17 in the light of Greek idiom," *New Testament Studies* 50, no. 4 (2004), 337–348.

Theissen, Gerd, *The Social Setting of Pauline Christianity: Essays on Corinth*, trans. John H. Schütz (Philadelphia: Fortress Press, 1982).

Thiselton, Anthony C., *The First Epistle to the Corinthians: A Commentary on the Greek Text*, NIGTC (Grand Rapids: Eerdmans, 2000).

New Horizons in Hermeneutics: The Theory and Practice of Transforming Biblical Reading (Grand Rapids: Zondervan, 1992).

The Two Horizons: New Testament Hermeneutics and Philosophical Description with Special Reference to Heidegger, Bultmann, Gadamer, and Wittgenstein (Exeter: The Paternoster Press, 1980).

Thomas, Matthew J., *Early Perspectives on Works of the Law: A Patristic Study*, WUNT II (Tübingen: Mohr Siebeck, 2018).

Thomassen, Einar, *The Spiritual Seed: The Church of the "Valentinians,"* NHMS 60 (Leiden: Brill, 2006).

Thüsing, Wilhelm, "'Milch' und 'feste Speise' (1Kor 3,1f und Hebr 5,11–6,3): Elementarkatechese und theologische Vertiefung in neutestamentlicher Sicht," in Thomas Söding (ed.), *Studien zur neutestamentlichen Theologie*, WUNT I/82 (Tübingen: Mohr Siebeck, 1995), pp. 23–56.

Tloka, Jutta, *Griechische Christen – Christliche Griechen. Plausibilisierungsstrategien des antiken Christentums bei Origenes und Johannes Chrysostomos*, STAC 30 (Tübingen: Mohr Siebeck, 2005).

Tomson, Peter J., *Paul and the Jewish Law: Halakha in the Letters of the Apostle to the Gentiles*, CRINT 3:1 (Assen: Van Gorcum; Minneapolis: Fortress Press, 1990).

Torjesen, Karen Jo., "The Alexandrian tradition of the inspired interpreter," in L. Perrone (ed.), *Origeniana Octava: Origen and the Alexandrian Tradition/ Origene e la Tradizione Alessantrina*, vol. 1, BETL 166 (Leuven: Leuven University Press, 2003), pp. 287–299.

Hermeneutical Procedure and Theological Structure in Origen's Exegesis, PTS 28 (Berlin: De Gruyter, 1985).

"Pedagogical soteriology from Clement to Origen," In Lothar Lies (ed.), *Origeniana Quarta. Die Referate des 4. Internationalen Origenskongresses*, Innsbrucker theologische Studien 19 (Innsbruck: Tyrolia, 1987).

Tracy, James D., *Erasmus of the Low Countries* (Berkeley: University of California Press, 1996).

Trigg, Joseph W., *Origen*, The Early Church Fathers (London: New York: Routl edge, 1998).

Origen: The Bible and Philosophy in the Third-Century Church (Atlanta: John Knox, 1983).

Trobisch, David, *Die Entstehung der Paulusbriefsammlung. Studien zu den Anfängen christlicher Publizistik* (Göttingen: Vandenhoeck & Ruprecht, 1989).

Tuckett, Christopher M., "The *Didache* and the Synoptics once more: a response to Aaron Milavec," *Journal of Early Christian Studies* 13, no. 4 (2005), 509–518.

"The *Didache* and the writings that later formed the New Testament," in Andrew F. Gregory and Christopher M. Tuckett (eds.), *The Reception of the New Testament in the Apostolic Fathers* (Oxford: Oxford University Press, 2005), pp. 83–127.

Turck, A., "Aux origines du catéchuménat," *Revue des sciences philosophiques et théologiques* 48 (1964), 20–31.

"Catéchein et *catéchésis* chez les premiers pères," *Revue des sciences philosophiques et théologiques* 47, no. 3 (1963), 361–372.

Turner, John D., "From baptismal vision to mystical union with the One: the case of the Sethian Gnostics," in April D. De Conick, Gregory Shaw, and John Douglas Turner (eds.), *Practicing Gnosis: Ritual, Magic, Theurgy, and Liturgy in Nag Hammadi, Manichaean and Other Ancient Literature. Essays in Honor of Birger A. Pearson*, NHMS 85 (Leiden: Brill, 2013), pp. 411–431.

Turner, Martha Lee, *The Gospel According to Philip: The Sources and Coherence of an Early Christian Collection* (Leiden and New York: Brill, 1996).

Ulrich, Jörg, "What do we know about Justin's 'school' in Rome?" *Zeitschrift für Antikes Christentum* 16, no. 1 (2012), 62–74.

Usacheva, A., "The exegetical requirements in Origen's late works: mystical and intellectual aspects of perfection according to Origen and his followers," in Anders-Christian Jacobsen (ed.), *Origeniana Undecima: Origen and Origenism in the History of Western Thought. Papers of the 11th International Origen Congress, Aarhus University*, BETL 279 (Leuven: Peeters, 2016), pp. 871–883.

Vakula, Oleksandra, "Spiritual progress and a disciple of Christ as a model of the perfect Christian in Origen," *Studia Patristica* 51 (2011), 45–59.

Vanveller, Courtney Wilson, "Paul's therapy of the soul: a new approach to John Chrysostom and anti-Judaism," unpublished Ph.D. thesis, Boston University (2015).

Viciano, Alberto, "Das Bild des Apostels Paulus im Kommentar zu den paulinischen Briefen des Theodoret von Kyros," *Studia Patristica* 25 (1993), 176–188.

Völker, Walther, "Paulus bei Origenes," *Theologische Studien un Kritiken* 102 (1930), 258–279.

Das Vollkommenheitsideal des Origenes. Eine Untersuchung zur Geschichte der Frömmigkeit und zu den Anfängen christlicher Mystik, BHT 7 (Tübingen: Mohr Siebeck, 1931).

Der wahre Gnostiker nach Clemens Alexandrinus, TU 57 (Berlin: Akademie Verlag, 1952).

Vollenweider, Samuel, "Paulus zwischen Exegese und Wirkungsgeschichte," in Moisés Mayordomo-Marín (ed.), *Die prägende Kraft der Texte. Hermeneutik und Wirkungsgeschichte des Neuen Testaments*, Stuttgarter Bibelstudien 199 (Stuttgart: Verlag Katholisches Bibelwerk, 2005), pp. 15–37.

Vööbus, Arthur, *History of Asceticism in the Syrian Orient: A Contribution to the History of Culture in the Near East*, 5 vols. (Louvain: Secrétariat du Corpus SCO, 1958).

Vos, Johan S., *Die Kunst der Argumentation bei Paulus. Studien zur antiken Rhetorik*, WUNT 149 (Tübingen: Mohr Siebeck, 2002).

Voss, Florian, *Das Wort vom Kreuz und die menschliche Vernunft. Eine Untersuchung zur Soteriologie des 1. Korintherbriefes*, FRLANT 199 (Göttingen: Vandenhoeck & Ruprecht, 2002).

Watson, Francis, *Gospel Writing: A Canonical Perspective* (Grand Rapids: Eerdmans, 2013).

Wechsler, Andreas, *Geschichtsbild und Apostelstreit. Eine forschungsgeschichtliche und exegetische Studie über den antiochenischen Zwischenfall (Gal 2, 11–14)*, BZNW 62 (Berlin: De Gruyter, 1991).

Wehn, Beate, "'Selig die Körper der Jungfräulichen': Überlegungen zum Paulusbild der Thekla-Akten," in C. Janssen, L. Schottroff, and B. Wehn (eds.), *Paulus. Umstrittene Tradition – lebendige Theologie. Eine feministische Lektüre* (Gütersloh: Kaiser, 2001), pp. 182–198.

Weiss, Hans-Friedrich, *Der Brief an die Hebräer*, 15th edn, KEK 13 (Göttingen: Vandenhoeck & Ruprecht, 1991).

Weiss, Johannes, *Der erste Korintherbrief*, 9th rev. edn. KEK 5 (Göttingen: Vandenhoeck & Ruprecht, 1910).

Werner, J., *Der Paulinismus des Irenaeus*, TU 6.2 (Hinrichs, 1889).

Westerhoff, Matthias, *Das Paulusverständnis im Liber Graduum*, PTS 64 (Berlin: De Gruyter, 2008).

Weyel, Birgit, "Ferdinand Christian Baur und die praktische Theologie," in Martin Bauspiess, Christof Landmesser, and David Lincicum (eds.), *Ferdinand Christian Baur und die Geschichte des frühen Christentums*, WUNT I/333 (Tübingen: Mohr Siebeck, 2014), pp. 405–424.

White, Adam G., *Where is the Wise Man? Graeco-Roman Education as a Background to the Divisions in 1 Corinthians 1–4*, LNTS 356 (London: Bloomsbury, 2015).

White, Benjamin L., *Remembering Paul: Ancient and Modern Contests over the Image of the Apostle* (New York: Oxford University Press, 2014).

"The traditional and ecclesiastical Paul of 1 Corinthians," *Catholic Biblical Quarterly* 79, no. 4 (2017), 651–669.

White, Devin L., *Teacher of the Nations: Ancient Educational Traditions and Paul's Argument in 1 Corinthians 1–4*, BZNW 227 (Berlin: De Gruyter, 2017).

Wiles, Maurice F., *The Divine Apostle: The Interpretation of St. Paul's Epistles in the Early Church* (Cambridge: Cambridge University Press, 1967).

Wilken, Robert Louis, *John Chrysostom and the Jews: Rhetoric and Reality in the Late 4th Century* (Berkeley: University of California Press, 1983).

Willard, Louis Charles, *A Critical Study of the Euthalian Apparatus*, ANT 41 (Berlin: De Gruyter, 2009).

Winter, Bruce W., *Philo and Paul Among the Sophists*, SNTSMS 96 (Cambridge: Cambridge University Press, 1997).

Wire, Antoinette Clark, *The Corinthian Women Prophets: A Reconstruction Through Paul's Rhetoric* (Minneapolis: Fortress Press, 1990).

Wolter, Michael, *Der Brief an die Römer*, EKK 6,1 (Neukirchen-Vluyn: Neukirchener Theologie; Ostfildern: Patmos Verlag, 2014).

Paulus. Ein Grundriss seiner Theologie (Neukirchen-Vluyn: Neukirchener, 2011).

Wright, N. T., *Paul and the Faithfulness of God*, 2 vols., Christian Origins and the Question of God 4 (Minneapolis: Fortress Press; (London: SPCK, 2013).

Wyrwa, Dietmar, *Die christliche Platonaneignung in den Stromateis des Clemens von Alexandrien*, AzKG 53 (Berlin: De Gruyter, 1983).

"Religiöses Lernen im zweiten Jahrhundert und die Anfänge der alexandrinischen Katechetenschule," in Beate Ego and Helmut Merkel (eds.), *Religiöses Lernen in der biblischen, frühjüdischen und frühchristlichen Überlieferung*, WUNT I/180 (Tübingen: Mohr Siebeck, 2005), pp. 271–306.

Yarnold, Edward J., "Baptismal catechesis," in Cheslyn Jones, Geoffrey Wainwright, and Edward Yarnold (eds.), *The Study of Liturgy* (London: SPCK, 1978), pp. 59–60.

"Baptism and the pagan mysteries in the fourth century," *Heythrop Journal* 13 (1972), 247–267.

"The fourth and fifth centuries," in Cheslyn Jones, Geoffrey Wainwright, and Edward Yarnold (eds.), *The Study of Liturgy* (London: SPCK, 1978), pp. 95–110.

Young, Frances M., *Biblical Exegesis and the Formation of Christian Culture* (Cambridge: Cambridge University Press, 1997).

Zachhuber, Johannes, *Theology as Science in Nineteenth-Century Germany: From F. C. Baur to Ernst Troeltsch*, Changing Paradigms in Historical and Systematic Theology (Oxford: Oxford University Press, 2013).

Zahl, Simeon, "Non-competitive agency and Luther's experiential argument against virtue," *Modern Theology* 34 (2018), 1–24 (Early View access at https://doi.org/10.1111/moth.12410).

Zeller, Dieter, *Der erste Brief an die Korinther*, KEK 5 (Göttingen: Vandenhoeck & Ruprecht, 2010).

Zuiddam, Benno A., "Early orthodoxy: the scriptures in Clement of Alexandria," *Acta Patristica et Byzantina* 21, no. 2 (2010), 307–319.

Reference Index

Modern Author Index

Subject Index